Symbiotic Intelligence

Advancing Forecasting Through Human-AI Collaboration

Editors

Hamid Jahankhani
Northumbria University London
London, UK

Gordon Bowen
Anglia Ruskin University,
Cambridge, UK

Nitsa J. Herzog
Northumbria University London Campus
London, UK

David J. Herzog
Computer Science, London Campus of Ulster
Solent and Roehampton Universities, UK

CRC Press
Taylor & Francis Group
Boca Raton London New York

CRC Press is an imprint of the
Taylor & Francis Group, an **informa** business
A SCIENCE PUBLISHERS BOOK

First edition published 2026
by CRC Press
2385 NW Executive Center Drive, Suite 320, Boca Raton FL 33431

and by CRC Press
4 Park Square, Milton Park, Abingdon, Oxon, OX14 4RN

CRC Press is an imprint of Taylor & Francis Group, LLC

Library of Congress Cataloging-in-Publication Data (applied for)

ISBN: 978-1-032-86768-7 (hbk)
ISBN: 978-1-032-88926-9 (pbk)
ISBN: 978-1-003-54037-3 (ebk)

DOI: 10.1201/9781003540373

Typeset in Times New Roman
by Prime Publishing Services

Preface

Innovation in technologies is moving at great speed and changing the business and technological landscape. AI has become an invaluable tool in the technological landscape with its many applications to improve business forecasting and thus improving business strategy and improving competitive advantage of many businesses across the different industries and sectors.

The book charts the areas of AI Demand from data driven futures to forecasting, insightful intelligence, business strategy in the AI Demand ecosystem and cyber security in general. The areas identified are important in driving the AI cycle from a productivity tool to a source for intelligent decision making that drives organizational strategies forward to be inclusive of stakeholders. Businesses will adapt AI Demand applications to become an enabler of sustainable competitive advantage and speed up accuracy of information and decision making. AI Demand applications are tools to enable better understanding of business environments that are uncertain, volatile and dynamic.

To further the aim of the book it consists of the chapter below with a brief discussion on the central purpose of the book chapters:

Chapter 1 focuses on the clinical medical industry and its growing expenditure; OECD countries medical expenditure is 8–12% of GDP. The high expenditure is ripe for technological innovation such as AI. Within the chapter there is discussion on the range of clinical activities where AI can contribute ranging from medical diagnostics, clinic research, robotic surgery to the type of decision support reasoning tools.

The theme of medical diagnostics is continued in Chapter 2 with the discussion on diagnosing autism with the aid of deep learning. The chapter starts with a review of traditional diagnosis of autism and then delves into how deep learning can aid in the diagnosis through facial recognition based on primary research data.

In Chapter 3, the focus is on cybersecurity and the role of predictive analytics and AI in minimising cybersecurity breaches. Many high-profile breaches have occurred recently in the UK in the retail sector and this chapter is a timely discussion on how AI and machine learning can spot predictive trends in the cybersecurity ecosystems of organisations.

Within Chapter 4 the discussion is about deep learning and machine language and how it is a driver of AI. Deep learning has overcome technological challenges and one such area is cryptocurrency (BTC) to model price fluctuation due to the dynamic and volatile nature of cryptocurrency ecosystem. Methodologies such as BERT a deep learning model is applied to understand the sentiment towards BTC on the social network X (Twitter) to further understand this behaviour by the collection of primary.

Chapter 5 looks at data engineering technologies to automate flow of raw data. The engineering and design of the data pipeline systems from extraction of the raw data to processing the extracted data and then the analysis. The technique can be applied to many business requirements from job seekers, recruiters, governmental and organisational policymakers need for real-time data that can be analysed in a timely and effective manner.

The strategic focus of Chapter 6 is on KPIs and how AI can improve the metrics. KPIs are important for businesses to succeed in business environments whose ecosystems includes uncertainty, dynamism and volatility. The deployment of AI developed and refined KPIs is another business tool for monitoring business performance rapidly, flexibly using a predictive AI instrument.

Industry 4.0 and 5.0 includes many technologies that Generative AI (GAI) has an influence upon. The application of Industry 5 categories includes digital transition (quantum computing, cloud computing, and edge computing) and human-centric (co-bots, automation, smart factories, and human system interaction). Furthermore, Chapter 7 discusses the disruptive nature of Industry 5.0 and the ethical issues required to safeguard the technologies in Industry 4.0 and 5.0.

Chapter 8 reviews the role of Industry 5.0 in data management to bring resilience and sustainability in managing data-driven application of AI. The discussion is enhanced with cases on healthcare, supply chain, automotive industry, environmental management in the context of AI and the challenges that this will create.

Vehicle forecasting from vehicle numbers to traffic volume with the application of intelligent traffic systems (ITS) is the focus of Chapter 9. The societal and economic impact of ITS will make traffic management smarter, reduce road injuries, traffic congestion and improved traffic light management. Improvement in ITS will reduce economic losses and be better for society overall.

The theme of forecasting is continued in Chapter 10 but this time it is related to agriculture. Related examples of agricultural forecasting are discussed and how machine learning assists in the development of the forecasting technique. The chapter is developed from primary research that creates a model that help agricultural forecasting to improve productivity and efficiency.

Supply chain and artificial intelligence is the central focus of Chapter 11. The role of Industry 4.0 technologies is positioned in the chapter to improve supply chain activities with the help of AI. Within the chapter there is discussion on the use of AI and machine language to improve sustainability in the supply.

Chapter 12 discussion is about scalability and security of blockchain with the application of quantum number random generator (QRNG) in the IoT healthcare industry. The data from IoT can convey valuable insights and benefits for all healthcare stakeholders from doctors to nurses, patients, researchers and policymakers. The application of QRNG is a tool that can help overcome the anxiety of the healthcare industry on privacy and security of data and information.

Financial cybersecurity crime is a growing challenge for authorities and businesses. Chapter 13 reviews the role of AI in combatting financial crime. The detection and forecasting of cybersecurity financial crime is an area of research that is gaining visibility. It appears the AI algorithms need to match the expertise of humans in combatting financial crime. The chapter then goes on to discuss the capability of AI in cybersecurity crime detection and combatting it.

Biomedical digital twins are the central thesis of Chapter 14 and the penultimate chapter. Furthermore, the discussion entails the application of AI in digital twin data solutions from data preparation and processing. The intersection of natural intelligence and artificial intelligence in the application of biomedical twins is another area of discussion.

The final chapter (Chapter 15) is about understanding London's housing market from trends to prediction with the use of primary research. The analysis of the London housing market applies XAI methodologies to expand stakeholder understanding of the model outcomes thus, ensuring transparency and ethical decision-making.

Contents

CHAPTER 1

Large Language Models

Strengths and Limitations of (Generative) AI Clinical Reasoning

David J. Herzog and *Nitsa J. Herzog**

1. Introduction

Healthcare represents a significant part of socio-economic endeavours, accounting for 8–12% of GDP expenditures in OECD countries (Anwar et al. 2023). There is a trend of growing healthcare expenditure per capita due to extended life longevity and ageing population in OECD and many other countries (Christiansen and Bech 2012). There are several ways to alleviate budgetary pressure and optimize the use of resources in order to provide a good level of healthcare. There are a number of strategies used to mitigate these challenges. Preventive care with regular health screenings and routine check-ups for early onset detection of hypertension, diabetes, malignancies, mental health and other pathological conditions is vital for adequate resource distribution and health improvement. Information on public health campaigns about healthy ageing, the promotion of healthy lifestyles, and general well-being is important for the general public.

Recommended vaccinations and boosters with a growing range for seasonal and epidemic infectious diseases are important for elderly and immunocompromised patients. Vaccination against influenza variants, pneumococcal vaccines, vaccination against Herpes Zoster for adults over 50, and Hepatitis A and B can be boosted by vaccination against meningococcal and some other infections, especially in the case when regular vaccination in earlier years was missing. Human papillomavirus (HPV) vaccine and Hepatitis B vaccines also can be seen as malignancy prophylactics of

Computer Science, London Campus of Ulster, Solent and Roehampton Universities.
* Corresponding author: nitsa.herzog@northumbria.ac.uk

DOI: 10.1201/9781003540373-1

certain types. Appropriate management of acute and chronic conditions is another significant part of healthcare governance. It includes high accessibility of hospital and ambulatory medical care, adequate home-based care solutions, effective daycare and walk-in centres, and a developed family general medicine network.

Technological solutions are instrumental in the modern healthcare system, and their importance is ever-growing. Diagnostic, therapeutic, monitoring, laboratory and supportive hospital and polyclinic medical equipment is crucial for contemporary healthcare. Home-based care can be enhanced by telemedicine, Ambient Assisted Living (AAL) and Electronic Health Records (EHR) updated in real-time. Wearable and standalone sensors and medical devices help to monitor vital signs and Activities of Daily Living (ADL), control medication intake and report emergency situations or signs of health deterioration. AAL and telemedicine elements are applicable for home-based chronic patients, rural and remote areas, healthcare support, and experimental, sport, expeditionary, and space medicine.

The development of telecommunications, information, and data technologies allows for remarkable improvement in several areas: diagnostics and prophylactics, efficient management of human resources and inventory administration, clinical research, and education. An integrated system of electronic health records allows quick data sharing and coordination across healthcare stakeholders and providers. Big Data flow formed by medical systems requires additional means of handling, which Artificial Intelligence provides. Figure 1 represents the roadmap of the chapter.

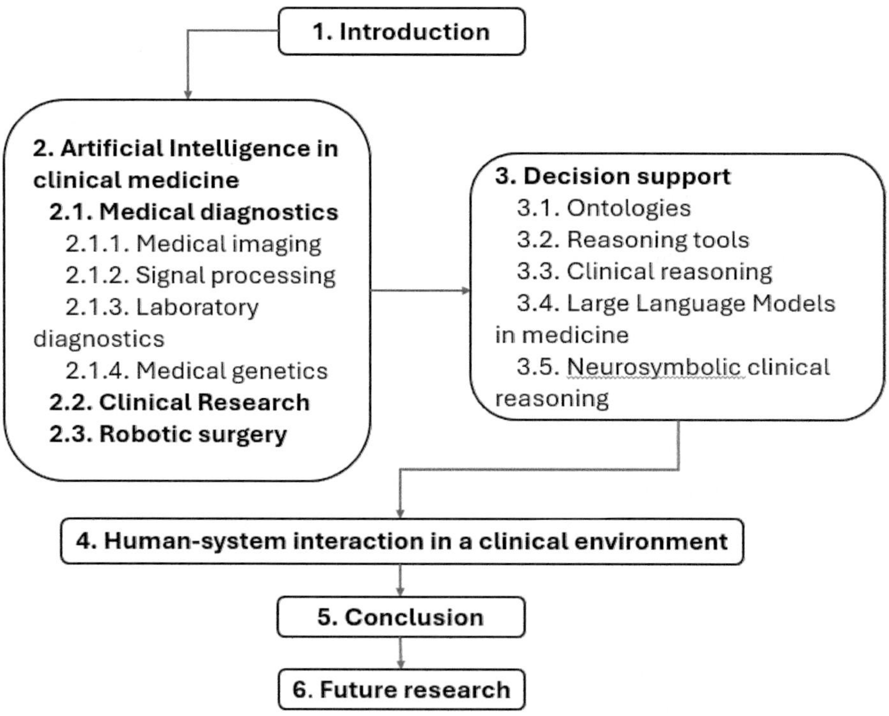

Figure 1: Chapter's roadmap.

2. Artificial Intelligence in Clinical Medicine

Artificial Intelligence (AI) has become a ubiquitous tool utilized across various domains. It is useful in handling voluminous, variable and high-velocity Big Data. AI allows quick pattern recognition, which is important in diagnostics. Modelling and predictive analysis are important in clinical research and prognostic public and individual health trends. Early AI-supported diagnostics is crucial in effective healthcare, differential diagnostics is vital for efficient treatment, and AI-powered decision support can empower healthcare professionals with potent tools. AI-supported Workflow optimization and resources management, scheduling follow-up, medical equipment and bed allocation are also important for effective healthcare.

2.1 Medical diagnostics

Medical diagnosis is a result of several key steps. First, data is usually provided by the patient, the patient's relatives or members of the public. It includes complaints and partial anamnesis. This data, including previous medical data, serves as a starting point for the diagnostic quest. The next step is usually the collection of vital signs, subject to the condition of the patient, physical and mental examination, and necessary laboratory and other technical diagnostic tests. Once the nature, area and extent of the health problem are determined and the differential diagnosis has offered additional insights, treatment can be started. The treatment outcomes also give further information, either supporting or refuting the preliminary diagnosis.

The initial steps substantially rely on human participation, from presenting the problem and complaints to gathering anamnestic details and conducting a physical examination. There are proposals to formalize these processes and make them machine-readable for optimization and AI involvement. However, the principal achievements in contemporary healthcare applications of ML and AI relate to diagnostic tools and laboratory tests when healthcare professionals have already collected and analysed initial data in the early stages. Medical imaging, genetics and other laboratory tests benefit from enhanced analytical techniques and Big Data. Big Data analysis might be important in uncovering trends in public health with possible applications for individual diagnosis or in quality control for automated results. Figure 2 shows the relationship between medical data sources and AI technologies.

2.1.1 Medical imaging

Medical imaging is quickly expanding diagnostic area, applied in many instrumental methods of visual recognition: radiologic X-ray, Computer Tomography (CT) scans, Magnetic Resonance Imaging (MRI), Positron-Emission Tomography (PET); ultrasound (US) imaging techniques, including echocardiography and Doppler sonography; ophthalmologic fundoscopy, gastroenterostomy, into operational angio-, entero-, laparo-, cardioscopy and some others. Picture comparative analysis in dermatology is another extensive field. Pathology and microscopic imaging of biopsies are important for quick and effective diagnosis. Every digitalized visual technique can benefit from AI-powered analysis of still images or video streaming.

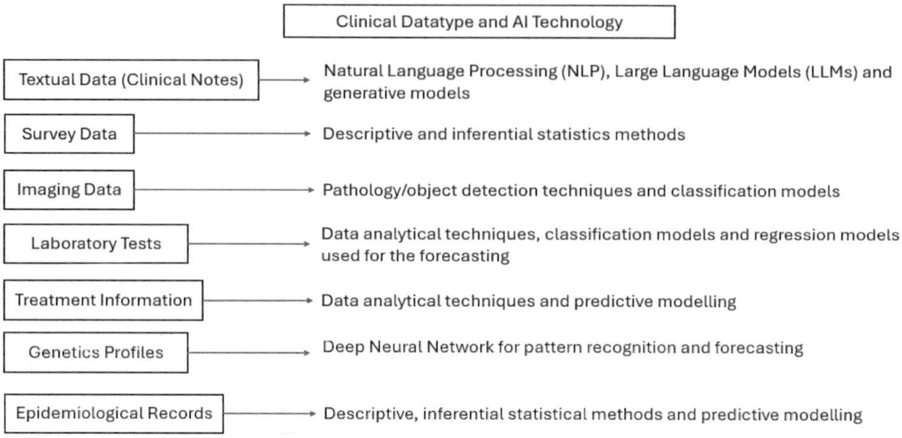

Figure 2: AI technologies applied in the healthcare industry.

Filtering, pattern recognition, classification, and preliminary diagnostic support are important steps in AI analysis and can be applied independently or in one complex. Numerous studies demonstrate the high effectiveness of AI-powered histopathology detection and diagnostics, whether employed independently or as a supportive tool for radiologists and pathologists.

2.1.2 Signal processing

AI pattern recognition is applied in many diagnostic techniques besides imaging. Signal processing is important in electrocardiography (ECG), electroencephalography (EEG), electromyography (EMG), electrodermal activity (EDA) registration, neural signal registration, high-speed video neural impulse propagation registration and many other methods. Signal denoising and filtering are important steps in signal processing and can be effectively done with the help of ML. The next step is pattern recognition, which helps with classification and anomaly detection. For example, ECG analysis can provide quick prediagnostic results in the case of tachycardia or bradycardia, connected to the focal localization of anomaly for prediction of myocardial, cardiac conductive system or valve pathology. This is effective as a prognostic tool and can be applied for real-time event monitoring.

2.1.3 Laboratory diagnostics

Biochemical, immunochemical, cytological and microbiological laboratory techniques applications are important in the diagnostic process. General biochemistry, electrolytes level, and blood or other corporeal fluid cell count are basic laboratory tests routinely applied in ambulatory and clinical medicine. In combination with blood coagulation tests, they can provide sufficient information about most somatic health emergencies, but not always with the necessary high accuracy. Particular analysis procedures, such as immunologic, immunochemical, hormone, medication, malignancy markers or other metabolites registration, help specify the pathological process behind these changes. AI enhances efficiency, accuracy, and speed but is also implemented in flow cytometry, especially with radio or fluorescent markers with pattern recognition and laser-based count. Quick tests for microbial, viral, fungal, and other parasites or immune reactions are empowered by AI with optimization and control of results. It also can be applied for remote real-time monitoring of signals from implanted glucose or other fluid marker sensors.

2.1.4 Medical genetics

2.1.4.1 Significance

Medical genetics has developed into a significant area of laboratory testing with the considerable importance of several diagnostic methods and engineering possibilities. Genes are double helix DNA polymers directly responsible for the particular protein production, with the help of one-chain RNA. In addition to exons and coding loci, Eukaryotic DNA also has regulatory parts, such as enhancers and silencers of gene expression. Proteins play a role as enzymes, transporters, hormones, signal transducers, receptors, antibodies and cellular and tissue structures. In this way, genes are responsible for living organisms' development, growth and reproduction.

2.1.4.2 Main tests

Genetic aberrations, such as chromosome aneuploidies, insertions or deletions, point mutations, Copy Number variations (CNV) and some others can result in disorders. Genetic testing allows diagnosis and prediction for different conditions. Prenatal genetic tests help to predict and, in some cases, prevent genetic disorders. Newborn and adult career screening tests help diagnose and predict multiple pathological conditions. An example is the Variant Annotation, Analysis, and Search Tool (VAAST) by Fabric Genomics. Diagnostic testing is an important part of the diagnostic process. Pharmacogenetic testing helps to check individual reactions to specific drugs, such as thiopurines, Selective Serotonin Reuptake Inhibitors (SSRI), antidepressant codeine and metabolites, abacavir, clopidogrel, omeprazole and many others. RightMed® by OneOme platform is an example. Endocrine and oncogenes testing platforms are helpful in the diagnosis and treatment control of malignant disorders.

2.1.4.3 AI applications

AI-powered Next-Generation Sequencing (NGS) Analysis and Whole Genome Sequencing (WGS) are powerful screening and testing procedures. RNA sequencing and metagenomics allow gene expression testing. Omics unification, such as genomics, proteomics, metabolomics, and cytomics, to list just a few, gives an opportunity for complex molecular and tissue analysis for diagnostic and various testing. AI-driven genomic databases are powerful tools for clinical research and medical support. AI models can predict the efficiency and effects of Clustered Regularly Interspaced Palindromic Repeats (CRISPR-Cas9) and other gene editing techniques.

2.2 Clinical research

The role of AI in clinical research is hard to underestimate. Every step, from hypothesis formulation and study preparation to the final analysis, prediction modelling, proposals and socio-economic adaptation, can be supported or designed by artificial intelligence and reasoning agents. Design, preliminary data search, molecular modelling *in-silico* run, or organ-on-a-chip (OoC) are included as essential elements. Data optimization and analysis, databases, advanced search unification and integrative research networks are indispensable supportive parts of modern clinical research.

Laboratory testing machinery and augmented reality molecular design tools require significant AI power. In more narrow, mundane terms, it accelerates drug and vaccine discovery, helps to implement precision medicine in clinical practice and provides a wide basis for future research. Immersive reality reinforced by molecular mechanics and kinetic simulation, molecular interaction and 3D folding prediction, with a virtual manipulation interface, helps to speed up novel designs. Pharmacokinetics and pharmacodynamics in simulative models and digital twins reduce biological models' exposure to the new active compounds. Real-time interaction with omics databases helps to create a highly effective integrative research environment shared across global centres.

2.3 Public health

Public health is important for the population's health and encompasses epidemiology, biostatistics, environmental and occupational health, behavioural and social science and effective healthcare organizations and management. The main goal of public medicine is to protect and improve public health through programmes that prevent, monitor, and control diseases. It includes epidemiological and biostatistical studies, real-time population health and environment monitoring, vaccination, wellness promotion and regulatory measures. Accessibility of the medical system for all members of the population, maximal information reach, and the ability to address environmental and social factors are important.

Artificial intelligence empowers public health with numerous data analytical instruments. The combination of various sources of information, such as Electronic Health Records, environmental data, health reports, and relevant biostatistical and clinical studies, helps to reflect a real public health picture and predict main trends qualitatively and quantitatively. Improved and enriched data helps address challenges and advise clinical and administrative specialists. Natural language processing can be applied to social network analysis to dynamically follow up on public health trends at the wide population level. Targeted automatic advice messaging can be coupled with NLP. AI helps to administrate available resources, propose effective policies, and have immediate reactions in the case of epidemics and environmental disasters.

2.4 Robotic surgery

Robotic surgery is a novel method of surgical intervention with the help of collaborative robots (cobots), telerobotic systems or, in some cases, autonomous task-automated machines. They have two main parts. The surgery robotic unit consists of robotic arm parts, with manipulators equipped with surgery tools, such as scalpels, scissors or graspers, effectors for irrigation, suction or electrocoagulation, cameras and measurement sensors. The remote interactive console includes a manipulation interface and visual control. Robotic surgery can be done in the room next to the operation theatre, saving time and effort for standard preoperative surgeon preparation and lowering workload per intervention. Improved telecommunication operations are also performed over distance, optimizing accessibility to top-quality healthcare options.

Artificial intelligence plays a significant, sometimes crucial, role in robotic surgery. Surgical navigation can be supported by augmented 3D reality, real-time image processing, and monitoring of vital signs and other parameters. Optimal manipulation decision support and instrument tracking enhance operational precision and improve outcomes. Gesture recognition, voice command interface, and haptic technology support effective interaction and micro-precision. Postoperative multimedia digital documentation backing and training enchantment are additional benefits of AI-powered robotic surgery.

3. Decision Support

Decision support tools are important software frameworks that automate some routine and statistically loaded parts of the decision-making process. While the front end has specific data intake forms and dashboards with visualization tools and real-time alerts, the back end includes a database management system, data processing elements, an integration architectural layer and some other components, such as a log system and cybersecurity integrands. There are several potential methods to support semiautomatic decision-making. The classical approach procedure includes specific ontological knowledge bases and reasoning rule-based tools. Statistically based AI-powered systems with analytical, model-building and predictive functions are seen as relatively advanced and usually require well-trained models, big data access, sophisticated architecture and the possibility of human readability. The most modern Large Language Models are actively tested for decision support, while hybrid neuro-symbolic systems combine knowledge base, reasoning tools and neural networks.

3.1 Ontologies

The ontological foundation of knowledge bases represents branching categories or classes and sub-classes with formal relationships and contextual backgrounds. Usually, a knowledge base is related to a certain domain as an expert system and structured in accordance with relation to existing human-readable ontologies. Ontologies possess standard domain vocabulary and syntax across the knowledge base to ensure consistency, scalability, data integration and interoperability with similar knowledge bases from the same domain or similarly organized knowledge bases. Classes or categories include specific instances and have certain properties and relationships. Ontology is based on rules which can form logic or formal language for potential reasoning.

XML-based Resource Description Framework (RDF) is one of the basic ontology standards. SPARQL Protocol and RDF Query Language Simple Knowledge (SPARQL) are used for RDF queries. Organization System (SKOS) is the W3C's principal standard for knowledge base organization of a simpler type. Web Ontology Language (OWL) is a more complex formal semantic web language for developed ontologies.

Domain-specific clinical ontology Systematized Medical Nomenclature for Medicine–Clinical Terminology (SNOMED CT) is widely used and has its own native format, Release Format 2 (RF2). Significant effort is being put into making SNOMED RDF convertable for the SPAQL application. OWL representation is also proposed to utilize complex ontology and various OWL reasoners. Logical Observation Identifiers Names and Codes (LOINC) is a universal medical laboratory standard that exists in tabular form and is also proposed for representation in RDF and OWL. International Classification of Diseases (ICD) also has its own tabular format, but ICD-11 also has OWL representation and complementary XML and JSON formats.

Another domain of vocabulary ontology is developed by the National Library of Medicine (NLM) in the USA. Unified Medical Language System (UMLS) integrates biomedical vocabulary and provides meta thesaurus, formal ontology and lexical tools. It also potentially could be OWL convertible for semantic web expressiveness and Linked Open Data (LOD) server functionality. RxNorm is also developed by NLM and provides a standard vocabulary for all medications in the US. It has a tabular form and is potentially convertible into RDF and OWL but without official distributives for it. Medical Subject Headings (MeSH) is a standalone vocabulary ontology for biomedical and health-related publications.

3.2 Reasoning tools

Automated reasoning is an important element built upon an ontological knowledge base or expert system. Reasoning is usually rule-based, and many reasoning tools are sufficiently effective when exploiting propositional logic with elements of First Order Logic (FOL). Symbolic logical representation is often employed in these types of reasoning, which allows machine and human readability. Inference engines utilize logic rules to make predictions. Alerts are produced, if necessary when the system reaches a certain condition. The axiomatic base of the reasoning can be extended; expert systems employ "if-then" rules to assist decision-making. Case-based reasoning systems are useful for more specific situations based on past cases. Expert systems are also updated by newly acquired expertise. Reasoning tools often check ontology on consistency, Protege-integrated plug-ins, such as HermiT or Pellet. The pellet is OWL Description Logic Reasoner, while HermiT is OWL hyper tableau calculus Reasoner. ELK is a Java-based existential type of Description Logic and can be applied in SNOMED CT. Apache Jena is a framework for semantic web building with a built-in inference engine. It also provides tools for handling RDF, RDF-Schema, OWL and SPARQL.

Symbolic reasoning can be enhanced by statistical methods such as Bayesian probabilistic reasoning. A statistical approach is fundamental for neural networks and is at the basis of most advanced AI systems today. While rule-based systems are relatively open for clear interpretation, more developed statistical systems, especially unsupervised learning and deep learning, have a tendency to appear as black boxes. Decision trees are relatively transparent and useful for decision-making. More complex statistical AI systems are useful for pattern recognition but could be less reliable in the case of strict diagnostic procedures, decision-making and medico-legal issues. Statistical reasoning systems can effectively handle uncertainty with probabilities, fuzzy logic and Dempster-Shafer Theory, but resulting uncertain ontologies are not always satisfactorily precise.

3.3 Clinical reasoning

Clinical reasoning is multifaceted and can be applied in many areas of clinical practice. Direct medical application is related to diagnostic assistance when rule-based systems and Bayesian networks are used to narrow down possible conditions towards a clearer ontologically related diagnosis. The differential diagnosis step is essential in most practically applied clinical reasoning frameworks, including semi-automated and automated. Medical domain-specific systems and follow-up and predictive modules enhance triage systems and primary care medical decision support systems (MDSS).

Supportive diagnostic procedures and tests can be proposed stepwise as a decision tree. Treatment planning closely follows the diagnostic procedure and can be part of it in the case of a registration reaction to a certain treatment with dependence on the underlying condition. The medication management system is coupled with vital signs registration and laboratory follow-up of biochemical signs and blood and fluid concentration levels. It can include the alert system and predictive analytics. Predictive models are also applied after diagnostic and treatment reasoning and might be useful for risk assessment of acute and chronic diseases.

(Administration of resources, electronic document support, and scheduling decision support are important in clinical medicine but are principal in public health. Epidemiological tracking and environment disaster prevention frameworks include automatically or semi-automatically triggered protocols for resource allocation, forces deployment, regulatory interventions, community mental health, social care institutions and healthcare system mobilization.)

3.4 Large Language Models in medicine

Integration of generative chatbot and Natural Language Processing (NLP) concepts led to the creation of Large Language Models (LLMs). NLP part is able to analyze and extract meaningful information from documents and human inputs through the tokenizer with related dance vector and embedding matrix, specific vocabulary set, contextual vectorization and Named Entity Recognition (NER). NER employs a rule-based approach, statistical Hidden Markov Models (HMMs), Conditional Random Fields (CRFs), and Maximum Entropy Models (MEM). With the application of Deep Learning (DL) and Long-Short Term Memory (LSTM), all these functions can be represented as transformer models. Transformer models are capable of unsupervised learning and self-learning with necessary clustering, association rules, and dimensionality reduction. In LLM, all these elements and functions are used to generate textual output, where input, trained model and output are integrated by residual connections to preserve consistency across the layers.

Various attempts have been made to employ LLMs and generative AI in clinical medicine (Lucas et al. 2024). The ability of trained LLMs to pass medical qualification and license exams has facilitated optimistic expectations (Katz et al. 2024).

LLMs can be useful is several areas. Enhanced chatbots are able to answer preliminary questions in the 24/7 healthcare information service and function as virtual assistants. Another possibility is automatically interpreting primary data from manual inputs and wearable devices. Diagnostic assistance helps to compare patient data with medical and scientific literature to facilitate efficient and quick diagnosis. It can also produce treatment recommendations and prognostic predictive analysis. LLMs can produce medical notes, discharge letters, administrative documents and medical bills. In the wider biomedical field, LLMs can enhance literature review, hypothesis generation and research data interpretation.

However, there are numerous concerns about the effective use of LLMs in medicine. The statistical nature of neural networks and the polysemy of natural languages do not allow a high level of precision and transparency, which is necessary in the biomedical and healthcare environment (institutions, organizations, systems). There is some evidence of obvious mistakes made by LLMs, which are unacceptable in the framework of rigorous requirements (Zakka et al. 2024).

LLMs were found unreliable with a number of clear clinical prompts. The reason is a tendency to "hallucinate", e.g., create invented content with false references and internal inconsistency. Similar problems of "hallucination" are seen in image-creative AI. Bias is numerous and difficult to remove. Fairness and privacy concerns are other issues with LLM applications in healthcare. In the contemporary state, it is hard to imagine HIPAA compliance for LLMs or easy, seamless integration of LLMs into EHR-handling systems or even extended chat. There is also a specific problem for ethical-sensitive areas of medicine. Any autonomous expert system does not easily overcome lack of genuine empathy and human experience (Ferrario and Biller-Andorno 2024).

There is evidence of poor medical coding capability for all main LLMs, with performance not higher than 45% in ChatGPT 4.0 and cases of fabricated information (Soroush et al. 2024). LLMs without deep domain training can produce mistakes. NER is not sufficiently effective in the case of some specific pathologies (Panagoulias et al. 2024). There is a potential significant medicolegal challenge for LLM applications in healthcare (Shumway and Hartman 2024).

There are underlying problems with model training that go beyond hallucination and other specific LLM problems. Training for effective autonomous LLM can never be sufficient to obtain high performance without serious pitfalls and streaming updates (Arvisais-Anhalt et al. 2024).

Much wider concerns are associated with potential healthcare providers de-skilling and declining professionalism (Choudhury and Chaudhry 2024).

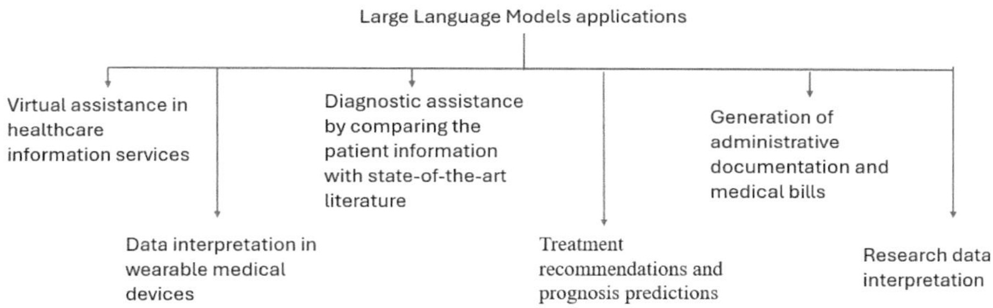

Figure 3: Areas of LLMs in healthcare.

The other potential problem is a shifted balance between retrieval and generative modes. If the last one is more prevalent than the first one, LLM, even in a specific framework, can lose its critical ability level to learn (Frisoni et al. 2024).

LLMs are transformational in medicine, including primary care. However, caution and proactive measures are necessary (Andrew 2024). Healthcare professionals have to be educated on the positive and problematic sides of LLMs (Cascella et al. 2023). Domain-specific training of LLMs can be a partial solution for underlying problems. However, there is an additional possibility of empowering clinical AI systems. Figure 3 illustrates the possible applications of LLMs in healthcare.

3.5 Neurosymbolic clinical reasoning

Neurosymbolic (NeSy) AI might be a better solution for clinical reasoning than LLMs, even domain-trained ones. NER can be improved in NeSy NLP applications (Barnes and Hutson 2024). Neurosymbolic AI combines all the functionality of data-driven neural networks with the power of knowledge-driven symbolic reasoning (Hitzler et al. 2022). Domain-trained transformers are integrated alongside ontological knowledge bases, expert systems and semantic webs, where rule-based, case-based and context-aware reasoning agents are applied (Oltramari et al. 2020).

Statistical systems are capable of effective pattern recognition and generative functions, while rule-based formalization limits the possibility of mistakes and restricts the creation of potentially inaccurate output. Neurosymbolic systems allow the creation of robust learning models with embedded symbolic reasoning. It is desirable to create neurosymbolic systems with a high degree of plasticity capable of goal-oriented architectural self-designing, but this task might have a steep slope. It is more feasible to have a pre-designed task-specific architecture.

There are several clinical spheres of potential neurosymbolic AI applications. In medical imaging and laboratory results, specific patterns are recognized by pre-trained neural networks and potential areas of concern are compared with existing ontologies introduced to reasoning layers. It could be effective in situations with minimal visual signs of tumours or other pathologies. Neurosymbolic Clinical Decision Support Systems (CDSS) might support the next step. A neural network registers and analyses continuous data flow, and data is produced using the rule-based decision-making framework. A personalized treatment plan might be based on the extensive analysis of pharmacogenetics and individual metabolomics, drug interactions, and optimal choice of the medication composition. Clinical symbolic reasoning is applied at the stage of clinical plan formalization, with standard clinical guidelines and patient personal choices on balance with efficacy. DL analysis identifies trends on the public health level, and additional reasoning is applied to adjust policies and organizational management.

Certain benefits exist in the clinical application of neurosymbolic systems. Accuracy, personalization, regulation compliance, and explainability are supposed to be higher than in NN-based AI. However, there are also challenges with data integration, computational complexity, and the necessity of regularly updating related ontologies. Unintended semantics and excessive reasoning shortcuts are other problems (Marconato et al. 2024).

There might be a place for more developed neurosymbolic declarative language with neural predicates (Hinnerichs et al. 2024).

There might still be an additional obstacle in the development of NeSy AI. It is highly likely that the symbolic element will enhance particular NLP-focused systems. However, more than one factor influences performance and the level of outcome. While the symbolic part enhances general results for NLP, the underlying logical system might significantly increase the effectiveness of language processing (Hamilton et al. 2024).

All components of the NLP, such as Natural Language Understanding (NLU), Natural Language Inference (NLI) and Natural Language Generation (NLG), are improving with the addition of a formalized logical framework. NLI outcome is supposed to correlate strongly with semantics, but even First Order Logic (FOL) benefits the outcome. The FOL is integrated into the process by tensorization (Ismail 2024). There is a way to create tensors from numerous lower-dimensional data vectors. A number of tensors can be combined into the tensor network. The tensor network effectively reduces dimensionality in the training model and can help replace standard neural network layers with matrix product operators (Jahromi and Orús 2024).

Logic can also be introduced via methods of horizontal and vertical hybrid learning (Hamilton et al. 2024 - above). Horizontal learning is a process that includes rule-based knowledge expertise data distributed across the knowledge domains, while vertical learning deals with the reasoning of symbolic and sub-symbolic types in one particular domain. Neuro-symbolic reasoning combines processes of learning and reasoning in a chosen proportion. The more extreme versions can be shifted towards heavy learning with a light reasoning counterpart or combine light learning with a heavy reasoning component. More sophisticated versions include the Markovian probabilistic process, applied to FOL, classical probabilistic process, or inductive logic. Knowledge graphs, produced in the process, can transfer semantic data into the trained model.

Despite the high promise of the NeSy network, there are some potential pitfalls based on underlying semantic simplifications (Marconato et al. 2024). The so-called deterministic reasoning shortcuts can undermine the outcome despite the implementation of a sufficient learning model and externally viable reasoning model. There are several ways to solve the problem. It can be knowledge-based, data-based, objective-based, architecture-based or heuristic approach in every case.

An interesting way of development can be opened by the weighted combination of different solution types to remove deterministic reasoning shortcuts from the neuro-symbolic system.

Neuro-symbolic reasoning is a robust tool with the potential for extension and complex development. There is strong evidence of high performance for NeSy systems, which analyze knowledge graphs generated from bioinformatics databases and built with OWL and RDF (Alshahrani et al. 2017). NeSy reasoning frameworks have been shown to be effective in understanding medical publications (Kang et al. 2021). Similar results are obtained from the NeSy reasoning system and applied to clinical data (Rivas et al. 2024).

Knowledge Graph Embedding (KGE) is important for successfully implementing a neuro-symbolic reasoning framework. It can be presented as a successful process of combining two fundamental AI approaches, such as statistical pattern recognition and rule-based neural networks, and semantically connected, ontologically empowered, human-readable traditional AI.

4. Human-System Interaction in a Clinical Environment

The modern healthcare system is rooted in technological development more than ever before. Every step of the patient, from primary contact through the diagnosis and treatment to the final discharge, is supported by multiple computerized devices and systems. Significant dependency on all procedural steps from the computerized equipment, ontological expert systems, pattern recognition models and reasoning agents shift the issue of the best potential outcome towards equipment calibration, model improvement and optimal system architecture. With quickly growing complexity, especially in AI-powered diagnostic systems, LLM-based clinical decision support and expanding knowledge base in molecular biology and all other omics applications of computerized systems are highly desirable yet lacking the necessary level of human readability and transparency. Due to highly sensitive issues of healthcare, including questions of regulatory medicolegal compliance, ethical considerations, standardization, the necessity of informed consent, and cultural and social contexts, there is a clear necessity for an expert human end-operator or administrator in any sophisticated computerized clinical system.

Additional dependence on human operators of these systems comes from necessary maintenance, upgrades and model retraining. The problem of the black box arises in many advanced NN techniques, especially DL. There are partial solutions such as grey box and Explainable AI (XAI) (Herzog and Herzog 2024).

While numerous efficient models are applicable to healthcare, the black box approach is not readable by human operators and is insufficiently transparent, even with the most profound explainability. Nevertheless, the explanatory power in XAI can be judged by the area of focus, stage and level of explainability. Partial XAI is narrowed to the layer, group of neurons or section of the system. A similar principle applies to the grey box, where some elements are intrinsically human-readable while others remain opaque black boxes. Ad hoc explainability is intrinsic and, in the white box, is usually related to the Random Forest (RF) self-supervised algorithm or monotonic linear regressions, such as simple Linear regression, Logistic Regression

(LR) or Least Absolute Shrinkage and Selection Operator regression, or LASSO. Simple probabilistic networks, such as Naive Bayes or Markov Models, also possess elements of explainability.

Clinical utilization of any AI-powered system, including LLMs and other transformers, requires highly competent operators in every case of interaction. It is insufficient to rely on medical knowledge, experience, or technical competence as separate entities. The modern healthcare shift is focused on joining the theoretical and practical areas of expertise. It goes from the combination of memorizing medical data compendium and routinizing practical tasks to the more complex amalgam of the ability to function professionally in a complex environment. This environment is enriched with diagnostic, supportive systems, LLMs, Augmented Reality tools with on-the-fly expert and patient data support, shared VR planning and training devices and haptic elements for distant diagnostics and procedures (Williams et al. 2024). Significant emphasis is placed on Big Data medical prognostication and analysis, personalized medicine and access to express diagnostic tools (Giansanti 2024).

The requirements of the specialists in the new era of cyber-physical healthcare might be concentrated around a smooth synergetic approach of expert-machine interaction, a deep understanding of underlying processes in relation to medical practice and successful implementation of related technologies. Biomedical digital twin, powered by bioinformatics, or organ-on-a-chip, cell culture, tissue, biomedical in-silico system with just-in-time interactions with supplementary data and diagnostic/treatment supporting tools are only a few possible additions to the array of kits, potentially available for future healthcare professionals. It is important to include significant elements of IT and NLP techniques and ontological and statistical approaches in professional education for a deep understanding of their capabilities and limitations. LLMs cannot be seen as separate sets of generative models applied in healthcare. They can be only an integrative part of highly technological healthcare and have to be balanced and attuned with all other available tools and systems.

5. Conclusion and Future Directions

The fast development of AI instruments, especially statistically based neural networks, inspired transformative changes in multiple spheres of human activity. Healthcare is a critical area in every society, and most observers see significant improvements in diagnostics, treatment methods, and administration as positive. Nevertheless, there are limitations to any AI method based on neural networks and statistical pattern recognition. Medical imaging results, LLMs, and decision support have restrictions from the very nature of data-driven AI. Besides expectable ethical problems and lack of instilled empathy, these AI tools are prone to bias, hallucinations, and unacceptable errors in clinical practice. However, it might be leveraged by several additional methods, applied separately or as a composite technique. Better model training in certain domains checked for even singular inconsistencies before practical application is a good standard for AI diagnostic and generative tools. Integrating neural networks with ontological expert systems and semantic webs, enhanced by reasoning agents, can create domain-specific neurosymbolic frameworks. It improves accuracy, transparency, ethical performance and regulation compliance. The necessity of a final arbiter, a human expert, can resolve the issue of medicolegal responsibility and apply lock for human-readable machine-generated errors. Human mistakes are also mitigated by the human-system interaction, where every controlling layer is at the same time empowered by a supportive system with a computerized error check or human-operated mistake search. Final approval by the clinical expert or panel of experts is a standard approach in clinical practice and is easily expandable to any machine-supported expert system. Future perspectives can also focus on using LLMs for policy generation in medical ethics and improving client services in primary and secondary healthcare (Ferrario and Biller-Andorno 2024, Andrew 2024).

References

Alshahrani, M., Khan, M.A., Maddouri, O., Kinjo, A.R., Queralt-Rosinach, N. and Hoehndorf, R. 2017. Neuro-symbolic representation learning on biological knowledge graphs. *Bioinformatics*, 33(17): 2723–2730.

Andrew, A. 2024. Potential applications and implications of large language models in primary care. *Family Medicine and Community Health*, 12(Suppl 1).

Anwar, A., Hyder, S., Mohamed Nor, N. and Younis, M. 2023. Government health expenditures and health outcome nexus: a study on OECD countries. *Frontiers in Public Health*, 11: 1123759.

Arvisais-Anhalt, S., Gonias, S.L. and Murray, S.G. 2024. Establishing priorities for implementation of large language models in pathology and laboratory medicine. *Academic Pathology*, 11(1): 100101.

Barnes, E. and Hutson, J. 2024. Natural language processing and neurosymbolic AI: the role of neural networks with knowledge-guided symbolic approaches. *Journal of Artificial Intelligence and Robotics*, 2(1).

Cascella, M., Montomoli, J., Bellini, V. and Bignami, E. 2023. Evaluating the feasibility of ChatGPT in healthcare: an analysis of multiple clinical and research scenarios. *Journal of Medical Systems*, 47(1): 33.

Choudhury, A. and Chaudhry, Z. 2024. Large language models and user trust: consequence of self-referential learning loop and the deskilling of health care professionals. *Journal of Medical Internet Research*, 26: e56764.

Christiansen, T. and Bech, M. 2012. *Demographic changes and aggregate health-care expenditure in Europe*. CEPS.

Giansanti, D. 2024. Joint expedition: exploring the intersection of digital health and AI in precision medicine with team integration. *Journal of Personalized Medicine*, 14(4): 388.

Ferrario, A. and Biller-Andorno, N. 2024. Large language models in medical ethics: useful but not expert. *Journal of Medical Ethics*, 50(9): 653–654.

Frisoni, G., Cocchieri, A., Presepi, A., Moro, G. and Meng, Z. 2024. To generate or to retrieve? on the effectiveness of artificial contexts for medical open-domain question answering. *arXiv preprint arXiv:* 2403.01924.

Hamilton, K., Nayak, A., Božić, B. and Longo, L. 2024. Is neuro-symbolic AI meeting its promises in natural language processing? A structured review. *Semantic Web*, 15(4): 1265–1306.

Herzog, D.J. and Herzog, N.J. 2020. Towards a potential paradigm shift in health data collection and analysis: Contemporary challenges of Human-Machine interaction. *Metaverse*. 2024; 5(1): 2690. https://doi.org/10.54517/m.v5i1.2690.

Hinnerichs, T., Manhaeve, R., Marra, G. and Dumancic, S. 2024. Towards a fully declarative neuro-symbolic language. *arXiv preprint arXiv:* 2405.09521.

Hitzler, P., Eberhart, A., Ebrahimi, M., Sarker, M.K. and Zhou, L. 2022. Neuro-symbolic approaches in artificial intelligence. *National Science Review*, 9(6), p.nwac035.

Ismail, A.M. 2024. The influential impact of tensor decompositions on biomedical sciences: a review. *J. of Clin. Bio. Med. Adv.*, 3(6): 01–06.

Jahromi, S.S. and Orús, R. 2024. Variational tensor neural networks for deep learning. *Scientific Reports*, 14(1): 19017.

Kang, T., Turfah, A., Kim, J., Perotte, A. and Weng, C. 2021. A neuro-symbolic method for understanding free-text medical evidence. *Journal of the American Medical Informatics Association*, 28(8): 1703–1711.

Katz, U., Cohen, E., Shachar, E., Somer, J., Fink, A., Morse, E. et al. 2024. GPT versus resident physicians—a benchmark based on official board scores. *NEJM AI*, 1(5): AIdbp2300192.

Lucas, H.C., Upperman, J.S. and Robinson, J.R. 2024. A systematic review of large language models and their implications in medical education. *Medical Education*, 58(11): 1276–1285.

Marconato, E., Teso, S., Vergari, A. and Passerini, A. 2024. Not all neuro-symbolic concepts are created equal: Analysis and mitigation of reasoning shortcuts. *Advances in Neural Information Processing Systems*, 36.

Oltramari, A., Francis, J., Henson, C., Ma, K. and Wickramarachchi, R. 2020. Neuro-symbolic architectures for context understanding. In *Knowledge Graphs for eXplainable Artificial Intelligence: Foundations, Applications and Challenges* (pp. 143–160). IOS Press.

Panagoulias, D.P., Virvou, M. and Tsihrintzis, G.A. 2024. Evaluating LLM—generated multimodal diagnosis from medical images and symptom analysis. *arXiv preprint arXiv:* 2402.01730.

Rivas, A., Collarana, D., Torrente, M. and Vidal, M.E. 2024. A neuro-symbolic system over knowledge graphs for link prediction. *Semantic Web*, 15(4): 1307–1331.

Shumway, D.O. and Hartman, H.J. 2024. Medical malpractice liability in large language model artificial intelligence: legal review and policy recommendations. *Journal of Osteopathic Medicine*, 124(7): 287–290.

Soroush, A., Glicksberg, B.S., Zimlichman, E., Barash, Y., Freeman, R., Charney, A.W. et al. 2024. Large language models are poor medical coders—benchmarking of medical code querying. *NEJM AI*, 1(5): AIdbp2300040.

Williams, R., Anderson, S., Cresswell, K., Kannelønning, M.S., Mozaffar, H. and Yang, X. 2024. Domesticating AI in medical diagnosis. *Technology in Society*, 76: 102469.

Zakka, C., Shad, R., Chaurasia, A., Dalal, A.R., Kim, J.L., Moor, M. et al. 2024. Almanac—retrieval-augmented language models for clinical medicine. *NEJM AI*, 1(2): AIoa2300068.

CHAPTER 2

Utilizing Deep Learning to Diagnose Autism in Children Through Facial Feature Analysis

Eboagu Chiamaka Chinwe and *Nitsa J. Herzog*★

1. Introduction

Autism spectrum disorder (ASD) is a complex neurodevelopmental disorder characterized by persistent impairment in reciprocal communication and social interactions as well as a restricted, repetitive pattern of behaviours, interests, or activities (Bernier and Dawson 2016). According to Zwaigenbaum et al. (2015), it is recommended to screen children for autism between 18 and 24 months to benefit from the option of early intervention therapies. Hence, early identification of Autism is essential since it enables early treatment and management of the condition to enhance the quality of life of the affected individuals. However, the traditional method for the diagnostic process mostly depends on behavioural observation assessments and clinical interviews, which tend to be lengthy, biased, and tasking, especially in the case of a young child (Hus and Segal 2021).

Recent developments in deep learning have created the way for new opportunities in the automated and unbiased examination of facial characteristics, which can contribute to the early detection of Autism Spectrum Disorder (ASD) (Awaji et al. 2023). In numerous studies, differences in facial structure, emotional expressions, and visual focus have been observed between children with Autism and other children without Autism (LI et al. 2011). People might not correctly identify autism spectrum disorder (ASD) from faces.

Faculty of Engineering & Environment, Northumbria University London Campus, UK.
* Corresponding author: nitsa.herzog@northumbria.ac.uk

DOI: 10.1201/9781003540373-2

Deep learning, especially Convolutional Neural Networks (CNNs), has proven effective in computer vision for image categorization, object detection and identification, and facial recognition (Aiman and Vishwakarma 2017). CNN can play a key role as it can extract features and successfully allow the development of systems that can analyse a child's facial image and effectively classify them as either typically developing (TD) or with Autism Spectrum Disorder (ASD).

The study suggests using deep CNN to train using a dataset of children with and without ASD facial images where transfer learning and data augmentation are employed for improved performance. The performance of the trained models was assessed by checking how accurately the models were able to classify facial images of subjects as autistic or non-autistic. Further, visualization techniques will be used to understand learned features and get insights about the relevant facial characteristics more significantly associated with ASD.

By accomplishing these goals, the current study will assist in the advancement of early screening using automated, nonintrusive techniques for individuals on the ASD spectrum, subsequently improving their quality of life.

2. Literature Review

It is important to identify autism in early childhood so that appropriate assistance may be offered. The traditional diagnostic tools that involve the use of behavioural rating scales are often qualitative, time-consuming, and also require the services of skilled personnel (Dawson and Sapiro 2019). The emergence of deep learning allows for the objective and quantitative diagnosis of the disease with the help of facial features, which are distinguishable and differ from typical samples in patients with ASD (Hosseini et al. 2022). This literature reviews traditional methods of detecting autism and explores existing literature that used facial images for the analysis.

2.1 Traditional methods of autism diagnosis

Traditional methods of diagnosing autism spectrum disorder (ASD) rely on observational assessments of a child's behaviour and developmental history (Dawson and Sapiro 2019). The important process in the traditional method for diagnosis of ASD is the observation of the relationship and interactions of the child with their parents/carer and unfamiliar person during parent-child observation and free play, as well as during structured play, and obtaining additional information on the child's development (Lord et al. 2020).

Despite the absence of standard screening instruments, national healthcare systems in diverse European countries, including Spain and Ireland, have programs for the early detection of children (18–30 months) with ASD (Blank et al. 2020). The two main traditional diagnostic tools used are:

- DSM-5 Criteria: The DSM-5 states that a child must exhibit consistent deficiencies in the following domains of social communication and interaction: social-emotional reciprocity, nonverbal communication, and developing, understanding, and maintaining relationships. Also, if alternative explanations of intellectual incapacity or developmental problems do not provide a better explanation for the symptoms, then ASD may be suspected.

- Modified Checklist for Autism in Toddlers (M-CHAT): M-CHAT is designed to screen infants from 16 to 30 months of age. It has 23 "yes/no" questions covering several developmental domains, together with a parent interview to help explain parent surveys and lower the risk of false positives (Zwaigenbaum and Penner 2018). This checklist does not rely on a professional's observations but on the parent's account of the child's skills and behaviours.

2.2 Challenges in traditional methods of autism diagnosis

Time-Consuming: Traditional methods of autism diagnosis usually entail in-person evaluations by medical specialists, including developmental paediatricians and psychologists (Micheletti et al. 2023). Despite the successes of these approaches, there are frequently drawbacks such as lengthy wait times, restricted access to specialists, and high costs. These obstacles may impede early intervention attempts and postpone diagnosis.

Subjectivity and Variability: Most traditional diagnosis techniques rely on subjective observations and assessments, which might add biases and variability. According to Mandell and Mandy (2015), the effectiveness of these screening methods has also been a matter of debate mainly because most children with ASD are not diagnosed through screening until their parents have noted delayed development. This subjectivity may result in an underdiagnosis or incorrect diagnosis, depriving people of the proper care and interventions.

Inconsistencies in diagnosis: These have been observed due to differences in how the DSM-5 and other diagnostic tools represent and interpret behavioural criteria (Evers et al. 2021). This has also led to diagnostic criteria varying across research centres leading to differences in diagnosis and symptoms and the failure in replicating research findings.

Cultural differences: The focus of autism research is primarily on high-income Western nations. The majority of people with autism worldwide reside in low- and middle-income environments, where there is a lack of culturally competent autism screening and diagnosis tools (de Leeuw et al. 2020). Especially in low- and middle-income nations where culturally appropriate screening and diagnostic tools are lacking, this might result in misinterpreting symptoms and making erroneous diagnoses. Also, cultural differences in behaviour and communication may not be sufficiently considered by the current diagnostic techniques for autism, which are mostly behaviourally defined (Norbury and Sparks 2013).

Limited Accessibility: Rural communities face significant issues when it comes to providing enough diagnostic, therapeutic, and supportive services for people with autism spectrum disorder (ASD) (Antezana et al. 2017). Several variables, such as the geographic distance between families and service providers, the lack of dependence on medical professionals, and cultural traits, all contribute to decreased accessibility and use of services. These characteristics increase the likelihood of delayed diagnosis and screening for ASD, which negatively affects functional and educational results.

2.3 The application of deep learning in autism diagnosis

The challenges identified in traditional methods of autism diagnosis led to research on other less subjective and more efficient ways of identifying autism, such as deep learning and facial recognition. The advancement of technology can help solve the challenges identified in traditional methods of diagnosing autism and lead to early and more accurate diagnoses.

Deep learning, a branch of machine learning, has transformed the domain of pattern identification and data abstraction, especially for high-dimensional and complex data sets like speech and images (Chen 2015). Its capacity to automatically identify complex patterns inside such data has resulted in notable progress across multiple fields, such as speech and picture identification, natural language comprehension, and multimodal processing. Unlike traditional methods, deep learning models can automatically find complex patterns in data by a collection of methods that enable systems to extract features from raw data and identify representations required for classifications or detection.

2.4 Methods for medical imaging using deep learning

Among the deep learning methods used in medical imaging, image classification is useful for using facial feature analysis to diagnose autism (Ker et al. 2018). Although deep learning has demonstrated impressive performance on a range of medical imaging applications, image classification techniques are best suited for the goal of using facial feature analysis to diagnose autism.

2.5 Image classification

In medical imaging, image classification is a relevant field that uses computational models for analysing and classifying different medical images which can help improve the efficiency of diagnosing methods in healthcare organizations (Gulshan et al. 2016). With regards to the diagnosis of autism, this involves classifying images of children's faces as either autistic or not autistic depending on the characteristics found by the deep learning model. According to Miranda et al. (2016) Image classification includes the following key steps:

- Feature Extraction: This is an important step in image classification. It allows for the accurate representation of the content of images. This stage focuses on the extraction of features in medical images that will help distinguish between different classes or categories.
- Feature Selection: This directly translates into a reduced time complexity to a large extent and gives improved results. It involves selecting features to be used in classification and removing irrelevant features. By selecting the relevant features, image systems can classify these images with accuracy, better

generalization, and lower computation. As a result, they provide appropriate diagnostic support for physicians.

- Classification: This involves using the features selected to categorize the images into different classes.

2.6 Facial features analysis for autism diagnosis

Facial features play an important role in detecting autism. It involves analyzing relevant data to reveal recurring patterns (Akter et al. 2021). Various papers have described certain facial features that seem to be typical for individuals with ASD in comparison with those without autism (Tan et al. 2020).

Hammond et al. (2008) analysed and contrasted the face morphology of boys who have ASD and their first-degree relatives with that of unrelated control subjects. They found that boys with ASD had a peculiar pattern of right-sided dominance in the supraorbital and periorbital areas of their faces, which are situated anterior to the frontal cerebral pole.

The study by Aldridge et al. (2011) sought to determine whether the face of a child diagnosed with ASD is, to some extent, immediately distinguishable from that of a typically developing child and whether there are categories of such phenotypes within the ASD category. They reported that statistically significant differences in facial morphology were observed between children with ASD and children without autism, including a notable increase in the breadth of the mouth, orbits, and upper face, along with a flattened nasal bridge and decreased height of the philtrum and maxillary region.

The paper by Obafemi-Ajayi et al. (2015) supports the hypothesis that facial morphology analysis may be useful as a biomarker in identifying various subtypes of ASD patients and that the presence of some facial features may predict the severity of the manifestations and developmental characteristics of the disorder.

2.7 Relevance of facial features in autism

2.7.1 Unique facial characteristics

Children with Autism Spectrum Disorder (ASD) have unique facial characteristics that distinguish them from other children (Patel et al. 2023). These include increased distances between the eyes and ears, larger distances between the right and left eyes and lips, greater right and left face height, smaller right and left face width, a flatter right nostril, smaller right and left face length, and a larger head girth. However, such facial differences may not be noticeable or easily discernible to parents or caregivers.

2.7.2 Potential for early detection

Finding specific facial features connected to autism can be useful for early detection. As with any disease, timely identification and management of autism can play a crucial role in ensuring that children receive appropriate attention and improve their quality of life. Currently, some technologies can be considered potential non-invasive methods of early identification.

2.7.3 Automated detection

In the case of computer vision, machine learning algorithms are trained to recognize some specific features of a face or distinguish between normal and an unusual facial structure (Liu et al. 2016). Recent studies have shown that machine learning models can be developed based on the training of several facial images to improve the accuracy in detecting autism (Sharma and Sharma 2023, Reddy 2024).

2.8 Anthropometric landmarks of the frontal face concerning autism

Anthropometric reference points are certain distinctive points of a person's face selected for studies concerning facial dimensions (Vezzetti and Marcolin 2012). These landmarks are important for detecting small differences in facial features that may relate to different conditions, such as autism. Several studies have established that ASD patients display different facial structures compared to typically developing (TD) individuals (Yi et al. 2014).

Figure 1 outlines some facial landmarks in the upper face region, mid-face, and lower face, which are the regions of the human face. A professional can identify the extent of face dysmorphology (if any) in the child by applying the Euclidean distance between landmarks.

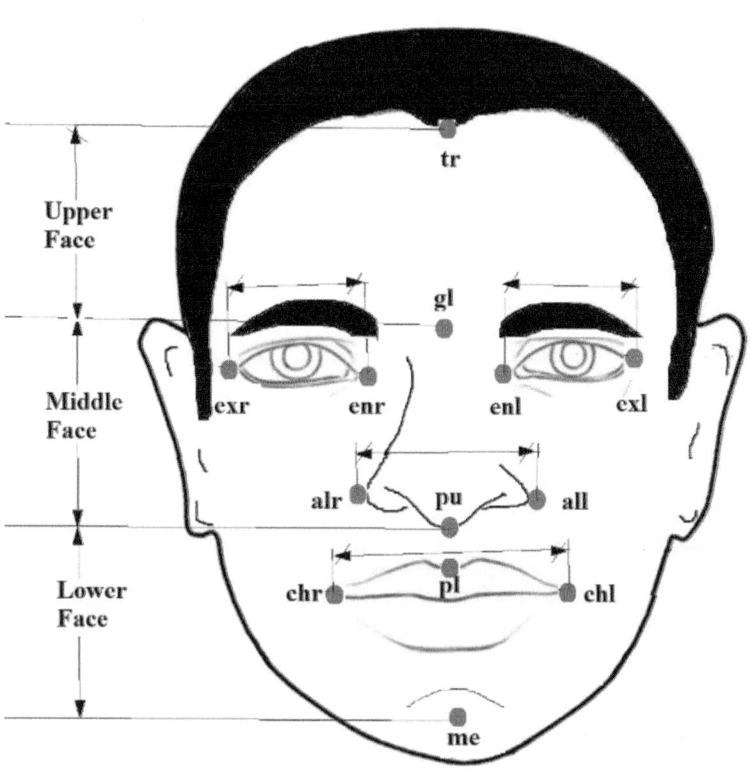

Figure 1: Anthropometric landmarks of frontal face.

Table 1: Facial landmarks and anthropometric measures.

Landmark 1	Landmark 2	Distance	Definition
Trichion (tr)	Glabella (gl)	Vertical	Upper facial height
Glabella (gl)	Upper philtrum (pu)	Vertical	Middle facial height
Upper part of philtrum (pu)	Menton (me)	Vertical	Lower facial height
Upper philtrum (pu)	Lower philtrum (pl)	Vertical	Philtrum
Endo canthion left, (enl)	Endo canthion right (enr)	Horizontal	Intercanthal width
Exo canthion left, (exl)	Exo canthion right (exr)	Horizontal	Binocular width
Alare left (all)	Alare right, (alr)	Horizontal	Nasal width
Ch Eilion left (chr)	Cheilion to right (chl)	Horizontal	Mouth width

Table 1 presents a brief description of the most important facial anthropometric measurements relevant to ASD.

CNN-based feature extractor with several digital filters is used to extract specific attributes from the input images. Each filter has a set of learnable parameters known as weights and biases to capture significant characteristics from the training images. The digital filters can use different combinations of weights and biases to gather elements from the photographs, including corners, contours, and edges (horizontal, vertical, and inclined); this is a difficult task for an expert to perform visually.

These anthropometric landmarks and measurements form the foundation upon which differences in the facial features of people with autism can be explained. They provide useful information about the differences in children with autism and may be useful alongside current diagnostic instruments.

2.9 Related works

According to Khosla et al. (2021), most of the work done in similar studies was conducted without removing duplicates, which affected the accuracy of previous studies. To improve accuracy in this study, exact duplicate images were checked from the dataset using the Message-Digest Algorithm 5 (MD5) hash, and it was discovered that the dataset does not have exact duplicates. The authors also checked for near-exact duplicates using the perceptual hashing (pHash) algorithm. It was found that there were 42 near-exact duplicates in the autistic dataset and 94 in the non-autistic dataset.

Three models were used in this study, comparing accuracy to determine which had the highest accuracy in detecting autism from images. The MobileNet model achieved a maximum accuracy of 87% in testing, while InceptionV3 and InceptionResNetV2 achieved accuracies of 86% and 84%, respectively. The maximum runtime for each model was also compared. The InceptionV3 model had a maximum runtime of 125 seconds, the MobileNet model had a maximum runtime of 97 seconds, and the InceptionResNetV2 model had a maximum runtime of 435 seconds per epoch. Given that MobileNet has fewer parameters than InceptionResNetV2 and InceptionV3, it trains much more quickly. Since InceptionResNetV2 uses the most parameters, its runtime is also the longest.

Akter et al. (2021) utilized 2D face images to identify children with Autism Spectrum Disorder in the early stages. They presented a structured transfer learning-based autism face recognition model that can accurately distinguish non-autistic children from autistic children of various origins. Face images of children were collected from the Kaggle data repository, and several transfer-learning-based pre-trained models, machine learning techniques, and deep learning classifiers were used. Different machine learning and deep learning classifiers were tested to determine which performed best. The results showed that, at 90.67%, MobileNet-V1 had the highest test accuracy. However, the suggested framework has certain drawbacks. For example, the quality of the few face images used was not promising.

Bidwe et al. (2023) evaluated the performance of transfer learning methods used for the non-clinical analysis of predicting autism. The dataset was collected from Zenodo, which differed from the datasets used in previous research papers. It included pictures of children's faces, focusing on areas of interest in an image. The study compared the performance of popular transfer learning models, including VGG16, VGG19, InceptionV3, AlexNet, and ResNet50, with the CNN model. Instead of classifying data, all models were utilized to predict autistic features after being fine-tuned for hyperparameters. With prediction accuracy on the test and validation datasets of 84.33% and 87.99%, respectively, InceptionV3 performed significantly better than the other proposed models.

Ruan (2020) presented an effective method for distinguishing between images captured by people with ASD and identifying abnormal visual attention in ASD from a distinct first-person viewpoint. A fine-tuned VGG16 was applied to categorize images of people, places, and objects into two groups: those taken by peers without ASD and those taken by individuals with ASD. All three types of images were well distinguished by the classifier, but pictures of people were especially well classified, with accuracy greater than 80%.

Additionally, they classified videos of the identical actions (brushing teeth and washing face) as coming from peers without ASD or from people with ASD using Graph Convolutional Networks (GCN) applied to the 2D skeleton sequence. This method achieved an accuracy of 80%. The results revealed an efficient and innovative way to determine whether a picture was taken by someone with ASD and to demonstrate abnormal visual attention in ASD from a distinct first-person viewpoint.

Wu et al. (2021) used a machine learning (ML) method to diagnose ASD from recordings of infants between 6 and 36 months to identify particular behaviors. The behaviors of interest included vocalization, directed gazing toward interesting faces or objects, and pleasant affect. The dataset comprised 2,000 three-minute videos in which these characteristics were manually coded by professional raters. Additionally, the dataset contained statistical variables such as the frequency and duration of the aforementioned behaviors in the collected videos, as well as physicians' independent diagnoses of ASD. A two-stage strategy was used to solve the ML challenge: behavior classification and ASD diagnosis prediction. The study achieved 82% accuracy in predicting ASD diagnosis.

Yang (2020) evaluated facial images as a potential screening test for autism using supervised machine learning and a convolutional neural network classifier. A total of 908 facial images obtained from Google search were used in this study; half of the images included photos of children labelled with autism, which may have included some developmental disorders with autistic features, while the other half featured children without autism. The primary finding of this study is that face photos classified as "autism" and normal controls belong to two separate manifolds. The deep learning model achieved an accuracy of 90%, and distinct patterns were discovered to be concentrated in the lips and eyes.

Kalaiselvi et al. (2021) compared four different CNN architectures to detect autism from facial expressions of children. The models used in this were VGG19, Resnet50, InceptionV3, and Neural Architecture Search Network (NASNetLarge) models. The NASNetLarge model gave the highest accuracy of 87.50% and a loss of 0.372 compared to the other three children. The dataset contained 1648 images of facial expressions of autistic and non-autistic children.

Table 2 displays an overview of previously discussed research studies, including their technique, datasets, results, and limitations.

2.10 Research gap covered by current study

Autism can be diagnosed both clinically and non-clinically (Bidwe et al. 2023). Clinical analysis is conducted by examining differences in the brain images of children. On the other hand, non-clinical analysis can be carried out through gaze analysis of the eyes, in which different characteristics such as attentiveness, eye movement, and posture are taken into account to determine autistic tendencies. There is no single universal medical test, such as a blood test, capable of classifying a person as autistic (Bauer and Msall 2011).

Thus, physicians observe how young children behave and pay attention to their parents' concerns. Traditional non-clinical analytic methods rely on the subjective assessments of individual clinicians, which can introduce bias and variability in diagnosing a patient. In contrast, deep learning models enable diagnostics to be conducted in a more systematic and precise manner, eliminating manual errors and providing much more accurate results. The application of deep learning in autism detection has the potential to accelerate the diagnostic process, even in low-income communities, because deep learning algorithms are capable of accurately identifying faces, thereby enhancing healthcare services.

The observed research gap shows that although some studies have explored the use of facial feature analysis and deep learning to diagnose autism in children, there is still room for improvement in making this method more effective. This study aims to improve the accuracy of existing deep learning models for detecting autism by customizing them to specific facial traits and behavioral characteristics.

Additionally, while many studies have achieved high accuracy, the specific facial features used by the models in detecting autism have not been clearly identified. This study intends to reveal the specific facial features that deep learning models utilize for autism detection.

Table 2: An overview of previously discussed research studies.

Author	Dataset	Methodology	Comments/ Accuracy	Limitation
Khosla et al. (2021)	Kaggle Dataset –2936 images	InceptionV3, InceptionResNetV2 and MobileNet	Near exact duplicate data was removed to improve the accuracy	The 87% accuracy, while good, still leaves room for misclassification
Akter et al. (2021)	2936 images	MobileNet-V1 Dense-Net121 ResNet50	90.67 % 83.67% 80%	Low-quality images used
Bidwe et al. (2023)	Zenodo images of children faces focused on an image	InceptionV3	84.33%	The accuracy can be improved
Ruan (2020)	1672 images	VGG16 Graph Convolutional Networks (GCN)	80%	The results revealed an innovative way to determine if a picture may have been taken by someone with ASD and demonstrate abnormal visual attention in ASD from a distinct first-person viewpoint.
Wu et al. 2021)	2000 videos	CNN	82%	The accuracy can be improved
Yang (2020)	Google images using search engine - 908 photographs (454 per group)	Convolutional Neural Network, Supervised machine learning	The author provided preliminary evidence of mood imagery for autism-like features using deep learning	The dataset is relatively small for deep learning applications.
Kalaiselvi et al. (2021)	1648 facial images	NASNetLarge	87.50%	Accuracy can be improved

3. Research Methodology and Planning

This section describes the research method and planning for utilizing deep learning to diagnose autism in children through facial feature analysis. The Convolutional Neural Network (CNN) is used in this study. It is a type of neural network that is highly effective in image detection. The CNN learns the filters that, in traditional algorithms, were hand-engineered. Significant progress has been made in pre-trained image classification algorithms in recent years, providing researchers with effective solutions (Livinus 2024).

A pre-trained model has undergone training to address a problem that is similar to the current one, utilizing a substantial benchmark dataset (Al-Banna and Al-Mashhadany 2023). Model weights and parameters are obtained using transfer learning for a pre-trained model, saving time and producing more accurate models faster than if the model were created from scratch. In this study, the following pre-trained models are adopted: DenseNet201, Xception, Visual Geometry Group (VGG) 19, ResNet-50, and InceptionV3. These models will be evaluated, and the model with the highest accuracy will be used to visualize the high-dimensional features of the images in a two-dimensional environment. Additionally, comprehensive insights into the decision-making process of each model will be provided. This study proposes modifying the CNN model for image detection to achieve higher accuracy.

3.1 Research design

Figure 2 shows the research design used in this study, and is explained below.

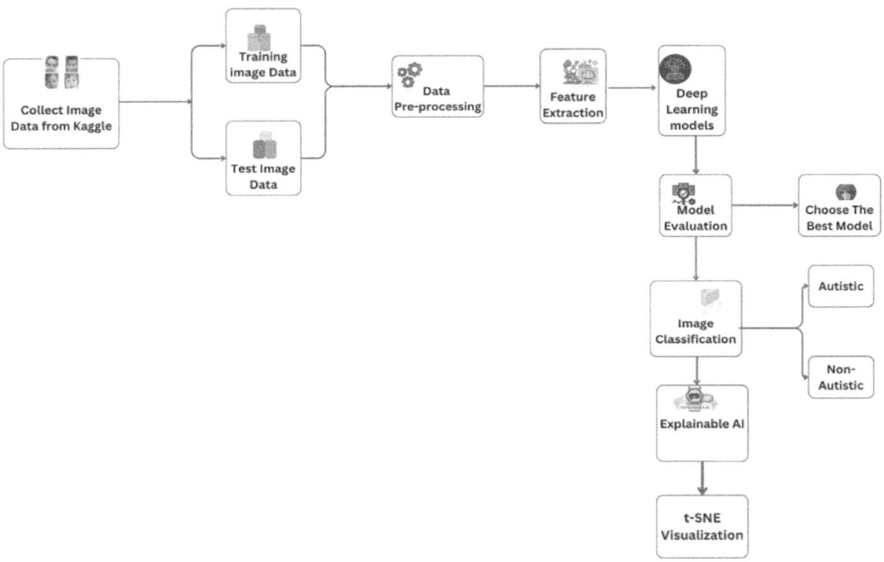

Figure 2: Research design for the Study.

a. Data collection

The dataset contains 2,886 colored 2D face images of children between the ages of 2 and 14, with the majority of the images representing children between the ages of 2 and 8. Some information is not included in the dataset, such as the child's socioeconomic status, ethnicity, ASD severity score, and clinical history. The dataset is divided into two subfolders, autistic and non-autistic, within each of the three folders: training, validation, and test. There are 2,526 images in the training set, while the test and validation datasets are evenly distributed, each containing 280 and 80 images, respectively.

b. Data preprocessing and augmentation

The first step in preparing data is data cleaning, which includes removing errors, duplicates, and outliers. It also includes removing unnecessary data points, adding structure to the information, and managing missing values (Kwak and Kim 2017). However, no values are missing in this dataset, and all duplicate data has been removed. The images are normalized and resized according to the requirements of each model. Preprocessing techniques were applied to the dataset to enhance analytical outcomes and ensure that the information was in the optimal format for the models. Data augmentation is a technique used to artificially increase the quantity of the dataset by manipulating images in different ways, such as flipping, rotating, or cropping them. This could enhance the model's robustness and applicability. The human eye can clearly distinguish that this is the same image even after certain changes have been done. However, the image will be viewed as a fresh sample by the models because the pixels are now in a different location.

c. Feature extraction from images

The technique of obtaining pertinent and significant characteristics or representations from unprocessed data is known as feature extraction (Salau and Jain 2019). Feature extraction is a crucial step in many data analysis domains, including image processing, natural language processing, and signal processing. It reduces data dimensionality, identifies significant patterns, and facilitates efficient machine learning or data analysis.

Deep Learning models such as CNNs can extract features from raw inputs and make accurate predictions. This excellent predictive capability and good feature extraction from raw data have made CNN popular, specifically in computer vision (Kuttichira et al. 2023). The study aims to find and extract useful features from facial images that correctly classify children's images. Facial traits such as eye-gazing patterns and facial expressions can provide important information that may be used to identify autistic children.

3.2 Deep learning models

There are various classifications for deep learning, but some of the main ones are Convolutional Neural Networks (CNN), Recurrent Neural Networks (RNNs), and Variants and Unsupervised Learning/Pretrained Networks (Alzubaidi et al. 2021). CNN models are used in this study because, in a variety of computer vision tasks—including semantic segmentation, object detection, and image classification—CNNs have demonstrated outstanding performance due to improvements in processing power, the availability of large training datasets, and the application of transfer learning for adaptable classification (McCann et al. 2017).

Transfer learning is a technique used in deep learning that allows models to use the knowledge they have learned from one task to perform better on related tasks (Ribani and Marengoni 2019). When applied to facial images, CNN models with a transfer learning approach can significantly enhance early screening for autism spectrum disorder.

Feature learning and classification processes are combined as the main goal of building a CNN (Rana and Chauhan 2021). Recently, pattern recognition and image categorization have seen notable advancements with CNNs. The following models will be used in this study.

DenseNet201

This model is made up of layers called "Dense blocks," where each block consists of multiple convolutional layers that are intimately connected to every layer that came before it (Pramesti et al. 2023). This makes it possible for all layers to obtain information from the network, which minimizes the need to manage features that are not necessary and improves information movement throughout the network. The DenseNet-201 uses a condensed network because of the capacity of subsequent layers to reuse features. This enables an incredibly parametrically efficient model that improves performance and increases diversity in the input of succeeding layers (Lee et al. 2019).

With 201 convolutional layers, DenseNet201 has the advantages of reduced parameters, good feature distribution, fewer vanishing-gradient difficulties, and feature reusability (Akhtar et al. 2022). In the DenseNet201 architecture, direct connections are provided from all previous layers to all subsequent layers to increase connectivity.

Downsampling occurs at Dense Blocks in DenseNet, which are separated by Transition Layers. Each Transition Layer consists of an average pooling layer with batch normalization (BN) and a 1×1 convolutional layer. Eventually, the transition layer's outputs flow into the dense layers. The average pooling layer is converted into a 2×2 max pooling layer to optimize network utility. Each convolutional layer undergoes prior BN (Batch Normalization), which helps reduce model complexity. The hyperparameter k represents the network growth rate, allowing DenseNet to achieve state-of-the-art results. The proposed detection layers are fully integrated and connected to the classification layers, with pooling layers removed.

Xception

Xception stands for the Extreme version of Inception, with a modified depthwise separable convolution. It replaces Inception modules with depthwise separable convolutions (Chollet 2017). Compared to InceptionV3, this update enables more efficient use of model parameters, leading to better performance in image classification tasks. The data passes through the entry flow initially, followed by the middle flow (which is repeated eight times) and the exit flow at the end. Batch normalization comes after each layer of convolution and separable convolution.

The architecture has residual connections implemented throughout, though the linear residual connections were only included in all the modules except for the first and the last (Chollet 2017). These skip connections also aid in the gradient flow, thus making it possible to train deeper networks and letting each block learn differences from the inputs.

The dimensions of the input image are $299 \times 299 \times 3$. The input is processed by the entry flow, which extracts features of $19 \times 19 \times 728$ dimensions. As the feature map passes through nine rounds of convolution layers in the central block, residual connections guarantee that each layer's output is the maximum value.

Visual Geometry Group (VGG) 19

The VGG19 architecture is a convolutional neural network that uses 3 × 3-dimensional small convolution filters. The network, which has 19 weighted layers and is a major advancement over earlier designs, exemplifies the advantages of deeper networks (Ravindaran et al. 2023). By increasing the network's depth, this architecture enables the model to extract more complex features from the images. The input images for this model must be in RGB format and have a size of 224 × 224. To prepare the image for output, all that needs to be done is subtract each pixel's mean RGB value from the training set. Each of the convolutional layers of the VGG19 architecture has a small 3 × 3 receptive field, and together they process input images. Five max-pooling layers are used for spatial pooling and applied after certain convolutional layers. Three completely linked layers are used after the convolutional layers. The depth of the convolutional layers varies based on the particular design.

The network consists of five max-pooling layers and sixteen convolutions with ReLUs in between. The number of filter maps in the convolutional layers increases from 64 to 512. After the convolutions, a linear classifier is used, consisting of three fully connected (fc) layers with dropout in between. The last layer has 1,000 features, while the first two have 4,096 each. A softmax function is applied in the final fc layer, converting values into probabilities for classification in 1,000 ImageNet categories (Srivastava et al. 2014).

ResNet-50

ResNet, which stands for Residual Network, refers to the residual blocks that form the architecture of the network. ResNet-50 consists of 50 layers, divided into five blocks, each containing multiple residual blocks. The network can learn more accurate representations of input data by using residual blocks, which allow information from previous layers to be retained (Koonce 2021). One important aspect of ResNet-50 is skip connections, also known as identity connections. A block diagram of the ResNet model's is shown.

This model's input size is 224 × 224, just like the VGG networks, where the convolutional layers are 3 × 3 filters, and they adhere to some straightforward designs: The output of the layers with the same number of filters is the same. To maintain the time complexity per layer, halving the convolved output size results in twice as many filters. A 1000-way fully-connected layer with softmax and an average pooling layer completes the model. Compared to VGG nets, this model has fewer filters and is less complex. ResNet101 and ResNet152 are two further variations of this model. Figure 5 displays the ResNet50 network's setup layers.

A residual connection links the output of an earlier convolutional layer to the input of a later convolutional layer, skipping several intermediate steps. The input of the mainstream model and the convolutional prior are combined using a simple summation. Skip connections allow outputs from earlier layers to be combined with outputs from later layers. From an architectural perspective, any layer that negatively affects model performance in a standard network is bypassed due to the presence of skip connections.

InceptionV3

The primary goal of Inception v3 is to reduce processing power consumption by altering the previous Inception architectures. Inception Networks (GoogLeNet/Inception v1) have demonstrated more computational efficiency than VGGNet concerning the quantity of parameters produced by the network and the economic cost (memory and other resources) spent (Szegedy et al. 2015). Several network optimization strategies have been proposed in an Inception v3 model to relax the constraints and facilitate model adaptability. Some methods used are factorized convolutions, regularization, dimension reduction, and parallelized calculations. InceptionV3 reduces the number of parameters by splitting the convolution into smaller convolutions. The pre-trained model Inceptionv3 took advantage of transfer learning, allowing the neural network's trained knowledge to be transferred to the new model in the form of parametric weights. It employs Google's 48-layer CNN architecture.

Inception-v1 (GoogLeNet) splits some 7×7 and 5×5 convolutional layers into multiple consecutive 3×3 convolutional layers. Inception-v3, which uses a similar concept, divides the symmetric $n \times n$ convolutional layers into two asymmetric layers, namely $1 \times n$ and $n \times 1$ convolutional layers. For instance, it splits the 3×3 convolutional layer into 1×3 and 3×1 convolutional layers, reducing the number of parameters from nine to six (Phumthong and Supratid 2021). This method of asymmetrical splitting can increase feature diversity, creating three new Inception modules.

The three Inception modules are combined to generate Inception-v3, which is then completed by running BN on all convolutional layers and fully connected layers of the auxiliary classification network, factorizing the first 7×7 convolutional layer in GoogLeNet into three 3×3 convolutional layers. The network increases categorization accuracy even more.

3.3 Explainable AI (XAI)

This is a field of AI research that aims to address the problem of transparency and interpretability in using Artificial Intelligence by creating models and algorithms that are simple for people to comprehend and use (Ribeiro et al. 2016). The purpose of XAI is to make the inner workings of AI systems transparent and understandable so that humans may better comprehend and make judgments based on the reasoning behind AI's decisions (Tiwari 2023).

The gradient-weighted class activation mapping (Grad-CAM) method is one of the more recent techniques that may provide an explanatory capacity for the CNN models. It generates heat maps that potentially explain the classification outcomes (Chien et al. 2022). Grad-CAM is useful for image classification tasks as it allows us to pinpoint the specific areas of an image that impacted the model's labelling choice.

3.4 t-SNE Visualization

A common method for reducing dimensionality and presenting high-dimensional data in a lower-dimensional environment is t-SNE (t-distributed Stochastic Neighbor Embedding) (Soni et al. 2020). It helps visualize clusters or patterns in complicated datasets because it attempts to maintain the local structures and interactions between data points. In this case, the retrieved features are flattened, transformed into a one-dimensional vector, and then scaled to a common value via normalization (Mukherjee 2017). The t-SNE algorithm, which maps high-dimensional features to a lower-dimensional space while maintaining the local structures and relationships between the features, is then applied to the reduced-dimensional features. The t-SNE algorithm iteratively optimizes a cost function to produce a low-dimensional embedding of the data after computing the pairwise similarity between data points based on their feature representations (Khot 2016). The reduced-dimensional representations are produced when the t-SNE algorithm projects the features onto a lower-dimensional space and are plotted using a visualization method like scatter plots. In the scatter plot, every data point is represented as a point, and the spatial proximity of the points indicates how similar they were in the initial high-dimensional feature space (Rosero-Montalvo et al. 2017). In a scatter plot, linkages between data points that might not be seen in the original high-dimensional space can be shown, and clusters or patterns of points might shed light on the underlying structure of the data.

3.5 Data source

The dataset used in this study consists of images, and the method of data collection is observation. This approach allows for the extraction of facial features and patterns that may indicate autism, providing data for deep learning algorithms. The images were obtained from Kaggle, an open-source platform with a large collection of image datasets.

3.6 Hardware and Software

An 11th Gen Intel(R) Core (TM) i5-1145G7 with a Dell XPS 15 9500 model laptop @ 2.60 GHz, 1.50 GHz, 64-bit operating system, and x64-based processor was used as local runtime.

Google Colab was used to create and execute the algorithms in Python with other deep learning frameworks like TensorFlow and Keras. OpenCV is used for image processing, while Matplotlib and Seaborn are used for visualization.

4. Methodology

This chapter presents the findings and key results obtained from the collected and preprocessed data using the proposed deep learning method for diagnosing autism in children by analyzing their facial features. The chapter aims to provide a detailed analysis of the results, share interpretations, and describe conclusions drawn in the context of autism diagnosis and the application of deep learning in healthcare. By employing deep learning techniques for facial characteristic recognition, this study aims to develop an efficient, non-intrusive, and precise screening tool for children with autism. Such an approach could significantly reduce the time required for the diagnostic process, increase the number of early interventions, and ultimately have a positive impact on the futures of children with ASD.

4.1 Dataset preparation and augmentation

As with any deep learning approach, the quality of the results depends on the quality of the data used for training the algorithm. Therefore, dataset preparation and augmentation are crucial steps in ensuring reliable model performance. This section describes the measures taken to enhance the dataset quality for training and testing. The steps for data preparation and augmentation are outlined to improve the performance of the proposed Convolutional Neural Network (CNN) model. Proper data preprocessing ensures that the model learns effectively and generalizes well to unseen data.

4.2 Data preparation

The process of converting raw image data into a format that can be used and understood is known as image preprocessing. This step enhances specific attributes necessary for computer vision applications while removing unwanted distortions. Preprocessing is a crucial initial step before supplying image data to deep learning models. The following techniques were used in preprocessing the images:

i. Normalization: The pixel values in the images were divided by 255 to bring them into the range of 0 to 1. The pixel values are normalized here to make them balanced and compatible with the models and algorithms that may be used.
ii. Resizing: The images are resized according to the dimensions required for the model. 224 × 224 pixels was applied to DenseNet201, ResNet50 and VGG19. While 299 × 299 was used for InceptionV3 and Xception.
iii. Shuffling: Shuffling was set to false for the validation and test sets to maintain consistency with the training phase and result replication. For the case of the training set, shuffling was made possible to allow for some level of randomness so that the machine could generalize well.

4.3 Data augmentation

Due to the training set's limited size, data augmentation is essential to increase the quantity of training samples. Several kinds of augmentation strategies were used to artificially create a larger set of images. Exposing the model to as many data variations as possible increases the chance that the model will generalize.

i. Shear Transformation: A shear range of 0.1 was applied, slightly slanting the images. This transformation is achieved by moving every pixel of the image in a specific direction to create a distortion effect that one gets when camera's angle of view is changed.

ii. Horizontal Flipping: Horizontal flipping was used for the images. A single-sided feature can sometimes lead to confusion during training because the human face is generally symmetrical. Understanding the features of both sides of the face is possible with a full horizontal flip.
iii. Zooming: A zoom range of 0.1 was used, allowing for slight zooming in or out of the images. This enables the model to differentiate between the objects in the images regardless of their size.

4.4 Model training

After preprocessing the data, the models were trained using various layers. Five pre-trained models—DenseNet201, Xception, VGG19, ResNet-50, and InceptionV3—were used, with their weights initialized from training on the ImageNet dataset. When working on image classification using deep learning models, the training process is divided into transfer learning and fine-tuning steps. All models were initialized with parameters obtained from pre-training on ImageNet, which provides a strong foundation for feature learning. The initial layers of these models were stripped off and fine-tuned to adapt them for binary classification tasks. Table 3 provides an overview of the parameters used for training the models.

Custom layers are added, including a flattening layer to convert the 2D feature maps into a vector, a dense layer consisting of 512 units with ReLU activation to introduce non-linearity, a dropout layer with a rate of 0.5 to prevent overfitting, and a final fully connected layer with a single node and a sigmoid activation function for binary classification.

The models are compiled using the Adam optimizer with a learning rate of 0.0001, with binary cross-entropy as the loss function and accuracy as the primary evaluation metric. Training is conducted for 100 epochs with 158 steps per epoch. Early stopping is used to monitor the validation loss and halt training if no improvement is observed for ten consecutive epochs. A model checkpoint callback saves the model with the lowest validation loss. Each model is evaluated based on accuracy, precision, F1 score, recall, best epoch, and training time to determine the most effective model for detecting autism from images. The results are presented in Table 3.

Table 3: Training parameters.

Parameter	Value
Number of Epoch	100
Steps per Epoch	158
Learning Rate	0.001
Loss function	Binary Crossentropy
Activation Function	Relu
Classification Layer	Sigmoid
Optimizer	Adam
Metric	Accuracy (acc)

5. Results

5.1 Prediction probability

The Table 4 shows the prediction probability for each model for both autistic and non-autistic images. The probability values represent the model's prediction for an image to belong to the autistic (ASD) or non-autistic (NASD) images. These probabilities capture how well each model performs; higher percentages indicate the model's greater confidence in the classification.

The ResNet and InveptionV3 showed a prediction of 1.00 indicating 100% probability for both autistic and non-autistic images. Meanwhile, VGG19, Xception and DenseNet201 predicted 100% probability for the non-autistic images and 99%, 92% and 90%, respectively, for the autistic images.

5.2 Evaluation metrics

ResNet50 demonstrates excellent performance across all evaluation metrics (see Table 5). With an accuracy of 0.971, it is the most accurate model in this evaluation. The high precision of 0.992 suggests a low rate of false positives, while the recall of 0.95 indicates strong identification of true positives. The balanced F1 score of 0.970 confirms the model's stability and overall performance. It achieves peak performance at epoch 22 and is highly efficient in terms of training time, making it the best model for classifying autism in this study.

In precision, InceptionV3 achieves the highest score of 1.0, which implies it has no false positive errors. The accuracy of the results is also satisfactory and amounts to 0.953; in addition, the obtained F1 score equals 0.951, which is also very high and proves the system's reliability. However, recall is less than the ResNet50, that is, 0.907, meaning some positive cases have been left out. Comparatively, InceptionV3 is the most efficient model in terms of training time duration, and it took 497.74 seconds. The model starts converging at epoch 18, which signifies that its performance has reached its peak. This model is best suited for situations where false positives are extremely unadvisable.

VGG19 has the highest recall of 0.964, meaning it minimizes false negatives and is highly effective in true identification. However, the precision of this model is only 0.894, indicating a higher percentage of type II errors, meaning more false samples were included in the set of positive results. Its accuracy is 0.925, and its F1 score is 0.927, which are both strong but not as high as some other models. VGG19 takes 2749.82 seconds to train and reaches peak performance at 87 epochs. Thus, it can be considered inefficient in terms of computational cost. In applications such as screening, where it is crucial to identify positives, this model is appropriate despite its higher number of false positives.

Xception model reached an accuracy of 90.3% while its precision was considered high at 97.5%, meaning it was very good at identifying non-autistic persons. However, it had the lowest recall at 82.9% among the various models, which shows the high rate of omitted diagnoses of autism. Xception required 100 epochs to fine-tune the model and had the highest training time of 3956.94 seconds. Though it

Table 4: Probability Prediction.

	ResNet50	InceptionV3	VGG19	Xception	DenseNet201
ASD	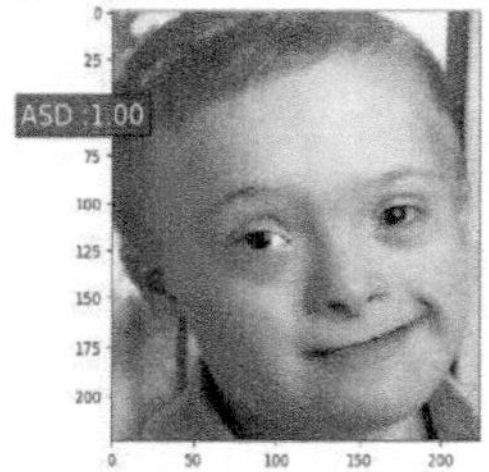	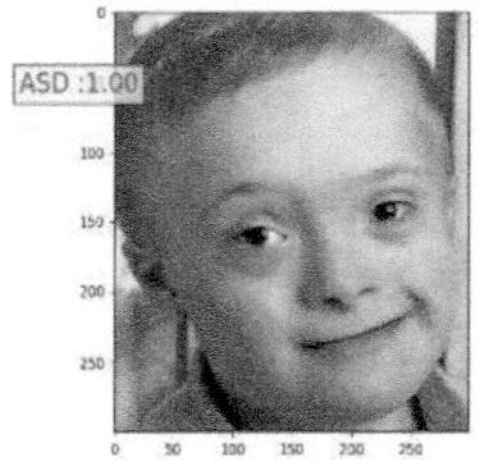	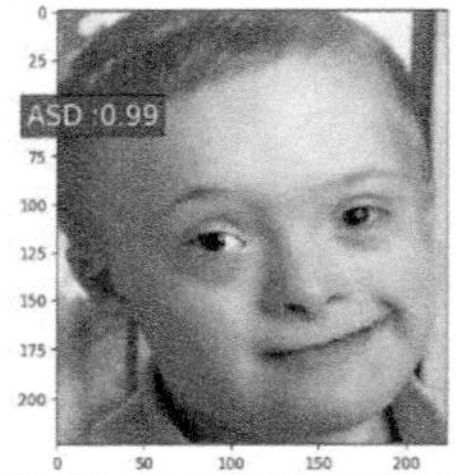	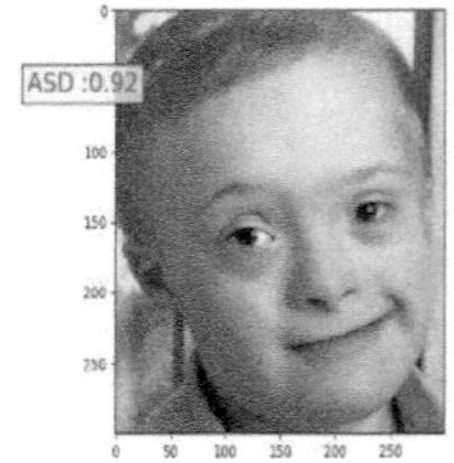	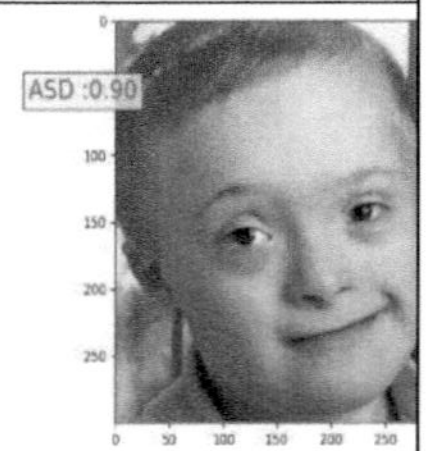
NASD	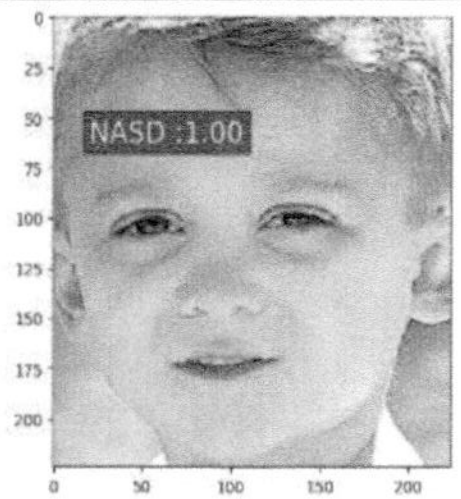	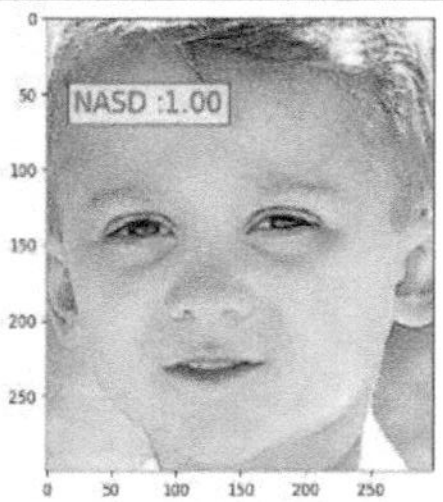	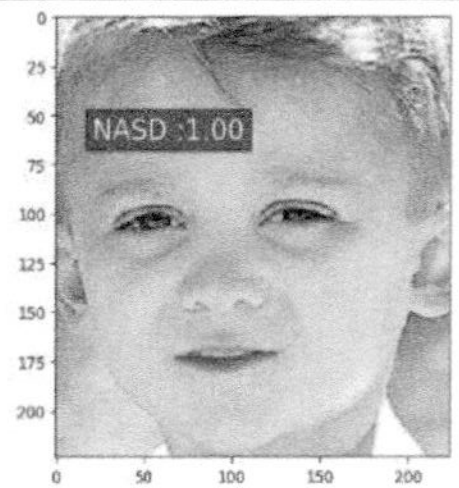	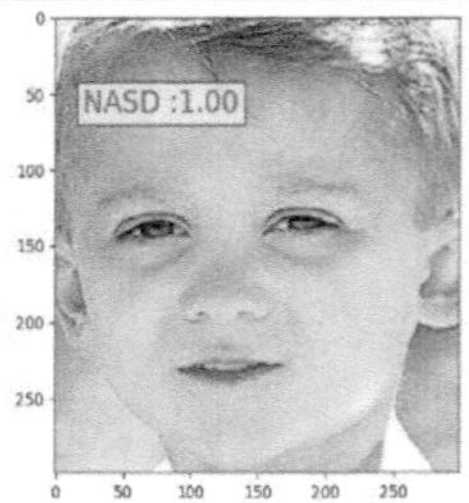	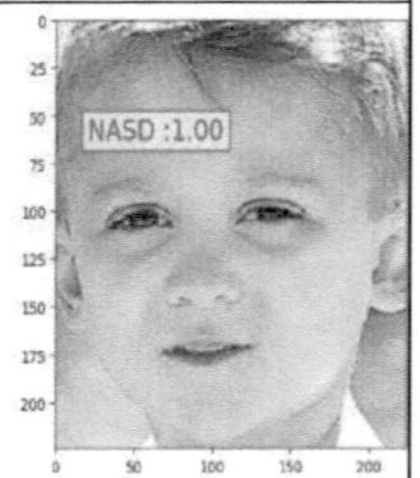

Table 5: Evaluation metrics for the models.

Algorithm	Accuracy	Precision	F1 score	Recall	Best Epoch	Training Time (seconds)
ResNet50	0.971	0.992	0.970	0.95	22	912.57
InceptionV3	0.953	1.0	0.951	0.907	18	497.74
VGG19	0.925	0.894	0.927	0.964	87	2749.82
Xception	0.903	0.975	0.896	0.829	100	3956.94
DenseNet201	0.939	0.977	0.936	0.9	76	2544.08

performs better in terms of precision, it has higher training time and comparatively lower recall values, and hence, it is not suitable in situations where all the cases of autism must be identified.

DenseNet201 exhibits reasonable prediction performance, with high precision (0.977) and relatively high recall (0.9), yielding an F1 score of 0.936 and an accuracy of 0.939. It requires significant training time and reaches its best performance after 76 epochs. Hence, DenseNet201 is a well-rounded model suitable for applications where precision and recall need to be balanced without excessively high computational demands.

5.3 Performance of the ResNet50 model

The training and validation loss are reflected in Figure 3. The plot indicates that loss has reduced over the epochs, which means the model is reducing errors and performing better for training and validation sets.

While Graph b shows the training accuracy curve is very high at the start of epochs and stays high throughout the entire epoch training period, such consistently high accuracy values for both training and valid sets mean that the model is again learning properly, and the model's performance will also be good on unseen data.

The higher training and validation accuracy value, combined with the lower and constant loss value, proves that the model is capable of learning from the data and performing well on the unseen data.

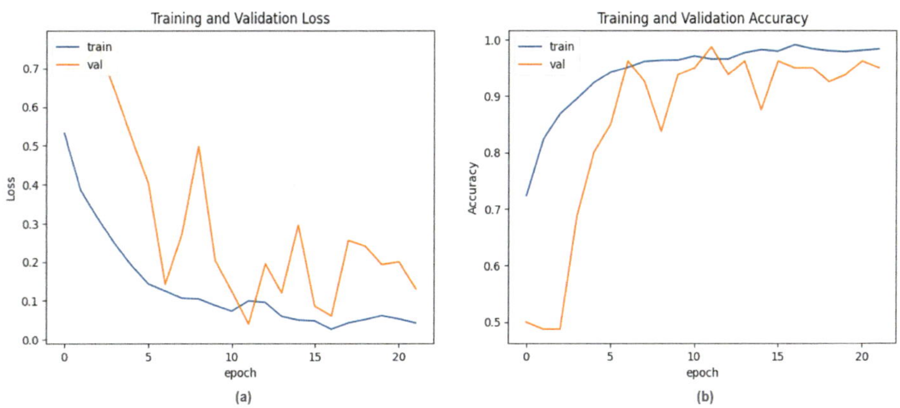

Figure 3: Performance of ResNet50. (a) Loss; (b) Accuracy.

ResNet50 has a high classification capability of accurately identifying individuals with autism and only a few missed cases. This helps to ensure that almost all people with autism are accurately diagnosed. ResNet50 offers a better result, with the least number of false positives among the other models, while yielding the highest true negative and remaining equally effective in detecting autism instances. This makes ResNet50 particularly beneficial in terms of accuracy and could help reduce unnecessary anxiety and follow-up medical visits due to misdiagnosis. The model also performs well in correctly predicting negative cases, reducing false positive rates and the resulting stress for individuals without autism.

5.4 Performance of the InceptionV3 model

The Graph a in Figure 4 shows fluctuation in the validation loss, especially when compared to training loss, which is relatively stable most of the time. This may indicate the model's overfitting to the training data and ability to generalize properly to unseen data in the validation data set.

Graph b shows that the training accuracy gradually increases, while the validation accuracy fluctuates. The initial rise in validation accuracy followed by fluctuations suggests that the model is learning; however, the continuous increase in training accuracy alongside inconsistent validation accuracy may indicate overfitting.

The confusion matrix for the test images provides a detailed breakdown of the InceptionV3 model's performance in classifying autistic and non-autistic individuals. The model correctly predicted 131 images as autistic, depicted in blue in the confusion matrix, meaning the model's predictions for autism matched the actual data 131 times. However, 9 images were wrongly classified by the inceptionV3 model as not belonging to the autistic class when they did. This falls under the category of False negative and is known as misclassification. The model correctly predicted 128 samples, which can be categorized as false negatives, for the non-autistic class. Additionally, only 12 images were incorrectly classified, referred to as false positive.

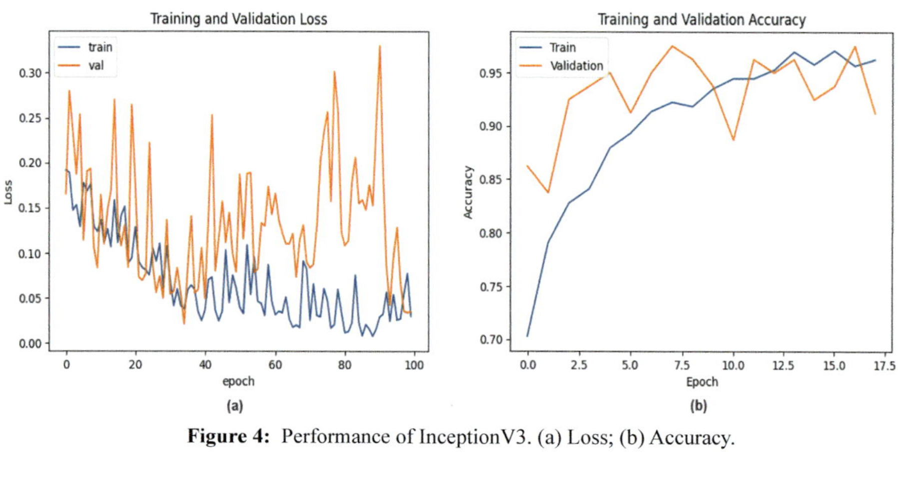

Figure 4: Performance of InceptionV3. (a) Loss; (b) Accuracy.

5.5 Performance of the VGG19 model

In Figure 5, Graph a shows that training loss is initially high but decreases continuously with each epoch. This suggests that the model is learning and improving its ability to predict outcomes for the training dataset. The validation loss initially follows the same decreasing trend but eventually plateaus and slightly increases, indicating that the model starts memorizing the training data. As a result, it performs well on the training set but struggles with the validation data.

In Graph b, the training accuracy rises from a low percentage and steadily increases to a high value, approaching but not reaching 100%. This indicates that during training, most of the data is correctly classified by the model. The validation accuracy also increases at first, stabilizes, and then slightly declines, suggesting overfitting—the model stops improving on independent validation data after a certain number of iterations and may even degrade in performance.

Out of 280 test images, the model correctly classified 133 images as autistic (true positives) and 136 images as non-autistic (true negatives). However, there were 4 false positives, where non-autistic individuals were incorrectly classified as autistic, and 7 false negatives, where autistic individuals were mistakenly labeled as non-autistic. Overall, the model performs strongly, achieving high accuracy in both autism identification and correct classification of non-autistic cases.

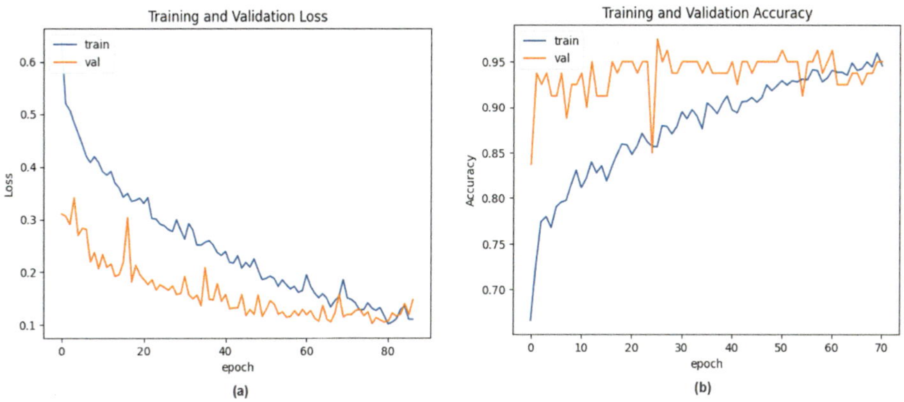

Figure 5: Performance of VGG19. (a) Loss; (b) Accuracy.

5.6 Performance of the Xception model

Graph a in Figure 6 shows a gradual decrease in loss as the model processes the training data. This downward trend indicates that the model's accuracy improves over time when applied to the training dataset. The validation loss curve follows a similar pattern, suggesting that the model performs well on new data.

Graph b in Figure 6 displays an upward trend, showing that with each epoch, the model becomes more accurate in predicting training samples. The validation accuracy curve also trends upward, indicating that the model correctly classifies an increasing number of validation samples over time.

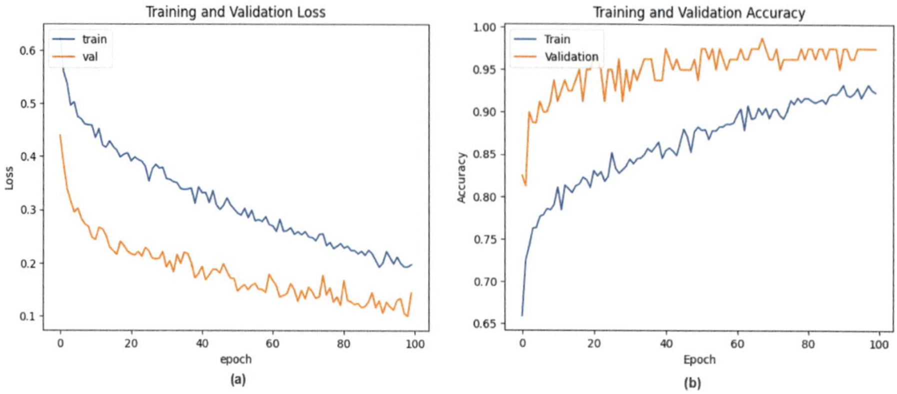

Figure 6: Performance of Xception. (a) Loss; (b) Accuracy.

The model correctly classified 137 images as autistic and wrongly classified 3 images as non-autistic. The low number of false negatives indicates that the model was able to correctly detect a significant number of children with autism. The model produced 24 false positives, representing the number of individuals incorrectly classified as having autism. While these false positives may lead to unnecessary further testing and anxiety, they are generally less critical than missing true cases of autism. A total of 116 individuals were correctly classified as not having autism, further demonstrating the model's effectiveness in identifying children without autism.

5.7 Performance of the DenseNet201

In Graph A, in Figure 7, the training loss continuously decreases, indicating that the model is learning from the training data. The validation loss also declines, though with some fluctuations across a few epochs. This is a normal occurrence, suggesting that while the model is learning, its performance may vary slightly across different validation batches.

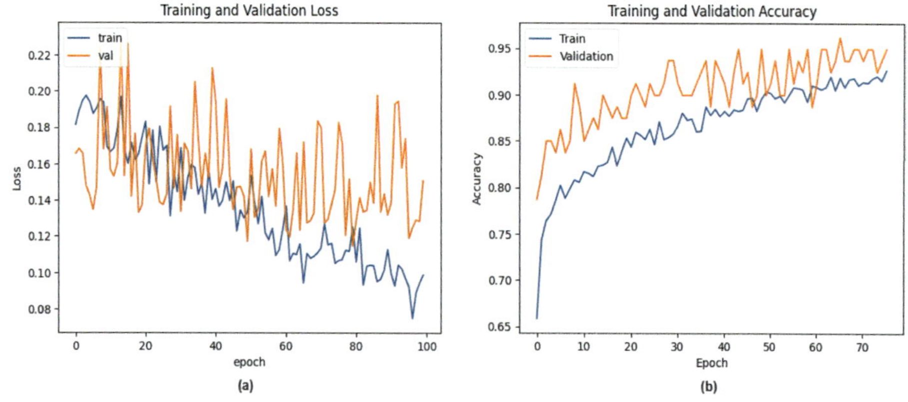

Figure 7: Performance of DenseNet201. (a) Loss; (b) Accuracy.

Graph b shows that the model achieved strong training and validation accuracy, indicating that it is effectively learning the unique features of the dataset. Both training and validation accuracy steadily increase and intersect, confirming that the model is not overfitting and performs well on new, unseen data.

DenseNet201 exhibits a high true positive rate and a low false negative rate, indicating strong accuracy in diagnosing autism. This suggests that the model rarely misses true autism cases, which is crucial for ensuring an accurate diagnosis for affected individuals. Although 14 cases were misclassified, labeling non-autistic individuals as autistic, these individuals can be referred for further testing and evaluation. Additionally, the model effectively rules out most cases that do not have autism, thereby reducing unnecessary concern and additional testing for those with a negative diagnosis.

5.8 Explainable AI using Grad-CAM

The term "explainable AI" refers to an AI system's ability to communicate its decision-making processes in a way that is understandable to humans. Visualization tools such as Grad-CAM help illustrate how neural networks make predictions by highlighting key areas of an input image that influence the classification outcome. By visualizing the model's learned knowledge, Grad-CAM aids in debugging transfer learning models and identifying their limitations.

Table 6 shows the facial feature region in people with autism. Samples were chosen at random from a total of 280 test samples. Grad-CAM indicates where the different models pick up the feature that identifies them as autistic. ResNet50 focuses mostly on the eyes, noses, and lips. The main focus region for InceptionV3 is in the space between the eyes, nose, and lips while the VGG19 model focuses on the lower part of the nose and lips. The Xception mainly concentrates on the areas of the lower nose, like the lips and lower nose. The DenseNet201 focuses on the eyes, the space between the eyes, forehead, and the noses.

5.9 t-SNE visualization

The visualization of data points using t-SNE (t-Distributed Stochastic Neighbor Embedding) is presented in Figure 8. This visualization represents the distribution of features extracted by the ResNet50 model, clearly distinguishing autism cases from non-autism cases. By reducing the high dimensionality of the ResNet50 model to two dimensions, t-SNE enables better interpretation of the data. The findings illustrate the strong classification performance of the ResNet50 model.

The plot divides the figure into two clusters, with blue points representing non-autism cases and red points representing autism cases. This clear separation further confirms that the ResNet50 model has successfully learned discriminative features for detecting autism. The distinction between the autism and non-autism clusters suggests that the model effectively differentiates between the two groups.

However, the t-SNE visualization also identifies a few overlapping cases, suggesting that the model may encounter difficulties in classifying certain instances.

Table 6: Grad-CAM feature map for autistic children using random images from the test dataset.

	Autistic Facial Image	Gradcam Heatmap	Main Focus Area
ResNet50	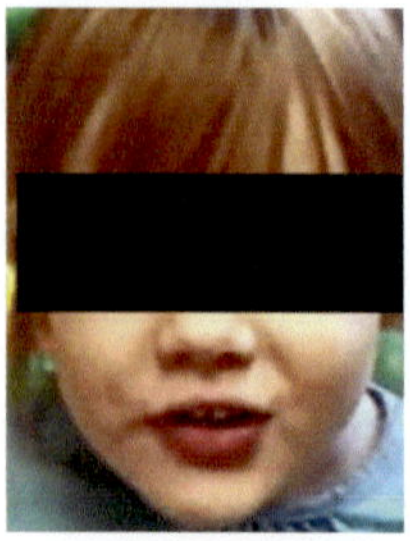	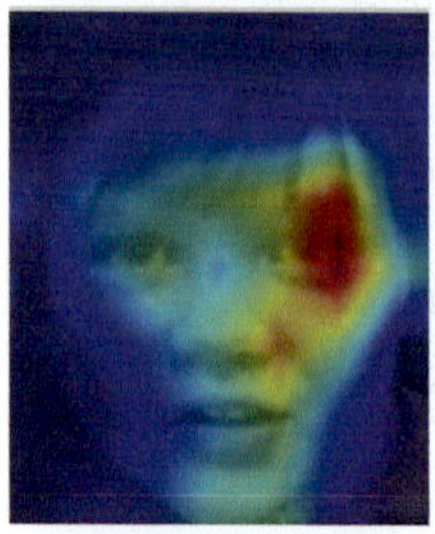	Eyes, nose, and lips
InceptionV3	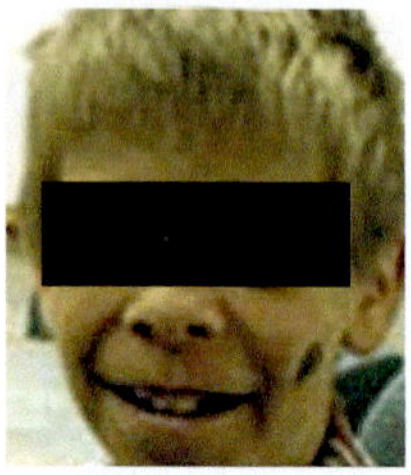	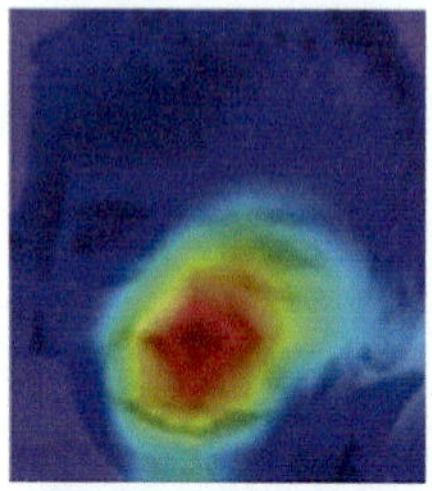	Space between eyes, nose, and lips
VGG19	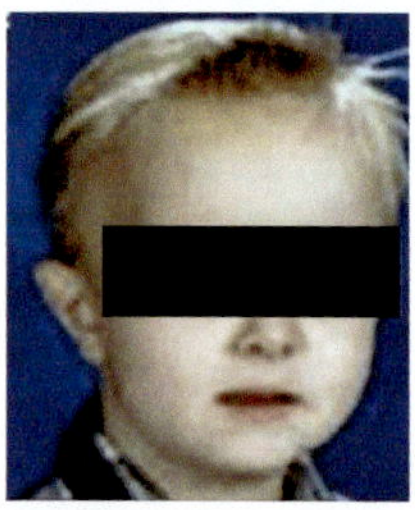	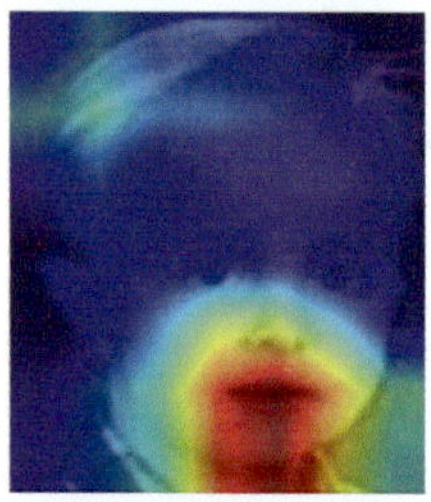	Lower part of the nose and lips
Xception		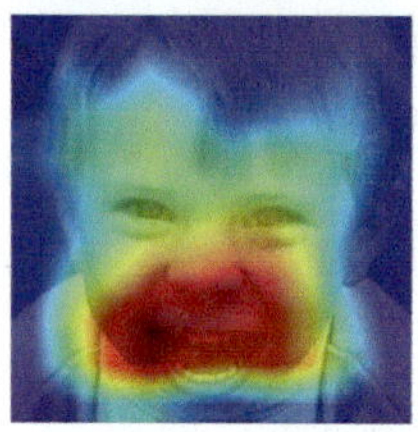	Lower nose and lips
DenseNet201	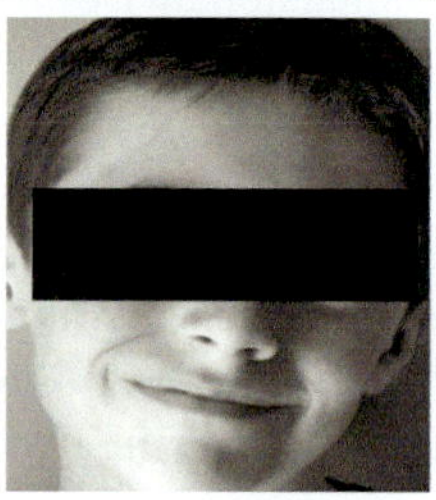	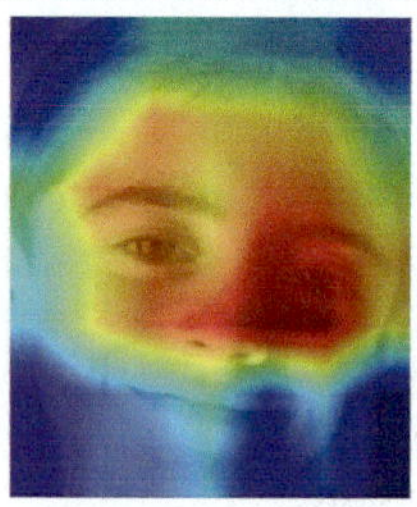	Eyes, space between the eyes, forehead, and the nose

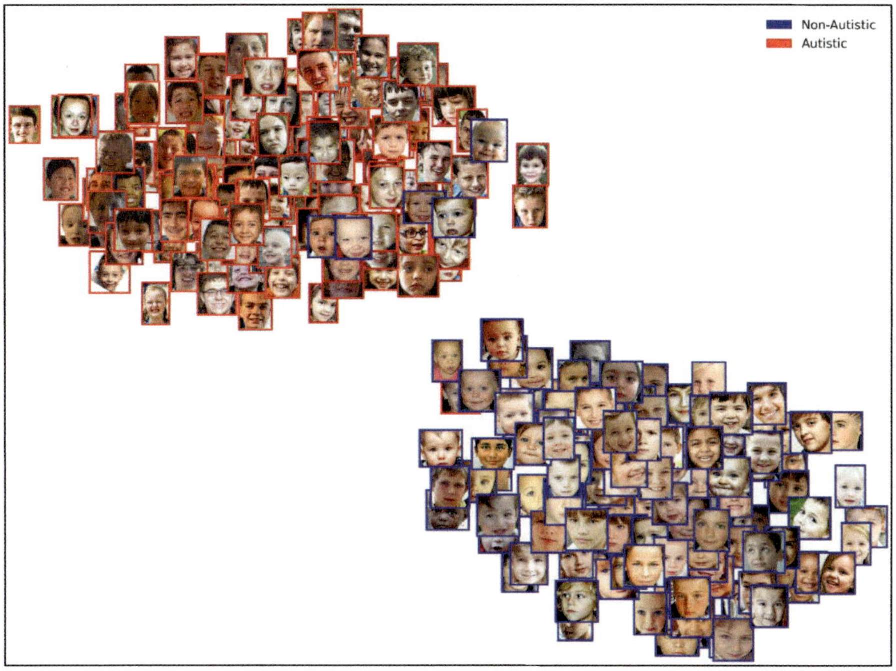

Figure 8: t-SNE Visualization for the ResNet50 model.

This is consistent with real-world medical diagnosis, where some cases exhibit borderline characteristics that can complicate classification.

6. Conclusion and recommendation

This study evaluated the performance of five CNN architectures in detecting autism from images. Five pre-trained models (ResNet50, DenseNet201, VGG19, Xception, and InceptionV3) were applied to the dataset, and the same finetuning layers and optimizers were applied to the model for accurate evaluation and comparison. Based on the evaluation metrics, the ResNet50 model was selected as the most effective model in this study. It achieved the highest accuracy (0.97%) and F1 score (0.97%), a good percentage for recall (0.95), with a relatively short training time (912.57 seconds) compared to the other models. InceptionV3 and DenseNet201 also had good results in the evaluation metrics, with inception having the lowest training time (497.74 seconds) and highest precision (1.0). VGG19 had the highest recall; the other metrics had lower values. Xception also had low evaluation values and a longer training time.

The Grad-CAM was used to visualise the key areas of the facial image that influence the neural network's prediction. ResNet50 focuses mainly on the eyes, noses, and lips. The central focus region for InceptionV3 is in the space between the eyes, nose, and lips, while the VGG19 model focuses on the lower part of the nose and lips. Xception mainly concentrates on the lower nose and lips. The DenseNet201 focuses on the eyes, the space between the eyes, the forehead, and the nose.

T-SNE reduces the high-dimensional feature space obtained from facial images to a lower-dimensional representation in 2D or 3D. This makes it easier to visualize and interpret complex data. The clustering effect for the characteristics collected from autistic and non-autistic classes is visualized using t-distributed Stochastic Neighbor Embedding (t-SNE) plots, which translate high-dimensional data into its two-dimensional equivalents. The ResNet50 model generated the t-SNE (t-Distributed Stochastic Neighbor Embedding) visualization. High-dimensional points are embedded in low dimensions using t-SNE when their relative similarities closely match the genuine labels. When using t-SNE on the high-dimensional features extracted by the ResNet50 model, a lower feature representation is obtained and plotted as a scatter plot. This plot can be interpreted to represent all images where each point refers to an image. Hence, the distance between such points shows the similarity of images or data points in the original high-dimensional space.

Recent research on detecting autism using the same facial images from Kaggle dataset is compared, and the detailed result is displayed in Table 7.

The proposed method in this study (ResNet50) outperformed other models from recent studies, achieving an accuracy of 97%. This is significantly higher than what has been reported for other models in similar research. Since the same Kaggle dataset was used in these studies, the comparison is fair and demonstrates that the proposed method improves accuracy in detecting autism.

However, this study has some limitations related to the dataset used. The Kaggle dataset is the only publicly available dataset, and a larger dataset would be beneficial for training and testing. Attempts to obtain additional datasets from health organizations were unsuccessful due to policy restrictions limiting access to larger and more diverse data sources. Despite this, the study provides valuable insights into developing an automated model that can assist doctors in identifying children with autism. Additionally, the ASD dataset has a non-symmetrical distribution concerning gender, emotions, and facial postures. Furthermore, no specific methodology or attention mechanism was applied in the data collection process. This makes it challenging to establish a normalized pattern or target face regions when evaluating the explainability of CNN models.

Future research could be done in partnership with hospitals or government agencies to provide a large dataset and other patient information. This partnership

Table 7: Comparison of the method with recent research.

Author	Dataset	Suggested Model	Accuracy
Ahmad et al. (2024)	Kaggle	ResNet50	92%
Alsaade and Alzahrani (2022)	Kaggle	Xception	91%
Shobana and Shaik (2021)	Kaggle	VGG19	85%
Kalaiselvi et al. (2021)	Kaggle	NASNEtLarge	87.5%
Khosla et al. (2021)	Kaggle	MobileNet	87%
Proposed Method	Kaggle	ResNet50	97%

can improve the dataset's quality, and the patient information can be used to expand the basis of the model by utilizing multi-modal data based on genetic, behavioral observation, and neuroimages.

Also, more advanced studies can involve participants from different age groups and various geographic regions to increase the effectiveness of the deep learning model. Using cross-sectional data from various developmental stages and geographical areas, researchers can pinpoint age-related biomarkers of autism. This will contribute to the development of a model that would be applicable to various populations and ages with the same level of efficiency, including longitudinal studies to offer additional insights into the progression of autism. Integrating this data with facial images can provide a deeper understanding of autism.

In addition, the range of uses should be expanded to include not only static facial images but also videos of the faces of the candidates. Compared to photo analysis, video analysis captures dynamic expressions and behaviors that are essential for diagnosing autism because they present patterns in expression, gaze, and social interaction that are optimally visible in motion. Incorporating information from the wider context of video data should improve the model's effectiveness in identifying autism-related features, creating a richer understanding of the subject.

References

Ahmad, I., Rashid, J., Faheem, M., Akram, A., Khan, N.A. and Amin, R.U. 2024. Autism spectrum disorder detection using facial images: A performance comparison of pretrained convolutional neural networks. *Healthcare Technology Letters*, 11(4): 227–239. Available at: https://doi.org/10.1049/htl2.12073.

Aiman, U. and Vishwakarma, V.P. 2017. Face recognition using modified deep learning neural network. In 2017 8th International Conference on Computing, Communication and Networking Technologies (ICCCNT). *IEEE*, pp. 1–5. Available at: https://doi.org/10.1109/ICCCNT.2017.8203981.

Akhtar, M.J., Mahum, R., Butt, F.S., Amin, R., El-Sherbeeny, A.M., Lee, S.M. et al. 2022. A robust framework for object detection in a traffic surveillance system. *Electronics*, 11(21): 3425. Available at: https://doi.org/10.3390/electronics11213425.

Akter, T., Ali, M.H., Khan, M.I., Satu, M.S., Uddin, M.J., Alyami, S.A. et al. 2021. Improved transfer-learning-based facial recognition framework to detect autistic children at an early stage. *Brain Sciences*, 11(6): 734. Available at: https://doi.org/10.3390/brainsci11060734.

Al-Banna, A.A. and Al-Mashhadany, A.K. 2023. Automatic Text summarization based on pre-trained models. In 2023 Al-Sadiq International Conference on Communication and Information Technology (AICCIT). *IEEE*, pp. 80–84. Available at: https://doi.org/10.1109/AICCIT57614.2023.10218006.

Aldridge, K., George, I.D., Cole, K.K., Austin, J.R., Takahashi, T.N., Duan, Y. et al. 2011. Facial phenotypes in subgroups of prepubertal boys with autism spectrum disorders are correlated with clinical phenotypes. *Molecular Autism*, 2(1): 15. Available at: https://doi.org/10.1186/2040-2392-2-15.

Alsaade, F.W. and Alzahrani, M.S. 2022. Classification and detection of autism spectrum disorder based on deep learning algorithms. *Computational Intelligence and Neuroscience*, pp. 1–10. Available at: https://doi.org/10.1155/2022/8709145.

Alzubaidi, L., Zhang, J., Humaidi, A.J., Al-Dujaili, A., Duan, Y., Al-Shamma, O. et al. 2021. Review of deep learning: concepts, CNN architectures, challenges, applications, future directions. *Journal of Big Data*, 8(1): 53. Available at: https://doi.org/10.1186/s40537-021-00444-8.

Antezana, L., Scarpa, A., Valdespino, A., Albright, J. and Richey, J.A. 2017. Rural trends in diagnosis and services for autism spectrum disorder. *Frontiers in Psychology*, 8. Available at: https://doi.org/10.3389/fpsyg.2017.00590.

Awaji, B., Senan, E.M., Olayah, F., Alshari, E.A., Alsulami, M., Abosaq, H.A. et al. 2023. Hybrid techniques of facial feature image analysis for early detection of autism spectrum disorder based on combined CNN features. *Diagnostics*, 13(18): 2948. Available at: https://doi.org/10.3390/diagnostics13182948.

Bauer, S.C. and Msall, M.E. 2011. Genetic testing for autism spectrum disorders. *Developmental Disabilities Research Reviews*, 17(1): 3–8. Available at: https://doi.org/10.1002/ddrr.131.

Bernier, R. and Dawson, G. 2016. Autism Spectrum Disorders. In Developmental Psychopathology. *Wiley*, pp. 1–35. Available at: https://doi.org/10.1002/9781119125556.devpsy303.

Bidwe, R.V., Mishra, S. and Bajaj, S. 2023. Performance evaluation of Transfer Learning models for ASD prediction using non-clinical analysis. In Proceedings of the 2023 Fifteenth International Conference on Contemporary Computing. New York, NY, USA: ACM, pp. 474–483. Available at: https://doi.org/10.1145/3607947.3608050.

Blank, M.S., Turner, J.B., Fisher, P.W., Guthrie, E.B. and Whitaker, A.H. 2020. The need for a clinically useful schema of social communication. *Journal of the American Academy of Child & Adolescent Psychiatry* 59(11): 1198–1200. Available at: https://doi.org/10.1016/j.jaac.2020.03.011.

Chen Philip. 2015. Deep learning for pattern learning and recognition. In 2015 IEEE 10th Jubilee International Symposium on Applied Computational Intelligence and Informatics. *IEEE*, pp. 17–17. Available at: https://doi.org/10.1109/SACI.2015.7208200.

Chien, J.C., Lee, J.D., Hu, C.S. and Wu, C.T. 2022. The usefulness of gradient-weighted CAM in assisting medical diagnoses. *Applied Sciences*, 12(15): 7748. Available at: https://doi.org/10.3390/app12157748.

Chollet, F. 2017. Xception: deep learning with depthwise separable convolutions. In 2017 IEEE Conference on Computer Vision and Pattern Recognition (CVPR). *IEEE*, pp. 1800–1807. Available at: https://doi.org/10.1109/CVPR.2017.195.

Dawson, G. and Sapiro, G. 2019. Potential for digital behavioral measurement tools to transform the detection and diagnosis of autism spectrum disorder. *JAMA Pediatrics*, 173(4): 305. Available at: https://doi.org/10.1001/jamapediatrics.2018.5269.

Evers, K., Maljaars, J., Carrington, S.J., Carter, A.S., Happé, F., Steyaert, J. et al. 2021. How well are DSM-5 diagnostic criteria for ASD represented in standardized diagnostic instruments? *European Child & Adolescent Psychiatry*, 30(1): 75–87. Available at: https://doi.org/10.1007/s00787-020-01481-z.

Gulshan, V., Peng, L., Coram, M., Stumpe, M.C., Wu, D., Narayanaswamy, A. et al. 2016. Development and validation of a deep learning algorithm for detection of diabetic retinopathy in retinal fundus photographs. *JAMA*, 316(22): 2402. Available at: https://doi.org/10.1001/jama.2016.17216.

Hammond, P., Forster-Gibson, C., Chudley, A.E., Allanson, J.E., Hutton, T.J., Farrell, S.A. et al. (2008). Face–brain asymmetry in autism spectrum disorders. *Molecular Psychiatry*, 13(6): 614–623. Available at: https://doi.org/10.1038/mp.2008.18.

Hosseini, M.P., Beary, M., Hadsell, A., Messersmith, R. and Soltanian-Zadeh, H. 2022. RETRACTED: deep learning for autism diagnosis and facial analysis in children. *Frontiers in Computational Neuroscience*, 15. Available at: https://doi.org/10.3389/fncom.2021.789998.

Hus, Y. and Segal, O. 2021. Challenges surrounding the diagnosis of autism in children. *Neuropsychiatric Disease and Treatment*, 17: 3509–3529. Available at: https://doi.org/10.2147/NDT.S282569.

Kalaiselvi, A., Nagarathinam, S., Paul, T.D. and Alagumeenaakshi, M., 2021. Detection of autism spectrum disorder using transfer learning. *Turkish Journal of Physiotherapy and Rehabilitation*, 32(2): 926–933.

Ker, J., Wang, L., Rao, J. and Lim, T. 2017. Deep learning applications in medical image analysis. *IEEE Access*, 6: 9375–9389. Available at: https://doi.org/10.1109/ACCESS.2017.2788044.

Khosla, Y., Ramachandra, P. and Chaitra, N. 2021. Detection of autistic individuals using facial images and deep learning. In 2021 IEEE International Conference on Computation System and Information Technology for Sustainable Solutions (CSITSS). *IEEE*, pp. 1–5. Available at: https://doi.org/10.1109/CSITSS54238.2021.9683205.

Khot, T. 2016. Visualizing high-dimensional data. XRDS: Crossroads, The ACM Magazine for Students, 23(2): 66–67. Available at: https://doi.org/10.1145/3021604.

Koonce, B. 2021. 'ResNet 50', in Convolutional Neural Networks with Swift for Tensorflow. *Berkeley, CA: Apress*, pp. 63–72. Available at: https://doi.org/10.1007/978-1-4842-6168-2_6.

Kuttichira, D.P., Azam, B., Verma, B., Rahman, A. and Wang, L. 2022. A novel explainable deep learning model with class specific features, in, pp. 62–74. Available at: https://doi.org/10.1007/978-3-031-25825-1_5.

Kwak, S.K. and Kim, J.H. 2017. Statistical data preparation: management of missing values and outliers. *Korean Journal of Anesthesiology*, 70(4): 407. Available at: https://doi.org/10.4097/kjae.2017.70.4.407.

Lee, Y., Hwang, J.W., Lee, S., Bae, Y. and Park, J. 2019. An energy and GPU-computation efficient backbone network for real-time object detection. In 2019 IEEE/CVF Conference on Computer Vision and Pattern Recognition Workshops (CVPRW). *IEEE*, pp. 752–760. Available at: https://doi.org/10.1109/CVPRW.2019.00103.

de Leeuw, A., Happé, F. and Hoekstra, R.A. 2020. A conceptual framework for understanding the cultural and contextual factors on autism across the globe. *Autism Research*, 13(7): 1029–1050. Available at: https://doi.org/10.1002/aur.2276.

Li, Y.M., Jing, J., Jin, Y., Zou, X.B., Igarashi, K. and Chan, R.C. 2011. Visual attention, emotional and behavioral responses to facial expression in young children with autism. *Psychologia*, 54(3): 156–165. Available at: https://doi.org/10.2117/psysoc.2011.156.

Liu, W., Li, M. and Yi, L. 2016. Identifying children with autism spectrum disorder based on their face processing abnormality: A machine learning framework. *Autism Research*, 9(8): 888–898. Available at: https://doi.org/10.1002/aur.1615.

Livinus, I.U. 2024. Survey of image classification models for transfer learning. *World Journal of Advanced Research and Reviews*, 21(1): 373–383. Available at: https://doi.org/10.30574/wjarr.2024.21.1.0006.

Lord, C., Brugha, T.S., Charman, T., Cusack, J., Dumas, G., Frazier, T. et al. 2020. Autism spectrum disorder. *Nature Reviews Disease Primers*, 6(1): 5. Available at: https://doi.org/10.1038/s41572-019-0138-4.

Mandell, D. and Mandy, W. 2015. Should all young children be screened for autism spectrum disorder? Autism, 19(8): 895–896. Available at: https://doi.org/10.1177/1362361315608323.

McCann, M.T., Jin, K.H. and Unser, M. 2017. Convolutional neural networks for inverse problems in imaging: a review. *IEEE Signal Processing Magazine*, 34(6): 85–95. Available at: https://doi.org/10.1109/MSP.2017.2739299.

Micheletti, M., Brukilacchio, B.H., Hooper-Boyle, H., Basiru, T., Brinster, M.I., Ravenscroft, S. et al. 2023. Evaluating the efficiency and equity of autism diagnoses via telehealth during COVID-19. *Journal of Autism and Developmental Disorders [Preprint]*. Available at: https://doi.org/10.1007/s10803-023-05986-9.

Miranda, E., Aryuni, M. and Irwansyah, E. 2016. A survey of medical image classification techniques. In 2016 International Conference on Information Management and Technology (ICIMTech). *IEEE*, pp. 56–61. Available at: https://doi.org/10.1109/ICIMTech.2016.7930302.

Mukherjee, S. 2017. t-SNE based feature extraction technique for multi-layer perceptron neural network classifier. In 2017 International Conference on Intelligent Computing, Instrumentation and Control Technologies (ICICICT). *IEEE*, pp. 660–664. Available at: https://doi.org/10.1109/ICICICT1.2017.8342641.

Naik, N. et al. 2022. Legal and ethical consideration in artificial intelligence in healthcare: who takes responsibility? *Frontiers in Surgery*, 9. Available at: https://doi.org/10.3389/fsurg.2022.862322.

Nicole, M.-M. 2019. What Are Important Ethical Implications of Using Facial Recognition Technology in Health Care? *AMA Journal of Ethics*, 21(2): E180–187. Available at: https://doi.org/10.1001/amajethics.2019.180.

Norbury, C.F. and Sparks, A. 2013. Difference or disorder? Cultural issues in understanding neurodevelopmental disorders. *Developmental Psychology*, 49(1): 45–58. Available at: https://doi.org/10.1037/a0027446.

Obafemi-Ajayi, T., Miles, J.H., Takahashi, T.N., Qi, W., Aldridge, K. et al. 2015. Facial structure analysis separates autism spectrum disorders into meaningful clinical subgroups. *Journal of Autism and Developmental Disorders*, 45(5): 1302–1317. Available at: https://doi.org/10.1007/s10803-014-2290-8.

Patel, K., Ramanuj, A., Sakhiya, S., Kumar, Y. and Rana, A. et al. 2023. Transfer learning approach for detection of autism spectrum disorder using facial images. In 2023 10th IEEE Uttar Pradesh Section

International Conference on Electrical, Electronics and Computer Engineering (UPCON). *IEEE*, pp. 247–253. Available at: https://doi.org/10.1109/UPCON59197.2023.10434861.

Phumthong, L. and Supratid, S. 2021. Impacts of kernel factorization on different resized images in object recognition base on inception convolutional neural network. In 2021 18th International Conference on Electrical Engineering/Electronics, Computer, Telecommunications and Information Technology (ECTI-CON). *IEEE*, pp. 31–34. Available at: https://doi.org/10.1109/ECTI-CON51831.2021.9454729.

Pramesti, E., Mutiara, A.B. and Refianti, R. 2023. Implementation of deep learning using convolutional neural network for skin disease classification with DenseNet-201 architecture. In 2023 Eighth International Conference on Informatics and Computing (ICIC). *IEEE*, pp. 1–6. Available at: https://doi.org/10.1109/ICIC60109.2023.10381915.

Rana, A. and Chauhan, K. 2021. Computer vision and machine learning for image recognition: A review of the convolutional neural network (CNN) model. *Asian Journal of Multidimensional Research*, 10(10): 1023–1029. Available at: https://doi.org/10.5958/2278-4853.2021.00920.4.

Ravindaran, R., Kasthuri, N., Preethi, S., Adithya, B., Sp, G., Dharanidharan, K. et al. 2023. Performance analysis of a VGG based deep learning model for classification of weeds and crops. In 2023 14th International Conference on Computing Communication and Networking Technologies (ICCCNT). *IEEE*, pp. 1–5. Available at: https://doi.org/10.1109/ICCCNT56998.2023.10307169.

Reddy, P. and J, A. 2024. Diagnosis of autism in children using deep learning techniques by analyzing facial features. In RAiSE-2023. *Basel Switzerland: MDPI*, p. 198. Available at: https://doi.org/10.3390/engproc2023059198.

Ribani, R. and Marengoni, M. 2019. A survey of transfer learning for convolutional neural networks. In 2019 32nd SIBGRAPI Conference on Graphics, Patterns and Images Tutorials (SIBGRAPI-T). *IEEE*, pp. 47–57. Available at: https://doi.org/10.1109/SIBGRAPI-T.2019.00010.

Ribeiro, M.T., Singh, S. and Guestrin, C. 2016. Why should i trust you? In Proceedings of the 22nd ACM SIGKDD International Conference on Knowledge Discovery and Data Mining. New York, NY, USA: ACM, pp. 1135–1144. Available at: https://doi.org/10.1145/2939672.2939778.

Rosero-Montalvo, P., Diaz, P., Salazar-Castro, J.A., Pena-Unigarro, D.F., Anaya-Isaza, A.J., Alvarado-Pérez, J.C. et al. 2017. Interactive data visualization using dimensionality reduction and similarity-based representations, in, pp. 334–342. Available at: https://doi.org/10.1007/978-3-319-52277-7_41.

Ruan, M. 2020. Image and Video-Based Autism Spectrum Disorder Detection via Image and Video-Based Autism Spectrum Disorder Detection via Deep Learning Deep Learning. Available at: https://researchrepository.wvu.edu/etd/7818.

Salau, A.O. and Jain, S. 2019. Feature extraction: a survey of the types, techniques, applications. In 2019 International Conference on Signal Processing and Communication (ICSC). *IEEE*, pp. 158–164. Available at: https://doi.org/10.1109/ICSC45622.2019.8938371.

Sharma, H. and Sharma, O. 2023. Performance analysis of transfer learning models for detecting autism spectrum disorder using facial images. In 2023 11th International Conference on Intelligent Systems and Embedded Design (ISED). *IEEE*, pp. 1–5. Available at: https://doi.org/10.1109/ISED59382.2023.10444603.

Shobana, P. and Shaik, J. 2021. Detecting autism from facial image. *International Journal of Advance Research, Ideas and Innovations in Technology*, 7. Available at: https://doi.org/10.13140/RG.2.2.35268.35202.

Smith, H., Manzini, A. and Ives, J. 2022. Inclusivity in TAS research: an example of EDI as RRI. *Journal of Responsible Technology*, 12: 100048. Available at: https://doi.org/10.1016/j.jrt.2022.100048.

Soni, J., Prabakar, N. and Upadhyay, H. 2020. Visualizing High-Dimensional Data Using t-Distributed Stochastic Neighbor Embedding Algorithm, in, pp. 189–206. Available at: https://doi.org/10.1007/978-3-030-43981-1_9.

Srivastava, N., Hinton, G., Krizhevsky, A., Sutskever, I. and Salakhutdinov, R. 2014. A simple way to prevent neural networks from overfitting. *Journal of Machine Learning Research*, 15: 1929–1958.

Szegedy, C., Liu, W., Jia, Y., Sermanet, P., Reed, S., Anguelov, D. et al. 2015. Going deeper with convolutions. In 2015 IEEE Conference on Computer Vision and Pattern Recognition (CVPR). *IEEE*, pp. 1–9. Available at: https://doi.org/10.1109/CVPR.2015.7298594.

Tan, D.W., Maybery, M.T., Gilani, S.Z., Alvares, G.A., Mian, A., Suter, D. et al. 2020. A broad autism phenotype expressed in facial morphology. *Translational Psychiatry*, 10(1): 7. Available at: https://doi.org/10.1038/s41398-020-0695-z.

Tiwari, R. 2023. Ethical and societal implications of ai and machine learning. *Interantional Journal of Scientific Research in Engineering and Management*, 07(01). Available at: https://doi.org/10.55041/IJSREM17519.

Vezzetti, E. and Marcolin, F. 2012. 3D human face description: landmarks measures and geometrical features. *Image and Vision Computing*, 30(10): 698–712. Available at: https://doi.org/10.1016/j.imavis.2012.02.007.

Wu, C., Liaqat, S., Helvaci, H., Chcung, S.C.S., Chuah, C.N., Ozonoff, S. et al. 2021. Machine learning based autism spectrum disorder detection from videos. In 2020 IEEE International Conference on E-health Networking, Application & Services (HEALTHCOM). *IEEE*, pp. 1–6. Available at: https://doi.org/10.1109/HEALTHCOM49281.2021.9398924.

Yang, Y. 2020. A preliminary evaluation of still face images by deep learning: a potential screening test for childhood developmental disabilities. *Medical Hypotheses*, 144: 109978. Available at: https://doi.org/10.1016/j.mehy.2020.109978.

Yi, L., Feng, C., Quinn, P.C., Ding, H., Li, J., Liu, Y. et al. 2014. Do individuals with and without autism spectrum disorder scan faces differently? A new multi-method look at an existing controversy. *Autism Research*, 7(1): 72–83. Available at: https://doi.org/10.1002/aur.1340.

Zanfir-Fortuna, G. 2020. Article 13 Information to be provided where personal data are collected from the data subject. In The EU General Data Protection Regulation (GDPR). Oxford University PressNew York, pp. 413–433. Available at: https://doi.org/10.1093/oso/9780198826491.003.0044.

Zwaigenbaum, L., Bauman, M.L., Fein, D., Pierce, K., Buie, T., Davis, P.A. et al. 2015. Early screening of autism spectrum disorder: recommendations for practice and research. *Pediatrics*, 136(Supplement_1): S41–S59. Available at: https://doi.org/10.1542/peds.2014-3667D.

Zwaigenbaum, L. and Penner, M. 2018. Autism spectrum disorder: advances in diagnosis and evaluation. *BMJ*, p. k1674. Available at: https://doi.org/10.1136/bmj.k1674.

CHAPTER 3

The Role of Predictive Analytics and Artificial Intelligence in Cybersecurity

Baba Shaheer

1. Introduction: An Overview of Predictive Intelligence in Cyber Security

Cybersecurity in today's rapidly growing digital world is a significant concern for organisations worldwide. The traditional security strategy based on response is no longer sufficient to protect valuable assets, as cyber-attacks are becoming more sophisticated and widespread. This necessitates the adoption of prediction-focused methods rather than mere reactive approaches. With the exponential growth of digital data and increasingly complex attack vectors, predictive intelligence is emerging as a transformative technique in cybersecurity. It applies advanced analytics, including artificial intelligence (AI) and machine learning (ML) algorithms, to provide predictive insights into cyber threats (Sarker 2022).

Prediction-based cybersecurity moves away from conventional security mechanisms that often react only after breaches occur. Instead, it enables organisations to detect early indicators of potential attacks before they materialise. This requires employing machine learning algorithms designed to identify abnormal behavioural patterns and leveraging big data analytics to process vast amounts of security-related information. AI-driven threat intelligence platforms significantly reduce the time gap between detection and response, enabling real-time prediction and mitigation of cyber risks (Welukar and Bajoria 2021).

Faculty of Engineering & Environment, Northumbria University London Campus, UK.
Email: baba.shaheer@northumbria.ac.uk

DOI: 10.1201/9781003540373-3

One of the major concerns in this field is the emergence of AI-driven threats. For instance, AI-generated malware poses significant risks due to its ability to adapt and evade traditional detection techniques. The use of deepfake technology to create highly realistic fake video or audio content has also added new dimensions to social engineering attacks. Additionally, threats such as AI steganography, which involves hiding malicious code within seemingly harmless AI-generated content, further complicate cybersecurity. These developments necessitate advanced predictive models capable of identifying and neutralising such sophisticated threats (Hartmann and Steup 2020, Papernot et al. 2016).

This paper examines the evolution of predictive analytics in cybersecurity, focusing on machine learning algorithms, big data analytics, and AI applications. It also evaluates the ethical concerns associated with AI in cybersecurity, including issues such as algorithmic bias. Furthermore, the study analyses case studies that demonstrate the successful implementation of these technologies in real-world scenarios, offering insights into their transformative potential. From all indications, a proactive, intelligence-driven approach that leverages predictive analytics appears to be the most effective way forward in cybersecurity (Dilek et al. 2015).

2. Predicting Cybersecurity with Artificial Intelligence

The incorporation of machine learning into cybersecurity prediction has been one of the most significant advancements in the field. By recognising and learning from patterns in network traffic, user behaviour, and attack vectors, machine learning models enable cybersecurity systems to anticipate potential threats before they cause harm (Liu et al. 2015a, Shen et al. 2018). The flexibility of machine learning is attributed to its capacity for adjusting and growing so that it constantly enhances its accuracy from time to time as new information gets added into it. This ability is especially helpful for spotting new or hidden threats—like zero-day attacks or advanced persistent threats—that usually slip past regular security systems.

Machine Learning Techniques can strengthen cybersecurity even more. Machine learning helps make cybersecurity stronger by spotting potential threats early. This gives security teams the chance to catch and deal with issues before they become serious. It works by using different types of algorithms that are specifically designed for handling cybersecurity challenges. It can be seen from the classification that the study defines what Cybersecurity Machine Learning is, along with its potential. Consequently, Cyberspace Machine Learning can be pursued with a great level of confidence. Many of the most used machine learning algorithms in cybersecurity are shown in Table 1.

One area where supervised learning is particularly useful in cybersecurity prediction is in training models using labelled data to enable an algorithm to identify benign versus malicious activities. This is seen in email filtering algorithms like IronPort, which use supervised learning to separate safe messages from phishing emails based on past examples (Fung and Hamaster Tactical Terrorists). In this context, supervised learning occurs when known labels guide the model, unlike unsupervised learning, where the model identifies patterns on its own. For large datasets without predefined labels, clustering or anomaly detection techniques may be employed

Table 1: Machine learning algorithms in cyber security.

Machine Learning Algorithm	Reference for State-of-the-Art Literature	Algorithm Application in Modern Cybersecurity
Supervised Learning (e.g., Decision Trees, SVM)	(Sarker 2022)	One way to find malware is by examining traffic patterns carefully. In other words, the analysis of relations between certain emails and certain links and classification of the setting is understood.
Unsupervised Learning (e.g., K-Means, DBSCAN)	(Papernot et al. 2016)	One of the popular examples for the use of anomaly detection is when applied for network traffic analysis. It aims to identify threats in a way that they have not been defined before.
Reinforcement Learning	(Shen et al. 2018)	Prompt response to security threats in cloud services which are prone to constant changing.
Deep Learning (e.g., CNNs, RNNs)	(Welukar and Bajoria 2021)	Category of malware and the use of statistical models to predict likely areas of attacks prior to actual harm.
Neural Networks (e.g., MLP, CNNs)	(Liu et al. 2015b)	Detection of botnet activity in network traffic, malicious file behaviour awareness for prevention and classification purposes.
Support Vector Machines (SVM)	(Gonzalez and Fernandez 2022)	The process of predicting a class (in the application domain of cyber-security): spam filtering or web traffic malicious URL detection.
Naive Bayes Classifier	(Shen et al. 2018)	Identifying phishing emails by sorting emails into different categories with features and, based on the statistical order model, screen emails on some safe levels.
Random Forest	(Hartmann and Steup 2020)	Spotting unusual activity and predicting attacks in real time by combining decisions from several different models.
K-Nearest Neighbors (KNN)	(Gonzalez and Fernandez 2022)	Identifying unusual patterns in system logs and grouping threats based on how closely they match previously known attacks.
Logistic Regression	(Papernot et al. 2016)	Working with situations where there is only one option or the other one is the main concerning issue when analyzing and predicting future events such as differentiating normal and malicious network activity.
Gradient Boosting Machines (e.g., XGBoost, LightGBM)	(Sarker 2022)	The identification and categorization of complex criminal methods implemented in connection with data, which can be used in particular to detect Kulayah practices like denial of service attacks that are initiated from within secure networks.
Clustering Algorithms (e.g., DBSCAN, K-Means)	(Liu and Zhang 2023)	When it comes to preparedness against such potential threats, it is essential to group similar types of cyberattacks, discover patterns from unstructured data and identify unknown attack types.
Dimensionality Reduction (e.g., PCA, t-SNE)	(Hartmann and Steup 2020)	The feature space of network traffic data is decreased so that the threat detection is not only quick but also reaches high accuracy levels.
Ensemble Learning (e.g., AdaBoost, Bagging)	(Welukar and Bajoria 2021)	Aggregating multiple weak models for our purpose combines weak models into a strong classifier. It does that by enhancing the detection prowess of the system by detecting such complex attacks as ransomware as well as advanced persistent threats (APTs).

(Biscubastic Artificial Botnet). These methods can detect sudden abnormal activity, such as unusually high data traffic or an increase in authentication failure attempts (Casas et al. 2012, González et al. 2022, Münz et al. 2017), which may indicate an ongoing brute-force attack and require immediate intervention (Sarker 2022).

Reinforcement learning (RL) is an evolving defence mechanism in which models learn from their interactions with the environment. These models are particularly useful in dynamic environments, such as cloud infrastructures, where security conditions change continuously (Sewak et al. 2022). One example involves IDS using reinforcement learning mechanisms to adapt to new attack techniques in real time.

One of the most remarkable applications of predictive cybersecurity using machine learning is detecting Advanced Persistent Threats (APTs). These attacks are highly sophisticated, long-term operations aimed at stealing confidential information, making them difficult for traditional security systems to detect. However, ML models can analyse vast amounts of historical attack data, revealing subtle patterns and behaviours indicative of APT activity. A notable example is the deployment of deep learning algorithms in banking systems, enabling faster responses to emerging threats (Nkashama et al. 2022, Aiyanyo et al. 2020).

Through these aspects of machine learning techniques, organisations can carry out their operations securely by detecting and mitigating threats as soon as they occur, often before they lead to significant impacts. However, there exist limitations such as large data requirements, overfitting risks, and the possibility of adversarial attacks on machine learning models, which necessitate further improvements in these areas.

There is no doubt that machine learning algorithms play a crucial role in real-time attack identification and limitation within an evolving cyber threat landscape. Malware detection is one application of supervised learning that has gained attention over time. For example, a cybersecurity model for identifying good from malicious documents would learn from previous classifications done manually on large datasets (Mohammed 2023, Li et al. 2021). Additionally, these systems are able to identify polymorphic malware, which alters its code to evade signature-based detection systems, by recognising patterns from one instance to another.

On the other hand, unsupervised learning has been extensively used for network anomaly detection. Such techniques are highly effective in detecting new attacks like DDoS, as they do not require labelled data points yet can still find outliers accurately (Truong-Huu et al. 2020). One approach involves clustering analysis coupled with Principal Component Analysis (PCA) aimed at identifying unusual patterns of activities not in line with established norms. As a result, using off-the-shelf modules for these tasks has also led to wider industry adoption and improved operational efficiency.

Convolutional Neural Networks (CNNs) and Recurrent Neural Networks (RNNs) have also been explored for analysing time-series data relevant to cybersecurity. CNNs play a crucial role in intrusion detection, where they analyse raw network traffic data. On the other hand, RNNs are best suited for identifying phishing attacks and other electronic warfare tactics because they can examine behavioural patterns in sequences (Kurniawan et al. 2022, Abbadi et al. 2021). This enables models to learn complex interactions between variables, achieving higher accuracy rates than conventional machine learning methods.

Yet another advancement is the use of Generative Adversarial Networks (GANs) in cybersecurity. Primarily used in generating images that are realistic, GANs have also been used to replicate cyber-attack contexts. This means that security teams can simulate AIs attacking their defenses so that when faced with the real situation, they will be more prepared (Lowry et al. 1951). Additionally, GAN-generated synthetic data in anomaly detection may help identify normal network behaviour, making it easier to detect deviations that could indicate a security breach.

However, despite these benefits, machine learning also introduces challenges. Adversaries may manipulate data inputs to mislead models, a practice known as adversarial machine learning. This involves intentional input modifications, including poisoning or evasion attacks (Burnyshev et al. 2023, Salman et al. 2020, Biggio et al. 2013). An example is injecting hidden malware samples that appear harmless, tricking the system into misclassifying them. Addressing these vulnerabilities is crucial for ensuring the robustness of machine learning-based cybersecurity systems.

Machine learning has become a key component of modern cybersecurity strategies, with its ability to analyse vast datasets, detect anomalies, and respond to threats in real time. However, as attackers develop increasingly sophisticated techniques, ongoing research is necessary to improve defences against adversarial attacks that attempt to deceive these models.

3. Big Data Analytics and Threat Intelligence

In the digital age, big data analytics has emerged as a fundamental element of contemporary cybersecurity due to the rapid growth of data. Big data analytics refers to the process of examining large amounts of structured and unstructured information to identify patterns, correlations, and trends that provide actionable insights. In the cybersecurity realm, big data analytics helps monitor network traffic, user actions, and external threat intelligence feeds with the aim of enabling real-time cyber threat detection (Sarker et al. 2023a, Kahwema and Hameed 2022, Hirve and Reddy 2019).

One of the main challenges organisations face today is the vast amount of information generated by their systems. According to IDC's projection, global data production is expected to reach 175 zettabytes by 2025, including data relevant for security purposes (Global DataSphere 2023). This volume encompasses logs from firewalls, intrusion detection systems (IDSs), antivirus programs, and information from external sources such as social media platforms, blogs, and the Dark Web. Manual analysis of this data is impractical, necessitating automated solutions for timely threat identification.

The ability of big data analytics to process vast amounts of data makes it easier for cybersecurity experts to determine patterns and trends unique to potential threats. However, while analytics offer valuable insights, challenges such as computational costs and data confidentiality concerns must be addressed. Table 2 outlines the benefits and challenges associated with utilising big data analytics for cybersecurity threat intelligence.

Big data analytics systems can process massive amounts of data at high speeds, enabling real-time threat detection. These systems leverage distributed computing frameworks such as Hadoop and Apache Spark, allowing data to be

Table 2: Implications and challenges of big data analytics in cybersecurity.

Successful Implications	Challenges
Detecting and addressing threats gradually in real time with the help of advanced Artificial Intelligence (AI) platforms and tools.	High computational costs associated with processing massive datasets
Predictive analytics to prevent cyber threats by recognising patterns in data.	Privacy concerns due to extensive data collection and surveillance requirements.
More precise detection of newly developed dangers, such as zero-day security risks.	Challenges in building, training, and validating threat detection models while managing false positives.
More efficient automation of security incident handling processes that lowers the incident response time.	Issues of data quality, in particular those related to the completeness or bias in dataset that affects the learning of the statistical model.
Decreasing the risk of incorrect threat recognition and following steps in security.	AI models should meet all required regulatory compliance standards, and also ease system interpretation and decision-making process.
Abilities to distinguish APTs and state of the art innovations.	Integration issues occur in many aspects due to variances in data sources and submission types.
Always learning and adjusting our models to accommodate new types of threats.	One of the problems of unstructured data in the field of feature selection is that it is complex.
Detecting anomalies in large data warehouses helps prevent data breaches by identifying unusual behavior patterns early.	Data elements are security and privacy risks that arise when the confidential information is shared between research organizations or their own groups.
Consolidating intelligence from different sources and the purpose of defense.	Processing petabytes of data in real-time has always been a challenge for the past few decades.
Predicting malicious insider threats by analysing employee behaviour.	Putting into consideration privacy laws (for example, the General Data Protection Regulation) when analyzing user and organizational data for potential insider threats.
Employing Artificial Intelligence systems to determine previously undetected malware in large data samples.	System performance, in view of these challenges, and the need for balanced performance is paramount, especially to societies that operate in resource constrained setups.
Enhanced decision-making skills through the power of predictive analysis.	The reason why machine learning models may become over specific is another source of weakness as far as machine learning deployment is concerned.

(Anderson and Patel 2022, Clark and White 2018, Jones and Thompson 2020, Lee and Garcia 2021, Miller and Zhao 2019, O'Neill and Foster 2019, Roberts and Green 2017, Smith and Nguyen 2022)

processed simultaneously across multiple nodes. This parallel processing capability is particularly useful in detecting complex, multi-vector attacks, where individual data fragments may appear harmless in isolation but indicate a coordinated attack when analysed collectively. Big data analytics can uncover correlated attacks by identifying seemingly unrelated events (Aniello et al. 2014, Janeja et al. 2014).

Another critical application of big data analytics in cybersecurity is the integration of threat intelligence feeds. Threat intelligence involves gathering and analysing information on cyber threats, including indicators of compromise (IoCs), attacker tactics, techniques, and procedures (TTPs), and known vulnerabilities. By incorporating threat intelligence feeds into big data analytics systems, organisations can gain insights into adversary strategies and proactively defend against potential attacks (Security Analytics to Identify the 12 Indicators of Compromise 2014).

The real-world impact of big data analytics in cybersecurity is evident in several successful implementations. IBM's QRadar Security Intelligence Platform, for example, utilises big data analytics to detect and respond to real-time security incidents. This approach has proven particularly effective in identifying insider threats, which often evade traditional security measures (Al-Muntaser et al. 2023, Brancik and Ghinita 2011).

However, despite its advantages, big data analytics presents certain challenges. One of the most pressing concerns is data privacy. Organisations must comply with regulations such as the EU General Data Protection Regulation (GDPR) and the California Consumer Privacy Act (CCPA) when collecting and analysing data for cybersecurity purposes. Additionally, the sheer volume of data generated by modern systems increases the risk of false positives, where benign activities are mistakenly flagged as threats. This can overwhelm security teams, leading to "alert fatigue" and reducing the effectiveness of threat detection (Gelman et al. 2023, Four Reasons for Alert Fatigue and How to Make It Stop 2023) .

In summary, real-time threat detection through big data analytics is crucial for modern cybersecurity, providing insights into the tactics of potential adversaries. The integration of machine learning and AI into big data analytics frameworks is expected to be one of the most effective defences against cybercrime as data volumes continue to grow. However, challenges related to data privacy and false positives must be carefully managed to unlock the full potential of big data analytics in cybersecurity.

By and large, the rise of Security Information and Event Management (SIEM) systems is one of the most successful applications of big data analytics in cybersecurity frameworks. SIEM platforms like Splunk, AlienVault, and LogRhythm collect data from multiple network sources to provide a unified view of an organisation's security posture. This enables analysts to monitor security incidents effectively and investigate potential threats almost immediately. For instance, Splunk is renowned for processing billions of data points daily and integrating machine learning-based anomaly detection systems to offer robust threat intelligence that many businesses rely on (Splunk for Enterprise Security featuring User Behavior Analytics 2016, Top 50 Cybersecurity Threats 2023, The Essential Guide to Security 2023).

One of the ways big data is used in cybersecurity is through threat hunting, which leverages large datasets to predict attacks before they occur. Instead of relying solely on automated tools, threat hunting is a proactive approach where security personnel actively search for abnormalities and signs of adversarial activity that have not yet been recognised by automatic detection methods. Big data analytics enhances threat hunting by enabling security teams to analyse massive datasets, identifying early indicators of compromise (IoCs). For example, organisations using CrowdStrike's Falcon Platform to examine endpoint data have been able to identify behaviours linked to different threat actor groups, significantly reducing detection times (FALCON INSIGHT: ENDPOINT DETECTION AND RESPONSE (EDR) n.d, Falcon Complete Uncovers Global Attack Campaign 2020).

A crucial aspect of big data analytics is the integration of internal and external data sources to generate predictive insights about future events and trends. Internally, organisations monitor their logs, network traffic, and user activity. Externally, threat intelligence feeds provide information on emerging threats worldwide. Combining these data streams allows organisations to forecast the most probable cyber-attacks, determining not only whether a specific threat exists but also when it might occur and its potential scale (Okutan et al. 2018, Winkler and Gomes 2017). FireEye's large-scale data-driven threat intelligence services, for instance, harvest information from millions of sources globally, enabling companies to stay ahead of sophisticated cyber adversaries (n.d).

The real-world impact of big data analytics in cybersecurity is evident in various sectors. A study on JP Morgan Chase, one of the world's largest financial institutions, demonstrates how the company utilises big data analytics to secure its extensive virtual infrastructure (How JPMorgan leverage Big Data Analytics? 2024). JP Morgan relies on advanced algorithms to analyse network traffic and employee behaviour patterns, helping it detect sophisticated threats that easily bypass traditional perimeter defences. Additionally, its security team integrates external threat intelligence feeds to monitor known vulnerabilities and exploits, ensuring they remain up to date with the latest information on potential threats (Kott et al. 2018).

However, despite its potential, implementing big data analytics in cybersecurity presents several challenges. False positives remain a significant issue, as big data systems generate a vast number of alerts, overwhelming security teams. Up to 85% of SIEM alerts are false positives, leading to "alert fatigue" and reducing analysts' ability to address genuine threats effectively (Quest 2019). To mitigate this, advanced big data analytics systems are being integrated with machine learning algorithms to enhance the filtering and prioritisation of security alerts, enabling security professionals to focus on the most critical threats while reducing the number of benign anomalies.

Data privacy is another major concern when employing big data for cybersecurity. The ingestion, storage, and processing of personal data must be transparent, and organisations failing to comply with regulations such as GDPR or CCPA risk severe fines and reputational damage. Privacy-preserving machine learning techniques, such as federated learning, offer a potential solution by balancing cybersecurity effectiveness with data protection requirements (Goldsteen et al. 2022). Additionally, some organisations are adopting data anonymisation techniques that allow big data analytics to be leveraged effectively without compromising user privacy.

All in all, big data analytics enables organisations to monitor vast datasets and detect patterns indicative of impending cyber-attacks. It allows security teams to analyse large amounts of data and identify trends suggesting potential threats. However, challenges such as false positives, data privacy concerns, and optimising threat intelligence remain areas for continuous improvement. As data volumes continue to expand and cyber threats grow more sophisticated, integrating big data analytics with advanced AI and machine learning systems will be essential in maintaining strong cybersecurity defences (Apurva et al. 2017).

4. AI-Driven Predictive Models and Real-World Applications

The convergence of artificial intelligence and cybersecurity has transformed how organisations approach threat detection and response. AI's real-time ability to process massive datasets and learn from them makes it an ideal tool for predicting and preventing cyber threats (Donepudi 2015). By combining historical attack data with real-time threat intelligence, predictive models can identify potential attack vectors, detect anomalies, and even automate responses to threats.

AI-powered platforms are now instrumental in countering modern cyber threats. These systems rely on complex algorithms to detect subtle data patterns that may indicate malicious activity, making them highly effective against zero-day attacks—threats that emerge before software developers release fixes. As cybercriminals continuously refine their tactics, AI systems evolve in parallel, ensuring they stay ahead of emerging threats (Podder et al. 2021, Hoffman and Kim 2023). AI-driven security tools adapt to cybercriminal strategies, identifying novel techniques used to bypass traditional security measures.

AI-driven systems have significantly improved in addressing the increasing sophistication of cyber threats. These technologies continuously learn from new data, making them more effective in identifying and mitigating evolving threats (Dilek et al. 2015). As a result, AI-powered security tools are capable of keeping pace with cybercriminals, who constantly develop new evasion techniques.

A leading example of AI in predictive cybersecurity is Darktrace, an autonomous cybersecurity platform that leverages unsupervised machine learning to detect and respond to emerging threats. Darktrace's AI algorithms develop a "pattern of life" for every user and device, identifying even the slightest deviations from normal behaviour. When an anomaly is detected, the system autonomously investigates and mitigates the threat before it escalates, reducing the need for human intervention. This approach has proven highly effective in countering advanced cyber threats such as insider attacks and polymorphic malware (Wallart 2024).

Predictive cybersecurity with AI tools goes beyond merely identifying threats; they are also highly effective in automating incident response. An example of this is Cortex XSOAR from Palo Alto Networks, which utilises SOAR (Security Orchestration, Automation, and Response) by integrating machine learning models into its software to analyse security incidents and automate their resolution. Cortex XSOAR assesses the severity of a potential threat by leveraging multiple threat intelligence feeds. Based on this intelligence, it can take various actions such as isolating infected devices, blocking malicious traffic, or applying patches to protect an organisation's information systems. AI-powered platforms such as Cortex XSOAR have significantly improved response times during cyber incidents by reducing manual interventions (How SOAR is transforming threat intelligence 2020, Paloalto 2023).

A significant branch of AI in cybersecurity is Natural Language Processing (NLP), which involves communication between humans and machines using everyday language (Jurafsky et al. 2009). NLP falls under Natural Language Understanding (NLU), which focuses on interpreting human communication. In the era of big data, where vast amounts of information are processed instantly, NLP advancements have led to improvements in speech recognition, machine translation, and question-answer systems. Stanford University, for instance, has worked on projects developing technology capable of transcribing real-time conversations between people speaking different languages (Oberteuffer 1995, Hayakawa et al. 2021). AI chatbots represent one of the more visible interfaces of computational linguistics—they help people and machines communicate more effectively using natural language. These dialogue systems support everyday tasks like making phone reservations or offering virtual companionship through computer-based interactions.

By focusing on user needs, web developers ensure a seamless and efficient experience. A user-centric approach enhances website functionality and overall effectiveness (Korgaonkar et al. 2009).

Real-world applications of AI-driven predictive cybersecurity highlight the tangible benefits these technologies offer. For instance, a tier-one financial institution implemented machine learning algorithms to process real-time transaction data for fraud detection, significantly reducing false positives and allowing security teams to focus on genuine threats (HSBC 2020). For instance, Microsoft Azure Security Center employs AI-based technology in monitoring cloud infrastructures for potential security breaches including identity thefts among others. This move by Microsoft has saved the company from several massive cloud attacks due to its robustness (Microsoft 2021).

Despite these advancements, applying AI to cybersecurity presents challenges. One major issue is the lack of interpretability in deep learning models, often referred to as "black boxes" due to their opaque decision-making processes. Cybersecurity analysts may struggle to understand why AI has reached a specific conclusion, making it difficult to validate the results. To address this, researchers are developing Explainable AI (XAI) techniques to improve the transparency of AI models, allowing security professionals to assess and trust AI-generated insights (Doshi-Velez and Kim n.d, Gunning et al. 2019, Samek et al. 2019).

This implies that cybersecurity is being revolutionised by the emergence of AI predictive models in the search for faster and more accurate ways to detect and respond to threats. Nevertheless, as these systems become more complex, there must be transparency, ethical considerations, and efforts to address any bias within their algorithms to ensure their effective contribution to cybersecurity.

Beyond incident response and anomaly detection, AI-driven predictive analytics is transforming how cyber-attacks are anticipated.

Predictive models can be developed using regression, time-series forecasting, and classification algorithms, which help detect attacks before they occur by identifying patterns. These models can determine the type, scale, and timing of an impending attack, enabling an organisation to strengthen its defences accordingly. Siemplify, a leading SOAR platform, incorporates AI-driven predictive analytics into its operations to help enterprises prioritise security alerts based on potential impact while also reducing alert fatigue and response times (Security Orchestration, Automation & Incident Response 2023).

Within the healthcare sector, significant progress has been made in using AI-driven cybersecurity solutions. For example, Stanford University recently partnered with Microsoft Azure AI to develop a predictive cybersecurity system aimed at preventing threats targeting medical devices. This system uses AI-driven predictive analytics to analyse network traffic and historical data to predict potential cyber-attacks. As a result, sensitive patient information has been secured, and critical healthcare systems have continued to operate without disruption (Center et al. n.d, Enhancing healthcare with data and responsible AI: New innovations from microsoft cloud for healthcare, n.d).

AWS has also been leveraging AI technology to enhance its GuardDuty service, which analyses tens of billions of event logs across all AWS accounts to detect threat signals. GuardDuty employs machine learning techniques and anomaly detection methods to identify abnormal activities within an account, such as unusual API calls or unauthorised data retrieval attempts. Since its launch, AWS has significantly improved its detection of compromised accounts and prevention of data breaches (AWS GuardDuty: Threat detection with AI and machine learning, n.d).

On the other hand, challenges remain in integrating AI into predictive cybersecurity. One major concern is the transparency of AI models, particularly deep learning systems, which often function as "black boxes" with limited explainability (Sarker et al. 2023a). Security analysts may struggle to validate AI-generated results due to the lack of insight into how decisions are made. To address this, Explainable AI (XAI) is being adopted to help analysts not only understand but also confidently approve recommendations from AI-driven systems.

In conclusion, cybersecurity has undergone a significant transformation due to AI-driven predictive models, which enable faster threat detection and response. However, as these systems become more advanced, it is crucial to address transparency issues, ethical concerns, and algorithmic bias to ensure AI continues to enhance cybersecurity efficiently and reliably.

AI does more than just detect threats; it also has an application in terms of how it uses past data to predict the future by analysing historical attack data. Predictive models using regression analysis, time-series forecasting, and classification algorithms can identify threats before they occur by recognising attack patterns. These models can determine the type, scale, and timing of an attack, allowing organisations to anticipate potential breaches. For example, Siemplify, a top SOAR provider, uses AI-driven predictive analytics to help companies focus on critical security alerts, reducing both notification fatigue and response times (Security Orchestration, Automation & Incident Response 2023, SOAR Implementation Pitfalls to Avoid 2023).

The increasing importance of AI in state security underscores its growing integration into national defence strategies. Governments now rely on AI-driven models to safeguard critical infrastructure. The United States Department of Defense (DoD), for example, employs AI-based techniques to counter cyber-attacks from advanced state-sponsored hacker groups targeting its military communication networks. The Joint Artificial Intelligence Center (JAIC) within the DoD is responsible for developing AI models to predict cyber espionage and cyber warfare incidents, helping to secure military networks against foreign adversaries (United States Department of Defense 2020, Joint Artificial Intelligence Center (JAIC) 2020).

AI-based predictive models powered by machine learning have become crucial for cybersecurity because they provide real-time threat detection, anticipate attacks proactively, and enable effective incident response. These models have applications across multiple sectors, with healthcare and defence being notable examples of their transformative potential. However, to fully realise AI's capabilities in cybersecurity, challenges such as adversarial machine learning and explainable AI must be addressed to ensure trust, reliability, and widespread adoption.

5. Ethical Worries and Problems in AI-Powered Cybersecurity

AI in cybersecurity presents not merely technical challenges but also important ethical issues. One essential concern involves the question of algorithmic transparency, as organisations increasingly depend on AI-driven models for monitoring networks, anomaly detection, and responding to threats. Numerous AI systems, particularly those based on deep learning, function like "black boxes," implying that users do not understand how they made decisions. Ethical concerns arise when such systems make security-related decisions with serious ramifications, such as blocking certain users or terminating access to the network (Mittelstadt et al. 2016, Goodman and Flaxman n.d).

One possible ethical challenge comes from the bias of AI algorithms. If there is any bias within the data used to train an AI model, then decisions made by it will reflect those biases. This could lead to automated security programs unfairly targeting some people or areas in cybersecurity. For instance, facial recognition technology sometimes fails to identify individuals from certain ethnic groups proportionally, which may translate into similar problems with AI-driven cybersecurity systems if not properly addressed (Sarridis et al. 2023, Atzori et al. 2022). Ensuring that AI models are trained on diverse and representative datasets helps prevent unfair treatment in cybersecurity.

Another major issue is data privacy. AI models usually require huge amounts of information to be effective, raising concerns regarding how this information is obtained, stored, and used. In the context of cybersecurity, AI models may analyse sensitive data such as personal details and financial records to detect potential threats, which means they can compromise individual privacy if mishandled or shared with unauthorised persons. This is why compliance with regulations such as the EU's General Data Protection Regulation (GDPR) and the California Consumer Privacy Act (CCPA) is important in ensuring that the privacy rights of individuals are not violated by such systems (California consumer privacy act (CCPA) of 2018, n.d, Voigt and Bussche 2017).

There are also challenges associated with autonomous AI systems that can operate without human intervention. While these systems can respond to cyber threats in real-time, concerns arise about who should be held accountable if humans are not directly involved. If an AI-based system mistakenly identifies a legitimate user as an intruder and denies them access to essential services, who is responsible for that error? It is important to involve human oversight in major security decisions to ensure AI systems remain accountable and trustworthy (Yazdanpanah et al. 2022, Ryan et al. 2024).

Moreover, there is the potential for the malicious misuse of AI. While AI is used to defend against cyber threats, it can also be weaponised by adversaries.

AI-powered malware and adversarial AI are emerging threats that can bypass security measures and adapt. Attackers may use AI to identify and exploit unknown software vulnerabilities, launch sophisticated phishing attacks, or create highly convincing deepfakes for social engineering purposes. The rise of AI-generated deepfakes has become a significant concern in cybersecurity, as such content can be used to manipulate individuals or groups, posing serious threats to trust and security in digital communications (Buo 2020, Increasing Threat of DeepFake Identities 2021, Ovadya and Whittlestone 2019).

To address these ethical concerns, several initiatives have been introduced to establish guidelines for the ethical use of AI in cybersecurity. For example, the European Commission's *Ethics Guidelines for Trustworthy AI* outlines principles aimed at ensuring AI technology is transparent, accountable, and respects fundamental rights. These guidelines stress that AI models in cybersecurity should be explainable so that individuals understand how decisions are made (EUR 2019, 2023, Universal Guidelines for AI 2024).

Furthermore, there is a growing need for policy frameworks to regulate AI in cybersecurity matters. Governments and international organizations are beginning to create guidelines concerning moral use of automation in relation to security. For example, U.S. National Security Commission on Artificial Intelligence (NSCAI) has recommended the development of standards and regulation that would ensure ethics and effectiveness in national defense related cases. Such rules are necessary to prevent situations where some people might have good intentions towards deploying these technologies but end up creating more harm than good due to unintended ethical repercussions (Morgan et al. 2020, Accessible et al. 2014).

In conclusion, even though it has significant potential in enhancing security online, applying AI systems needs strict ethical control as well as regulatory oversight mechanisms. Therefore, certain things like algorithmic transparency, data protection laws, accountability systems, and possibilities of malicious AI must be checked so that trustable cyber defense mechanisms are generated by means based on artificial intelligence approaches. As technology advances, ethical concerns will remain central to discussions on the best practices for using AI in cybersecurity to protect individuals, organisations, and critical infrastructure from cyber threats.

6. Case Studies in Predictive Cybersecurity

The use of predictive analytics in safeguarding internet security has gained immense acceptance recently, with several organisations already incorporating such technologies into their security strategies. This section presents various best practice cases showcasing the efficacy of predictive models in combating cyber threats across different sectors.

1. Case Study: JPMorgan Chase's Predictive Cybersecurity JPMorgan Chase

JPMorgan Chase has been at the forefront of using cutting-edge cybersecurity measures as one of the largest financial institutions worldwide. The bank employs a combination of AI-driven predictive analytics and big data to secure its vast online infrastructure. One of the pillars of JPMorgan's cybersecurity is its Global

Cybersecurity Fusion Center, which continually monitors network traffic, employee activities, and external threat intelligence sources. By using machine learning algorithms to identify unusual activities and predict potential risks, JPMorgan has drastically reduced the time taken to respond to security incidents. Through this proactive approach, the bank has been able to prevent data breaches and minimise the effects of cyber-attacks (JPMorgan Chase 2015, Technology 2022).

2. Case Study: IBM's QRadar and Predictive Threat Intelligence

IBM is a good example of how predictive analytics can be employed to strengthen IT security against cyber threats. The IBM QRadar Security Intelligence Platform integrates machine learning algorithms with real-time big data analytics, enabling it to identify threats to an organisation's information assets. QRadar operates by analysing logs, flow records, and threat intelligence feeds, allowing it to uncover anomalies that indicate potential attacks. This software has been applied across various sectors, including healthcare, finance, and government, to predict risks before they escalate into full-blown incidents. In one instance, a large healthcare provider leveraged QRadar to stop a ransomware attack in its early stages by recognising initial signs of intrusion (IBM 2021).

3. Case Study: CrowdStrike Falcon's Endpoint Protection

CrowdStrike's Falcon is another example of predictive model application in cybersecurity. Falcon uses AI-driven threat hunting to predict endpoint malfunctions in real time. At its core, Falcon's machine learning models detect the most evasive attackers by analysing abnormal events globally. In one particular incident, an APT group targeted a multinational corporation. CrowdStrike was able to identify their lateral movement throughout the organisation's network and initiate an automatic response, successfully preventing a data exfiltration attempt (CrowdStrike 2020).

4. Case Study: Microsoft's AI-Enhanced Cloud Security

Microsoft's Azure Security Center employs AI-driven analytics to safeguard cloud infrastructures against cyber threats. It uses machine learning to scan millions of cloud workloads for unusual activities such as identity theft and abnormal login patterns. For example, Azure's predictive functionality enabled a large manufacturing firm to thwart an internal attack by detecting suspicious login behaviour from a compromised account. This early warning mechanism allowed security personnel to take immediate action, preventing unauthorised access to confidential information. The success of these security measures has established Azure as a trusted platform for cloud security (Microsoft 2021).

5. Case Study: Palo Alto Networks' Cortex XDR for Incident Response

The Cortex (2021) article provides insight into how AI can improve incident response based on predictions provided by Cortex XDR developed by Palo Alto Networks. This involves employing artificial intelligence algorithms to collate data from different sources like cloud environments, endpoints, and network traffic, among others, to anticipate likely attack points. For example, in a retail organisation targeted by a phishing campaign that bypassed traditional email security controls, Cortex

XDR's machine learning-based intelligence detected abnormal email behaviour. This triggered an automated response, successfully blocking the phishing attempt before it could compromise critical systems (Cortex 2021).

These examples highlight the effectiveness of predictive analytics in enhancing cybersecurity across multiple sectors. From banking to cloud services, AI models play a crucial role in detecting and preventing incidents before they occur. As predictive technologies continue to evolve, they will play an even greater role in safeguarding valuable data and critical infrastructure.

7. Conclusion: The Future of Predictive Cybersecurity and AI

As cyber threats become more sophisticated, the significance of predictive cybersecurity cannot be understated. Organisations are increasingly shifting from reactionary approaches to proactive measures, thanks to the integration of artificial intelligence (AI), machine learning (ML), and big data analytics. By employing models that analyse real-time user behaviour, historical data, and current threats, companies can identify potential risks before they materialise, thereby reducing the likelihood of cyber-attacks.

The future of predictive cybersecurity may lie in advancements in explainable AI (XAI), which aim to make AI models more transparent. This is crucial for addressing issues of trust and accountability in automated security decisions. Additionally, progress in adversarial machine learning will help mitigate threats posed by adversaries attempting to manipulate AI systems. As a result, developing robust and resilient systems to counter these risks will remain a key area of focus for both researchers and cybersecurity practitioners (Goodfellow et al. 2018).

Moreover, the ethical dimensions of AI in cybersecurity require ongoing attention. Issues such as algorithmic bias and data privacy must be addressed within strong regulatory frameworks (Hunkenschroer and Luetge 2022). Governments and international bodies are beginning to establish legislative and policy frameworks for AI ethics, ensuring these technologies are deployed effectively and responsibly (NXP Ethical Framework for Artificial Intelligence 2020).

In conclusion, the future of digital defence lies in predictive cybersecurity. Organisations can stay ahead of emerging risks and protect their valuable assets by leveraging AI and predictive analytics. However, ethical and technical challenges must not be overlooked, ensuring AI remains a reliable and responsible tool in the fight against cybercrime.

References

Joint Artificial Intelligence Center (JAIC). (2020, January 1). AI in national defense: Enhancing cybersecurity capabilities. https://www.ai.mil/.

FireEye. (n.d.). CSO: Less secure than you think. http://www.cnmeonline.com/myresources/fireeye/fireeye-cso-less-secure-than-you-think.pdf.

Abbadi, M.A., Tareef, A. and Sarayreh, A. 2021, February 28. Hand side recognition and authentication system based on deep convolutional neural networks. *Blue Eyes Intelligence Engineering and Sciences Publication*, 10(4): 5–13. https://doi.org/10.35940/ijitee.d8430.0210421.

Accessible, I.G., Board, T., Law., Jl, C., Wf, B. and Hs, L. 2014, January 1. Emerging and Readily Available Technologies and National Security: A Framework for Addressing Ethical, Legal, and Societal Issues. https://www.ncbi.nlm.nih.gov/pubmed/25032403.

Aiyanyo, I.D., Samuel, H. and Lim, H. 2020, August 22. A systematic review of defensive and offensive cybersecurity with machine learning. *Multidisciplinary Digital Publishing Institute*, 10(17): 5811–5811. https://doi.org/10.3390/app10175811.

Al-Muntaser, B., Mohamed, M.A. and Tuama, A.Y. 2023, January 1. Real-time intrusion detection of insider threats in industrial control system workstations through file integrity monitoring. *Science and Information Organization*, 14(6). https://doi.org/10.14569/ijacsa.2023.0140636.

Anderson, C. and Patel, N. 2022. Predicting malicious insiders with big data analysis. *International Journal of Information Security and Privacy*, 300–315.

Aniello, L., Bondavalli, A., Ceccarelli, A., Ciccotelli, C., Cinque, M., Frattini, F. et al. 2014, January 1. Big data in critical infrastructures security monitoring: challenges and opportunities. *Cornell University*. https://doi.org/10.48550/arxiv.1405.0325.

Apurva, A., Ranakoti, P., Yadav, S., Tomer, S. and Roy, N R. 2017, October 1. Redefining Cyber Security With Big Data Analytics., 199–203. https://doi.org/10.1109/ic3tsn.2017.8284476.

Atzori, A., Fenu, G. and Marras, M. 2022, January 1. The more secure, the less equally usable: gender and ethnicity (Un)fairness of deep face recognition along security thresholds. Elsevier BV, 210, 212-217. https://doi.org/10.1016/j.procs.2022.10.139.

AWS GuardDuty: Threat detection with AI and machine learning. (n.d), undefined(undefined). https://aws.amazon.com/guardduty/.

Biggio, B., Corona, I., Maiorca, D., Nelson, B., Šrndić, N., Laskov, P. et al. 2013, January 1. Evasion Attacks against machine learning at test time. Springer Science+Business Media, 387–402. https://doi.org/10.1007/978-3-642-40994-3_25.

Brancik, K. and Ghinita, G. 2011, February 15. The Optimization of Situational Awareness for Insider Threat Detection. https://doi.org/10.1145/1943513.1943544.

Buo, S.A. 2020, January 1. The emerging threats of deepfake attacks and countermeasures. *Cornell University*. https://doi.org/10.48550/arxiv.2012.07989.

Burnyshev, P., Kostenok, E. and Zaytsev, A. 2023, January 1. Machine translation models stand strong in the face of adversarial attacks. *Cornell University*. https://doi.org/10.48550/arXiv.2309.

California consumer privacy act (CCPA) of 2018. (n.d), undefined(undefined). https://leginfo.legislature.ca.gov/faces/billTextClient.xhtml?bill_id=201720180AB375.

Casas, P., Mazel, J. and Owezarski, P. 2012, January 30. Unsupervised network intrusion detection systems: detecting the unknown without knowledge. *Elsevier BV*, 35(7): 772–783. https://doi.org/10.1016/j.comcom.2012.01.016.

Center, S., Artificial, I., Medicine, I. and Imaging, A. (n.d). Stanford AIMI center. , undefined(undefined). https://aimi.stanford.edu/.

Chase, J. 2015, March 16, undefined(undefined). https://www.jpmorganchase.com/content/dam/jpmc/jpmorgan-chase-and-co/documents/suppliers-documents/systems-monitoring.pdf.

Clark, S. and White, B. 2018. Data integration challenges in big data cybersecurity. *Computational Security Science*, 140–158.

Cortex. 2021, January 1. Cortex XDR: AI-Driven incident response for advanced threat protection, undefined(undefined). https://www.paloaltonetworks.com/cortex/cortex-xdr.

CrowdStrike. 2020, January 1. CrowdStrike falcon: AI-Driven endpoint protection and threat hunting, undefined(undefined). https://www.crowdstrike.com/products/endpoint-security/falcon-endpoint-protection/.

Defense, U S D O. 2020, January 1. The role of AI in national defense: Cybersecurity and threat prediction, undefined(undefined). https://www.defense.gov/Our-Story/Artificial-Intelligence/.

Dilek, S., Çakır, H. and Aydın, M. 2015, January 31. Applications of Artificial Intelligence Techniques to Combating Cyber Crimes: A Review, 6(1): 21–39. https://doi.org/10.5121/ijaia.2015.6102.

Donepudi, P.K. 2015, December 31. Crossing Point of Artificial Intelligence in Cybersecurity, 2(3): 121–128. https://doi.org/10.18034/ajtp.v2i3.493.

Doshi-Velez, F. and Kim, B. (n.d). Towards interpretable machine learning: A review, undefined(undefined). https://arxiv.org/abs/1702.08608.

Enhancing healthcare with data and responsible AI: New innovations from microsoft cloud for healthcare. (n.d), undefined(undefined). https://www.microsoft.com/en-us/industry/blog/healthcare/2024/10/10/enhancing-healthcare-with-data-and-responsible-ai-new-innovations-from-microsoft-cloud-for-healthcare/.

EUR. 2019, April 8. The title cannot be extracted from the provided text, undefined(undefined). https://eur-lex.europa.eu/legal-content/EN/TXT/?uri=CELEX%3A52019DC0168.

EUR. 2023, January 10, undefined(undefined). https://edps.europa.eu/sites/edp/files/publication/icdppc-40th_ai-declaration_adopted_en_0.pdf.

Falcon Complete Uncovers Global Attack Campaign. 2020, August 27. https://www.crowdstrike.com/blog/falcon-complete-uncovers-a-global-attack-campaign/.

FALCON INSIGHT: ENDPOINT DETECTION AND RESPONSE (EDR). (n.d). https://www.crowdstrike.com/wp-content/uploads/2020/02/crowdstrike-falcon-insight-data-sheet.pdf.

Four Reasons for Alert Fatigue and How to Make It Stop. 2023, December 19. https://cloudsecurityalliance.org/blog/2022/06/24/four-reasons-for-alert-fatigue-and-how-to-make-it-stop.

Gelman, B., Taoufiq, S., Vörös, T. and Berlin, K. 2023, January 1. That escalated quickly: an ml framework for alert prioritization. *Cornell University*. https://doi.org/10.48550/arxiv.2302.06648.

Global DataSphere. 2023, January 1. https://www.idc.com/getdoc.jsp?containerId=IDC_P38353.

Goldsteen, A., Ezov, G., Shmelkin, R., Moffie, M. and Farkash, A. 2022, January 1. Anonymizing Machine Learning Models. Springer Science+Business Media, 121–136. https://doi.org/10.1007/978-3-030-93944-1_8.

González, J., Huet, A. and Rossi, D. 2022, January 1. Rare yet popular: evidence and implications from labeled datasets for network anomaly detection. *Cornell University*. https://doi.org/10.48550/arxiv.2211.10129.

Gonzalez, M. and Fernandez, C. 2022. Applications of support vector machines in cybersecurity. *Cybersecurity Journal*, 98–115.

Goodfellow, I., McDaniel, P. and Papernot, N. 2018, June 25. Making machine learning robust against adversarial inputs. Association for Computing Machinery, 61(7): 56–66. https://doi.org/10.1145/3134599.

Goodman, B. and Flaxman, S. (n.d). European Union regulations on algorithmic decision-making and a "right to explanation", 38(undefined), 50. https://ojs.aaai.org/index.php/aimagazine/article/view/2741.

Gunning, D., Stefik, M., Choi, J., Miller, T., Stumpf, S. and Yang, G. 2019, December 18. XAI—Explainable artificial intelligence, 4(37). https://robotics.sciencemag.org/content/4/37/eaay7120.

Hartmann, T. and Steup, M. 2020. Random forest in cybersecurity: a comprehensive analysis. *Security and Privacy Journal*, 145–168.

Hartmann, K. and Steup, C. 2020, May 1. Hacking the AI - the Next Generation of Hijacked Systems. https://doi.org/10.23919/cycon49761.2020.9131724.

Hayakawa, A., Ishii, M., Kobayashi, Y., Nakamura, A., Narihira, T., Obuchi, Y. et al. 2021, January 1. Neural network libraries: a deep learning framework designed from engineers' perspectives. *Cornell University*. https://doi.org/10.48550/arXiv.2102.

Hirve, S.A. and Reddy, P. 2019, January 1. A survey on visualization techniques used for big data analytics. Springer Nature, 447–459. https://doi.org/10.1007/978-981-13-6861-5_39.

Hoffman, W. and Kim, H.M. 2023, March 1. Reducing the Risks of Artificial Intelligence for Military Decision Advantage. https://doi.org/10.51593/2021ca008.

HSBC. 2020, January 1. AI-driven cybersecurity in financial services, undefined(undefined).

Hunkenschroer, A.L. and Luetge, C. 2022, February 8. Ethics of AI-enabled recruiting and selection: a review and research agenda. *Springer Science+Business Media*, 178(4): 977–1007. https://doi.org/10.1007/s10551-022-05049-6.

IBM. 2021, January 1. IBM QRadar security intelligence platform: Predictive analytics in cybersecurity, undefined(undefined). https://www.ibm.com/security/security-intelligence/qradar.

Increasing Threat of DeepFake Identities. 2021, August 11. https://www.dhs.gov/sites/default/files/publications/increasing_threats_of_deepfake_identities_0.pdf.

Janeja, V.P., Azari, A., Namayanja, J. and Heilig, B. 2014, October 1. B-dids: Mining anomalies in a Big-distributed Intrusion Detection System. https://doi.org/10.1109/bigdata.2014.7004484.

Jones, A. and Thompson, R. 2020. Privacy concerns in big data analytics for cybersecurity. *Journal of Information Security*, 87–104.

Jurafsky, D. and Martin, J.H. 2009, January 1. Speech and Language Processing. Pearson Prentice Hall, undefined (undefined).

Kahwema, P. and Hameed, T. 2022, January 5. Review of the IT Integration Framework for a University's Institutional Performance Setting in Zimbabwe, 12(1). https://doi.org/10.6007/ijarbss/v12-i1/12054.

Korgaonkar, P., O'Leary, B. and Silverblatt, R. 2009, October 1. Critical factors to successful website development. *IGI Global*, 5(4): 39–54. https://doi.org/10.4018/jebr.2009040603.

Kott, A., Mancini, L.V., Ron, P.T., Ar, M.D., Dushku, E., Nther, H.G. et al. 2018, March 1. Initial Reference Architecture of an Intelligent Autonomous Agent for Cyber Defense. https://apps.dtic.mil/sti/pdfs/AD1049300.pdf.

Kurniawan, K., Sedayu, B.B., Hakim, A.R. and Erawan, I.M.S. 2022, January 1. Classification of Rastrelliger kanagurta and Rastrelliger brachysoma using Convulational Neural Network (CNN). IOP Publishing, 969(1): 012017–012017. https://doi.org/10.1088/1755-1315/969/1/012017.

Lee, M. and Garcia, M. 2021. Automating cybersecurity with big data analytics. *Journal of Automation in Cybersecurity*, 40–59.

Li, Y., Wang, X., Shi, Z., Zhang, R., Xue, J. and Wang, Z. 2021, May 16. Boosting training for PDF malware classifier via active learning. *Wiley*, 37(4): 2803–2821. https://doi.org/10.1002/int.22451.

Liu, Q. and Zhang, T. (2023). Deep learning technology of computer network security detection based on artificial intelligence. *Computers and Electrical Engineering*, 110: 108813. https://doi.org/10.1016/J.COMPELECENG.2023.108813.

Liu, Y., Sarabi, A., Zhang, J., Naghizadeh, P., Karir, M., Bailey, M. et al. 2015a, August 12. Cloudy with a Chance of Breach: Forecasting Cyber Security Incidents, 1009–1024.

Liu, Y., Li, Z., Zhang, J., Chen, W., Zhao, X. and Wang, M. 2015b. Botnet detection using machine learning approaches. *Journal of Computer Networks*, 78: 200–215.

Lowry, O.H., Rosebrough, N., Farr, A. and Randall, R.J. 1951, November 1. Protein measurement with the folin phenol reagent. *Elsevier BV*, 193(1): 265–275. https://doi.org/10.1016/s0021-9258(19)52451-6.

Microsoft. 2021, January 1. Microsoft azure security center: AI-Driven analytics for cloud security, undefined(undefined). https://azure.microsoft.com/en-us/services/security-center/.

Microsoft. 2021, January 1. Microsoft Azure Security Center: Protecting cloud infrastructure with A, undefined(undefined).

Miller, D. and Zhao, W. 2019. Zero-day threats and big data analytics in cybersecurity. *Cyber Defense Review*, 65–80.

Mittelstadt, B., Allo, P., Taddeo, M., Wachter, S. and Floridi, L. 2016, December 1. The ethics of algorithms: Mapping the debate, 3(undefined), 1. https://journals.sagepub.com/doi/10.1177/2053951716679679.

Mohammed, K. 2023, January 1. Harnessing the speed and accuracy of machine learning to advance cybersecurity. *Cornell University*. https://doi.org/10.48550/arxiv.2302.12415.

Morgan, F., Boudreaux, B.D., Lohn, A.J., Ashby, M., Curriden, C., Klima, K. et al. 2020, January 1. Military Applications of Artificial Intelligence: Ethical Concerns in an Uncertain World. https://doi.org/10.7249/rr3139-1.

Münz, G., Li, S. and Carle, G. 2017, August 8. Traffic Anomaly Detection Using K-Means Clustering. https://www.semanticscholar.org/paper/Traffic-Anomaly-Detection-Using-K-Means-Clustering-M%C3%BCnz-Li/634e2f1a20755e7ab18e8e8094f48e140a32dacd.

Nkashama, D.K., Soltani, A., Verdier, J., Frappier, M., Tardif, P. and Kabanza, F. 2022, January 1. Robustness evaluation of deep unsupervised learning algorithms for intrusion detection systems. *Cornell University*. https://doi.org/10.48550/arXiv.2207.

NXP Ethical Framework for Artificial Intelligence. 2020, December 11. https://www.nxp.com/docs/en/white-paper/AI-ETHICAL-FRAMEWORK-WP.pdf.

Oberteuffer, J.A. 1995, October 24. Commercial applications of speech interface technology: an industry at the threshold. National Academy of Sciences, 92(22): 10007–10010. https://doi.org/10.1073/pnas.92.22.10007.

Okutan, A., Yang, S.J. and McConky, K. 2018, January 1. Forecasting cyber attacks with imbalanced data sets and different time granularities. *Cornell University*. https://doi.org/10.48550/arxiv.1803.09560.

O'Neill, S. and Foster, G. 2019. Balancing GDPR compliance and cybersecurity. *Data Protection and Privacy Journal*, 112–127.

Ovadya, A. and Whittlestone, J. 2019, January 1. Reducing malicious use of synthetic media research: Considerations and potential release practices for machine learning. *Cornell University*. https://doi.org/10.48550/arXiv.1907.

Paloalto. 2023, January 1. Cortex XSOAR. paloaltonetworks, undefined (undefined).

Papernot, N., McDaniel, P., Sinha, A. and Wellman, M.P. 2016, January 1. Towards the science of security and privacy in machine learning. *Cornell University*. https://doi.org/10.48550/arxiv.1611.03814.

Papernot, N., McDaniel, P., Sinha, A. and Wellman, M. 2016. Towards the science of security and privacy in machine learning. *IEEE Symposium on Security and Privacy*, 493–508.

Podder, P., Bharati, S., Mondal, M.R.H., Paul, P.K. and Köse, U. 2021, January 1. Artificial neural network for cybersecurity: a comprehensive review. *Cornell University*. https://doi.org/10.48550/arXiv.2107.

Projectpro. 2024, January 1. How JPMorgan leverage Big Data Analytics?. Blog, undefined(undefined).

Quest. 2019, October 21, undefined(undefined). https://www.quest.com/docs/how-to-improve-your-siem-s-roi-and-threat-hunting-potential-white-paper-27276.pdf.

Roberts, P. and Green, L. 2017. Anomaly detection in large data warehouses for cybersecurity. *Journal of Cyber Intelligence*, 202–218.

Ryan, P., Porter, Z., Al-Qaddoumi, J., McDermid, J. and Habli, I. 2024, January 1. What's my role? Modelling responsibility for AI-based safety-critical systems. Cornell University. https://doi.org/10.48550/arxiv.2401.09459.

Salman, H., Ilyas, A., Engstrom, L., Vemprala, S., Mądry, A. and Kapoor, A. 2020, January 1. Unadversarial examples: designing objects for robust vision. *Cornell University*. https://doi.org/10.48550/arXiv.2012.

Samek, W., Montavon, G., Vedaldi, A., Hansen, L.K. and Müller, K. 2019, January 1. Explainable AI: Interpreting, explaining and visualizing deep learning, undefined(undefined). https://arxiv.org/abs/1708.08296.

Sarker, I.H. 2022, September 19. Machine learning for intelligent data analysis and automation in cybersecurity: current and future prospects. *Springer Science+Business Media*, 10(6): 1473–1498. https://doi.org/10.1007/s40745-022-00444-2.

Sarker, I.H. 2022. Machine learning and cybersecurity: applications and challenges. *ACM Computing Surveys*, 45–67.

Sarker, I.H., Janicke, H., Mohammad, N., Watters, P. and Nepal. 2023a, January 1. AI potentiality and awareness: a position paper from the perspective of human-AI teaming in cybersecurity. *Cornell University*. https://doi.org/10.48550/arXiv.2310.

Sarker, I.H., Janicke, H., Μαγλαράς, Λ. and Camtepe, S. 2023b, January 1. Data-driven intelligence can revolutionize today's cybersecurity world: a position paper. *Cornell University*. https://doi.org/10.48550/arXiv.2308.

Sarridis, I., Koutlis, C., Papadopoulos, S. and Diou, C. 2023, January 1. Towards fair face verification: an in-depth analysis of demographic biases. Cornell University. https://doi.org/10.48550/arxiv.2307.10011.

Security Analytics to Identify the 12 Indicators of Compromise. 2014, March 23. https://www.slideshare.net/21CTinc/12-indicatorsofcompromiseslideshare.

Security Orchestration, Automation & Incident Response. 2023, February 6. https://www.slideshare.net/Siemplify/security-orchestration-automation-incident-response.

Sewak, M., Sahay, S.K. and Rathore, H. 2022, January 1. Deep reinforcement learning for cybersecurity threat detection and protection: a review. *Springer Science+Business Media*, 51–72. https://doi.org/10.1007/978-3-030-97532-6_4.

Shen, S. and others. 2018. Reinforcement learning in cloud security. *Journal of Cloud Computing*, 102–113.

Shen, Y., Mariconti, E., Vervier, P. and Stringhini, G. 2018, October 15. Tiresias: Predicting Security Events Through Deep Learning. https://arxiv.org/pdf/1905.10328.pdf.

Smith, J. and Nguyen, A. 2022. Artificial intelligence platforms for real-time cybersecurity. *International Journal of Big Data Analytics*, 120–138.

SOAR Implementation Pitfalls to Avoid. 2023, February 6. https://www.slideshare.net/Siemplify/5-soar-implementation-pitfalls-to-avoid.

Splunk for Enterprise Security featuring User Behavior Analytics. 2016, June 1. https://www.slideshare.net/Splunk/splunk-for-enterprise-security-featuring-user-behavior-analytics-63031519.

Technology. (2022, January 1). https://www.jpmorgan.com/technology.

The Essential Guide to Security. 2023, January 1. https://www.splunk.com/en_us/form/the-essential-guide-to-security.html?_bk=&_bt=430953495794&_bm=&_bn=&_bg=78879557673&gclid=CjwKCAjwx9_4BRAHEiwApAt0zsFFRabAqdcffC2W49JcZLryc7Mkf0Ac524Imhml_T0fvAdL7SVWtBoC1qoQAvD_BwE.

Top 50 Cybersecurity Threats. 2023, January 1. https://www.splunk.com/en_us/form/top-50-security-threats.html.

Truong-Huu, T., Dheenadhayalan, N., Kundu, P.P., Ramnath, V., Jingyi, L., Teo, S.G. et al. 2020, October 6. An Empirical Study on Unsupervised Network Anomaly Detection using Generative Adversarial Networks. https://doi.org/10.1145/3385003.3410924.

Universal Guidelines for AI. 2024, June 1. https://www.caidp.org/universal-guidelines-for-ai.

Velasquez, J. 2020, October 1. How SOAR is transforming threat intelligence. https://library.idgcommunications.net/idgcampaigns/documents/uploaded_data/f6c/82c/db-/original/cortex-xsoar.pdf.

Voigt, P. and Bussche, A.V.D. 2017, August 7. The EU general data protection regulation (GDPR): A practical guide, undefined(undefined). https://link.springer.com/book/10.1007/978-3-319-57959-7.

Wallart, L. 2024, January 1. Darktrace. (2023). devoteam.com, undefined(undefined).

Welukar, A. and Bajoria, K. 2021. Deep learning methods in cybersecurity. *Springer Nature Computer Science*, 321–342.

Welukar, J.N. and Bajoria, G.P. 2021, December 15. Artificial intelligence in cyber security - a review. *Technoscience Academy*, 488–491. https://doi.org/10.32628/ijsrst218675.

Winkler, I. and Gomes, A.T. 2017, January 1. What is threat intelligence? Elsevier BV, 143–150. https://doi.org/10.1016/b978-0-12-809316-0.00012-9.

Yazdanpanah, V., Gerding, E.H., Stein, S., Dastani, M., Jonker, C.M., Norman, T.J. et al. 2022, December 2. Reasoning about responsibility in autonomous systems: challenges and opportunities. *Springer Nature*, 38(4): 1453–1464. https://doi.org/10.1007/s00146-022-01607-8.

CHAPTER 4

Application of Deep Learning (BERT model) to Predict Bitcoin Sentiment Using X (Twitter) Data

Dilek Celik,[1,*] *Niloufar Karimian*[1] and *Ahmet Celik*[2]

1. Introduction

Deep learning (DL), a specialized domain within the expansive realm of machine learning, harnesses the capabilities of artificial neural networks characterized by their multi-layered architecture, enabling them to discern complex patterns within data and make informed predictions or decisions (LeCun et al. 2015). Deep learning research has driven the rapid progress in Artificial Intelligence (AI) research leading to remarkable breakthroughs in addressing longstanding issues in various fields such as computer vision (He et al. 2016), natural language processing (Devlin et al. 2019), recommendation systems, drug discovery, and beyond. Deep learning methodologies have catalyzed transformative breakthroughs, offering novel solutions to longstanding challenges.

Bitcoin (BTC) emerges as a pioneering force within the realm of cryptocurrencies, embodying both a symbol of innovation and a coveted financial asset for investors. Yet, the dynamic and volatile nature of BTC renders predicting its price a formidable challenge, necessitating the development of innovative methodologies to navigate its

[1] Faculty of Engineering & Environment, Northumbria University London Campus, UK.
Email: niloufar.karimian@northumbria.ac.uk

[2] Computer Engineering, Khoja Akhmet Yassawi International Kazakh-Turkish University, Turkey.
Email: ahmet.celik@ogr.yesevi.edu.tr

* Corresponding author: dilek.celik@northumbria.ac.uk

DOI: 10.1201/9781003540373-4

erratic fluctuations. Notably, the periodic event of BTC halving, occurring roughly every four years and entailing a reduction in block rewards, exerts significant influence on its price dynamics. With the next BTC halving slated for 2024, anticipation ripples through social media platforms like X (formerly Twitter), which have emerged as potent channels for gauging cryptocurrency sentiment and price trends.

Using X data to forecast BTC and cryptocurrency prices using cutting-edge DL technologies has become an important phenomenon and there is a growing body of literature on this subject. X is a dynamic hub for real-time opinions, conversation and discussion, usually reflecting the collective sentiment of the community of cryptocurrency. Considering the wealth of information embedded in X's discussions, this research aims to take the power of the DL models to analyze and interpret the sentiments expressed by influencers in X about BTC.

The primary aim of this study is to scrutinize the impact of sentiment expressed in tweets—whether positive, negative, or neutral—on Bitcoin (BTC) prices, elucidating their potential influence on future price fluctuations. To achieve this, advanced DL models incorporating Twitter sentiment analysis will be meticulously developed to forecast BTC sentiment accurately. The specific objectives of this research are as follows:

1. To delineate the efficacy of Twitter sentiment analysis in predicting BTC prices, elucidating the mechanisms through which sentiment impacts price dynamics.
2. To conduct a comprehensive analysis aimed at identifying the key variables crucial for making precise predictions regarding BTC price movements.
3. To devise and refine a robust DL model tailored specifically for BTC price prediction, integrating insights gleaned from sentiment analysis and variable analysis.

The subsequent section of this paper will furnish an exhaustive review of contemporary literature pertaining to BTC prediction methodologies employing diverse DL models. Following this, the methodology employed in this study will be explicated in Section 3, while Section 4 will present the empirical findings. A thorough discussion of the results will ensue in Section 5, culminating in conclusive remarks and recommendations for future research endeavors in Section 6. The study will also be placed in a broad context to highlight its importance.

2. Literature Review

The rapid proliferation of web-based applications, including blogs and social media platforms, has catalyzed the emergence of reviews and commentaries on various aspects of daily life. Capturing and assessing people's sentiments, opinions, and attitudes across a spectrum of subjects, products, and services constitutes the essence of sentiment analysis. Utilizing such data for informed decision-making holds significant value for businesses, governments, and individuals alike (Wankhade et al. 2022). Deep Learning (DL) models, in the realm of sentiment analysis, demonstrate notable advantages over conventional feature-based methodologies, offering enhanced performance and nuanced representation capabilities (Alsayat 2022).

The landscape of DL has witnessed the swift emergence of diverse techniques, manifesting promise across multiple domains encompassing audio, image, and natural language processing (Peng et al. 2022). DL algorithms adeptly extract insights from raw inputs, such as textual data or tweets, employing a gamut of algorithms to encode this information within specific model architectures (AlBadani et al. 2022).

2.1 Sentiment analysis in financial markets

Financial markets represent one of the myriad domains where sentiment analysis finds application (Yekrangi and Abdolvand 2021). While traditional financial theory posits that stock prices hinge solely on fundamental value and assumes market efficiency, behavioral finance theory suggests that non-fundamental factors like investor sentiment can influence future returns (Naeem et al. 2021). Investors are keenly attuned to market behaviors, often becoming emotionally swayed and driven to buy or sell shares (Valle-Cruz et al. 2022). In today's landscape, investors face the critical task of continuously gauging and monitoring sentiments conveyed in news and social media posts to inform timely investment decisions, given the significant impact these sentiments wield on stock prices and brand perception (Mishev et al. 2020). In the nascent stages of conducting financial sentiment analysis, many studies resort to the lexicon-based approach. This method relies heavily on word weighting and lexicon/dictionary usage. While lexicon-based approaches excel with high-dimensional data and boast user-friendly interfaces, they falter in analyzing positional information and may overlook crucial nuances. Conversely, conventional machine learning techniques such as Support Vector Machines (SVM), Decision Trees, Random Forests, Lasso Regressions, Ridge Regressions, and Naïve Bayes demonstrate superior efficiency compared to lexicon-based methods.

2.2 Twitter as a source of financial sentiment

Investor sentiment and reactions are often influenced by information disseminated through social media platforms, potentially affecting their decisions regarding financial assets, particularly stocks (Man et al. 2019). Regardless of its accuracy, news propagated via social media platforms can instigate fluctuations in global stock market indices (Jiao et al. 2020).

Recent research has shown that Twitter sentiment can serve as a predictor for the performance of cryptocurrencies such as Bitcoin, Bitcoin Cash, and Litecoin. This predictive capability was established through the integration of financial data, lexicon-based sentiment analysis techniques, and bilateral Granger-causality testing (Kraaijeveld and De Smedt 2020). Notably, an event involving Elon Musk, currently the wealthiest individual globally, exemplifies this phenomenon. On January 29, 2021, Musk modified the bio of his Twitter account to include "#bitcoin". Subsequently, within a short span of time, the price of Bitcoin surged from over \$32,000 to over \$38,000, resulting in a remarkable increase of \$111 billion in the asset's market capitalization (Ante 2023).

2.3 Sentiment analysis for cryptocurrency prices

Research by (Gurrib and Kamalov 2022) aimed to predict fluctuations in Bitcoin (BTC) prices by amalgamating sentiment analysis with Linear Discriminant Analysis (LDA). Data encompassing daily BTC values and OHLC (Open, High, Low, Close) was sourced from Coinmarketcap.com, spanning June 2016 to April 2021. Employing Support Vector Machine (SVM), Linear Discriminant Analysis (LDA), and VADER sentiment analysis, the investigation revealed that SVM utilizing news sentiment and asset-specific data achieved the highest accuracy (0.585). Both LDA and SVM outperformed random conjectures in comparison to baseline models, with SVM demonstrating superior accuracy. Identifying a research gap, the study proposed enriching the model by incorporating other cryptocurrencies and integrating additional classifiers like Decision Trees and Long Short-Term Memory (LSTM).

In a separate study, (Vo 2019) examined the impact of news reports on forecasting Ethereum (ETH) price fluctuations. The dataset, acquired from NewsNow and Poloniex-API, underwent manual sentiment labeling (–1, 0, 1). Adopting a two-stage approach integrating semantic and syntactic vectors with sentiment analysis, the study utilized a Long Short-Term Memory (LSTM) network for sentiment prediction and a Recurrent Neural Network (RNN) for price prediction. The model achieved an MAE of 1.36, indicating efficacy compared to prior models solely reliant on pricing data. The study underscored areas for further exploration, including the incomplete coverage of cryptocurrencies and the neglect of real-time temporal considerations.

Pano and Kashef (2020) endeavored to elucidate preprocessing methodologies linking sentiment scores with Bitcoin prices, focusing on VADER-based sentiment analysis of BTC-related tweets during the COVID-19 period. Data collection involved the Twitter API and CryptoCompare API. Exploring 13 intermediate preprocessing steps, the study assessed their correlation with BTC closing values using Pearson correlation. Notably, an unexpected polarity association with considerable strength emerged from analyzing daily data. The paper proposed abbreviated Twitter text as a viable option for real-time prediction systems. Future research could delve into datasets with minute-level timespans and evaluate machine learning algorithm performance based on preprocessing techniques, as Twitter sentiments may fluctuate post-COVID-19.

Lastly, Valencia et al. (2019) advocated leveraging social media data and machine learning techniques to forecast cryptocurrency price changes. Integrating sentiment analysis using Valence Aware Dictionary and Sentiment Reasoner (VADER) with historical market data from 65 Bitcoin exchanges and raw tweets from Twitter, the study assessed three models: Random Forests (RF), Support Vector Machines (SVM), and Multi-Layer Perceptrons (MLP). The MLP model, leveraging both Twitter and market data, emerged as the best fit for Bitcoin and Ethereum. For Ripple, the optimal model was once again an MLP utilizing solely market data, while the SVM model proved most effective for Litecoin when considering both market data and Twitter sentiment. Notably, market movements could be predicted solely through Twitter data by implementing the MLP and RF models. To enhance predictive capabilities, the study recommended deploying specialized models such as Long Short-Term Memory Networks (LSTMs), exploring additional data sources, and further researching content quality improvement.

2.4 Integration of deep learning and twitter for cryptocurrency price prediction

The investigation conducted by (Aslam et al. 2022) employs tweet analysis to predict public sentiments and attitudes toward the Bitcoin industry. Employing a supervised machine learning approach, the authors utilize an ensemble model incorporating Gated Recurrent Unit (GRU) and Long Short-Term Memory (LSTM) networks. The data collection process involves extracting specific tags from Twitter, followed by sentiment and emotion annotation using the TextBlob and Text2Emotion packages. Various deep learning and machine learning models, including LR, RF, DT, KNN, SVM, and GNB, are employed for sentiment analysis and emotion identification. Notably, the ensemble LSTM-GRU model outperforms other models in sentiment analysis, achieving an accuracy score of 0.99. However, the study observes a potential vulnerability in the performance of the LSTM-GRU model related to dataset balancing.

Similarly (Ye et al. 2022), utilize price data, technical indicators, and sentiment indices from Twitter to propose a novel ensemble deep learning model for Bitcoin value prediction. This model employs a stacking ensemble approach with GRU and LSTM networks. Data collection involves harvesting tweets and obtaining Bitcoin price data from Binance.com, while technical indicators are computed using the TA-Lib module, and basic sentiment scores are derived from the VADER Python library. Results indicate that the stacking ensemble model, utilizing opinions expressed on Twitter, outperforms other models and consumes fewer resources when predicting Bitcoin values. The study underscores the significance of social media sentiment analysis for additional short-term price prediction, affirming the efficacy of the proposed model.

Addressing the enhancement of action suggestion models in the cryptocurrency domain, (Park and Seo 2023) propose an adjustment approach based on Twitter sentiment analysis. The study utilizes Bitcoin price data and employs a deep learning model based on LSTM to recommend actions. Sentiment analysis is conducted on Twitter data across different time spans (one, three, and seven days). The adjustment strategy involves exploring thresholds for modification and updating model outputs based on positive or negative tweets. The proposed modification technique demonstrates a notable enhancement, resulting in a 3% increase in accuracy (81.31%) and F1 score (77.86%) compared to the original model. Performance measures indicate superiority over existing models, particularly in 1-day sentiment analysis. Statistical validation through the F-test and heteroscedasticity t-test further confirms the method's accuracy, surpassing traditional approaches. Despite its effectiveness in optimizing investment profits, the study acknowledges certain limitations, such as an emphasis on short-term effectiveness and a sole focus on sentiment from Twitter without exploring other factors.

3. Materials and Methods

Data is gathered from publicly available data published in (Jahanbin et al. 2023). The dataset comprised tweets of over 50 expert accounts for a market analysis of 40 cryptocurrencies. For this study, we only considered the tweets and sentiment about BTC from January 1, 2023, to June 12, 2023. 11988 rows of data are used for training and testing.

Data cleaning comprised tokenizing, removing punctuation, eliminating stopwords, and lemmatization. All these methods are applied to clean the data. The data has been divided into Train (70%), Validation (15%), and Test sets (15%).

Bidirectional Encoder Representations from Transformers (BERT) is a natural language processing model based on the transformer architecture, recognized for its significant improvement over previous state-of-the-art models. BERT (shown in Figure 1) was introduced by researchers at Google [3]. Tokenization is the process of splitting raw texts into tokens and encoding the tokens into numeric data. This study implemented the BERT tokenizer with "bert-base-uncased." For tokenization, we first initialized the BERT tokenizer and then created a function for encoding.

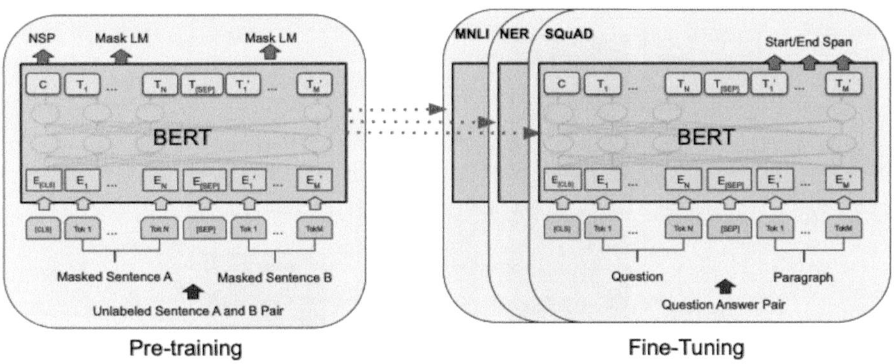

Figure 1: Bert Model (Jacob et al. 2018).

Pytorch Dataset and DataLoader are used to split data into catchers.

Bert For Sequence Classification Model is initiated using Jupyter Notebook.

AdamW optimizer with a learning rate of 2e-6 is used.

The model has been trained in ten epochs.

Classification reports with precision, recall, accuracy, and f1-score are used as measure metrics. The equations for these metrics are given below.

$$Precision = \frac{TruePositives}{TruePositives + FalsePositives} \tag{1}$$

$$Recall = \frac{TruePositives}{TruePositives + FalseNegatives} \tag{2}$$

$$Accuracy = \frac{TruePositives + TrueNegatives}{TotalExamples} \tag{3}$$

$$F1 = \frac{2 \times Precision \times Recall}{Precision + Recall} \tag{4}$$

4. Results

4.1 Data

Figure 2 provides a quantitative representation of the frequency of each sentiment type in the dataset. The sentiment types are categorized as negative, neutral, and positive. Specifically, it reveals that out of the total texts analyzed:

Negative: 2030 texts were categorized as expressing a negative sentiment.

Neutral: 3491 texts were classified as having a neutral sentiment.

Positive: 6467 texts were identified as conveying a positive sentiment.

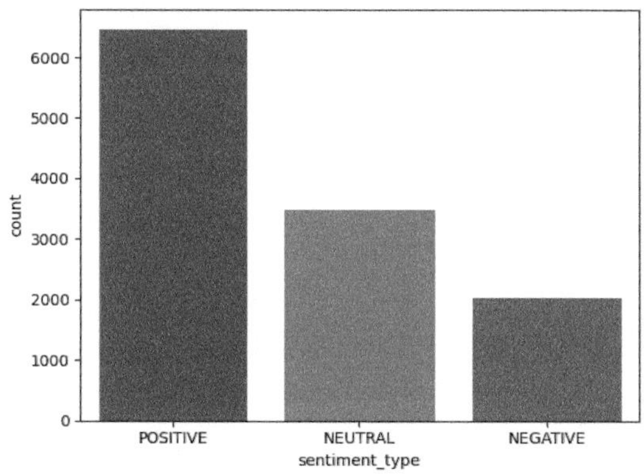

Figure 2: Count of sentiment types.

Table 1 provides a breakdown of individual texts within the dataset, along with their corresponding sentiment types. Each row in the table represents a specific text sample, and the columns are labelled as "full_text" and "sentiment_type." The full_text column contains excerpts of the analyzed texts. Each row corresponds to a unique text sample. Sentiment_type column categorizes each text sample based on its sentiment into one of three classes: negative, neutral, or positive.

Table 1: Sample text and sentiment type.

	full_text	sentlment_type
4760	rt bitcoin crypto company complained directly ...	NEGATIVE
7295	breaking jack dorsey donates million fund bitc ...	NEUTRAL
8017	rt casahodl ever wondered safe bitcoin btc sti...	POSITIVE
7998	rt crypto update daily coinbase ethereum stall...	NEGATIVE
5811	bnb mark zuckerberg ceo launched raised bnb pi...	POSITIVE

4.2 Training and validation loss

Overall, the decreasing trend in both training and validation losses indicates that the model is learning and improving its performance over the epochs as presented in Figure 3.

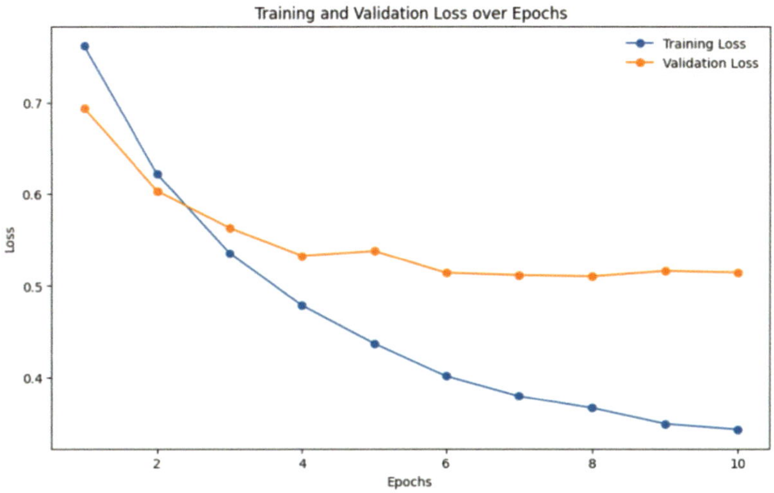

Figure 3: Training and validation loss.

4.3 Confusion matrix

Figure 4 shows the confusion matrix for a classification model. In the confusion matrix, the rows represent the actual classes, and the columns represent the predicted classes. Each cell in the matrix contains the proportion or percentage of instances belonging to a particular actual class that were predicted to be in a particular predicted class.

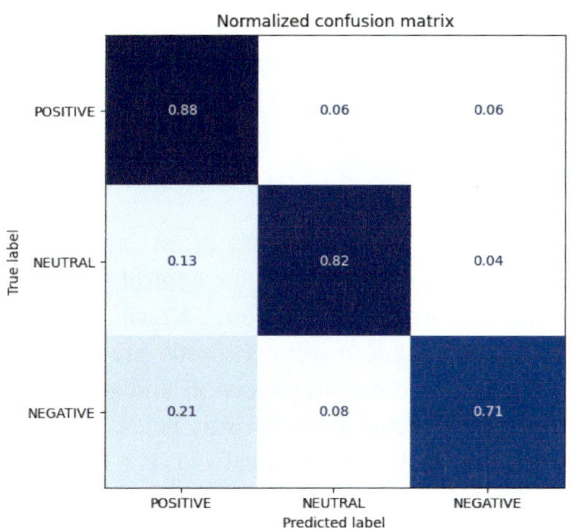

Figure 4: Confusion matrix.

According to the confusion matrix:

Actual positive:

Predicted Positive (True Positive Rate - Recall): 0.88. This indicates that 88% of instances that were actually positive were correctly predicted as positive.

Predicted Neutral: 0.06. This suggests that 6% of instances that were actually positive were incorrectly predicted as neutral.

Predicted Negative: 0.06. This means that 6% of instances that were actually positive were incorrectly predicted as negative.

Actual neutral:

Predicted Positive: 0.13. About 13% of instances that were actually neutral were incorrectly predicted as positive.

Predicted Neutral (True Negative Rate - Specificity): 0.82. This shows that 82% of instances that were actually neutral were correctly predicted as neutral.

Predicted Negative: 0.04. About 4% of instances that were actually neutral were incorrectly predicted as negative.

Actual negative:

Predicted Positive: 0.21. Around 21% of instances that were actually negative were incorrectly predicted as positive.

Predicted Neutral: 0.08. Approximately 8% of instances that were actually negative were incorrectly predicted as neutral.

Predicted Negative (True Negative Rate - Specificity): 0.71. This indicates that 71% of instances that were actually negative were correctly predicted as negative.

4.4 Evaluation metrics

Table 2 presents the results of the evaluation metrics including precision, recall, f1-score and accuracy. In Table 2, the Precision for positive (0.88) indicates that out of all instances predicted as positive, 88% were actually positive. Precision for neutral (0.82) means that 82% of instances predicted as neutral were actually neutral. Precision for negative (0.71) signifies that 71% of instances predicted as negative were actually negative.

Recall for positive (0.85) means that out of all actual positive instances, 85% were correctly predicted as positive. Recall for neutral (0.84) indicates that 84% of actual neutral instances were correctly predicted. Recall for negative (0.75) signifies that 75% of actual negative instances were correctly predicted.

F1-Score is the harmonic mean of precision and recall. F1-Score for positive (0.86) balances precision and recall for the positive class. F1-Score for neutral (0.83) balances precision and recall for the neutral class. F1-Score for negative (0.73) balances precision and recall for the negative class.

Table 2: Classification Report.

	Precision	Recall	F1-score	Support
POSITIVE	0.88	0.85	0.86	953
NEUTRAL	0.82	0.84	0.83	532
NEGATIVE	0.71	0.75	0.73	314
Accuracy			0.83	1799
Macro avg.	0.80	0.81	0.81	1799
Weighted avg	0.83	0.83	0.83	1799

In Table 1, support indicates the actual number of occurrences of each class in the dataset. There are 953 instances of positive, 532 instances of neutral, and 314 instances of negative.

In Table 1, we can see that the overall accuracy of the model is 0.83 or 83%, meaning that 83% of all instances were correctly classified.

Macro Avg provides the unweighted average of precision, recall, and F1-Score across all classes. Macro Avg Precision is 0.80, Recall is 0.81, and F1-Score is 0.81.

Weighted Avg considers the contribution of each class to the overall score, weighted by the number of samples in each class. Weighted Avg Precision is 0.83, Recall is 0.83, and F1-Score is 0.83.

The model performs well in terms of precision especially for the positive and neutral classes, indicating that when it predicts a class, it is often correct. The negative class shows a balanced precision and recall, with a reasonable F1-Score.

It's crucial to consider the specific goals of the classification task. If equal importance is given to precision and recall, then the F1-Score becomes a critical metric for evaluating overall model performance. If different priorities exist, precision or recall may be emphasized based on the task requirements.

5. Discussion and Conclusion

This study explores the application of deep learning, specifically the BERT model, for sentiment analysis on Twitter data regarding Bitcoin (BTC) before the 2024 halving. The dynamic nature of the price of BTC, especially affected by events like halving, makes prediction challenging. Leveraging advanced deep learning models on Twitter data aims to capture sentiments that may serve as indicators for BTC price movements.

The literature review highlights the importance of sentiments expressed on Twitter as indicators of cryptocurrency price movements. It also provides a comprehensive overview of the role of sentiment analysis in financial markets, particularly in the context of cryptocurrency. Studies demonstrate that sentiments expressed on Twitter can have predictive capabilities for cryptocurrency returns. Various techniques, including lexicon-based approaches and deep learning models, have been used to analyze sentiments from social media, emphasizing the significance of integrating sentiment analysis with market data.

The developed BERT-based model shows promise, achieving 83% accuracy in predicting BTC sentiment using Twitter data. The classification report provides a detailed assessment of the model's performance. According to the results, the model achieves high precision, particularly for positive and neutral sentiments.

The study identifies areas for future research, such as exploring additional deep learning models, incorporating more classifiers, and addressing potential shortcomings in existing models. It emphasizes the need for continuous investigation into sentiment analysis for cryptocurrency prices.

Suggestions for Future Works:

Enhanced Model: Develop and refine the existing model to improve recall for positive and neutral sentiments. Experiment with different deep learning architectures and fine-tuning strategies to optimize performance.

Real-Time Analysis: Explore real-time sentiment analysis to capture instantaneous shifts in Twitter discussions. This can provide timely insights into evolving sentiments and their potential impact on cryptocurrency prices.

Extended Dataset: Expand the dataset to include a broader range of influencers, diverse opinions, and additional cryptocurrencies. A more extensive dataset can enhance the model's ability to generalize to various market conditions.

In summary, while the current study lays the foundation for sentiment analysis using the BERT model on Twitter data for BTC, future research should focus on refining the model, expanding datasets, and exploring real-time analysis to further advance the understanding of cryptocurrency sentiment dynamics.

This section may be divided by subheadings. It should provide a concise and precise description of the experimental results, their interpretation, as well as the experimental conclusions that can be drawn.

Author Contributions: In this research, Dilek Celik was responsible for the conceptualization of the study. Literature Review is performed by Niloufar Karimian. The methodology, model development, and formal analysis were primarily carried out by Dilek Celik. Validation of the results involved contributions from Dilek Celik and Ahmet Celik. Dilek Celik also led the investigation, resources management, data curation, writing of the original draft, and visualization of the results. All authors were actively involved in the writing, review, and editing process and have read and agreed to the published version of the manuscript.

Data Availability Statement: The data can be downloaded at: https://data.mendeley.com/datasets/8fbdhh72gs/5.

References

AlBadani, B., Shi, R. and Dong, J. 2022. A novel machine learning approach for sentiment analysis on twitter incorporating the universal language model fine-tuning and SVM. *Applied System Innovation*, 5(1). doi: 10.3390/asi5010013.

Alsayat, A. 2022. Improving sentiment analysis for social media applications using an ensemble deep learning language model. *Arabian Journal for Science and Engineering*, 47(2). doi: 10.1007/s13369-021-06227-w.

Ante, L. 2023. How Elon Musk's Twitter activity moves cryptocurrency markets. *Technological Forecasting and Social Change*, 186. doi: 10.1016/j.techfore.2022.122112.

Aslam, N., Rustam, F., Lee, E., Washington, P.B. and Ashraf, I. 2022. Sentiment analysis and emotion detection on cryptocurrency related tweets using ensemble LSTM-GRU Model. *IEEE Access*, 10. doi: 10.1109/ACCESS.2022.3165621.

Devlin, J., Chang, M.W., Lee, K. and Toutanova, K. 2019. BERT: Pre-training of deep bidirectional transformers for language understanding. *NAACL HLT 2019 - 2019 Conference of the North American Chapter of the Association for Computational Linguistics: Human Language Technologies - Proceedings of the Conference*, vol. 1.

Gurrib, I. and Kamalov, F. 2022. Predicting bitcoin price movements using sentiment analysis: a machine learning approach. *Studies in Economics and Finance*, 39(3). doi: 10.1108/SEF-07-2021-0293.

He, K., Zhang, X., Ren, S. and Sun, J., 2016. Deep residual learning for image recognition. *Proceedings of the IEEE Computer Society Conference on Computer Vision and Pattern Recognition*, 2016-December. doi: 10.1109/CVPR.2016.90.

Jahanbin, K., Zare, C., Mohammad, A. and Rahmanian, F. 2023. Database of influencers' tweets in cryptocurrency (2021–2023). *Mendeley Data*, 5.

Jiao, P., Veiga, A. and Walther, A. 2020. Social media, news media and the stock market. *Journal of Economic Behavior and Organization*, 176. doi: 10.1016/j.jebo.2020.03.002.

Kraaijeveld, O. and De Smedt, J., 2020. The predictive power of public Twitter sentiment for forecasting cryptocurrency prices. *Journal of International Financial Markets, Institutions and Money*, 65. doi: 10.1016/j.intfin.2020.101188.

LeCun, Y., Bengio, Y. & Hinton, G., 2015. Deep learning. *Nature*, 521, pp.436–444.

Man, X., Luo, T. and Lin, J. 2019. Financial sentiment analysis (FSA): A survey. *Proceedings of the IEEE International Conference on Physics of Data Science (ICPHYS)*. doi: 10.1109/ICPHYS.2019.8780312.

Mishev, K., Gjorgjevikj, A., Vodenska, I., Chitkushev, L.T. and Trajanov, D., 2020. Evaluation of sentiment analysis in finance: from lexicons to transformers. *IEEE Access*, 8. doi: 10.1109/ACCESS.2020.3009626.

Naeem, M.A., Mbarki, I. and Shahzad, S.J.H. 2021. Predictive role of online investor sentiment for cryptocurrency market: Evidence from happiness and fears. *International Review of Economics & Finance*, 73. doi: 10.1016/j.iref.2021.01.008.

Pano, T. and Kashef, R. 2020. A complete vader-based sentiment analysis of bitcoin (BTC) tweets during the ERA of COVID-19. *Big Data and Cognitive Computing*, 4(4). doi: 10.3390/bdcc4040033.

Park, J. and Seo, Y.S. 2023. Twitter sentiment analysis-based adjustment of cryptocurrency action recommendation model for profit maximization. *IEEE Access*, 11. doi: 10.1109/ACCESS.2023.3273898.

Peng, S., Cao, L., Zhou, Y., Ouyang, Z., Yang, A., Li, X. et al. 2022. A survey on deep learning for textual emotion analysis in social networks. *Digital Communications and Networks*, 8(5): 745–762. doi: 10.1016/j.dcan.2021.10.003.

Valencia, F., Gómez-Espinosa, A. and Valdés-Aguirre, B. 2019. Price movement prediction of cryptocurrencies using sentiment analysis and machine learning. *Entropy*, 21(6). doi: 10.3390/e21060589.

Valle-Cruz, D., Fernandez-Cortez, V., López-Chau, A. and Sandoval-Almazán, R. 2022. Does twitter affect stock market decisions? Financial sentiment analysis during pandemics: a comparative study of the H1N1 and the COVID-19 periods. *Cognitive Computation*, 14(1). doi: 10.1007/s12559-021-09819-8.

Vo, A.D. 2019. Sentiment analysis of news for effective cryptocurrency price prediction. *International Journal of Knowledge Engineering*, 5(2). doi: 10.18178/ijke.2019.5.2.116.

Wankhade, M., Rao, A.C.S. and Kulkarni, C. 2022. A survey on sentiment analysis methods, applications, and challenges. *Artificial Intelligence Review*, 55(7). doi: 10.1007/s10462-022-10144-1.

Ye, Z., Wu, Y., Chen, H., Pan, Y. and Jiang, Q. 2022. A stacking ensemble deep learning model for bitcoin price prediction using twitter comments on bitcoin. *Mathematics*, 10(8). doi: 10.3390/math10081307.

Yekrangi, M. and Abdolvand, N. 2021. Financial markets sentiment analysis: developing a specialized Lexicon. *Journal of Intelligent Information Systems*, 57(1). doi: 10.1007/s10844-020-00630-9.

CHAPTER 5

Data Pipeline Modelling and Implementation for Real-Time Processing of Job Listings from Online Platforms

Adnane Elmotassadeq and *Dilek Celik**

1. Introduction

Data Engineering involves applying various technologies and skills to automate and manage the flow of raw data into formats suitable for analysis. This project offers a comprehensive overview of these techniques, focusing on designing and developing a data pipeline for extracting, processing, and analyzing data. By evaluating multiple architectural structures against recent technologies, the study addresses the challenges of dynamic and evolving domains, such as the job market. The efficient collection and analysis of real-time or near-real-time job portal data from diverse online sources significantly benefits stakeholders, including job seekers, recruiters, and policymakers at both organizational and governmental levels. This project aims to build a data pipeline that scrapes job information from websites and public APIs, cleans the data, and derives actionable insights. This section outlines the project's aims, background, objectives, and methodology while providing an overview of the report structure.

The motivation for this project arises from the dynamic nature of the job market, which necessitates real-time data analysis to track job trends and demands. Traditional data processing methods struggle to manage the vast volume of daily

Faculty of Engineering & Environment, Northumbria University London Campus, UK.
Emails: adnane.elmotassadeq@northumbria.ac.uk
* Corresponding author: dilek.celik@northumbria.ac.uk

DOI: 10.1201/9781003540373-5

job listings and the demand for instantaneous insights. To address these challenges, this project develops an optimized data pipeline capable of processing and analyzing real-time job data, supporting evidence-based decision-making for stakeholders.

Recent literature underscores the significance of stream processing in managing large-scale, real-time data efficiently. For instance, Intorruk and Numnonda (2019) highlight the capabilities of distributed messaging systems such as Apache Kafka for stream processing. Similarly, Corbone et al. (2015) designed a stream-processing data pipeline based on Apache Flink, focusing on scalable architectures for real-time analytics in high-throughput data streams. Their approach evaluated system performance based on latency and throughput, confirming enhanced data processing capabilities and accuracy. These findings reinforce the effectiveness of combining batch processing technologies with real-time analytics for dynamic data environments like the job market.

The primary goal of this research is to design, implement, and evaluate a data pipeline that processes job listings by efficiently collecting, cleaning, and analyzing data from public websites and APIs. The system aims to generate actionable insights for job seekers, employers, and policymakers, enabling informed, data-driven decision-making.

This research addresses the following key questions:

1. What is the most efficient data pipeline architecture for processing job listings and delivering timely insights?
2. Which technologies are most suitable for implementing such a pipeline in the job market domain?
3. What trends and insights can be extracted from processed job data to inform stakeholders?

To achieve the central goal, this project is guided by the following objectives:

- Develop a scalable and efficient data pipeline architecture for processing job listing information.
- Integrate real-time data processing technologies with batch processing and a storage system optimized for efficient querying and analysis.
- Evaluate the pipeline's performance and accuracy using predefined metrics such as data processing speed and correctness.

The remainder of this paper is organized as follows: Section 2 reviews related work, discussing existing literature and techniques relevant to data pipeline development. Section 3 outlines the methodology adopted for designing and implementing the pipeline, including the choice of tools and technologies. Section 4 focuses on the implementation phase, detailing processes such as web scraping, data cleaning, and real-time data processing. Section 5 presents the evaluation results, analyzing the pipeline's performance and effectiveness against predefined metrics. Finally, Section 6 provides a discussion of the findings, addresses limitations, and proposes directions for future research and development.

2. Literature Review

This section provides an extensive review of relevant literature on data pipeline architectures, technologies, and their application in real-time data processing, particularly for job listings. The section serves as a guide to understanding the existing knowledge base and technological frameworks that informed the project's methodology for this research.

2.1 Data pipeline architectures: a study and comparison

A data pipeline architecture is crucial in efficiently managing and processing data, particularly for real-time applications such as job listings. The architecture plays a pivotal role in ensuring the efficiency, scalability, and reliability of data flow from its source to the end-user. This section examines different data pipeline architectures, analyzing their advantages and limitations within the context of processing job-related data.

2.1.1 Batch processing vs. stream processing

Batch processing and stream processing represent two fundamental paradigms in data pipeline architectures. Batch processing involves accumulating data in batches and processing it at scheduled intervals. Apache Hadoop has been a leading technology in this domain, though newer innovations have since emerged (Zaharia et al. 2010). Batch processing is resource-efficient and relatively simple to manage, making it a practical choice for many applications. However, it may lack responsiveness in environments with rapidly changing data. Despite this, the trade-off is less significant in the context of job listings, where trends typically do not shift dramatically on a minute-by-minute basis.

In contrast, stream processing processes data in real-time, enabling immediate analysis and response. Widely adopted technologies for this approach include Apache Kafka and Apache Pulsar. Stream processing is particularly advantageous for applications requiring real-time insights, such as financial transactions or fraud detection, where minimizing latency is critical (Akanbi and Masinde 2020). However, this paradigm comes with significant challenges. The complexity and resource demands of stream processing necessitate continuous resource allocation, which can be both costly and difficult to scale sustainably over the long term.

When applied to job market analysis, where data updates occur at a moderate pace rather than continuously, the advantages of stream processing diminish. The additional complexity and overhead associated with stream processing cannot be justified. In such cases, batch processing offers a more suitable alternative by providing timely updates without unnecessary resource consumption, making it a better fit for the specific requirements of job listing data analysis.

2.1.2 Lambda architecture

The Lambda architecture combines batch and stream processing to deliver a robust solution for managing large-scale data. It is structured into three key layers: the batch layer, which processes historical data to ensure comprehensive and accurate computations; the speed layer, which handles real-time data for immediate insights; and the serving layer, which integrates outputs from both the batch and speed layers to provide unified, comprehensive insights (Kiran et al. 2015).

Despite its strengths in balancing the accuracy of batch processing with the immediacy of stream processing, Kiran et al. (2015) highlight significant challenges associated with Lambda architecture. One notable drawback is its complexity, particularly in maintaining and managing a codebase that spans across its multiple layers.

2.1.3 Kappa Architecture

Kappa architecture simplifies data processing by focusing solely on stream processing. It eliminates the batch layer, relying entirely on the speed layer to handle both historical and real-time data. This architecture is suitable for applications where real-time processing is paramount, and batch processing can be bypassed (Kreps 2014).

Given the moderate pace at which job market data updates, Kappa architecture's exclusive reliance on real-time processing was unnecessary and potentially inefficient for this application as the data stream will not be continuous.

2.1.4 Extract, Load, Transform (ELT) architecture

ELT architecture, a variant of the traditional ETL (Extract, Transform, Load) approach, involves extracting data from sources, loading it into a data storage system, and then transforming it as needed. This approach leverages the power of modern data warehousing solutions like Snowflake and Google BigQuery, which can handle large-scale transformations efficiently within the data warehouse (Hellerstein et al. 2017).

The ELT approach's flexibility and scalability make it an attractive choice for many data-intensive applications. However, it also shifts much of the transformation workload to the database layer, which can strain system resources if not properly managed.

2.2 Recent tools and technologies for data pipeline development

The choice of technology significantly impacts the efficiency, scalability, and ease of integration with existing systems of a data pipeline. This section critically reviews some contemporary technologies that facilitate the development of robust and scalable data pipelines.

2.2.1 Python for data ingestion and transformation

Python has become a dominant language in data engineering due to its simplicity, extensive libraries, and community support. Libraries such as Requests, BeautifulSoup, and Pandas are particularly useful for data ingestion and transformation tasks. According to McKinney (2022), the author of "Python for Data Analysis," Python's libraries offer powerful tools for cleaning, transforming, and analysing data, making it an excellent choice for building data pipelines.

Despite its strengths, Python is not without limitations. Its performance can lag when handling very large datasets, particularly in comparison to more optimized languages like Java or C++. Python's extensive ecosystem and strong community support still justify its use for job-marked data processing research.

2.2.2 Apache Kafka

Apache Kafka is a distributed streaming platform capable of handling high-throughput, low-latency data streams. It is designed to be fault-tolerant and scalable, making it an ideal choice for real-time data processing (Kreps et al. 2011). Although Kafka excels at real-time processing, the nature of job market data—which is not continuously streamed—necessitates relying solely on Kafka's batch processing capabilities.

2.2.3 Apache Pulsar

Apache Pulsar is a cloud-native, distributed messaging and streaming platform. It supports multi-tenancy and geo-replication, making it a robust choice for global-scale data streaming applications (Kjerrumgaard 2021). Pulsar's features can be considered for deploying the system on the cloud for future expansion and project scalability.

2.2.4 Google Cloud Dataflow

Google Cloud Dataflow is a fully managed service for stream and batch processing. It allows users to develop data pipelines using the Apache Beam SDK, providing a unified model for both types of processing. Dataflow's integration with other Google Cloud services enhances its capabilities and scalability. Dataflow's versatility makes it an attractive option for more complex data processing needs (Akidau et al. 2015).

2.2.5 PostgreSQL for Data Storage

PostgreSQL is renowned for its reliability and flexibility, particularly in handling complex queries and maintaining data integrity. Petrov (2019) highlights PostgreSQL's robustness in supporting large datasets and its adaptability in various applications.

However, PostgreSQL's performance can be a limiting factor when dealing with very high write loads or when scaling horizontally across distributed systems. In this project, these limitations are not critical within the scope, as the batch processing model and the nature of the job listings data did not require extreme scalability or high-frequency writes. PostgreSQL's strengths lie in data consistency, rich feature set, and strong community support.

2.2.6 Snowflake

Snowflake is a data warehousing solution designed for cloud environments. Its architecture supports ELT workflows, allowing for efficient data storage and transformation within the warehouse. Snowflake's scalability and performance make it suitable for handling large-scale data pipelines (Kashyap 2023). Data warehousing should also be considered for future iterations of the project where enhanced data storage capabilities and computing may be required.

2.2.7 Tableau for data visualization

Tableau is a leading tool in data visualization, known for its user-friendly interface and powerful capabilities for creating interactive dashboards. Murray (2013) notes that Tableau excels in handling large datasets and providing intuitive visualizations that can easily be shared and understood by stakeholders.

Despite its many advantages, Tableau can be expensive for large-scale deployments, and its integration with certain data sources can require additional configuration and management. In this project, Tableau's benefits outweighed these concerns, particularly because it provided an effective means to visualize and communicate the insights derived from the job listing data. Its ability to connect seamlessly with PostgreSQL and the ease with which dashboards could be created and shared, in addition to a pack of tools that support other functions like Tableau prep for processing data and Tableau server for connectivity, offers students a free trial version to work with.

2.3 Web scraping techniques, technologies, and ethics

The internet contains a wealth of information, exponentially increasing. A researcher could always turn to the web to identify and extract real data for projects. Getting that data manually is very laborious though and becomes ridiculous when aiming to continuously obtain live Big Data. That is when Web Scraping practices come into play, either through screen scraping or Application Programming Interfaces (APIs). Web scraping is a critical component of the data pipeline for collecting job listings from various online sources. This section explores the techniques and technologies used in web scraping, as well as the ethical considerations involved.

2.3.1 Web Scraping techniques

Web scraping involves extracting data from websites using automated scripts. Techniques include HTML parsing, DOM manipulation, and API interactions. Tools like Beautiful Soup and Scrapy are popular for web scraping due to their ease of use and powerful capabilities (Mitchell 2018).

2.3.2 Technologies for web scraping

Beautiful Soup: A Python library for parsing HTML and XML documents. It creates parse trees for web pages, which can be used to extract data easily.

Scrapy: In the open-source web-crawling framework for Python. It provides a comprehensive environment for building and running web spiders (Scrapy 2023).

Selenium: A tool for automating web browsers. It is used for web scraping when dealing with dynamic content that requires interaction (SeleniumHQ 2023).

2.3.3 Ethical considerations in web scraping

Ethical web scraping involves adhering to the terms of service of websites, respecting robots.txt files, and avoiding actions that could harm the website's performance. It is crucial to ensure that scraping activities do not violate legal guidelines or infringe on intellectual property rights (Krotov et al. 2020).

2.4 Job market landscape and the need for streamlined data analysis

The job market is dynamic, with continuous fluctuations influenced by various factors such as economic conditions, technological advancements, and changing industry demands. Real-time data analysis is essential for stakeholders to stay updated and make informed decisions.

2.4.1 The dynamic nature of the job market

The job market is characterized by rapid changes in job availability, required skills, and salary trends. Analysing real-time job listings provides insights into current market demands, helping job seekers align their skills with industry requirements (Carnevale et al. 2013).

2.4.2 The role of streamlined data analysis

Streamlined data analysis enables quick and efficient processing of large volumes of job data. By leveraging advanced data pipelines, stakeholders can access up-to-date information, facilitating timely decisions. Employers can identify skill gaps, job seekers can find relevant opportunities, and policymakers can address labour market challenges effectively (Chui et al. 2016).

2.5 Conclusion

This literature review has provided a comprehensive analysis of data pipeline architectures, technologies, and their applications in processing real-time job listing data. The review critically examined batch and stream processing paradigms, highlighting their respective advantages and limitations, and explored hybrid approaches such as Lambda and Kappa architectures. The importance of contemporary tools like Python, Apache Kafka, Snowflake, and PostgreSQL for efficient pipeline development was emphasized, alongside the role of visualization platforms like Tableau in delivering actionable insights. Additionally, ethical considerations in web scraping and the dynamic nature of the job market were discussed, underscoring the need for streamlined data analysis to support stakeholders in navigating this ever-changing domain. Collectively, these insights form the foundation for developing an optimized data pipeline tailored to the specific requirements of job market analysis.

3. Research Methodologies

This study adopts the Design Science Research Methodology (DSRM) as its overarching framework. DSRM provides a problem-solving paradigm focused on the creation and evaluation of artefacts designed to address specific problems (Geerts 2011). In the design and development of the data pipeline artefact, Agile and CRISP-DM (Cross-Industry Standard Process for Data Mining) methodologies are implemented to structure the development process and ensure robust data processing and analysis.

By leveraging the iterative nature of Agile and the systematic data-focused approach of CRISP-DM, the methodology provides a flexible yet structured path for designing, developing, and evaluating the pipeline. This integration ensures consistency, adaptability, and rigorous adherence to best practices.

3.1 Design Science Research Methodology (DSRM)

DSRM provides the foundation for the entire research process. Its six stages—problem identification, objective definition, design and development, demonstration, evaluation, and communication—align with Agile and CRISP-DM methods to achieve the research goals.

1. Problem Identification and Motivation: The research addresses the challenge of real-time processing and analysis of job listings to provide actionable insights for job seekers, employers, and policymakers.
2. Objective Definition: The primary objective is to design a pipeline capable of real-time data ingestion, cleaning, storage, and visualization while ensuring adaptability and efficiency.
3. Artefact Development: The data pipeline artefact is developed iteratively using Agile sprints, guided by the CRISP-DM phases for data processing tasks.
4. Demonstration: The pipeline is tested with real-world data scraped from public websites.
5. Evaluation: The artefact is evaluated using metrics such as accuracy, efficiency, reliability, and scalability.
6. Communication: Results and methodologies are documented comprehensively for replication and dissemination.

3.2 Agile framework

Agile methodology was selected for its iterative and incremental nature, making it particularly suited for projects involving complex data processing and evolving requirements. Agile facilitates regular updates and refinements based on feedback, ensuring the development of a robust and efficient data pipeline.

3.2.1 Sprint planning

The project was divided into eight sprints, each lasting two weeks. Each sprint focused on specific tasks and deliverables:

- Sprint 1: Requirement gathering, initial setup, and architecture design.
- Sprint 2: Development of web scraping and API request scripts while searching for sources that allow it.

- Sprint 3: Integration of data extraction and schema design for job listings with common columns between sources.
- Sprint 4: Implementation of data cleaning and transformation processes, focusing on structuring and preparing raw data.
- Sprint 5: Testing and optimization of batch data ingestion processes.
- Sprint 6: Data loading and integration into PostgreSQL, followed by validation.
- Sprint 7: Creation of Tableau dashboards for visualization and initial testing.
- Sprint 8: Evaluation of pipeline performance, system integration, and final adjustments.

3.2.2 Daily stand-ups

Daily stand-up meetings are conducted to review progress, address challenges, and plan the day's activities. These meetings ensured continuous communication and quick resolution of issues. However, this project is individual work and with daily meetings with the supervisor not being possible, this would be done by self-reflection on progress and a weekly review with the supervisor.

3.2.3 Sprint reviews and retrospectives

At the end of each sprint, a review meeting showcased completed work and gathered feedback. Retrospective meetings followed to discuss what went well, what could be improved, and how to enhance the process in the next sprint.

3.3 CRISP-DM model integration

The CRISP-DM model was integrated within the Agile framework to provide a structured approach to data mining and processing. This model consists of six phases: Business Understanding, Data Understanding, Data Preparation, Modelling, Evaluation, and Deployment. This structure helps with the data analysis side of the research ensuring adherence to best practices.

3.3.1 Business understanding

In this phase, the project objectives were defined, and the requirements for the data pipeline were gathered. The goal was to understand the specific needs of job seekers, employers, and policymakers in accessing real-time job market data (Brzozowska et al. 2023). These stakeholders in the job market domain could benefit from key variables insights such as salary ranges, job title popularity, activity in certain domain categories or geographic spread of job activity.

3.3.2 Data understanding

This phase involves collecting initial data samples, exploring the data, and identifying any quality issues. Job listings are gathered from various public websites. The collected data is examined to understand its structure and content (Mitchell 2018).

This phase is critical in deciding the pipeline architecture to follow and choosing appropriate technologies to capture meaningful changes in job data.

3.3.3 Data preparation

Data preparation involves cleaning and transforming the collected data to ensure it is suitable for analysis. Python's Pandas library was used extensively to standardize the data format and ensure consistency across job sources. This included:

- Removing duplicates and irrelevant information.
- Standardizing formats for job titles, company names, and locations.
- Handling missing values and outliers.
- Error checking and validation (Rahm and Do 2020).

These steps are fundamentally how data is transformed, but further detailed changes may be required for specific formatting exceptions that generate faulty data.

3.3.4 Modelling

The data pipeline architecture was designed and modelled to handle the core tasks of data ingestion, transformation, and storage. Batch processing was chosen as the primary mode of operation, supported by scheduled extraction intervals. The modelling phase focused on:

- Implementing Python libraries such as pandas and NumPy to transform and analyse data.
- Setting up a database for storing and querying processed data and deploying it on a local server.
- Link Tableau Desktop to the database server for automatic access to data and capturing changes that reflect on visualizations.

3.3.5 Evaluation

The evaluation phase focused on assessing the performance and accuracy of the data pipeline. Key metrics used to evaluate the pipeline include efficiency, reliability of data extraction, processing, speed, accuracy, and system stability. Error handling and safety measures were also put to ensure the pipeline met the needs of stakeholders (Akanbi and Masinde 2020). Performance profiling tools (e.g., Python's cProfile) were used to identify bottlenecks and ensure that the pipeline was optimized for efficiency, given the moderate size of the job data and the batch-based approach.

3.3.6 Deployment

In the deployment phase, the fully developed data pipeline was deployed to a production environment locally. This phase is mainly reliant on running the Python script, setting up a PostgreSQL database server on localhost and linking Tableau to it, as well as setting up email notifications. Continuous monitoring and maintenance were implemented to ensure the pipeline's ongoing performance and to accommodate any necessary updates or improvements.

3.4 Detailed process description

Step 1: Requirement Gathering and Initial Setup

- Conducted research on the domain to gather requirements for stakeholders.
- Defined project scope, objectives, and deliverables.
- Set up the development environment on the chosen IDE, including necessary tools and technologies.

Step 2: Architecture Design

- Designed the overall architecture of the data pipeline, incorporating ETL principles or other desired models.

  Selected appropriate technologies (e.g., Python, PostgreSQL, Snowflake) (Carbone et al. 2015).

Step 3: Development of Data Extraction Scripts

- Using public APIs, when possible, with the Python request library.
- Developed web scraping scripts using requests, Beautiful Soup and Scrapy libraries.
- Ensured scripts adhered to ethical standards and website terms of service, and respected the API rate limit (Mitchell 2018).

Step 4: Data Cleaning and Transformation

- Cleaned and transformed the extracted data to ensure consistency and accuracy. Pandas were used extensively for this part following best practices to handle missing values, removing duplicates and standardizing position and salary.

Step 5: Data Storage

- Stored in a flexible database system locally for recording and analysis with schema validation to ensure integrity (Rahm and Do 2020).

Step 6: Visualization and Reporting

- Exploring loaded data with analytics and visualization tools to mine insights and create dashboards relevant to the stakeholders.

Step 7: System Testing, Evaluation and Refinement

- Conducted unit tests, integration tests, and performance tests to ensure the pipeline's functionality.
- Evaluated the system using profiling tools to identify bottlenecks. In addition to evaluating the data itself and ensuring it checks the three main criteria of CIA (confidentiality, integrity and availability).
- Adjust the script to fix anomalies in pipeline functioning or data quality.
- Integrated all components into a cohesive system (Akanbi and Masinde 2020).

Step 8: Documentation and Deployment

- Documented the entire development process, including code, configurations, user guides and dashboards for insights.
- Deployed the data pipeline to the production environment (Kashyap 2023).

3.5 Conclusion

This methodology provides a comprehensive and structured approach to designing, developing, and evaluating a data pipeline for real-time job listings. By integrating Agile practices with the CRISP-DM model, the methodology ensures flexibility, continuous improvement, and robust data processing capabilities. These methodologies overlap in several steps and all fall within the DSRM, not to signal redundancy in tasks but rather that they complete each other in the context of the research. This detailed process description ensures that the study can be replicated, allowing for consistent results and further enhancements.

4. Design and Implementation of Data Pipeline

With project objectives set, and a comparative review of state-of-the-art technologies and domains studied, the following step is to design and build the data pipeline and leverage it to move data from raw format in source to sink, where it would be clean and ready for analysis. This section details the development of this system and justifications for the chosen approach and technologies.

4.1 Preliminary overview

Considering the existence of many architectural designs and technologies to be used as mentioned in comparative studies, it is apparent that this project could be designed and executed in numerous ways using different technologies and solutions available. Therefore, a wise approach to deciding on a specific architecture that is best for this specific case requires a reflection on the objectives, requirements and limitations of this research.

Firstly, the goal of this pipeline is to handle job listings from different sources, process the data efficiently, and produce useful insights. Simplicity is key, especially with limited resources, a narrow time schedule, and no need for complex designs. Therefore, the pipeline should be simple and concise, using open-source technologies that offer both robust solutions to handling data and minimal computational expenses and that can be paired up smoothly with each other, ensuring the efficiency of the pipeline and low maintenance.

Moreover, while the idea of streaming real-time data constantly through the pipeline to catch job listings as soon as they are posted sounds appealing, this research fails to justify this real-time approach for the following reasons.

Firstly, the research aims to monitor the state and fluctuations in the job market using current data. Those changes would not be noticeable live or not even daily or weekly, except in extremely rare cases of a big event that delivers instant impact on the job market. And so, in the absence of the need to react to this data in real-time, using batch streaming at scheduled intervals makes more sense and is close enough to real-time without following real-time structure.

Furthermore, while the websites used, among others, do offer public access to those job offers to developers through their API, there is a delay between the time when the job was posted and when it was made available in the API. On the

RemoteOK website, for instance, you can see some job postings less than a day old advertised, but they do not appear on the API yet. Understandably, the website keeps to itself a lead in advertising the jobs for about 24 hours before allowing third parties to grab them—unless they do so without permission using web crawlers/scrapers and violating the terms of service instead of using the API endpoint. In addition, the API rate limit from websites like Reed only allows a maximum of 100 returns per request. Therefore, the main motive behind real-time extraction is already not plausible.

Other reasons for this choice include the fact that the data sources do not provide a constant flow of data, and stream processing may result in data inconsistencies as the data needs thorough formatting, cleaning, and structuring from all sources—for which batch processing is better equipped. Evidently, stream processing also requires more resources and more complex structures.

4.2 Pipeline architecture

When designing the pipeline, the aim was to balance efficiency and practicality. The pipeline was broken down into three main components: data ingestion, data transformation, and data loading (ETL architecture). An analysis layer was also added. Each component was tailored to meet our specific needs, focusing on getting the job done right rather than using the fanciest tools (see Figure 1).

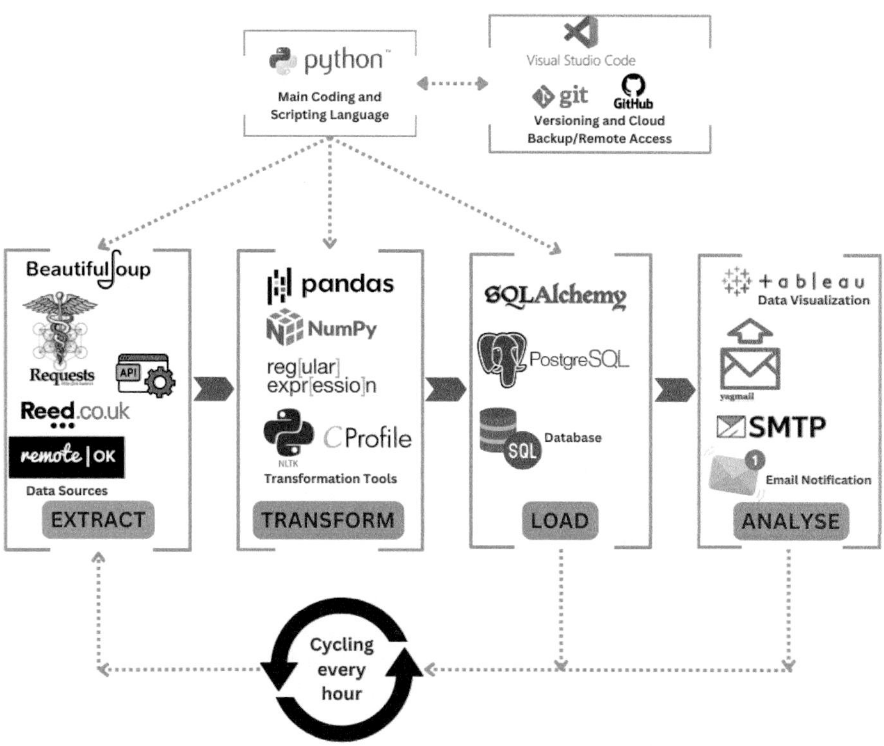

Figure 1: The Data Pipeline Architecture.

The ETL (Extract, Transform, Load) and Analysis pipeline (see Figure 1) leverages a combination of tools to ensure seamless data acquisition, processing, storage, and analysis, which are critical for real-time insights. Each stage and the use of the tools are explained in further detail in the sections below.

4.2.1 Extract

The extraction phase involved pulling job listings from two online sources. "RemoteOK" and "Reed" offer public APIs, which were used to gather job data. The goal was to collect as much relevant data as possible without being overwhelmed by unnecessary details, excessive requests, or overloading the database and requiring more resources.

For sourcing job data, Python's requests library and BeautifulSoup were utilized. These tools were selected for their simplicity and effectiveness, ensuring minimal setup requirements while maintaining ethical compliance with data providers (Richardson 2020). Although more advanced frameworks like Scrapy could have been used, the straightforward approach was better suited for this project. Python's requests library was used to send GET requests to these APIs, which may include parameters to filter the data requested, such as retrieving only certain domain jobs. The responses were parsed using BeautifulSoup to extract the relevant job listings. Each job listing was then stored in a structured format, typically a list of dictionaries, where each dictionary represented a job post.

4.2.2 Transform

The data transformation step was essential for cleaning the data, formatting it, and ensuring that data from different sources was structured appropriately. This ensured that the data was useful and consistent and that the pipeline ran smoothly without demanding excessive processing power or development time (Wang et al. 2020). Python served as the primary scripting language, supported by pandas for data manipulation and cleaning, NumPy for numerical computations and array handling, and regular expressions (re) for data cleaning tasks. These libraries were chosen for their user-friendliness and powerful functionality, avoiding the complexities of heavier frameworks like Apache Spark (McKinney 2022). Pandas was extensively used in this part for the transformations, which included:

- Structuring: Converting raw data into a well-defined format (e.g., a DataFrame), ensuring that all relevant fields (job title, company, location, salary, etc.) were captured accurately, matching columns from both websites accordingly, and dropping extra columns that contained unnecessary information or were not present in both sources.
- Cleaning: Removing duplicates, filling in missing values (e.g., replacing salaries with mean when absent), and correcting errors (e.g., standardizing date formats or cleaning up location names).
- Formatting: Ensuring that all data was in a consistent format, such as standardizing salary columns to use the same currency, making it easier to load into the PostgreSQL database and use for further analysis.

Additionally, a simple logic was implemented to flag potential fraudulent postings based on criteria such as overly frequent reposts, bulk job submissions from a single source, and suspicious words in descriptions (e.g., "easy cash" or unusually high salaries). This logic used a point-based system, where each suspicious criterion contributed one or more points. Based on the total score, job postings were classified into categories: safe, low risk, medium risk, high risk, or extremely high risk.

4.2.3 Load

The next step in the data pipeline was loading the cleaned and structured data into a PostgreSQL relational database. PostgreSQL was chosen for its reliability, robust documentation, and adaptability, which reduced project risks and provided flexibility to handle unexpected challenges (Stonebraker and Kemnitz 2020). The database interaction was streamlined using SQLAlchemy, a Python library that allowed efficient communication with PostgreSQL.

The schema for the database was designed to be straightforward, with a table to store essential job listing information. The job ID served as the primary key, while other fields included company, position, date, location, salary, and application URLs.

4.2.4 Analyse

In the final stage of the pipeline, a side process was set up to email job listings that meet defined criteria, such as jobs in specific locations, accept graduates or within a certain salary range. This was automated to run as part of the pipeline as a side use-case of the pipeline, so relevant job listings would be delivered directly to email and notify the interested person as soon as the job advertisement is available through the API. Automated email notifications were integrated using yagmail and smtplib to ensure timely updates to stakeholders.

Finally, the PostgreSQL database was linked to Tableau running on a local server to create interactive dashboards. The tool's ease of use, availability of a trial version for students, and ability to present findings in a visually engaging manner made it an ideal choice for this project (Murray 2013). This connection allowed Tableau to automatically update and visualize the data on dashboards, which were created to show key insights extracted from the data and monitor changes.

4.3 Environment setup

The development environment was crucial for streamlining the workflow and managing the project efficiently. Visual Studio Code (VS Code) IDE was used for writing scripts and managing the codebase. VS Code's flexibility and extensive range of extensions made it easy to integrate various tools and streamline development, in contrast to cloud-based options such as Google Colab, which appeared to be limiting. Version control was handled using Git, allowing us to track changes and manage different versions of scripts, while the GitHub repository served as a cloud backup to restore progress or access the project elsewhere if needed. The entire process operates cyclically on an hourly basis, ensuring data freshness and supporting continuous analytical insights.

- Create a Git repository and initiate the project.
- Set up VS code with necessary extensions.
- Install Python along with necessary libraries like requests, pandas, and SQLalchemy using pip.
- Set up PostgreSQL on a local server to handle database requirements.
- Link Tableau with the PostgreSQL database on the local server to create real-time visualizations.

4.4 Error handling and data validation

Robust error-handling mechanisms were critical to safeguarding the reliability of the pipeline. Various error-handling codes were implemented to manage errors and validate data at each stage, ensuring that the pipeline continued running if an error occurred at a certain step. Additionally, logs were generated to pinpoint exactly where the error happened, simplifying pipeline maintenance and ensuring efficiency:

- Extraction Errors: Handled by retrying failed requests and logging errors for manual review. If fetching data from a website fails, the pipeline does not stop running and continues extracting from other sources.
- Data Validation: Ensured data integrity by implementing checks for duplicate entries, invalid data formats, and missing values during the transformation phase. This prevents job postings from being re-entered into the database and filters out invalid entries.
- Data Load: If a failure occurs at this stage, it indicates that the database is not connected, preventing the pipeline from loading the data. The script continuously attempts to reconnect to the database while remaining operational. If new data arrives, it may replace the data waiting to be loaded. However, this is not a major issue since unloaded data can still be retrieved from the website once the loading process is fixed.

These measures ensured that the data flowing through the pipeline remained accurate and reliable while isolating errors at specific points to prevent them from compromising the entire system.

4.5 Data privacy and security considerations

Handling job listing data responsibly was paramount. No sensitive personal information was processed. Security was ensured by restricting access to the PostgreSQL database and the Tableau dashboards under authentication. Additionally, compliance with relevant data protection regulations, such as GDPR where applicable, and adherence to the terms of service of websites providing the data were maintained. These measures helped preserve the confidentiality and integrity of the data processed by the pipeline.

4.6 Conclusion

In this section, we have detailed the design and implementation of the data processing pipeline. By focusing on simplicity, efficiency, and practicality, the project successfully produced a working system to streamline data flow from source to sink. The chosen architecture and technologies were suitable for this research; however, many alternatives exist, and their selection should be based on a critical evaluation of the use case, objectives, resources, and limitations.

5. Implementation of the data pipeline

This section highlights the functionality of the data pipeline, demonstrating its ability to achieve research objectives. Each step of the pipeline is illustrated with figures to track the transformation of data from its raw format to actionable insights that can be visualized effectively.

5.1 Data flow

5.1.1 Extract

Using the 'RemoteOK' website as an example, job listings are accessed via the API available at https://remoteok.com/api. Each job posting begins with a unique identifier, the "slug," which serves as a marker. All subsequent data associated with the "slug" represents the job details that need to be extracted.

The next step involves defining the table schema (see Figure 2). The selected columns represent the key information that is commonly found across most job

Figure 2: Table Schema.

advertising websites. This approach ensures seamless integration of data when extracting from multiple sources. The ID column is assigned a primary key constraint to maintain data integrity and prevent duplicate rows or faulty data. While additional constraints, such as ensuring the date is later than the current date or enforcing NOT NULL constraints, could be applied to other columns, these validations have been incorporated into the Python script for data cleaning and integrity checks. Consequently, duplicating these checks in SQL was deemed unnecessary.

The extracted raw data, displayed in Figure 3, is beginning to take shape but requires further cleaning and standardization to ensure usability. Key tasks include standardizing dates to a consistent format, converting salary rates into annualized values, unifying location names, removing HTML tags from the description text, and addressing missing values, particularly in critical fields like location and salary. These steps are essential to refining the dataset for reliable analysis.

5.1.2 Transform

The next step in the pipeline involves transforming the received data and adhering to standard data-cleaning practices. The primary focus is to ensure that data from the two sources is structured into one homogeneous dataset. The transformation process begins by retaining only the common columns from the two sources and standardizing their names to maintain consistency.

Critical columns such as ID, date, and company are essential for valid job listings; therefore, missing values in these columns are dropped, as their absence likely indicates errors that cannot be resolved or replaced. In contrast, missing or zero values in the salary column, often due to companies not disclosing salary information, are replaced with the mean salary to avoid skewing the analysis. Additionally, salaries reported in non-annual formats—hourly, daily, weekly, or monthly—are standardized to annual figures. For instance, hourly salaries under 100 are multiplied by 1,920 (assuming 40 hours per week), daily salaries under 1,000 are multiplied by 365, and monthly salaries are multiplied by 12 to estimate annual compensation accurately.

Cleaning functions for date, location, and description columns are defined separately to standardize these fields. Dates and locations are converted into consistent, accepted formats, while the description column is cleaned using the BeautifulSoup library to remove HTML tags, retaining only the relevant textual content.

Additional transformation steps include creating new columns for analysis, such as a "fraud score" to identify potentially suspicious job advertisements. Indicators of fraudulent listings include unusually high salaries, a company posting multiple similar advertisements in a short time frame, or poorly written descriptions with shady phrases like "easy cash". Each of these criteria assigns 2 or 3 points, and the total score categorizes the listing as "Safe," "Low," "Medium," "High," or "Extremely High" risk. These steps ensure the dataset is both clean and enriched for meaningful analysis.

The final dataset reflects a clean, consistent, and standardized format, ready for further data analysis. Each record has undergone rigorous processing to address missing values, ensure data uniformity, and enrich the dataset with derived features

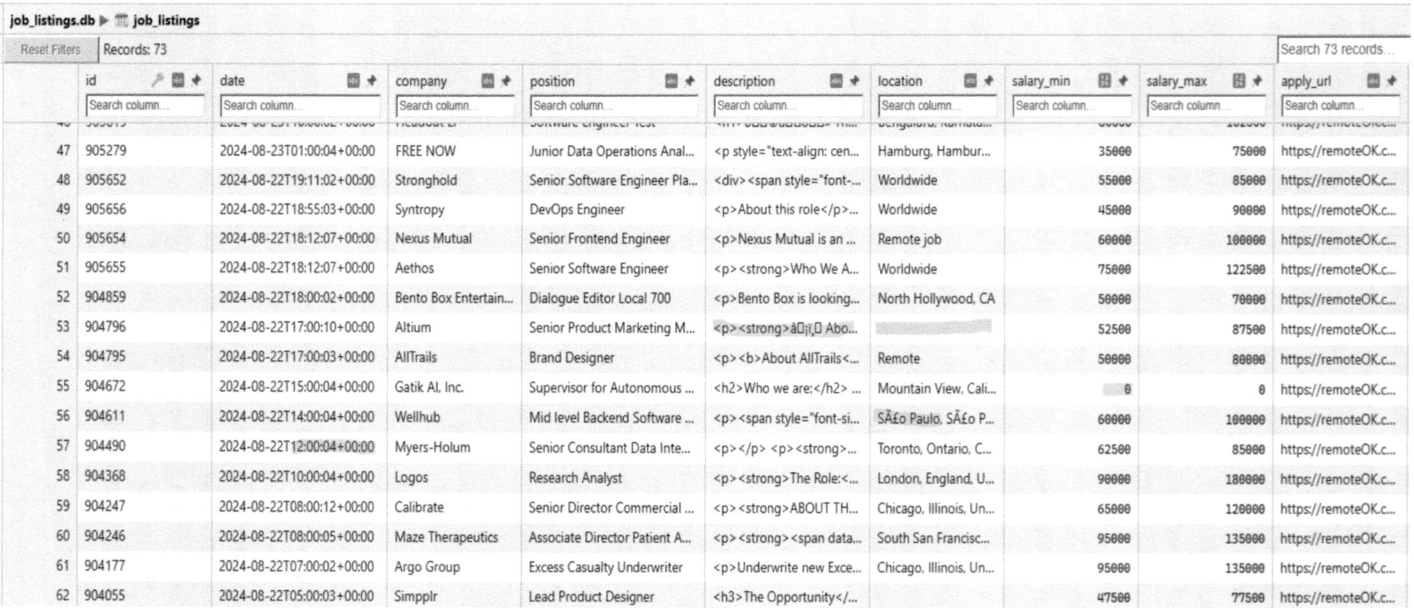

job_listings.db ▶ job_listings

Reset Filters | Records: 73 | Search 73 records...

	id	date	company	position	description	location	salary_min	salary_max	apply_url
47	905279	2024-08-23T01:00:04+00:00	FREE NOW	Junior Data Operations Anal...	<p style="text-align: cen...	Hamburg, Hambur...	35000	75000	https://remoteOK.c...
48	905652	2024-08-22T19:11:02+00:00	Stronghold	Senior Software Engineer Pla...	<div><span style="font-...	Worldwide	55000	85000	https://remoteOK.c...
49	905656	2024-08-22T18:55:03+00:00	Syntropy	DevOps Engineer	<p>About this role</p>...	Worldwide	45000	90000	https://remoteOK.c...
50	905654	2024-08-22T18:12:07+00:00	Nexus Mutual	Senior Frontend Engineer	<p>Nexus Mutual is an ...	Remote job	60000	100000	https://remoteOK.c...
51	905655	2024-08-22T18:12:07+00:00	Aethos	Senior Software Engineer	<p><strong>Who We A...	Worldwide	75000	122500	https://remoteOK.c...
52	904859	2024-08-22T18:00:02+00:00	Bento Box Entertain...	Dialogue Editor Local 700	<p>Bento Box is looking...	North Hollywood, CA	50000	70000	https://remoteOK.c...
53	904796	2024-08-22T17:00:10+00:00	Altium	Senior Product Marketing M...	<p><strong>â□¡□ Abo...		52500	87500	https://remoteOK.c...
54	904795	2024-08-22T17:00:03+00:00	AllTrails	Brand Designer	<p><b>About AllTrails<...	Remote	50000	80000	https://remoteOK.c...
55	904672	2024-08-22T15:00:04+00:00	Gatik AI, Inc.	Supervisor for Autonomous ...	<h2>Who we are:</h2> ...	Mountain View, Cali...	0	0	https://remoteOK.c...
56	904611	2024-08-22T14:00:04+00:00	Wellhub	Mid level Backend Software ...	<p><span style="font-si...	SÃ£o Paulo, SÃ£o P...	60000	100000	https://remoteOK.c...
57	904490	2024-08-22T12:00:04+00:00	Myers-Holum	Senior Consultant Data Inte...	<p></p> <p><strong>...	Toronto, Ontario, C...	62500	85000	https://remoteOK.c...
58	904368	2024-08-22T10:00:04+00:00	Logos	Research Analyst	<p><strong>The Role:<...	London, England, U...	90000	180000	https://remoteOK.c...
59	904247	2024-08-22T08:00:12+00:00	Calibrate	Senior Director Commercial ...	<p><strong>ABOUT TH...	Chicago, Illinois, Un...	65000	120000	https://remoteOK.c...
60	904246	2024-08-22T08:00:05+00:00	Maze Therapeutics	Associate Director Patient A...	<p><strong><span data...	South San Francisc...	95000	135000	https://remoteOK.c...
61	904177	2024-08-22T07:00:02+00:00	Argo Group	Excess Casualty Underwriter	<p>Underwrite new Exce...	Chicago, Illinois, Un...	95000	135000	https://remoteOK.c...
62	904055	2024-08-22T05:00:03+00:00	Simpplr	Lead Product Designer	<h3>The Opportunity</...		47500	77500	https://remoteOK.c...

Figure 3: Initial Fetched Data Viewed on Sqliteviewer.

such as fraud risk scores. Key transformations include standardizing salary data to annualized figures, converting dates and locations into uniform formats, and cleaning job descriptions to remove HTML tags. This figure demonstrates the effectiveness of the transformation pipeline, illustrating how disparate raw data from multiple sources has been harmonized into a cohesive dataset that supports seamless integration and accurate analysis.

5.1.3 Load

Once the data has successfully passed through the transformation phase, it is prepared to be loaded into the database, which for this project is PostgreSQL. To interactively manage the PostgreSQL database, PgAdmin is used as the primary tool. As shown in Figure 4, the PostgreSQL database and server monitoring are managed and visualized using PgAdmin, providing a comprehensive interface for database administration and query execution.

A server named "job_pipeline" was created and hosted on localhost to enable other applications to access the database. It also facilitates monitoring database transactions and assessing their operational state via the dashboard, with access to error logs for troubleshooting if required. Additionally, it provides an SQL query interface for altering tables and managing data directly.

As illustrated in Figure 5, data that satisfies the criteria defined in the check_conditions function is automatically sent via email to notify interested parties, including details such as the position, location, salary, and application URL.

5.1.4 Running pipeline and performance metrics

The data frame is printed before and after cleaning the data from each source for troubleshooting purposes. In this pipeline cycle, we notice that the pipeline inserted 27 new records from RemoteOK and then 100 new records from Reed, which is the API rate limit of the website that cannot be exceeded per request. The pipeline cycle was completed in 6.09 seconds, which is quite fast and not too troublesome for an hourly cycle. If the pipeline does not find any new data, the cycle is completed in 4.29 seconds, meaning that most of the time taken by the cycle is used by import and printing functions rather than the actual ETL functions.

When storing the results of the script profiling done with the cProfile library in the profile_results.prof file, those results can be viewed with the command python -m, allowing interaction with the file in the terminal. After sorting the results by cumulative time and displaying the first 20, it is noticeable that while the pipeline function takes one of the highest cumulative times, it is only called once per run and therefore does not slow the script. In contrast, built-in methods and library imports take considerably more time. The pipeline completes each run in 4 to 6 seconds, depending on the data available, which is considered an acceptable runtime for a script executed on an hourly basis. Given this performance, further optimization is not deemed necessary for the current use case.

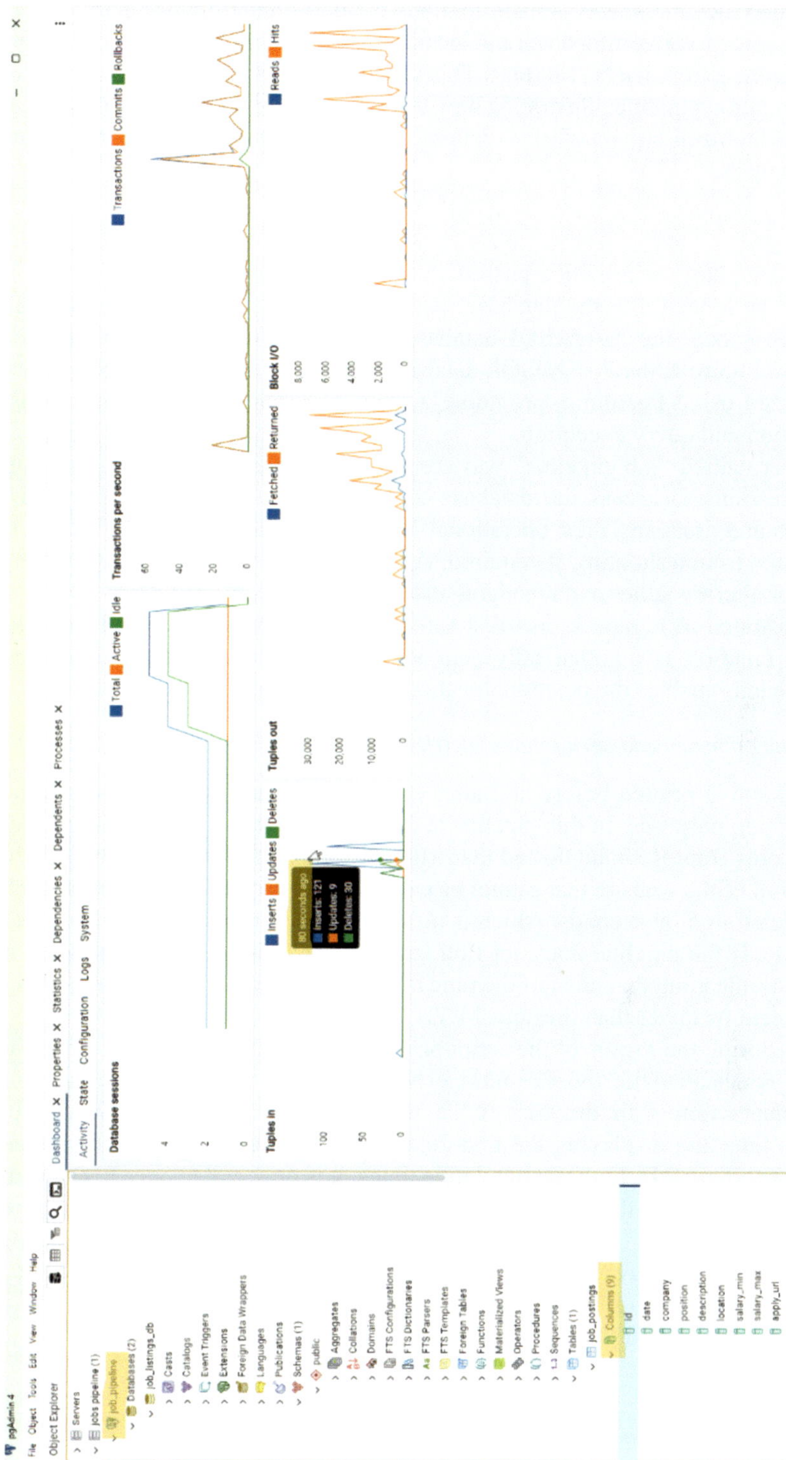

Figure 4: PostgreSQL Database and Server Monitoring Viewed on PgAdmin.

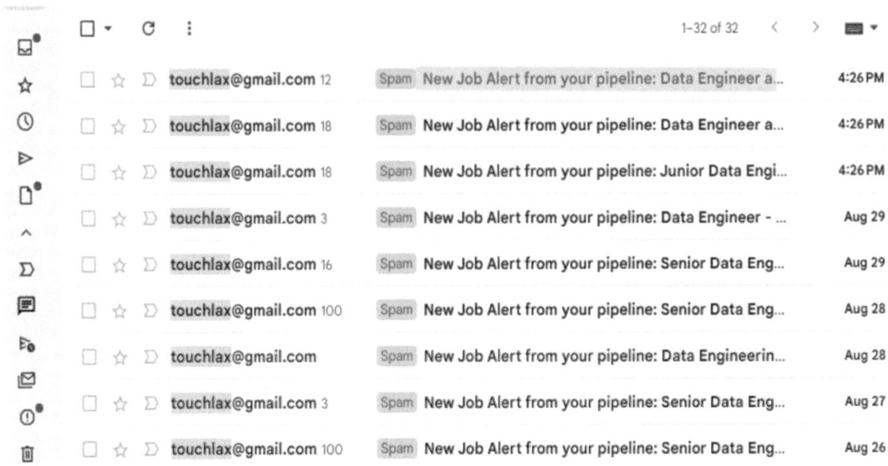

Figure 5: Sample Email Alerts Received from the Pipeline.

5.2 Data insights

Tableau software for data analysis and visualization is used to present the findings with a clear and user-friendly interface, tailored to showcase only the necessary information for users without technical complexities.

Tableau is connected to the PostgreSQL database on the localhost server and can communicate with it, fetching data directly and automatically as soon as it is available. This allows for monitoring near real-time changes in our dashboard when new data is entered.

Similar to accessing the database from PgAdmin, users are required to authenticate before viewing the results on Tableau to prevent unauthorized access to the data.

The developed dashboard, presented in Figure 6, visualizes the dispersion of job listings based on location alongside the total number of jobs available. It is noticeable that London is a clear outlier, holding more than half of the listings. This is due to London having the most active job market in the UK, but also because sourcing the data initially focused on London as a filter, meaning the dataset was primarily fed with London-based jobs for a period of time. The dashboard can also be filtered by other columns, such as salary or job title, to observe how they are distributed on the map.

Company activity and company overview chats aim to observe which companies have been more active, using a bubble chart of companies based on the number of jobs they advertised and a horizontal bar chart showing their average salary across job listings (see Figure 6).

Market activity, suspicious activity, and average salary charts present the overall state of the job market. A timeline graph illustrates market activity throughout the year, though it currently only shows activity from August onward, as that is when the pipeline began running. Additionally, a bar chart displays average salaries, with most

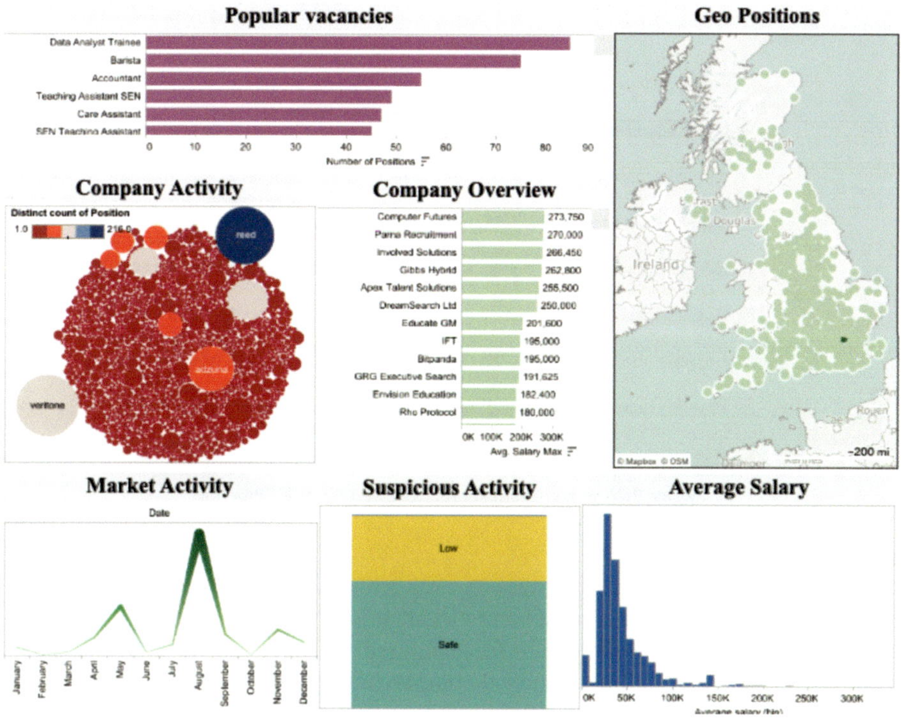

Figure 6: Job listings dashboard.

salaries falling in the £24,000 range. Finally, a stacked bar chart monitors the number of suspicious job advertisements.

The word cloud (see Figure 7) highlights the most frequently occurring job titles within our dataset. Notably, "Data Analyst Trainee" appears to be the most common job title since data collection began.

Aside from these examples, numerous other visualizations can be created, and the data can be explored in various ways depending on user needs.

5.3 Conclusion

The implementation of the data pipeline demonstrated its capacity to achieve the research objectives by efficiently transforming raw job listing data into actionable insights. Through the extraction, transformation, and loading (ETL) processes, the pipeline structured data from multiple sources into a cohesive and enriched dataset, ready for analysis and visualization. The pipeline's ability to process data in cycles under six seconds ensures timely updates while maintaining resource efficiency, making it suitable for hourly execution. Integration with PostgreSQL facilitated secure storage and management of the data, while Tableau dashboards offered user-friendly visualizations, enabling stakeholders to derive insights into job market trends, company activity, and suspicious advertisements. These dashboards showcased the pipeline's utility in monitoring job market dynamics in near real-time, providing tailored insights for users. The system's performance metrics and

Figure 7: Word Cloud Figure Showing Most Apparent Positions in the Data.

visualization outputs affirm its reliability and scalability for applications in job market analysis and beyond.

6. Discussions

The results of this study align with and expand upon existing literature on data pipeline architectures and their application in real-time data processing. Previous research, such as Kiran et al. (2015) and Carbone et al. (2015), emphasizes the utility of hybrid approaches like Lambda and stream-centric Kappa architectures for managing large-scale data. However, this study demonstrates that batch processing, while considered less responsive in dynamic environments, is a more practical and efficient approach for job market data. This finding is consistent with Zaharia et al. (2010), who highlight the simplicity and resource efficiency of batch processing for applications where immediate real-time updates are unnecessary. By adopting a batch-oriented approach, the pipeline avoided the complexities and resource demands associated with stream processing, effectively addressing the moderate pace of job market data updates.

The study's findings also support the flexibility and modularity of the ETL framework, as noted by Hellerstein et al. (2007). The implementation of Python for data extraction and transformation mirrors McKinney's (2022) discussion on Python's dominance in data engineering due to its simplicity and rich ecosystem of libraries. PostgreSQL's robust handling of structured data proved effective, reinforcing observations by Petrov (2019) on its reliability and adaptability. However, unlike studies advocating for cloud-native solutions (e.g., Akidau et al. 2015), this pipeline's local deployment highlighted the trade-offs between resource constraints and scalability. The results suggest that while local deployment meets the requirements of this research, cloud-based solutions could further enhance scalability and enable integration with additional data sources.

The ethical and practical challenges of web scraping, as discussed by Krotov et al. (2020), were also evident in this study. While the use of public APIs ensured compliance with website policies, the limited accessibility and delayed updates from these APIs highlighted a key constraint. Addressing this limitation through direct partnerships with data providers or the careful deployment of ethical web scraping technologies could significantly enrich the dataset. Moreover, the inclusion of fraud detection mechanisms and dynamic visualization dashboards aligns with Akanbi and Masinde's (2020) focus on using enriched datasets for actionable insights, demonstrating the potential for integrating machine learning models to further enhance predictive capabilities in future iterations of the pipeline.

7. Conclusions, Limitations, Future Works

This section summarizes the key findings of the project and discusses their potential academic impact and use cases. It also addresses the limitations encountered during the research and development process and proposes possible directions for future work. The goal is to provide a comprehensive conclusion by reflecting on the study's outcomes, acknowledging its constraints, and exploring opportunities for further development and enhancement.

7.1 *Research impact and potential use-cases*

The research presented in this dissertation contributes to the academic understanding of data processing pipelines within the context of job market analysis. By leveraging open-source tools to design a practical and efficient pipeline, this work provides a framework that can be adapted and expanded for various academic research areas. Researchers can modify this pipeline to automate data gathering and processing based on their specific needs.

Furthermore, the pipeline's design emphasizes modularity and adaptability, allowing for applications beyond the academic sphere. The results from this system could be utilized in related fields such as economic forecasting, labour market studies, and human resource management. These fields could benefit from monitoring trends in job availability, salary ranges, and employment patterns across different industries and regions, providing insights that can inform policy decisions, business strategies, and workforce planning.

Companies and recruitment agencies could implement similar systems to streamline the aggregation and analysis of job postings, enhancing their talent acquisition strategies. Labour market researchers and economists could use this pipeline as a foundation for developing more comprehensive models that incorporate additional data sources. By purchasing rights from websites and obtaining API permissions, researchers could integrate data from other regulated environments, such as social media or economic indicators, to provide a richer, multi-faceted view of employment trends. The adaptability and robustness of the system ensure that it can be tailored to various research and practical needs, making it a valuable tool for both academic inquiry and real-world applications.

Lastly, on an individual scale, job seekers may use the pipeline to automate the job search process, making it more efficient, less stressful, and less time-consuming. Individuals could receive direct notifications of job listings that match their criteria while also monitoring market trends in skills, active companies, and salary ranges. This would help them better plan for entering the workforce or transitioning to new positions. The system's low resource requirements make it feasible to run on local machines with minimal maintenance, depending on the number of data sources and database storage capacity.

7.2 *Limitations*

While the project achieved its primary objectives, several limitations were encountered that impacted the scope and outcomes of the research.

7.2.1 Data availability and quality

The project relied heavily on public APIs for data collection. Not all job listings were immediately accessible through the APIs, leading to potential delays in capturing data. Additionally, the data provided by these sources was sometimes incomplete or inconsistent, requiring extensive cleaning and transformation. Moreover, many other data sources were discarded due to ethical considerations regarding web scraping or deploying web crawlers on their pages, which limited the research to relying solely on public APIs. These limitations affected the timeliness and comprehensiveness of the data and required considerable time to research, review website robots.txt files and terms of service, and contact websites for access to their data.

7.2.2 Resource constraints

The project was designed with limited computational and budgetary resources in mind, which influenced the choice of tools and the overall pipeline architecture. While this approach ensured that the system was resource-efficient and could achieve its objectives even with multiple data sources, it also meant that the pipeline could struggle under heavier data loads over time or more complex processing tasks. Despite this, the system successfully automated data collection and monitored job market insights from multiple sources seamlessly. However, scalability remains limited and would require upgrading the architecture and tools.

7.2.3 Time management and upskilling

Data engineering tools and techniques were not only new territory for me but also highly extensive and complex. Getting familiar with new technologies in a limited time was a significant challenge and required careful selection of tools with a reasonable learning curve and a large user community to benefit from shared knowledge and troubleshooting support. The flexibility of the system allowed for changing technologies used in each step with minimal adjustments to the others, ensuring adaptability as needed.

7.3 Future works

Building on the foundation established by this project, several avenues for future work can be explored to enhance the pipeline's functionality, address its limitations, and expand the scope of the analysis.

7.3.1 Expanding data sources

Two sources were used to demonstrate the system's functionality; however, for practical use, adding more data sources is recommended to enrich the dataset. This could be achieved by incorporating additional public APIs, premium APIs requested from websites, or web crawlers to scrape data where permitted. Integrating new sources into the pipeline would require adding the script to the "Extract" phase and ensuring column names and formatting remain consistent. Alternatively, a separate script could be used to feed data into the same database if properly transformed. Major data sources in the domain that could be considered include "LinkedIn" and "Indeed".

7.3.2 Enhancing data processing capabilities

Upscaling the architecture and technologies used is necessary to handle a "Big Data" level of load. While the scripts may remain fundamentally similar, the architecture needs to be reinforced with new technologies, particularly at the "Transform" and "Load" levels, to process data more efficiently. Cloud solutions stand out in this area, offering a wide range of tools for distributed computing and scalable storage.

This advancement could open new opportunities for the pipeline, such as integrating a machine learning component to predict job market trends, identify emerging roles and skills, and extract deeper insights from the data.

7.3.3 Conclusion

In conclusion, this project successfully demonstrated the potential of a well-designed data processing pipeline to transform raw job listings into valuable insights about the job market. While the project encountered some limitations, the overall success of the pipeline indicates that the chosen approach and technologies were well-suited to the task. Looking ahead, there are numerous opportunities to build on this work, from expanding data sources and enhancing processing capabilities to applying more sophisticated analytical techniques. By pursuing these avenues, future iterations of the pipeline could offer even greater insights and serve as a powerful tool for understanding and navigating the complexities of the job market.

References

Akanbi, A. and Masinde, M. 2020. A distributed stream processing middleware framework for real-time analysis of heterogeneous data on big data platform: Case of environmental monitoring. *Sensors*, 20(11): 3166.

Akidau, T., Bradshaw, R., Chambers, C., Chernyak, S., Fernández-Moctezuma, R.J., Lax, R. et al. 2015. The dataflow model: A practical approach to balancing correctness, latency, and cost in massive scale, unbounded, out-of-order data processing. *Proceedings of the VLDB Endowment*, 8(12): 1792–1803.

Brzozowska, J., Pizoń, J., Baytikenova, G., Gola, A., Zakimova, A. and Piotrowska, K. 2023. Data engineering in CRISP-DM process production data–case study. *Applied Computer Science*, 19(3).

Carbone, P., Katsifodimos, A., Ewen, S., Markl, V., Haridi, S. and Tzoumas, K. 2015. Apache Flink™: stream and batch processing in a single engine. *IEEE Data Engineering Bulletin*, 43(4): 28–38.

Carnevale, A.P., Smith, N. and Strohl, J. 2013. Recovery: Job growth and education requirements through 2020. Georgetown University Center on Education and the Workforce.

Chui, M., Manyika, J. and Miremadi, M. 2016. Where machines could replace humans—and where they can't (yet). McKinsey Quarterly.

Geerts, L. 2011. A design science research methodology and its application to accounting information systems research. *International Journal of Accounting Information Systems*, 12(2): 142–151.

Hellerstein, J.M., Stonebraker, M. and Hamilton, J. 2007. Architecture of a database system. *Foundations and Trends in Databases*, 1(2): 141–259.

Intorruk, S. and Numnonda, T. 2019. A comparative study on performance and resource utilization of real-time distributed messaging systems for big data. 20th IEEE/ACIS International Conference on Software Engineering, Artificial Intelligence, Networking and Parallel/Distributed Computing (SNPD), Toyama, Japan, 2019, pp. 102–107, doi: 10.1109/SNPD.2019.8935759.

Kashyap, R. 2023. Data sharing, disaster management, and security capabilities of snowflake a cloud datawarehouse. *International Journal of Computer Trends and Technology*, 71(2): 78–86.

Kiran, M., Murphy, P., Monga, I., Dugan, J. and Baveja, S.S. 2015. Lambda architecture for cost-effective batch and speed big data processing. In 2015 IEEE International Conference on Big Data (Big Data) (pp. 2785–2792). *IEEE.*

Kjerrumgaard, D. 2021. Apache Pulsar in action. Simon and Schuster.

Kreps, J., Narkhede, N. and Rao, J. 2011. Kafka: A distributed messaging system for log processing. In Proceedings of the NetDB (Vol. 11, pp. 1–7).

Kreps, J. 2014. I Heart Logs: Event Data, Stream Processing, and Data Integration. O'Reilly Media.

Krotov, V., Johnson, L. and Silva, L. 2020. Tutorial: Legality and Ethics of Web Scraping.

McKinney, W. 2022. Python for data analysis. "O'Reilly Media, Inc."

Mitchell, R. 2018. Web Scraping with Python: Collecting Data from the Modern Web. O'Reilly Media, Inc.

Murray, D. 2013. Tableau Your Data!: Fast and Easy Visual Analysis with Tableau Software. 2nd edn. Hoboken: John Wiley & Sons.

Petrov, A. 2019. Database Internals: A Deep Dive into How Distributed Data Systems Work. Sebastopol: O'Reilly Media, Inc.

Rahm, E. and Do, H.H. 2000. Data cleaning: problems and current approaches. *IEEE Data Engineering Bulletin*, 23(4): 3–13.

Scrapy, 2023. Scrapy: An Open Source and Collaborative Web Crawling Framework for Python. Available at: https://scrapy.org/.

SeleniumHQ, 2023. Selenium: Web Browser Automation. Available at: https://www.selenium.dev/.

Zaharia, M., Chowdhury, M., Franklin, M.J., Shenker, S. and Stoica, I. 2010. Spark: Cluster computing with working sets. In 2nd USENIX workshop on hot topics in cloud computing (HotCloud 10).

CHAPTER 6

Using Generative AI Artificial Intelligence to Re-Shape Key Performance Indicators (KPIs)

Alnassarwin, Muawia Salman S.,[1,*] *Bowen, Gordon*[2] and *Alnasraween, Mo'en Salman S.*[3]

1. Introduction

According to Sibanda (2022), leaders find that traditional key performance indicators (KPIs) do not provide the data and insights they require to succeed. They must be up to standard regarding monitoring development, coordinating procedures, setting priorities, and promoting responsibility. In addition to reducing operational efficiencies, these errors make it harder to achieve strategic goals (Mouton 2021). Key performance indicators (KPIs) need to be demonstrably more intelligent and capable, according to sophisticated firms worldwide. Organizations must make their performance metrics more thoughtful, flexible, and predictive, consequently investing money into algorithmic advancements. Key performance indicators (KPIs) enabled by artificial intelligence (AI) go beyond being basic metrics for strategic differentiation and start creating value themselves. AI applications can improve and radically alter performance. Businesses that use algorithms to improve and challenge assumptions regarding growth, profitability, and performance have a better chance of seeing significant financial gains than those that do not. Schrage et al. (2024) found that results improve when key performance indicators are more intelligent.

[1] DBA Candidate, Anglia Ruskin University.
[2] DBA, Professor (Associate) Management at Anglia Ruskin University.
[3] Associate Professor of educational psychological sciences, Yarmouk University.
* Corresponding author: msa247@pgr.aru.ac.uk

DOI: 10.1201/9781003540373-6

Key performance indicators (KPIs) are extensively utilized in several sectors to gauge and enhance corporate performance. Below are pertinent facts and trends concerning the use of key performance indicators (KPIs) and their incorporation with artificial intelligence (AI). According to a study by Schrage et al. (2023), published in the MIT Sloan Management Review, more than 90% of firms across different industries use key performance indicators (KPIs) to monitor and manage performance. Furthermore, regarding key performance indicators (KPIs) and the integration of artificial intelligence (AI), a poll conducted by McKinsey found that 22% of participants reported that AI accounted for more than 5% of their total revenues (Gudigantala et al. 2023). Kirova and colleagues (2023) stated that, based on Gartner's findings, by 2025, half of the firms that utilize key performance indicators (KPIs) will have incorporated fully AI-driven analytics to automate the tasks of establishing, monitoring, and modifying KPIs in real time.

There have been significantly more cases of intelligent machines augmenting human work than cases of complete automation across various real-world usage scenarios. Predictions indicate that this pattern will persist for some time. Results from an international survey of 3,200 executives and in-depth interviews with 18 prominent industry figures show that CEOs and CFOs worldwide are struggling to find the optimal balance where key performance indicators (KPIs) for the present and future can coexist (Schrage and Kiron 2018).

The way executives utilize key performance indicators (KPIs) to track and encourage growth is impacted by the rapid development of machine learning (ML), which refers to a machine's capacity to enhance its performance by analyzing past data (Tambare et al. 2021). Digital dashboards of the future will likely be modeled after next-generation predictive algorithms, which are increasingly used in business process design and planning. As a result, key performance indicators will not only provide a retrospective analysis but also offer actionable insights for the future. Companies that are data-driven and take advantage of these advancements by rethinking their key performance indicators will gain a competitive edge (Schrage and Kiron 2018). According to research by Kassies (2022), businesses across various sectors are reevaluating their key performance indicators (KPIs) and uncovering previously unrecognized aspects of performance by leveraging AI. Company leaders can improve their capacity to achieve intended results by discovering, redefining, and communicating more intelligent metrics through their strategic measurement systems (Schrage et al. 2022). Intelligent key performance indicators do more than reveal unexplored opportunities for value creation and differentiation; they also help avoid unfavorable outcomes that may arise from failing to routinely review the assumptions behind traditional key performance indicators.

Due to algorithmic improvements in their KPIs, businesses are reevaluating performance measurement, KPI functionality, and the strategic value of metrics. Prior research, such as that of Medne et al. (2022) and Imran et al. (2021), shows that such reevaluations often lead to innovative approaches in KPI design and alignment with strategic objectives. One of the primary goals of implementing AI-driven key performance indicators (KPIs) is to improve strategic alignment. This study explores the following topics: the existing literature on organizational KPIs, their evolution with AI, how AI enhances KPIs, and how organizations achieve operational, organizational, and strategic value through smart KPIs. Lastly, the study examines the limitations of AI in the workplace.

The primary objective of this review article is to examine how generative artificial intelligence (AI) might redefine key performance indicators (KPIs) to better align with the changing demands of modern business environments. This article discusses the limitations of traditional key performance indicators (KPIs), illustrates how artificial intelligence (AI) can improve these measures, and explores the potential of AI-powered KPIs to enhance competitiveness at different organizational levels. Additionally, it offers a comprehensive analysis of the advantages and challenges of incorporating AI into KPI frameworks, providing an impartial perspective on the future of performance evaluation in business.

To meet the needs of contemporary corporate contexts, the article is structured to provide an in-depth explanation of how generative AI might transform key performance indicators (KPIs). The section "Introducing Key Performance Indicators (KPIs)" establishes a framework for monitoring and guiding company performance. Various business models use key performance indicators (KPIs) to align operations with strategic objectives, which is explored in "KPIs for Business Models." The section "Challenges in Legacy KPIs" identifies the limitations of conventional KPIs, such as their rigidity and lack of adaptability to changing business conditions. The section "Enhancing Current KPIs with AI" examines how generative AI can make key performance indicators more dynamic, predictive, and context-sensitive. The section "Competitiveness by Value Creation: Operationally, Organizationally, and Strategically Using KPIs" details how AI-enhanced KPIs can drive value creation and improve competitiveness across various business levels. Finally, "AI in the Workplace: Limitations" discusses both the positive and negative aspects of integrating AI into KPI frameworks, including potential biases, resource requirements, and the risks of excessive reliance on AI technologies.

2. Literature Review

2.1 Key Performance Indicators (KPIs)

KPIs, or key performance indicators, are crucial metrics that reveal how effectively a company is achieving its most important goals. Measurable values, carefully chosen to align with the company's strategic objectives, serve as indicators that provide a clear picture of success across different processes and departments (Setiawan and Purba 2020). A company's ability to make rational choices to improve efficiency and effectiveness directly correlates with its ability to monitor key performance indicators (KPIs). Financial performance, customer satisfaction, employee engagement, and operational efficiency are among the areas measured by key performance indicators (KPIs), enabling a comprehensive assessment of the company's success (Uddin et al. 2021).

Since their inception, key performance indicators (KPIs) have undergone substantial evolution. Initially, companies relied on simple financial indicators, such as sales growth and profit margins, to evaluate performance. However, as corporate environments became increasingly complex, the need for more precise and comprehensive performance metrics arose. Advances in data analytics, technological breakthroughs, and a deeper understanding of organizational dynamics have all contributed to this evolution. Modern KPIs now encompass a broad range of factors, from supply chain efficiency and environmental impact to customer experience and employee satisfaction (Mourad et al. 2020). With the development of modern data analysis and collection methods, businesses can now monitor key performance indicators (KPIs) in real time, providing insights that were previously impossible to obtain (Claramunt 2024).

Key performance indicators (KPIs) are more critical than ever in today's fast-paced, technology-driven business world. Organizations rely heavily on them for strategic planning, as they help define goals and track performance (Ngure 2021). The proliferation of data and sophisticated analytics allows businesses to leverage key performance indicators (KPIs) to gain deeper insights into their operations, identify trends, and make data-driven decisions. Additionally, key performance indicators (KPIs) are essential for fostering transparency and accountability within organizations, as they provide a quantifiable and measurable method for evaluating performance across all levels (Ali 2024). At a time when flexibility and responsiveness are crucial to success, key performance indicators (KPIs) help organizations maintain focus, align their activities with strategic objectives, and promote continuous improvement (Cruz Villazón et al. 2020).

2.2 KPIs for business models

Modern business models have diversified dramatically in response to the rapidly shifting market landscape and technological innovations. Contemporary business models include subscription-based models, such as Netflix and Spotify, where users pay a recurring fee for continuous access to products or services (Freed et al. 2022). Another prevalent concept is the platform-based approach, exemplified by companies such as Uber and Airbnb. Businesses like LinkedIn and Dropbox have successfully adopted the freemium model, which offers basic services for free while charging for premium features (Panda 2020). The growth of online shopping and the decline of traditional retail channels have also contributed to the rise of e-commerce and direct-to-consumer models. Tripathi (2023) argues that contemporary business models prioritize adaptability, customer-centricity, and the use of technology to enhance efficiency and scalability.

Key performance indicators (KPIs) are essential for evaluating and guiding these various business models (van de Ven et al. 2022). They provide a structured approach to measuring success, monitoring performance, and facilitating decision-making. For instance, Rodríguez García et al. (2022) highlight that in a subscription-based model, key performance indicators (KPIs) such as customer acquisition cost (CAC), churn rate, and lifetime value (LTV) are crucial for understanding customer retention and profitability. In platform-based models, performance indicators (KPIs) include user engagement, transaction volume, and network growth. The financial health of freemium models is assessed by tracking the conversion rate of free users to paying customers and the average revenue per user (ARPU). By aligning key performance indicators (KPIs) with specific business model objectives, organizations can monitor performance, identify areas for improvement, and adjust strategies to meet evolving market demands (Erlebach 2021).

Iranian et al. (2023) note significant challenges in evaluating new business models using traditional KPIs. Conventional key performance indicators (KPIs), originally designed for more traditional business processes, often fail to capture the nuances and distinct characteristics of modern models. For example, subscription-based businesses may prioritize recurring revenue and customer retention over traditional sales KPIs. Similarly, platform-based models depend on network effects and user engagement, which legacy key performance indicators (KPIs) may not fully reflect (Pirro 2024). Outdated metrics can lead to misaligned priorities and missed optimization opportunities. To ensure that key performance indicators (KPIs) remain relevant and effective in guiding strategic decisions, organizations must develop and implement new KPIs that accurately reflect the success factors of modern business models (Mtau and Rahul 2024).

2.3 Challenges in legacy KPIs

Traditional key performance indicators (KPIs) struggle to keep up with the complexity and continuously shifting nature of today's business climate. In the digital era, intangible assets such as brand equity, customer loyalty, and staff engagement are vital but difficult to assess (Schrage et al. 2022). These outdated metrics were developed for an era when tangible assets and simple financial indicators were sufficient. Since intangible assets are the primary drivers of value in certain industries, relying solely on legacy KPIs to assess a company's performance and prospects is risky (Kankaanpää 2024).

Another challenge with legacy KPIs is their rigidity and lack of flexibility. Traditional KPIs are becoming obsolete due to their inability to adapt to rapid changes and novel business realities (Girod and Králik 2021). Instead, firms are shifting toward more agile and innovative models. For instance, traditional key performance indicators (KPIs) often overlook essential metrics in subscription-based models, such as customer churn and lifetime value. Due to this discrepancy, businesses risk making decisions based on inaccurate or incomplete information, which may hinder growth and reduce competitiveness (Kankaanpää 2024). To measure performance effectively, companies must continuously innovate their performance evaluation frameworks (Mio et al. 2022).

Additionally, in today's fast-paced market, successful decision-making typically requires real-time information and granularity, neither of which are provided by legacy KPIs. While these traditional metrics help track performance over time, they generally lack the predictive power to identify trends and make proactive strategic adjustments (Singh et al. 2023). The advent of big data and advanced analytics has further exposed the limitations of traditional key performance indicators (KPIs), as they frequently fail to utilize the vast amounts of data now available. According to Aljumah et al. (2021), businesses may miss out on valuable insights into customer behaviour, industry tendencies, and areas for improvement.

By enhancing data analysis, boosting predictive capabilities, and providing real-time insights, AI has the potential to revolutionize how KPIs are approached.

AI can sift through vast amounts of data from multiple sources using machine learning algorithms and sophisticated analytics to identify trends and patterns that conventional KPIs might overlook (Hurry 2024). As a result, companies can develop key performance indicators (KPIs) that are more relevant to their needs and adaptable to changing market conditions. AI-powered real-time monitoring and notifications enable businesses to respond swiftly to emerging concerns or opportunities. AI-driven insights can help organizations shift from a reactive to a proactive stance through predictive maintenance, customer behaviour forecasting, and more strategic resource allocation (Khan et al. 2024). Gudigantala et al. (2023) found that businesses significantly benefit from improved decision-making, innovation, and performance when AI is incorporated into KPI development and monitoring.

2.4 Enhancing current KPIs with AI

According to Goodhart's law, a metric loses its usefulness when it becomes a target. While Goodhart's warning is valid, improving metrics is essential for long-term operational success and aligns with his concerns. The continuous enhancement of key performance indicators (KPIs) must remain a priority (Clubb et al. 2022). A compelling example of this approach is CBS, the media giant. One executive questioned whether AI could provide better insights than intuition and expertise in identifying performance drivers. The CEO wanted to determine whether the company had the correct key performance indicators (KPIs) for predicting the success of TV programs, so she supplied AI teams with 50 years' worth of data on key performance indicators and consumer research. AI was then used to validate existing KPIs and discover new ones, improving the company's experimental evaluation process (Proksch et al. 2024).

In their study, Sutikno et al. (2019) demonstrate how Tokopedia has improved its key performance indicators (KPIs) by implementing AI algorithms to reassess and refine performance metrics. As one of Indonesia's largest marketplaces, Tokopedia prioritizes reliable merchants to ensure customer satisfaction. More than 85% of its 14 million merchants are first-time business owners, collectively selling 1.8 billion products daily. While many vendors offer high-quality items, poor inventory management negatively impacts platform performance metrics, such as fulfilment rates, customer satisfaction, and total sales. To address this issue, Tokopedia began analyzing and synthesizing data points from millions of retailers and customers. AI-driven analysis led to the development of an improved key performance indicator (KPI) for merchant quality, resulting in a grading system. This system enhanced market efficiency by helping low-scoring merchants improve operations and improving customer service by connecting buyers with high-quality sellers. Tokopedia, its merchants, and customers all benefited from this AI-enhanced KPI framework, which contributed to a more credible and effective marketplace.

Key performance indicators (KPIs), both strategic and operational, are traditionally defined by human leadership teams. However, several studies have demonstrated that AI can suggest and even generate new key performance indicators (KPIs) to guide executive decision-making. For example, research by Gudigantala et al. (2023) and Stone et al. (2020) highlights AI's potential in KPI development. Additionally, studies such as Neirotti et al. (2021) show that executives use AI algorithms to identify meaningful performance metrics from data patterns too complex for human analysis. These AI-generated KPIs are essential for both strategic planning and operational efficiency. Research conducted by Schrage et al. (2024) using survey data confirms that businesses experience numerous advantages when they employ AI to develop new key performance indicators (KPIs) compared to those that do not. Organizations that integrate AI-driven KPIs report greater alignment, collaboration, effectiveness, financial gains, and efficiency. Specifically, 34% of surveyed organizations that used AI to create new key performance indicators experienced significant benefits.

Nair et al. (2023) identified a growing demand for AI-driven key performance indicators (KPIs). For example, researchers at Region Halland Health System in Sweden developed and trained an algorithm to improve predictions of sudden cardiac death (SCD) within one year of an electrocardiogram (ECG). This algorithm was trained using data from death certificates, government documents, and electronic medical records. According to a study by Chugh et al. (2008), SCD affects 300,000 individuals in the United States and millions worldwide each year. Although the use of AI in identifying reliable SCD predictors is still in its early stages, researchers remain optimistic about the technology's potential to develop early warning indicators for other diseases. Obermeyer notes that the ability to transform complex biological signals into predictive indicators is a powerful advancement.

Smart KPI projects are complex but essential, according to Schrage et al. (2024), who interviewed executives and found that everyone agreed. Key performance indicators (KPIs) are now mainly the purview of algorithmic advancements, which previously required human knowledge and judgement. The human monopoly on key performance indicator (KPI) generation, management, and governance is fading, making this more of a disruption than a shift. The study by Schrage et al. (2024) outlines six changes from the current state of legacy KPIs to the state of algorithmically informed KPIs. To meet these objectives, leadership teams must upgrade legacy KPIs to Smart KPIs, incorporating AI into their development and usage. According to research by Schrage et al. (2024), organisations can take six approaches to upgrade their key performance indicators (KPIs) using artificial intelligence. Below, we explore these transformations in greater detail.

From static benchmarks to dynamic predictors, smarter key performance indicators (KPIs) that more accurately predict market conditions, supply chains, and customer behaviour are replacing outdated benchmarking approaches. To account for the impact of weather volatility on trade-offs among key performance indicators (KPIs) related to energy costs, distributive load-balancing risks, and carbon footprints, Schneider Electric models dynamic KPIs (Schneider 2022). Businesses are encouraged to respond more effectively to changing environments by using dynamic key performance indicators. Executives are increasingly coordinating data flows and workflows to make key performance indicators more predictive and adaptive, according to research by Hassan and Mhmood (2021). Markets for programmatic advertising and high-frequency algorithmic trading also exhibit such predictive dynamism, according to research by Sazu (2022). Markets that are constantly evolving pose challenges to static key performance indicators.

Secondly, executives have traditionally used their knowledge, past performance, and current market conditions to develop and define key performance indicators (KPIs). This human exclusivity can be broken, and unimaginable metrics can be created by combining generative AI with other intelligent algorithms. The most cutting-edge measures for coordinating and evaluating critical performance in the future might very well be created by machines. The capabilities of "machine-made" measures must be explained, and businesses that uphold a responsible AI approach must publicly promote interpretability and transparency. From a business perspective, intelligent KPIs should reflect the company's principles and goals. Strategic and operational metrics must be created, refined, aligned, and communicated differently. Algorithmic insight and prediction should be complemented and guided by human oversight.

Thirdly, from KPI management to innovative KPI governance, improved key performance indicator (KPI) management emphasises targeted results, while KPI governance ensures that results are well-aligned and maximised (Jansen 2020). Maximising performance against individual metrics, typically at the team or unit level, is essential to managing key performance indicators. KPI governance, on the other hand, necessitates enterprise-level monitoring and active improvement of complete KPI portfolios. The research conducted by Schrage (2024) reveals that a significant number of executives still prioritise key performance indicator (KPI) administration over KPI governance. Key performance indicators (KPIs) are essential for businesses because they provide logical measures and standards for evaluating the KPIs' efficacy, efficiency, and alignment. A meta-level strategy is required to develop KPIs that ensure the continuous improvement of the performance measurement system. These meta-key performance indicators are shaped by better governance, not merely by better data science (Putte et al. 2023).

Fourthly, from KPI concentration to KPI dialogues and discussions, the development of more comprehensive, aesthetically appealing, and insightful dashboards has made it easier and more beneficial for managers worldwide to focus on key performance indicators (KPIs) throughout the day. Intelligent algorithms, however, transform visually appealing dashboards into machine learning platforms that enable, facilitate, and empower managers to engage in real-time conversations with their key performance indicators. Managers can instruct dashboards to generate alternative scenarios for financial planning or inventory management, for instance, by integrating generative AI capabilities into KPIs. These hypothetical situations can be refined into decision-making and collaboration-friendly narratives through iterative processing with large language models (Dias 2021).

Fifthly, from strategy with KPIs to strategy for KPIs, key performance indicators (KPIs) are a part of conventional strategic management frameworks; they represent the observable, quantifiable goals set by company executives. Strategy requires measurable objectives to guide actions, communicate goals, and hold individuals accountable. Strategy and operations are connected through key performance indicators. This constitutes a critical performance indicator strategy. A new paradigm is necessary for intelligent KPIs, as these metrics require a plan for their continuous improvement. Companies may optimise their strategy through their smartest key performance indicators and vice versa. By planning with and for KPIs, strategists are more likely to focus on measurable targets and continuously improve KPIs (Sibanda 2022).

Sixthly, from tracking performance to redefining performance, evaluating progress towards established performance goals remains a key function of KPIs. The primary historical value of key performance indicators (KPIs) has been their role in keeping score, reflecting their long-standing use in business. However, research conducted by Weiss and Hartle (2023) suggests that tracking historical KPIs alone may yield diminishing returns on investment. Executives can gain fresh insights into performance assessment and its key drivers by leveraging innovative tools, technologies, and data flows. The real return on investment for AI-enhanced KPIs lies not merely in improving performance assessments based on old metrics but in redefining performance itself.

2.5 Competitiveness with smart KPIs

Now more than ever, value creation is the key to success in the corporate world. Gaining a competitive edge in the market is possible for organizations that can generate value on three levels: operational, organizational, and strategic. Organizations can generate value operationally, organizationally, and strategically using key performance indicators (KPIs), according to this study and a review of several studies in the literature, including those of Zerfass and Link (2022) and Karavokiris (2020).

To create value within organisations, they must realign data governance to enable measurably smarter KPIs. Robust, dependable, and intelligent data governance is a crucial enabler for smarter KPIs. Data must be improved measurably to enhance critical performance. Every piece of data, no matter how small, should be considered a strategic asset. Data quality, accuracy, timeliness, and contextual relevance are the four pillars upon which the successful development of intelligent key performance indicators rests, according to research by Kiron et al. (2023). Simply put, what goes in must come out. Smarter key performance indicators (KPIs) generally rely on data that is extremely accurate and collected frequently, as they pointed out.

According to Kankaanpää (2024), many steps need to be taken to improve data governance for better key performance indicators. First, ensure that key performance indicators (KPIs) such as customer lifetime value (CLV), new recurring revenue, and employee experience are in sync with data governance frameworks and capabilities. The key performance indicators (KPIs) that data sets contribute to, whether directly or indirectly, should not be regulated in a vacuum. The data that represents performance and informs performance monitoring should be identified and labelled as part of data governance. Second, data owners and stewards should be involved in providing oversight and input. Their participation is crucial from a technical, organisational, and cultural perspective. Effective metadata management is essential for capturing, analysing, and improving performance excellence standards using smart key performance indicators (KPIs) with predictive and prescriptive capacities. Lastly, organisations must improve data governance across departments. Smarter key performance indicators (KPIs) require data and metadata to be considered business assets rather than departmental, functional, or segregated assets. Data interpretation and prioritisation can be influenced by bias when data governance is determined at the departmental level, leading to skewed key performance indicator measures.

Furthermore, enhancing KPI metrics through digital twins is crucial in the new business environment. According to research by Honghong et al. (2023), testing is necessary when using machine learning to define new or improved performance measurements. Digital twins, representations of actual systems in a digital format, provide a foundation for intelligent key performance indicator (KPI) development and can enhance current digital twin efforts. Organisations should improve their key performance indicators with digital twins by identifying the right critical indicators for algorithmic augmentation and twinning. Additionally, workflows and key performance indicator dataflows must be mapped. How do digital twins get their data, and where do these sources come from? Creating digital twins that faithfully represent real-world scenarios relies on thorough mapping. Lastly, cross-functional collaboration and data science teams should be incorporated into digital twinning. The company's leadership should set a good example by utilising and sharing intelligent KPI twins in all aspects of strategic planning and operational management.

Smarter key performance indicators (KPIs) require the following actions from the management team: First, recognise and prepare for any organisational resistance to smart KPI adoption. Setting a good example is essential for those who want to pioneer cultural change genuinely. Demonstrating how intelligent metrics encourage value creation and better decision-making is a part of this process. Second, it is essential to anticipate and address any emerging power dynamics that may arise when smarter KPIs reveal interdependent, organisationally sensitive processes, operations, and departments. Lastly, senior management should become familiar with algorithms that augment and improve critical performance indicator production and continuous improvement. Managers could benefit from a "dialogue with dashboards" executive education course to support more informed decision-making.

Developing smart key performance indicators (KPIs) in a networked firm requires harmonizing people, processes, and technology to help connect strategic goals with strategic performance. Smart KPIs require distinct strategies; therefore, end-users should consider doing these to boost strategy alignment, according to Kirton et al. (2023). First, begin with the company's declared plan and select KPIs that senior executives believe will illustrate how far the company has progressed towards its goals. Second, analyse best-, worst-, and most-likely-case scenarios using these KPIs. The strategic KPIs' relative importance and ranking may shift depending on the scenario. They would influence management decisions more effectively if they incorporated new data or superior analytics. It is essential to determine whether novel intelligent key performance indicator (KPI) capabilities—descriptive, predictive, or prescriptive—could enhance efficiency, strategy alignment, or strategic outcomes. Mariani and Nambisan (2021) found that algorithmic innovation helps CEOs create new, more detailed strategic KPIs. A critical step is mapping the interdependencies and development pathways of smart KPIs. These maps should highlight strategic goals and tell their story. Senior management must evaluate growth, workforce, products, and profitability under interrelated strategic criteria. Rather than relying solely on data or human judgement, strategic goals should now be quantitatively measured.

2.6 Limitations of AI in the workplace

After reviewing the literature on key performance indicators (KPIs) and artificial intelligence (AI) in the workplace, this study concludes that human intervention remains necessary for AI-enabled KPIs and tasks. Companies should continue investing in employee education and training, and those working in the field should expect stable employment in the near future. As AI gains capabilities over time, there is an ongoing debate regarding what machines can and cannot do in real-world work environments. However, organisations must not overestimate AI's capabilities. Below, we examine some of the major current limitations.

According to Wilkens (2020), the first limitation of AI in the workplace is its inability to comprehend context. Artificial intelligence is still developing its ability to grasp the broader business landscape and the tasks at hand. Second, AI struggles to prioritise notifications. Regardless of the problem's nature—whether security, health, or machinery-related—computerised systems, sensors, and AI-driven image and audio analysis frequently generate excessive alerts. In a case study involving a large mall linked to Changi Airport in Singapore, Sreenath et al. (2021) found that human oversight was required to sort and prioritise security alerts. Artificial intelligence systems often fail to differentiate between critical alerts and non-urgent or false alarms in complex and dynamic environments. While AI surveillance systems are highly effective at detecting patterns, human security personnel and system operators remain essential for consistently prioritising the most pressing alerts.

Additionally, Rana et al. (2022) analysed AI's limitations in the workplace and identified its inability to evaluate subjective variables as a major drawback. Although AI may eventually develop the capability to analyse voice patterns and facial expressions to assess trustworthiness, assessments influenced by cultural, contextual, and subjective factors still require human judgement. According to Sturm's (2023) study, subjective human evaluations should complement AI-driven, data-based algorithmic assessments. Both humans and AI systems are susceptible to biases. Moreover, machine learning systems can inadvertently inherit human biases. One approach to mitigating bias is to have humans review machine-generated decisions and vice versa.

AI also struggles when assessing and selecting optimal solutions for business applications. While artificial intelligence excels at making data-driven predictions, human oversight remains necessary for final decision-making, particularly in high-stakes situations. This was evident at Morgan Stanley, where a machine learning-based "next best action" algorithm identified tailored investment opportunities for clients. However, financial advisors made the ultimate decision regarding which recommendations to present to their clients (Korteling et al. 2021).

3. Discussion

This study examines how managers and executives utilise AI to enhance strategic measurement and drive progress towards strategic outcomes. It explores how firms have adapted KPIs and even developed new ones using AI to define and achieve superior measurable performance. Strategic measurement and KPIs play a crucial role in evaluating a company's effectiveness. They provide quantifiable criteria for assessing progress, identifying areas for improvement, and ensuring that strategies align with intended outcomes. In today's rapidly evolving corporate landscape, data-driven insights are essential. As businesses continuously refine their key performance indicators and strategic measurement frameworks, these metrics serve as navigational tools, guiding organisations towards their objectives. Key performance indicators track critical business metrics such as operational efficiency, customer satisfaction, market share, and profitability. These measures also monitor progress and ensure accountability. Well-designed strategic measurement procedures lead to improved performance, more efficient resource allocation, and well-informed decision-making, ultimately providing long-term competitive advantages. This study reviews the literature on AI's potential to enhance key performance indicators (KPIs) and strategic measurement, drawing from examples of leading businesses.

This analysis concludes that AI specialists should collaborate with executives and staff to clarify AI's capabilities and limitations if performance metrics are to become more intelligent. Given AI's numerous potential applications, discussions should focus on specific business use cases and domains. In most scenarios, AI implementation should involve close cooperation between technical specialists and management teams. Everyone involved in AI implementation—including developers, future users, and their managers—must recognise the importance of AI-driven change management. Organisations should allocate resources for change management interventions and assessments while ensuring that teams include members with the appropriate change management expertise.

This study has profound implications for organisations by shedding light on the key performance indicators (KPIs) that are being reshaped by generative AI and their ability to monitor, manage, and optimise performance. Organisations can use this study to motivate them to reshape their KPIs to attain a higher level of precision by utilising AI-driven KPIs, enabling real-time analysis and predictive insights that promote more flexible and informed decision-making. This study also provides evidence from previous literature on the connection between performance measurements and strategic goals. Moreover, to ensure these sophisticated tools are used ethically and effectively, organisations must manage this shift carefully, balancing AI's advantages with the necessity of human supervision.

For stakeholders, including employees, customers, investors, and regulators, the study focuses on the idea that integrating generative AI into KPI frameworks presents both opportunities and challenges. Employees may experience changes in how their performance is evaluated, with AI-driven metrics offering more objective assessments while potentially increasing expectations and accountability. Customers could benefit from enhanced service quality and product innovation as organisations become more responsive and efficient. With AI providing more accurate and timely data, investors might gain greater transparency and confidence in organisational performance. However, there are also concerns for regulators and the broader public, particularly regarding data privacy, bias, and the ethical implications of AI-driven decision-making. Ensuring that AI-enhanced KPIs are implemented fairly, transparently, and with accountability will be crucial to maintaining stakeholder trust and avoiding potential negative impacts.

4. Conclusion

The present KPI design and review methods are outdated, and executives who recognise the value of AI-enabled KPIs acknowledge this reality. To address this challenge, an increasing number of firms are incorporating governance processes and activities to monitor the development of key performance indicators. KPI quality is not an afterthought but rather an explicit consideration, supported by governance mechanisms that ensure precise, accurate, and relevant performance data over time. Executives and their boards can enhance their understanding of strategy, ambition, and responsibility by replacing static measurements with more intelligent, dynamic, and accurate key performance indicators. Smart key performance indicators (KPIs) enable data-driven organisational dynamism at previously unimaginable levels. From the insights shared by CEOs already investing in intelligent KPIs, it is evident that this is not mere hype—it is what AI now makes possible.

By applying AI methods to key performance indicators (KPIs), we aim to gain a deeper understanding of the interplay between operational drivers, contextual variables, and strategic outcomes. The result of this work could be a new KPI, an improved version of an existing one, or the establishment of clear causal relationships between KPIs. Ultimately, the outcome should be a leading indicator of strategic results that is both more reliable and dynamic.

The advantages of AI-driven strategy outweigh the disadvantages, aside from the ethical, operational, organisational, and cultural concerns discussed in previous research on AI's ability to enhance KPIs. Intelligent key performance indicators (KPIs) necessitate a shift in company culture towards stronger collaboration between skilled professionals and the tools they use. Lastly, this study poses the following critical question for future research on AI and KPIs: "How leaders learn from and with their smartest KPIs will determine the success of both."

This article can be expanded by exploring future research directions that examine the relationship between generative AI and key performance indicators. Future studies could investigate advanced AI techniques such as deep learning and reinforcement learning to develop key performance indicators (KPIs) that can better adapt to evolving business conditions and optimise themselves. Additionally, research might explore how AI-driven KPIs could be customised to meet the specific needs of various industries, considering the opportunities and risks each sector faces. Further studies into the effects of AI-enhanced key performance indicators (KPIs) on company culture and decision-making could provide insight into how these innovative measures influence worker conduct and output. To guarantee fairness and openness in KPI systems, additional investigation into ethical concerns, such as bias in data created by AI, is necessary. Longitudinal studies might be useful to determine whether AI-enhanced KPIs successfully drive sustainable company performance over the long term. Also, a promising subject for future research could be optimizing key performance indicators (KPIs) by combining AI with new technologies like the Internet of Things (IoT) and blockchain. Comparative studies between AI-generated and human-centric KPIs and investigations into regulatory and compliance challenges would provide a comprehensive understanding of the benefits and limitations of AI in KPI development, guiding future business practices.

References

Ali, F. 2024. Measuring Success: Key Performance Indicators for Business Managers. *Journal of Accounting & Business Archive Review*, 1(03): 17–28.

Aljumah, A.I., Nuseir, M.T. and Alam, M.M. 2021. Traditional marketing analytics, big data analytics and big data system quality and the success of new product development. *Business Process Management Journal*, 27(4): 1108–1125.

Alsaid, L.A.Z.A. and Ambilichu, C.A. 2024. Performance measurement in urban development: unfolding a case of sustainability KPIs reporting. *Journal of Accounting in Emerging Economies*, 14(1): 48–74.

Chalvantzis, N., Vontzalidis, A., Kassela, E., Spyrou, A., Nikitas, N., Provatas, N. et al. 2024. IW-NET BDA: A big data infrastructure for predictive and geotemporal analytics of inland waterways. *IEEE Access*, PP(99): 1-1.

Chugh, S.S., Reinier, K., Teodorescu, C., Evanado, A., Kehr, E., Al Samara, M. et al. 2008. Epidemiology of sudden cardiac death: clinical and research implications. *Progress in Cardiovascular Diseases*, 51(3): 213–228.

Claramunt, M. 2024. Process Performance Improvement through a Successful KPI System.

Clubb, J., Allen, S.V. and Yung, K.K. 2022. Selection of key performance indicators for your sport and program: proposing a complementary process-driven approach. *Strength & Conditioning Journal*, 10–1519.

Cruz Villazón, C., Sastoque Pinilla, L., Otegi Olaso, J.R., Toledo Gandarias, N. and López de Lacalle, N. 2020. Identification of key performance indicators in project-based organisations through the lean approach. *Sustainability*, 12(15): 5977.

de Oliveira, H.C., You, J. and Coelho, A.P. 2021. Governing coalitions and key performance indicators of port governance. *Maritime Transport Research*, 2: 100023.

Dias, V.M. 2021. Smart KPI-ORIENTED decision support Dashboard for measuring the Digital Transformation success (Master's thesis, University of Twente).

Erlebach, A.M. 2021. The impact of ongoing monetization tools on the sustainability of online free-to-play game services.

Freed, L., Bishop, L., Gregory, D., Kolachina, V., Shteynberg, E., Sultana, F. et al. 2022. Implications of the Subscription Economy. Varun and Shteynberg, Emily and Sultana, Faiza and Zhang, Derrick and Bhalala, Darsh, Implications of the Subscription Economy (January 2, 2022).

Garud, R., Kumaraswamy, A., Roberts, A. and Xu, L. 2022. Liminal movement by digital platform-based sharing economy ventures: The case of Uber Technologies. *Strategic Management Journal*, 43(3): 447–475.

Girod, S.J. and Králik, M. 2021. Resetting management: Thrive with agility in the age of uncertainty. Kogan Page Publishers.

Gudigantala, N., Madhavaram, S. and Bicen, P. 2023. An AI decision-making framework for business value maximization. *AI Magazine*, 44(1): 67–84.

Hassan, A. and Mhmood, A.H. 2021. Optimizing network performance, automation, and intelligent decision-making through real-time big data analytics. *International Journal of Responsible Artificial Intelligence*, 11(8): 12–22.

Heilig, T. and Scheer, I. 2023. Decision Intelligence: Transform Your Team and Organization with AI-Driven Decision-Making. John Wiley & Sons.

Hodges, J. 2024. People-centric Organizational Change: Engaging Employees with Business transformation. *Kogan Page Publishers.*

Honghong, S., Gang, Y., Haijiang, L., Tian, Z. and Annan, J. 2023. Digital twin enhanced BIM to shape full life cycle digital transformation for bridge engineering. *Automation in Construction*, 147: 104736.

Hurry, B. 2024. Transforming Workforce Management: Leveraging Advanced Analytics, AI, and Integrated Approaches for Performance Forecasting (No. 12704). EasyChair.

Imran, F., Shahzad, K., Butt, A. and Kantola, J. 2021. Digital transformation of industrial organizations: Toward an integrated framework. *Journal of Change Management*, 21(4): 451–479.

Irani, Z., Abril, R.M., Weerakkody, V., Omar, A.and Sivarajah, U. 2023. The impact of legacy systems on digital transformation in European public administration: Lesson learned from a multi case analysis. *Government Information Quarterly*, 40(1): 101784.

Jansen, S. 2020. Machine learning for algorithmic trading: predictive models to extract signals from market and alternative data for systematic trading strategies with Python. Packt Publishing Ltd.

Kankaanpää, K. 2024. Key Performance Indicators to Enhance Customer Success Management in IT Service Delivery.

Karamthulla, M.J., Malaiyappan, J.N.A., Muthusubramanian, M. and Tillu, R. 2024. From theory to practice: implementing ai technologies in project management. *International Journal for Multidisciplinary Research*, 6(2): 1–11.

Karavokiris, A. 2020. Strategic Management in Small Liberal Arts Colleges: The Use of the Strategic Success Model as Framework for Success (Doctoral dissertation, Alliant International University).

Kassies, H.R.W. 2022. A Framework for Artificial Intelligence Capabilities for Challenges in the Supply Chain for Business-to-Business Companies (master's thesis, University of Twente).

Khan, R., Usman, M. and Moinuddin, M. 2024. From raw data to actionable insights: navigating the world of data analytics. *International Journal of Advanced Engineering Technologies and Innovations*, 1(4): 142–166.

Kiron, D., Schrage, M., Candelon, F., Khodabandeh, S. and Chu, M. 2023. Governance for smarter KPIs. *MIT Sloan Management Review*, 65(1): 1–6.

Kiron, D., Schrage, M., Candelon, F., Khodabandeh, S. and Chu, M. 2023. Strategic alignment with AI and smart KPIs. *MIT Sloan Management Review*, 65(1): 1–6.

Kirova, V.D., Ku, C.S., Laracy, J.R. and Marlowe, T.J. 2023. The ethics of artificial intelligence in the era of generative AI. *Journal of Systemics, Cybernetics and Informatics*, 21(4): 42–50.

Korteling, J.H., van de Boer-Visschedijk, G.C., Blankendaal, R.A., Boonekamp, R.C. and Eikelboom, A.R. 2021. Human-versus artificial intelligence. *Frontiers in Artificial Intelligence*, 4: 622364.

Mio, C., Costantini, A. and Panfilo, S. 2022. Performance measurement tools for sustainable business: A systematic literature review on the sustainability balanced scorecard use. *Corporate Social Responsibility and Environmental Management*, 29(2): 367–384.

Medne, A., Lapiņa, I. and Zeps, A. 2022. Challenges of uncertainty in sustainable strategy development: Reconsidering the key performance indicators. *Sustainability*, 14(2): 761.

Mourad, A., Yang, R., Lehne, P.H. and De La Oliva, A. 2020, March. Towards 6G: Evolution of key performance indicators and technology trends. In 2020 2nd 6G wireless summit (6G SUMMIT) (pp. 1–5). *IEEE.*

Mouton, C. 2021. Performance measurement of policy priorities: Tracking government performance (Doctoral dissertation, Stellenbosch: Stellenbosch University).

Mtau, T.T. and Rahul, N.A. 2024. Optimizing Business Performance through KPI Alignment: A Comprehensive Analysis of Key Performance Indicators and Strategic Objectives. *American Journal of Industrial and Business Management*, 14(1): 66–82.

Nair, M., Andersson, J., Nygren, J.M. and Lundgren, L.E. 2023. Barriers and enablers for implementation of an artificial intelligence–based decision support tool to reduce the risk of readmission of patients with heart failure: Stakeholder interviews. *JMIR Formative Research*, 7(1): e47335.

Neirotti, P., Pesce, D. and Battaglia, D. 2021. Algorithms for operational decision-making: An absorptive capacity perspective on the process of converting data into relevant knowledge. *Technological Forecasting and Social Change*, 173: 121088.

Ngure, S.W. 2021. The balance score card as a strategic plan monitoring and evaluation tool: A practical approach.

Nguyen, Q.C., Li, D., Meng, H.W., Kath, S., Nsoesie, E., Li, F. et al. 2016. Building a national neighborhood dataset from geotagged Twitter data for indicators of happiness, diet, and physical activity. *JMIR Public Health and Surveillance*, 2(2): e5869.

Panda, B.K. 2020. Application of business model innovation for new enterprises: A case study of digital business using a freemium business model. *Journal of Management Development*, 39(4): 517–524.

Pirro, D.N. 2024. Dynamic Value Networks Theory (DVN): Harnessing Interconnected Relationships for Value Creation. Available at SSRN 4818195.

Proksch, M., Paliwal, N. and Bielert, W. 2024. The secrets of AI value creation: a practical guide to business value creation with artificial intelligence from strategy to execution. John Wiley & Sons.

Putte, H.V., van der Voordt, T. and van Bortel, G. 2023. Performance measurement in the built environment.

Rana, N.P., Chatterjee, S., Dwivedi, Y.K. and Akter, S. 2022. Understanding dark side of artificial intelligence (AI) integrated business analytics: assessing firm's operational inefficiency and competitiveness. *European Journal of Information Systems*, 31(3): 364–387.

Rodríguez García, M., Núñez Fernández, A., González Romero, I. and Prado Prado, J.C. 2022. Examining the business model of replenishment subscriptions: a longitudinal case study. Dirección y Organización.

Sazu, M.H. 2022. How machine learning can drive high frequency algorithmic trading for technology stocks. *International Journal of Data Science and Advanced Analytics*, 4(4): 84–93.

Schneider, G. 2022. Health Data Pools: Case-Studies and Involved Interests. In Health Data Pools Under European Data Protection and Competition Law: Health as a Digital Business (pp. 61–135). Cham: Springer International Publishing.

Schrage, M. and Kiron, D. 2018. Leading with next-generation key performance indicators. MIT Sloan Management Review.

Schrage, M., Muttreja, V. and Kwan, A. 2022. How the wrong KPIs doom digital transformation. *MIT Sloan Management Review*.

Schrage, M., Kiron, D., Candelon, F., Khodabandeh, S. and Chu, M. 2023. AI is helping companies redefine, not just improve, performance. *MIT Sloan Management Review*, 64(3): 1–7.

Schrage, M., Kiron, D., Candelon, F., Khodabandeh, S. and Chu, M. 2024. The Future of Strategic Measurement: Enhancing KPIs with AI. Future.

Setiawan, I. and Purba, H.H. 2020. A systematic literature review of key performance indicators (KPIs) implementation. *Journal of Industrial Engineering & Management Research*, 1(3): 200–208.

Sibanda, J. 2022. Investigating the changing role of key performance indicators for technology and project management entities (Doctoral dissertation, North-West University (South Africa)).

Singh, H., Singh, M., Kumar, R. and Khan, S. (2023, September). Dynamically Visualizing Key Performance Indicators for Informed Business Decision-Making. In Proceedings of the 2023 6th International Conference on Robot Systems and Applications (pp. 321–325).

Sreenath, S., Sudhakar, K. and Yusop, A.F. 2021. Sustainability at airports: Technologies and best practices from ASEAN countries. *Journal of Environmental Management*, 299: 113639.

Stone, M., Aravopoulou, E., Ekinci, Y., Evans, G., Hobbs, M., Labib, A. et al. 2020. Artificial intelligence (AI) in strategic marketing decision-making: a research agenda. *The Bottom Line*, 33(2): 183–200.

Sturm, T. 2023. Exploring Human and Artificial Intelligence Collaboration and Its Impact on Organizational Performance: A Multi-Level Analysis.

Sutikno, B., Sanjaya, M.D., Hanamaria, S.J. and Xaveria, V. 2019. Tokopedia: Dissecting the unicorn marketplace's magic for national domination.

Tambare, P., Meshram, C., Lee, C.C., Ramteke, R.J. and Imoize, A.L. 2021. Performance measurement system and quality management in data-driven Industry 4.0: A review. *Sensors*, 22(1): 224.

Tripathi, A. 2023. The impact of e-commerce on international business: a comparative study of traditional and online business models.

Uddin, S., Popesko, B., Papadaki, Š. and Wagner, J. 2021. Performance measurement in a transitional economy: unfolding a case of KPIs. *Accounting, Auditing & Accountability Journal*, 34(2): 370–396.

van de Ven, M.R., Machado, P.L., Athanasopoulou, A., Aysolmaz, B. and Türetken, O. 2022. Key performance indicators for business models: a review of literature. In 30th European Conference on Information Systems (ECIS 2022): New Horizons in Digitally United Societies (p. 126). AIS Electronic Library.

Verhaelen, B., Mayer, F., Peukert, S. and Lanza, G. 2021. A comprehensive KPI network for the performance measurement and management in global production networks. *Production Engineering*, 15: 635–650.

Weiss, T. and Hartle, F. 2023. Reengineering performance management breakthroughs in achieving strategy through people. CRC Press.

Wilkens, U. 2020. Artificial intelligence in the workplace–A double-edged sword. *The International Journal of Information and Learning Technology*, 37(5): 253–265.

Zerfass, A. and Link, J. 2022. Communication management: Structures, processes, and business models for value creation through corporate communications. In Research handbook on strategic communication (pp. 237–258). Edward Elgar Publishing.

CHAPTER 7

Reimagining Industry 5.0

Generative Artificial Intelligence as the Enabling Technology

Amin Hosseinian-Far,[1,*] *Maryam Farsi,*[2] *Koorosh Gharehbaghi,*[3] *Hamid Jahankhani*[4] and *Alireza Daneshkhah*[5]

1. Introduction

Industry 5.0 (I5.0) represents a paradigm shift from its predecessor, Industry 4.0, emphasizing a few 'leading characteristics', including a human-centric approach, sustainability, and resilience (Leng et al. 2022). Although these principles are critical, the true driving force behind this new industrial revolution is the advent and integration of Artificial Intelligence (AI), particularly Generative AI (GenAI) (Mohammed and Skibniewski 2023). GenAI, with its ability to generate, innovate, and optimize, is a transformative force reshaping industries and societal norms (Feuerriegel et al. 2024). From manufacturing (Doanh et al. 2023) to healthcare (Zhang and Kamel Boulos 2023), finance (Chen et al. 2023) to retail (Ooi et al. 2023), GenAI's disruptive capabilities are redefining how businesses operate and

[1] Department of Business Analytics and Systems, University of Hertfordshire, AL10 9EU, UK.
[2] Centre for Digital Engineering and Manufacturing, Cranfield University, Cranfield MK43 0AL, UK.
Email: maryam.farsi@cranfield.ac.uk
[3] School of Property, Construction and Project Management, RMIT University, Melbourne 3000, Australia.
Email: koorosh.gharehbaghi@rmit.edu.au
[4] Faculty of Engineering and Environment, Northumbria University London, London E1 7HT, UK.
Email: hamid.jahankhani@northumbria.ac.uk
[5] Faculty of Mathematics and Data Science, Emirates Aviation University, Dubai P.O. Box 53044, United Arab Emirates.
Email: alireza.daneshkhah@eau.ac.ae
* Corresponding author: a.hosseinian-far@herts.ac.uk

DOI: 10.1201/9781003540373-7

how people interact with technology (Huang 2023). This chapter explores the significant impact of GenAI on I5.0, arguing that while sustainable, resilience, and a human-centric view are essential constructs in the current industrial revolution, it is GenAI that stands at the forefront, steering us into a new era of industrial and societal evolution. Accordingly, through a thematic narrative literature review, we highlight several instances where GenAI technologies demonstrate their disruptive nature across various contexts. Furthermore, we explore the concept of 'disruption' to support our argument that the 'true' Industry 5.0—characterized by significant impacts on individuals' lives and business operations—is now being realized with the increasing adoption of GenAI technologies.

The following sections provide an overview of Industry 5.0 and the role of GenAI within the I5.0 context, followed by explicit examples of the disruptive nature of GenAI, highlighting its innovative application, value, and impact on business and society. The notions of sustainability and resilience are also presented and discussed within this chapter. Moreover, the security and ethical concerns of developing GenAI systems are reviewed. In addition, the swift expansion of embedded systems and Internet of Things (IoT) technologies is discussed and considered as an additional construct within the I5.0 era. Finally, the notion of disruptiveness in industrial revolutions is briefly examined to consolidate our argument that I5.0 is now realised in the GenAI era.

2. An Overview of Industry 5.0

Industry 5.0 integrates sustainable development goals with digitalisation, building on the advancements of Industry 4.0. It focuses on human-centric solutions, bio-inspired technologies, and cyber-safe data transmission to create an innovative, resilient, and socio-centred industry that minimises negative environmental and social impacts while promoting economic growth and prosperity (Farsi et al. 2021, Kasinathan et al. 2022). The six key technologies that enable the I5.0 vision are human-machine interactive technologies, smart materials and bio-inspired technologies, digital twins and real-time simulations, energy-efficient data management technologies, AI, and renewable energy technologies for storage and autonomy (European Commission 2021).

The European Commission outlines three drivers for the I5.0 transition: the green transition, the digital transition, and the competitive transition. The green transition focuses on avoiding climate change and environmental degradation, promoting clean energy, a circular economy, resource efficiency, sustainable mobility, and zero pollution. The digital transition supports the circular economy by advancing digital skills, data, technologies, and infrastructures. The competitive transition aims to enhance marketing policies and regulations to create more value for businesses and society. Technologies from Industry 4.0, such as IoT, AI, and automation, support the I5.0 vision by providing human-centric solutions and enhancing human-machine integration, exemplified by innovative materials with recyclability features and energy-efficient automation in smart factories (European Commission 2021).

Industry 4.0 revolutionised industrial operations by enhancing productivity through data-driven remote monitoring and control of machines, traditionally

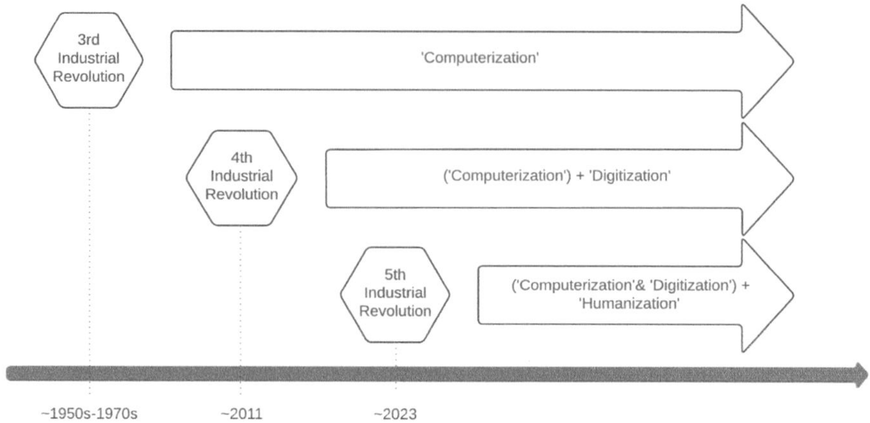

Figure 1: An Overview of Industry 5.0 - adapted from (Raja Santhi and Muthuswamy 2023).

accessed via dashboards (Tambare et al. 2021). In contrast, Industry 5.0 emphasises a human-centric approach, leveraging advancements in auto-regressive Large Language Models (LLMs) to develop Intelligent Cognitive Assistants (ICAs) for natural language interactions (Figliè et al. 2024). Figure 1 presents an overview of Industry 5.0.

The transition to Industry 5.0 integrates human factors into automated decision-making processes, enhancing Industry 4.0 operations with technologies such as cyber-physical systems, AI, and big data analytics. Industry 5.0 emphasises transparent and interpretable AI models to ensure autonomy and efficiency in industrial processes (Trivedi et al. 2024).

Existing literature on Industry 5.0 also highlights social sustainability and the need for capacity building, including upskilling and reskilling personnel to integrate human expertise with advanced technology (Fraile et al. 2023). Research indicates that the application of techniques such as Large Language Models (LLMs) and deep learning can enhance data analysis accuracy with real-time processing, leading to energy savings, efficiency improvements, and better quality outcomes (Shchepkina et al. 2024).

As already noted, Industry 5.0 represents a progressive development in the landscape of industrial production, signifying a notable departure from the principles established by Industry 4.0. While the latter primarily emphasises automation, data interchange, and the integration of the Internet of Things (IoT) to facilitate the creation of intelligent manufacturing environments, Industry 5.0 advances this framework by prioritising human-centric approaches, sustainability, and resilience within businesses and industries. This evolution offers a fundamental transformation in the perception of the links between human labour, technological innovation, and sustainable production practices. According to current literature and as noted earlier, the primary attributes of Industry 5.0 revolve around embedding sustainability, enhancing resilience, and particularly reinstating the human element in various disciplines. In contrast to Industry 4.0's predominant focus on automating and digitising operations, Industry 5.0 aims to embrace collaborative systems where human workers and machines enhance each other's capabilities. Additionally, a strong commitment to sustainable methodologies is integral to Industry 5.0, as it addresses the ecological and societal implications of industrial activities by optimising resource utilisation, curtailing waste, and lowering the carbon emissions associated with manufacturing processes. The aspect of resilience is further reinforced in Industry 5.0, which aims to establish solid foundations for production systems capable of enduring and adapting to various disruptions and external and internal shocks, including natural disasters, pandemics, or cyber threats. This is achieved by developing flexible supply chains and agile manufacturing strategies that can swiftly adjust to fluctuations in market demands or operational conditions. This evolution entails a transition from a focus solely on efficiency to an emphasis on value creation, as well as a shift from linear to circular economic models to address various forms of accumulating waste. While the ramifications of Industry 5.0 differ across sectors, the most significant challenges arise from the need for innovative business models and the establishment of suitable policies and regulations. Such a substantial paradigm shift is integral to industrial production, transitioning towards a more human-centred, sustainable, and resilient framework.

Between 2018 and 2022, the early basis of AI-related research focused on the role of AI in sustainability, data management, and healthcare applications. These studies established the groundwork for more advanced applications of AI, including GenAI, in various sectors. In 2023, GenAI began to take centre stage, with research focusing on its applications in content generation, personalisation, and human-like outputs. Ethical considerations and energy consumption challenges also started to emerge during this period. In more recent literature published in 2024, a tremendous number of studies explore the application of GenAI together with I4.0 and 5.0 technologies across multiple industries, including manufacturing, healthcare, supply chains, and finance, with a focus on improvement. This research work reviews some of the main literature in detail in the following section. The centric role of GenAI across Industry 5.0 and 4.0 technologies is illustrated schematically in Figure 2.

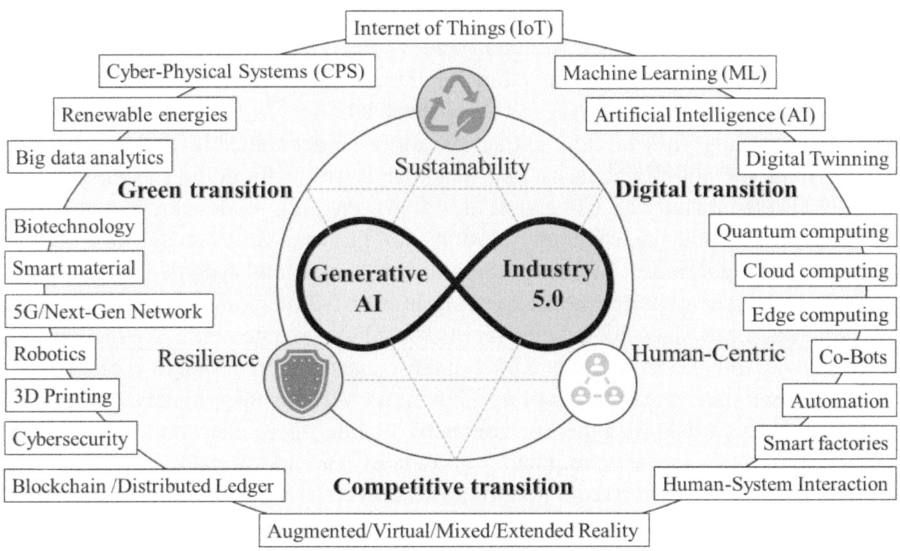

Figure 2: Gen-AI and Industry 5.0 Technologies (authors' own elaboration).

3. The Role of Generative AI in Industry 5.0

Generative AI, a subset of AI, goes beyond sole automation, data analysis, prediction, classification, and recommendations (Banh and Strobel 2023), and it entails sophisticated algorithms capable of generating new content, designs, and solutions. These AI technologies learn from large datasets (Banh and Strobel 2023), identifying patterns (Ooi et al. 2023), generating human-like outputs (Bandi et al. 2023), and extending human creativity (Zhou and Lee 2024).

In the context of business, GenAI is revolutionizing processes by optimizing supply chains (Fosso Wamba et al. 2024), personalising customer experiences (Abrokwah-Larbi 2023), and devising sustainable and predictive maintenance strategies in manufacturing (Ghobakhloo et al. 2024). Over the past few years, there have also been numerous studies examining the role of GenAI in other sectors. For instance, in healthcare, GenAI can analyse medical records to generate personalised treatment plans (Loh 2024), potentially saving countless lives. In finance, it can create models that predict market trends with unprecedented accuracy, providing businesses with a competitive edge (Linkon et al. 2024). Moreover, it is argued that GenAI will have a transformative role in the hospitality and tourism industry, impacting both businesses and individuals (Dwivedi et al. 2024).

Kernan Freire et al. (2023) explored the use of cognitive assistants (CAs) with LLMs in manufacturing to enhance knowledge transfer and worker performance. They identified critical challenges such as data security, privacy, and the reliability of LLMs in high-stakes environments. Addressing these concerns through proper design guidelines can unlock their potential benefits (Kernan Freire et al. 2023). In manufacturing, traditional methods of collecting customer requirements have limitations in accurately capturing customer needs and driving innovation, especially in product-service system business models, where feedback is intangible. The application of GenAI can enable the extraction of actionable insights from customer-service interactions, providing valuable real-time data for agile decision-making (Shahin et al. 2024). Kiangala and Wang (2024) presented the design of a hybrid AI and generative AI chatbot for human-machine interaction to mitigate equipment downtime in factories. The chatbot interacts with operators in natural language, making information extraction more understandable and augmenting factory data for additional tasks like machine learning modelling (Kiangala and Wang 2024). In a study by Cónego et al. (2024), the authors developed chatbots to generate customised gamification solutions for Industry 5.0, focusing on human-technology collaboration. These chatbots utilise Virtual and Augmented Reality to enhance employee experiences by creating immersive, personalised environments. This approach promises advancements in workplace engagement, satisfaction, and performance, integral to Industry 5.0's human-centric vision (Cónego et al. 2024).

In operational research, adopting Generative AI can raise several challenges, such as perceived risk, data quality, connectivity, interoperability, data privacy, user acceptance, legacy systems, regulatory guidelines, and additional concerns specific to ChatGPT, including job reduction, linguistic diversity, and ethical considerations. Nevertheless, addressing these challenges leads to improvements in the effectiveness and efficiency of operations and provides opportunities for roles requiring critical thinking and creativity, leading to better decision-making (Dewasiri et al. 2024). Ghobakhloo et al. developed a strategic roadmap to show how generative AI can enhance responsible manufacturing in Industry 5.0. They argued that the application of generative AI promotes sustainability, offering data-driven insights and resilience. By leveraging these functions synergistically, manufacturers can maximise benefits, advancing Industry 5.0's sustainability goals through enhanced human-technology collaboration (Ghobakhloo et al. 2024).

The impact of GenAI extends beyond business applications. It is transforming our daily lives, from intelligent virtual assistants that manage our schedules to AI-driven platforms that curate personalised content and recommendations (Boulus-Rødje et al. 2024). Boulus-Rødje et al. (2024) even argue that such systems should be viewed as human partners rather than just tools. This rapidly expanding integration of GenAI is enhancing convenience yet also fundamentally altering the fabric of human interactions and decision-making processes. By reimagining Industry 5.0 through the lens of GenAI, we recognise its incomparable potential to drive innovation, enable and enhance growth, and address the complex challenges of the modern world while maintaining a sustainable, resilient, and human-centric mindset. As we traverse this new industrial landscape, it is imperative to employ the power of GenAI responsibly, ensuring that its benefits are equitably distributed and aligned with the principles of sustainability and resilience. These aspects are further explored in the following sections of the chapter.

4. GenAI Transforming Business and Society

The transformative and disruptive nature of generative AI extends across various sectors, fundamentally altering business operations and societal interactions. In manufacturing, GenAI optimizes design and performance (Grech La Rosa et al. 2024), and in the energy sector, it reduces energy waste, and enhances quality control through predictive analytics and automated decision-making (Poland et al. 2024). Siemens is using GenAI to enhance its predictive maintenance solutions (Hörmann 2024), whilst Accenture reported in 2024 a significant increase in innovative disruption, providing numerous examples of improved efficiency and productivity in a range of sectors (Azagury et al. 2024).

Precision medicine, also referred to as personalised medicine, is "an innovative approach to tailoring disease prevention and treatment that takes into account differences in people's genes, environments, and lifestyles" (US FDA 2018), often linked to predictions based on an individual's genome (Ni Ki et al. 2022). In healthcare, GenAI is revolutionising diagnostics and personalised medicine, and AI algorithms can analyse medical images with remarkable accuracy, often surpassing human capabilities (The Lancet Regional Health – Europe 2023). Moreover, GenAI is deemed to enhance surgical precision (Rajaratnam et al. 2024). An instance of GenAI in healthcare includes IBM's Watson X system, which uses AI to provide oncologists with evidence-based treatment recommendations, significantly improving patient outcomes (IBM 2024). Several other domains are also impacted, with GenAI enabling advanced fraud detection (Kumar et al. 2023), empowering developers (Ulfsnes et al. 2024), and enhancing customer care (Huang and Rust 2024). AI-driven chatbots and virtual assistants handle customer inquiries, process transactions, and offer financial advice, streamlining operations and enhancing customer satisfaction (Bhuiyan 2024).

Beyond business applications, GenAI is reshaping societal dynamics. Education systems are integrating AI to provide personalised learning experiences, adapting content to individual students' needs and pacing (Kumar et al. 2024). In this context, several challenges are also reported within the literature, necessitating further examination through empirical studies (Law 2024). The widespread accessibility of GenAI platforms, including OpenAI's ChatGPT, Bard, and Microsoft Co-Pilot, has led to the adoption of this technology among students. However, this raises several concerns for lecturers, schools, and universities regarding the authenticity of assessments and the impact on students' learning (Chan and Colloton 2024). The use of GenAI in learning and teaching is in its infancy, yet it is already generating several competing perspectives (Rudolph et al. 2024). Further research will be required to examine the responsible use of the technology by students, educators, and educational institutions.

In daily life, AI influences how we interact with technology (Lee et al. 2023). Virtual assistants like Amazon's Alexa, Apple's Siri, and Google Assistant manage our schedules, control smart home devices, and provide instant information, seamlessly integrating into our routines (Mauny et al. 2021). This ubiquitous presence of AI is redefining convenience and efficiency in our personal lives. By revolutionising business processes and societal interactions, GenAI has the potential to enhance productivity and innovation (Kanbach et al. 2024). This pervasive influence and disruptive nature highlight the central role of GenAI in I5.0, driving forward a new era of technological and societal advancement and making changes to the way we create, innovate, and live.

5. Integrating Sustainability and Resilience with GenAI

While generative AI stands at the forefront of Industry 5.0, its integration with sustainability and resilience is crucial for a holistic approach to future industrial advancements. GenAI's capabilities offer innovative solutions to some of the most pressing environmental and social challenges. Although the current literature on this is scarce, this can include creating inferences in contexts characterized by deep uncertainty, including climate change, just transitions, and global social disruptions (Luccioni et al. 2021, Rane 2023). From a dissimilar perspective, GenAI technologies themselves consume significant amounts of energy and have a carbon footprint, thus considerations will need to be placed on minimizing and reducing the rising adoption of GenAI platforms and technologies (Chien et al. 2023).

AI technologies are driving significant advancements in energy efficiency and resource management (Waltersmann et al. 2021). AI-powered systems optimise energy consumption in buildings and industrial processes (Yussuf and Asfour 2024), reducing carbon footprints and operational costs (Tseng and Lin 2024). For instance, Google has implemented deep AI to manage the cooling systems in its data centres, resulting in a 40% reduction in energy use (Shead 2018). Although the role of general

AI systems in reducing energy consumption, managing carbon footprints, and optimising systems is well covered within the literature, the role of GenAI systems is an underexplored area and will necessitate further research.

AI also plays an important role in environmental conservation (Balsalobre-Lorente et al. 2023). Machine learning algorithms analyse satellite imagery to monitor deforestation, track wildlife populations, and predict natural disasters (Raihan 2023). These insights enable timely interventions and more effective conservation strategies. Digital Twin technologies provide a digital replica of a physical system or context, enabling the adoption and application of advanced AI technologies for monitoring, transparency, devising maintenance strategies, optimisation, and informed decision-making (Ofosu et al. 2022). Accordingly, Jouan and Hallot (2020) have examined the role that a Digital Twin can play in supporting preventative environmental conservation policies.

Resilience, another core principle of I5.0, is enhanced through AI's predictive and adaptive capabilities (Sindhwani et al. 2022). AI-driven predictive maintenance in manufacturing and infrastructure prevents failures and reduces downtime, ensuring continuous operations even in the face of disruptions (Daneshkhah et al. 2017). During the COVID-19 pandemic, AI-powered models helped predict infection trends (Jamshidi et al. 2022) and optimise resource allocation (Alam et al. 2021), demonstrating the critical role of AI in crisis management (Onder and Uzun 2022).

Furthermore, GenAI aids in developing resilient supply chains (Ahmed et al. 2023). By analyzing vast amounts of data, AI identifies vulnerabilities and suggests optimization strategies, enhancing supply chain agility and robustness (Abaku et al. 2024). This capability is crucial in a world where geopolitical tensions and climate change increasingly threaten global supply networks. GenAI can also positively disrupt supply chain systems in the coming years; this is achieved through accurate demand forecasting for inventory management, supply chain design and innovation, supplier relationship management, quality control, predictive maintenance of critical assets in the supply chain, personalisation and customer care and support, promoting a circular economy, supply chain risk management, automation, and data-informed decision-making (Ghadge et al. 2020, Jackson et al. 2024, Fosso Wamba et al. 2024).

Considering these insights and examples within the literature, it is evident that AI, and particularly GenAI, is playing an instrumental role in transforming every aspect of business and life, including efforts to promote or adapt to sustainable practices. Nonetheless, the impact of the swift adoption of GenAI may, itself, have sustainability implications, and this aspect remains underexplored to date.

6. Security Concerns and Ethical Considerations

As Generative AI becomes a central component of Industry 5.0, addressing security concerns and ethical considerations is imperative to ensuring its responsible development and deployment. The extensive use of AI brings forth significant challenges related to data privacy, cybersecurity, and ethical decision-making, and accordingly, we argue that security and ethical considerations should be viewed as another set of characteristics in the I5.0 era. The narrative below presents several examples where security can become a sensitive and concerning area when AI, and particularly GenAI technologies, are adopted.

AI technologies often rely on vast amounts of data, raising concerns about data privacy and protection (Manheim and Kaplan 2019). Ensuring that personal and sensitive information is securely stored and processed is critical to maintaining public trust. Implementing robust encryption techniques and adhering to data protection regulations, such as the GDPR, are essential steps in safeguarding privacy (Jimenez and Jahankhani 2020, Jahankhani and Hosseinian-Far 2017). Cybersecurity is another major concern, as AI systems and technologies are both targets and tools in cyber warfare (Seify et al. 2022, Chakraborty et al. 2023). Chakraborty et al. (2023) discuss this within the context of Industry 4.0; nonetheless, Generative AI adds the dimension of generation to this, and therefore, we argue that cybersecurity would remain a major consideration in I5.0, enabled through Generative AI technologies.

Adversarial attacks, where malicious entities manipulate AI algorithms, pose significant risks to system integrity and reliability (Liu et al. 2021). Developing resilient AI models that can detect and counter such attacks is crucial for maintaining the security of AI-driven infrastructures. Xu et al. (2020), in a survey and review of existing attacks and countermeasures, provide insights into AI-based algorithms that form the basis of adversarial attacks and present countermeasures. The cybersecurity landscape is also being disrupted by Generative AI, given its capabilities to generate text, sound, image, and other media, and its ability to support adversaries in sophisticated cyber-attacks (Gupta et al. 2023, Huang et al. 2024). Thus, security and ethics, in our view, should still be regarded as additional key characteristics of I5.0.

Ethical considerations play an instrumental role in the development and deployment of GenAI systems. AI technologies, in general, must be designed to operate transparently and fairly, avoiding biases that can lead to discriminatory outcomes (Ferrer et al. 2021, Varona and Suárez 2022). Moreover, diversity in training datasets and implementing rigorous testing protocols can help mitigate these risks (Hort et al. 2024, Petersen et al. 2022). In addition to these, a survey of the literature highlights the need for the establishment of pertinent ethical frameworks for the development, deployment, and use of AI technologies, similar to frameworks available in other fields such as medicine (Prem 2023). These frameworks should address issues such as accountability, fairness, transparency, and the ethical implications of AI decisions (Akinrinola et al. 2024, Femi Osasona et al. 2024). Engaging diverse stakeholders, including ethicists, technologists, researchers, end users, and policymakers, is essential to creating comprehensive and inclusive guidelines. The call for the establishment of ethical frameworks for GenAI technologies, specifically, is also discussed within pertinent literature (Zohny et al. 2023, Kirova et al. 2023).

7. Expansion of Embedded Systems and IoT

Espina-Romero et al. (2023), through a bibliometric analysis, presented some of the key terms in the literature from 2019 to 2022 related to I5.0. According to this bibliometric analysis, the term IoT appears to be the most repeated key term, along with AI, followed by sustainable development. The argument being put forward here is not the adoption of IoT technologies, but rather the swift diffusion and adoption of technology at rates never seen before. Accordingly, it is forecasted that the number of IoT connections will double by 2033 compared to a decade earlier (Vailshery 2024). The expansion of embedded systems and the Internet of Things (IoT) is a critical feature of Industry 5.0, complementing the advancements brought by GenAI. The integration of AI with IoT and embedded systems creates a network of intelligent devices that communicate and collaborate, driving unprecedented levels of automation and innovation. This rapid adoption and expansion are moving us closer to the true realisation of 'smart' concepts.

Embedded systems, which are specialized computing systems designed to perform dedicated functions, are increasingly equipped with AI capabilities (Oliveira et al. 2024). These systems are found in various applications, from smart home devices and wearable technology to industrial machinery and automotive systems (Hosseinian-Far et al. 2018). By incorporating AI, these devices can perform complex tasks, make autonomous decisions, and learn from their environments (Singh and Singh 2024). IoT, which connects physical devices to the internet, allows for seamless data exchange and real-time monitoring (Jahankhani and Hosseinian-Far 2017). The convergence of AI and IoT leads to the creation of smart environments, where devices interact intelligently to enhance efficiency and user experience. For instance, in smart cities, AI-powered IoT systems manage traffic flow (Javaid et al. 2018), optimise energy usage (Maier 2016), and enhance public safety through detection and monitoring (Sha et al. 2022), creating more liveable and sustainable urban environments (Lim et al. 2021). In agriculture, AI-driven IoT devices monitor soil conditions and weather patterns, improving irrigation and crop health, enabling precision farming, and reducing resource consumption (Pandey and Mukherjee 2022). In healthcare, wearable devices track vital signs and provide real-time health analytics, empowering individuals to manage their health proactively (Kazanskiy et al. 2024).

The alignment and linkage between IoT devices and Generative AI drive the massive expansion of interconnected technologies, transforming various sectors and enhancing people's lives. This alignment further accelerates the adoption of smart technologies, resulting in more creative and innovative solutions, and creating new opportunities for economic growth and societal advancement. Accordingly, the disruptive nature of GenAI is further explored in the next section.

8. Disruptiveness of GenAI and Implications for I5.0

GenAI is characterised by the fusion of a wide range of technologies and represents a significant advancement in AI. This convergence of GenAI with human-centric approaches, the prioritisation of sustainability and ethics, and the rapid expansion of IoT technologies form a robust foundation for viewing GenAI as the core of the 5th Industrial Revolution. This technological convergence, coupled with rising automation and productivity, as well as data-driven decision-making and strategies, is truly disrupting traditional industries. "Disruptive innovation is a powerful means of broadening and developing new markets and providing new functionality, which, in turn, may disrupt existing market linkages" (Christensen 1997, Yu and Hang 2010). Although the focus of this chapter is not necessarily on the notion of disruptiveness,

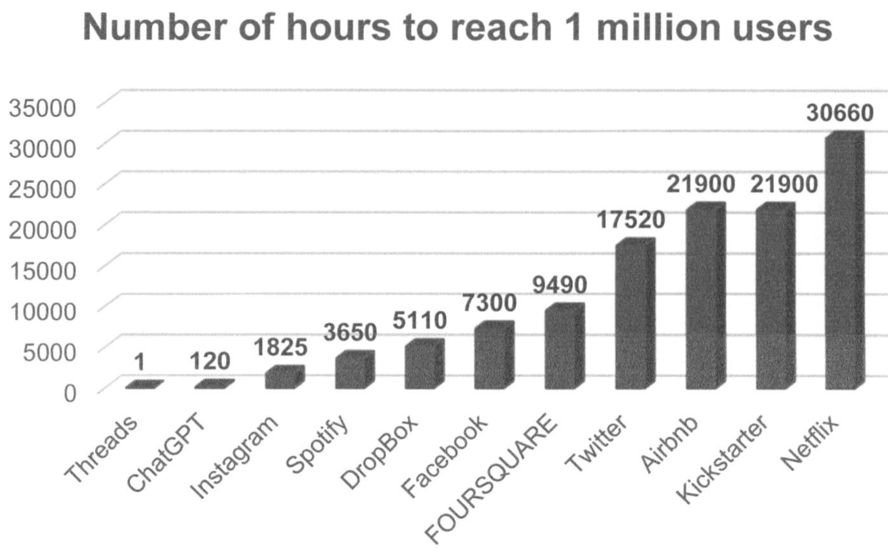

Figure 3: Number of hours required to reach a 100 million users - data derived from (Buchholz 2023).

and despite the criticisms of disruptive theory, we will exclusively discuss how GenAI has been altering the way people live and how businesses operate.

GenAI is revolutionising the personalisation trends that began in the 4th Industrial Revolution, profoundly impacting sectors ranging from journalism and software development to art and logistics. By opening new markets, GenAI has also spurred the emergence of innovative business models that harness the power of large language models and generative AI as a whole. The adoption of the technology among typically non-technical users was astonishing, with OpenAI's ChatGPT reaching 100 million users in just five days (Figure 3).

GenAI is increasingly integrating into the ecosystem of advanced technologies across various sectors, as discussed in this chapter, and has the potential to make a significant global socio-economic impact in the coming years. Considering this, we argue that GenAI possesses many characteristics required to be considered the backbone of a new industrial revolution, whilst embracing the previously defined characteristics of I5.0, such as sustainability, human-centredness, and resilience. Figure 4 outlines I5.0 with GenAI at the core, along with surrounding elements that characterise this new industrial revolution.

Industry 5.0 represents a significant advancement beyond Industry 4.0, focusing on a manufacturing paradigm that prioritises human involvement, sustainability, and resilience. The role of GenAI within this context is deemed fundamental, as it has the potential to transform various sectors, business frameworks, and societal expectations. As illustrated in Figure 4, the impact of GenAI on Industry 5.0 encompasses a range of aspects, including resilience and security. The incorporation of GenAI into this model brings forth several important considerations. Firstly, it enhances resilience and adaptability by enabling the prediction of potential disruptions and the formulation of proactive strategies, which are essential for the flexible and robust systems that characterise I5.0. Secondly, the human-centric nature of I5.0 necessitates a strong

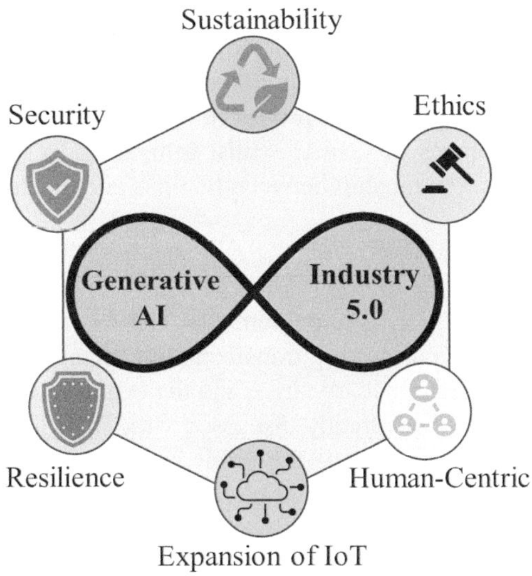

Figure 4: Industry 5.0 Hexagon with GenAI at its Core (authors' own elaboration).

emphasis on ethical issues, such as privacy, security, and bias, highlighting the need for the deployment of AI technologies to be transparent, equitable, and respectful of human rights—vital for embracing and nurturing trust and ensuring the successful integration of these systems. Moreover, the capabilities of GenAI, when integrated with the human-centred principles of Industry 5.0, offer a distinctive opportunity to revolutionise various sectors by emphasising efficiency, customisation, and sustainability. Nevertheless, this integration also introduces challenges concerning ethical considerations, workforce adjustments, and societal implications that require meticulous management to fully leverage the potential advantages.

The emergence of GenAI introduces a variety of challenges that carry profound consequences for I5.0. These challenges primarily revolve around ethical considerations, the evolving dynamics of employment, the interconnections and interactions between humans and machines, and the broader societal effects. In summary, the ramifications and potential pitfalls of these challenges include:

- Security risks. The utilization of GenAI presents opportunities for the creation of deepfakes, the alteration of information, and the execution of cyberattacks, thereby introducing considerable security threats to individuals, organizations, and broader societal structures,
- Originality and authenticity. The capacity of GenAI to produce contents that closely resemble human creativity poses significant challenges to conventional understandings of originality and authenticity, hence prompting apprehensions regarding the worth and acknowledgment of works created by humans,
- Loss of human touch. The integration of AI-generated responses in fields such as healthcare, education, and customer service could result in a diminished capacity for empathy, understanding, and trust, as it replaces traditional human interaction.

The challenges presented by GenAI may represent considerable obstacles to the realization of I5.0; however, they simultaneously offer a chance to build a future in which technology amplifies human potential and aids in the creation of a more just and sustainable society. By taking a proactive approach to these challenges, I 5.0 can leverage the advantages of GenAI whilst mitigating its associated risks, thus promoting a synergistic relationship between humans and machines.

9. Conclusion

As we reimagine Industry 5.0, it is evident that GenAI stands at the vanguard of this new industrial revolution, driving transformative changes across industries and societies. Sustainability, resilience, security, and the expansion of embedded systems and IoT are crucial features as already discussed within the literature; however, the disruptive nature of GenAI makes it the predominant force shaping the new era. Previous industrial revolutions were not without flaws. The past century, with advances in automation and the increasing energy demand, led to significant reliance on fossil fuels, resulting in massive greenhouse gas (GHG) emissions, global warming, and changes in the Earth's climate. Accordingly, while we are entering a new industrial revolution, the ethics and responsible development and adoption of innovation reliant on GenAI technologies must be dealt with caution. By employing the power of GenAI responsibly, integrating it with sustainable practices, and addressing security and ethical concerns, we can unlock the full potential of Industry 5.0, ensuring the sustainable, resilient, equitable, and ethical adoption of technology. The future trajectory of Industry 5.0 promises to be dynamic and transformative, with GenAI technologies and applications at the forefront. The rapid adoption of this technology in recent years further illustrates its desirability and impact across industries and societies.

The existing literature suggests how Generative AI is reshaping Industry 5.0 to date. In terms of the 'sustainability' pillar, GenAI is enabling sustainable innovations in manufacturing, energy management, and environmental conservation. In terms of the 'resilience' pillar, GenAI enhances resilience by enabling predictive capabilities, improving operational agility, and addressing cybersecurity challenges. Finally, the existing literature focuses on the 'human-centric' pillar and the role of GenAI in improving human interactions, worker engagement, and decision-making by integrating human experience into AI-driven systems.

There are several research pathways to this work. Further exploring the impacts of GenAI technologies in various industries is deemed to be increasingly important in the coming years, and further pertinent research will be required. Moreover, an examination of the energy consumption and greenhouse gas (GHG) emissions of GenAI systems is needed. In addition to this, the level of disruption caused by GenAI within the I5.0 context will provide a nuanced assessment of I5.0. The rising adoption of GenAI in various sectors necessitates a deep understanding of the skills required for workers to proactively address the impacts of the technology on the labour market and the upskilling and reskilling needs. Finally, further research on the full autonomy of AI systems and Artificial General Intelligence (AGI) will be imperative, given the rapid development and expansion of the field.

References

Abaku, E.A., Edunjobi, T.E. and Odimarha, A.C. 2024. Theoretical approaches to AI in supply chain optimization: pathways to efficiency and resilience. *International Journal of Science and Technology Research Archive*, 6(1): 092–107. https://doi.org/10.53771/ijstra.2024.6.1.0033.

Abrokwah-Larbi, Kwabena. 2023. The role of Generative Artificial Intelligence (GAI) in Customer Personalisation (CP) Development in SMEs: A Theoretical Framework and Research Propositions. *Industrial Artificial Intelligence*, 1(1): 11. https://doi.org/10.1007/s44244-023-00012-4.

Ahmed, Tazim, Chitra Lekha Karmaker, Sumaiya Benta Nasir, Md. Abdul Moktadir and Sanjoy Kumar Paul. 2023. Modeling the artificial intelligence-based imperatives of industry 5.0 towards resilient supply chains: A Post-COVID-19 pandemic perspective. *Computers & Industrial Engineering*, 177(March): 109055. https://doi.org/10.1016/j.cie.2023.109055.

Akinrinola, O., Okoye, C.C., Ofodile, O.C. and Ugochukwu, C.E. 2024. Navigating and reviewing ethical dilemmas in AI development: strategies for transparency, fairness, and accountability. *GSC Advanced Research and Reviews*, 18(3): 050–058. https://doi.org/10.30574/gscarr.2024.18.3.0088.

Alam, Furqan, Ahmed Almaghthawi, Iyad Katib, Aiiad Albeshri and Rashid Mehmood. 2021. IResponse: An AI and IoT-Enabled framework for autonomous COVID-19 pandemic management. *Sustainability*, 13(7): 3797. https://doi.org/10.3390/su13073797.

Azagury, Jack, Muqsit Ashraf, Oliver Wright, Karen Grant and Mike Moore. 2024. Reinvention in the Age of Generative AI. Https://Www.Accenture.Com/Gb-En/Insights/Consulting/Total-Enterprise-Reinvention. January 12, 2024.

Balsalobre-Lorente, Daniel, Jaffar Abbas, Chang He, Ladislav Pilař and Syed Ale Raza Shah. 2023. Tourism, urbanization and natural resources rents matter for environmental sustainability: the leading role of AI and ICT on sustainable development goals in the digital era. *Resources Policy*, 82(May): 103445. https://doi.org/10.1016/j.resourpol.2023.103445.

Bandi, Ajay, Pydi Venkata Satya Ramesh Adapa and Yudu Eswar Vinay Pratap Kumar Kuchi. 2023. The Power of generative AI: A review of requirements, models, input–output formats, evaluation metrics, and challenges. Future Internet, 15(8): 260. https://doi.org/10.3390/fi15080260.

Banh, Leonardo and Gero Strobel. 2023. Generative artificial intelligence. *Electronic Markets*, 33(1): 63. https://doi.org/10.1007/s12525-023-00680-1.

Bhuiyan, Mohammad Shafiquzzaman. 2024. The role of AI-enhanced personalization in customer experiences. *Journal of Computer Science and Technology Studies*, 6(1): 162–69. https://doi.org/10.32996/jcsts.2024.6.1.17.

Boulus-Rødje, Nina, Jocelyn Cranefield, Cathal Doyle and Benedicte Fleron. 2024. GenAI and Me: the hidden work of building and maintaining an augmentative partnership. *Personal and Ubiquitous Computing*, May. https://doi.org/10.1007/s00779-024-01810-y.

Buchholz, Katharina. 2023. Threads Shoots Past One Million User Mark at Lightning Speed. Https://Www.Statista.Com/Chart/29174/Time-to-One-Million-Users/. July 7, 2023.

Chakraborty, Abhilash, Anupam Biswas and Ajoy Kumar Khan. 2023. Artificial Intelligence for Cybersecurity: Threats, Attacks and Mitigation. In, 3–25. https://doi.org/10.1007/978-3-031-12419-8_1.

Chan, Cecilia Ka Yuk and Tom Colloton. 2024. Generative AI in Higher Education. London: Routledge. https://doi.org/10.4324/9781003459026.

Chen, Boyang, Zongxiao Wu and Ruoran Zhao. 2023. From fiction to fact: the growing role of generative AI in business and finance. *Journal of Chinese Economic and Business Studies*, 21(4): 471–96. https://doi.org/10.1080/14765284.2023.2245279.

Chien, Andrew A., Liuzixuan Lin, Hai Nguyen, Varsha Rao, Tristan Sharma and Rajini Wijayawardana. 2023. Reducing the carbon impact of generative AI inference (Today and in 2035). In Proceedings of the 2nd Workshop on Sustainable Computer Systems, 1–7. New York, NY, USA: ACM. https://doi.org/10.1145/3604930.3605705.

Christensen, Clayton M. 1997. The Innovator's Dilemma : When New Technologies Cause Great Firms to Fail. The Management of Innovation and Change Series. Boston, Mass.: Harvard Business School Press.

Cónego, Leonor, Rui Pinto and Gil Gonçalves. 2024. Digital transformation in manufacturing: the synergy of chatbots and tailored gamification strategies. *Procedia Computer Science*, 237: 171–78. https://doi.org/10.1016/j.procs.2024.05.093.

Daneshkhah, Alireza, Amin Hosseinian-Far and Omid Chatrabgoun. 2017. Sustainable maintenance strategy under uncertainty in the lifetime distribution of deteriorating assets. In Strategic Engineering for Cloud Computing and Big Data Analytics, 29–50. Cham: Springer International Publishing. https://doi.org/10.1007/978-3-319-52491-7_2.

Dewasiri, Narayanage Jayantha, Karunarathnage Sajith Senaka Nuwansiri Karunarathna, Mananage Shanika Hansini Rathnasiri, D. G. Dharmarathne and Kiran Sood. 2024. Unleashing the challenges of chatbots and ChatGPT in the banking industry: evidence from an emerging economy. In The Framework for Resilient Industry: A Holistic Approach for Developing Economies, 23–37. Emerald Publishing Limited. https://doi.org/10.1108/978-1-83753-734-120241002.

Doanh, Doung Cong, Zdenek Dufek, Joanna Ejdys, Romualdas Ginevičius, Pawel Korzynski, Grzegorz Mazurek et al. 2023. Generative AI in the manufacturing process: theoretical considerations. *Engineering Management in Production and Services*, 15(4): 76–89. https://doi.org/10.2478/emj-2023-0029.

Dwivedi, Yogesh K., Neeraj Pandey, Wendy Currie and Adrian Micu. 2024. Leveraging ChatGPT and Other Generative Artificial Intelligence (AI)-based applications in the hospitality and tourism industry: practices, challenges and research Agenda. *International Journal of Contemporary Hospitality Management*, 36(1): 1–12. https://doi.org/10.1108/IJCHM-05-2023-0686.

Espina-Romero, Lorena, Jesús Guerrero-Alcedo, Niria Goñi Avila, José Gregorio Noroño Sánchez, Humberto Gutiérrez Hurtado and Aura Quiñones Li. 2023. Industry 5.0: Tracking scientific activity on the most influential industries, associated topics, and future research agenda. *Sustainability*, 15(6): 5554. https://doi.org/10.3390/su15065554.

European Commission, Directorate-General for Research, Innovation, M. Breque, L. De Nul and A Petridis. 2021. Industry 5.0 – Towards a Sustainable, Human-Centric and Resilient European Industry. Publications Office of the European Union. https://doi.org/doi/10.2777/308407.

Farsi, Maryam, Rohita Kumar Mishra and John Ahmet Erkoyuncu. 2021. Industry 5.0 for sustainable reliability centered maintenance. *SSRN Electronic Journal*. https://doi.org/10.2139/ssrn.3944533.

Femi Osasona, Olukunle Oladipupo Amoo, Akoh Atadoga, Temitayo Oluwaseun Abrahams, Oluwatoyin Ajoke Farayola and Benjamin Samson Ayinla. 2024. Reviewing the ethical implications of ai in decision making processes. *International Journal of Management & Entrepreneurship Research*, 6(2): 322–35. https://doi.org/10.51594/ijmer.v6i2.773.

Ferrer, Xavier, Tom van Nuenen, Jose M. Such, Mark Cote and Natalia Criado. 2021. Bias and discrimination in AI: A cross-disciplinary perspective. *IEEE Technology and Society Magazine*, 40(2): 72–80. https://doi.org/10.1109/MTS.2021.3056293.

Feuerriegel, Stefan, Jochen Hartmann, Christian Janiesch and Patrick Zschech. 2024. Generative AI. *Business & Information Systems Engineering*, 66(1): 111–26. https://doi.org/10.1007/s12599-023-00834-7.

Figliè, Roberto, Tommaso Turchi, Giacomo Baldi and Daniele Mazzei. 2024. Towards an LLM-based intelligent assistant for industry 5.0. In Proceedings of the 1st International Workshop on Designing and Building Hybrid Human–AI Systems (SYNERGY 2024). Arenzano, Italy: CEUR Workshop Proceedings.

Fosso Wamba, Samuel, Cameron Guthrie, Maciel M. Queiroz and Stefan Minner. 2024. ChatGPT and generative artificial intelligence: an exploratory study of key benefits and challenges in operations and supply chain management. *International Journal of Production Research*, 62(16): 5676–96. https://doi.org/10.1080/00207543.2023.2294116.

Fraile, Francisco, Foivos Psarommatis, Faustino Alarcón and Jordi Joan. 2023. A methodological framework for designing personalised training programs to support personnel upskilling in Industry 5.0. *Computers*, 12(11): 224. https://doi.org/10.3390/computers12110224.

Ghadge, Abhijeet, Hendrik Wurtmann and Stefan Seuring. 2020. Managing climate change risks in global supply chains: a review and research agenda. *International Journal of Production Research*, 58(1): 44–64. https://doi.org/10.1080/00207543.2019.1629670.

Ghobakhloo, Morteza, Masood Fathi, Mohammad Iranmanesh, Mantas Vilkas, Andrius Grybauskas, and Azlan Amran. 2024. Generative artificial intelligence in manufacturing: opportunities for actualizing industry 5.0 sustainability goals. *Journal of Manufacturing Technology Management*, 35(9): 94–121. https://doi.org/10.1108/JMTM-12-2023-0530.

Grech La Rosa, Andrea, Peter Simpson and Ryan Zammit. 2024. Exploring the opportunities of generative artificial intelligence in concept ship design. *International Marine Design Conference*, May. https://doi.org/10.59490/imdc.2024.752.

Gupta, Maanak, Charankumar Akiri, Kshitiz Aryal, Eli Parker and Lopamudra Praharaj. 2023. From ChatGPT to ThreatGPT: impact of generative AI in cybersecurity and privacy. *IEEE Access*, 11: 80218–45. https://doi.org/10.1109/ACCESS.2023.3300381.

Hörmann, Fabiane. 2024. Generative Artificial Intelligence Takes Siemens' Predictive Maintenance Solution to the next Level. Https://Press.Siemens.Com/Global/En/Pressrelease/Generative-Artificial-Intelligence-Takes-Siemens-Predictive-Maintenance-Solution-Next. February 5, 2024.

Hort, Max, Zhenpeng Chen, Jie M. Zhang, Mark Harman and Federica Sarro. 2024. Bias mitigation for machine learning classifiers: a comprehensive survey. *ACM Journal on Responsible Computing*, 1(2): 1–52. https://doi.org/10.1145/3631326.

Hosseinian-Far, Amin, Muthu Ramachandran and Charlotte Lilly Slack. 2018. Emerging trends in cloud computing, big data, fog computing, iot and smart living. In Technology for Smart Futures, 29–40. Cham: Springer International Publishing. https://doi.org/10.1007/978-3-319-60137-3_2.

Huang, Yuxuan. 2023. The future of generative AI: How GenAI would change human-computer co-creation in the next 10 to 15 Years. In Companion Proceedings of the Annual Symposium on Computer-Human Interaction in Play, 322–25. New York, NY, USA: ACM. https://doi.org/10.1145/3573382.3616033.

Huang, Ken, Ben Goertzel, Daniel Wu and Anita Xie. 2024. GenAI Model Security. In, 163–98. https://doi.org/10.1007/978-3-031-54252-7_6.

Huang, Ming-Hui and Roland T. Rust. 2024. The caring machine: feeling ai for customer care. *Journal of Marketing, March*. https://doi.org/10.1177/00222429231224748.

IBM. 2024. Meet Watson X. Https://Shorturl.at/R4XMS. 2024.

Jackson, Ilya, Dmitry Ivanov, Alexandre Dolgui and Jafar Namdar. 2024. Generative artificial intelligence in supply chain and operations management: a capability-based framework for analysis and implementation. *International Journal of Production Research*, 62(17): 6120–45. https://doi.org/10.1080/00207543.2024.2309309.

Jahankhani, Hamid and Amin Hosseinian-Far. 2017. Challenges of cloud forensics. In, 1–18. https://doi.org/10.1007/978-3-319-54380-2_1.

Jamshidi, Mohammad Behdad, Sobhan Roshani, Jakub Talla, Ali Lalbakhsh, Zdeněk Peroutka, Saeed Roshani, Fariborz Parandin et al. 2022. A review of the potential of artificial intelligence approaches to forecasting COVID-19 spreading. *AI* 3(2): 493–511. https://doi.org/10.3390/ai3020028.

Javaid, Sabeen, Ali Sufian, Saima Pervaiz and Mehak Tanveer. 2018. Smart traffic management system using internet of things. In 2018 20th International Conference on Advanced Communication Technology (ICACT), 393–98. *IEEE*. https://doi.org/10.23919/ICACT.2018.8323770.

Jimenez, Jaime Ibarra and Hamid Jahankhani. 2020. Bring your own device: GDPR compliant or headache? *The Human Aspect in Security and Privacy*. In Cyber Security Practitioner's Guide, 239–73. WORLD SCIENTIFIC. https://doi.org/10.1142/9789811204463_0007.

Jouan, Pierre and Pierre Hallot. 2020. Digital Twin: research framework to support preventive conservation policies. *ISPRS International Journal of Geo-Information*, 9(4): 228. https://doi.org/10.3390/ijgi9040228.

Kanbach, Dominik K., Louisa Heiduk, Georg Blueher, Maximilian Schreiter and Alexander Lahmann. 2024. The GenAI is out of the bottle: generative artificial intelligence from a business model innovation perspective. *Review of Managerial Science*, 18(4): 1189–1220. https://doi.org/10.1007/s11846-023-00696-z.

Kasinathan, Padmanathan, Rishi Pugazhendhi, Rajvikram Madurai Elavarasan, Vigna Kumaran Ramachandaramurthy, Vinoth Ramanathan, Senthilkumar Subramanian et al. 2022. Realization of sustainable development goals with disruptive technologies by integrating industry 5.0, society 5.0, smart cities and villages. *Sustainability*, 14(22): 15258. https://doi.org/10.3390/su142215258.

Kazanskiy, Nikolay L., Svetlana N. Khonina and Muhammad A. Butt. 2024. A review on flexible wearables – recent developments in non-invasive continuous health monitoring. *Sensors and Actuators A: Physical*, 366(February):114993. https://doi.org/10.1016/j.sna.2023.114993.

Kernan Freire, Samuel, Mina Foosherian, Chaofan Wang and Evangelos Niforatos. 2023. Harnessing large language models for cognitive assistants in factories. In Proceedings of the 5th International Conference on Conversational User Interfaces, 1–6. New York, NY, USA: ACM. https://doi.org/10.1145/3571884.3604313.

Kiangala, Kahiomba Sonia and Zenghui Wang. 2024. An experimental hybrid customized AI and generative AI Chatbot human machine interface to improve a factory troubleshooting downtime in the context of industry 5.0. *The International Journal of Advanced Manufacturing Technology*, 132(5-6): 2715–33. https://doi.org/10.1007/s00170-024-13492-0.

Kiran Deep Singh and Prabhdeep Singh. 2024. Fog cloud computing and IoT integration for AI enabled autonomous systems in robotics. *EAI Endorsed Transactions on AI and Robotics*, 3(March). https://doi.org/10.4108/airo.3617.

Kirova, Vassilka D., Cyril S. Ku, Joseph R. Laracy and Thomas J. Marlowe. 2023. The ethics of artificial intelligence in the era of generative AI. *Journal of Systemics, Cybernetics and Informatics*, 21 (4): 42–50. https://doi.org/10.54808/JSCI.21.04.42.

Kumar, Keshaw, Kuldeep and Bharat Bhushan. 2023. Augmenting cybersecurity and fraud detection using artificial intelligence advancements. In 2023 International Conference on Computing, Communication, and Intelligent Systems (ICCCIS), 1207–12. *IEEE*. https://doi.org/10.1109/ICCCIS60361.2023.10425069.

Kumar, Tajinder, Ramesh Kait, Ankita and Anu Malik. 2024. The role of generative artificial intelligence (GAI) in education: a detailed review for enhanced learning experiences. In, 195–207. https://doi.org/10.1007/978-981-97-1682-1_17.

Law, Locky. 2024. Application of generative artificial intelligence (GenAI) in language teaching and learning: a scoping literature review. *Computers and Education Open*, 6(June): 100174. https://doi.org/10.1016/j.caeo.2024.100174.

Lee, Sunok, Minha Lee and Sangsu Lee. 2023. What if artificial intelligence become completely ambient in our daily lives? Exploring Future Human-AI Interaction through High Fidelity Illustrations. *International Journal of Human–Computer Interaction*, 39(7): 1371–89. https://doi.org/10.1080/10447318.2022.2080155.

Leng, Jiewu, Weinan Sha, Baicun Wang, Pai Zheng, Cunbo Zhuang, Qiang Liu et al. 2022. Industry 5.0: Prospect and Retrospect. *Journal of Manufacturing Systems*, 65(October):279–95. https://doi.org/10.1016/j.jmsy.2022.09.017.

Lim, Tian Kuay, Abbas Rajabifard, Victor Khoo, Soheil Sabri and Yiqun Chen. 2021. The smart city in singapore: how environmental and geospatial innovation lead to urban livability and environmental sustainability. In Smart Cities for Technological and Social Innovation, 29–49. Elsevier. https://doi.org/10.1016/B978-0-12-818886-6.00003-4.

Linkon, A.A., Shaima, M., Sarker, M.S.U., Badruddowza, B., Nabi, N., Rana, M.N.U. et al. 2024. Advancements and applications of generative artificial intelligence and large language models on business management: a comprehensive review. *Journal of Computer Science and Technology Studies*, 6(1): 225–32. https://doi.org/10.32996/jcsts.2024.6.1.26.

Liu, Ninghao, Mengnan Du, Ruocheng Guo, Huan Liu and Xia Hu. 2021. Adversarial Attacks and Defenses. *ACM SIGKDD Explorations Newsletter*, 23(1): 86–99. https://doi.org/10.1145/3468507.3468519.

Loh, Erwin. 2024. ChatGPT and generative AI chatbots: challenges and opportunities for science, medicine and medical leaders. *BMJ Leader*, 8(1): 51–54. https://doi.org/10.1136/leader-2023-000797.

Luccioni, Alexandra, Victor Schmidt, Vahe Vardanyan and Yoshua Bengio. 2021. Using artificial intelligence to visualize the impacts of climate change. *IEEE Computer Graphics and Applications*, 41(1): 8–14. https://doi.org/10.1109/MCG.2020.3025425.

Maier, Stephan. 2016. Smart energy systems for smart city districts: case study reininghaus district. *Energy, Sustainability and Society*, 6(1): 23. https://doi.org/10.1186/s13705-016-0085-9.

Manheim, Karl and Lyric Kaplan. 2019. Artificial intelligence: risks to privacy and democracy. *Yale Journal of Law & Technology*, 21: 106+. https://link.gale.com/apps/doc/A587366495/AONE?u=anon~25b26c35&sid=googleScholar&xid=b28c4049.

Mauny, Harsh, Devarsh Panchal, Meet Bhavsar and Nidhi Shah. 2021. A prototype of smart virtual assistant integrated with automation. In 2021 Third International Conference on Inventive Research in Computing Applications (ICIRCA), 952–57. *IEEE*. https://doi.org/10.1109/ICIRCA51532.2021.9544101.

Mohammed, Moyassar Y. and Mirosław J. Skibniewski. 2023. The role of generative AI in managing industry projects: transforming industry 4.0 Into Industry 5.0 Driven Economy. *Law and Business*, 3(1): 27–41. https://doi.org/10.2478/law-2023-0006.

Ni Ki, Chong, Amin Hosseinian-Far, Alireza Daneshkhah and Nader Salari. 2022. Topic modelling in precision medicine with its applications in personalized diabetes management. *Expert Systems*, 39(4). https://doi.org/10.1111/exsy.12774.

Ofosu, Rosemary, Amin Hosseinian-Far and Dilshad Sarwar. 2022. Digital Twin Technologies, Architecture, and Applications: A Comprehensive Systematic Review and Bibliometric Analysis. In, 105–42. https://doi.org/10.1007/978-3-030-98225-6_5.

Oliveira, Franklin, Daniel G. Costa, Flávio Assis and Ivanovitch Silva. 2024. Internet of intelligent things: a convergence of embedded systems, edge computing and machine learning. *Internet of Things*, 26(July): 101153. https://doi.org/10.1016/j.iot.2024.101153.

Onder, Murat and Mehmet Metin Uzun. 2022. Roles of Artificial Intelligence (AI) on COVID-19 pandemic crisis management policies. *International Journal of Public Administration in the Digital Age*, 8(2): 1–13. https://doi.org/10.4018/IJPADA.294122.

Ooi, Keng-Boon, Garry Wei-Han Tan, Mostafa Al-Emran, Mohammed A. Al-Sharafi, Alexandru Capatina, Amrita Chakraborty et al. 2023. The potential of generative artificial intelligence across disciplines: perspectives and future directions. *Journal of Computer Information Systems*, October, 1–32. https://doi.org/10.1080/08874417.2023.2261010.

Pandey, Amit Kumar and Arpita Mukherjee. 2022. A review on advances in IoT-Based technologies for smart agricultural system. In, 29–44. https://doi.org/10.1007/978-981-16-6210-2_2.

Petersen, Eike, Yannik Potdevin, Esfandiar Mohammadi, Stephan Zidowitz, Sabrina Breyer, Dirk Nowotka, et al. 2022. Responsible and regulatory conform machine learning for medicine: a survey of challenges and solutions. *IEEE Access*, 10: 58375–418. https://doi.org/10.1109/ACCESS.2022.3178382.

Poland, Shaun, Siddhartha Sharad and Gus Wigen-Toccalino. 2024. Powering innovation: the comprehensive impact of generative AI. *Climate and Energy*, 40 (7): 1–11. https://doi.org/10.1002/gas.22385.

Prem, Erich. 2023. From ethical AI frameworks to tools: a review of approaches. *AI and Ethics*, 3(3): 699–716. https://doi.org/10.1007/s43681-023-00258-9.

Raihan, Asif. 2023. Artificial intelligence and machine learning applications in forest management and biodiversity conservation. *Natural Resources Conservation and Research*, 6(2): 3825. https://doi.org/10.24294/nrcr.v6i2.3825.

Rajaratnam, Vaikunthan, Steffi Tan Shih May and J. Terrence Jose Jerome. 2024. Precision at Hand: revolutionising surgery with generative AI. *Journal of Hand and Microsurgery*, 16(3): 100090. https://doi.org/10.1016/j.jham.2024.100090.

Rane, Nitin. 2023. Roles and challenges of ChatGPT and similar generative artificial intelligence for achieving the sustainable development goals (SDGs). *SSRN Electronic Journal*. https://doi.org/10.2139/ssrn.4603244.

Raja Santhi, A. and Muthuswamy, P. 2023. Industry 5.0 or industry 4.0S? Introduction to industry 4.0 and a peek into the prospective industry 5.0 technologies. *Int. J. Interact. Des. Manuf.*, 17 947–979 https://doi.org/10.1007/s12008-023-01217-8.

Rudolph, Juergen, Fadhil Mohamed Mohamed Ismail and Stefan Popenici. 2024. Higher education's generative artificial intelligence paradox: the meaning of chatbot mania. *Journal of University Teaching and Learning Practice*, 21(06). https://doi.org/10.53761/54fs5e77.

Seify, Mahdi, Mehran Sepehri, Amin Hosseinian-Far and Aryana Darvish. 2022. Fraud detection in supply chain with machine learning. *IFAC-PapersOnLine*, 55(10): 406–11. https://doi.org/10.1016/j.ifacol.2022.09.427.

Sha, Yutian, Mohan Li, Huikun Xu, Shaohan Zhang and Tianxin Feng. 2022. Smart city public safety intelligent early warning and detection. *Scientific Programming*, 2022(June): 1–11. https://doi.org/10.1155/2022/7552601.

Shahin, Mohammad, F. Frank Chen and Ali Hosseinzadeh. 2024. Harnessing customized AI to create voice of customer via GPT3.5. *Advanced Engineering Informatics*, 61(August): 102462. https://doi.org/10.1016/j.aei.2024.102462.

Shchepkina, Natalia, Awadhesh Chandramauli, Suniana Ahuja, P. Prathibha Swaraj and Rajiv Ranjan. 2024. Deep learning algorithms in industry 5.0: A comprehensive experimental study. *BIO Web of Conferences*, 86(January):01067. https://doi.org/10.1051/bioconf/20248601067.

Shead, Sam. 2018. Google trusts DeepMind AI to manage data centre cooling. Https://Www.Forbes.Com/Sites/Samshead/2018/08/18/Google-Trusts-Deepmind-Ai-to-Manage-Data-Centre-Cooling/. August 18, 2018.

Sindhwani, Rahul, Shayan Afridi, Anil Kumar, Audrius Banaitis, Sunil Luthra and Punj Lata Singh. 2022. Can Industry 5.0 revolutionize the wave of resilience and social value creation? A multi-criteria framework to analyze enablers. *Technology in Society*, 68(February):101887. https://doi.org/10.1016/j.techsoc.2022.101887.

Tambare, Parkash, Chandrashekhar Meshram, Cheng-Chi Lee, Rakesh Jagdish Ramteke and Agbotiname Lucky Imoize. 2021. Performance measurement system and quality management in data-driven industry 4.0: A Review." *Sensors*, 22(1): 224. https://doi.org/10.3390/s22010224.

The Lancet Regional Health – Europe. 2023. Embracing Generative AI in Health Care. The Lancet Regional Health - Europe 30(July):100677. https://doi.org/10.1016/j.lanepe.2023.100677.

Trivedi, Chandan, Pronaya Bhattacharya, Vivek Kumar Prasad, Viraj Patel, Arunendra Singh, Sudeep Tanwar et al. 2024. Explainable AI for Industry 5.0: Vision, architecture, and potential directions. *IEEE Open Journal of Industry Applications*, 5: 177–208. https://doi.org/10.1109/OJIA.2024.3399057.

Tseng, Cheng-Jui and Shih-Yen Lin. 2024. Role of artificial intelligence in carbon cost reduction of firms. *Journal of Cleaner Production*, 447(April):141413. https://doi.org/10.1016/j.jclepro.2024.141413.

Ulfsnes, Rasmus, Nils Brede Moe, Viktoria Stray and Marianne Skarpen. 2024. Transforming software development with generative AI: Empirical insights on collaboration and workflow. In Generative AI for Effective Software Development, 219–34. Cham: Springer Nature Switzerland. https://doi.org/10.1007/978-3-031-55642-5_10.

US FDA. 2018. Precision Medicine. Https://Www.Fda.Gov/Medical-Devices/in-Vitro-Diagnostics/Precision-Medicine. September 27, 2018.

Vailshery, Lionel. 2024. Number of IoT Connections Worldwide 2022-2033, with Forecasts to 2030. Https://Www.Statista.Com/Statistics/1183457/Iot-Connected-Devices-Worldwide/. June 12, 2024.

Varona, Daniel, and Juan Luis Suárez. 2022. Discrimination, Bias, Fairness, and Trustworthy AI. *Applied Sciences*, 12(12): 5826. https://doi.org/10.3390/app12125826.

Waltersmann, Lara, Steffen Kiemel, Julian Stuhlsatz, Alexander Sauer and Robert Miehe. 2021. Artificial intelligence applications for increasing resource efficiency in manufacturing companies—A Comprehensive Review. *Sustainability*, 13(12): 6689. https://doi.org/10.3390/su13126689.

Xu, Han, Yao Ma, Hao-Chen Liu, Debayan Deb, Hui Liu, Ji-Liang Tang and Anil K. Jain. 2020. Adversarial Attacks and defenses in images, graphs and text: a review. *International Journal of Automation and Computing*, 17(2): 151–78. https://doi.org/10.1007/s11633-019-1211-x.

Yu, Dan and Chang Chieh Hang. 2010. A reflective review of disruptive innovation theory. *International Journal of Management Reviews*, 12(4): 435–52. https://doi.org/10.1111/j.1468-2370.2009.00272.x.

Yussuf, Raheemat O. and Omar S. Asfour. 2024. Applications of artificial intelligence for energy efficiency throughout the building lifecycle: an overview. *Energy and Buildings*, 305(February): 113903. https://doi.org/10.1016/j.enbuild.2024.113903.

Zhang, Peng and Maged N. Kamel Boulos. 2023. Generative AI in medicine and healthcare: promises, opportunities and challenges. *Future Internet*, 15(9): 286. https://doi.org/10.3390/fi15090286.

Zhou, Eric and Dokyun Lee. 2024. Generative artificial intelligence, human creativity, and art. *PNAS Nexus*, 3(3). https://doi.org/10.1093/pnasnexus/pgae052.

Zohny, Hazem, John McMillan and Mike King. 2023. Ethics of generative AI. *Journal of Medical Ethics*, 49(2): 79–80. https://doi.org/10.1136/jme-2023-108909.

CHAPTER 8

Data-Driven Future

A Review of Technologies and Applications in the Era of Industry 5.0

Idowu Mosaku, Opeyemi Ajewole, Seun Adegoke* and *Amin Hosseinian-Far*

1. Introduction

The rapid advancements in data analytics and the exponential adoption of analytics and artificial intelligence technologies have led to the emergence of various digital business models. These models enable data-driven collection, preparation, analysis, reporting, and decision-making. This trend is mirrored at the individual level, where social media generates vast amounts of diverse content. The rise in transactional data, surging adoption of IoT-based systems, and advancements in big data analytics technologies and artificial intelligence, namely machine learning, are undoubtedly triggers of data-led services and analytics (Hosseinian-Far et al. 2017). The rise in content creation is further accelerated by Generative AI (GenAI) technologies. The future is, without doubt, data-driven, where connections, interactions, and decisions are strongly influenced by data analysis and reporting.

This chapter explores these technologies that play a significant role in managing and analysing vast quantities of data, arriving at varying speeds and in different types. The chapter begins with an overview of Industry 5.0, highlighting the fundamental role of these technologies in enhancing sustainability and resilience and the necessity for embracing a human-centric approach to analytics. Section 3 succinctly outlines these key technologies. Section 4 provides a sector-specific discussion of how these technologies are transforming industries such as healthcare, supply chain

Department of Business Analytics and Systems, University of Hertfordshire, AL10 9EU, UK.
* Corresponding author: i.mosaku@herts.ac.uk

DOI: 10.1201/9781003540373-8

management, the automotive sector, and environmental management. Considering its potential for disruption, GenAI is discussed in Section 5. The ethical implications of AI, particularly GenAI, are also addressed at the end of Section 5. The chapter concludes in Section 6.

2. Industry 5.0

The concept of Industry 5.0 (I-5.0) has been presented and defined in different ways by many scholars, thus posing a challenge in finding a perfect definition for this new industrial revolution. However, Sachsenmeier (2016) discussed the inevitable symbiotic relationship between humans and the Industry 4.0 (I-4.0) capabilities that are taking place. This means a total backtrack from complete dependence on technologies that drive I-4.0 and more human-machine intervention that caters for sustainability. I- 5.0's latest key constructs include "Sustainability, Human-centricity and Resilience" (Renda et al. 2021), even though some may view the role of GenAl as the key disruptor in I-5.0. Industry 5.0 is an extension that complements I-4.0 paradigm through research and innovation to implement these key concepts (Xu et al. 2021). Following this background, we can define Industry 5.0 as,

> "*a value-driven industry revolution leap from industry 4.0 that seeks to rebalance its sustainability with human touch and drive technological transformation of people, planet and prosperity.*"

Industry 5.0 signifies a major shift from the automation-centric approach in I-4.0. It emphasises the combination of human creativity, innovation, and advance technologies in industrial processes (Mourtzis 2024). Contrary to I-4.0, which focused on complete digitalisation and automation of production processes through technologies like the Internet of things (IoT), Artificial intelligence (AI) and Big Data, I-5.0 revolves around a human-centred approach (Dabo and Hosseinian-Far 2023). Its goal is to harmonise the capabilities of smart machines with the distinct quality of human workers, promoting a collaboration between human and technology rather than substitution.

3. Key Technologies Enabling Data-Driven Futures

The convergence of Artificial Intelligence, data analytics, and human creativity is a transformative force shaping the future of societies, industries, and governance structures. With data at the centre of a data-driven future, AI-driven data analytics provide tools to connect this information for more informed and efficient decision-making, while human creativity focuses on ensuring the sustainability of this AI-driven process (Pedersen and Wilkinson 2019, Schmitt 2023). The foundation of a data-driven future lies in the advanced technologies from I-4.0 that enable the efficient collection, storage, processing, and analysis of big data (Hosseinian-Far et al. 2018). These technologies include big data infrastructure, cloud computing, artificial intelligence, the Internet of Things, and blockchain (Raja Santhi and Muthuswamy

2023). All of these technologies play a pivotal role in realising the full potential of data-driven systems. A non-exhaustive list of these techniques is provided below:

- Big Data Infrastructure: The emergence of big data, often defined by its 5Vs (volume, variety, veracity, velocity, value), is a paradigm associated with a variety of complex large-scale data that exceeds the computing power of traditional software and databases (Chen and Wang 2018, Hosseinian-Far et al. 2018). This has necessitated the development of scalable and resilient solutions for handling big data. Parallel processing databases, scalable storage systems, and distributed computing frameworks, such as Apache Hadoop and Apache Spark, allow organisations to manage and process large datasets (Ankam 2016). Not-only SQL (NoSQL) databases, such as MongoDB and Cassandra, are highly scalable, non-relational databases designed to store semi-structured and unstructured data, which are commonly used by businesses and individuals in today's digital age (Anusha et al. 2021). These technologies are leveraged by big data analytics to manage the sheer amount of data generated by IoT devices, social media platforms, and digital transactions (Kumar et al. 2021).
- Cloud Computing: Cloud computing is defined as the delivery of networking and computing services solutions over the internet (Raja Santhi and Muthuswamy 2023). Cloud computing revolutionises data-driven technologies by providing scalable and cost-efficient solutions for data analytics. The pay-per-use model for enabling convenient, on-demand network access to computing resources provides organisation with the ability to store, process and analyse data without the need for upfront investments in physical infrastructure (Avram 2014). Cloud computing has two distinct operating models: deployment model and service model. The deployment model is classified into three categories: private, public and hybrid cloud, while the service model is classified into Infrastructure-as-a-service (IaaS), Platform-as-a-service (PaaS) and Software-as-a-Service (SaaS) (Hosseinian-Far et al. 2018). Examples of all this service models include Amazon web services (AWS), Google Compute Engine, Microsoft Azure, MapReduce and Hadoop (O'Driscoll et al. 2013).
- Artificial Intelligence: Another key concept and enabler of data-driven futures is Artificial Intelligence, which is defined by (Haenlein and Kaplan 2019) as "a system's ability to interpret external data correctly, to learn from such data, and to use those learnings to achieve specific goals and tasks through flexible adaptation". In other words, AI systems use algorithmic intelligence to extract actionable insights from big data, automate decision-making processes, and perform human-like tasks through various statistical learning techniques and algorithms.
- Machine Learning: Machine learning is a subclass of Artificial Intelligence that directs AI systems to automatically learn from datasets and predict outcomes based on training of the historical datasets. There are three main approaches of machine learning (Morales and Escalante 2022). These are:
    - Supervised Learning: This is a method used by AI systems to enable the classification and regression model of historical data to predict the outcome

of a related data based on its experience or learning of the historical data. This method is also known as predictive modelling. Typical algorithms include KNN, Logistic Regression, Decision Tree, etc.

- Unsupervised Learning: This is a method used by AI systems to identify patterns in big data through clustering or association analysis thereby grouping similar data together. This method is also known as descriptive modelling. Typical algorithms include, K-means, Probabilistic clustering methods, etc.
- Reinforcement Learning: This learning method facilitates decision-making in a complex environment. AI system automatically learns and develops a model/policy by interacting with the environment, receiving feedback, and gradually improving the model over time (Johnson et al. 2000). The AI system's (agent) goal is to maximise its long-term reward by learning the best sequence of actions. Typical algorithms include Q-learning, Deep Q-Networks, Policy Gradient methods, etc.

▪ Internet of Things: The Internet of Things (IoT) is a key enabler of data-driven futures through the generation of huge volumes of real-time data from connected devices (Ge et al. 2018). IoT devices are classified as devices or systems that are integrated with technologies that allow them to connect and communicate with each other using the Internet (Ang et al. 2022). These devices, ranging from smart home appliances to industrial sensors, continuously collect real-time data on a variety of metrics. This data is essential for AI-driven analytics systems that rely on real-time inputs to optimise operations, predict failures, and enhance user experiences. As IoT networks expand, the volume of data generated will continue to grow, driving the demand for more advanced data processing and AI systems capable of extracting actionable insights.

▪ Blockchain Technology: Blockchain technology is also a key enabler of a data-driven future, as it offers trust, transparency, and automation across critical industries (Lezzi et al. 2024). This technology provides a decentralised, transparent, and secure framework for managing data (Raja Santhi and Muthuswamy 2023). Unlike centralised systems where data or transactions are controlled by a single entity, blockchain distributes authority across a network, ensuring resilience and reducing the risk of breaches. Its immutability ensures that once data is recorded, it cannot be altered, making blockchain ideal for sectors like healthcare, finance, and the supply chain, where verifiable, tamper-proof records are critical (Yli-Huumo et al. 2016). A key innovation of blockchain technology is the use of smart contracts (Jahankhani et al. 2021, Laryea et al. 2024). These are self-executing agreements with terms directly encoded into code. They automate processes such as transactions and data exchanges when predefined conditions are met, reducing reliance on intermediaries and ensuring secure, efficient automation (Macrinici et al. 2018). For example, in supply chains, smart contracts can automatically trigger payments once goods are delivered and verified, streamlining the entire operation. Blockchain also enhances data privacy and ownership. Individuals maintain control over their data through encryption and cryptographic keys, deciding who can access their information (Sedlmeir et al. 2020, Weking et al. 2020). This is crucial in sectors such as healthcare, where patients can securely share their medical records with authorised providers (Attaran 2022).

In addition to these technologies, there are other recent innovations that are shaping the future of artificial intelligence and data analytics. These technologies are also enablers of data-driven futures:

- Digital Twins: A combination of AI, IoT and Big Data Analytics has also led to developments such as Digital Twins, where digital replicas of physical systems are created using real-time or semi-real-time data from sensory systems. Furthermore, advanced analytics can provide invaluable insights for decision-making by enhancing system transparency, improving visibility and safety, and developing appropriate sustainable maintenance strategies (Farsi et al. 2024, Ofosu et al. 2022). Zhang (2024) states that "Digital Twins are accurate digital replicas of a real-world objects across multiple granularity levels". This is achievable due to semantic technologies, which allow for interoperability for heterogeneous data and information (Zheng et al. 2022). In the context of data-driven futures, Digital Twins provide valuable opportunities for organisations to enhance operations such as forecasting, structure monitoring, decision-making, and maintenance (Saunila et al. 2024). There are three main components in a Digital Twin: the physical system, the virtual model, and the data. In today's world that is increasingly driven by data, Digital Twins can allow organisations to leverage data for smarter and more sustainable decisions. Other applications of Digital Twins are in aviation, intelligent transportation, and healthcare (Ofosu et al. 2022, Zhang 2024).
- Deep Learning Architectures: With advances in AI and ML, deep learning has built on this advancement. While Machine Learning is a subgroup of Artificial Intelligence, Deep Learning is a subgroup of Machine Learning that is motivated by neural networks to model and understand complex data (Halbouni et al. 2022, Patterson and Gibson 2017). Deep Learning is more sophisticated than Machine Learning because of the number of learning layers known as Artificial Neural Networks (ANNs). As data size increases, Machine Learning models may encounter limitations in performance and fail to provide adequate insights (Taye 2023). However, due to representation learning, deep learning provides a higher-performing model as the size of data increases (Taye 2023). This is particularly useful in a data-driven future where significantly greater volumes of data are being produced and there is a requirement to extract actionable insights from them (Patterson and Gibson 2017):
    - Unsupervised pretrained network,
    - Convolutional neural networks,
    - Recurrent neural networks, and
    - Recursive neural networks.

It is worth noting that novel approaches to Machine Learning are being introduced daily, improving the efficiency, accuracy, and speed of computational inference. A novel example of these advancements in the field of deep learning includes Physics-Informed Neural Networks (PINNs), which can provide accurate and efficient predictions despite incomplete models or data (Raissi et al. 2019).

The following section presents some of the applications of data analytics technologies, particularly artificial intelligence, in different sectors.

4. Application of Data Analytics and Artificial Intelligence

4.1 Big data and AI in the healthcare industry

The raw data available in the healthcare industry is voluminous and there is a rising need to leverage on big data analytics and machine learning algorithms to obtain useful insights (Dinov 2016). Considering the volume, variety, and velocity of data in healthcare sector, the data is sufficient to be called big data. The healthcare data is from different sources and could either be structured or unstructured. According to Batko and Ślęzak (2022), big data in healthcare sector could be biometric data, clinical data, scientific research data, financial data, and social media data. The application of big data analytics and machine learning is resulting in significant improvement in healthcare industry and the analytics could be descriptive, predictive or discovery-based (Arowoogun et al. 2024, Batko and Ślęzak 2022). Mirbabaie et al. (2021) argue that the use of AI diagnostic systems has led to a reduction in detection errors and accelerated disease detection. Unlike the traditional approach, which relied on the experience of healthcare professionals and was susceptible to human error, the use of machine learning and data analytics tools in the analysis of medical data offers speed and accuracy (Kaur et al. 2020). As such, patients receive earlier treatment with better outcomes through the use of AI algorithms.

The application of AI to improve public health cannot be overemphasised. The use of AI in predictive modelling helps utilise data to forecast future results, as it combines machine learning techniques and statistical models (Olawade et al. 2023). Alowais et al. (2023) emphasised that the application of AI in the analysis of healthcare big data leads to a significant reduction in healthcare expenses and a better patient experience. The revolutionary trend in precision medicine, which allows a particular patient to receive an effective and specific treatment, is made possible by the application of data analytics and ML algorithms (Batko and Ślęzak 2022). Sahu et al. (2022) reiterated that with artificial intelligence and ML, there is a better understanding of disease pathology, which has led to improvements in drug development and design. The application of recent technologies has enhanced drug design and development, enabling precision medicine. The application of machine learning algorithms for precision medicine is yielding positive results in areas such as risk prediction, clinical study of chronic diseases, dose-treatment responses, and drug repurposing (Peng et al. 2021).

Telemedicine is enhanced through the application of data analytics and artificial intelligence. Uddin and Koo (2024) explained that patients are monitored remotely using technologies that collect patient health data related to their conditions, and these data are analysed with a high level of accuracy using data analytics and ML algorithms. Kothamali et al. (2024) concluded that the application of AI in telemedicine has resulted in higher levels of satisfaction among patients.

The application of AI in pharmacovigilance has shown immense benefits. According to Bate and Stegmann (2023), ML is applied in pharmacoepidemiology to monitor the risks and benefits of humans taking a particular drug in a real-life situation. Liang et al. (2022) mentioned that the benefits of AI application in pharmacovigilance include evidence generation networks, automatic detection, integration of different source datasets, and standardisation. In medical research, these technologies improve the quality of studies, leading to better outcomes.

4.2 Big data analytics and AI in supply chain management

Considering economic globalisation, there has been a significant increase in the complexity of supply chain management. Supply chains (SC) generate large volumes of data from sources such as warehousing, sales, transportation, inventory, distribution, and manufacturing (Pradhan et al. 2022, Seyedan and Mafakheri 2020). The analysis of big data from SC has become more complex than ever when relying on traditional approaches, hence the shift towards AI. Zamani et al. (2023) stated that the application of big data analytics and ML has led to improved visibility and transparency along the SC. AI helps in collecting critical information related to the operating environment and operation status and processing the data collected (Belhadi et al. 2024). With improved visibility and transparency, decision-making also becomes more effective. Zouari et al. (2021) revealed that AI and big data analytics are resulting in significant improvements in supply chain responsiveness. By applying big data analytics, information sharing is facilitated among all partners involved in the supply chain, leading to improved responsiveness.

Supplier selection is seen as one of the major functions carried out by firms and the success of this process goes a long way in affecting the profitability of the firm. Multi-criteria decision-making (MCDM) techniques are used to make decisions when multiple criteria and alternatives are involved (Ali et al. 2023, Liou et al. 2021). In some cases, there are situations where the set of alternatives and number of suppliers are large to the extent of having an unsatisfactory result from MCDM. ML has proven to give more reliable results than MCDM when there are large alternatives and suppliers, using techniques like DT (Decision Trees) and SVM (Support Vector Machine).

Risk refers to the combination of the probability of a defined hazard and the magnitude of its occurrence (Christopher 2023, Tummala and Schoenherr 2011). The vulnerability of supply chains to disruption has increased due to trends such as outsourcing and globalisation (Christopher 2023), highlighting the need for greater attention to supply chain risk management (SCRM). Tirkolaee et al. (2021) stated that AI techniques are applicable in SCRM for identifying and assessing supply chain risks. In risk identification, machine learning algorithms like SVM and decision trees (DT) have now been applied with improved outcomes. In risk assessment, ML algorithms such as artificial neural networks (ANNs) and big data analytics are now used for risk assessment modelling.

Machine learning (ML) and deep learning (DL) algorithms are applied to inventory management to reduce the inefficiency of traditional approaches. Given that the cost of inventory management may be up to 50% of the total invested capital

(Ivanov et al. 2021), AI technologies should be applied to reduce costs and ensure better customer service (Tirkolaee et al. 2021). The application of machine learning and deep learning to inventory management has resulted in a more efficient and flexible system (Lin et al. 2022). Moreover, the capacity of big data analytics and AI to collect and analyse voluminous SC data from different points has reduced errors in demand forecasting (Albayrak Ünal et al. 2023).

4.3 Data analytics and AI in automotive industry

The recent transformation in automotive industry is a result of the combination of technologies such as edge computing, artificial intelligence and IoT (Khayyam et al. 2020). Autonomous vehicles are self-driving vehicles that have an automatic system, which react to environmental situations in a regulated manner while considering safety (Gupta et al. 2021). According to Bachute and Subhedar (2021), autonomous vehicles significantly reduce human intervention, and are largely the product of the application of machine learning and deep learning. However, autonomous vehicles make use of sensor networks and varieties of signals received from the environment (Biswas and Wang 2023, Fényes et al. 2019). Cheng et al. (2018) revealed that the vehicular communication network is generating high volumes, and varieties of data needed for autonomous, intelligent, and safe transportation networks. Moreover, emerging technologies such as machine learning algorithms are used to analyse the data, thereby enhancing the self-driving vehicle experience.

Predictive maintenance of vehicles is a major application of big data analytics and AI in the automotive industry. Arena et al. (2021) highlighted that with the application of AI techniques to the voluminous condition monitoring data from the sensor network of a vehicle, there is a likelihood of preventing failures of vehicle parts or systems. Theissler et al. (2021) corroborated this by concluding that ML is a major approach when it comes to maintenance modelling and is the best possible candidate for predictive maintenance. The potential benefits of adopting AI-based predictive maintenance strategies include higher efficiency, cost reduction, improved safety, and higher overall reliability (Ucar et al. 2024).

The application of ML algorithms in manufacturing has led to significant improvements in efficiency, sustainability, and productivity. Predictive maintenance of manufacturing equipment using ML has significantly reduced downtime in the industry (Plathottam et al. 2023). According to Goh et al. (2021), additive manufacturing is used to fabricate major parts of complex systems, and there has been a noticeable improvement in the manufacturing workflow with the application of ML. These improvements in the sector also enhance the quality of production, thereby improving customer satisfaction.

Sustainability is an essential consideration in the production of energy needed by vehicles, given the damaging impact of energy derived from fossil fuels on human health and the planet (Ahmed et al. 2021). Rauf et al. (2024) extensively examined smart electric vehicle (EV) charging technology aimed at boosting a sustainable environment. From a conceptual perspective, the Internet of Vehicles (IoV) connects EVs, renewable energy, people, power grids, utilities, and computer and communication infrastructures. Rimal et al. (2022) demonstrated that the combination of IoT, edge, and cloud computing in the Fourth Industrial Revolution has resulted in improved benefits of IoV.

4.4 Application of data analytics and AI to environmental management

The human habitat is under significant threat due to human activities, which highlights the need for sustainable environmental management through the use of recent and effective technologies. The positive impacts that have resulted from the application of data analytics and artificial intelligence to environmental management cannot be over-emphasised. The application of these technologies (Jones et al. 2024) is improving the monitoring, collection and analysis of big environmental data. The application of ML, Deep Learning and data analytics in environmental monitoring enables the collection and processing of voluminous and varieties of data that are generated by remote sensors and satellites. AI technologies such as Convolutional Neural Networks (CNNs) provide an extraordinary efficiency to data processing (Dahake et al. 2024). Ncube and Ngulube (2024) reported that the use of recent machine learning algorithms and big data analytics has led to the earlier detection of environmental issues compared to traditional approaches. Moreover, the application of data analytics in environmental management helps to make sound and data-driven decisions. The combination of big data analytics and Geographic Information Systems (GIS) gives an improved framework for assessing and managing risk (Sharma et al. 2018). A recent example of application of advanced analytics is conducted by Donnelly et al. (2024) ion, in which they examine flood risk modelling using PINNs.

With the increasing global population, there is an urgent need to boost agricultural production significantly. The application of AI in various aspects of agriculture is gradually replacing traditional methods with technology-driven approaches, leading to higher yields. Modern AI-based equipment is increasing farm production and enabling real-time monitoring of farm operations. Talaviya et al. (2020) reported that AI in agriculture has enabled the use of drones to apply herbicides and insecticides, automated irrigation systems, and sensors for remote monitoring of soil moisture. These advancements ultimately increase food production and lead to a higher number of job opportunities in the agricultural sector. Javaid et al. (2023) explained that ML-based models are used for monitoring and forecasting the impact of climate change on agricultural produce, and the combination of IoT and AI in agriculture is improving precision farming (Sharma et al. 2023).

Natural disasters cause huge economic losses every year. In 2023, statistics from Statista revealed that \$113.12 billion was lost due to natural disasters. Abid et al. (2021) acknowledged that geographic information systems (GIS) and remote sensor tools are opening new avenues for understanding emergencies. Linardos et al. (2022) outlined the breakthroughs of machine learning and deep learning in disaster management, including hazard and disaster prediction, risk assessment, natural disaster detection, early warning systems, disaster monitoring, damage assessment, and post-disaster response development.

Salvia et al. (2021) referred to the waste management challenge as a wicked problem due to the astronomical increase in global waste, which poses significant negative impacts on both human life and the environment. The research conducted by

Chidepatil et al. (2020) demonstrated that the application of AI in waste management leads to improvements in efficiency in waste recycling. Olawade et al. (2024) highlighted genetic algorithms (GAs), support vector machines (SVMs), artificial neural networks (ANNs), and decision trees (DTs) as some of the AI techniques that can be applied in waste management. They further argued that AI plays an important role in waste collection (including smart bin systems, route optimisation, dynamic waste collection scheduling, and demand prediction), waste sorting, and waste recycling.

In the next section, we will explore the newly emerged technology known as the Generative Artificial Intelligence and examine the role it can play in shaping the data-driven future.

5. The Role of Generative AI

Humans are often faced with decision-making daily, which involves thinking about choices of actions among alternatives (Taylor 2013). Garrett (2017) suggests that 50.3% of Americans 'trust their guts' when making decisions. A report by McKinsey (2023) indicates that managers surveyed across over 1,200 global businesses spend, on average, nearly 40% of their time on decision-making, with many experiencing 'decision fatigue'. Unfortunately, most of these decisions are complex and cannot be based on intuition or emotions because there are huge financial and, sadly, sometimes human costs associated with ineffective decision-making (Abubakar et al. 2019). Hence, there is a need for data-driven decisions. In this section, we focus on the role of Generative AI (GenAI) in decision-making, examining the application of GenAI in the process and the benefits and challenges that it brings.

5.1 Background and historical context

As highlighted earlier within this chapter, the vast array of data available and its complexities in terms of volume, velocity, variety, and variability can be overwhelming (Kitchin and McArdle 2016). To deal with these complexities, Generative Artificial Intelligence comes to the fore. This is because, unlike a human decision, which might be tainted with bias, Generative AI leverages analytics for strategic and insightful decision-making based on available data. According to Feuerriegel et al. (2024), Generative AI refers to deep learning models and computational techniques that are capable of taking raw data to learn and, when prompted, generate new content such as images, texts, and speech similar, but not identical, to the training data.

Historically, GenAI has evolved over the years with the advent of computers and AI using statistical rule-based approaches to develop decision trees and Bayesian networks (Feuerriegel et al. 2024). This formed the basis for more sophisticated decision-making and data generation, paving the way for machine learning algorithms that enable systems to learn from data without predefined rules (Cao et al. 2023). Moreover, the giant leap in 2010 saw the introduction of deep learning with generative models such as Generative Adversarial Networks (GANs) and Variational Autoencoders (VAEs). These formed the building blocks for producing digital assistants and chatbots. In addition, the 2020s saw smarter chatbots with scalable capabilities, combining Large Language Models (LLMs) with generative AI, giving rise to ChatGPT (Generative Pre-trained Transformer) and Copilot. Bommasani et al. (2021) observe that with the foundation model, these systems can model data output across specific domains with a high degree of accuracy, adapting to a wider range of tasks. Furthermore, through human interaction and prompting, Large Language Models (LLMs) that utilise Natural Language Processing (NLP) enable GenAI to unleash its capability to understand human preferences through strategic dialogues, stating clear roles, context, tone, and purpose (Bozkurt and Sharma 2023), thus producing authentic texts, music, virtual environments, and images.

5.2 Application of GenAI in decision making

There are various applications of GenAI in decision-making. These include, but are not limited to, (1) Enhancing predictive models, (2) Decision support in complex systems, (3) Creative problem-solving and innovation, and (4) Facilitating ethical and inclusive decision-making. These are subsequently discussed in more detail.

5.2.1 Enhancing predictive analytics

In the era of an ever-dynamic business landscape and big data, it has become necessary for businesses to adopt GenAI for decision-making. Most businesses that desire to maintain their competitive edge are required to study trends, make predictions, and mitigate potential risks (Syed and Bawazir 2021). According to Dhoni (2023), one of the most prominent applications of GenAI in decision-making is predictive analytics. By learning from historical data, generative models can forecast potential outcomes and generate multiple scenarios for decision-makers to evaluate. This is particularly useful in business strategy development, risk management, and financial planning. Moreover, GANs have been used to simulate various market conditions in financial sectors, enabling more informed investment decisions (Che et al. 2024). These models can generate plausible future market conditions that go beyond traditional statistical methods, helping organisations anticipate risks and prepare for different possibilities. Similarly, the use of GenAI is evident in the service industry and after-sales service in the manufacturing sector, among other examples. Bi (2023) observes that GenAI, based on data prompts provided, can anticipate customers' problems and provide authentic solutions in real-time, saving staff costs and mitigating human limitations. Evidently, GenAI is situated in organisations to deliver value to stakeholders while solving business problems (Feuerriegel et al. 2024).

Generative AI has applications in other sectors as well. In healthcare, for instance, GenAI can predict the progression of diseases by generating potential trajectories based on patient data (Topol 2019). In addition, Shokrollahi et al. (2023) acknowledge the crucial role of generative models in analysing diverse data forms, including medical imaging, clinical decision support, protein structure prediction, molecular representation, and drug synthesis. However, there are concerns about how this would impact the patient-doctor relationship and whether these advancements would improve or deteriorate this relationship.

5.2.2 Decision support in complex systems

Generative AI plays a crucial role in supporting decisions in complex and dynamic systems. In areas such as supply chain management, urban planning, and environmental management, decision-makers face a high number of variables and uncertainty (Fosso Wamba et al. 2023, Yandrapalli 2023). Generative models can synthesise vast datasets and generate multiple scenarios to help decision-makers evaluate different strategies. For instance, in urban planning, GenAI can model different layouts and configurations of a city or transport network, simulating their potential impacts on traffic, pollution, and energy consumption based on predetermined criteria (Ooi et al. 2023). By offering a range of potential outcomes and alternative scenarios, these models assist policymakers in assessing probable outcomes and selecting the most sustainable and efficient solutions. It is critical to note that there are challenges related to human barriers, cultural shifts, and the integration of multiple systems to handle the many stakeholders and variables associated with each complex system (Yandrapalli 2023).

5.2.3 Creative problem-solving and innovation

According to Shrestha et al. (2021), the product development phase can be challenging because designers are limited to focusing on a few iterations. This process is tedious and time-consuming, as it requires the evaluation of a pool of proposed solutions. The ability of generative models to produce creative outputs is particularly valuable in innovation and problem-solving. Garbuio and Lin (2021) opined that by generating new ideas, designs, or solutions, AI can assist in overcoming cognitive biases and offering perspectives that may not be obvious to human decision-makers. In product development, for instance, GenAI can generate multiple design prototypes based on initial inputs, helping companies optimise their offerings (Hyunjin 2020).

Furthermore, GenAI can assist in scientific research by generating hypotheses and models that lead to new discoveries. In drug discovery, for instance, AI offers the promise to revolutionise drug development by producing potential molecular structures and testing their viability. This can significantly accelerate the process of identifying new treatments and overcoming obstacles in the drug discovery pipeline (Malandraki-Miller and Riley 2021).

5.3 Challenges and ethical considerations

5.3.1 Data privacy and security

The evolution of GenAI has been an impressive advancement in the technology space, and its significant contributions to different sectors are notable, with immense potential in decision-making (Golda et al. 2024). However, its widespread adoption raises significant concerns about data privacy and security. Many generative models rely on vast amounts of data, including sensitive personal information. According to Abadi et al. (2016), if these models are not carefully managed, they can inadvertently expose private data or generate outputs that reveal confidential information. Privacy-preserving techniques, such as differential privacy and federated learning, are essential to address these risks.

5.3.2 Lack of interpretability and control

GenAI models, particularly, deep learning-based ones, are often considered "black boxes" due to their complexity and lack of transparency (Yang et al. 2022). Many of the machine learning algorithms cannot manifest how and why a decision has been made. This can be problematic in decision-making contexts, where the rationale behind a decision is crucial for trust and accountability (Tredinnick and Laybats 2023). For example, a healthcare provider may hesitate to rely on a generative model if the model's decision-making process is unclear, even if it produces accurate predictions. This highlights the need for research on explainability in generative models to ensure they are interpretable and can be trusted by human decision-makers (Doshi-Velez and Kim 2017).

5.3.3 Ethical implications of GenAI

The creative capacity of GenAI also raises ethical questions. AI-generated content, such as deepfakes or fabricated news, can be used maliciously to manipulate decision-making processes or deceive individuals (Danry et al. 2022, Romero Moreno 2024). This highlights the importance of regulation and ethical frameworks to ensure GenAI is used responsibly (Floridi et al. 2018). Consequently, decision-makers must also consider the potential for AI to reinforce existing biases, especially if the training data reflect societal inequalities.

6. Conclusion

The integration of advanced analytics and artificial intelligence is rapidly reshaping industries and personal interactions. This is resulting in a data-led present and leading to a data-driven future. This chapter succinctly presented the key technologies enabling efficient handling, analysis, and utilisation of high-volume and diverse data sources. The chapter started by briefly introducing Industry 5.0, which embraces sustainability, resilience, and human-centric analytics. Considering some of the sector-specific applications outlined in this chapter, it is evident that AI and analytics are critical for enhancing decision-making, optimising processes, and driving innovation. The rising diffusion of GenAI, with its disruptive capabilities, presents new opportunities and challenges, such as the importance of ethical considerations in its development and deployment. As data continues to grow in scale and complexity, the need for robust, scalable, and ethical AI systems will only intensify. Embracing these technologies thoughtfully and responsibly is essential to unlocking their full potential while mitigating risks and potential unintended consequences.

We envisage several future research pathways from this review chapter. Future research could focus on improving data integration techniques to offer seamless integration of data often derived from various sources. This can include developing more advanced tools for real-time or semi-real-time data processing and ensuring data accuracy across multiple platforms. Moreover, as AI systems become more autonomous, there will be a growing need for frameworks that ensure transparency, fairness, and accountability. Future work should aim to establish clearer guidelines and ethical standards for the deployment of AI technologies, particularly in critical sectors such as healthcare and finance. In addition to this, the shift toward Industry 5.0 presents the necessity of collaboration between humans and AI systems. Future studies could explore the development of AI systems that are more intuitive, adaptable, and designed to enhance human decision-making rather than replace it. Moreover, as GenAI matures as a technology, further research can focus on ways to make it more accurate, reliable, and safe. It is envisaged that more research on AI biases, misinformation, deepfakes, and privacy will continue to grow. Finally, there is a growing awareness and concern regarding the environmental impacts of AI technologies, particularly the vast decentralised adoption of GenAI platforms. Examining the environmental impacts, and potentially social impacts (digital divide, equality and fairness in access, among others), of these technologies could offer a clearer picture of the scale of the potential challenges and pave the way for finding pertinent solutions.

References

Abadi, M., Chu, A., Goodfellow, I., McMahan, H.B., Mironov, I., Talwar, K. et al. 2016. Deep learning with differential privacy. Proceedings of the 2016 ACM SIGSAC Conference on Computer and Communications Security, 308–318. https://doi.org/10.1145/2976749.2978318.

Abid, S.K., Sulaiman, N., Chan, S.W., Nazir, U., Abid, M., Han, H. et al. 2021. Toward an integrated disaster management approach: how artificial intelligence can boost disaster management. *Sustainability*, 13(22): 12560. https://doi.org/10.3390/su132212560.

Abubakar, A.M., Elrehail, H., Alatailat, M.A. and Elçi, A. 2019. Knowledge management, decision-making style and organizational performance. *Journal of Innovation & Knowledge*, 4(2): 104–114. https://doi.org/10.1016/j.jik.2017.07.003.

Ahmed, M., Zheng, Y., Amine, A., Fathiannasab, H. and Chen, Z. 2021. The role of artificial intelligence in the mass adoption of electric vehicles. *Joule*, 5(9): 2296–2322. https://doi.org/10.1016/j.joule.2021.07.012.

Albayrak Ünal, Ö., Erkayman, B. and Usanmaz, B. 2023. Applications of artificial intelligence in inventory management: a systematic review of the literature. *Archives of Computational Methods in Engineering*. https://doi.org/10.1007/s11831-022-09879-5.

Ali, Md. R., Nipu, S. Md. A. and Khan, S.A. 2023. A decision support system for classifying supplier selection criteria using machine learning and random forest approach. *Decision Analytics Journal*, 7: 100238. https://doi.org/10.1016/j.dajour.2023.100238.

Alowais, S.A., Alghamdi, S.S., Alsuhebany, N., Alqahtani, T., Alshaya, A.I., Almohareb, S.N. et al. 2023. Revolutionizing healthcare: the role of artificial intelligence in clinical practice. *BMC Medical Education*, 23(1): 689. https://doi.org/10.1186/s12909-023-04698-z.

Ang, L.-M., Seng, K.P. and Wachowicz, M. 2022. Embedded intelligence and the data-driven future of application-specific Internet of Things for smart environments. *International Journal of Distributed Sensor Networks*, 18(6): 155013292211023. https://doi.org/10.1177/15501329221102371.

Ankam, V. 2016. Big Data Analytics. Packt Publishing.

Anusha, K., Rajesh, N., Kavitha, M. and Ravinder, N. 2021. Comparative study of MongoDB vs Cassandra in big data analytics. 2021 5th International Conference on Computing Methodologies and Communication (ICCMC), 1831–1835. https://doi.org/10.1109/ICCMC51019.2021.9418441.

Arena, F., Collotta, M., Luca, L., Ruggieri, M. and Termine, F.G. 2021. Predictive Maintenance in the Automotive Sector: A Literature Review. *Mathematical and Computational Applications*, 27(1): 2. https://doi.org/10.3390/mca27010002.

Arowoogun, J., Babawarun, O., Chidi, R., Adeniyi, A. and Okolo, C. 2024. A comprehensive review of data analytics in healthcare management: Leveraging big data for decision-making. *World Journal of Advanced Research and Reviews*, 21(2): 1810–1821. https://doi.org/10.30574/wjarr.2024.21.2.0590.

Attaran, M. 2022. Blockchain technology in healthcare: Challenges and opportunities. *International Journal of Healthcare Management*, 15(1): 70–83. https://doi.org/10.1080/20479700.2020.1843887.

Avram, M.G. 2014. Advantages and challenges of adopting cloud computing from an enterprise perspective. *Procedia Technology*, 12: 529–534. https://doi.org/10.1016/j.protcy.2013.12.525.

Bachute, M.R. and Subhedar, J.M. 2021. Autonomous driving architectures: insights of machine learning and deep learning algorithms. *Machine Learning with Applications*, 6: 100164. https://doi.org/10.1016/j.mlwa.2021.100164.

Bate, A. and Stegmann, J.-U. 2023. Artificial intelligence and pharmacovigilance: What is happening, what could happen and what should happen? *Health Policy and Technology*, 12(2): 100743. https://doi.org/10.1016/j.hlpt.2023.100743.

Batko, K. and Ślęzak, A. 2022. The use of Big Data Analytics in healthcare. *Journal of Big Data*, 9(1): 3. https://doi.org/10.1186/s40537-021-00553-4.

Belhadi, A., Mani, V., Kamble, S.S., Khan, S.A.R. and Verma, S. 2024. Artificial intelligence-driven innovation for enhancing supply chain resilience and performance under the effect of supply chain dynamism: an empirical investigation. *Annals of Operations Research*, 333(2–3): 627–652. https://doi.org/10.1007/s10479-021-03956-x.

Bi, Q. 2023. Analysis of the application of generative AI in business management. *Advances in Economics and Management Research*, 6(1): 36. https://doi.org/10.56028/aemr.6.1.36.2023.

Biswas, A. and Wang, H.-C. 2023. Autonomous vehicles enabled by the integration of IoT, Edge Intelligence, 5G, and Blockchain. *Sensors*, 23(4): 1963. https://doi.org/10.3390/s23041963.

Bommasani, R., Hudson, D.A., Adeli, E., Altman, R., Arora, S., von Arx, S. et al. 2021. On the Opportunities and Risks of Foundation Models. ArXiv, abs/2108.07258. https://api.semanticscholar.org/CorpusID:237091588.

Bozkurt, A. and Sharma, R.C. 2023. Generative AI and prompt engineering: The art of whispering to let the genie out of the algorithmic world. *Asian Journal of Distance Education*, 18(2): i–vii.

Cao, Y., Li, S., Liu, Y., Yan, Z., Dai, Y., Yu, P.S. et al. 2023. A Comprehensive survey of AI-Generated Content (AIGC): A history of generative AI from GAN to ChatGPT. ArXiv, abs/2303.04226. https://api.semanticscholar.org/CorpusID:257405349.

Che, C., Huang, Z., Li, C., Zheng, H. and Tian, X. 2024. Integrating generative AI into Financial Market Prediction for Improved Decision Making. https://arxiv.org/abs/2404.03523.

Chen, J. and Wang, H. 2018. Guest editorial: big data infrastructure II. *IEEE Transactions on Big Data*, 4(3): 299–300. https://doi.org/10.1109/TBDATA.2018.2855558.

Cheng, N., Lyu, F., Chen, J., Xu, W., Zhou, H., Zhang, S. et al. 2018. Big data driven vehicular networks. *IEEE Network*, 32(6): 160–167. https://doi.org/10.1109/MNET.2018.1700460.

Chidepatil, A., Bindra, P., Kulkarni, D., Qazi, M., Kshirsagar, M. and Sankaran, K. 2020. From Trash to Cash: How Blockchain and Multi-Sensor-Driven Artificial Intelligence Can Transform Circular Economy of Plastic Waste? *Administrative Sciences*, 10(2): 23. https://doi.org/10.3390/admsci10020023.

Christopher, M. 2023. Logistics and supply chain management. Pearson Education.

Dabo, A.-A. A. and Hosseinian-Far, A. 2023. An integrated methodology for enhancing reverse logistics flows and networks in industry 5.0. Logistics, 7(4): 97. https://doi.org/10.3390/logistics7040097.

Dahake, R., Metre, K., Kale, N., B J, D. and Mahankale, N. 2024. AI-Powered environmental monitoring and conservation strategies. *International Journal of Engineering Trends and Technology*, 72(8): 1–7. https://doi.org/10.14445/22315381/IJETT-V72I8P101.

Danry, V., Leong, J., Pataranutaporn, P., Tandon, P., Liu, Y., Shilkrot, R. et al. 2022. AI-generated characters: putting deepfakes to good use. CHI Conference on Human Factors in Computing Systems Extended Abstracts, 1–5. https://doi.org/10.1145/3491101.3503736.

Dhoni, P. 2023. Exploring the Synergy between Generative AI, Data and Analytics in the Modern Age. https://doi.org/10.36227/techrxiv.24045792.v1.

Dinov, I.D. 2016. Volume and value of big healthcare data. Journal of Medical Statistics and Informatics, 4(1): 3. https://doi.org/10.7243/2053-7662-4-3.

Donnelly, J., Daneshkhah, A. and Abolfathi, S. 2024. Physics-informed neural networks as surrogate models of hydrodynamic simulators. *Science of The Total Environment*, 912: 168814. https://doi.org/10.1016/j.scitotenv.2023.168814.

Doshi-Velez, F. and Kim, B. 2017. Towards A Rigorous Science of Interpretable Machine Learning. https://arxiv.org/abs/1702.08608.

Farsi, M., Namoano, B., Latsou, C., Subhadu, V.V., Deng, H., Sun, Z. et al. 2024. Digital Twin Architecture for a Sustainable Control System in Aircraft Engines (pp. 93–123). https://doi.org/10.1007/978-3-031-62987-7_5.

Fényes, D., Németh, B. and Gáspar, P. 2019. A predictive control for autonomous vehicles using big data analysis. *IFAC-PapersOnLine*, 52(5), 191–196. https://doi.org/10.1016/j.ifacol.2019.09.031.

Feuerriegel, S., Hartmann, J., Janiesch, C. and Zschech, P. 2024. Generative AI. *Business & Information Systems Engineering*, 66(1): 111–126. https://doi.org/10.1007/s12599-023-00834-7.

Floridi, L., Cowls, J., Beltrametti, M., Chatila, R., Chazerand, P., Dignum, V. et al. 2018. AI4People—An ethical framework for a good AI Society: opportunities, risks, principles, and recommendations. *Minds and Machines*, 28(4), 689–707. https://doi.org/10.1007/s11023-018-9482-5.

Fosso Wamba, S., Queiroz, M.M., Chiappetta Jabbour, C.J. and Shi, C. (Victor). 2023. Are both generative AI and ChatGPT game changers for 21st-Century operations and supply chain excellence? *International Journal of Production Economics*, 265: 109015. https://doi.org/10.1016/j.ijpe.2023.109015.

Garbuio, M. and Lin, N. 2021. Innovative idea generation in problem finding: Abductive reasoning, cognitive impediments, and the promise of artificial intelligence. *Journal of Product Innovation Management*, 38(6): 701–725. https://doi.org/10.1111/jpim.12602.

Garrett, R.K. (2017, September 28). Should we worry that half of Americans trust their gut to tell them what's true?, The Conversation. The Conversation: Https://Theconversation.Com/Should-We-Worry-That-Half-of-Americans-Trust-Their-Gut-to-Tell-Them-Whats-True-84259.

Ge, M., Bangui, H. and Buhnova, B. 2018. Big data for internet of things: a survey. *Future Generation Computer Systems*, 87: 601–614. https://doi.org/10.1016/j.future.2018.04.053.

Goh, G.D., Sing, S.L. and Yeong, W.Y. 2021. A review on machine learning in 3D printing: applications, potential, and challenges. *Artificial Intelligence Review*, 54(1): 63–94. https://doi.org/10.1007/s10462-020-09876-9.

Golda, A., Mekonen, K., Pandey, A., Singh, A., Hassija, V., Chamola, V. et al. 2024. Privacy and security concerns in generative AI: A comprehensive survey. *IEEE Access*, 12: 48126–48144. https://doi.org/10.1109/ACCESS.2024.3381611.

Gupta, S., Amaba, B., McMahon, M. and Gupta, K. 2021. The evolution of artificial intelligence in the automotive industry. 2021 Annual Reliability and Maintainability Symposium (RAMS), 1–7. https://doi.org/10.1109/RAMS48097.2021.9605795.

Haenlein, M. and Kaplan, A. 2019. A brief history of artificial intelligence: on the past, present, and future of artificial intelligence. *California Management Review*, 61(4): 5–14. https://doi.org/10.1177/0008125619864925.

Halbouni, A., Gunawan, T.S., Habaebi, M.H., Halbouni, M., Kartiwi, M. and Ahmad, R. 2022. Machine learning and deep learning approaches for cyberSecurity: A Review. *IEEE Access*, 10: 19572–19585. https://doi.org/10.1109/ACCESS.2022.3151248.

Hosseinian-Far, A., Ramachandran, M. and Sarwar, D. 2017. Strategic engineering for cloud computing and big data analytics (A. Hosseinian-Far, M. Ramachandran, & D. Sarwar, Eds.). Springer International Publishing. https://doi.org/10.1007/978-3-319-52491-7.

Hosseinian-Far, A., Ramachandran, M. and Slack, C.L. 2018. Emerging trends in cloud computing, big data, fog computing, iot and smart living. In Technology for Smart Futures (pp. 29–40). Springer International Publishing. https://doi.org/10.1007/978-3-319-60137-3_2.

Hyunjin, C. 2020. A study on application of generative design system in manufacturing process. IOP Conference Series: Materials Science and Engineering, 727(1): 012011. https://doi.org/10.1088/1757-899X/727/1/012011.

Ivanov, D., Tsipoulanidis, A. and Schönberger, J. 2021. Inventory Management (pp. 385–433). https://doi.org/10.1007/978-3-030-72331-6_13.

Jahankhani, H., Kendzierskyj, S. and Colin, A. 2021. Blockchain as a tool for transparency and governance in the delivery of development aid. In Strategy, Leadership, and AI in the Cyber Ecosystem (pp. 93–111). Elsevier. https://doi.org/10.1016/B978-0-12-821442-8.00006-9.

Javaid, M., Haleem, A., Khan, I.H. and Suman, R. 2023. Understanding the potential applications of Artificial Intelligence in Agriculture Sector. *Advanced Agrochem*, 2(1): 15–30. https://doi.org/10.1016/j.aac.2022.10.001.

Johnson, J. D., Li, J. and Chen, Z. 2000. Reinforcement Learning: An Introduction. Neurocomputing, 35(1-4): 205–206. https://doi.org/10.1016/S0925-2312(00)00324-6.

Jones, J., Harris, E., Febriansah, Y., Adiwijaya, A. and Nuril Hikam, I. 2024. AI for sustainable development: applications in natural resource management, agriculture, and waste management. *International Transactions on Artificial Intelligence (ITALIC)*, 2(2): 143–149. https://doi.org/10.33050/italic.v2i2.549.

Kaur, S., Singla, J., Nkenyereye, L., Jha, S., Prashar, D., Joshi, G.P. et al. 2020. Medical diagnostic systems using Artificial Intelligence (AI) algorithms: principles and perspectives. *IEEE Access*, 8, 228049–228069. https://doi.org/10.1109/ACCESS.2020.3042273.

Khayyam, H., Javadi, B., Jalili, M. and Jazar, R.N. 2020. Artificial intelligence and internet of things for autonomous vehicles. In Nonlinear Approaches in Engineering Applications (pp. 39–68). Springer International Publishing. https://doi.org/10.1007/978-3-030-18963-1_2.

Kitchin, R. and McArdle, G. 2016. What makes Big Data, Big Data? Exploring the ontological characteristics of 26 datasets. *Big Data & Society*, 3(1). https://doi.org/10.1177/2053951716631130.

Kothamali, P.R., Banik, S., Dandyala, S.S.M. and kumar Karne, V. 2024. Advancing telemedicine and healthcare systems with AI and machine learning. *International Journal of Machine Learning Research in Cybersecurity and Artificial Intelligence*, 15(1): 177–207.

Kumar, E.S., Kesavan, S., Naidu, R. Ch. A., Kumar R, S. and Latha. 2021. Comprehensive analysis of cloud based databases. *IOP Conference Series: Materials Science and Engineering*, 1131(1), 012021. https://doi.org/10.1088/1757-899X/1131/1/012021.

Laryea, E., Nwakile, E., Daneshkhah, A. and Hosseinian-Far, A. 2024. The Revolutionary Impact of Verified Plastic Credit Schemes: A Catalyst for Sustainable Business Practices and Community Empowerment in Developing Countries (pp. 103–116). https://doi.org/10.1007/978-3-031-62474-2_8.

Lezzi, M., Del Vecchio, V. and Lazoi, M. 2024. Using blockchain technology for sustainability and secure data management in the energy industry: implications and future research directions. *Sustainability*, 16(18): 7949. https://doi.org/10.3390/su16187949.

Liang, L., Hu, J., Sun, G., Hong, N., Wu, G., He, Y. et al. 2022. Artificial intelligence-based pharmacovigilance in the setting of limited resources. *Drug Safety*, 45(5): 511–519. https://doi.org/10.1007/s40264-022-01170-7.

Lin, H., Lin, J. and Wang, F. 2022. An innovative machine learning model for supply chain management. *Journal of Innovation & Knowledge*, 7(4): 100276. https://doi.org/10.1016/j.jik.2022.100276.

Linardos, V., Drakaki, M., Tzionas, P. and Karnavas, Y. 2022. Machine learning in disaster management: recent developments in methods and applications. *Machine Learning and Knowledge Extraction*, 4(2): 446–473. https://doi.org/10.3390/make4020020.

Liou, J.J.H., Chang, M.-H., Lo, H.-W. and Hsu, M.-H. 2021. Application of an MCDM model with data mining techniques for green supplier evaluation and selection. *Applied Soft Computing*, 109: 107534. https://doi.org/10.1016/j.asoc.2021.107534.

Macrinici, D., Cartofeanu, C. and Gao, S. 2018. Smart contract applications within blockchain technology: A systematic mapping study. *Telematics and Informatics*, 35(8): 2337–2354. https://doi.org/10.1016/j.tele.2018.10.004.

Malandraki-Miller, S. and Riley, P.R. 2021. Use of artificial intelligence to enhance phenotypic drug discovery. *Drug Discovery Today*, 26(4): 887–901. https://doi.org/10.1016/j.drudis.2021.01.013.

Mckinsey. (2023, March 13). What is decision making? McKInsey.Com:Https://Www.Mckinsey.Com/Featured-Insights/Mckinsey-Explainers/What-Is-Decision-Making.

Mirbabaie, M., Stieglitz, S. and Frick, N.R.J. 2021. Artificial intelligence in disease diagnostics: A critical review and classification on the current state of research guiding future direction. *Health and Technology*, 11(4): 693–731. https://doi.org/10.1007/s12553-021-00555-5.

Morales, E.F. and Escalante, H.J. 2022. A brief introduction to supervised, unsupervised, and reinforcement learning. In Biosignal Processing and Classification Using Computational Learning and Intelligence (pp. 111–129). Elsevier. https://doi.org/10.1016/B978-0-12-820125-1.00017-8.

Mourtzis, D. 2024. Challenges and opportunities of the transition from Industry 4.0 to Industry 5.0. In Manufacturing from Industry 4.0 to Industry 5.0 (pp. 97–131). Elsevier. https://doi.org/10.1016/B978-0-443-13924-6.00004-1.

Ncube, M.M. and Ngulube, P. 2024. Enhancing environmental decision-making: a systematic review of data analytics applications in monitoring and management. *Discover Sustainability*, 5(1): 290. https://doi.org/10.1007/s43621-024-00510-0.

O'Driscoll, A., Daugelaite, J. and Sleator, R.D. 2013. 'Big data', Hadoop and cloud computing in genomics. *Journal of Biomedical Informatics*, 46(5): 774–781. https://doi.org/10.1016/j.jbi.2013.07.001.

Ofosu, R., Hosseinian-Far, A. and Sarwar, D. 2022. Digital Twin Technologies, Architecture, and Applications: A Comprehensive Systematic Review and Bibliometric Analysis (pp. 105–142). https://doi.org/10.1007/978-3-030-98225-6_5.

Olawade, D.B., Wada, O.J., David-Olawade, A.C., Kunonga, E., Abaire, O. and Ling, J. 2023. Using artificial intelligence to improve public health: a narrative review. *Frontiers in Public Health*, 11. https://doi.org/10.3389/fpubh.2023.1196397.

Olawade, D.B., Fapohunda, O., Wada, O.Z., Usman, S.O., Ige, A.O., Ajisafe, O. et al. 2024. Smart waste management: A paradigm shift enabled by artificial intelligence. *Waste Management Bulletin*, 2(2): 244–263. https://doi.org/10.1016/j.wmb.2024.05.001.

Ooi, K.-B., Tan, G.W.-H., Al-Emran, M., Al-Sharafi, M.A., Capatina, A., Chakraborty, A. et al. 2023. The potential of generative artificial intelligence across disciplines: perspectives and future directions. *Journal of Computer Information Systems*, 1–32. https://doi.org/10.1080/08874417.2023.2261010.

Patterson, J. (Consultant) and Gibson, A. 2017. Deep learning : a practitioner's approach. O'Reilly. https://cir.nii.ac.jp/crid/1130000796727490688.

Pedersen, J.S. and Wilkinson, A. 2019. The promise, application and pitfalls of big data. In Big Data. Edward Elgar Publishing. https://doi.org/10.4337/9781788112352.00005.

Peng, J., Jury, E.C., Dönnes, P. and Ciurtin, C. 2021. Machine learning techniques for personalised medicine approaches in immune-mediated chronic inflammatory diseases: applications and challenges. *Frontiers in Pharmacology*, 12. https://doi.org/10.3389/fphar.2021.720694.

Plathottam, S.J., Rzonca, A., Lakhnori, R. and Iloeje, C.O. 2023. A review of artificial intelligence applications in manufacturing operations. *Journal of Advanced Manufacturing and Processing*, 5(3). https://doi.org/10.1002/amp2.10159.

Pradhan, I., Sarwar, D. and Hosseinian-Far, A. 2022. Impact of predictive analytics on the strategic business models of supply chain management. In Integrated Business Models in the Digital Age (pp. 207–249). Springer International Publishing. https://doi.org/10.1007/978-3-030-97877-8_6.

Raissi, M., Perdikaris, P. and Karniadakis, G.E. 2019. Physics-informed neural networks: A deep learning framework for solving forward and inverse problems involving nonlinear partial differential equations. *Journal of Computational Physics*, 378: 686–707. https://doi.org/10.1016/j.jcp.2018.10.045.

Raja Santhi, A. and Muthuswamy, P. 2023. Industry 5.0 or industry 4.0S? Introduction to industry 4.0 and a peek into the prospective industry 5.0 technologies. *International Journal on Interactive Design and Manufacturing (IJIDeM)*, 17(2): 947–979. https://doi.org/10.1007/s12008-023-01217-8.

Rauf, M., Kumar, L., Zulkifli, S.A. and Jamil, A. 2024. Aspects of artificial intelligence in future electric vehicle technology for sustainable environmental impact. *Environmental Challenges*, 100854. https://doi.org/10.1016/j.envc.2024.100854.

Renda, A., Schwaag Serger, S., Tataj, D., Morlet, A., Isaksson, D., Martins, F. et al. 2021. Industry 5.0, a transformative vision for Europe – Governing systemic transformations towards a sustainable industry. Publications Office of the European Union. https://doi.org/doi/10.2777/17322.

Rimal, B., Kong, C., Poudel, B., Wang, Y. and Shahi, P. 2022. Smart electric vehicle charging in the era of internet of vehicles, emerging trends, and open issues. *Energies*, 15(5): 1908. https://doi.org/10.3390/en15051908.

Romero Moreno, F. 2024. Generative AI and deepfakes: a human rights approach to tackling harmful content. *International Review of Law, Computers & Technology*, 38(3): 297–326. https://doi.org/10.1080/13600869.2024.2324540.

Sachsenmeier, P. 2016. Industry 5.0—The relevance and implications of bionics and synthetic biology. *Engineering*, 2(2): 225–229. https://doi.org/10.1016/J.ENG.2016.02.015.

Sahu, M., Gupta, R., Ambasta, R.K. and Kumar, P. 2022. Artificial intelligence and machine learning in precision medicine: A paradigm shift in big data analysis (pp. 57–100). https://doi.org/10.1016/bs.pmbts.2022.03.002.

Salvia, G., Zimmermann, N., Willan, C., Hale, J., Gitau, H., Muindi, K. et al. 2021. The wicked problem of waste management: An attention-based analysis of stakeholder behaviours. *Journal of Cleaner Production*, 326: 129200. https://doi.org/10.1016/j.jclepro.2021.129200.

Saunila, M., Holopainen, M., Nasiri, M., Ukko, J. and Rantala, T. 2024. Digital transformation with digital twins - distinct mechanisms of enabling and controlling uses. *Technology Analysis & Strategic Management*, 36(6): 1323–1336. https://doi.org/10.1080/09537325.2022.2090917.

Schmitt, M. 2023. Automated machine learning: AI-driven decision making in business analytics. *Intelligent Systems with Applications*, 18: 200188. https://doi.org/10.1016/j.iswa.2023.200188.

Sedlmeir, J., Buhl, H.U., Fridgen, G. and Keller, R. 2020. The energy consumption of blockchain technology: beyond myth. *Business & Information Systems Engineering*, 62(6): 599–608. https://doi.org/10.1007/s12599-020-00656-x.

Seyedan, M. and Mafakheri, F. 2020. Predictive big data analytics for supply chain demand forecasting: methods, applications, and research opportunities. *Journal of Big Data*, 7(1): 53. https://doi.org/10.1186/s40537-020-00329-2.

Sharma, A., Sharma, A., Tselykh, A., Bozhenyuk, A., Choudhury, T., Alomar, M.A. et al. 2023. Artificial intelligence and internet of things oriented sustainable precision farming: Towards modern agriculture. *Open Life Sciences*, 18(1). https://doi.org/10.1515/biol-2022-0713.

Sharma, R., Kamble, S.S. and Gunasekaran, A. 2018. Big GIS analytics framework for agriculture supply chains: A literature review identifying the current trends and future *perspectives. Computers and Electronics in Agriculture*, 155: 103–120. https://doi.org/10.1016/j.compag.2018.10.001.

Shokrollahi, Y., Yarmohammadtoosky, S., Nikahd, M.M., Dong, P., Li, X. and Gu, L. 2023. A Comprehensive Review of Generative AI in Healthcare. https://arxiv.org/abs/2310.00795.

Shrestha, P.R., Timalsina, D., Bista, S., Shrestha, B.P. and Shakya, T.M. 2021. Generative design approach for product development. 020008. https://doi.org/10.1063/5.0065031.

Syed, A.M. and Bawazir, H.S. 2021. Recent trends in business financial risk – A bibliometric analysis. *Cogent Economics & Finance*, 9(1). https://doi.org/10.1080/23322039.2021.1913877.

Talaviya, T., Shah, D., Patel, N., Yagnik, H. and Shah, M. 2020. Implementation of artificial intelligence in agriculture for optimisation of irrigation and application of pesticides and herbicides. *Artificial Intelligence in Agriculture*, 4, 58–73. https://doi.org/10.1016/j.aiia.2020.04.002.

Taye, M.M. 2023. Understanding of machine learning with deep learning: architectures, workflow, applications and future directions. *Computers*, 12(5): 91. https://doi.org/10.3390/computers12050091.

Taylor, D.W. 2013. Decision Making and Problem Solving1. In Handbook of Organizations (RLE: Organizations) (pp. 48–86). Routledge.

Theissler, A., Pérez-Velázquez, J., Kettelgerdes, M. and Elger, G. 2021. Predictive maintenance enabled by machine learning: Use cases and challenges in the automotive industry. *Reliability Engineering & System Safety*, 215: 107864. https://doi.org/10.1016/j.ress.2021.107864.

Tirkolaee, E.B., Sadeghi, S., Mooseloo, F.M., Vandchali, H.R. and Aeini, S. 2021. Application of machine learning in supply chain management: a comprehensive overview of the main areas. *Mathematical Problems in Engineering*, 2021, 1–14. https://doi.org/10.1155/2021/1476043.

Topol, E.J. 2019. High-performance medicine: the convergence of human and artificial intelligence. *Nature Medicine*, 25(1): 44–56. https://doi.org/10.1038/s41591-018-0300-7.

Tredinnick, L. and Laybats, C. 2023. Black-box creativity and generative artifical intelligence. *Business Information Review*, 40(3): 98–102. https://doi.org/10.1177/02663821231195131.

Tummala, R. and Schoenherr, T. 2011. Assessing and managing risks using the Supply Chain Risk Management Process (SCRMP). *Supply Chain Management: An International Journal*, 16(6): 474–483. https://doi.org/10.1108/13598541111171165.

Ucar, A., Karakose, M. and Kırımça, N. 2024. Artificial intelligence for predictive maintenance applications: key components, trustworthiness, and future trends. *Applied Sciences*, 14(2): 898. https://doi.org/10.3390/app14020898.

Uddin, R. and Koo, I. 2024. Real-time remote patient monitoring: a review of biosensors integrated with multi-Hop IoT systems via cloud connectivity. *Applied Sciences*, 14(5): 1876. https://doi.org/10.3390/app14051876.

Weking, J., Mandalenakis, M., Hein, A., Hermes, S., Böhm, M. and Krcmar, H. 2020. The impact of blockchain technology on business models – a taxonomy and archetypal patterns. *Electronic Markets*, 30(2): 285–305. https://doi.org/10.1007/s12525-019-00386-3.

Xu, X., Lu, Y., Vogel-Heuser, B. and Wang, L. 2021. Industry 4.0 and Industry 5.0—Inception, conception and perception. *Journal of Manufacturing Systems*, 61: 530–535. https://doi.org/10.1016/j.jmsy.2021.10.006.

Yandrapalli, V. 2023. Revolutionizing supply chains using power of generative AI. *International Journal of Research Publication and Reviews*, 4(12): 1556–1562. https://doi.org/10.55248/gengpi.4.1223.123417.

Yang, G., Ye, Q. and Xia, J. 2022. Unbox the black-box for the medical explainable AI via multi-modal and multi-centre data fusion: A mini-review, two showcases and beyond. *Information Fusion*, 77: 29–52. https://doi.org/10.1016/j.inffus.2021.07.016.

Yli-Huumo, J., Ko, D., Choi, S., Park, S. and Smolander, K. 2016. Where is current research on blockchain technology?—A Systematic Review. *PLOS ONE*, 11(10): e0163477. https://doi.org/10.1371/journal.pone.0163477.

Zamani, E.D., Smyth, C., Gupta, S. and Dennehy, D. 2023. Artificial intelligence and big data analytics for supply chain resilience: a systematic literature review. *Annals of Operations Research*, 327(2): 605–632. https://doi.org/10.1007/s10479-022-04983-y.

Zhang, Y. 2024. Digital Twin (Vol. 16). Springer Nature Switzerland. https://doi.org/10.1007/978-3-031-51819-5.

Zheng, X., Lu, J. and Kiritsis, D. 2022. The emergence of cognitive digital twin: vision, challenges and opportunities. *International Journal of Production Research*, 60(24): 7610–7632. https://doi.org/10.1080/00207543.2021.2014591.

Zouari, D., Ruel, S. and Viale, L. 2021. Does digitalising the supply chain contribute to its resilience? *International Journal of Physical Distribution & Logistics Management*, 51(2): 149–180. https://doi.org/10.1108/IJPDLM-01-2020-0038.

CHAPTER 9

Traffic Analysis Framework

Vehicle Counting and Traffic Volume Forecasting

Omar Gamal AbdElKhalek Mohamed ElSherbiny and *Nitsa J. Herzog*★

1. Introduction

Intelligent Traffic Systems are crucial components of road monitoring and management systems, especially in urban areas. These systems provide numerous services to enable smarter transportation management, which can benefit countries in various ways. With the rapid rise of vehicles in multiple areas, ITS has improved transport communication and vehicle tracking (Zhou et al. 2023).

Chand et al. (2021) mention that road traffic accidents cause various damages, including injuries and economic losses. Traffic congestion increases due to these accidents and the rise in the number of vehicles, subsequently affecting the lifestyle of drivers and passengers (Zheng et al. 2020, Shepelev et al. 2022). Therefore, designing a full end-to-end model that improves the monitoring system to reduce traffic jams can indirectly create a safer road environment.

The technique of identifying the count of vehicles on a specific road can help manage the road more efficiently and may help decrease traffic congestion. It can also assist in managing a smart traffic light system more effectively and could recommend whether the road needs to be managed differently or if a highway needs more lanes.

The research aimed to design an effective, flexible monitoring system to reduce traffic congestion. The system uses deep learning algorithms to process and analyse

Faculty of Engineering & Environment, Northumbria University London Campus, UK.
* Corresponding author: nitsa.herzog@northumbria.ac.uk

DOI: 10.1201/9781003540373-9

traffic images from various locations. Subsequently, the system forecasts the number of vehicles expected to appear in the image an hour after its capture time, thus improving traffic monitoring systems.

1.1 Background

In this section, the discussions will focus on the problems that ITS aims to combat, as well as the projects deployed by different countries to address these problems. Firstly, Choy et al. (2020) addressed the global status report, which shows that road traffic injuries have become a significant problem and have increased drastically since 2000. To combat these problems, strategies to deploy applications are expected to control traffic and collect information describing the performance of roadway systems. The objective was to improve efficiency and avoid the misuse of resources.

Furthermore, traffic jams have affected roads until now, causing economic losses to countries. Effective traffic monitoring and prediction systems aid in avoiding these problems for any country. As addressed by Rocha Filho et al. (2020), traffic congestion causes several types of environmental pollution, including an increase in CO_2 emissions and noise.

Many advancements have been made in enabling real-time data gathering to handle the data collection challenge. These new capabilities allow for immediate data analysis from the systems, which has had a significant impact on transport operations (Lusikka et al. 2020). Moreover, keeping track of citizens' needs and developing new approaches to creating a safer and faster transportation system can help make a country more economically efficient.

For many years, ITS relied heavily on Global Navigation Satellite Systems (GNSS) for positioning and navigation. However, GNSS signals are incredibly weak and vulnerable to many threats and faults, including satellite and receiver problems (Du et al. 2021). Additionally, accurate recommendations and actions are required to ensure safer and more efficient road management. According to Karthikeyan and Usha (2023), the UK has initiated three ITS projects to set up an intelligent transport system with vast hardware installations, such as CCTV cameras, Advanced Traveller Management Systems, sensors, and monitoring and detection systems. This demonstrates the importance of improving ITS and highlights how crucial it is for countries to have such systems.

The main problems are mostly the same across all cities, as mentioned by Rudskoy et al. (2021) and can be divided as follows:

Objective problems cities face:

- Vehicle-to-population ratio increase
- Increase in citizen transportation use
- Decrease in citizen transportation efficiency
- Increasing movement needs of city residents
- Pollution (Rocha Filho et al. 2020)

Subjective problems:

- Management of traffic is way too complex for an imperfect system
- Funding for the development of roads and transport has become insufficient
- Human factors are impacted negatively

The management system would solve the following (Zadobrischi 2022, Zheng et al. 2020):

- Traffic flow efficiency
- Traffic monitoring and management
- Accident Prevention
- Pollution control
- Reduction in traffic congestion
- Reduced human workloads (Mandal et al. 2020).

According to Rao et al. (2022), machine learning applications allow vehicles to avoid unforeseen problems by detecting objects in real-time. In recent years, machine learning algorithms have advanced to better understand practical data and identify potential irregularities. With large amounts of data collected daily from different systems, deep learning has become crucial for performing better computation and learning.

This paper's purpose is to contribute to traffic congestion reduction and the advancement of traffic monitoring services. This will not only benefit countries around the world, but it will also provide a challenging concept in a real-world scenario.

2. Literature Review

2.1 Chapter overview

This part of the paper will address recent developments in dealing with road jams. The primary goal is to examine the techniques used in recent studies and understand the problem.

2.2 Traffic volume prediction

First, it is important to discuss the advancements in volume prediction and the benefits of such projects for countries. Smart cities have become more relevant and are rapidly developing, so implementing these systems will undoubtedly create a promising future for traffic management (Xiang et al. 2023). Such systems will maximise the resources used in traffic control and anticipate future traffic, thus minimising the waiting time for drivers (Zou et al. 2023). To achieve such a system, one needs to consider the type of data collected from traffic systems. Numerous authors have focused on forecasting models that predict the number of vehicles on a particular road (Mahdavian et al. 2021). Such systems have been successful and can be achieved in many ways.

2.3 Traffic volume prediction methods

Parametric models: These are widely used for traffic flow prediction, with their parameters determined in advance, as these models are mathematically configured. The parameters are chosen primarily based on the characteristics of the input data. Thus, understanding the data is crucial for researchers to ensure the model works as intended. Various methods have been used to improve these models. For instance, Tao et al. (2019) and Wang and Boukerche (2021) used SARIMA with an adjacency matrix representing the delay ratio to enhance the model's performance.

Other parametric models are ARIMA, the Kalman Filter, etc.

Non-Parametric models: As the name implies, there are no pre-determined parameters to describe the input data's characteristics, making these models more flexible. As mentioned by Sun et al. (2020) and Wang and Boukerche (2021), the models use machine learning algorithms which employ various techniques to learn the data patterns. This flexibility can aid the non-parametric model in achieving what parametric models do, and as will be discussed later, they can often achieve even better performance.

Non-parametric models are Random Forest, K Nearest Neighbors, and Neural Network architectures.

2.4 Related work

Since some researchers have focused on specific aspects of the project, this section will be divided into three subsections: those who focused on vehicle counting, those who focused on forecasting the vehicle count, and those who developed a complete end-to-end system.

2.4.1 Vehicle counting methods

Dai et al. (2019) conducted a study focused on vehicle object detection and counting using a video dataset. The dataset consisted of videos recorded at intersections and urban roads using Miovision cameras. The authors categorised the dataset based on whether the image was taken at a crossroad, T-junction, or standard road. Comparisons were made using precision and recall metrics to evaluate selected models: Faster R-CNN, SSD-300 with Inception architecture, SSD-512 with VGG16 architecture, and YOLOv3 with Darknet-19 architecture. Despite Faster R-CNN achieving overall better performance, it had the slowest running speed at seven frames per second. Meanwhile, YOLOv3 was chosen due to its speed, with an average precision of nearly 88% and a recall of 79.2%.

Singh et al. (2021) devised a system for vehicle detection and accident prediction during sand or dust storms. The dataset comprised videos and photos captured in different weather conditions from various locations, including China, Arizona, Kuwait, and Saudi Arabia. The dataset was classified into four categories, indicating dense traffic or accidents. The YOLOv3 model was fed one image at a time, even for video data, with image preprocessing techniques applied to improve clarity. For prediction, the study used the same model to provide a probabilistic outcome indicating whether the given image contained dense traffic or an accident. The reports indicated an overall accuracy of 85% and a mostly balanced F1 score, although the model was less accurate in predicting accidents. The results included a confusion matrix along with a classification report.

2.4.2 Vehicle count forecasting techniques

A study by Xu et al. (2013) used Kalman Filter, KNN and CART models to predict the traffic state and traffic volumes using historical traffic data. The study used the traffic volume data from the PORTAL FHWA Test Data Set for model testing and evaluation. Additional preprocessing techniques were applied to segment the data into 15-minute intervals. The metric used for comparison was MAPE, which indicated that non-parametric techniques performed better than parametric techniques by a significant margin. The MAPE percentage difference between non-parametric and parametric methods showed that KNN and CART achieved around 9%, while Kalman reached 12%. As for the final model selection, the authors chose the CART model due to its overall better performance.

An advancement in forecasting the traffic flow was made by Lartey et al. (2021). The study applied XGBoost with Lasso regularization to traffic data from an open-source UCI Machine Learning Repository by the Minnesota Department of Transportation. Additionally, the data was merged with weather data collected from OpenWeatherMap. Data preprocessing techniques were employed to handle outliers and missing values by filling them based on their average. Implementing feature engineering was crucial to producing additional features which would describe the peak periods and weekends. The authors also implemented K-fold cross-validation to get an overall better performance model, taking hyperparameters into account. For evaluation, metrics such as MAE, RMSE, and R-squared were used to compare multiple models, including SVM, KNN, DT, RF, GBM, FCDNN, LSTM, XGBoost with Ridge, and XGBoost with Lasso. The results showed that XGBoost with Lasso performed best overall, achieving an R-squared of 0.9802, an RMSE of 0.1406, and an MAE of 0.0902. Additionally, the study conducted further analysis to assess model execution time and performed statistical analysis to validate the significance of the model's results.

2.4.3 The fully integrated traffic prediction systems

A full end-to-end urban traffic volume prediction system was created by Peppa et al. (2021) using CCTV image series to forecast traffic in the next 30 minutes. The tests were conducted on a dataset provided by the Northeast Combined Authority Travel and Transport Data. The process used a pre-trained Faster R-CNN to estimate vehicle counts, followed by preparing traffic volume data for the forecasting model. The project compared various architectures of Faster R-CNN and selected the most appropriate one, while the authors noted that SSD and MobileNet were not used due to the harmonic means of R-CNN achieving better performance. For the forecasting component, the project implemented SARIMAX, RF, and LSTM. The researchers divided the dataset into training, validation, and test sets over specific periods. After various tests, the machine learning approaches outperformed SARIMAX, with RF

Table 1: Summary of Popular Methods used in each Subsection.

Sub-Section	Data Used	Programming Language	Model	Metrics	Preprocessing Techniques
Vehicle Counting Methods	Images	Python	YOLOv3, Faster RCNN	Accuracy, Precision, Recall, F1 score	Image preprocessing for a clearer image
Vehicle Count Forecasting Techniques	Tabular datasets with related data	Python	SVR, RF, XGBoost, LSTM	MSE, MAE, MAPE, RMSE, R-Squared	Feature selection, handling outliers and missing values
Integrated Traffic Prediction Systems	Both images, and tabular datasets	Python, Tensorflow	Faster RCNN, YOLOv4, CLSTM, SARMIAX	MAE, MAPE, RMSE	Segmenting data, statistical analysis

being the most consistent of the three, achieving 1.10 MAE, 0.16 MAPE, and 1.42 RMSE. Some challenges were encountered in the study, such as missing data and gaps in traffic data due to weather conditions or other unspecified reasons. To address the challenge of camera views per location, the study used the average vehicle count over a period, which proved to be an effective solution.

Another study (Zheng et al. 2022) conducted a full video implementation system, which used a dataset from China. It implemented a lightweight DCN-MultiNet-YOLO for the counting component of the system, following the YOLOv4 architecture on video data. The output was then processed statistically before being fed into a CLSTM model. The loss metrics used were RMSE, MAE, and MAPE. The system was implemented using TensorFlow 1.13.1 and Keras 2.3.1 on an Ubuntu operating system to utilise GPU CUDA 10 capabilities. When comparing systems like MobileNet with the authors' proposed architecture, the study showed that the proposed architecture performed better overall and was faster. For the forecasting component, the authors employed KNN, LSTM, convolutional LSTM, and CLSTM, comparing them using various metrics. They selected CLSTM as it best satisfied the project requirements.

2.5 Ethical, Legal, and Social Considerations

2.5.1 Ethical issues

Several ethical issues need to be considered when developing this project to ensure fair use of the application. If deployed in a real-world scenario, the forecasted data collected should only be used for its intended purpose—reducing traffic congestion. To provide a fair system, training the model on data from different roads can help avoid bias.

2.5.2 Legal issues

The implementation of this project must comply with the legal system of the country in which it is deployed. Data protection is of utmost importance to ensure compliance with regulations. An authentication process is needed to verify the staff's identity, as there may be individuals who seek to cause harm or negatively affect the system. Another vital legal consideration involves clarifying responsibilities and liabilities in the event of a system malfunction, where the model fails to predict vehicle counts correctly. Finally, ensuring ownership of the product used is essential.

2.5.3 Social issues

Nowadays, it is crucial to raise public awareness of the system. Given concerns about AI replacing human jobs, it is important to train employees to understand, manage, and monitor the model effectively, thus it will not reduce any hires. Also, it is vital to ensure that the model deployed to reduce traffic jams will provide a safer environment for the drivers.

3. Research Methodology

Since this project is divided into two parts, a discussion in this section is about the tools used, along with the data and model procedures to implement the project and get the data ready for analysis and model training.

3.1 Proposed materials

These are the components that will be used in the project:

1. Video Traffic Footage and Forecasting data: Collected from the internet.
2. Object Detection model: Used to detect objects in an image and provide a class for each object.
3. Tracking Algorithm: Used to keep track of the objects detected from the object detection model to prevent counting the same vehicle twice.
4. Forecasting Model: Utilized to forecast the vehicle count on a certain road after an hour.
5. Web Interface: Employed to connect to the full system and forecast the road footage shown.

3.2 Vehicle counting and detection

A challenge was determining whether to train an object detection model using transfer learning on datasets collected from the internet or to use a pre-trained model immediately. Given the limitations, training the model for better overall performance on a general dataset seemed impractical compared to using models already trained on the COCO dataset. These models require days to train on large datasets like COCO.

This phase of the project must be able to track and count vehicles for each lane. The output of this part must follow the format of the forecasting data, which will be fed into the final phase of the project—forecasting the vehicle count on the road shown in the next hour.

3.2.1 COCO dataset

The dataset used to pre-train the object detection model is the COCO dataset, which stands for Common Objects in Context. COCO is a large-scale object detection, segmentation, and captioning dataset containing over 200,000 labelled images and 80 object categories. It is supported by CVDF, Microsoft, Facebook, and Mighty AI and developed through collaboration with various industry experts.

In the research paper (Lin et al. 2014), COCO aims to advance and improve object recognition by providing a broader understanding. For example, COCO includes approximately 100,000 instances of cars, which are relevant to this project. This makes the dataset more general and enhances the model's ability to handle unseen data compared to smaller datasets.

3.2.2 YOLO v8

You Only Look Once version 8 (YOLOv8) is a CNN model and one of the latest iterations in the YOLO family, created by Glenn Jocher, Ayush Chaurasia, and Jing Qiu. In January 2023, Ultralytics introduced YOLOv8, the most recent stable version (Hussain 2024). Many recent studies, such as the one conducted by Talaat and ZainEldin (2023), have used YOLOv8 to improve fire detection systems in smart cities. It processes images or frames by detecting objects through bounding boxes and estimating the probability of the most likely object within each box.

According to the Ultralytics website, YOLOv8's architecture is made of three main components:

1. Backbone: A deep CNN responsible for extracting features and contextual information from the input image. It follows CSPDarknet53 architecture while focusing on feature extraction. The goal is to optimize computation, reduce the model size, and enhance the network's ability to handle various tasks.
2. Neck: Takes the output of the backbone and uses a combination of FPN and PAN, which combines the high-level semantic features with low level spatial information. This results in an improvement in the detection of smaller objects.
3. Head: The output of the YOLOv8, where class probabilities and bounding boxes are created. The real improvement for this version compared to others is the introduction of dynamic anchor assignment and intersection over union loss function. These improvements enhance the model's ability to match bounding boxes to the objects during training and address limitations by handling overlapping objects better.

YOLOv8 was selected for this project due to its overall better performance and speed on the COCO dataset compared to its previous versions, YOLOv5, YOLOv6, and YOLOv7, via this link https://docs.ultralytics.com/models/yolov8/.

After using the inference from the model library, a tracking algorithm will be utilised to avoid counting the same vehicle more than once and to provide a more comprehensive and accurate output. Since the model used is pre-trained on the COCO dataset, which contains various unnecessary labels, only specific classes such as cars and trucks were selected.

3.2.3 Byte tracker

Multi-object tracking algorithms (MOT) are utilized in computer vision tasks to track objects within a video. MOT can be viewed as identifying an object across different angles or frames and assigning a tracker ID to the object to track it, thus avoiding counting the same object twice in a video. According to Beard et al. (2020), the objective of MOT is to calculate the path of each object after time has passed, which would demand high computational resources. However, there are various tracking algorithms to choose from.

As mentioned by Luo et al. (2021), there are two categories of MOT, depending on how the objects are identified. Decision-free Tracking requires manual identification, meaning the user identifies the objects that need to be tracked in an image. Decision-based Tracking uses an object detection model to detect the object. The process after is to use the frames within the image and an MOT algorithm to keep track of the objects detected.

The algorithm which will be used for this project is BYTETrack algorithm, which is an evolution of SORT and DeepSORT tracking algorithms. BYTETrack introduces innovations to track low-confidence objects, ensuring small object tracking is not ignored. It first focuses on high-confidence objects in the frame and then considers the remaining objects that were not tracked. BYTETrack excels in tracking multiple objects, and using the Multiple Object Tracking Accuracy (MOTA) metric, it has demonstrated both speed and accuracy on the MOT17 dataset (Zhang et al. 2022).

BYTETrack has proven its practicality, as it was used to track the development of dairy cows in significant areas (Zheng et al. 2023). Another study (Yasir et al. 2024) used satellite-based synthetic aperture radar to monitor ships, effectively sending rescue teams and improving the overall resilience of maritime transportation systems. Thus, using this algorithm appears to be beneficial.

3.3 Traffic volume forecasting

This section discusses how to understand the forecasting data and identify the theories and models that were trained.

3.3.1 Data collection

The data was collected from the Minnesota Department of Transport via this link: https://www.dot.state.mn.us/traffic/data/reports-hrvol-atr.html. Traffic volume data from 2019 to 2023 was downloaded, containing hourly data from numerous automatic traffic recorder stations. The data was collected from major roadways such as highways, local roads (e.g., county roads), and other roads like airport roads. The volume data is gathered from sensors and loop detectors by MnDOT's central office.

Table 2: Data Description.

Column	Description
station_id	Unique identifier describing the station [ATR] in which the traffic counting took place. It describes the road's location.
dir_of_travel	Direction of travel code, 1 being North, 3 being East, 5 being South, and 7 being West
lane_of_travel	Lane of travel code, 1: Driving in the rightmost lane, 2 being left of 1, etc.
date	Date when the count was taken
columns from "1" to "24"	Identifies the interval hour when the count was taken and has the count values within that interval. For instance, 1 identifies 12 am to 1 am, while 24 identifies 11 pm to 12 am.

3.3.2 Data understanding

Understanding the data is a vital step before implementing any transformations or cleaning processes. The dataset consists of 28 columns across five Excel files, all sharing the same structure. As previously mentioned, the data was collected to provide raw traffic counts for each hour of the day, categorised by station (location), direction of travel, and lane of travel. The table below describes each column within the dataset. The descriptions are drawn using the traffic mapping application on the website, which indicates the location of each station in Minnesota.

3.3.3 Forecasting models

There are several models to choose from; however, the decision was made to use the most well-known and advanced algorithms at the time of writing. The selection also considered the limitations of the available hardware and software.

3.3.3.1 Ensemble learning algorithms

Ensemble is one of the most popular techniques in machine learning, as it merges the outputs of several models to make a single, more accurate decision. According to Sagi and Rokach (2021), the effectiveness of these algorithms is likely due to multiple models working together to improve overall predictive performance.

XGBoost

XGBoost is an implementation of gradient tree boosting, a method used for both regression and classification tasks. Experimentally, XGBoost is faster than many other ensemble methods, such as AdaBoost. XGBoost's popularity has grown due to its success in numerous competitions, particularly on platforms like Kaggle. Its features include parallel computing, which speeds up the training process, and regularisation techniques that prevent overfitting.

The process of XGBoost begins with a decision tree regressor making predictions. The model then identifies and weighs the errors. This adjusted data is fed into another decision tree regressor, and this process continues until all estimators are completed (Budholiya et al. 2022). Finally, every model is combined to produce a single, more accurate model. Additionally, parallel computation enhances speed, while regularisation techniques and subsampling prevent overfitting. XGBoost also has built-in capabilities to handle missing values and perform cross-validation.

2.3.3.2 Artificial neural network algorithms

LSTM

RNNs were designed to process sequential data across time steps Sequential data is input into cells corresponding to time steps, with each cell passing a hidden state to the next, containing information from that time step. However, traditional RNNs often suffer from vanishing gradients, which affects the accuracy of the output. LSTM networks were developed to address this issue. Their effectiveness is further supported by Wang et al. (2021), who found them superior in maintaining trend characteristics in forecasting compared to RNNs.

LSTM adds gating mechanisms that control the information passed through time steps (Landi et al. 2021). Within each LSTM cell, gates determine which information to retain and which to minimise. The gates are calculated using input data and previous states. In addition to the hidden state, LSTM introduces a cell state that passes through the network, controlled by three gates: the forget gate, the input gate, and the output gate.

As illustrated in Figure 1, the forget gate adjusts the weight of the previous cell state, which decides how much information to preserve from the previous cell state. The input gate calculates the new cell state, which determines what information to retain. Subsequently, these outputs are combined to calculate the new cell state. Finally, the output gate uses the new cell state, the input and the previous hidden state to produce the new hidden state.
The following equation calculates the candidate cell state:

$$z^{(t)} = g(W_z x(t) + R_z y^{(t-1)} + b_z) \tag{1}$$

where Wz and Rz are the weights associated with x(t) and y(t-1) bz is a biased weight vector

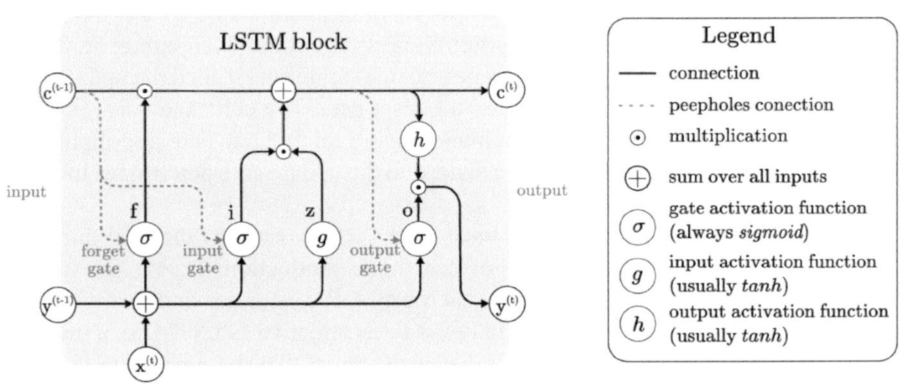

Figure 1: LSTM Architecture (Houdt et al. 2020).

The following equation calculates the input gate:

$$i^{(t)} = \sigma(W_i x^{(t)} + R_i y^{(t-1)} + p_i \cdot c^{(t-1)} + b_i) \tag{2}$$

where · is the point-wise multiplication of two vector Wi, Ri and pi are the weights associated with x(t), y(t-1) and c(t-1) bi is a bias vector

The following equation calculates the forget gate:

$$f^{(t)} = \sigma(W_f x^{(t)} + R_f y^{(t-1)} + p_f \cdot c^{(t-1)} + b_f) \tag{3}$$

where Wf, Rf and pf are the weights associated with x(t), y(t-1) and c(t-1) bf is a bias vector

The following equation calculates the new cell state:

$$c^{(t)} = z^{(t)} \cdot i^{(t)} + c^{(t-1)} \cdot f^{(t)} \tag{4}$$

The following equation calculates the output gate:

$$o^{(t)} = \sigma(W_o x^{(t)} + R_o y^{(t-1)} + p_o \cdot c^{(t-1)} + b_o) \tag{5}$$

where Wo, Ro and po are the weights associated with x(t), y(t-1) and c(t-1) bo is a bias vector

The following equation calculates the new hidden state:

$$y^{(t)} = g(c^{(t)}) \cdot o^{(t)} \tag{6}$$

The outputs of LSTM can be sequential or a single value. For a single output, the final hidden state of the last cell is used, while if sequential, every hidden state is sent as input to the next layer. A deep LSTM can be created by connecting the outputs of each LSTM cell to the inputs of the next LSTM, forming a more complex architecture.

GRU

GRU is another variant of RNN with a very similar architecture to LSTM. It was designed to optimize the LSTM by simplifying its structure (Mahjoub et al. 2022). GRU merges the input gate and forget gate into one single gate, called the update gate. Meanwhile, the forget gate is known as the reset gate. The cell state was removed, but GRU calculates the retained information using the hidden state and input. The reset gate produces a candidate hidden state, and the update gate determines the final hidden state.

Studies such as Jia et al. (2020) have used GRU to forecast the coal mine gas concentration to improve the safety of coal mine production. Due to its simpler network and fewer calculations within each cell, GRU is easier and faster to train than LSTM. However, GRUs may not always be as effective as LSTM, as it depends on the application and data. The study has also shown that the more data is fed to GRU, the better its accuracy.

ConvLSTM

ConvLSTM is a hybrid that combines CNN with LSTM to handle spatiotemporal data. Unlike traditional LSTM, which uses matrix multiplication within each cell, ConvLSTM sometimes uses convolutional operators. Due to the integration of CNN architecture within each LSTM cell, the parameters used are going to be different. Instead of focusing on the number of units like GRU and LSTM, ConvLSTM uses parameters such as the number of filters, kernel size and padding. Each filter convolves around the input data entered. The kernel size determines the number of weights within each filter. Finally, the padding parameter ensures no data points are missing and that the final shape is similar to the input one.

A study done by Moishin et al. (2021) used ConvLSTM to forecast future flood events in Fiji. The study showed that ConvLSTM has performed better than LSTM across all forecast windows.

4. Data analysis and preprocessing

This section discusses how the data was handled before being fed into the models and the preprocessing techniques implemented for model training.

4.1 Data cleaning & preprocessing

The goal of this project is to forecast the vehicle count on a road after an hour has passed. Each record in the dataset is identified by a combination of station ID, direction, and lane, which specifies the road's full location and separates the multi-time series data. Managing these unique identifiers is essential for accurate analysis and forecasting.

To ensure data suitability for time series forecasting, it was necessary to maintain continuous hourly records and address any date gaps by generating the required data for each unique identifier. After filling the gaps and performing necessary transformations, the data was reshaped, checked for duplicates, and prepared for further enrichment and processing.

4.2 Data enrichment

Considering ways to enrich the dataset, numerous ideas emerged on how to make the data more informative for the model. The aim was to identify additional external features that might impact traffic volume. While station ID, direction of travel, and lane of travel act as spatial attributes, adding external factors such as weather data could improve the model's overall performance. For example, precipitation could reduce vehicle speed, thus affecting traffic flow.

Weather data was collected from two sources: "https://www.dnr.state.mn.us/climate/twin_cities/listings.html" and "https://meteostat.net/en/place/us/minnesota-lake?s=KACQ0&t=2024-07-12/2024-07-19". One source provides information on precipitation, temperature, and snow, while the other offers air pressure, wind speed, and wind direction. The weather data was cleaned, for example, by setting trace

Table 3: New Columns Description.

Column	Description
Maximum Temperature degrees (F)	An estimate of the maximum temperature of the day in Fahrenheit
Minimum Temperature degrees (F)	An estimate of the minimum temperature of the day in Fahrenheit
Precipitation (inches)	Amount of rainfall or snowfall in inches that has occurred over the day
Snow (inches)	Amount of snowfall over the day, measured in inches
Snow Depth (inches)	Total snow thickness of the snow layer collected on the ground over the day, measured in inches
wdir	Wind direction indicates the direction from which the wind is coming, measured in degrees
wspd	Wind speed indicates the rate at which the wind is moving, measured in kilometres per hour
pres	Air pressure is the force produced by the weight of the air above sea level, measured in hPa
is_holiday	Indicates if the day was a holiday for the state

precipitation values to zero and interpolating missing wind data. After cleaning, the weather data was merged with the traffic dataset to align with the same time structure.

Feature engineering added additional variables, such as a holiday indicator to account for potential changes in traffic on public holidays, and time components to capture the cyclic nature of traffic patterns. Before further processing, the final dataset consisted of 21 million records and 15 columns, including the target variable, traffic volume. After final checks for duplicates, the dataset was ready for analysis.

4.3 Data analysis techniques

Various techniques were implemented to address the research questions and gain insights from data distribution. Due to hardware limitations and restrictions in Kaggle notebooks, the dataset was reduced. The data was reduced to concentrate on stations located within the twin cities of Minneapolis and St. Paul, Minnesota. This selection was made using the traffic mapping application from the source website to ensure relevant stations were identified. This step reduced the dataset to around 8 million records. Time components, such as the day of the week, day of the month, week number, month, and year, were extracted from the date column.

Traffic volume ranged from 0 to 2,000 vehicles per hour, with some values reaching up to 4,000. A sample of three stations was analyzed: one with the highest average volume, one with the lowest, and one near the median. The lowest average station showed variability, while the highest had consistent distribution, and the median station exhibited the most outliers.

Analysis indicated that south and west travel directions had higher volumes. Additionally, lanes 1 and 2 recorded the highest volumes, whereas lanes 4 and 5 showed lower counts. Further analysis also revealed that non-holiday days had higher vehicle counts compared to holidays, despite only a 100-vehicle difference in median values.

Finally, the relationship between weather features and traffic volume revealed a low correlation, with the hypothesis test strengthening this finding. Meanwhile, the date attribute confirmed the dataset's cyclic nature and the time sensitivity of traffic volume.

4.4 Data splitting

When splitting the data, several considerations were taken into account to ensure efficient processing within the available hardware constraints. After the data analysis, it was decided to include weather features in the model, as these could enhance its performance. A suitable approach was chosen for the data split, as data from all years before 2023 were taken as the training set, while data from 2023 was divided evenly between the validation and test sets.

To prepare the data for deep learning, LSTM, and GRU models, a function was implemented to reshape the data appropriately, treating each unique ID as its own time series. The transformed data was then saved in NumPy format files to speed up the model's data feeding process, preventing unnecessary processing time.

With this split, the training set contained approximately 6 million records, while the validation and test sets contained around 1 million records each. This distribution may not be ideal, but the hardware's constraints and limitations forced this solution.

4.5 Forecasting preprocessing methods

Before feeding data into forecasting models, it was necessary to prepare the data to align with the forecasting task. Unlike regression problems, where inputs like weather features are used to predict traffic volume directly, forecasting models must account for past traffic volume to predict future trends. In this project, the model will use the traffic volume in the past 3 hours to forecast the volume for the next hour.

To achieve this, lagging methods were applied to the target column. Since the dataset consists of unique identifiers representing different time series, applying lagging methods separately for each unique identifier was necessary. The data was also sorted by date and hour in ascending order to maintain the correct sequence of events. As a result, the first records for each unique identifier contained null values, as there was no prior traffic data to generate lags.

Another preprocessing approach was to feature engineers by capturing the seasonality and cyclic nature of the data. This was done by extracting the year, month, week, day of week and day of month from the date attribute. Finally, to emphasize the cyclic nature of the data, trigonometric transformations were applied to certain time components. Specifically, the sine and cosine of the hour, day of the week, week, and month were estimated. This transformation assists the model to identify periodic patterns in the data.

4.6 Data preprocessing tools for model training

An effective data preprocessing tool is vital for training models efficiently, especially when dealing with data that contain numerical, categorical, and string data types. The split data was used for imputation techniques, standard scaling, one hot encoding, and dimensionality reduction tools before being fed into the models.

4.7 Final configuration

This step involves connecting the object detection and forecasting models to implement the final project. The final setup involves feeding the output from the vehicle counting phase into the forecasting model, which then generates the predicted vehicle count. Moreover, some additions, such as getting the weather features and the location, need to be considered. However, the location features will be provided in a web interface for testing.

5. Results & discussion

The first priority is answering the research questions. This will be done in order, starting with visualizations and data analysis, followed by model training and evaluation. Finally, a full discussion about the challenges faced and potential future improvements is conducted.

5.1 Research questions

The first research question to be answered is: "How do the weather and time impact the traffic flow and the number of vehicles in an area?".

This question can be addressed from two perspectives: the weather side and the time side. From the weather side, correlation analysis indicates a surprisingly weak relationship between weather conditions and traffic flow. Even when focusing on precipitation, which was expected to significantly impact vehicle volume, only a small effect was observed.

As for the time side, the components showed more significant effects on traffic flow, as shown in Figure 2. Over the years, there was an increase in the average number of vehicles across all stations. Throughout the months, traffic volumes increased from May to October, while volumes decreased in the other months, and the reason behind this trend is still unclear. Moreover, weekdays exhibited higher average traffic volumes compared to weekends. Traffic rose during the mornings for hours, peaking between 4 and 6 pm. Meanwhile, the lowest volumes occurred during the nighttime. Additionally, holidays exhibited fewer volumes than non-holidays, as shown in the "Data Analysis" sub-section.

To summarize, the weather exhibited low impact, while the time components, including year, month, day, and hour, impacted traffic flow and vehicle count.

The second research question to be addressed is: "Does traffic congestion increase more in the center of an area/city compared to the rest of the city?"

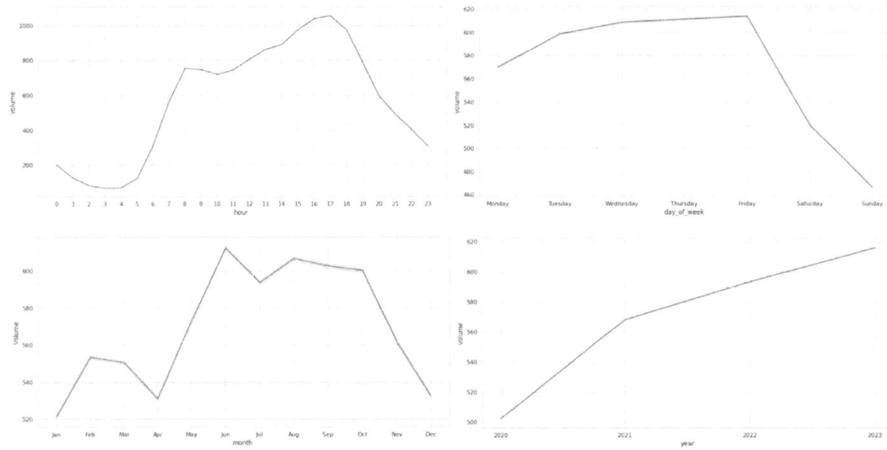

Figure 2: Time Components Impact.

Due to the lack of longitude and latitude data, the analysis involved some randomness in station selection. However, the data source provided a map showing the location of the station, allowing for a fair comparison. Station 10800, which represented a station close to the center of the city of Minneapolis, did exhibit more vehicle volumes compared to stations farther from the center. The comparison was conducted by examining the stations far from the center with the same number of lanes to have a fairer comparison between both stations in distribution.

The third research question to be answered is: "How does the number of lanes impact the vehicle count within the road?"

After implementing techniques to categorise every station depending on its lane count, one station from each category was randomly chosen, and the results are illustrated in Figure 3. In the figure, station 11179 has 5 lanes, while 11517 has 4 lanes and so on. It seems that stations with more lanes exhibit more vehicles, as

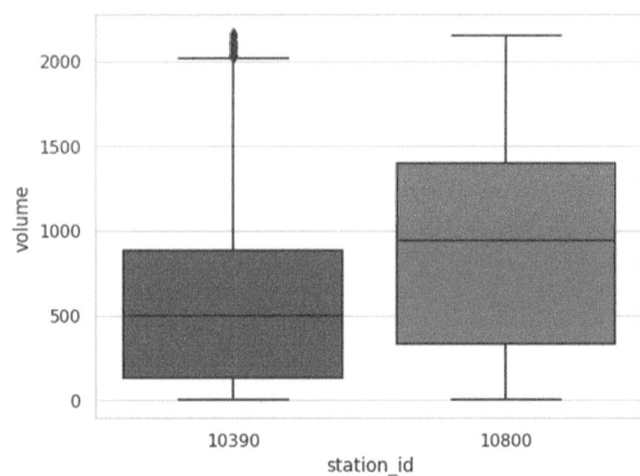

Figure 3: Far From Center Station v Center Station.

the distribution does widen more with stations with more lanes. Additionally, the averages also increase with the number of lanes.

5.2 Models implementation and results

5.2.1 Tracking model

As previously discussed, YOLOv8, pre-trained on the COCO dataset, was used for vehicle detection. It was integrated and connected with BYTETrack to track vehicles using the same video. A random video focused on the road, sourced from the internet, was utilized to test the model. The test was satisfactory overall for the task given. The YOLOv8 model was implemented only to identify cars, buses, and trucks using the Ultralytics library, while BYTETrack used the supervision library. YOLOv8x was used, which was trained on 640 pixels and had a 53.9 mAP 50-95 validation on the COCO dataset and 479.1 ms speed on a CPU ONNX. This performance is better and faster than YOLOv5x, which has a 53.2 mAP 50-95 validation and 763.2 ms speed on a CPU ONNX.

The count was calculated using the tracker ID assigned to vehicles by the BYTETrack algorithm and detected by the YOLO model. Additionally, a feature for the counting system was implemented to count vehicles in each lane to be consistent with the forecasting data. This was achieved by providing each lane's tracking algorithm with polygonal rectangles/zones. These zones were estimated using tools available on the supervision website, as the tool's goal is to provide the necessary x and y coordinates to define the zones correctly. Another advantage of the zones is that they can exclude vehicles on different roads heading in different directions to ensure only vehicles from a certain road are counted. In the final output, the vehicle count for each lane was saved in variables and displayed in the upper corners of the output video, as shown in Figure 4, with some boxes indicating cars and others indicating buses and trucks.

The third research question to be answered is: "Does the object detection model fully recognize all necessary objects in an image?" This question was answered using the test data, as the model exhibited some limitations in recognizing vehicles that were distant or blurred in the video. This was taken into consideration when defining the zones to ensure accurate results and detection from the camera.

5.2.2 Forecasting mModel

This second phase and most time-consuming part of the project focused on training the models after preparing and understanding the data, as discussed in the Methodology section. The data was fed into four different models: XGBoost, LSTM, GRU, and ConvLSTM. The metrics used for evaluation were MSE, MAE, MAPE, and R^2 score. The models were trained in a Kaggle notebook environment with a GPU P100 accelerator, which has a limit of 30 hours per week. XGBoost was implemented using its own library, xgb, while the deep learning models were built with TensorFlow.

Before feeding the models, a preprocessing pipeline was implemented using the sci-kit library to extract the cyclic nature, sine, and cosine of time components.

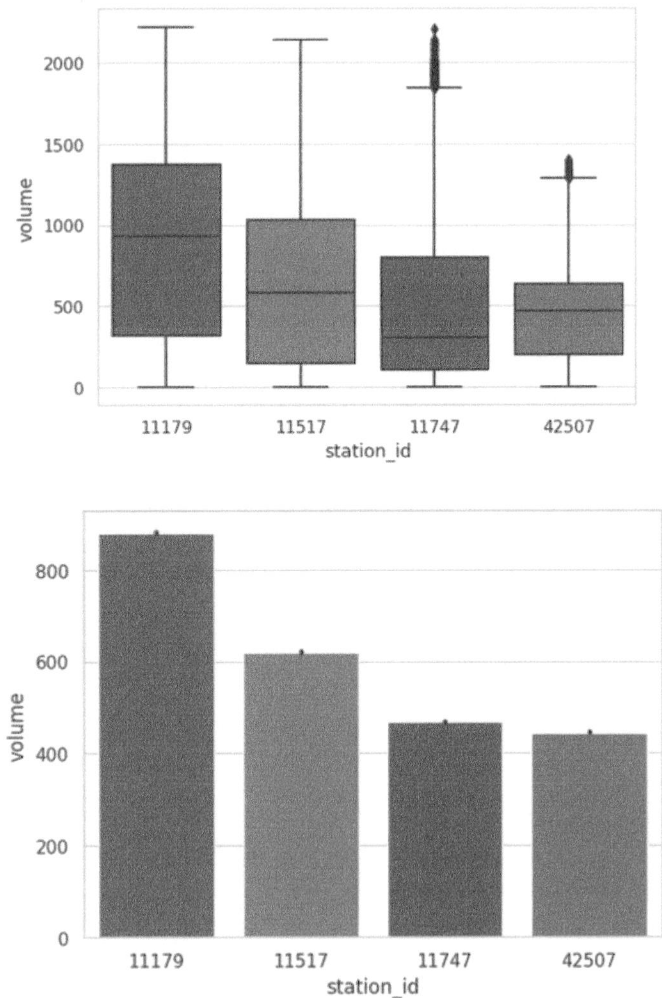

Figure 4: Number of Lanes Impact.

One-hot encoding was applied to the categorical columns, and numerical features were standardized. Additionally, NumPy files were created to reduce the time consumed for feeding the deep learning algorithms, as the data needed to be reshaped.

Among the models, XGBoost took the least time to train, while ConvLSTM took the longest. Various architectures were tested for deep learning models, and increasing layers with these models would lead to over-complication. Thus, numerous batch sizes and fully connected layers were experimented with, specifically for LSTM. A cosine decay algorithm was applied to control the learning rate of the Adam optimizer to ensure smoother convergence. Additionally, LSTM performed slightly better with weather features than without, indicating feature effectiveness.

Surprisingly, after all the experiments, XGBoost outperformed the other models in both speed and performance, which could be due to the reduction of the data. PCA

Figure 5: Tracking Model Output.

was applied to the weather features, which slightly improved XGBoost's performance. The number of PCA components was determined by examining the variance, which indicated that three components were sufficient to describe all the weather features. The output from XGBoost with PCA achieved the following results:

- Training: 46.7502 MAE, 0.9741 R2 score, 5691.072897 MSE, and 20.63% MAPE
- Validation: 50.3497 MAE, 0.9746 R2 score, 6069.407161 MSE, and 20.60% MAPE

These close training and validation results indicate good generalization. In comparison, the GRU model with 16 units, 128 batch sizes and 3 fully connected layers, achieved the overall most acceptable deep learning results:

- Training: 43.228 MAE, 0.9774 R2, 4967.6787 MSE, and 22.48% MAPE
- Validation: 59.7528 MAE, 0.9689 R2, 7443.4272 MSE, and 21.65% MAPE

```
Total number of vehicles in Zone 1: 91
Total number of vehicles in Zone 2: 76
```

Figure 6: Tracking Model Count Output.

This comparison (Appendix A) indicates that XGBoost achieved better generalization, even though GRU and LSTM achieved better training results. Finally, the next step was to take the model and train it on the train and validation sets to fully test it on the test set, which achieved 52.9777 MAE, 22.30% MAPE, and a 0.9711 R^2 score, thus indicating great generalization and forecasting accuracy.

5.3 Web interface

The interface was designed using the Dash library, which connected both models and provided a separate tab for the forecasting model. This interface includes instructions to guide users in interacting with the system and offers a clear presentation of the data

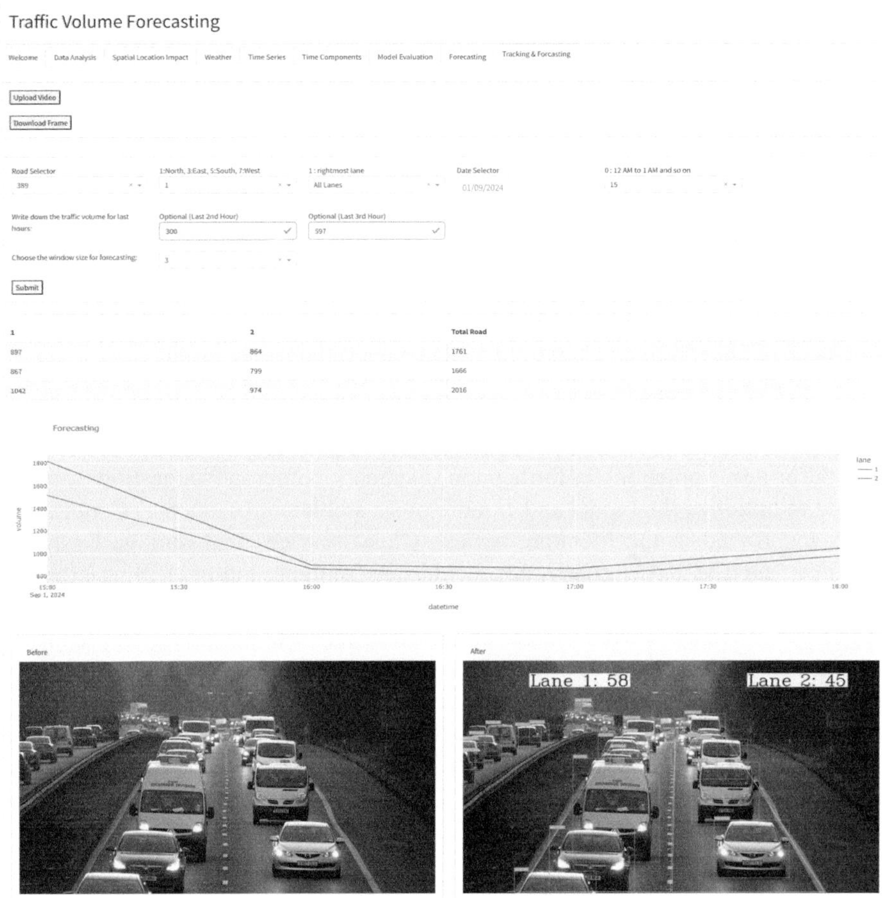

Figure 7: Web Interface.

analysis and answers to the research questions. Visualizations were created using the Seaborn and Plotly libraries, including the performance curves for the forecasting data and the analysis of the data. A sample of the interface is shown in Figure 7, with and without entering the requested inputs.

5.4 Challenges faced

Due to the complexity of the project, various challenges were faced. Some were solved, while others posed a significant challenge:

1. Finding a suitable data source was challenging because this data is mostly confidential and not easily accessible online. Some available sources had significant gaps in the time series, which made those data unsuitable for analysis and forecasting. A more complete dataset would have been preferable.
2. When the data was found, its size was difficult to handle due to the available hardware not being capable of processing it. Data manipulation and preprocessing were both time-consuming and computationally expensive.
3. Even after data preprocessing, feeding the entire dataset into the model was difficult due to RAM limitations on the available hardware, including Kaggle notebooks, which also had constraints. To proceed with model training, it was necessary to reduce the data size, which may have impacted the overall performance.
4. Identifying an optimal model was both time-consuming and computationally expensive. Hardware limitations and time restrictions affected the project's ability to experiment with more models, configurations, and architectures to find the best fit for the data.

Even with these challenges, the project addressed them to the best of its ability, using the available hardware and time to achieve a satisfactory result.

5.5 Future work

Given the project's potential for further improvements, numerous suggestions can still be made to optimize the model and explore more architectures, such as Conditional LSTM, mentioned in the literature review. Cloud services that remove hardware limitations, such as RAM constraints, could help mitigate the overfitting problem observed in deep learning models trained on this dataset. Additionally, improving the tracking functionality to work on real-time footage rather than waiting for the model to process each frame from the video would enhance efficiency. Enhancing the web interface design to make it more user-friendly and intuitive would also be beneficial. Finally, implementing an unsupervised algorithm to categorize the forecasted values and identify high and low traffic flows could provide additional recommendations for the traffic management system.

6. Recommendations & Conclusion

6.1 Recommendations

Based on the data analysis and the understanding of the data, numerous recommendations can be applied to improve traffic flow in the city. First, a schedule for the traffic lights can be devised to reduce the traffic using the data provided by CCTV footage or sensors. By using the forecasting of the model, the city can ensure smoother traffic movements depending on the roads and directions with more vehicles. In addition, some considerations can be taken; for instance, if a road experiences fewer vehicles than expected during specific times, it may indicate severe congestion. Thus, traffic management can enhance and address potential congestion using the forecasting model and data.

Furthermore, analysis of the lanes indicated that lanes 1 to 3 consistently exhibited higher vehicle volumes than other lanes, particularly in locations with more than three lanes. To address this, efforts can be made to minimize obstructions in these lanes at specific times and ensure that roads with these lanes are well-maintained to facilitate smoother traffic flow. The traffic management system should also consider the direction of travel and the number of lanes as critical factors influencing traffic flow. These insights can help in planning infrastructure projects to ensure roads are capable of handling expected traffic volumes and reducing congestion.

6.2 Conclusion

The objective of this project was to develop a method for reducing traffic congestion in a city to enable citizens and workers to carry out their daily activities with minimal disruption. By implementing a YOLOv8 model integrated with BYTETrack, the project successfully counted the number of vehicles on the road, providing the necessary data for the forecasting phase. The use of the XGBoost model to predict the number of vehicles in the following hour allowed for valuable recommendations and insights into traffic management. These recommendations can help traffic control systems prepare for congestion before it occurs, minimizing its impact. Ultimately, this project presents a method for improving traffic flow, reducing congestion, and enhancing overall quality of life.

References

Beard, M., Vo, B.T. and Vo, B.-N. 2020. A solution for large-scale multi-object tracking. *IEEE Transactions on Signal Processing*, 68: 2754–2769. doi:10.1109/tsp.2020.2986136.

Budholiya, K., Shrivastava, S.K. and Sharma, V. 2022. An optimized XGBoost based diagnostic system for effective prediction of heart disease. *Journal of King Saud University - Computer and Information Sciences*, 34(7): 4514–4523. doi:10.1016/j.jksuci.2020.10.013.

Chand, A., Jayesh, S. and Bhasi, A.B. 2021. Road traffic accidents: An overview of data sources, analysis techniques and contributing factors. *Materials Today: Proceedings*, 47: 5135–5141. doi: 10.1016/j.matpr.2021.05.415.

Choy, J.L., Wu, J., Long, C. and Lin, Y.-B. 2020. Ubiquitous and low power vehicles speed monitoring for Intelligent Transport Systems. *IEEE Sensors Journal*, 20(11): 5656–5665. doi:10.1109/jsen.2020.2974829.

Dai, Z., Song, H., Wang, X., Fang, Y., Yun X. and Zhang, Z. 2019. Video-based vehicle counting framework. *IEEE Access*, 7: 64460–64470. doi:10.1109/access.2019.2914254.

Du, Y., Wang, J., Rizos, C. and El-Mowafy A. 2021. Vulnerabilities and integrity of precise point positioning for intelligent transport systems: Overview and analysis. *Satellite Navigation*, 2(1). doi:10.1186/s43020-020-00034-8.

Hussain, M. 2024. Yolov1 to V8: Unveiling each variant–a comprehensive review of Yolo. *IEEE Access*, 12: 42816–42833. doi:10.1109/access.2024.3378568.

Jia, P. et al. 2020. Research on a mine gas concentration forecasting model based on a GRU network. *IEEE Access*, 8: 38023–38031. doi:10.1109/access.2020.2975257.

Karthikeyan, H. and Usha, G. 2023. A secured IOT-based Intelligent Transport System (IOT-its) framework based on Cognitive Science. *Soft Computing* [Preprint]. doi:10.1007/s00500-023-08410-7.

Lartey, B., Homaifar, A., Girma, A., Karimoddini, A. and Opoku, D. 2021. XGBoost: A tree-based approach for traffic volume prediction. *2021 IEEE International Conference on Systems, Man, and Cybernetics* (SMC) [Preprint]. doi:10.1109/smc52423.2021.9658959.

Lin, T.-Y., Maire, M., Belongie, S., Hays, J., Perona, P., Ramanan, D. et al. 2014. Microsoft coco: common objects in context. *Lecture Notes in Computer Science*, pp. 740–755. doi:10.1007/978-3-319-10602-1_48.

Luo, W., Xing, J., Milan, A., Zhang, X., Liu, W. and Kim, T.-K. 2021. Multiple object tracking: A literature review. *Artificial Intelligence*, 293: 103448. doi:10.1016/j.artint.2020.103448.

Lusikka, T., Kinnunen, T.K. and Kostiainen, J. 2020. Public transport innovation platform boosting intelligent transport system value chains. *Utilities Policy*, 62: 100998. doi:10.1016/j.jup.2019.100998.

Landi, F., Baraldi, L., Cornia, M. and Cucchiara, R. 2021. Working memory connections for LSTM. *Neural Networks*, 144: 334–341. doi:10.1016/j.neunet.2021.08.030.

Mahdavian, A., Shojaei, A., Salem, M., Laman, H., Eluru, N. and Oloufa, A.A. 2021. A universal automated data-driven modeling framework for truck traffic volume prediction. *IEEE Access*, 9: 105341–105356. doi:10.1109/access.2021.3099029.

Mahjoub, S., Chrifi-Alaoui, L., Marhic, B. and Delahoche, L. 2022. Predicting energy consumption using LSTM, multi-layer gru and drop-gru neural networks. *Sensors*, 22(11): 4062. doi:10.3390/s22114062.

Mandal, V., Mussah, A. R., Jin, P. and Adu-Gyamfi, Y. 2020. Artificial intelligence-enabled traffic monitoring system. *Sustainability*, 12(21): 9177. doi:10.3390/su12219177.

Moishin, M., Deo, R.C., Prasad, R., Raj, N., and Abdulla, S. 2021. Designing deep-based learning flood forecast model with ConvLSTM hybrid algorithm. *IEEE Access*, 9: 50982–50993. doi:10.1109/access.2021.3065939.

Peppa, M.V., Komar, T., Xiao, W., James, P., Robson, C., Xing, J., and Barr, S. et al. 2021. Towards an end-to-end framework of CCTV-based urban traffic volume detection and prediction. *Sensors*, 21(2): 629. doi:10.3390/s21020629.

Rao, M.G., Priyanka, H., Kumar, A.P. and Divakarala, U. 2022, September. A Deep Learning Approach Towards Building Intelligent Transport System. *In 2022 Second International Conference on Computer Science, Engineering and Applications (ICCSEA)* (pp. 1–6). IEEE.

Rocha Filho, G.P., Meneguette, R.I., Torres Neto, J.R., Valejo, A., Weigang, L., Ueyama, J. et al. 2020. Enhancing intelligence in traffic management systems to aid in vehicle traffic congestion problems in Smart Cities. *Ad Hoc Networks*, 107: 102265. doi:10.1016/j.adhoc.2020.102265.

Rudskoy, A., Ilin, I. and Prokhorov, A. 2021. Digital Twins in the Intelligent Transport Systems. *Transportation Research Procedia*, 54: 927–935. doi:10.1016/j.trpro.2021.02.152.

Sagi, O. and Rokach, L. 2021. Approximating XGBoost with an interpretable decision tree. *Information Sciences*, 572: 522–542. doi:10.1016/j.ins.2021.05.055.

Shepelev, V., Zhankaziev, S., Aliukov, S., Varkentin, V., Marusin, A., Marusin, A. et al. 2022. Forecasting the passage time of the queue of highly automated vehicles based on neural networks in the services of Cooperative Intelligent Transport Systems. *Mathematics*, 10(2): 282. doi:10.3390/math10020282.

Singh, A., Kumar, D.P., Shivaprasad, K., Mohit, M. and Wadhawan, A. 2021. Vehicle detection and accident prediction in sand/dust storms. *2021 International Conference on Computing Sciences* (ICCS) [Preprint]. doi:10.1109/iccs54944.2021.00029.

Sun, P., Aljeri, N. and Boukerche, A. 2020. Machine learning-based models for real-time traffic flow prediction in Vehicular Networks. *IEEE Network*, 34(3): 178–185. doi:10.1109/mnet.011.1900338.

Talaat, F.M. and ZainEldin, H. 2023. An improved fire detection approach based on Yolo-V8 for smart cities. *Neural Computing and Applications*, 35(28): 20939–20954. doi:10.1007/s00521-023-08809-1.

Tao, Y., Sun, P. and Boukerche, A. 2019. A hybrid stacked traffic volume prediction approach for a sparse road network. *2019 IEEE Symposium on Computers and Communications (ISCC)* [Preprint]. doi:10.1109/iscc47284.2019.8969710.

Wang, J. and Boukerche, A. 2021. Non-parametric models with optimized training strategy for vehicles traffic flow prediction. *Computer Networks*, 187: 107791. doi:10.1016/j.comnet.2020.107791.

Wang, Z., Su, X. and Ding, Z. 2021. Long-term traffic prediction based on LSTM encoder-decoder architecture. *IEEE Transactions on Intelligent Transportation Systems*, 22(10): 6561–6571. doi:10.1109/tits.2020.2995546.

Xiang, C., Yang, P., Xiao, F., and Fan, X. 2023. Urban traffic application: Traffic volume prediction. *Multi-dimensional Urban Sensing Using Crowdsensing Data*, pp. 113–150. doi:10.1007/978-981-19-9006-9_5.

Xu, Y., Kong, Q.-J. and Liu, Y. 2013. Short-term traffic volume prediction using classification and regression trees. *2013 IEEE Intelligent Vehicles Symposium* (IV) [Preprint]. doi:10.1109/ivs.2013.6629516.

Yang, H., Zhang, Y., Zhang, Y., Meng, H., Li, S. and Dai, X. 2021. A fast vehicle counting and traffic volume estimation method based on Convolutional Neural Network. *IEEE Access*, 9: 150522–150531. doi:10.1109/access.2021.3124675.

Yasir, M., Shanwei, L., Mingming, X., Jianhua, W., Hui, S., Nazir, S. et al. 2024. Yolov8-byte: Ship tracking algorithm using short-time sequence SAR images for disaster response leveraging geoai. *International Journal of Applied Earth Observation and Geoinformation*, 128: 103771. doi:10.1016/j.jag.2024.103771.

Zadobrischi, E. 2022. Intelligent traffic monitoring through heterogeneous and autonomous networks dedicated to traffic automation. *Sensors*, 22(20): 7861. doi:10.3390/s22207861.

Zhang, Y. et al. 2022. ByteTrack: Multi-object tracking by associating every detection box. *Lecture Notes in Computer Science*, pp. 1–21. doi:10.1007/978-3-031-20047-2_1.

Zheng, Y., Li, X., Xu, L. and Wen, N. 2022. A deep learning–based approach for moving vehicle counting and short-term traffic prediction from video images. *Frontiers in Environmental Science*, 10. doi:10.3389/fenvs.2022.905443.

Zheng, Z., Wang, Z., Zhu, L. and Jiang, H. 2020. Determinants of the congestion caused by a traffic accident in Urban Road Networks. *Accident Analysis & Prevention*, 136: 105327. doi:10.1016/j.aap.2019.105327.

Zheng, Z., Li, J. and Qin, L. 2023. Yolo-byte: An efficient multi-object tracking algorithm for automatic monitoring of Dairy Cows. *Computers and Electronics in Agriculture*, 209: 107857. doi:10.1016/j.compag.2023.107857.

Zhou, Z., Li, Y., Li, J., Yu, K., Kou, G. and Wang, M. 2023. Gan-siamese network for cross-domain vehicle re-identification in Intelligent Transport Systems. *IEEE Transactions on Network Science and Engineering*, 10(5): 2779–2790. doi:10.1109/tnse.2022.3199919.

Zou, X., Chung, E., Zhou, Y., Long, M. and Lam, W.H.K. 2023. A feature extraction and deep learning approach for network traffic volume prediction considering detector reliability. *Computer-Aided Civil and Infrastructure Engineering*, 39(1): 102–119. doi:10.1111/mice.13062.

Chapter 10

Agriculture Forecasting
Predicting Commodity Producer Prices and Yield

Amela Karmaj and *Nitsa J. Herzog**

1. Introduction

The agricultural sector is a vital aspect of global economies, ensuring a proper food supply and, for some primary-based countries, playing a crucial role in economic growth and sustaining livelihoods. However, the inherent volatility in agricultural commodity prices poses significant challenges, affecting both producers and consumers alike. To attain better results in terms of production and sustainability, it has become vital to forecast factors such as commodity yield and price as accurately as possible.

Through previous research, it can be deduced that various statistical methods of agricultural forecasting have been implemented, for example, Autoregressive (AR), Moving Average (MA), Autoregressive Moving Average (ARMA), Autoregressive Integrated Moving Average (ARIMA), and Exponential Smoothing (ES) (Reddy and Sureshbabu 2020). These forecasting algorithms have been proven useful in various situations; however, in terms of agricultural forecasting, due to its overwhelming nature, they have failed to provide highly accurate readings. Presently, the focus has shifted towards Machine Learning (ML), Time Series (TS), and Deep Learning (DL) algorithms. With their introduction, better accuracy and scalability objectives can be met. Adapting to such algorithms enables the analysis of vast amounts of historical data, which is essential for agricultural forecasting and enables stakeholders to make informed decisions in an ever-evolving market landscape.

Faculty of Engineering & Environment, Northumbria University London Campus, UK.
* Corresponding author: nitsa.herzog@northumbria.ac.uk

DOI: 10.1201/9781003540373-10

Even with technological advancements in forecasting algorithms, several obstacles remain. These are either directly related to the algorithm's capability or bound to the user's selection process. Examples include the selection of forecasting datasets and the optimization of machine learning algorithms to meet the forecast's requirements. Moreover, the unpredictability of agricultural commodity prices, influenced by factors ranging from climate change to geopolitical events, further complicates the forecasting process.

These persisting problems within agricultural forecasting highlight the need for a better and more capable method of forecasting, one that can predict commodity yield and price with greater efficiency. Integrating machine learning, statistical analysis, deep learning, and historical data offers a promising avenue for achieving this goal. By implementing modern technology and analytics, it is possible to gain valuable insights into market dynamics, enabling production optimization, minimizing waste, and reducing risks associated with price volatility.

This chapter provides insight into how to enhance productivity and efficiency in the agricultural sector through the implementation of advanced forecasting methodologies, specifically focusing on machine learning, time series analysis, and deep learning algorithms. By leveraging these cutting-edge techniques, the study aims to provide stakeholders with accurate predictions of agricultural yield and price fluctuations, enabling them to make informed decisions and optimize their operations. Through a comprehensive analysis of historical data and the application of sophisticated forecasting models, this study seeks to identify market trends and help drive strategic growth initiatives in the European agricultural economy. By emphasizing the integration of modern forecasting methodologies, the study aims to contribute to the advancement of agricultural forecasting practices, ultimately leading to greater efficiency and competitiveness in the agricultural sector. There will be a wide range of forecasting models leveraging diverse techniques, including time series analysis, machine learning algorithms, and deep learning algorithms. Time series analysis will be utilized to identify patterns and trends in historical data, providing valuable insights into future demand and price movements. Machine learning algorithms, such as decision trees, support vector machines, and neural networks, will be employed to capture nonlinear relationships and extract complex patterns from large datasets. Deep learning algorithms, such as convolutional neural networks and recurrent neural networks, will enable the extraction of high-level features from sequential data, further enhancing forecasting accuracy. Through rigorous experimentation and comparative analysis, the strengths and weaknesses of each forecasting technique will be assessed across diverse agricultural commodities and market conditions. Performance metrics such as the R-Squared score and Mean Squared Error (MSE) will be used to quantify the predictive capabilities of each model. By identifying the most effective forecasting models for specific scenarios, agricultural stakeholders can make informed decisions and implement strategies to optimize productivity, minimize risk, and enhance price efficiency in the agricultural market.

In summary, this chapter will provide an understanding of advancements in the field of agricultural forecasting by developing and implementing innovative models for predicting both yield and price fluctuations of agricultural commodities.

By leveraging a combination of time series analysis and advanced machine learning techniques, this research seeks to empower stakeholders with actionable insights, ultimately contributing to improved productivity, profitability, and sustainability within the agricultural sector.

2. Related Works

2.1 Forecasting onion price using machine learning approach

Hasan et al. (2020) study focuses on the use of machine learning forecast models due to instability in the agricultural commodity market. It is important to emphasize that similar studies have been conducted since the gap between the literature and practical application is yet to be corrected. This study revolves around the use of Artificial Neural Network (ANN), Support Vector Machine (SVM), and Random Forest (RF) and criticizes prior statistical methods since machine learning models have been proven to provide better accuracy.

2.2 IoT-based smart agriculture for crop price prediction

Rana (2019) took a step toward a solution to the immense variables found in agricultural forecasting. By using sensors and various computing hardware, he sought to introduce an IoT-based smart agriculture system aimed at forecasting crop prices. This would be achieved by placing sensors throughout the fields and collecting real-time data. Moreover, through the integration of the sensor-derived data and market trends, the forecasted price would be the output. This study contrasts with various others due to its predictive nature regarding the volatile factors found in agricultural forecasting; however, it is differentiated by the use of IoT devices. Nonetheless, there is still a long way to go toward its practical implementation, leaving room for more literature and practical opportunities within the field.

2.3 Ensemble learning for financial forecasting

The study by (Zhu et al. 2019) encompasses the use of ensemble methods to forecast various financial decisions. It seeks to combine multiple models to reach its purpose. This study, unlike those focused on agriculture, diverts toward finance; however, a similar model can be implemented in the agriculture sector. Other studies (Babu and Mallikharjuna 2022) have found that using a combination of methods usually leads to complexity within the algorithm; however, it results in higher accuracy if done correctly. Such models are also considered costly, but several authorities within agricultural forecasting may seek to use such models if needed. This study portrays similar methodologies within different fields and how they could potentially improve forecasting performance.

2.4 Crop prediction through the utilisation of machine learning

Elbasi et al. (2023) emphasizes the worldwide importance of agriculture, deeming it to be the sole field that tackles the greatest human need for food while highlighting advancements in data processing and decision-making algorithms. The main concept discussed in this study is how ML algorithms aid in sustainable farming by optimizing crop production. This is derived through an efficient decision-making process that provides numerical values to each agricultural process and forecasts the best possible outcomes with the given data so agricultural stakeholders can plan accordingly. Like various studies, setbacks and future implications are also discussed by the author, who used 15 different algorithmic approaches with a high percentage of accuracy throughout the study. Even though several other studies have mentioned minimizing crop waste, this study provides a solution through Bayes Net and Bayes Classifier algorithms. Apart from the different algorithms, the focus of my study was on factors such as weather, whereas this study includes factors such as disease detection, which are not widely researched. Ultimately, the conclusion of the study states that the integration of these algorithms, as the author states, will "revolutionize" the agricultural commodity market.

2.5 Machine learning for large-scale crop yield forecasting

Paudel et al. (2021) explores a similar approach to ours, where they seek to implement ML algorithms to forecast yield; however, there is no mention of its effect on price. The study revolves around large-scale agricultural forecasting since even notable departments such as the European Commission's MARS Crop Yield Forecasting System (MCYFS) have yet to implement ML algorithms. The author comments on the gap identified between research and real-life use of these methods. To the author's knowledge, the European Commission does not lack the resources to implement ML models; however, their current system, MCYFS, accesses data through statistical models. The use of two models, multiple linear regression and principal component analysis, is employed by MCYFS. The author persists that in the future, if MCYFS implements ML algorithms, there will be a significant increase in its practical use in agricultural forecasting, assisting in modernizing the agricultural commodity markets. It is to be noted, however, that results varied slightly from country to country, so the algorithms are yet to be perfected. Hence, their practical implementation would be effective in increasing the accuracy of future research.

2.6 Patterns, similarities, differences in utilization of machine learning

Most of the studies have been conducted using machine learning models, signifying the importance of data-driven methods. Forecasting solutions employ different models such as XGBoost, XGBRFBoost, Random Forest, Prophet, and LSTM networks, with ensemble methods utilized across the studies, demonstrating the versatility of machine learning in different forecasting domains.

Diverse application domains

While some studies focus specifically on agricultural forecasting, others explore forecasting in financial markets and other domains. Despite the differences in application domains, the methodologies and techniques employed are common, indicating the transferability and adaptability of forecasting methods across different domains.

Addressing market instability

Another commonality among the studies is the instability of the agricultural market and the aim to challenge it through forecasting. Stakeholders in the agricultural market can make more informed decisions using machine learning models, as the forecasted results provide a basis for their decisions.

Integration of IoT

The use of IoT devices is a relatively new concept in crop price prediction. It focuses on using sensors to gather real-time data. This data can be processed and used through the implementation of machine learning models to provide forecasted factors that assist in the decision-making process, which in turn benefits overall crop yield.

To summarize the findings, the majority of the studies focused on machine learning models to tackle different forecasting needs aimed at reducing the effects of volatility in the agricultural market. Even though there are discrepancies within the datasets used or the fields of application, each study contributes to advancing forecasting algorithms for better accuracy and timely results.

3. Methods and materials

3.1 Tools and techniques

This research uses Python as a programming language for model development and analysis with the Jupiter Notebook environment. Several libraries, such as scikit-learn, Keras, NumPy, pandas, and matplotlib, are used for visualizations, algorithm implementation, and data manipulation and preparation.

Principal Component Analysis (PCA)

PCA is a linear unsupervised method for feature extraction that reduces the dimensionality of the dataset. It identifies correlations between features in the dataset and transforms the data by reducing its dimensions. This process simplifies the dataset for visualizations and training models (Uddin et al. 2021).

One-Hot Encoding

One-Hot Encoding is one of the most popular encoding methods used before algorithm design. It converts categorical data into binary format and creates new binary features for each unique category. This ensures that all values of the same categorical feature are represented as being equally distinct from each other, preventing the model from assuming an order between the categorical values (Yu et al. 2022).

StandardScaler

StandardScaler is a technique for data preprocessing before designing models. It ensures that all features in the dataset have a standard distribution with a mean of 0 and a standard deviation of 1. This technique improves the overall model performance by ensuring that all features have an equal influence on the model (Aldi et al. 2023).

3.2 Models

Initially, the dataset is split into three subsets: training, testing, and validation, consisting of 76%, 9%, and 15% of the dataset, respectively. To develop accurate predictive models, various algorithms, such as XGBoost, XGBRFBoost, Random Forest, LSTM, and Prophet, are used for both yield and price datasets. At the beginning of the process, the models are trained using the training data, which is also the largest portion of the dataset. During training, the model parameters are adjusted to learn patterns in the data, enabling more accurate predictions for future unseen data.

Extreme Gradient Boosting XGBoost

As the name suggests, XGBoost is a gradient boosting model focused on greater efficiency in the use of decision tree machine learning algorithms. The name stands for "Extreme Gradient Boosting," and it is among the most widely used machine learning libraries worldwide (Wade and Glynn 2020). It employs multiple decision trees simultaneously, with the process beginning with a plain model during the initial run. However, with the use of the gradient descent technique, the loss is minimized. This process is repeated until the loss cannot be minimized further. This suggests that a greater number of repetitions would result in greater accuracy. The concept behind this is that multiple decision trees will outperform a single one (Azmi and Baliga 2020). Hence, each decision tree that is formed may initially provide an inaccurate result, but after several iterations, the results become more efficient.

$$\hat{y}_i = \sum_{k=1}^{K} f_k(x_i), f_k \in \varphi \quad (1)$$

$$\varphi = \{f(x) = w_s(x)\} \; (s{:}R^m \rightarrow T, w_s \in R^T) \quad (2)$$

Equations (1) and (2) are for the result of sample prediction, where $\hat{y}_i$ is the predicted value, x_i represents the independent features and $f_k(x_i)$ is the predicted score at a data point i. φ is a set of regression tree with structure parameters s, f(x) and w present the weight of the leaves and number of leaves, respectively.

Random Forest

Random Forest is an ensemble machine learning method used for classification and regression. It was first developed in 1995 and has been continuously improving since then. The main concept involves building a large collection of decision trees during training. For classification, the final prediction is the class that most trees select, while for regression, the output is the average prediction of individual trees (Li et al. 2021). The algorithm was further improved by Breiman and Cutler in 2007, using bootstrap sampling to train multiple CART decision trees on sub-training datasets. It assesses feature importance through metrics such as the total decrease in node impurity.

The RF algorithm gets the final prediction outcome by averaging the results from several decision trees using mean square error (MSE) for evaluation.

Prophet

Prophet is an algorithm developed by Facebook's Core Data Science team, and it is an open-source model designed to forecast time series data. It incorporates yearly, weekly, and daily seasonality alongside holiday effects, making it ideal for forecasting datasets with strong seasonal patterns (Zunic et al. 2020). Furthermore, Prophet is resilient to missing data, outliers, and trend shifts, ensuring accurate and reliable forecasting for real-world scenarios. It uses a user-friendly interface and is adaptable to different data settings, making it a popular choice among data scientists for time series forecasting.

LSTM

Long Short-Term Memory (LSTM) falls within the subset of Recurrent Neural Networks (RNNs) and is designed to overcome the limitations of RNNs. RNNs have difficulties learning long-term dependencies in sequential data and time series datasets, while LSTM does not have this problem because it incorporates memory cells with gates to control the information flow. LSTMs use these gates to remember relevant information from the past and make accurate predictions based on historical data. Initially, LSTM was designed to provide a solution to the vanishing gradient problem (Gu et al. 2022). Apart from its agricultural use within our research, LSTM has several applications in daily life, ranging from entertainment purposes to medical applications.

4. Data Analysis and Results

4.1 Dataset description

Collecting accurate data is essential for analyzing and training machine learning algorithms. The main factors that impact the accuracy of forecasting models are the quality and size of the dataset (Elbasi et al. 2023). Therefore, it is significant that the dataset is derived from a reliable source. The data for this project is gathered from two websites: the agricultural data is sourced from Food and Agriculture Data (FAOSTAT 2024) (https://www.fao.org/faostat/en/#data), and the data containing the weather conditions is taken from The World Bank website (The World Bank 2024) (https://databank.worldbank.org/).

Initially, there were six datasets, including data for yield, price, pesticides, import-export, average mean temperature, and average precipitation for the countries of Europe. The data covers yearly entries. These datasets are later merged into one dataset to undergo the pre-processing step. The merging is done based on common features such as area, year, and item, resulting in a more coherent dataset. After merging, the data undergoes pre-processing and analysis phases. The merged dataset includes 14 features and 17,195 records. Table 1 shows the description of the dataset.

Table 1: Dataset Description.

Name of the Attribute	Type	Description
Area	Categorical	Shows the European country for which the data applies, 37 countries in total.
Year	Numerical	Years ranging from 1990 to 2022.
Item	Categorical	The agricultural commodity. 13 commodities were chosen: Apples, Cherries, Potatoes, Tomatoes, Wheat, Barley, Cabbages, Carrots and turnips, Cucumbers and gherkins, Maize (corn), Oats, Pears, and Rye.
Area harvested (ha)	Numerical	Total area of land harvested in hectares for a specific commodity.
Production (t)	Numerical	Total commodity production in tonnes.
Yield (100 g/ha)	Numerical	Crop yield per unit area, expressed in units of 100 grams per hectare.
Producer Price (USD/tonne)	Numerical	Price of the commodity per tonne in US Dollars.
Export Quantity (t)	Numerical	Quantity of the agricultural commodity exported in tonnes.
Export Value (1000 USD)	Numerical	Value of exports in thousands of US Dollar.
Import Quantity (t)	Numerical	Quantity of the agricultural commodity imported in tonnes.
Import Value (1000 USD)	Numerical	Value of imports in thousands of US Dollar.
Pesticides (t)	Numerical	Total amount of pesticides used in tonnes within a year.
Annual Mean_temp	Numerical	Annual mean temperature in degree Celsius.
Annual Mean_prec	Numerical	Annual mean precipitation in millimetres.

4.2 Data pre-processing

The pre-processing stage is crucial to ensuring the quality and reliability of results in analysis and model training. Several steps are taken to prepare the dataset for analysis, such as dealing with missing values, checking for duplicates and handling them, and managing outliers.

Data adjustment

Some countries in the dataset no longer exist due to being divided into other nations, such as the USSR, Yugoslav SFR, Belgium-Luxembourg, and Czechoslovakia. Due to this, the data from these countries is distributed among the existing countries they were split into, and the non-existing countries are removed from the dataset. Andorra and the Holy See are removed from the dataset as they do not have enough data for analysis.

Handling missing values

Initially, the dataset contained missing values for some features. Agricultural commodities with more than 25% missing data are deemed unreliable and dropped from the dataset. Most of the missing values are from the years 1990–1997, likely due to a lack of data collection, as technological advancements were not as prevalent during that period. For the remaining missing values, appropriate techniques are applied to fill them based on detected patterns in the features. The missing values for pesticides occur only in one year; therefore, interpolation with spline order 2 is used to fill these gaps. The same interpolation method is used for missing producer price values, as the data is missing for some countries in certain years.

For import and export data, missing values are filled with zero because there was no trade of commodities during those years for some countries. For example, if a country did not produce enough of a product, it would not have had enough to meet domestic demand and export it; therefore, there was no export of that commodity. Similarly, if a country overproduced a commodity, it did not need to import that product, so the import value was zero. Political reasons have also prevented trade in certain years, resulting in missing values being filled with zero.

Handling outliers

By checking the statistics of the dataset, some outliers are found, such as in Production (t), Export Quantity (t), and Export Value (1000 USD). The extreme outlier is the Russian Federation for the wheat product. Research is conducted to verify these values, concluding that the information is correct. In that year, the Russian Federation had a large amount of wheat produced. Because of overproduction, the export of this commodity was also very high, which directly affected the export value. In conclusion, it is revealed that the outliers are legitimate data points caused by overproduction.

Data splitting

Machine learning models retain information on the datasets they were trained on, either through the models' predictions or even by the model itself. Therefore, it is crucial to prevent data leakage, especially when dealing with sensitive information (Hannun et al. 2021). To prevent data leakage and ensure the integrity of the predictive models, the dataset is split into two sets: yield and price. This separation allows the target variables to be predicted independently without mixing information from the other, which could cause data leakage and inaccurate results. The split is done based on research, and the datasets are created containing their respective target feature and the relevant features that affect them, removing any other irrelevant features.

4.3 Feature engineering

4.3.1 Feature selection and feature importance

Feature selection is essential in improving model performance by utilizing only the most important and relevant features. Evaluating feature importance effectively removes irrelevant features and helps determine which features contribute most significantly to the predictive performance of the models. By removing irrelevant data and less important columns with very little information, machine learning models train better and produce more accurate results for unseen data (Otchere et al. 2022).

Variance threshold is used to identify features with low variance and determine which features contain very little information, as they do not contribute significantly to training and predictions. Features with low information will not be selected for model training and forecasting. Variance is checked for both datasets, yield and price. Since it is not possible to determine feature importance just by looking at their variance, Random Forest is used to provide a clearer understanding of the results.

Random forest is used as a feature selection tool to select input features, improving forecasting accuracy. It creates multiple decision trees for regression tasks. Random Forest works by randomly selecting features and data points, leading to better performance and results in training models and predictions (Otchere et al. 2022).

Recursive Feature Elimination (RFE) is a feature selection technique that uses a Random Forest Regression (RFR) estimator to identify the most important features of the dataset by ranking them. RFE reduces model complexity and avoids overfitting. RFE was used to remove the least important features after checking their rank scores. After reviewing the ranking scores, it became evident which features are most important for each dataset.

For the yield dataset, area harvested and pesticides are the most important, ranking first and second, respectively. The least important feature is annual mean precipitation. Meanwhile, for the price dataset, the most important features are area harvested, import value, annual mean temperature, and yield, while the least important are import quantity and annual mean precipitation.

4.3.2 Dimensionality reduction with Principal Component Analysis (PCA)

Datasets with too many features can be challenging for model training, so this problem is addressed by reducing the number of features while keeping only the most important ones. Principal Component Analysis (PCA) is used to perform the reduction and retain only the most relevant features. PCA is chosen because most of the data is numerical, and PCA captures the most informative variations in the data. This process reduces model complexity and improves performance. After PCA is applied, it becomes apparent which features carry the most information in the datasets.

PCA revealed the number of features with the most significance in the datasets. It was determined that five features in the price dataset hold the most information, and for yield, there is one key feature. When the model is trained, only these features will be used to avoid data leakage.

4.4 Data analysis and insights

4.4.1 Yield and producer prices over time

Overall, yield and producer prices have a positive correlation for most commodities, as shown in Table 2. This indicates that both increase and decrease together over time, with some exceptions. Additionally, the correlation between yield and producer price for each commodity over the years was analyzed.

Table 2: Correlation of Yield and Producer Prices.

Item	Correlation Value
Apples	0.510057
Barley	0.411466
Cabbages	0.676244
Carrots and Turnips	0.788042
Cherries	–0.698792
Cucumber and Gherkins	0.0730428
Maize(Corn)	0.019248
Oats	0.321419
Pears	–0.600185
Potatoes	0.531171
Rye	0.224972
Tomatoes	0.872816
Wheat	0.248728

In general, throughout most of the years, most commodities have a positive correlation, as both yield and price change in the same way. However, there are some exceptions, such as cherries and pears, which, according to the graphs and correlation scores, have a negative correlation with yield. This indicates that when the yield is high for these products, the price decreases, and when the yield is lower, the price increases. A few reasons for this are that cherries and pears are perishable fruits, meaning if there is a surplus, the market will be flooded, and they will need to be sold quickly due to their short shelf life, causing a drop in price. Additionally, these products might not have high demand, further affecting their prices. When there is a low yield of cherries and pears, prices rise because demand exceeds production.

For the rest of the commodities, prices increase and decrease in line with the yield. This is because these commodities are important and in high demand from the food industries and serve as primary ingredients for in many food products. Therefore, an increase in yield does not necessarily result in price drop. However, there are still instances where the opposite occurs, such as barley from 2014 to 2020. In these years, yield increased, but the price decreased. Another notable change is in maize (corn) between 2019 and 2022, where yield significantly increased while price sharply declined. Similarly, rye from 1990 to 1995 experienced a small increase and decrease in yield, but the price dropped significantly over those five years.

Another factor affecting price changes is production costs, including fuel price fluctuations, fertilizer costs, and transportation expenses. Additionally, import and export restrictions imposed by governments can influence market prices, leading to situations where yield and price do not always change in tandem. Lastly, based on the graphs, both price and yield have been increasing over time. The main reasons for this are population growth, increased demand, and price inflation.

4.4.2 The impact of pesticide usage on production

Figure 1 shows a scatterplot of the relationship between pesticide usage and production for all European countries. It is noticeable that production tends to be higher in regions where pesticide usage exceeds 60,000 tonnes, though this relationship is not consistent. There are instances where pesticide usage is high, but production is lower, and vice versa. These anomalies might be due to other factors such as soil quality, climate, and pest resistance.

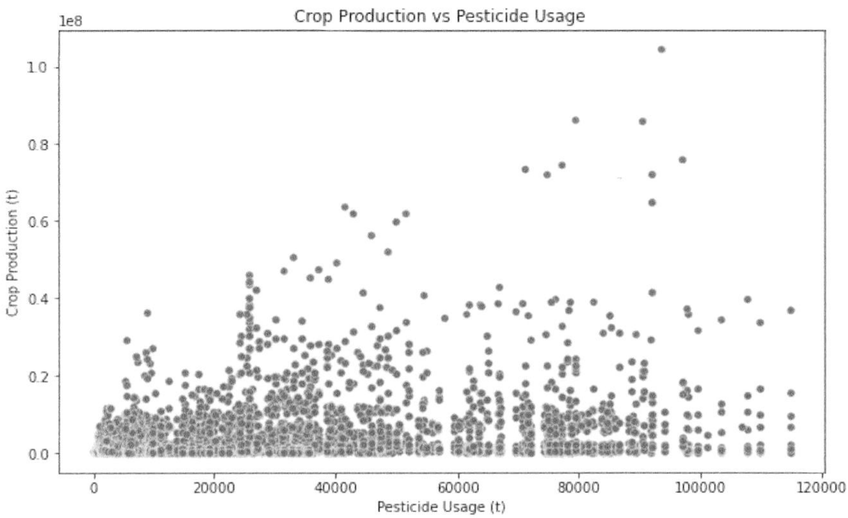

Figure 1: Scatterplot of Production (t) by Pesticide Usage (t).

4.4.3 The top 5 most-produced commodities in Europe

Europe's top five most-produced commodities are wheat, potatoes, maize, barley, and rye (see Figure 2). Wheat production is significantly higher than that of other commodities, standing at 6.7 million tonnes. Meanwhile, potatoes and maize appear to be produced in similar quantities, with barley slightly less than these two. Rye, on the other hand, even though it is one of the top five most-produced commodities on average, is produced considerably less than the other four, at 7.89 million tonnes. There are several reasons why these products dominate in Europe. All five commodities are suitable for European regions as they are adaptable to most climates and soils. Wheat ranks first due to its versatility in the food industry and high global demand. Potatoes and maize (corn) are also highly important for the food industry, but potatoes have a shorter storage life, and maize performs better in slightly warmer areas. These limitations contribute to their lower production quantity compared to wheat. Barley and rye are mainly used for animal feed and specific products such as beer (barley) and bread (rye); however, they are in lower demand than wheat.

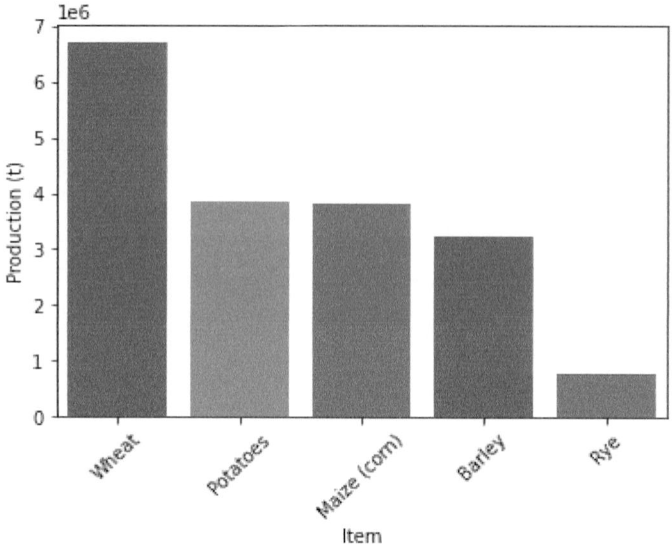

Figure 2: Top Five Most Produced Commodities.

4.4.4 Production and producer price analysis

An analysis of producer prices and production quantities reveals a strong correlation between the two, implying that agricultural commodities with lower production quantities have higher prices. Cherries stand out with a significantly higher price, surpassing other commodities, while also having the lowest production quantity. Interestingly, cherries, pears, cucumbers, and gherkins are among the commodities with the highest prices and lowest production quantities. This suggests that low production quantity is a primary factor influencing price increases. Their low production levels may be due to lower demand compared to other products. As a result, their prices tend to be higher due to lower availability.

Tomatoes and apples are also among the commodities with the highest producer prices. The reason for their high prices can be attributed to several factors. Both tomatoes and apples are widely consumed and in high demand across various food industries, ensuring that their prices remain high in the market.

Additionally, four out of the five commodities with the lowest producer prices are among the most-produced items in Europe. This highlights the impact of high production quantities on producer prices. Due to an oversupply in the market and the fact that these crops are among the most commonly consumed, their prices remain low. Although not one of the top five most-produced commodities, oats have the second-lowest producer price due to global market conditions, as they are widely produced in other regions.

4.4.5 Hypothesis analysis

The relationship between producer prices and export and import quantities was analysed to test the following hypothesis.

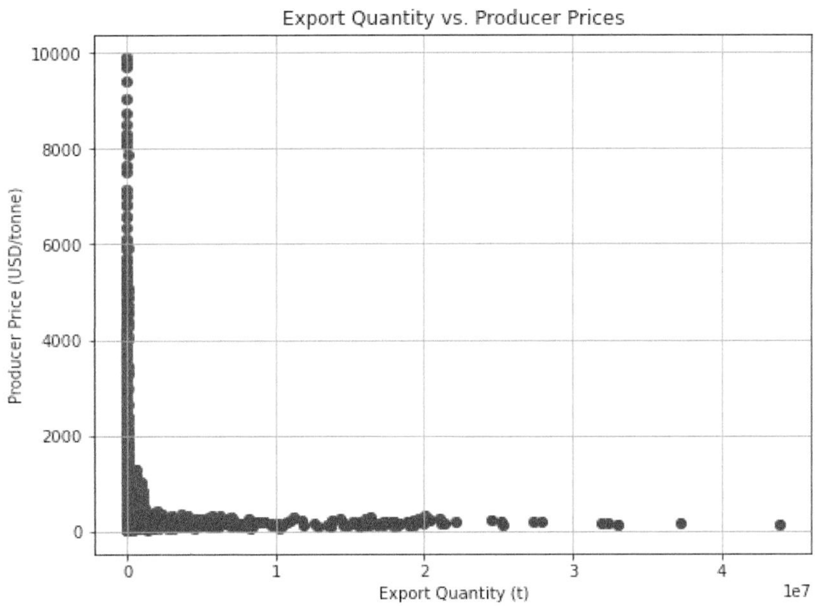

Figure 3: Scatterplot Producer Price (USD/tonne) by Export Quantity (t).

Null Hypothesis: There is no significant correlation between export quantity, import quantity and producer prices.

Alternative Hypothesis: There is a significant correlation between export quantity, import quantity and producer prices.

The analysis revealed weak correlations between producer price and both export and import quantities, with coefficients of –0.062 and –0.083, respectively. Meanwhile, there is a weak positive correlation (0.07) between import quantity (t) and export quantity (t). These findings suggest that there is no significant relationship among the variables; therefore, further analysis was conducted to better understand the results.

Figure 3 shows that when export quantity is low, prices are high, but as exports increase, prices tend to stabilize. Similarly, when import quantities are low, prices are high, and as imports increase, prices become more stable, as seen in Figure 4.

The analysis concluded that there might be a slight decrease in producer price when export quantity increases, but producer prices and import quantity do not appear to be strongly related. In conclusion, even though there is a correlation between producer prices and export quantity, the correlation is very weak. Therefore, the null hypothesis is accepted, meaning there is no significant correlation between export quantity and import quantity with producer prices. This suggests that other factors could influence prices besides export or import quantities.

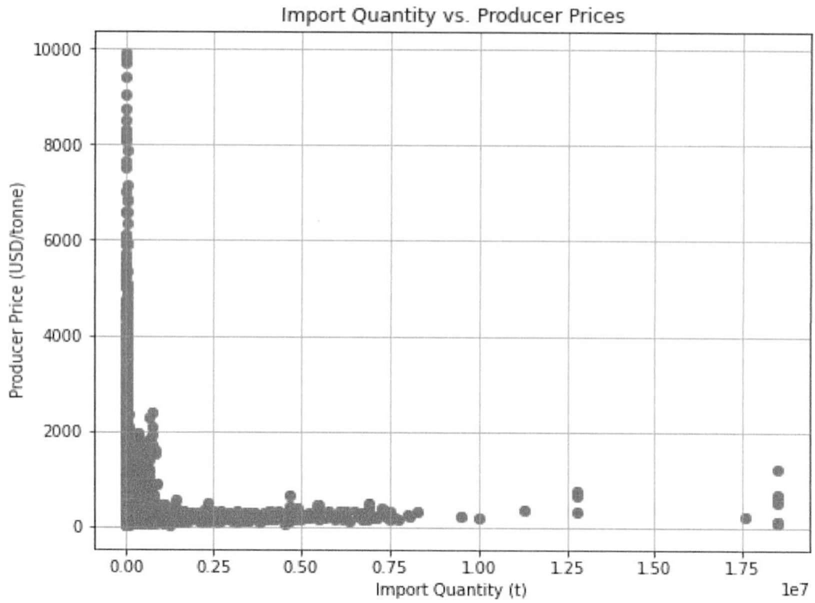

Figure 4: Scatterplot Producer Price (USD/tonne) by Import Quantity (t).

4.5 Model selection and evaluation

Data analysts utilize models and machine learning techniques to forecast outcomes and gain better insight into data. However, it is important to choose the most suitable model to ensure the most accurate results. Therefore, model selection is a crucial step in research (Ding and Yang 2018).

After completing feature engineering and data analysis, the next step is model selection, where several different algorithms are evaluated for their accuracy in predicting commodity yields and prices. Since the datasets contain historical data and are primarily numerical, the algorithms used in this project include XGBoost, XGBRegressor, Prophet, Random Forest, and LSTM. Each algorithm is trained and evaluated using Mean Squared Error (MSE) (3) and the R-squared Score (4).

$$MAE = \frac{\sum_{i=1}^{n} |y_i - x_i|}{n} \tag{3}$$

y_i = prediction value

x_i = true value

n = total number of data points

$$R^2 = 1 - \frac{\sum_{i=1}^{n} (y_i - \hat{y}_i)^2}{\sum_{i=1}^{n} (y_i - \bar{y})^2} \tag{4}$$

y_i is the actual value of the dependent feature for i iteration.

$\hat{y}_i$ is the predicted value of the dependent feature for i iteration.

$\bar{y}$ is the mean of the actual values for the dependent feature.

Σ is the sum over all iterations from 1 = 1 to n.

4.5.1 Data preparation

To develop effective prediction models, data needs to be split into training, testing, and validation sets. As mentioned in the methodology, the datasets were split into three sets before training: training, testing, and validation, consisting of 76%, 9%, and 15% of the data, respectively. This division ensures that the model is properly evaluated and prevents overfitting.

The Standard Scaler technique was applied to scale the data, ensuring that all features have a standard deviation of one and a mean of zero. This makes the features comparable and improves model performance.

Additionally, since the dataset contains categorical variables such as Area and Item, One-Hot Encoding was applied to convert the categorical data into binary format, allowing the models to interpret them. This ensures that there will not be any bias in the models caused by the categorical values.

4.5.2 Model Evaluation and Performance Analysis

XGBoost Regressor

The XGBoost Regressor was used on both the yield and price datasets. Two pipelines were employed to ensure consistency and achieve better results. One pipeline incorporated PCA to evaluate model performance with dimensionality reduction. Meanwhile, the other pipeline was used without PCA and included all the training features. Both pipelines were trained on their respective training datasets. MSE and R^2 scores were calculated on both validation and training sets in both cases. Based on the scores in Table 3, XGBoost performed better with PCA implementation in both datasets, exhibiting a lower MSE score, even though the R^2 score was slightly lower. When the model did not use PCA, there seemed to be overfitting. XGBoost performed significantly better for the price dataset than for the yield dataset.

Table 3: XGBoost Regressor Evaluation Metric Scores.

	Price		**Yield**	
	PCA	**No PCA**	**PCA**	**No PCA**
MSE Train	7166.36	2774.05	6.57e+09	1.65e+09
MSE Validation	61762.83	57297.68	1.6e+10	1.85e+10
R^2 Score Train	0.98	0.99	0.99	0.99
R^2 Score Validation	0.9	0.92	0.98	0.97

XGBRF Regressor

XGBRF Regressor is a variant of the XGBoost algorithm, which is also part of the gradient boosting algorithms. It is known for its good performance in handling large datasets. Like XGBoost, two pipelines were implemented for the XGBRF Regressor: one with PCA and one without PCA.

Based on the results in Table 4, the XGBRF Regressor performed better when the pipeline had no PCA in both datasets. In both cases, the MSE score was lower, and the R^2 score was higher when PCA was not implemented. Additionally, it achieved a better score for the price dataset compared to the yield dataset. Overall, XGBRF Regressor performed worse than XGBoost.

Table 4: XGBRF Regressor Evaluation Metric Scores.

	Price		**Yield**	
	PCA	**No PCA**	**PCA**	**No PCA**
MSE Train	61323.5	40410.53	9.19e+10	2.89e+10
MSE Validation	135153.68	104750.85	1.42e+11	6.54e+10
R^2 Score Train	0.82	0.82	0.76	0.94
R^2 Score Validation	0.78	0.82	0.68	0.89

Random Forest

Random Forest combines multiple decision trees to make predictions. Similar to the previous algorithms, Random Forest was evaluated using two pipelines: one with PCA and one without. Once the model was trained, MSE and R^2 scores were calculated in Table 5. The results show that Random Forest performed better when PCA was not used. Comparing the scores, it can be observed that Random Forest without PCA, for the yield dataset, was less prone to overfitting due to the decrease from train prediction to validation prediction. Overall, for both datasets, Random Forest demonstrated better performance without PCA.

Table 5: Random Forest Evaluation Metric Scores.

	Price		**Yield**	
	PCA	**No PCA**	**PCA**	**No PCA**
MSE Train	4498.19	3171.09	3.45e+09	1.50e+09
MSE Validation	76453.76	65122.92	1.46e+10	2.08e+10
R^2 Score Train	0.99	0.99	0.99	0.99
R^2 Score Validation	0.88	0.90	0.99	0.96

LSTM

For the LSTM model, the input data was reshaped into a 3D array because LSTM expects the data to be in the shape of (samples, time steps, and features). A sequential model was created, and two layers were added. The first layer had 50 units, took the reshaped input data as input, and returned sequences. The second layer had 30 units and also returned sequences. After the two LSTM layers, a Dense Layer with one unit was added; this layer was responsible for producing the regression output. When the model was trained, the epoch was set to 200, meaning the model was trained over 200 iterations on the whole dataset. The batch size was set to 1, indicating the model updated after each sample. Verbose was set to 2 and displayed progress during model training. After training, predictions were made on validation and training sets. As shown in Table 6, the MSE score was lower for the price dataset, but even though the MSE for yield was high, the R^2 score was very high, indicating the model was able to explain a large portion of the dataset. The R^2 score was similar for the training set of both datasets.

Table 6: LSTM Evaluation Metric Scores.

	Price	**Yield**
MSE Train	5852.05	4.66e+09
MSE Validation	57575.44	1.23e+10
R^2 Score Train	0.99	0.99
R^2 Score Validation	0.91	0.98

Prophet

To prepare the data for Prophet, the datasets for price and yield were copied to two other variables, but the column 'Year' was renamed to 'ds', and the name of the target variable was changed to 'y'. The renaming of these two columns was necessary for Prophet because it requires the input data to have a specific format where 'ds' represents the time variable, and 'y' is the target variable the model will predict. In this model, PCA with one component was used to reduce the dimensionality of the numerical features and improve the model's performance by keeping only the most important information. Additionally, the One-Hot Encoder was applied to the categorical features to ensure the dataset was compatible with the model. At the end, the MSE and R^2 scores were calculated. Based on Table 7, the MSE score was extremely high in both the yield and price datasets, and the R^2 score was negative; therefore, this model had very little predictive power.

Table 7: Prophet Evaluation Metric Scores.

	Price	**Yield**
MSE Train	7.20e+05	7.39e+11
MSE Validation	1.01e+06	9.50e+11
R^2 Score Train	–1.57	–2.22
R^2 Score Validation	–2.77	–3.17

4.5.3 Final model optimization

Based on the performance of the used models, it was concluded that the Long Short-Term Memory (LSTM) model was the best choice for both yield and price datasets. The LSTM model outperformed the other models, having the lowest Mean Squared Error (MSE) score and the highest R^2 Score. However, to further enhance the model's performance, hyperparameter tuning was implemented to identify the best combination of parameters.

Hyperparameter tuning

The LSTM model needs several parameters to be set, such as the number of input neurons, the number of hidden neurons, the optimizer, the number of hidden layers and the dropout rate. For a number of input neurons and a number of hidden neurons, values of 30, 40 and 50 were explored. For a number of hidden layers, we used the values 0, 1 and 2. For the optimizer, 'adam' and 'adadelta' were considered. Values of 0, 0.1 and 0.2 were used for the dropout rate. For epochs, the options 200 and 300 were explored, and lastly, for batch 1, 32 and 64 were used. Once the hyperparameters are set, RandomizedSearchCV was employed to perform a randomized search across the parameter grid. RandomizedSearchCV evaluated the performance of the model by using cross-validation in order to identify the best-performing parameter combination.

Both training and validation sets are processed similarly, and MSE and R^2 scores are used to indicate the accuracy of the prediction. The best parameters identified were: 'optimizer': 'adam', 'number_hidden': 2, 'neurons_input': 40, 'neurons_hidden': 30, 'epochs': 300, 'drop_out': 0.2, 'batch_size': 1.

Model training

Once the best hyperparameters were identified, they were used to train the model for yield and price on both the training and testing sets. The LSTM model was then used on the full dataset, and the performance results of the model are summarised in Table 8.

Table 8: Final LSTM Model Evaluation Metric Scores.

	Price		**Yield**	
	MSE	**R^2 Score**	**MSE**	**R^2 Score**
Train	18698.90	0.96	9.07e+09	0.98
Test	59271.21	0.93	3.76e+10	0.95
Full	11568.96	0.98	6.10e+09	0.99

4.5.4 Predictions

To predict the target features for the years 2023, 2024, and 2025, two techniques were utilized to handle the missing data of the independent features for these years: Interpolation and Prophet. These methods were used to fill in the missing independent features for these years, enabling the LSTM model to predict the target features.

Interpolation

For producer price, a new dataset was created, including the three future years to be predicted, with all other features initially set to null for these years. All columns except 'Producer Price (USD/tonne)' column, were filled by using various interpolation techniques, such as linear and spline (order 1 and 2). Once the dataset was prepared, the LSTM model was used to predict producer prices for the future.

Prophet

The other approach used to predict the missing independent values for the future years was Prophet. Similar to interpolation, a dataset for the future years was created, and the dataset was grouped by area and item. For each unique combination of area and item, Prophet was applied to predict the missing values of the independent features. Prophet was trained on the given dataset, which was then used to predict future prices. Finally, the missing values for producer prices and yield were predicted using the respective LSTM models for the datasets.

5. Results

Out of all the models used to predict producer prices and yield, LSTM was found to work the best and was the most effective for both datasets, making it the chosen model for prediction. This indicates that the LSTMs captured underlying patterns better than the other models. Even though LSTM showed promising results, there is still potential for further improvement by increasing the complexity of the model.

Based on the comparison of the evaluation metrics (MSE and R^2) in Table 8, it is concluded that the LSTMs effectively capture the data, especially when trained on the full dataset.

$$MSE_{Total} < MSE_{Train} < MSE_{Test}$$

$$R^2_{Total} > R^2_{Train} > R^2_{Test}$$

While predicting the future values for the target features, the interpolation technique for independent feature filling, the LSTM, did not give promising results on either of the datasets, as the predicted values deviated significantly from the pattern of the data.

Prophet was used as an alternative approach. It was the most effective prediction model for both datasets, giving satisfying results.

The most suitable technique for filling in missing data depends on the patterns and characteristics of the dataset. This research's analysis showed that interpolation was not an effective approach, while Prophet performed better for both datasets.

6. Conclusion

This research aimed to improve the standards of agricultural forecasting algorithms through the use and analysis of various models, such as XGBoost and Long Short-Term Memory (LSTM), by forecasting commodity yield and prices within the European agricultural sector. Such algorithms provided stakeholders with accurate forecasts, allowing for better decision-making, which led to greater yield control. Advanced algorithms give insights into the market to enable strategic growth within the field. This study introduced various forecasting algorithms, such as those mentioned above, to enable the reader to understand the complexities of agricultural forecasting. The focus shifted to machine learning algorithms due to the competitive edge they provide. Moreover, each algorithm displayed certain characteristics that allowed it to remain effective in different conditions.

Through a series of experiments, this study analysed the strengths and weaknesses of various forecasting models under several different conditions. Performance metrics such as Mean Squared Error (MSE) and R^2 scores were used to quantify the predictive capabilities of each model, and as a result, LSTM emerged as the most effective model, particularly for capturing underlying patterns in the data. However, while LSTM delivered the best results in this study, there is still room for improvement. To achieve more accurate forecasting results, additional data, such as soil temperature, water supply, and fertiliser usage, would be essential. More complex forecasting models would also help improve results.

In essence, this study fulfils its purpose of advancing agricultural forecasting through the implementation of a diverse network of algorithms, providing price and commodity yield forecasts. The introduction of machine learning models also provides positive insight into future improvements within such models and assists in improving current forecasts to a greater capacity.

References

(FAOSTAT, 2024) https://www.fao.org/faostat/en/#data

(The World Bank, 2024) https://databank.worldbank.org/

Aldi, F., Hadi, F., Rahmi, N.A. and Defit, S. 2023. Standardscaler's potential in enhancing breast cancer accuracy using machine learning. *Journal of Applied Engineering and Technological Science* (JAETS), 5(1): 401–413.

Azmi, S.S. and Baliga, S. 2020. An overview of boosting decision tree algorithms utilizing AdaBoost and XGBoost boosting strategies. *Int. Res. J. Eng. Technol.*, 7(5): 6867–6870.

Babu, K.S. and Mallikharjuna Rao, K. 2022, February. Onion price prediction using machine learning approaches. In Proceedings of International Conference on Computational Intelligence and Data Engineering: ICCIDE 2021 (pp. 175–189). Singapore: Springer Nature Singapore.

Ding, J., Tarokh, V. and Yang, Y. 2018. Model selection techniques: An overview. *IEEE Signal Processing Magazine*, 35(6): 16–34.

Elbasi, E., Zaki, C., Topcu, A.E., Abdelbaki, W., Zreikat, A.I., Cina, E. et al. 2023. Crop prediction model using machine learning algorithms. *Applied Sciences*, 13(16): 9288.

Gu, Y.H., Jin, D., Yin, H., Zheng, R., Piao, X. and Yoo, S.J. 2022. Forecasting agricultural commodity prices using dual input attention LSTM. *Agriculture*, 12(2): 256.

Hannun, A., Guo, C. and van der Maaten, L. 2021, December. Measuring data leakage in machine-learning models with fisher information. *In Uncertainty in Artificial Intelligence* (pp. 760–770). PMLR.

Hasan, M.M., Zahara, M.T., Sykot, M.M., Hafiz, R. and Saifuzzaman, M. 2020, July. Solving onion market instability by forecasting onion price using machine learning approach. In 2020 International conference on computational performance evaluation (ComPE) (pp. 777–780). *IEEE.*

Li, X., Geng, T., Shen, W., Zhang, J. and Zhou, Y. 2021. Quantifying the influencing factors and multi-factor interactions affecting cadmium accumulation in limestone-derived agricultural soil using random forest (RF) approach. *Ecotoxicology and Environmental Safety*, 209: 111773.

Otchere, D.A., Ganat, T.O.A., Ojero, J.O., Tackie-Otoo, B.N. and Taki, M.Y. 2022. Application of gradient boosting regression model for the evaluation of feature selection techniques in improving reservoir characterisation predictions. *Journal of Petroleum Science and Engineering*, 208: 109244.

Paudel, D., Boogaard, H., de Wit, A., Janssen, S., Osinga, S., Pylianidis, C. et al. 2021. Machine learning for large-scale crop yield forecasting. *Agricultural Systems*, 187: 103016.

Rana, S. 2019. AI Based Precision and Intelligent Farming System. Information Technology in Industry, 7(3): 31–37.

Reddy, P.C.S. and Sureshbabu, A. 2020. An applied time series forecasting model for yield prediction of agricultural crop. In Soft Computing and Signal Processing: Proceedings of 2nd ICSCSP 2019 2 (pp. 177–187). Springer Singapore.

Reddy, T., RM, S.P., Parimala, M., Chowdhary, C.L., Hakak, S. and Khan, W.Z. 2020. A deep neural networks-based model for uninterrupted marine environment monitoring. *Computer Communications*, 157: 64–75.

Uddin, M.P., Mamun, M.A. and Hossain, M.A. 2021. PCA-based feature reduction for hyperspectral remote sensing image classification. *IETE Technical Review*, 38(4): 377–396.

Wade, C. and Glynn, K. 2020. Hands-on gradient boosting with XGBoost and scikit-learn: Perform accessible machine learning and extreme gradient boosting with Python. Packt Publishing Ltd.

Yu, L., Zhou, R., Chen, R. and Lai, K.K. 2022. Missing data preprocessing in credit classification: One-hot encoding or imputation? *Emerging Markets Finance and Trade*, 58(2): 472–482.

Zhu, Y., Zhou, L., Xie, C., Wang, G.J. and Nguyen, T.V. 2019. Forecasting SMEs' credit risk in supply chain finance with an enhanced hybrid ensemble machine learning approach. *International Journal of Production Economics*, 211: 22–33.

Zunic, E., Korjenic, K., Hodzic, K. and Donko, D. 2020. Application of facebook's prophet algorithm for successful sales forecasting based on real-world data. arXiv preprint arXiv:2005.07575.

CHAPTER 11

Supporting Sustainable Supply Chains with Explainable Artificial Intelligence

Elias Pimenidis[1,*] and *John Patsavellas*[2]

1. Introduction

Supply Chain 4.0 is the way in which products and services are generated with the use of a mix of disruptive technologies properly interoperable. The main Industry 4.0's technologies include Internet of Things, Cloud Computing, Artificial Intelligence, Big Data Analytics, Additive Manufacturing, Robotics, Blockchain and Augmented Reality. When effectively integrated, these technologies enhance supply chain processes in terms of efficiency, integration, collaboration, responsiveness, flexibility, quality, and transparency. The concept was tested and proved effective during the recent pandemic and the limitations it created. Artificial Intelligence played a significant role, with machine learning making a major contribution to supporting the management of supply chains at both national and international scales.

This worldwide emergency taught supply chain managers and participating companies valuable lessons on how to survive in circumstances far from normal. These lessons can be further integrated into existing processes and practices to support supply chains in increasing efficiency, developing added flexibility, and becoming more sustainable—both in terms of business stability and environmental impact.

[1] University of the West of England, Bristol, BS16 1QY, United Kingdom.
[2] Cranfield University, Cranfield, MK43 0AL, United Kingdom.
Email: John.Patsavellas@cranfield.ac.uk
* Corresponding author: elias.pimenidis@uwe.ac.uk

DOI: 10.1201/9781003540373-11

Sustainable supply chains need the collaboration between large corporate partners, with access and collaboration to worldwide chains, and smaller partners operating at national and even local level, to be successful. The smaller, more localised members of the supply chain contribute added flexibility while also fostering sustainable supply chains, strengthening national and local business bases, and supporting a more sustainable global environment.

In previous work, the authors discussed the use of blockchain technologies with the support of Intelligent Agents to provide an efficient, effective, and sustainable supply chain that integrates both local and global partners (Pimenidis et al. 2021). At the time, the world was experiencing considerable restrictions due to the Covid-19 pandemic, making local partners essential, while large organisations assumed additional costs that smaller entities might not have been able to bear. In a normally operating and competitive world, however, smaller companies might find themselves at a disadvantage. Large organisations benefit from an abundance of data that allows them to run complex machine learning algorithms, effectively supporting decision-making at various operational levels. In contrast, smaller partners often manage small volumes of specialist data that complex, data-hungry algorithms cannot process effectively. This often prevents them from benefiting from the wealth of data shared across a blockchain, potentially leading to their exclusion from regular collaboration with large supply chains. Such an impact on smaller partners reduces the flexibility and sustainability of the supply chain, limits the benefits of machine learning, and disrupts the chain, ultimately affecting the sustainability of local societies, business environments, and individual organisations.

Large manufacturing organisations, where decision-making models are complex, rely heavily on advanced data analytics. These data enable managers to make efficient and effective business and operational decisions using tools, techniques, and processes—including algorithms that help businesses organise, visualise, and curate data (McManus 2020). The emphasis is on the speed and accuracy of decision-making. However, using vast volumes of data and data-hungry algorithms poses risks to the entire supply chain, creating imbalances in information sharing and disrupting the synchronous functionality of the chain (De Lara and Grech 2018).

This does not only threaten the survival of small partners in the supply chain but also impacts local-level sustainability, which, in the long term, could weaken the larger supply chains. As a result, when flexible and efficient local services are required, they may no longer be available.

To enable small but essential supply chain companies to become regular contributors, machine learning algorithms need to be optimised for processing smaller volumes of data. This work proposes how explainable artificial intelligence can contribute to more efficient, flexible, and adaptive supply chains, ultimately fostering sustainable business environments, societies, and economies.

2. Previous work

The authors had previously addressed the challenges of supply chain management in the modern era through the use of blockchain technology combined with the intelligence of Autonomous Agents, as shown in Figure 1. In this concept, Federated Blockchains

Figure 1: A diagrammatic representation of a Blockchain and Intelligent Agents enabled Supply Chain (Pimenidis et al. 2021).

provide a secure environment for connecting companies and organisations within a closed group of collaborating supply chain members. These members support each other in achieving a seamless supply chain, backed by the wealth of data stored in the secure ledger at the centre of any blockchain. Such a system enhances the resilience of the entire supply chain, acting as an insurance mechanism against disruptions that could compromise its functionality and efficiency (Runkaporta 2023). The blockchain ledger securely records all transactions within the supply chain and can feed this data to Machine Learning Algorithms to support supply chain management. Intelligent Agents, deployed at each node, facilitate communication between blockchain nodes, enabling automated contract negotiations that ensure the smooth operation of the supply chain (Demertzis et al. 2022, 2021).

The above concept of supply chain management is inspired by a much older work by one of the authors, where the concept of a digitally supported supply chain management system was built upon the theory of Value-Added Communities. These are groupings of members of integrated supply chains where each member feeds information to other members directly related to them as the next link in the chain (Pimenidis et al. 2002). These were systems that depended on technologies predominant in the mid-1990s to the early 2000s when the internet was still slow, storage systems were expensive and difficult to manage, and communication systems for sharing data were costly to acquire and use. Information flowed from one partner to another, as shown in Figure 2, but was not stored and shared as in blockchain. Each partner could be the weakest link in terms of security. ML algorithms were rather slow and of low performance at the time. The improvement introduced in supporting decision-making was based on the speed of information received and its

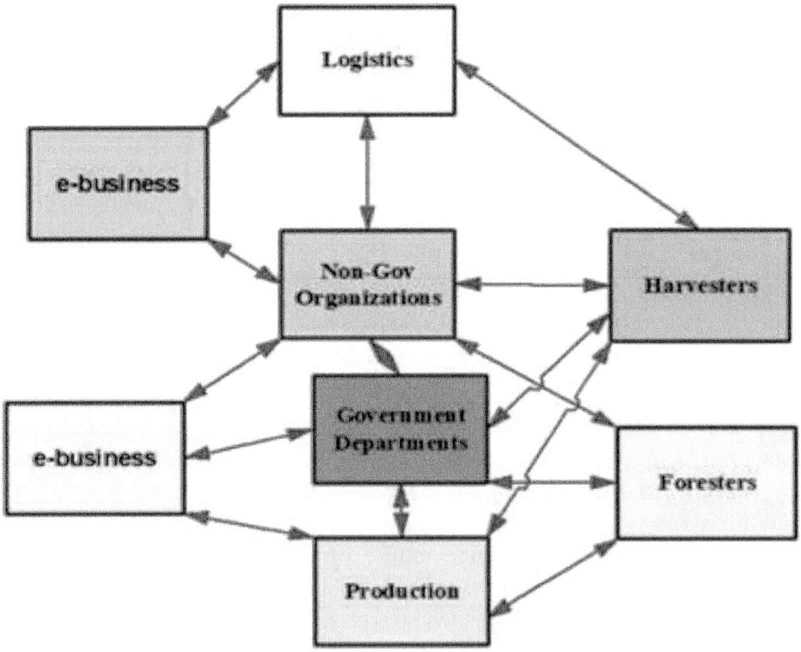

Figure 2: Value-Added Communities in Supply Chain (Pimenidis and Iliadis 2003).

reflection of current demands on the partners. Intelligent Agents were used to plan operations over a longer life cycle (Pimenidis and Iliadis 2003).

The wisdom of the supply chain is based on Machine Learning (ML) providing intelligence in managing, sequencing, and distributing orders and operations among members. Thus, ML contributes to optimising the supply chain by processing data in the shared secure ledger. ML algorithms are often data-hungry, requiring large volumes of data to train models and even more to seek solutions and draw conclusions that support decision-making in managing the supply chain (Han and Zhang 2020).

3. Explainable Artificial Intelligence

ML algorithms can support decision-making in a wide range of applications. They use large datasets to train models such as Neural Networks, which are subsequently utilised to solve problems related to the same datasets based on their ability to process very large volumes of data. Such systems are often seen as black box systems that offer no transparency in their processing, leading to concerns about the accuracy, consistency, and reproducibility of results achieved.

Over the past two decades, AI has enjoyed great successes, but these have come with additional costs and responsibilities. The most successful methods are often so complex that it is difficult for humans to retrace, understand, and interpret how a certain result was achieved. Therefore, explainability, interpretability, and understandability are motivated by the lack of transparency in black-box AI approaches.

This black box culture in AI supports and inflates issues of trust and acceptance, particularly in ML-based decision-making, where results are questioned.

Furthermore, increasing legal and data protection challenges related to the origins, use, and lack of transparency in handling data by ML-based systems are arising. For instance, the European General Data Protection Regulation (GDPR), in force since May 2018, complicates the use of black-box approaches, particularly in domains that affect human life, such as healthcare (Holzinger et al. 2022). Similarly, in the U.S.A., the government introduced the Algorithmic Accountability Act, which requires companies to assess their machine learning systems for bias and discrimination, necessitating corrective measures. Such regulations pose challenges for many organisations that rely heavily on ML but struggle with explainability, which is an inherent requirement of American legislation (Islam and Eberle 2021).

The concept of explainability is not new—it is inherent in human nature to understand the mechanisms through which results are obtained, decipher their logic, and adapt and reuse them in different situations. The goal is to enable human experts to understand why an AI decision has been made. This is highly relevant for causal understanding, thus enabling ethical, responsible AI and transparent, verifiable machine learning in decision support (Holzinger et al. 2022).

The international scientific community has developed a wide range of different methods and approaches to provide ample opportunities for explainability, but selecting and applying the right approach depends on the nature of the problem and the types of data available. Despite such progress, open challenges remain, including the quantification of explainability, compromises in performance, and information sacrifices.

Explainability refers to the details and reasons a model provides to make its functioning clear or easy to understand. The literature distinguishes between models that are interpretable by design and those that require external methods for explainability. Explainable AI (XAI) techniques are increasingly used across multiple fields in industry and academia (Saleem et al. 2022).

This work does not attempt to analyse different XAI techniques but instead focuses on supply chain problems, which typically involve structured and tabular data. While such data appears easily interpretable, it requires complex processing. Different XAI applications use various approaches to logically induce explanations into the black-box nature of ML.

One such approach is domain knowledge infusion, proposed by Islam and Eberle (2021). This method enhances explainability by incorporating domain knowledge into black-box models, reducing the level of information sacrifice while improving the explainability score. In their research on intrusion detection, they applied proxy task-based explainability quantification, demonstrating that their approach yielded better explainability scores than models that did not integrate domain knowledge. Although intrusion detection data may resemble supply chain data, the complexity of the problems differs.

Another widely used XAI method is Anchors. The core idea is to explain individual predictions of any black-box classification model by finding a decision rule that sufficiently anchors the prediction. The explanations are in the form of IF-THEN statements, defining regions in the feature space. The predictions in these regions are "anchored" to the class of the data point to be explained. The classification remains the same no matter how much the other feature values of the data point, that are not part of the anchor, are changed.

Good anchors have high precision and high coverage. Precision is the proportion of data points in the region defined by the anchor that have the same class as the data point being explained. Coverage describes how many data points an anchor's decision rule applies to. Consequently, the more data points an anchor covers, the better, because the anchor then covers a larger area of the feature space and thus represents a more general rule.

Anchors is a model-agnostic explanation method. It can be applied to any prediction model without requiring knowledge about the internals. Search and construction of decision rules is done by reinforcement learning in combination with a modified beam search, a heuristic search algorithm that extends the most promising nodes in a graph. The anchors algorithm cycles through different steps to produce candidate anchors, select the best candidates, and then use beam search to extend the anchor rules. To select the best candidate, it is necessary to call the model many times, which can be viewed as an exploration or multi-armed bandit problem. Although anchors are model-independent and can be applied to different domains such as tabular data, images, and text, the easiest applications are for tabular and text data (Islam and Eberle 2021).

4. Sustainable Data Systems

Present-day business environments follow the trend towards greater product variety and customisation. This development has accentuated the need for agile and reconfigurable production systems to cope with the increasing range of products and product families. To design and optimise production systems, as well as to choose the optimal product matches, product analysis methods are required. This inevitably leads to the continuous evolution of efficient comparison and selection of appropriate product family combinations for production systems. In turn, this generates the need for enhanced tools that analyse products based on their functional features and physical architectures to support the optimisation of existing production lines. This continuous improvement process in production design and optimisation inevitably raises the challenge of enhancing operations and aligning them with complementary services and processes within the supply chain. This ensures that all partners' operations are synchronised to deliver efficiency and effectiveness (Kaur et al. 2022).

The need for continuous analysis and improvement across a supply chain raises the urgency for AI and ML algorithms to evolve and address these challenges. This is not always easy to achieve, as any supply chain engages organisations of varying sizes and complexities. The differences among these entities result in data that varies in nature, size, complexity, and degree of integrity. To enable ML models to operate accurately and generate effective results that drive the entire supply chain towards excellence and success, data must undergo the same level of processing. The challenge of achieving this with smaller but equally important partners raises sustainability concerns within the supply chain. Explainable AI (XAI) presents a potential solution for advancing sustainable development in supply chains, with its impact extending beyond the strict confines of the supply chain.

4.1 Sustainability goal 9

In 2015, all United Nations Member States adopted the 2030 Agenda for Sustainable Development, providing a shared blueprint for peace and prosperity for people and the planet, both now and in the future. At the core of the agenda are 17 Sustainable Development Goals (SDGs), each further divided into actions designed to build initiatives that support a global partnership for sustainable environments, workplaces, and societies worldwide. The overarching goal is to eradicate poverty and other deprivations by executing strategies that improve health and education, reduce inequality, and drive economic growth, all while addressing climate change and preserving oceans and forests (United Nations 2015).

Goal 9 is particularly relevant to this work: "Build resilient infrastructure, promote inclusive and sustainable industrialisation, and foster innovation." The challenge lies in balancing industrialisation and quality of life. In the context of this research, the focus is on the impact of AI on industrial sustainability and how XAI can moderate this impact to ensure that the overarching sustainability focus is maintained. The most relevant target (9.4) aims to upgrade infrastructure and retrofit industries to enhance sustainability, with a focus on resource-use efficiency and the adoption of clean, environmentally sound technologies and industrial processes. Efficiency in resource use and the effectiveness of employed technologies are central to this study.

4.2 Data centres and their impact on energy consumption

Mass data consumption is a characteristic of complex and otherwise efficient AI systems. This leads to the need for large and electric power-hungry data centres that house vast collections of data that are continuously processed by very powerful servers. The consumption of electricity leads to the need for all these complex and sensitive system to be kept under controlled environments and cool temperatures. This then leads to further demands, such as natural resources used to constantly cool the systems.

A major concern with data centres is that industry trends show an annual growth in demand of 15%, for the foreseeable future (Cliford-Chance 2023). Such an increase in usage brings sustainability concerns, since data centres already use 1.5 percent of global electricity consumption, making providers a key player in the hunt for net zero. Improving data centre cooling energy efficiency presents many challenges to the data centre industry. At the heart of such challenge lies the implementation of efficient and sustainable data centre cooling solutions. The average modern data centre uses around 40 percent of its power for cooling, to provide a secure, high-quality service, by keeping processors and other hardware in optimal conditions. The future of data centre cooling techniques must bring methods that remove this excess heat in a more environmentally friendly way. Addressing the cooling challenge in data centres is crucial for sustainable operations (Osaka 2023). In seeking alternative to electricity-based cooling systems, data centre designers have opted for natural cool air that leads to free cooling.

Despite the obvious advantages of energy and cost savings, such systems come with restrictions related to locality and other disadvantages that can be summarised as follows: limited to regions with colder climates or cold seasons, variability in external conditions affecting performance, and the potential need for backup cooling solutions in case of unexpected changes. Other major cooling systems include liquid cooling. These may not consume as much energy as electricity-based ones and can overcome some of the limitations of air cooling systems, but they come with their own major challenge—massive usage of water resources. These systems often tap into potable water sources, and the world is already facing considerable challenges with potable water becoming scarce in warmer months across many regions globally. In 2021, global trends indicated that the availability and quality of water were growing concerns. Projections suggested that water demand would increase by 55% between 2000 and 2050 due to growth from manufacturing (+400%), thermal power generation (+140%), and domestic use (+130%) (Digital Reality n.d.).

ICT and data centres are another sector contributing to this demand. The trend does not appear to be changing so far. Figure 3 below shows the continuing trend of energy consumption by data centres at present and in the near future. Addressing the

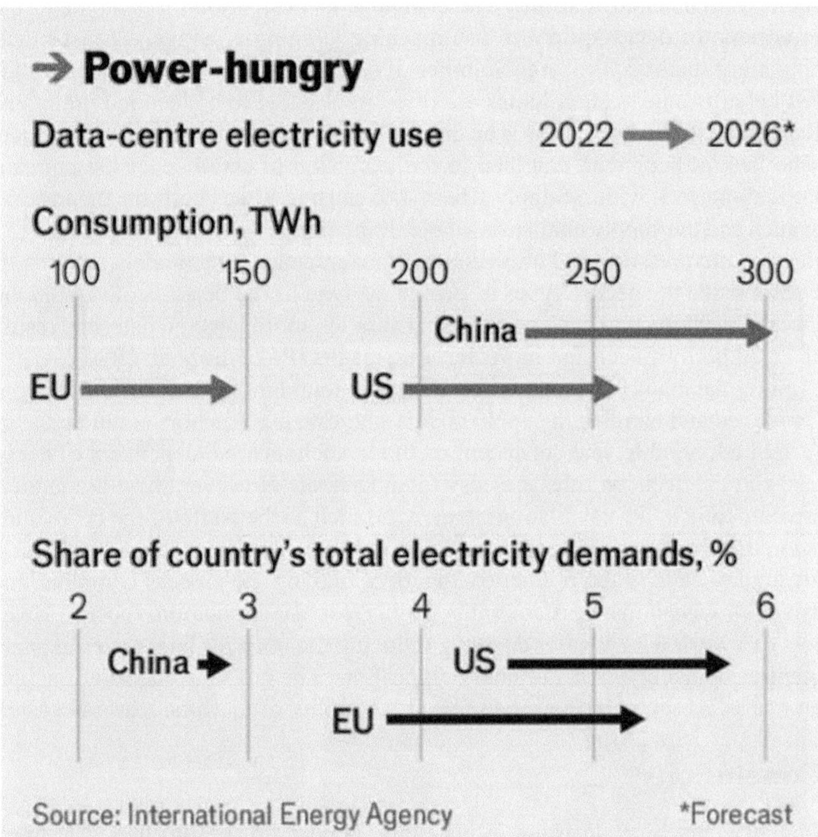

Figure 3: Power Hungry Data Centres, (The Economist 2024).

challenge of data-hungry algorithms and, consequently, power-hungry data centres is a major challenge for the future of AI and a sustainable world.

4.3 Taming data hungry algorithms with XAI

Supply Chain 4.0 is the way in which products and services are generated using a mix of disruptive technologies that are properly interoperable. The main Industry 4.0 technologies include the Internet of Things, Cloud Computing, Artificial Intelligence, Big Data Analytics, Additive Manufacturing, Robotics, Blockchain, and Augmented Reality. When effectively integrated, these technologies enhance supply chain processes in terms of efficiency, integration, collaboration, responsiveness, flexibility, quality, and transparency. The concept was tested and proved effective during the recent pandemic and the limitations it created. Artificial Intelligence played a significant role, with machine learning making a major contribution in supporting the management of supply chains at global and national levels.

The impact of machine learning is not always evident in the operations and performance of small companies, which are often essential in supporting local supply chains. Small specialist component manufacturers, in particular, may struggle to benefit from machine learning. The challenge is mostly non-monetary and relates to the volume of data required to use machine learning effectively. Most machine learning algorithms require large volumes of data to perform optimally and yield the desired benefits, and such volumes are often impossible to collect and maintain for small organisations whose focus is on day-to-day survival rather than data production.

The lack of such data can lead to the exclusion of small specialist companies from collaborations within Supply Chain 4.0, causing losses both for the individual companies and the supply chain as a whole. Explainable Artificial Intelligence (XAI) enables the interpretation and intervention of machine learning models, making them more responsive to specific types of problems. One of the benefits of XAI is that it produces algorithms that can operate using smaller, more targeted datasets, resulting in enhanced performance and more accurate results (Polatidis et al. 2020).

Among the many XAI methods and models found in the literature, the nature of data produced and handled in supply chains suggests that Anchors could be the most easily applied, reliable, and consistent method. Anchors are independent of decision models, and the decision rules are easy to understand. However, there are numerous hyperparameters in the calculation of anchors, such as the width of the beam and the precision threshold, which need to be tuned individually. The calculation of anchors requires many calls to the prediction function, making the process computationally intensive. This can impact sustainability by increasing computational costs. However, anchors can work with smaller datasets, reducing the need for large, ever-expanding data centres by using less data-hungry algorithms. The quality of decisions achieved remains satisfactory, contributing to the sustainability of machine learning systems.

5. Conclusions

Data-hungry machine learning algorithms appear to be driving AI towards technological solutions that could create inequalities in benefits across different companies. This could lead to imbalances in supply chains and, eventually, underperformance. At the same time, smaller organisations may face exclusion from complex supply chains due to insufficient data, preventing them from participating as equal partners.

Using explainable AI, machine learning algorithms can offer enhanced decision-making solutions for supply chains, regardless of company size, data availability, or structural complexity. The tabular data commonly available in supply chain systems can benefit from the XAI method Anchors. This approach allows sustainable supply chains to incorporate both small and large organisations, supporting local environments and societies. Small datasets processed by machine learning systems will require less data storage and, consequently, fewer data centres, leading to reduced resource wastage and contributing to a more sustainable world.

References

Cliford-Chance. 2023. Data Centre Trends 2023, https://www.cliffordchance.com/content/dam/cliffordchance/briefings/2023/02/data-centre-trends-in-2023.pdf [Accessed 28 November 2024].

De Lara, S. and Grech, C. 2018. Blockchain and Transaction Regulation, ITNOW, Volume 60, Issue Winter 2018, Pages 24–25, https://doi.org/10.1093/itnow/bwy094.

Demertzis, K., Iliadis, L., Pimenidis, E., Tziritas, N., Koziri, M., Kikiras, P. et al. 2021. Federated blockchained supply chain management: a cybersecurity and privacy framework. Proceedings of the17th IFIP WG 12.5 International Conference, AIAI 2021, Crete, Greece, 25 – 27 June, 2021 pp 769-779. https://doi.org/10.1007/978-3-030-79150-6_60.

Demertzis, K., Iliadis, L., Kikiras, P. and Pimenidis, E. 2022. An explainable semi-personalized federated learning model. *Integrated Computer-Aided Engineering*, 29(4): 335–350. https://doi.org/10.3233/ICA-220683.

Digital Reality. (n.d.). The Future of Data Centre Cooling: Innovations for Sustainability, https://www.digitalrealty.co.uk/resources/articles/future-of-data-center-cooling [Accessed 28 November 2024].

Han, C. and Zhang, Q. 2020. Optimization of supply chain efficiency management based on machine learning and neural network. *Neural Computing and Applications*. https://doi.org/10.1007/s00521-020-05023-1(2020).

Holzinger, A., Saranti, A., Molnar, C., Biecek, P. and Samek, W. 2022. Explainable AI methods - a brief overview. *In*: Holzinger, A., Goebel, R., Fong, R., Moon, T., Müller, KR. and Samek, W. (eds.). xxAI - Beyond Explainable AI. xxAI 2020. Lecture Notes in Computer Science, vol 13200. Springer, Cham. https://doi.org/10.1007/978-3-031-04083-2_2.

Islam, S.R. and Eberle, W. 2021. Implications of combining domain knowledge in explainable artificial intelligence. *In*: Martin, A., Hinkelmann, K., Fill, H.-G., Gerber, A., Lenat, D., Stolle, R. et al. (eds.). Proceedings of the AAAI 2021 Spring Symposium on Combining Machine Learning and Knowledge Engineering (AAAI-MAKE 2021) – Stanford, University, Palo Alto, California, USA, March 22–24, 2021. https://ceur-ws.org/Vol-2846/paper32.pdf.

Kaur, R., Patsavellas, J., Haddadb, Y. and Salonitis, K. 2022. Carbon accounting management in Complex Manufacturing Supply Chains: A structured framework approach. *Procedia CIRP*, 107(2022): 869–875. 55th CIRP Conference on Manufacturing Systems.

McManus, J. 2020. Competing in the Digital Age, ITNOW, 62, Issue (3): 52–53, https://doi.org/10.1093/itnow/bwaa084.

Osaka, S. 2023. A new front in the water wars: Your internet use, Washington Post, 25 April 2023 https://www.washingtonpost.com/climate-environment/2023/04/25/data-centers-drought-water-use/ [Accessed 20 November 2024].

Pimenidis, E., Patsavellas, J. and Tonkin, M. 2021. Blockchain and artificial intelligence managing a secure and sustainable supply chain. *In*: Jahankhani, H., Jamal, A. and Law-son, S. (eds.). Cybersecurity, Privacy and Freedom Protection in the Connected World. Advanced Sciences and Technologies for Security Applications. Springer, Cham. https://doi.org/10.1007/978-3-030-68534-8_23.

Pimenidis, E., Miller, C.J. and MacEachen, C.F. 2002. A new look at project estimation for E-business. *In*: Proceedings the International Conference on Project Management. Breakthrough with Project Management – In the Era of Global Revolution by IT (ProMAC2002), 31 July – 2 August 2002, Singapore, pp. 353–358.

Pimenidis, E. and Iliadis, L. 2003. E-collaboration in the rural Areas. *In*: Proceedings of itafe'03 – International Congress on Information Technology in Agriculture, Food and Environment, 7 – 10 October 2003, Ege University, Izmir, Turkey, pp. 80–84.

Polatidis, N., Papaleonidas, A., Pimenidis, E. and Iliadis, L. 2020. An explanation-based approach for experiment reproducibility in recommender systems. *Neural Computing & Applications*, 32: 12259–12266. https://doi.org/10.1007/s00521-019-04274-x.

Runkaporta, T. 2023. Right Story, Wrong Story, pp. 83–84, The Text Publishing Company, Melbourne, Australia.

Saleem, R., Yuan, B., Kurugollu, F. Ashiq Anjum, F.A. and Liu, L. 2022. Explaining deep neural networks: A survey on the global interpretation methods. *Neurocomputing*, 513: 165–180, http://creativecommons.org/licenses/by/4.0/.

The Economist. 2024. The very real constraints on artificial intelligence in 2025, https://www.economist.com/search?q=The+very+real+constraints+on+artificial+intelligence+in+2025 [Accessed 20 November 2024].

United Nations. 2015. The 17 Sustainable Goals, https://sdgs.un.org/goals [Accessed 25 November 2024].

CHAPTER 12

QRNG-Powered Quantum-resistant Blockchain for Secure and Scalable IoT Healthcare Machine Learning models

Osama Hussien, Anil Kaya, Hamid Jahankhani* and *Abdul Salih*

1. Introduction

IoT healthcare systems are emerging as a promising paradigm for improving the quality and efficiency of healthcare services and outcomes by enabling the collection and analysis of large-scale health data from various sources and devices, such as sensors, wearables, smartphones, and medical records (Pradhan et al. 2021).

IoT healthcare data can provide valuable insights and benefits for various healthcare stakeholders, such as patients, doctors, nurses, researchers, and policymakers (Islam et al. 2015, Kaur et al. 2021), by facilitating personalized and preventive healthcare, remote monitoring and diagnosis, disease detection and prediction, treatment optimization and evaluation, and healthcare policy making and regulation (Singh et al. 2023, Nissar et al. 2024). However, IoT healthcare data sharing also poses several challenges, such as data security, privacy, scalability, and quantum computing threats, which need to be addressed to ensure the trustworthiness and usability of the IoT healthcare systems (Awotunde et al. 2021).

Data security and privacy are essential for protecting sensitive health data from unauthorized access and disclosure, which can cause serious harm and damage to

Northumbria University London, UK.
Emails: anil.kaya@northumbria.ac.uk; hamid.jahankhani@northumbria.ac.uk; abdul.salih@northumbria.ac.uk
* Corresponding author: ossama.akram@northumbria.ac.uk

DOI: 10.1201/9781003540373-12

data owners and users, such as identity theft, fraud, discrimination, and reputation loss (Douglass 2022, Rosner and Kenneally 2019). Data security and privacy also require the preservation of data integrity and provenance, which ensure the accuracy and authenticity of the data and its sources. Scalability is another challenge for IoT healthcare data sharing, as it requires support for high-volume and high-velocity data transactions, which can overwhelm existing data storage and processing infrastructures, such as centralized servers or cloud platforms. Scalability also requires support for data interoperability and standardization, which enable seamless and consistent data exchange and integration among different data formats, protocols, and platforms.

Quantum computing threats are a new and emerging challenge for IoT generally and in healthcare specifically. The potential of quantum computers can lead to the breaking of existing cryptographic schemes that secure data and blockchain transactions, such as public-key encryption, digital signatures, and hash functions (Thomasian and Adashi 2021, Faruk et al. 2022). Quantum computers can exploit the quantum phenomena, such as superposition and entanglement, to perform parallel and exponential computations, which can outperform the classical computers and algorithms (Ramezani et al. 2020). Quantum computing threats can compromise the data security and privacy, as well as the blockchain security, which can undermine the trust and confidence of the IoT healthcare systems (Althobaiti and Dohler 2020, Cui et al. 2020).

Data poisoning attacks are a specific type of data security and integrity threat, where malicious actors inject false or corrupted data into the system to compromise its functionality and reliability. Data poisoning attacks can target data sources, such as sensors or devices; data transmission, such as wireless or wired networks; or data processing, such as servers or cloud platforms. These attacks can have various goals and impacts, such as manipulating data analysis and inference, disrupting data communication and coordination, or sabotaging data quality and reputation. Data poisoning attacks can also affect machine learning models that are trained and enhanced using IoT healthcare data, rendering the model's predictions faulty and jeopardizing healthcare outcomes (Ahmed and Kashmoola 2022, Newaz et al. 2020, Huang et al. 2022).

In response to the challenges faced by IoT healthcare systems, this research put forth a solution in the form of a quantum-resistant blockchain platform called Omnipoint Secure Suite Platform or OssPlat for short. This platform is designed specifically for IoT healthcare data sharing and utilizes quantum-resistant cryptographic primitives, including lattice-based schemes, to safeguard both the data and the blockchain transactions. We also introduce a novel concept of mutual trust between the server and the client. This concept is instrumental in preventing data poisoning attacks by ensuring that data is verified and validated both before and after transmission and processing. This does not only maintain the integrity and provenance of the data but also upholds its quality and reputation.

By leveraging the decentralized, transparent, and immutable characteristics of blockchain technology in the backbone of OssPlat, it allows for the creation and maintenance of a shared and immutable record of transactions among multiple parties without the need for a trusted central authority (Talukder et al. 2023, Notheisen et al.

2017). This technology brings several benefits to IoT healthcare data sharing. It ensures the integrity and authenticity of the data, making it virtually impossible for any unauthorized alterations to go unnoticed (Lai et al. 2021). Furthermore, it enhances the security of the data by providing a robust mechanism against common cyber threats, thereby fostering trust among the participating entities (Lai et al. 2021). It also facilitates seamless and efficient data exchange across different healthcare institutions, promoting interoperability and collaboration for improved patient care (Lai et al. 2021).

OssPlat employs quantum-resistant cryptographic primitives, which are cryptographic schemes capable of resisting quantum attacks. These schemes use complex mathematical problems that even quantum computers find hard to solve, such as lattice-based problems. These primitives provide quantum-proof data security and privacy, as well as quantum-proof blockchain security and consensus, thereby securing data and transactions from quantum adversaries.

The concept of mutual trust between the server and the client in OssPlat is a unique feature that helps prevent data poisoning attacks. This is achieved by establishing a trust relationship between the server (the data provider or processor) and the client (the data requester or consumer). The trust relationship is based on the verification and validation of the data before and after data transmission and processing.

OssPlat is designed to enhance the efficiency and scalability of the blockchain network by implementing a blockchain-based PKI infrastructure that uses post-quantum cryptography. We also discuss the strengths and weaknesses of OssPlat, along with future work and improvements.

The rest of the paper is organized as follows: Section 2 presents the related work and the research gap, Section 3 describes the methodology and the implementation details of OssPlat, Section 4 reports and analyzes the evaluation results and findings, and Section 5 concludes the paper and provides some directions for future research.

2. Related Works

In this section, we review the current IoT healthcare systems, blockchain technology, quantum computing, and data poisoning attacks, and identify the research gap that motivates our work. IoT healthcare systems are widely studied and applied in various domains and applications, such as chronic disease management, telemedicine (Dadkhah et al. 2021), smart hospitals (Uslu et al. 2020), and wearable devices (Dwivedi et al. 2022). IoT healthcare systems can offer many advantages, such as improving the accessibility and affordability of healthcare services, enhancing the quality and efficiency of healthcare delivery, and empowering the patients and caregivers with more control and information. However, IoT healthcare systems also face many challenges, such as data security, privacy, scalability, and interoperability, which require effective solutions and standards (Abounassar et al. 2022, Bhuiyan et al. 2021). Blockchain technology is a promising solution for addressing some of the challenges of IoT healthcare data sharing, as it can provide data security, privacy, integrity, provenance, interoperability, and standardization, by using cryptographic schemes and smart contracts. Several studies have proposed and implemented

Table 1: Related Works Table.

This paper at (Li et al. 2022) proposes an efficient and reliable two-way authentication scheme for federated chains, using elliptic curves and bilinear pairs, without relying on a centralized CA (Certification Authority).	Researcher at (Li et al. 2022) proposes a two-way authentication scheme for federated chains. This scheme, which employs elliptic curves and bilinear pairs as cryptographic primitives, aims to improve the security of identity authentication in federated chains. It directly performs membership authentication through smart contracts, addressing the issues of one-way authentication and the vulnerability of centralized Certification Authority (CA). The paper also introduces a scheme using Lagrangian interpolation for key recovery and update. On the other hand, this research proposes a quantum-resistant blockchain platform for IoT healthcare data sharing. This platform uses lattice-based schemes and true random number generation for nonce generation as quantum-resistant cryptographic primitives. It introduces the concept of mutual trust between the server and the client, which can prevent data poisoning attacks. The platform is designed to resist quantum attacks and prevent data poisoning attacks from untrusted sources as it is based on a quantum-resistant algorithm (NTRU and HarakaV2). The paper evaluates the performance, security, and usability of OssPlat using real-world healthcare IoT data and scenarios.
This paper at (Boyen et al. 2021) presents a novel scheme called decentralized PKI transparency (DPKIT), which aims to improve the security and transparency of the existing public key infrastructure (PKI) model.	The scheme leverages a blockchain-based ledger to store and verify certificates and revocations, as well as Merkle binary search trees to provide efficient and privacy-preserving proofs of membership for clients. The scheme is compatible with the current PKI and does not require any changes from the certificate authorities or the domain owners. The scheme also supports multiple certificates and multiple domain names per certificate and provides a reliable revocation mechanism. The paper defines the security properties of DPKIT, such as non-removability, proof consistency, and revocation reveal, and proves that they are satisfied under the ideal-ledger assumption. The proposed system differs from the DPKIT scheme in several aspects, such as the application domain, the source of randomness, the type of blockchain, and the trust model. While DPKIT focuses on certificate transparency for any domain using an associative distributed ledger, our proposal aims to achieve data integrity and privacy for healthcare data using a QRNG-based blockchain and lattice-based schemes. Moreover, DPKIT does not require any mutual trust between the server and the client, which can cause data poisoning attacks whereas our proposed work establishes mutual trust verification that helps prevent such attacks by ensuring both data sources and recipients are authenticated through the blockchain-based PKI infrastructure.

Researchers at (Fei et al. 2020) propose a method for establishing network trust in the industrial Internet. The method extends the network connection object from human to machine equipment, industrial products, and industrial services, providing a safe and credible environment for the development of the industrial Internet and a trust guarantee for cross-enterprise entities and data sharing.	In terms of similarities, both our research and research at (Fei et al. 2020) propose solutions that leverage blockchain technology to enhance data security and establish trust in their respective domains. Both recognize the importance of trust in the context of data sharing and propose methods to establish and maintain this trust. However, the paper differs in its focus areas and the specific challenges they address. The (Fei et al. 2020) proposal is focused on the industrial Internet and discusses the challenges of establishing trust in a fully interconnected industrial system. Our proposal, meanwhile, is focused on IoT healthcare systems and addresses the challenges of data security, privacy, scalability, quantum computing threats, and data poisoning attacks in these systems. It proposes a quantum-resistant blockchain platform to secure data and transactions from quantum attacks and prevent data poisoning attacks.
Researchers at (Pietro et al. 2018) present a distributed trust model for the IoT that leverages existing trust domains to create end-to-end trust between IoT devices. It introduces a new cryptographic primitive, the obligation chain, designed as a credit-based blockchain with a built-in reputation mechanism. The primary challenge it addresses is establishing trust in IoT systems, particularly between service providers and consumers.	In terms of methodology, the authors at (Pietro et al. 2018) proposed a protocol that involves creating, downloading, and fulfilling obligations according to the terms set by the service provider. However, our proposal leverages quantum-resistant cryptographic primitives and introduces the concept of mutual trust between the server and the client to secure IoT healthcare data sharing. Both papers address the challenge of establishing trust in IoT systems, but research at (Pietro et al. 2018) focuses particularly on trust between service providers and consumers, where obligations are created, downloaded, and fulfilled according to the terms set by the service provider. Both pieces of research contribute valuable insights and solutions to the ongoing development of secure and efficient IoT systems.

blockchain-based platforms for IoT healthcare data sharing, such as MedRec (Azaria et al. 2016), HealthChain (Rahoof and Deepthi 2020), and MedBlock (Fan et al. 2018). These platforms can enable secure and efficient data sharing among various healthcare stakeholders, such as patients, doctors, hospitals, insurers, and researchers, and support various healthcare applications, such as electronic health records, medical insurance, clinical trials, and drug supply chain. However, most of these platforms rely on the conventional cryptographic schemes, such as Elliptic Curve Cryptography (ECC), which are vulnerable to quantum attacks.

In this section, we review the current existing literature on the topics of IoT healthcare systems, blockchain technology, quantum computing, and data poisoning attacks, and identify the research gap that motivates our work. IoT healthcare systems are widely studied and applied in various domains and applications, such as chronic disease management, telemedicine (Dadkhah et al. 2021), smart hospitals (Uslu et al. 2020), and wearable devices (Dwivedi et al. 2022). IoT healthcare systems can offer many advantages, such as improving the accessibility and affordability of healthcare services, enhancing the quality and efficiency of healthcare delivery, and empowering patients and caregivers with more control and information. However, IoT healthcare systems also face many challenges, such as data security, privacy, scalability, and interoperability, which require effective solutions and standards (Abounassar et al. 2022) (Bhuiyan et al. 2021). Blockchain technology is a promising solution for addressing some of the challenges of IoT healthcare data sharing, as it can provide data security, privacy, integrity, provenance, interoperability, and standardization, by using cryptographic schemes and smart contracts. Several studies have proposed and implemented blockchain-based platforms for IoT healthcare data sharing, such as MedRec (Azaria et al. 2016), HealthChain (Rahoof and Deepthi 2020), and MedBlock (Fan et al. 2018)

Quantum computing is an emerging field that poses a serious threat to the security of blockchain networks and IoT healthcare data, as it can break the existing cryptographic schemes that secure the data and transactions. Several studies have analyzed the impact of quantum computing on blockchain technology, such as (Fernández-Caramès and Fraga-Lamas 2020, Selvi and Thamilselvan 2022), and suggested the need for quantum-resistant blockchains. Quantum-resistant blockchains are blockchains that employ post-quantum cryptographic algorithms, which are designed to be secure against quantum attacks. Some examples of post-quantum cryptographic algorithms are lattice-based cryptography, code-based cryptography, multivariate cryptography, and hash-based cryptography. However, there are few studies that have proposed and implemented quantum-resistant blockchains for IoT healthcare data sharing, such as (Zeydan et al. 2022, Farouk et al. 2022), and they have some limitations, such as large key sizes, high computational costs, and lack of data poisoning attack prevention. Data poisoning attacks are a specific type of data security and integrity threat, where malicious actors inject false or corrupted data into the system to compromise its functionality and reliability. Data poisoning attacks can target IoT healthcare data sources, transmission, or processing, and can affect the machine learning models that are trained and enhanced using IoT healthcare data. Several studies have investigated data poisoning attacks on machine learning in IoT environments, such as (Butt et al. 2023, Baracaldo et al. 2018), and proposed some detection and defense mechanisms, such as anomaly detection, data filtering, and data verification. However, most of these mechanisms rely on centralized servers or cloud platforms, which can introduce additional security and privacy risks and do not leverage blockchain technology, which can provide a distributed and immutable ledger for data verification and validation.

IoT healthcare systems are a promising paradigm that has emerged with the aim of enhancing the quality and efficiency of healthcare services. These systems enable the collection and analysis of large-scale health data from various sources and devices, such as sensors, wearables, smartphones, medical records, and electronic health records. Simultaneously, the use of these healthcare systems can completely transform care, remote monitoring, diagnosis, and treatment. This transformation ultimately leads to increased patient satisfaction (Delsi Robinsha and Amutha 2023).

IoT health data can provide valuable insights and benefits for various healthcare stakeholders, including doctors, nurses, researchers, and policymakers, as well as elderly patients who are at the highest risk of contracting illnesses and require specialized medical care and close health monitoring solutions. This facilitates personalized and preventive healthcare services. Additionally, it can offer valuable insights and benefits for elderly patients who do not have regular access to healthcare centers (Thaduangta et al. 2016). In this context, IoT technology can save time and achieve accurate results at low costs for many diseases that require regular monitoring by human medical staff, such as hypertension, diabetes, and hyperlipidemia (Elkahlout et al. 2020). However, the sharing of IoT health data also brings various challenges, such as data security, privacy, scalability, and threats from eavesdropping attacks, as well as quantum computing threats. These challenges need to be addressed to ensure the reliability and usability of IoT health systems (Sivakumaran et al. 2023).

Data security and privacy are of vital importance in protecting sensitive health data in the digitized healthcare industry, which has led to a paradigm shift. This is crucial to prevent serious harm that may arise from unauthorized access and disclosures. Among these potential harms are identity theft, fraud, discrimination, and reputation loss (Patil and Seshadri 2014). Data security and privacy also require the preservation of data integrity and provenance, ensuring the accuracy and authenticity of the data and its sources. Scalability is another challenge for IoT healthcare data sharing, as it demands support for high-volume and high-velocity data transactions, such as clinical, financial, genomic, social, and environmental data. This demand can overwhelm existing data storage and processing infrastructures, such as centralized servers or cloud platforms (Patil and Seshadri 2014).

Quantum computing threats pose a new and emerging challenge for IoT healthcare data sharing, as they refer to the potential of quantum computers to break existing encryption schemes. This includes cryptographic methods like public-key encryption, digital signatures, and hash functions (Dwivedi et al. 2023, Hussien et al. 2024). Quantum computers can perform parallel and exponential computations by utilizing quantum phenomena such as superposition and entanglement, surpassing classical computers and algorithms. Quantum computing threats can jeopardize data security, privacy, as well as blockchain security and consensus, undermining the trust and reliability of IoT healthcare systems (Arun and Mishra 2014).

The research gap that motivates our work is the lack of a comprehensive and efficient quantum-resistant blockchain platform for IoT healthcare data sharing, which can secure the data and transactions from quantum attacks and prevent data poisoning attacks by introducing the concept of mutual trust between the server and the client, using the blockchain ledger to ensure data integrity and provenance, as well as data quality and reputation. In the next section, we present the methodology and the implementation details of the proposed platform.

3. Methodology

The proposed system architecture for a large-scale deployment of secure IoT devices in a hospital setting is shown in Figure 1. It consists of three main components: the IoT devices (clients), the edge servers, and the cloud server. Each IoT device collects and transmits various sensor data, such as heart rate, blood pressure, temperature, and oxygen level, to an edge server. The IoT device also receives feedback from the edge server, such as alerts, recommendations, or instructions. The edge server processes the data from its cluster of IoT devices and applies a local machine learning model for data analysis. The edge server also sends the results to the cloud server, where a master machine learning model is trained and inferred. The cloud server also sends feedback to the edge server, which communicates it back to the relevant IoT devices.

In the given scenario, the depicted adversary has the potential to target a multitude of servers within the network architecture. This includes, but is not limited to, any of the peripheral edge servers or the central cloud server. The adversary can adopt multiple strategies to compromise the system. One such strategy involves the attacker masquerading as an IoT node and transmitting falsified data to the edge server, which will, in turn, send this data to the cloud server. Alternatively, the attacker can impersonate an edge server and propagate counterfeit data to the cloud.

Both of these strategies culminate in what are known as data poisoning attacks. These attacks involve the injection of false or misleading data into the system with

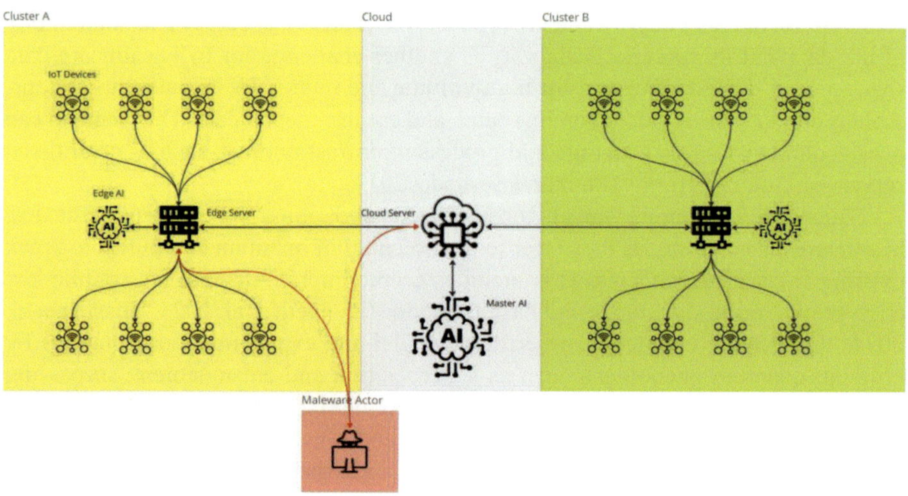

Figure 1: Simulated System Architecture.

the intent to corrupt or disrupt its normal functioning. The implications of such attacks are particularly severe in the context of machine learning models running on the cloud server. These models rely on the integrity and accuracy of the input data for their performance. Data poisoning attacks can lead to the models making incorrect predictions or decisions, thereby jeopardizing their reliability.

In a healthcare data-sharing environment, the consequences of such attacks can be catastrophic. Given the critical nature of healthcare data and the reliance on machine learning models for decision-making, data poisoning attacks can lead to incorrect diagnoses, inappropriate treatment recommendations, and other adverse outcomes. Therefore, it is of utmost importance to implement robust security measures to detect and mitigate such attacks.

3.1 Protocol design and implementation

The system is not dependent on an edge server, and the patient's health could be monitored from outside of the hospital if needed. The outside cluster of IoT devices can connect to the cloud server directly or through another edge server, as shown in Figure 2.

The proposed system uses a secure communication protocol between the IoT devices (clients) and the edge servers, based on quantum-resistant cryptographic primitives and blockchain technology. The protocol consists of the following steps, as shown in Figure 3:

- The server sends its FALCON-signed certificate that is hashed using Haraka-v2 to ensure the client is connecting to an authentic server ("Server Certificate with server shaking key").
- The client receives this information and connects to the blockchain node to verify the server's identity. If the server is who it claims to be, the node will confirm this with the client and continue the communication flow. The client then sends a simple challenge ("Encrypted Validation Challenge and temporary public key") to the server, encrypted with the client's validated public key alongside its own public key.
- If the server answers the challenge successfully, the client sends its own public certificate, as the server did.
- The server verifies the legitimacy of the certificate received from the client with another blockchain node responsible for this verification process, alongside sending another challenge. Once verified, secure data transmission between the client and the server commences.

The implementation of the blockchain system is designed to be resistant to modification of the data as well as being quantum-resistant and is used as a public, decentralized key infrastructure. It is the technology underlying applications that requires robustness and integrity, such as in financial services. It is mainly designed with two main components: the `Block` and the `Blockchain`.

The `Block` is the fundamental unit of the blockchain. It contains a set of transactions, a reference to the previous block via its hash, a timestamp indicating when the block was created, and a unique identifier called a nonce. The block is

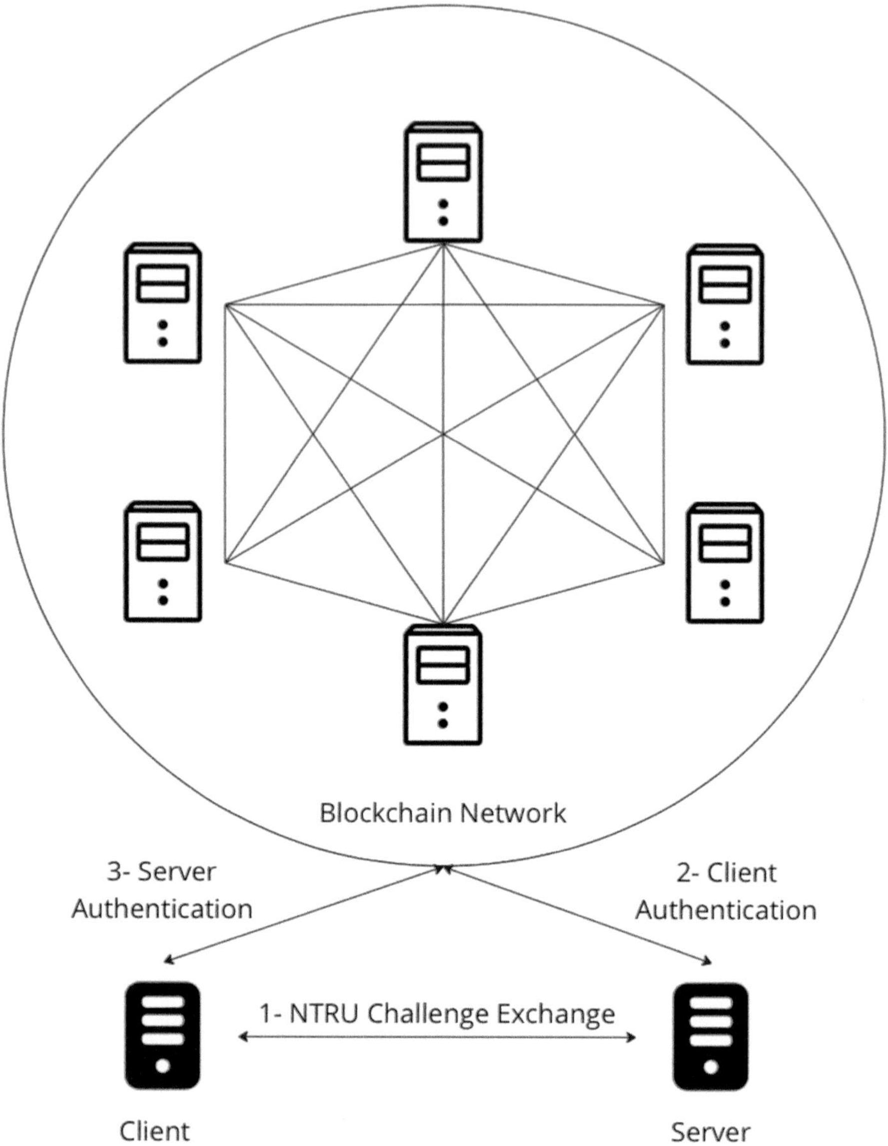

Figure 2: Blockchain Network Architecture.

created with a specific difficulty level, which determines how much computational work must be done to add the block to the blockchain. This process, known as mining, involves finding a hash that meets certain criteria. The hash function used in this code is Haraka v2, an efficient short-input hashing function for post-quantum applications that is designed to be fast and secure.

The `Blockchain` is a chain of blocks, where each block references the previous one, creating a linked list. The blockchain maintains a list of all blocks and pending transactions waiting to be added to the blockchain. The blockchain also maintains

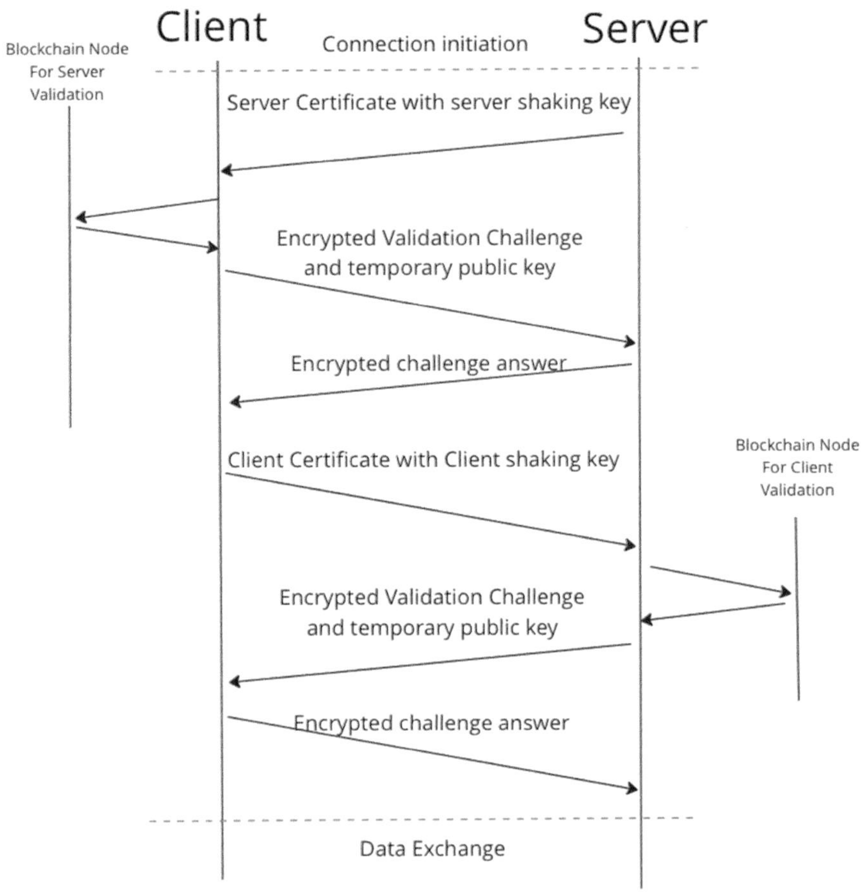

Figure 3: Blockchain PKI with Mutual Trust connection flow.

a set of nodes, representing other participants in the network. The blockchain has a consensus algorithm, which ensures that all nodes in the network agree on the contents of the blockchain. If a node finds a longer valid chain, it will replace its own chain with the longer one. This mechanism ensures the integrity and robustness of the blockchain.

This blockchain system mainly acts as a decentralized public key infrastructure (PKI) for the client and the server, in which digital certificates are used to verify the ownership of the NTRU public keys. These certificates are typically issued by a central authority. However, in a decentralized PKI, the blockchain can be used to store these certificates. Each transaction in a block represents a certificate, and the process of adding a block to the blockchain could represent the issuance of a certificate. This approach removes the need for a central authority and makes the PKI more resilient to attacks or failures.

The Haraka v2 hash function, used in the provided blockchain code, is a critical component of the system's security and efficiency. Haraka v2 is a cryptographic hash function designed for high-speed hashing on short inputs, making it an excellent choice for blockchain applications where efficiency is paramount.

In the context of post-quantum computing, the Haraka v2 cryptographic hash function, specifically the "Haraka512256" variant, is used in our blockchain system implementation to safeguard it from potential quantum attacks. Quantum computers, with their superior computational capabilities, pose a significant threat to classical cryptographic systems as they can efficiently solve problems such as integer factorization and discrete logarithms, which are computationally hard for classical computers. However, Haraka v2, with its unique design and properties, stands resilient against such threats. This variant focuses on inputs of 512 bits (64 bytes) and produces an output of 256 bits, making it particularly efficient for handling key and hash values, a common requirement in both blockchain technology and a decentralized PKI. The speed of Haraka v2, especially on platforms supporting AES-NI (Advanced Encryption Standard New Instructions), can significantly reduce the time required to mine a block, thereby increasing the overall efficiency of the blockchain. This speed is crucial in blockchain applications, where the time required to mine a block can directly impact the system's usability. Moreover, Haraka512256 has been optimized for short messages, reducing the number of rounds within the hashing process, which further enhances its speed. Furthermore, Haraka v2's resistance to preimage and collision attacks, which are types of attacks that quantum computers could potentially excel at, ensures the integrity and authenticity of data within the blockchain. This is particularly important in a decentralized PKI, where certificates are represented as transactions within a block. Therefore, the use of Haraka v2 in a blockchain provides a robust defense mechanism against the threats posed by quantum computing, thereby enhancing the security and reliability of blockchain-based systems in the era of quantum computing. These attributes make Haraka v2 an excellent choice for applications that require fast, secure hashing of short inputs.

In a decentralized PKI, each certificate could be represented as a transaction within a block. The Haraka v2 hash function would then be used to generate a unique identifier for each block (which includes the certificate data), linking it to the previous block in the chain. This creates an immutable record of all issued certificates, enhancing the robustness and reliability of the PKI. Moreover, the use of a blockchain for storing certificates eliminates the need for a centralized authority, which is a single point of failure in traditional PKI systems. Instead, trust is distributed across the network of nodes participating in the blockchain. This decentralization enhances the resilience and fault tolerance of the PKI.

3.2 Protocol simulation and testing

This section presents the simulation environment comprising three key components: a client device (Raspberry Pi 4 with IP 192.168.68.139), a server (Raspberry Pi 4 with IP 192.168.68.143) running Debian Linux, and a blockchain node operating on a Windows 11 Pro machine (IP 192.168.0.8). Table 2 displays the Wireshark packet capture data illustrating the communication flow between these components during the protocol execution.

Table 2: Blockchain node connection and server verification and trust process.

No.	Time	Source	Destination	Protocol	Length	Info
11	0.962930	192.168.68.143	192.168.0.18	TCP	74	46892 → 5000 [SYN] Seq=0 Win=64240 Len=0 MSS=1460 SACK_PERM TSval=2673182207 TSecr=0 WS=128
12	0.963579	192.168.0.18	192.168.68.143	TCP	58	5000 → 46892 [SYN, ACK] Seq=0 Ack=1 Win=64240 Len=0 MSS=1460
13	0.963950	192.168.68.143	192.168.0.18	TCP	60	46892 → 5000 [ACK] Seq=1 Ack=1 Win=64240 Len=0
14	0.964225	192.168.68.143	192.168.0.18	HTTP	492	GET /chain_details_get?hashid=%5B9513,%208537,%20932,%204492,%20 2761,%2011599,%2010238,%205271,%201619,%2064,%201122,%20 11931,%202474,%2010832,%209653,%2010723,%202991,%202071,%20 10133,%206203,%20814,%206893,%2012258,%2010357,%206798,%20 3856,%209597,%205809,%207453,%203553,%2012020,%2099%5D HTTP/1.1
15	0.964388	192.168.0.18	192.168.68.143	TCP	54	5000 → 46892 [ACK] Seq=1 Ack=439 Win=64240 Len=0
16	0.967066	192.168.0.18	192.168.68.143	HTTP/ JSON	902	HTTP/1.1 200 OK , JavaScript Object Notation (application/json)
17	0.967457	192.168.68.143	192.168.0.18	TCP	60	46892 → 5000 [ACK] Seq=439 Ack=849 Win=63600 Len=0
18	0.968205	192.168.68.143	192.168.0.18	TCP	60	46892 → 5000 [FIN, ACK] Seq=439 Ack=849 Win=63600 Len=0
19	0.968353	192.168.0.18	192.168.68.143	TCP	54	5000 → 46892 [ACK] Seq=849 Ack=440 Win=64239 Len=0
20	0.970451	192.168.0.18	192.168.68.143	TCP	54	5000 → 46892 [FIN, PSH, ACK] Seq=849 Ack=440 Win=64239 Len=0
21	0.970811	192.168.68.143	192.168.0.18	TCP	60	46892 → 5000 [ACK] Seq=440 Ack=850 Win=63600 Len=0

Analysis of Table 2 reveals the communication protocol sequence. The process begins with a standard TCP three-way handshake between the client and blockchain node (packets 11-12). Following successful connection establishment, in packet 13, the client initiates a request to the blockchain node to retrieve validation information for a specific server's digital certificate, identified by the included hash value.

```
“0000   00 50 56 e3 7c 3b 00 0c 29 94 41 88 08 00 45 00    .PV.|;..).A...E.
0010    01 de a1 3e 40 00 40 06 d1 e9 c0 a8 44 8f c0 a8    ...>@.@.....D...
0020    00 12 b7 2c 13 88 02 bb a5 d6 0c f3 62 69 50 18    ...,........biP.
0030    fa f0 f8 60 00 00 47 45 54 20 2f 63 68 61 69 6e    ...`..GET /chain
0040    5f 64 65 74 61 69 6c 73 5f 67 65 74 3f 68 61 73    _details_get?has
0050    68 69 64 3d 25 35 42 39 35 31 33 2c 25 32 30 38    hid=%5B9513,%208
0060    35 33 37 2c 25 32 30 39 33 32 2c 25 32 30 34 34    537,%20932,%2044
0070    39 32 2c 25 32 30 32 37 36 31 2c 25 32 30 31 31    92,%202761,%2011
0080    35 39 39 2c 25 32 30 31 30 32 33 38 2c 25 32 30    599,%2010238,%20
0090    35 32 37 31 2c 25 32 30 31 36 31 39 2c 25 32 30    5271,%201619,%20
00a0    36 34 2c 25 32 30 31 31 32 32 2c 25 32 30 31 31    64,%201122,%2011
00b0    39 33 31 2c 25 32 30 32 34 37 34 2c 25 32 30 31    931,%202474,%201
00c0    30 38 33 32 2c 25 32 30 39 36 35 33 2c 25 32 30    0832,%209653,%20
00d0    31 30 37 32 33 2c 25 32 30 32 39 39 31 2c 25 32    10723,%202991,%2
00e0    30 32 30 37 31 2c 25 32 30 31 30 31 33 33 2c 25    02071,%2010133,%
00f0    32 30 36 32 30 33 2c 25 32 30 38 31 34 2c 25 32    206203,%20814,%2
0100    30 36 38 39 33 2c 25 32 30 31 32 32 35 38 2c 25    06893,%2012258,%
0110    32 30 31 30 33 35 37 2c 25 32 30 36 37 39 38 2c    2010357,%206798,
0120    25 32 30 33 38 35 36 2c 25 32 30 39 35 39 37 2c    %203856,%209597,
0130    25 32 30 35 38 30 39 2c 25 32 30 37 34 35 33 2c    %205809,%207453,
0140    25 32 30 33 35 35 33 2c 25 32 30 31 32 30 32 30    %203553,%2012020
0150    2c 25 32 30 39 39 25 35 44 20 48 54 54 50 2f 31    ,%2099%5D HTTP/1
0160    2e 31 0d 0a 48 6f 73 74 3a 20 31 39 32 2e 31 36    .1..Host: 192.16
0170    38 2e 30 2e 31 38 3a 35 30 30 30 0d 0a 55 73 65    8.0.18:5000..Use
0180    72 2d 41 67 65 6e 74 3a 20 70 79 74 68 6f 6e 2d    r-Agent: python-
0190    72 65 71 75 65 73 74 73 2f 32 2e 32 38 2e 31 0d    requests/2.28.1.
01a0    0a 41 63 63 65 70 74 2d 45 6e 63 6f 64 69 6e 67    .Accept-Encoding
01b0    3a 20 67 7a 69 70 2c 20 64 65 66 6c 61 74 65 2c    : gzip, deflate,
01c0    20 62 72 0d 0a 41 63 63 65 70 74 3a 20 2a 2f 2a    br..Accept: */*
01d0    0d 0a 43 6f 6e 6e 65 63 74 69 6f 6e 3a 20 6b 65    ..Connection: ke
01e0    65 70 2d 61 6c 69 76 65 0d 0a 0d 0a                ep-alive....”
```

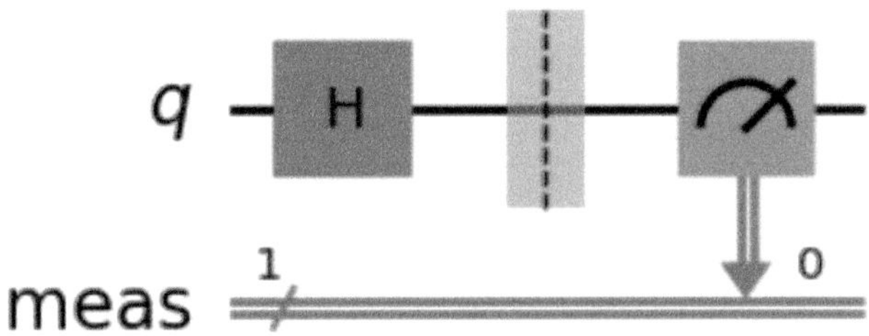

Figure 4: Proposed Nonce generation Quantum Circuit.

The packet communication between client/server and the blockchain node is transmitted as unencrypted HTTP traffic, implemented solely for demonstration and analysis purposes. In a production environment, secure HTTPS protocol would be enforced to maintain data confidentiality and integrity. For this simulation implementation, predefined constant values were utilized instead of true quantum random numbers due to limited access to QISKIT functionality resulting from recent software updates. In a production deployment, actual quantum random number generation would be implemented.

In packet number 16, the node sends a positive result of the digital certificate sent by the server with all of the necessary validation info, such as country, state code, state, organisation name and unit, cname, email and the same public key certificate sent by the server, which confirms that the server identity matches with the blockchain's block as shown below:

"{"chain":["{\"block_number\": 2, \"transactions\": {\"country\": \"EG\", \"state_code\": \"CA\", \"state\": \"Cairo\", \"org\": \"OssTech\", \"org_unit\": \"RND\", \"cname\": \"exp.osslayer.os\", \"email\": \"ossama@osslayer.os\", \"pub_key_s_h\": [9513, 8537, 932, 4492, 2761, 11599, 10238, 5271, 1619, 64, 1122, 11931, 2474, 10832, 9653, 10723, 2991, 2071, 10133, 6203, 814, 6893, 12258, 10357, 6798, 3856, 9597, 5809, 7453, 3553, 12020, 99]}, \"previous_hash\": \"a60d12d96d344fa71c2a20bf56f012528486dcb2af3901f2ce66b49346d4220e\", \"nonce\": 0, \"hashid\": \"a619b70305d0d06b870b286d8ecdc2014466030d948c53312232608d16bee5c3\", \"timestamp\": \"2023-11-20 19:58:53\"}"],"len":1}"

Following successful certificate verification, the client initiates the mutual trust establishment protocol by sending a cryptographic challenge to the server. This challenge consists of an encrypted array ([1340313, 453713, 264646, 226857, 37792, 151277]) that has been encrypted using the server's NTRU public key, as visible in the data snippet. The client also transmits its own public key alongside this challenge. Upon receipt, the server must decrypt the challenge using its private key, compute a hash of the challenge data using the Haraka-v2 algorithm, and return

Table 3: Continued blockchain node connection, server verification, and trust process.

22	2.556255	192.168.68.143	192.168.68.139	IPv4	636	any private encryption scheme (99)
23	2.605962	192.168.68.139	192.168.0.18	TCP	74	36042 → 6000 [SYN] Seq=0 Win=64240 Len=0 MSS=1460 SACK_PERM TSval=951602247 TSecr=0 WS=128
24	2.606401	192.168.0.18	192.168.68.139	TCP	58	6000 → 36042 [SYN, ACK] Seq=0 Ack=1 Win=64240 Len=0 MSS=1460
25	2.606726	192.168.68.139	192.168.0.18	TCP	60	36042 → 6000 [ACK] Seq=1 Ack=1 Win=64240 Len=0
26	2.606927	192.168.68.139	192.168.0.18	TCP	493	36042 → 6000 [PSH, ACK] Seq=1 Ack=1 Win=64240 Len=439 [TCP segment of a reassembled PDU]
27	2.607049	192.168.0.18	192.168.68.139	TCP	54	6000 → 36042 [ACK] Seq=1 Ack=440 Win=64240 Len=0
28	2.608739	192.168.0.18	192.168.68.139	X11	886	Event: <Unknown eventcode 72>, <Unknown eventcode 103>, <Unknown eventcode 44>, <Unknown eventcode 101>, <Unknown eventcode 101>, <Unknown eventcode 115>, <Unknown eventcode 92>, <Unknown eventcode 116>, MappingNotify, <Unknown eventcode 114>, ColormapNotify, <Unknown eventcode 92>, <Unknown eventcode 98>, <Unknown eventcode 53>, <Unknown eventcode 53>, <Unknown eventcode 49>, <Unknown eventcode 50>, <Unknown eventcode 44>, <Unknown eventcode 56>, <Unknown eventcode 97>, <Unknown eventcode 102>, <Unknown eventcode 51>, <Unknown eventcode 104>, <Unknown eventcode 100>, <Unknown eventcode 100>, <Unknown eventcode 50>
29	2.609138	192.168.68.139	192.168.0.18	TCP	60	36042 → 6000 [ACK] Seq=440 Ack=833 Win=64064 Len=0
30	2.610415	192.168.68.139	192.168.0.18	TCP	60	36042 → 6000 [FIN, ACK] Seq=440 Ack=833 Win=64064 Len=0
31	2.610574	192.168.0.18	192.168.68.139	TCP	54	6000 → 36042 [ACK] Seq=833 Ack=441 Win=64239 Len=0
32	2.612268	192.168.0.18	192.168.68.139	TCP	54	6000 → 36042 [FIN, PSH, ACK] Seq=833 Ack=441 Win=64239 Len=0
33	2.612482	192.168.68.139	192.168.0.18	TCP	60	36042 → 6000 [ACK] Seq=441 Ack=834 Win=64064 Len=0
34	2.637469	192.168.68.139	192.168.68.143	IPv4	60	any private encryption scheme (99)
35	2.693479	192.168.68.139	192.168.68.143	IPv4	60	any private encryption scheme (99)
36	6.094825	VMware_94:41:88	VMware_e3:7c:3b	ARP	60	Who has 192.168.68.2? Tell 192.168.68.143
37	6.094890	VMware_e3:7c:3b	VMware_94:41:88	ARP	42	192.168.68.2 is at 00:50:56:e3:7c:3b
38	6.392374	192.168.68.143	192.168.68.139	IPv4	388	any private encryption scheme (99)
39	6.645845	192.168.68.139	192.168.68.143	IPv4	436	any private encryption scheme (99)
40	10.528182	192.168.68.143	192.168.68.139	IPv4	388	any private encryption scheme (99)
41	11.393321	192.168.68.139	192.168.68.143	IPv4	436	any private encryption scheme (99)

this hash value to the client. After completing this verification step, the server then initiates a reciprocal trust verification sequence whereby the client must validate the server's identity through the same challenge-response mechanism.


```
“0000   00 0c 29 94 41 88 00 0c 29 9e 1d cc 08 00 45 00   ..).A...).....E.
0010    00 60 00 01 00 00 40 63 6f cf c0 a8 44 8b c0 a8   .`....@co...D...
0020    44 8f 00 00 00 00 00 00 00 00 00 00 00 00 00 00   D..............
0030    00 00 00 00 00 18 20 00 00 00 00 00 5b 31 2c 20   ...... .....[1,
0040    33 34 30 33 31 33 2c 20 34 35 33 37 31 33 2c 20   340313, 453713,
0050    32 36 34 36 34 36 2c 20 32 32 36 38 35 37 2c 20   264646, 226857,
0060    33 37 37 39 32 2c 20 31 35 31 32 37 37 5d         37792, 151277]”
```


In packet number 22, the server sends the client its digital public certificate, so that the client can verify the identity of the server from the blockchain nodes. The data packet contains the following data:


```
“0000 00 0c 29 9e 1d cc 00 0c 29 94 41 88 08 00 45 00   ..).....).A...E.
0010  02 6e 00 01 00 00 40 63 6d c1 c0 a8 44 8f c0 a8   .n....@cm...D...
0020  44 8b 00 00 00 00 00 00 00 00 00 00 00 00 00 00   D..............
0030  00 00 00 00 00 18 20 00 00 00 00 00 7b 22 6e 6f   ...... .....{“no
0040  6e 63 65 22 3a 20 22 73 73 73 73 73 73 73 73 73   nce”: “sssssssss
0050  73 73 73 73 73 73 73 22 2c 20 22 68 65 61 64 65   sssssss”, “heade
0060  72 22 3a 20 22 59 32 78 70 5a 57 35 30 58 32 68   r”: “Y2xpZW50X2h
0070  68 63 32 67 3d 22 2c 20 22 63 69 70 68 65 72 74   hc2g=”, “ciphert
0080  65 78 74 22 3a 20 22 6a 4f 6e 70 79 50 6a 4a 4d   ext”: “jOnpyPjJM
0090  35 72 4e 52 6b 7a 39 54 75 33 4b 34 33 32 39 31   5rNRkz9Tu3K43291
00a0  5a 37 2f 36 4a 75 47 72 67 77 73 4b 42 35 56 31   Z7/6JuGrgwsKB5V1
00b0  75 42 31 57 32 35 78 5a 34 37 43 77 70 4e 6a 65   uB1W25xZ47CwpNje
00c0  52 6d 4c 44 79 51 38 53 74 63 4c 71 65 77 59 73   RmLDyQ8StcLqewYs
00d0  4b 54 74 4e 30 34 57 30 79 6a 67 71 48 4b 6b 43   KTtN04W0yjgqHKkC
00e0  79 70 34 78 47 33 39 47 78 7a 4f 70 39 44 6a 48   yp4xG39GxzOp9DjH
00f0  49 4c 59 42 39 62 75 49 42 34 34 6f 4c 4b 64 44   ILYB9buIB44oLKdD
0100  36 72 58 37 7a 34 62 53 5a 34 47 2b 2f 6c 2b 70   6rX7z4bSZ4G+/l+p
0110  4f 49 31 30 47 31 53 75 61 4f 47 56 32 46 68 70   OI10G1SuaOGV2Fhp
0120  76 37 37 52 34 54 68 47 72 76 35 53 6e 30 62 6c   v77R4ThGrv5Sn0bl
0130  44 4a 48 37 37 54 2b 44 64 61 4d 54 59 54 38 57   DJH77T+DdaMTYT8W
0140  48 4a 32 33 76 78 73 34 71 4f 48 51 34 6d 71 52   HJ23vxs4qOHQ4mqR
0150  79 47 5a 4e 52 55 6b 78 5a 67 30 48 4d 41 32 33   yGZNRUkxZg0HMA23
0160  53 68 7a 61 66 49 67 78 5a 6e 71 49 58 57 4a 35   ShzafIgxZnqIXWJ5
0170  44 54 55 66 75 50 73 39 6e 74 72 46 5a 6d 4f 31   DTUfuPs9ntrFZmO1
0180  64 30 7a 77 2b 39 47 57 30 58 61 6a 63 5a 35 38   d0zw+9GW0XajcZ58
0190  76 69 58 57 38 2b 38 2f 54 56 2b 47 30 61 4f 46   viXW8+8/TV+G0aOF
01a0  41 52 73 48 4f 44 77 68 51 4d 45 76 39 6a 32 30   ARsHODwhQMEv9j20
01b0  30 4d 2f 37 76 48 4e 38 76 6d 59 4d 7a 55 4b 4b   0M/7vHN8vmYMzUKK
01c0  76 59 52 37 44 42 47 38 65 49 39 77 30 30 67 47   vYR7DBG8eI9w00gG
```

```
01d0  67 78 77 55 47 4d 44 54 6c 56 6e 45 63 46 4c 49  gxwUGMDTlVnEcFLI
01e0  65 34 30 4a 56 6e 49 77 62 46 2f 42 75 53 50 75  e40JVnIwbF/BuSPu
01f0  54 68 34 65 71 78 47 38 41 35 49 4b 74 37 6b 53  Th4eqxG8A5IKt7kS
0200  43 56 6f 68 46 56 4b 76 55 74 42 6d 58 53 44 6f  CVohFVKvUtBmXSDo
0210  71 7a 2f 2f 44 77 32 6c 71 6a 51 4e 6b 54 48 75  qz//Dw2lqjQNkTHu
0220  36 39 36 6d 78 69 78 2b 53 61 69 79 32 79 4f 57  696mxix+Saiy2yOW
0230  6e 71 61 69 31 39 31 4b 33 51 78 6e 64 65 2f 67  nqai191K3Qxnde/g
0240  62 75 38 34 67 47 49 6e 31 51 61 42 75 54 2f 69  bu84gGIn1QaBuT/i
0250  55 4c 34 55 78 48 49 22 2c 20 22 74 61 67 22 3a  UL4UxHI", "tag":
0260  20 22 67 47 56 6f 75 7a 31 32 46 35 38 79 33 65  "gGVouz12F58y3e
0270  38 49 30 7a 47 64 55 51 3d 3d 22 7d              8I0zGdUQ=="}"
```


The clients takes this and communicates with the blockchain node, as shown below. To verify the identity of the server, the communication currently uses traditional TCP and HTTP connection, as this demo is just for simulation and evaluation and is not intended for production right now; in the production version, it will make use of the OssLayer and HTTPS on top of it.

After this, both the client and the server can trust each other. The proposed protocol can prevent data poisoning attacks, where malicious actors inject false or corrupted data into the system to compromise its integrity and reliability. The protocol can also resist quantum attacks, where quantum computers can break the conventional cryptographic schemes that secure the data and the transactions. The protocol leverages quantum-resistant cryptographic, such as NTRU, FALCON and Haraka-v2, which are based on lattice-based and hash-based problems, respectively. The protocol also uses blockchain technology, which provides a distributed and immutable ledger for data verification and validation.

4. Discussion

In this section, we discuss the main results and findings of our research and compare them with previous studies and the working hypotheses. We also discuss the implications and limitations of our research and suggest some future research directions.

Our research proposed and implemented a quantum-resistant blockchain platform for IoT healthcare data sharing, which leverages quantum-resistant cryptographic primitives and blockchain technology to secure the data and transactions from quantum attacks and data poisoning attacks. We also introduced the concept of mutual trust between the server and the client, which can ensure data integrity and provenance, as well as data quality and reputation, based on blockchain technology.

Our research results support our working hypotheses, which are:

- H0: Nonces generated by Qiskit simulation are considered constant, but in real-world scenarios, they can never be constant.
- H1: Quantum-resistant cryptographic primitives can provide quantum-proof data security and privacy, as well as quantum-proof blockchain security and consensus, for IoT healthcare data sharing.

- H2: A blockchain network for mutual trust between the server and the client can prevent data poisoning attacks, by verifying and validating the data before and after the data transmission and processing, for IoT healthcare data sharing.

Our research extends and contributes to the existing literature by addressing the new and emerging challenges of quantum computing and data poisoning attacks, which have not been adequately explored and solved by existing solutions. It also has several implications for the theory and practice of IoT healthcare systems, blockchain technology, quantum computing, and data poisoning attacks. For theory, our research provides a novel and comprehensive framework for designing and implementing quantum-resistant blockchain platforms for IoT healthcare data sharing, which can be applied and adapted to other domains and applications. For practice, our research provides a practical and efficient solution for securing and scaling IoT healthcare data sharing, which can improve the quality and efficiency of healthcare services and outcomes, especially in the face of quantum computing threats and data poisoning attacks.

Our research also has some limitations, which needs to be acknowledged and addressed in the future research. Some of the limitations are:

- The OssPlat has not been fully deployed and tested in a real-world hospital setting, which may limit its generalizability and applicability.
- The OssPlat relies on the availability and reliability of the PKI nodes, which may introduce some security and privacy risks, such as single point of failure or collusion attacks.
- The OssPlat uses some specific quantum-resistant cryptographic primitives, such as FALCON and Haraka-v2, which may have some drawbacks, such as large key sizes, high computational costs, or lack of standardization.

5. Conclusions

In this paper, we proposed and implemented a quantum-resistant blockchain platform for IoT healthcare data sharing, which leverages quantum-resistant cryptographic primitives and blockchain technology to secure the data and transactions from quantum attacks and data poisoning attacks. We also introduced the concept of mutual trust between the server and the client, which can ensure data integrity and provenance, as well as data quality and reputation, using blockchain technology. The results and findings of this research have been discussed, along with the implications and limitations of our research, and some future research directions have been suggested.

The OssPlat is a promising and innovative solution for IoT healthcare data sharing, which can address the new and emerging challenges of quantum computing and data poisoning attacks and improve the quality and efficiency of healthcare services and outcomes. We hope that our research can inspire and inform future research and practice in this field.

References

Abounassar, Eman M., Passent El-Kafrawy and Ahmed A. Abd El-Latif. 2022. Security and interoperability issues with internet of things (IoT) in healthcare industry: a survey. Security and Privacy Preserving for IoT and 5G Networks: Techniques, Challenges, and New Directions 159–189.

Ahmed, Ibrahim M. and Manar Younis Kashmoola. 2022. Threats on machine learning technique by data poisoning attack: a survey. ACeS 2021: Advances in Cyber Security 586–600.

Althobaiti, Ohood Saud and Mischa Dohler. 2020. Cybersecurity challenges associated with the internet of things in a post-quantum world. *IEEE Access* 8: 157356–157381.

Arun, G. and Mishra, V. 2014. A review on quantum computing and communication. 2014 2nd International Conference on Emerging Technology Trends in Electronics, Communication and Networking 1–5.

Awotunde, Joseph Bamidele, Rasheed Gbenga Jimoh, Sakinat Oluwabukonla Folorunso, Emmanuel Abidemi Adeniyi, Kazeem Moses Abiodun and Oluwatobi Oluwaseyi Banjo. 2021. Privacy and security concerns in IoT-based healthcare systems. *The Fusion of Internet of Things, Artificial Intelligence, and Cloud Computing in Health Care* 105–134.

Azaria, Asaph, Ariel Ekblaw, Thiago Vieira and Andrew Lippman. 2016. MedRec: Using Blockchain for Medical Data Access and Permission Management. 2016 2nd International Conference on Open and Big Data (OBD) 25–30.

Baracaldo, Nathalie, Bryant Chen, Heiko Ludwig, Amir Safavi and Rui Zhang. 2018. Detecting poisoning attacks on machine learning in IoT environments. 2018 IEEE International Congress on Internet of Things (ICIOT) 57–64.

Bhuiyan, Mohammad Nuruzzaman, Md Mahbubur Rahman, Md Masum Billah and Dipanita Saha. 2021. Internet of Things (IoT): A Review of Its Enabling Technologies in Healthcare Applications, Standards Protocols, Security, and Market Opportunities. *IEEE Internet of Things Journal*, 8(13): 10474–10498.

Boyen, Xavier, Udyani Herath, Matthew McKague and Douglas Stebila. 2021. Associative Blockchain for Decentralized PKI Transparency. *Cryptography* 5(2).

Butt, Usman Javed, Osama Hussien, Krison Hasanaj, Khaled Shaalan, Bilal Hassan and Haider al-Khateeb. 2023. Predicting the Impact of Data Poisoning Attacks in Blockchain-Enabled Supply Chain Networks. Algorithms 16(549).

Cui, Wei, Tong Dou and Shilu Yan. 2020. Threats and opportunities: blockchain meets quantum computation. *2020 39th Chinese Control Conference* (CCC) 5822–5824.

Dadkhah, Mehdi, Mohammad Mehraeen, Fariborz Rahimnia and Khalil Kimiafar. 2021. Use of internet of things for chronic disease management: an overview. *J. Med. Signals Sens.*, 11(2): 138–157.

Douglass, Robert. 2022. Use and Abuse of IoT: Challenges and Recommendations. IoT for Defense and National Security 397–465.

Dwivedi, A., Saini, G.K., Musa, U.I. and Kunal. 2023. Cybersecurity and prevention in the quantum era. *2023 2nd International Conference for Innovation in Technology* (INOCON) 1–6.

Dwivedi, Ruby, Divya Mehrotra and Shaleen Chandra. 2022. Potential of Internet of Medical Things (IoMT) applications in building a smart healthcare system: A systematic review. *Journal of Oral Biology and Craniofacial Research*, 12(2): 302–318.

Elkahlout, M., M.M. Abu-Saqer, A.F. Aldaour, A. Issa and M. Debelijak. 2020. IoT-based healthcare and monitoring systems for the elderly: a literature survey study. *2020 International Conference on Assistive and Rehabilitation Technologies* (iCareTech) 92–96.

Fan, Kai, Shangyang Wang, Yanhui Ren, Hui Li and Yintang Yang. 2018. MedBlock: Efficient and Secure Medical Data Sharing Via Blockchain. *Journal of Medical Systems*, 42(136).

Farouk, Ahmed, Amal Alahmadi, Shohini Ghose and Atefeh Mashatan. 2022. Blockchain platform for industrial healthcare: Vision and future opportunities. *Computer Communications*, 5(4): 223–235.

Faruk, Md Jobair Hossain, Sharaban Tahora, Masrura Tasnim, Hossain Shahriar and Nazmus Sakib. 2022. A Review of Quantum Cybersecurity: Threats, Risks and Opportunities. 2022 1st International Conference on AI in Cybersecurity (ICAIC) 1–8.

Fei, Song, Shi Yuanbing and Huang Minghao. 2020. A method of industrial internet entity mutual trust combining PKI and IBE technology system. 2020 3rd International Conference on Artificial Intelligence and Big Data (ICAIBD) 304–308.

Fernández-Caramès, Tiago, M. and Paula Fraga-Lamas. 2020. Towards post-quantum blockchain: a review on blockchain cryptography resistant to quantum computing attacks. *IEEE Access*, 8: 21091–21116.

Huang, Mingyuan, Sheng Cao, Xiong Li, Ke Huang and Xiaosong Zhang. 2022. Defending data poisoning attack via trusted platform module and blockchain oracle. *ICC 2022 - IEEE International Conference on Communications* 1245–1250.

Hussien, Osama A.A.M., Isuru, S.W. Arachchige and Hamid Jahankhani. 2024. Strengthening security mechanisms of satellites and UAVs against possible attacks from quantum computers. International Conference on Global Security, Safety, and Sustainability 1–20.

Islam, S.M. Riazul, Daehan Kwak, M.D. Humaun Kabir, Mahmud Hossain and Kyung-Sup Kwak. 2015. The internet of things for health care: a comprehensive survey. *IEEE Access*, 3: 678–708.

Kaur, Kushwant, Sahil Verma and Ankit Bansal. 2021. IOT big data analytics in healthcare: benefits and challenges. *2021 6th International Conference on Signal Processing, Computing and Control* (ISPCC) 176–181.

Li, Yue, Mingcheng Xu and Gaojian Xu. 2022. Blockchain-based mutual authentication protocol without CA. *The Journal of Supercomputing*, 78: 17261–17283.

Newaz, Akm Iqtidar, Nur Imtiazul Haque, Amit Kumar Sikder, Mohammad Ashiqur Rahman and A. Selcuk Uluagac. 2020. Adversarial attacks to machine learning-based smart healthcare systems. GLOBECOM 2020 - 2020 *IEEE Global Communications Conference* 1–6.

Nissar, Gousia, Riaz A. Khan, Saba Mushtaq, Sajaad A. Lone, and Ayaz Hassan Moon. 2024. IoT in healthcare: a review of services, applications, key technologies, security concerns, and emerging trends. *Multimedia Tools and Applications* 83(33): 80283-80283.

Patil, Kupwade H. and Seshadri, R. 2014. Big data security and privacy issues in healthcare. *2014 IEEE International Congress on Big Data* 762–765.

Pietro, Roberto Di, Xavier Salleras, Matteo Signorini and Erez Waisbard. 2018. A blockchain-based trust system for the internet of things. *Proceedings of the 23nd ACM on Symposium on Access Control Models and Technologies* 77–83.

Pradhan, Bikash, Saugat Bhattacharyya and Kunal Pal. 2021. Medical Internet of Things (IoT) devices. *Journal of Healthcare Engineering*, 2021: 18.

Rahoof, T.P. Abdul and V.R. Deepthi. 2020. HealthChain: A secure scalable health care data management system using blockchain. *Distributed Computing and Internet Technology*, 11969.

Ramezani, Somayeh Bakhtiari, Alexander Sommers, Harish Kumar Manchukonda, Shahram Rahimi and Amin Amirlatifi. 2020. Machine learning algorithms in quantum computing: a survey. 2020 International Joint Conference on Neural Networks (IJCNN) 1–8.

Robisha, S. Delsi and Amutha, B. 2023. IoT revolutionizing healthcare: a survey of smart healthcare system architectures. 2023 International Conference on Research Methodologies in Knowledge Management, Artificial Intelligence and Telecommunication Engineering (RMKMATE) 1–5.

Rosner, Gilad and Erin Kenneally. 2019. Clearly opaque: privacy risks of the internet of things. IoT Privacy Forum.

Selvi, K. Tamil and Thamilselvan, R. 2022. Post-quantum cryptosystems for blockchain. Quantum Blockchain: An Emerging Cryptographic Paradigm 173–200.

Singh, Bhagvender, Sachin Sharma and Anupriya Jain. 2023. Internet of Things (IoT) in health care—a review. *Artificial Intelligence and Machine Learning in Healthcare*, 65–78.

Sivakumaran, A.R., Almusawi, M., Kumar, B.V., Almoussawi, Z.A. and Velumani, J. 2023. Detecting attackers during quantum key distribution in IoT networks using quantum-based secure and lightweight transmission. *2023 International Conference on Integrated Intelligence and Communication Systems* (ICIICS) 1–4.

Thaduangta, B., Choomjit, P., Mongkolveswith, S., Supasitthimethee, U., Funikul, S. and Triyason, T. 2016. Smart Healthcare: Basic health check-up and monitoring system for elderly. *2016 International Computer Science and Engineering Conference* (ICSEC) 1–6.

Thomasian, Nicole M. and Eli Y. Adashi. 2021. Cybersecurity in the internet of medical things. *Health Policy and Technology*, 10(3): 100549.

Uslu, Banu Çalış, Ertuğ Okay and Erkan Dursun. 2020. Analysis of factors affecting IoT-based smart hospital design. *Journal of Cloud Computing*, 9(67).

Zeydan, Engin, Yekta Turk, Bugrahan Ozturk, S., Hakan Mutlu and Anil Dundar, A. 2022. Post-quantum blockchain-based data sharing for IoT service providers. *IEEE Internet of Things Magazine*, 5(2): 96–101.

Chapter 13

Symbiotic Intelligence in Forecasting Cyber-Enabled Financial Crime

Natasha Omezi and *Hamid Jahankhani**

1. Introduction

The Digital/Information Age, which began in the 1940s, has evolved into the Age of Intelligence, where understanding, analysing, and processing data have increased in importance and paved the way for artificial intelligence (AI) to gradually become intertwined in our day-to-day lives.

While the concept of artificial intelligence generates both optimism and concern in almost equal measure, it is fast becoming an integral part of modern-day living. Even the most die-hard technophobe would have encountered AI in some form or another. For instance, anyone who has a mobile phone may have encountered predictive text/autocorrect, which utilises the principle of the "random forest" machine learning algorithm to understand the context of the message being typed and make accurate predictions. Additionally, voice assistants such as Siri and Alexa; image face recognition for face-unlock in mobile phones; drones; self-driven vehicles (driverless vehicles); assembly line robots; and, generally, the Internet of Things (IoT) are just some ways that artificial intelligence has stealthily crept into our lives. Most people have interacted with chatbots at some point. These are all practical examples of AI in action. Artificial intelligence is not just present in our day-to-day lives; it has almost become a way of life and is prevalent in various sectors such as the automobile, gaming, and financial sectors, to name a few.

Northumbria University London.
Emails: natashaomezi@gmail.com
* Corresponding author: Hamid.jahankhani@northumbria.ac.uk

DOI: 10.1201/9781003540373-13

In the financial sector, this prevalence is particularly significant as it addresses the digitalisation of financial crimes, which have transformed traditional crimes into sophisticated digital threats, where white-collar crime has transitioned into virtual-collar crime (crimes that are perpetrated entirely in cyberspace).

2. Financial Crimes and Their Evolving Nature in the Digital Age

Financial crimes have existed for as long as humanity has, ranging from petty theft to white-collar crimes such as fraud, large-scale embezzlement, and money laundering, to mention just a few. With the advent of digitalisation, these crimes have grown increasingly complex, pervasive, and interconnected, showing an almost linear correlation between technological advancement and financial crime sophistication.

Cybercriminals leverage online platforms such as social media networks to harvest personal information through the use of social engineering and fake profiles. This harvested information can then be used to access online banking portals or to send phishing emails impersonating trusted organisations or individuals. E-commerce websites are exploited through the use of fraudulent transactions, services, or products to steal payment details and other financial data. Encrypted messaging apps such as WhatsApp, iMessage, and Signal, which are beneficial for legitimate users who value privacy, can be exploited by cybercriminals who use them to coordinate illicit activities, share sensitive information, and conduct financial transactions.

3. The Impact of Financial Crime

Financial crime impacts economies, businesses and individuals and encompasses a broad range of illegal activities including money laundering, bribery, corruption, terrorist financing, and cybercrime.

3.1 Global scale of financial crime

Financial crime continues to be a leading threat globally. According to Nasdaq's 2024 Global Financial Crime report, an estimated \$3.1T (£2.4T)[1] in illicit funds flowed through the global financial system in 2023. Money laundering accounted for the funding of a range of destructive crimes to the tune of trillions of dollars, including an estimated \$346.7B (£262.5B) in human trafficking, \$782.9B (£592.8B) in drug trafficking, and \$11.5B (£8.7B) in terrorist financing. Fraud scams and bank fraud schemes totalled \$485.6B (£367.7B) in projected losses globally (Nasdaq 2024). Account takeover fraud has risen over 72% since 2022. The scale and complexity of financial crime highlights the urgent requirement for innovative solutions including Artificial Intelligence to combat and mitigate these pervasive threats.

[1] Conversion as of 24 August 2024.

4. The Role of Artificial Intelligence in Combatting Crime

Artificial intelligence is transforming various industries through automation, advanced analytics, and predictive capabilities. For instance, AI enables effective law enforcement resource allocation by analysing existing crime data and predicting high-risk areas for potential crimes. In the healthcare sector, AI systems aid in detecting insurance fraud and identifying counterfeit pharmaceutical products. AI is also used in the retail sector to identify potential shoplifters through real-time behavioural analysis and to detect supply chain fraud. AI is used in cybersecurity across industries for various purposes, including threat detection by continuously monitoring for network vulnerabilities, unusual activities, or breaches. Furthermore, AI is used in incident response, where the speed of detection and response to cyberattacks is greatly enhanced, thereby minimising damage and reducing response time.

In the financial sector, fraud and anti-money laundering (AML) detection capabilities are greatly enhanced by AI-powered tools. These tools also enhance the detection and mitigation of phishing and malware attacks, for which financial institutions are particularly targeted. The use of AI-powered tools strengthens fraud and AML detection, but to further enhance its abilities, it should be combined with human expertise—a collaboration known as Symbiotic Intelligence.

While AI systems excel at processing vast amounts of data, pattern recognition, and task repetition with high accuracy at top speeds, humans are creative, intuitive, and bring contextual and ethical understanding and judgement to situations. For instance, in financial crime prediction, AI can identify suspicious transactions in a large dataset and in real time, which can then be investigated by human experts. This collaboration helps enhance the speed and efficiency of detecting financial crimes—a huge benefit with the rise of digital banking and online transactions and the accompanying increase in data volumes.

5. Purpose of the Chapter

The purpose of this chapter is to explore how symbiotic intelligence can enhance the forecasting and, consequentially, the prevention of financial crime. As financial crimes have become increasingly complex, often outpacing traditional detection methods, this chapter aims to highlight the critical role of a human-AI collaboration in combatting these threats. It aims to address the challenges, benefits, and potential to revolutionise financial crime prevention strategies.

6. Convergence of Financial Crime and Cybersecurity

6.1 Financial crime meets cybercrime

The rise in the complexity of financial crime is largely driven by the advancement of technology and its pervasive integration into modern living through digitalisation. A consequence of this reliance on technology is the increasing intersection of financial crime with cybercrime, as more traditional financial crimes, such as fraud and money laundering, now often intersect with cybercrime. One example of this occurred as far back as 2013.

One of the most notorious cybercrime syndicates, the Carbanak gang, carried out a string of highly sophisticated financial crimes using a blend of cyber techniques and automation between 2013 and 2018. Targeting over 100 financial institutions in more than 40 countries, their activities resulted in cumulative losses exceeding €1 billion. They started with the Anunak malware, which evolved into Carbanak, and then shifted to using Cobalt malware developed from Cobalt Strike penetration testing software. Bank employees were sent spear-phishing emails, which, once downloaded, allowed criminals remote access to internal banking networks and ATM control servers, where they silently observed employees' actions over time (sniffing). Once they understood the workflows, they sent remote ATM instructions, dispensing cash to accomplices on-site. They also transferred funds to criminal accounts and temporarily inflated balances in customers' accounts to transfer stolen funds. Profits were then laundered through cryptocurrencies via prepaid cards linked to cryptocurrency wallets.

Although this was a full-fledged example of the convergence of financial crime with cybercrime, it also reflected a form of human-machine collaboration, where the gang used automation to scale their crimes, bypass human controls, and evade detection for years. It also became a precursor to more AI-driven financial crimes due to the "learning" aspect of the malware and its ability to simulate legitimate transactions.

7. Evolving Threat Landscape

The Carbanak incident highlights how the threat landscape for financial systems has become increasingly complex and dynamic, bearing in mind that this began over ten years ago. Two significant trends illustrate this evolution: ransomware attacks targeting financial systems and the exploitation of digital platforms such as financial services platforms (e.g., online banking, digital payment gateways); e-commerce platforms (e.g., Amazon, Etsy); social media platforms (e.g., Instagram, LinkedIn, WhatsApp Pay); cloud-based collaboration platforms (e.g., Dropbox, Zoom); IoT and connected device platforms (e.g., Alexa, Fitbit, Siemens MindSphere); entertainment platforms (e.g., Spotify, Xbox Live); education and learning platforms (e.g., Udemy, Moodle); and digital advertising platforms such as Google Ads. These platforms illustrate how nearly every aspect of modern life is permeated by digitalisation, creating opportunities for efficiency but lending themselves to new vulnerabilities for exploitation and, in particular, data harvesting due to poor user password practices (such as password reuse, weak passwords, etc.).

Other emerging trends in cybercrime are in the areas of supply chain vulnerabilities, and the Internet of Things (IoT).

Supply Chain Attacks—These are attacks on third-party vendors connected to financial institutions with the aim of gaining access to critical systems by exploiting vulnerabilities in the supply chain (Reuters 2024).

Internet of Things—The National Institute of Standards and Technology (NIST) has identified types of cyberattacks that pose a significant risk to financial services, including the risk of adversarial attacks on AI systems that are used for fraud detection, transaction monitoring, credit scoring, etc. For instance, tactics like evasion (manipulating inputs to bypass fraud detection), poisoning (introducing corrupt data during AI training), privacy breaches (extracting sensitive information), and abuse (misleading AI with compromised legitimate sources). NIST cautions against claims of foolproof AI security, adding that significant progress is still required to protect AI from exploitation.

8. Challenges in Detection and Forecasting Cyber-Enabled Financial Crime

The convergence of financial crime and cybercrime lends a level of complexity to the detection and forecasting of financial crimes. Criminals exploit technology, and the volume, speed, and complexity of these crimes overwhelm traditional detection systems. This makes forecasting particularly challenging as new methods evolve faster than existing defences. It is the age-old dilemma of cops and robbers, with the robbers moving faster than the cops, or cat and mouse, with attackers and defenders engaged in an ongoing battle of wit, subterfuge, evasion, and analysis. It is critical to understand these challenges in order to develop effective strategies for combatting this growing threat.

Complexity: Traditional financial crimes such as fraud and money laundering are now intertwined with cybercrimes such as phishing, ransomware, and hacking. Adding to that, criminals layer transactions across multiple jurisdictions and leverage anonymous digital currencies. This level of complexity is fast becoming the norm. Additionally, these methods evolve rapidly, making it difficult to build predictive models that stay relevant.

Data Volume and Speed: Massive transaction volumes typically seen in financial institutions require real-time detection, which is not always possible, thereby making it hard for irregularities to be detected quickly enough. Additionally, legitimate high-volume activity can lead to increased false positive detection, making it hard to predict.

Technology Barriers: Planning and execution of cybercrimes are carried out using encrypted messaging apps and dark web platforms, which makes detection harder.

AI as a Tool for Criminals—Cybercriminals are increasingly using AI to automate attacks and identify system vulnerabilities, thereby enhancing the sophistication of their attacks, and evading detection. For instance, AI is used in polymorphic malware generation in which the malware continuously alters its code, making it difficult for traditional signature-based systems to identify malicious patterns, as it appears as benign software.

AI-enhanced botnets autonomously change their attack strategies, making them more resilient against countermeasures. The proliferation of Deep Fake technology is also on the rise and becoming a familiar concept. AI-generated deep fakes are being increasingly used in social engineering attacks, particularly in CEO fraud (impersonating executives so that fraudulent transactions are authorised).

Another challenge in detection where technology is concerned is in the evasion of anomaly detection systems. AI-driven attacks can mimic normal behaviour by enabling malicious network traffic blend with legitimate traffic, effectively bypassing security protocols designed to detect irregular activities.

Cybercriminals also leverage AI to craft highly convincing phishing emails increasing the likelihood of successful data theft. Fast disappearing are the typo-ridden phishing emails.

System Integration Challenges—Many institutions struggle with the integration of financial crime detection systems with cybersecurity measures for a plethora of reasons, including:

i. Integration Issues – Many financial institutions are slow to adapt to new technology, making it difficult to integrate modern cybersecurity solutions. Additionally, it becomes very challenging to develop a unified defence strategy due to the existence of data silos within organisations, as fragmented information hinders effective threat detection and response.
ii. Regulatory and Compliance Challenges – For financial institutions, ensuring compliance with regulations across different jurisdictions while maintaining robust security protocols requires significant resources and coordination, which further complicates the integration of detection systems with cybersecurity measures.
iii. Resource Constraints – Effective system integration is hampered by the shortage of skilled professionals in both financial crime and cybersecurity.

Addressing these challenges will enable institutions to enhance their resilience against the threats borne out of the convergence of financial crime and cybersecurity. However, it would require a holistic and collaborative approach between AI and humans.

9. Symbiotic Intelligence: A New Paradigm

The longstanding argument about whether AI will replace or complement human beings has given rise to the new watchword – "symbiosis". Symbiosis leverages the distinct strengths of human expertise and artificial intelligence systems, giving rise to Symbiotic Intelligence.

9.1 Defining symbiotic intelligence

In the context of this topic, Symbiotic Intelligence refers to the collaborative integration of human expertise and artificial intelligence to enhance decision-making and forecasting. In this relationship, each compensates for the other's limitations.

10. The Role of AI vs. The Role of Human Expertise

AI systems excel in data processing and pattern recognition, automation of repetitive tasks, predictive analytics, and real-time monitoring.

Data Processing and Pattern Recognition: The sheer volume of data that AI can process exceeds human capabilities, particularly when you consider the speed at which it does this, and its ability to uncover patterns and correlations that could be overlooked by humans.

Automation of Repetitive Tasks: Humans can 'free up' time to focus on strategic thinking by automating routine and repetitive processes, which AI can do at high speed.

Predictive Analytics: AI is particularly effective in analysing historical data to forecast future trends and potential risks. It is, therefore, a critical tool in sectors such as finance and healthcare.

Real-Time Monitoring: AI enables quicker responses by continuously monitoring systems and flagging anomalies and potential risks at high speed and in real time.

Humans, on the other hand, contribute contextual understanding, ethical judgment, creativity, innovation and emotional intelligence.

Contextual Understanding: Humans can interpret results within the situational and cultural context, which AI cannot grasp.

Ethical Judgement: Humans mitigate potential ethical risks posed by AI by ensuring decisions align with societal and organisational values.

Creativity and Innovation: Humans can think creatively and innovatively, offering novel solutions to complex problems: they can 'think outside the box'.

Emotional Intelligence: In fields where empathy or negotiation are required, humans have an understanding of interpersonal dynamics that AI does not have.

11. Why Symbiosis Matters in Financial Crime Prevention

Symbiosis matters in financial crime prevention, as a symbiotic approach combines the strengths of both artificial intelligence and human expertise. Neither alone can effectively address the complexities involved, as both AI and humans have limitations on their own.

AI-Only Limitations

- *Lack of Contextual Understanding* – AI systems often lack contextual awareness. For instance, in identifying suspicious transactions, AI systems could process vast datasets and identify patterns. However, they do not understand content, context, and concepts the way humans do. In the context of financial crime, AI can monitor large volumes of transactions in real time but might flag a high-value transaction as suspicious without understanding its legitimate business context. As it does not have the contextual awareness to distinguish between legitimate and illicit activities, this could lead to false positives or negatives. Purportedly, one can surmise that this is a similar issue to that experienced with traditional rules-based transaction monitoring systems. The difference is that the results of human intervention can gradually be used to teach AI to make those decisions on its own moving forward.

- *Transparency and Explainability Issues* – Many AI models, particularly deep learning algorithms (such as neural networks), exhibit a high degree of opacity and are often referred to as "black boxes" because their internal workings and decision-making processes are difficult to interpret, even by experts. They involve complex architectures with multiple layers and parameters, which, though highly accurate, do not provide clear explanations for how decisions are made. In fraud detection, for example, a transaction could be flagged by a deep learning model as suspicious without providing any rationale for flagging it.

Human-Only Limitations

- Scalability – In transaction monitoring, the sheer volume of transactions processed daily by financial institutions makes it impractical for human analysts to process the data in a timely manner, resulting in delayed detection and response to fraudulent activities. The natural human ability means that analysts can only process and analyse a finite number of tasks within a given timeframe. Even with the best of intentions, it is not possible for human teams to thoroughly review each transaction for signs of financial crime.

Human-only systems are unable to cope with the requirement for financial crime to be immediately detected and responded to in order to prevent further fund transfers or damage. Real-time analysis is hindered by natural human limitations. For instance, time-sensitive international wire transfers are at risk of not being flagged promptly, allowing illicit activities to progress. A team of analysts cannot feasibly review the thousands of potential financial crime alerts that can be generated in the course of a day, increasing the risk of missing red flags.

Additionally, during peak trading hours, for instance, an over-reliance on human analysts can create bottlenecks, thereby reducing operational efficiency.

- *Human Error* – Manual processes could potentially allow suspicious activities to go undetected, or legitimate transactions could be wrongly flagged due to errors and inconsistencies. These issues can be further exacerbated by cognitive biases and fatigue. Repetitive tasks can be the breeding ground for error, as humans could overlook subtle or hidden patterns in data due to fatigue. For instance, small incremental transactions could be fraudulent, but because they mimic normal transactional behaviour, they could escape detection without technological assistance.

Confirmation bias is also another tendency exhibited by human analysts, who may focus on familiar patterns of fraud while unintentionally ignoring emerging or unfamiliar schemes. Certain anomalies could be dismissed by an analyst because they do not align with their preconceptions of fraud.

Human inconsistencies can occur across teams where different analysts apply subjective criteria to the same transaction, leading to inconsistent decisions, resulting in compliance gaps or unnecessary alert escalation.

Overall, human-only systems can lead to delayed detection of fraud, overwhelmed resources, and regulatory risks, as errors in manual reviews can result in non-compliance with regulations, leading to penalties or fines.

The limitations of AI-only or human-only approaches highlight the need for collaboration between the two, where human intuition is combined with AI's speed and scalability, ensuring more efficient and effective fraud detection and mitigation. This collaborative approach is already in motion, as there are advanced solutions already in existence.

12. AI Applications in Forecasting Financial Crimes

In the fight against money laundering and financial crimes, AI systems enhance the ability of financial institutions to identify and mitigate illicit activities by leveraging machine learning algorithms, natural language processing, and predictive analytics. Overall, the role of AI in AML/Financial crime prevention is to provide a more sophisticated and automated approach while reducing the burden on financial institutions (Sanction Scanner 2024). Achieving this level of automation in financial crime prevention depends on the training of the AI systems, and is about ensuring that the right kind of information is available to learn from.

12.1 Training Machine Learning (ML) models

Models need to be trained to distinguish between legitimate and fraudulent transactions. This employs two primary methods: supervised learning and unsupervised learning.

Supervised Learning: In this type of learning, models learn from a dataset where transactions have already been labelled as 'fraudulent' or 'legitimate', i.e., the analysis has already been done, and the model is trained on known outcomes. This enables new transactions to be classified based on already known and recognised patterns.

One of the main applications of supervised learning is in the retail sector. Jeff Wilke, who leads Amazon's consumer business, says that supervised learning systems have largely replaced the memory-based filtering algorithms that were used to make personalised recommendations to customers.

Such is the power of supervised learning.

Unsupervised Learning: This approach deals with unlabelled data and aims to identify anomalies or patterns that deviate, in general, from the norm. It uses techniques such as clustering[2] and anomaly detection to flag unusual transactions that may indicate fraud. Unsupervised learning is particularly beneficial for detecting unknown or novel fraud that lacks historical labelled data, and this is where it trumps rule-based detection techniques,[3] which are almost always based on known factors.

Financial crime and fraud detection systems can be enhanced by combining both supervised and unsupervised learning, each contributing uniquely to identifying and mitigating fraudulent activities. In practice, financial institutions have already begun to implement these machine learning techniques to identify suspicious activities in real time.

13. Current AI Solutions in Fraud Detection, Transaction Monitoring, and Anti-Money Laundering

Currently, a few financial institutions have adopted AI technologies in their financial crime prevention processes, utilising Machine Learning algorithms, behavioural analytics, and anomaly detection.

JP Morgan Chase: In 2021, JP Morgan Chase adopted an AI-driven system to enhance its anti-money laundering (AML) initiatives. Leveraging machine learning (ML) algorithms, the system identifies potential risks by analysing customer data. Whilst traditional fraud detection methods focus on transaction amounts or account specifics, JP Morgan's AI solution uses a behaviour-centric approach for fraud detection. In this approach, it examines user-account interactions and utilises graph-based models to uncover patterns and irregularities indicative of fraud.

JP Morgan saw remarkable results, including a 95% decrease in false positives in their AML programme, freeing up resources to oversee more effective monitoring. They also saw a significant improvement in trade monitoring in real time, as they were able to identify suspicious activities and mitigate financial crime risks more quickly.

Danske Bank: In 2018, Danske Bank utilised AI technology to detect suspicious transactions by analysing customer data and transaction patterns in real-time, resulting in a notable 60% reduction in false positives.

HSBC: HSBC adopted an AI-powered system in 2019 and achieved reduced AML review times, improved programme accuracy, and annual cost savings of $400K. HSBC has gone further to partner with Google Cloud to develop and implement an

[2] Clustering is an unsupervised machine learning technique that groups data points into clusters based on their similarity, allowing patterns or structures in the data to emerge without prior labelling.

[3] Rule-based detection techniques in financial crime/fraud detection rely on predefined sets of conditions or thresholds, such as transaction amounts or frequency, to flag suspicious activities for further investigation.

AI solution (AML AI) capable of recognising suspicious activity on its own without being told what to look for (unsupervised learning), resulting in more accurate risk detection, reduction in processing time, and the ability to identify criminal networks from suspicious pattern detection.

Standard Chartered Bank: In 2020, Standard Chartered adopted an AI-driven system to automate their AML procedures and achieved a remarkable 40% reduction in the time required for compliance reviews and enhanced accuracy of their AML programme.

Commonwealth Bank of Australia (CBA): Commonwealth Bank of Australia (CBA) has implemented AI-driven technology to enhance scam and fraud prevention on its digital banking platforms. The system utilises machine learning to monitor and learn customers' usual interaction patterns, device usage, keystrokes, and mouse movements to detect deviations that may indicate compromised accounts or unauthorised activity. This is part of CBA's broader strategy of "protect, detect, and resolve", which aims to identify irregularities, stop scammers, and safeguard customers from potential threats.

13.1 Network analysis

Financial Institutions are also increasingly employing AI in network analysis to combat complex money laundering schemes. It involves mapping relationships between entities to uncover illicit activities involving multiple accounts and transactions and can lead to the uncovering of organised criminal networks as seen with HSBC and CBA (whose AI system creates visual maps linking transactions).

13.2 Automated Suspicious Activity Reports (SARs)

Comprehensive reports for regulatory compliance can be generated using Natural Language processing algorithms. For example, Google Cloud's AML AI helps financial institutions increase detection accuracy, thereby reducing alert volumes.

13.3 Know Your Customer (KYC)

AI can be used to verify identities and assess risk profiles, thereby streamlining the KYC processes employed in financial institutions. This automaton of customer due diligence (CDD) enhances compliance with AML regulations. CBA, in addition to previous mentioned processes, has also implemented AI technologies to automate customer onboarding and due diligence.

ComplyAdvantage offers real-time AML screening and monitoring solutions, which utilise AI and ML, enabling financial institutions to automate CDD.

14. Gaps in Current AI-Driven Approaches

AI has undeniably and significantly advanced financial crime detection. However, several challenges persist which are outlined in the section below.

False Positives: It is a known fact that traditional rule-based models often produce excessive false alerts, overwhelming compliance teams and diverting resources from genuine threats. However, AI systems can also generate a high number of false positives, particularly in their early stages of implementation. This is usually due to factors such as (i) imbalanced or poor-quality training data; (ii) over-sensitivity; or (iii) dynamic fraud tactics.

If the training data is unrepresentative of real-world scenarios or inaccurate in any way, the model may flag legitimate transactions as suspicious. Also, as AI models are trained to err on the side of caution, anomalies that deviate from learned patterns could be flagged, leading to false positives. Lastly, as fraudsters frequently adapt their methods, AI models trained by supervised learning could miss these transactions or misclassify new but legitimate actions as fraudulent, leading to false positives.

Adversarial Attacks: The integrity of AI-driven fraud detection systems can be compromised due to adversarial attacks, where malicious actors manipulate inputs to deceive the system. AI models are susceptible to these types of attacks, where, for instance, attackers may introduce subtle data modifications to evade detection.

Lack of Explainability: As mentioned earlier, many AI models function as "black boxes", making it difficult to interpret their decision-making processes and posing challenges in regulatory compliance. In compliance, justification for decision-making is crucial as evidence to regulators.

Data Quality and Availability: One of the gaps that have been highlighted is the lack of complete or biased data that AI is trained on. AI models are only as good as the data they are trained on. For instance, datasets used for financial crime detection could contain outdated or incomplete information, leading to fraudulent activities in underrepresented geographic regions going undetected.

Additionally, some financial systems lack the infrastructure to provide AI with real-time transactional data leading to fraudulent transactions proceeding without being flagged immediately.

Adaptability to Emerging Threats: The rapid evolution of financial crime presents a challenge as the data that the AI could have been trained on may already be outdated, such as those involving cryptocurrencies (Adhikari et al. 2024). Also, AI systems that are not updated may become ineffective as financial crime tactics evolve, leading to a decrease in detection accuracy.

Scalability: There could be infrastructure limitations, particularly with smaller financial institutions that may lack the necessary computational resources to implement sophisticated AI systems.

Integration Challenges: There can be integration challenges, such as incompatibility of AI systems with outdated financial systems. Additionally, a lack of integration between various systems such as KYC, AML, and transaction monitoring systems can limit AI's ability to provide a comprehensive overview.

Overreliance on Automation: Excessive reliance on AI may lead to human judgement being gradually eroded due to a lack of use, causing contextual factors to be overlooked. For instance, undue trust could be placed in AI-generated alerts, even when incorrect, leading to improper actions and potential regulatory risks.

Ethical and Privacy Concerns: The extensive data required by AI models raises data privacy concerns. Also, AI systems may inadvertently perpetuate biases present in the data, such as unfairly flagging certain demographics for higher fraud risks.

Regulatory and Legal Challenges: There could be global compliance variations due to financial institutions operating across jurisdictions with varying regulations, which could complicate the deployment of standardised AI solutions. For instance, AML laws differ significantly between the European Union (EU), US, and Asia. Attempting to standardise an AI solution across these three regions will pose significant challenges: the EU's risk-based frameworks would require tailoring AI models to individual countries; US' rules-based system with its emphasis on BSA/Patriot Act requirements such as real-time reporting and SAR thresholds would make standardisation difficult. The wide variability in AML frameworks in Asia would mean the solution must handle highly developed systems and weaker infrastructures in emerging markets. This would mean that AI solutions must be highly customisable to meet local compliance standards leading to complexities and possible operational inefficiencies.

There are also other challenges such as conflicting data protection laws, which would require decentralised or hybrid cloud infrastructure as well as jurisdiction-specific AI models.

Cost and Resource Barriers: The cost of developing and deploying AI systems can act as a barrier to smaller organisations. Currently, the relative shortage of AI expertise in the workforce limits the ability of financial institutions to design, implement and manage AI solutions effectively.

Cybersecurity Vulnerabilities: Beyond specific adversarial attacks, AI systems are vulnerable to broader cybersecurity risks such as insider threats, supply chain attacks, and model inference attacks where attackers attempt to infer sensitive information about the model's decision-making logic and use this knowledge to craft more effective attacks (Shokri et al. 2017).

Lack of Standardisation: The current absence of standardised frameworks and practices for AI in financial crime detection could lead to inconsistent results and interoperability issues.

These gaps underscore the need for human expertise and input.

15. The Role of Human Expertise in Financial Crime Forecasting

Cybercriminals exploit digital vulnerabilities to perpetrate traditional financial crimes such as money laundering, fraud, terrorist and proliferation financing. Despite the brilliance of Artificial Intelligence, and machine learning systems, human expertise remains a critical component in financial crime forecasting such as pattern detection, risk prediction, and suspicious activity flagging. Human expertise complements the abilities of AI with nuanced analysis, ethical oversight, and contextual understanding.

15.1 *Human intuition in contextual analysis of cyber-enabled financial crime*

AI excels in pattern detection in cyber-enabled financial crime such as phishing schemes, and other fraudulent transactions. However, human expertise is essential for interpreting nuanced, context-specific threats.

Analysing Complex Cybercrime Behaviours: Cybercriminals often adapt their methods to exploit vulnerabilities, such as using malware or ransomware to divert financial transactions or exploiting decentralised finance (DeFi) platforms for money laundering. In such cases, human analysts have the ability to draw on contextual or domain-specific knowledge, recognising unusual combinations of cyber and financial activity, which AI may misinterpret as unrelated anomalies.

For instance, a spike in transactions from IP addresses linked to a recent cyberattack may indicate coordinated money laundering efforts. Human analysts can correlate these patterns with external events, whereas AI might flag each transaction individually as an attempt at money laundering.

As noted by Belanger et al. (2021), human analysts excel at synthesising multi-domain insights, such as linking phishing campaigns to financial fraud outcomes (Belanger et al. 2021).

Cultural and Geopolitical Context: Financial cybercrime often reflects regional differences in technology usage, regulatory environments etc. For example, a sudden increase in cryptocurrency transactions in a sanctioned jurisdiction may be an indication of cybercriminals leveraging loopholes to bypass sanctions. In cases like this, human expertise is required to evaluate whether these patterns are legitimate or part of cyber-enabled financial crime.

15.2 *Ethical oversight and bias mitigation in AI for detection*

Human oversight is invaluable in ensuring that detection systems remain ethical, resilient and effective, as AI used to forecast financial crimes can inherit biases or be subject to adversarial manipulation.

Identifying Algorithmic Blind Spots: AI systems trained on historical financial crime datasets are prone to confirmation bias. These 'blind spots' can be exploited by cybercriminals by introducing synthetic identities that fall outside AI's detection thresholds, and leveraging "clean" financial history to bypass automated fraud checks. These blind spots can be identified and addressed by human experts and can assist in further training the AI model in the future. For instance, AI-driven trading bots can be fraudulently used to launder proceeds through micro-transactions across global markets, and manage to evade AI detection, without the use of human expertise to review anomalous trading patterns. Without human oversight, AI models cannot remain robust against adversarial manipulation.

Fairness: Human analysts can validate AI-driven decisions to avoid unfair targeting as automated systems may flag transactions disproportionately from certain geographies or demographics based on training data. Human analysts are able to review each case on an individual bases and can also advocate for inclusive training datasets that reflect diverse transaction behaviours.

15.3 The role of humans in real-time threat mitigation

In the cyber-enabled financial crime landscape, threats often emerge rapidly and dynamically, requiring real-time incident response. AI can flag unusual activities, such as massive data breaches or coordinated ransomware attacks, but human intervention is required to analyse the broader impact, such as secondary fraud attempts targeting financial systems. Cyber and financial crime human response teams can also coordinate to contain threats.

Additionally, cybercriminals often use techniques such as polymorphic malware or "as-a-service" platforms to obscure their activities. Human analysts can bring contextual understanding to uncover hidden links between cyberattacks and financial crime schemes (Anderson and Moore 2020).

15.4 Privacy, security, transparency and accountability

Human oversight ensures that AI-driven systems respect data privacy and ethical standards by ensuring that data used in cyber-financial crime detections complies with data privacy laws, and that AI systems avoid overreach, such as intrusive surveillance that could undermine customer trust or violate ethical norms.

Furthermore, regulators demand financial institutions provide explainable outcomes, particularly where legal and reputational stakes are high. Human expertise is critical in these instances to validate AI-driven insights before they are escalated to enforcement and ensure there is transparency in the decision-making processes.

Consequentially, human expertise cannot be discarded but rather is invaluable, if not critical, to providing contextual interpretation, ethical oversight, and adaptive thinking needed to address these multifaceted challenges, of which only a few have been provided here. By fostering collaboration between humans and AI, organisations can build resilient systems capable of staying ahead of cyber-enabled financial crime.

16. Building Symbiotic Intelligence in Practice

Building Symbiotic Intelligence in practice within financial institutions requires a structured framework to foster human-AI collaboration, involving workflow design, decision-making processes, and accountability structures.

A proposed framework, as depicted in Figure 1 below, would involve a split of the workflow into various units such as: (i) data collection and pre-processing; (ii) anomaly detection; (iii) decision-making and escalation; and (iv) regulatory reporting. In each of these steps, AI and humans would utilise their respective strengths to harness and improve the data and the entire process.

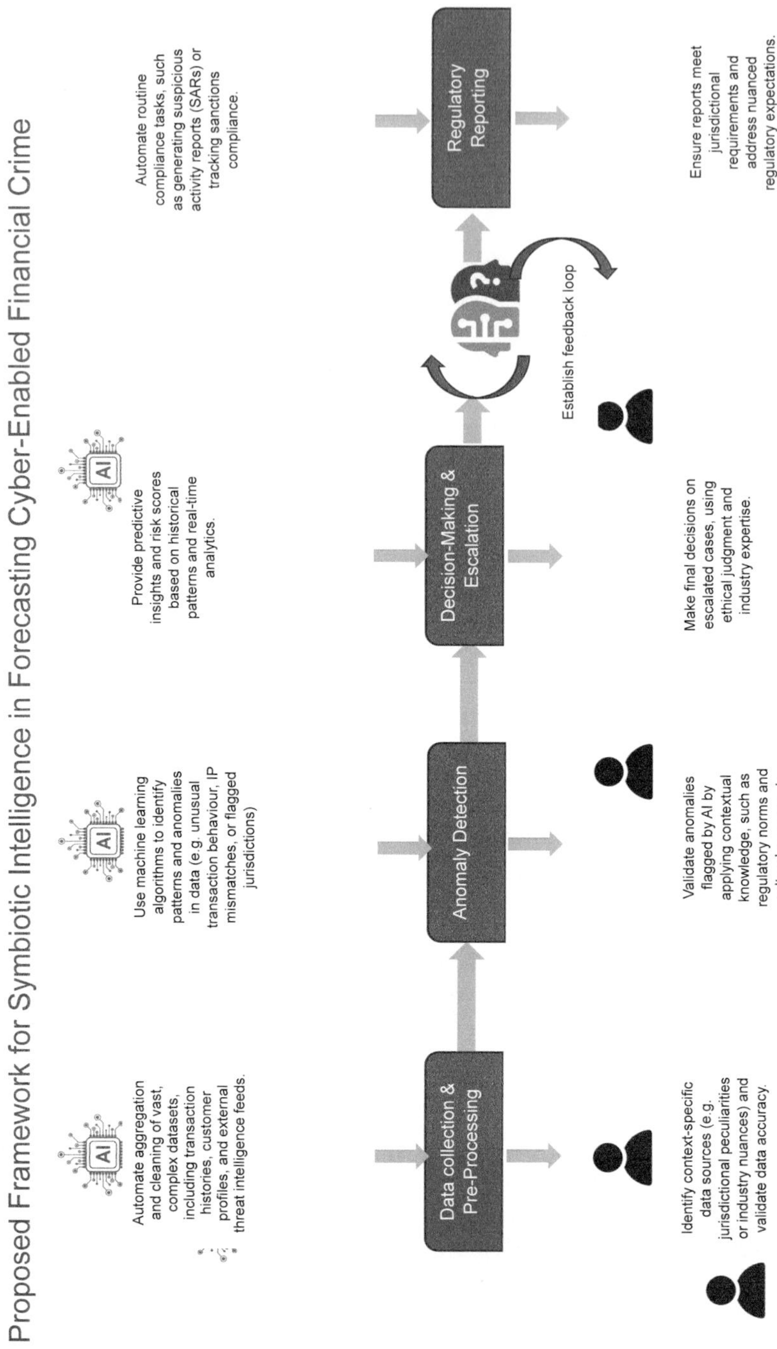

Figure 1: Proposed symbiotic framework.

Data Collection and Pre-Processing: Vast complex data sets can be aggregated and cleaned by AI. This will include transaction histories, customer profiles, and external threat intelligence feeds. AI capabilities mean this process can be automated.

The human role would be to validate data accuracy and identify context-specific data sources such as jurisdictional peculiarities or industry nuances.

Anomaly Detection: Using machine learning algorithms, AI can identify patterns and anomalies in data such as unusual transaction behaviour, IP mismatches etc. Again, the human role would be to validate the anomalies flagged by applying contextual knowledge, to distinguish genuine threats from false positives.

Decision-Making and Escalation: At this stage, AI can provide predictive insights and risk scores based on historical patterns and real-time analytics. Here, the human analyst will make the final decisions on all escalated cases applying contextual and ethical judgement, and industry expertise. A feedback loop should then be established where the outcome of human analysis should feed back into the AI models, which would improve system accuracy over time.

Regulatory Reporting: An important part of regulated financial institution operations, regulatory reporting can then be automated such that routine compliance tasks are carried out by AI. Prior to submitting to the regulators, the human analyst would review and ensure the reports meet jurisdictional requirements with a particular focus on addressing nuanced regulatory expectations (particularly with subjective regulations – 'grey areas').

Proposed Framework for Symbiotic Intelligence in Forecasting Cyber-Enabled Financial Crime

Workflows and Decision-Making Processes: Integrating symbiotic intelligence into daily operations should involve institutions adopting workflows that promote shared responsibilities. This can be done by applying any of one of these categories: (i) tiered review systems as evidenced in the process flow above; (ii) collaboration platforms.

Collaboration Platforms – These are unified spaces that bridge the gap between AI capabilities and human expertise, enhancing the speed, accuracy and effectiveness of decision-making in financial crime prevention. Collaboration platforms aggregate data from AI systems and display in an intuitive, visual format accessible to all stakeholders. These platforms typically include integrated communication tools such as instant messaging or video conferencing, which facilitate discussions between compliance teams, decision makers and data analysts. Examples of collaboration platforms already in use are Salesforce Financial Services Cloud, which integrates dashboards and tools for compliance and fraud detection teams to collaborate on cases; IBM Watson Studio, and Actimize by NICE.

Governance and Accountability: To avoid overlaps in human-AI collaboration, it is important that roles and responsibilities are clearly defined. AI owners should be assigned to monitor system performance and updates, while human experts should be designated to oversee ethical concerns and strategic decisions.

17. Technology and Training Requirements

To effectively implement symbiotic intelligence systems, financial institutions need to develop the necessary technological infrastructure and ensure that employees are equipped to work effectively alongside AI (Brynjolfsson and McAfee 2017). Consequently, core AI capabilities will need to be developed, ensuring interoperability, strengthening cybersecurity, and enhancing integration.

Core AI Systems: The requirement for core AI systems is critical and will include the deployment of machine learning models which will provide the requisite analytical power for financial crime analytics, detection and prediction.

Natural Language Processing (NLP): NLP-powered tools lend their strength to analysing unstructured data such as emails, contracts, etc., to extract meaningful insights.

Integration Platforms: Financial institutions must adopt platforms that allow seamless integration of AI systems with existing tools and systems including regulatory reporting systems, customer relationship management (CRM) tools, and core banking applications. This will facilitate a unified data flow between legacy systems and advanced AI technologies.

Cybersecurity Measures: The importance of robust cybersecurity measures cannot be downplayed, as AI systems must be protected from data poisoning, evasion tactics and any other form of adversarial attacks. Additional security measures such as end-to-end encryption and multi-factor authentication are critical for securing data flows and maintaining the integrity of AI-driven decision-making processes.

Interoperability: In order to foster a cohesive global operation, to any degree, technological infrastructure must prioritise the ability for AI systems to communicate and collaborate across departments and jurisdictions, ensuring that differences such as those in compliance or cybersecurity nuances are effectively addressed.

Focusing on these foundational technological elements, financial institutions can develop an ecosystem that supports and enhances the effectiveness of symbiotic intelligence systems in addressing modern cyber-enabled financial crime.

18. Future of Symbiotic Intelligence in Forecasting Cyber-Enabled Financial Crime

As cyber-enabled financial crimes evolve in sophistication, and prevention mechanisms scramble to catch up, symbiotic intelligence promises revolutionary advancements in predictive capabilities. This could finally see prevention mechanisms outpacing cybercriminals, particularly with the employment of unsupervised learning. Key emerging technologies include Explainable AI (XAI), Reinforcement Learning (RL), and Quantum Computing.

18.1 Emerging technologies

The integration of advanced AI technologies is set to redefine the landscape for forecasting cyber-enabled financial crime.

Explainable AI (XAI) – XAI provides clear, interpretable insights into how AI systems make decisions, offering transparency. In the context of financial crime forecasting, XAI can explain the reasons for flagging certain transactions or behaviours, enabling analysts and subsequently regulators to justify AI predictions. This will have a positive impact on the financial industry as a whole, as it will foster trust due to improved auditability.

Reinforcement Learning (RL) – RL is a type of machine learning where an AI model learns to make decisions by interacting with an environment in real time. It is based on the principle of trial and error, where an AI model takes actions, observes the outcomes, and adjusts its behaviour to maximise rewards or minimise penalties over time. The ability of RL to adapt to dynamic, complex environments makes it a powerful tool for tackling challenges in financial systems, among others. It differs from traditional machine learning models as it can learn from its interactions in a dynamic environment.

Advantages of RL include its ability to excel in environments where conditions change over time, such as evolving fraud tactics. RL can adapt its decision-making 'on the fly' as new data becomes available. This capability is crucial for identifying new and evolving cyber-enabled fraud tactics, such as phishing scams targeting banking apps or ransomware attacks. RL systems allow financial institutions to respond proactively to emerging threats and maintain a competitive edge over cybercriminals.

Quantum Computing – The most exciting one yet! Quantum computing represents a transformative leap in computational power. It offers the ability to process massive datasets and solve complex problems far beyond the capabilities of classical computing.

How it works – Quantum computing relies on quantum bits (qubits), which can exist in multiple states simultaneously (superposition) unlike classical bits which are either 0 or 1. These qubits allow for exponential increases in computational capacity enabling quantum systems to analyse multiple data points and patterns simultaneously, perform complex calculations at a fraction of the time required by classical computers, and solve optimisation and graph-related problems, which are crucial in uncovering financial crime networks. As forecasting ability is partially dependent on detection capabilities, the applications of quantum computing in financial crime detection will be introduced first.

Applications in Financial Crime Detection – (i) Rapid analysis of transactional data: Quantum systems could analyse millions of international transactions and detect unusual fund transfers indicative of layering in money laundering schemes.

(ii) Pattern recognition in fraud networks: Quantum computing can be used to detect the central nodes in a complex fraud ring by analysing transaction graphs and identifying the most influential accounts or entities. This is vital, as money laundering and cyber-enabled fraud often involve interconnected entities and transactions spread across jurisdictions – the bane of the anti-financial crime professional.

(iii) Quantum algorithms can improve the optimisation of AI and machine learning models used for fraud detection, enabling RL models to predict new types of cyber-enabled financial crimes with higher precision.

(iv) Quantum computing can also be used to break cryptographic protocols. While this is beneficial for detection, it is also a risk, particularly if deployed by cyber criminals, and used to break encryption methods used in financial systems. This highlights the need for quantum-safe encryption.

(v) Global collaboration – Quantum computing can therefore support international efforts to combat financial crime by facilitating the processing of global financial data.

As amazing as quantum computing is, it is incredibly difficult for humans to interpret. Symbiotic intelligence can therefore make quantum computing more actionable.

For instance, quantum computing can process complex datasets and identify patterns in financial data that traditional AI systems may struggle to detect. It could also solve optimisation problems, such as identifying the shortest path for detecting money laundering across global transactions. Despite this, human intervention will be required to provide contextual understanding and validate quantum predictions.

Despite the challenges, as quantum computing matures, its integration into symbiotic intelligence systems will redefine how financial institutions combat and forecast cyber-enabled financial crimes.

Applications in Financial Crime Forecasting – Quantum computing can enhance forecasting by enabling predictive models to anticipate emerging trends and detect potential threats more effectively than classical computing systems.

i. Predictive modelling – Quantum computing can process vast and complex datasets, enabling the detection of subtle and previously hidden correlations between financial transactions, entities, or activities. This can be used, for instance, in forecasting the likelihood of cyber-enabled fraud rings based on historical trends and cross-border financial flows, among other factors.
ii. Dynamic risk predictions – Financial institutions can dynamically adjust their forecasting models based on real-time data, identifying vulnerabilities before they are exploited by leveraging quantum optimisation algorithms.
iii. What-if Scenarios – Quantum computing can simulate millions of "what-if" scenarios simultaneously, allowing institutions to forecast the potential impact of new financial crime techniques or regulatory changes. This is useful, for instance, in predicting how cybercriminals could exploit upcoming technological advancements or regulatory changes with undiscovered loopholes.

iv. Quantum computing could also be used in the early detection of emerging threats by identifying and flagging anomalies indicative of new types of financial crimes, such as the rise of fraud schemes that target AI-driven financial platforms.

v. Regulatory Compliance - Quantum computing can be used to forecast regulatory risks based on emerging compliance trends due to its ability to simulate and analyse diverse legal frameworks. For instance, it can be used to anticipate the impact of new AML laws on transaction monitoring requirements.

Quantum computing, in collaboration with human capabilities, can empower financial institutions to anticipate emerging threats and design proactive countermeasures, reshaping financial crime prevention from reactive defence to predictive forecasting.

18.2 Global collaboration

Cyber-enabled financial crimes are global in nature; therefore, international cooperation is critical. This is not a novel thought, as most anti-financial crime initiatives since the beginning of globalisation and digitalisation have referred to global collaboration as a means of combatting international crime, particularly digital crime.

Real-Time Data Sharing – Establishing global frameworks for data sharing between financial institutions, regulators, and law enforcement will strengthen crime forecasting capabilities. Real-time collaboration will enable faster identification of cross-border cyber-enabled crimes, such as coordinated ransomware attacks or international money laundering.

Global standards for data interoperability and security should be utilised, as several international frameworks, principles, and regulations serve as guidelines, such as International Standards for Data Operability (ISO/IEC 27001 – Information Security Management Systems, ISO/IEC 11179 – Metadata Registries, ISO/TC 68 – Financial Services Standards).

Public-Private Partnerships – Governments and private sector organisations should collaborate to harness AI's full potential in combatting financial crimes. Programmes like the UK's Joint Money Laundering Intelligence Taskforce (JMLIT) illustrate how public-private partnerships can integrate cutting-edge technologies with human expertise. These collaborations enable comprehensive responses to complex crimes, as shared intelligence and advanced AI tools are leveraged.

Standardisation of AI Regulations – Establishing international standards for AI deployment and governance will reduce the barriers that impede collaboration, such as variations in data protection and AML regulations across jurisdictions.

A standardised regulatory framework will foster global cooperation, ensuring consistent and effective financial crime forecasting.

18.3 Ethical considerations

Symbiotic intelligence in forecasting cyber-enabled financial crimes raises critical ethical questions such as data privacy, algorithmic accountability, transparency vs security, and the human-AI balance, among others.

Data Privacy – AI systems require access to extensive datasets that often contain sensitive information, and a key challenge is balancing the need for data availability with privacy laws such as GDPR.

Ensuring compliance with privacy regulations while maintaining AI efficiency is essential for protecting individual rights.

Algorithmic Accountability - With AI systems increasingly influencing financial crime prevention, financial institutions must implement mechanisms to identify and mitigate biases, ensuring fair treatment across all demographic groups. Accountability for errors, biases, and unintended consequences must be clearly defined..

Transparency vs. Security – XAI solves the problem of lack of explainability. However, excessive transparency could expose vulnerabilities in fraud detection models, inadvertently aiding cybercriminals. Therefore, balancing transparency for compliance with security measures to protect AI systems from exploitation is crucial.

Human-AI Balance – The most touted concern relating to AI is job displacement in every sector, including compliance and financial crime detection roles. However, these systems are most effective when paired with human expertise.

Institutions must focus on redefining roles to enhance human-AI collaboration rather than replacing human input entirely.

19. Conclusion

The future of symbiotic intelligence in forecasting cyber-enabled financial crime hinges on advancements in technology, strengthened global cooperation, and ethical foresight. Emerging tools like XAI, reinforcement learning, and quantum computing offer transformative capabilities, while international partnerships and regulatory alignment ensure that these tools are deployed effectively. By addressing ethical considerations, financial institutions can harness symbiotic intelligence to predict and prevent complex cyber-enabled financial crimes, safeguarding the global financial ecosystem.

19.1 Call to action

The financial ecosystem faces increasingly sophisticated threats that require collaborative and innovative solutions. Stakeholders must embrace symbiotic intelligence to safeguard against financial crimes.

- Financial Institutions should invest in AI-powered tools for fraud detection, predictive modelling, and risk assessment while ensuring comprehensive training for employees to collaborate effectively with these technologies.

- Policymakers and Regulators should develop frameworks that encourage the ethical use of AI while balancing privacy and security concerns. International data-sharing agreements should also be facilitated to combat cross-border financial crimes effectively.
- Technologists should create scalable, user-friendly AI tools tailored to the unique needs of the financial sector. The focus should be on integrating AI with existing systems, ensuring interoperability and adaptability across different financial institutions and jurisdictions.

This collaborative effort among financial institutions, regulators, policymakers, and technologists can establish a safer and more resilient global financial ecosystem, forecasting and detecting financial crime effectively.

20. Vision for the Future

It is increasingly apparent that the future of financial crime forecasting lies in human-AI collaboration, where symbiotic intelligence becomes the cornerstone of financial crime prevention. By blending human creativity and judgement with AI's speed and scalability, the financial sector can move beyond reactive defences to proactive and predictive solutions.

Imagine a world where:

- Advanced AI systems forecast emerging fraud trends months in advance, providing actionable insights to prevent major financial crimes.
- Global cooperation and data-sharing networks powered by symbiotic intelligence dismantle cross-border financial crime syndicates.
- Ethical AI frameworks ensure fairness and transparency in fraud detection, fostering trust among regulators, institutions, and customers.

This optimistic vision highlights the transformative potential of symbiotic intelligence. By embracing it, financial institutions and their partners can redefine the fight against financial crime.

21. Future Considerations for Further Research on Symbiotic Intelligence in Financial Crime Forecasting

Enhancing Explainability in AI Systems - While Explainable AI (XAI) is a promising advancement, further research is needed to develop models that balance explainability with performance. Future studies could explore how to make AI decisions more transparent to regulators and users without compromising detection accuracy.

Real-Time Data Integration - Research could focus on developing infrastructure for seamless real-time data sharing across institutions and jurisdictions while addressing data privacy and security concerns. This includes leveraging blockchain for secure, auditable data exchanges.

AI Resilience to Adversarial Attacks - As cybercriminals increasingly use AI to evade detection, more research is needed to strengthen AI systems against adversarial attacks, such as data poisoning and evasion tactics, particularly in dynamic financial environments.

Quantum Computing Applications - Quantum computing holds immense potential for financial crime forecasting. However, further research is required to address its practical challenges, such as high implementation costs, cryptographic vulnerabilities, and integration with existing systems.

Dynamic Fraud Typologies - Studies could investigate how symbiotic intelligence can adapt to rapidly evolving fraud typologies, such as cryptocurrency fraud, decentralised finance (DeFi) exploits, and AI-driven phishing scams.

Cross-Border Collaboration Frameworks - Future research should explore standardised frameworks for international collaboration, enabling financial institutions and regulators to share insights and best practices effectively across jurisdictions.

Ethical AI in Financial Crime Detection - Research should focus on mitigating biases in AI models, ensuring unbiased outcomes across demographics, and addressing ethical concerns related to data usage, such as the tension between security and privacy.

Human-AI Workflows - More studies are needed to optimise human-AI collaboration workflows, focusing on how human intuition and contextual expertise can complement AI's speed and scalability in financial crime forecasting.

Scalability for Smaller Institutions - Current AI solutions often favour large institutions with substantial resources. Research could focus on developing cost-effective, scalable AI solutions tailored to smaller financial institutions with limited infrastructure.

Integration of IoT and Edge Computing - As financial services increasingly rely on IoT devices and edge computing for transactions, future studies could explore their integration with AI systems for real-time fraud detection and prevention.

Behavioural Analysis and AI Synergy - Research could delve deeper into how AI can model human behaviours in financial systems, detecting subtle deviations indicative of fraud while preserving customer experience.

These areas of research hold the potential to address existing gaps and unlock new opportunities for symbiotic intelligence in forecasting and preventing financial crimes. By investing in these avenues, financial institutions and regulators can stay ahead of emerging threats while ensuring ethical and effective use of AI.

References

Adhikari, P., Hamal, P. and Jnr, F.B. 2024. Artificial Intelligence in fraud detection: Revolutionizing financial security. *International Journal of Science and Research Archive*, 1457–1472.

AI.business. (2024, March 26). 95% Fewer False Alarms: JPMorgan Chase Uses AI to Sharpen Anti-Money Laundering Efforts. Retrieved from AI Business: https://ai.business/case-studies/ai-to-improve-anti-money-laundering-procedures/.

Ali, A., Razak, S.A., Othman, S.H., Eisa, T.A., Al-Dhaqm, A., Nasser, M. et al. 2022. Financial fraud detection based on machine learning: a systematic literature review. *Applied Sciences*, 12: 9637. https://doi.org/10.3390/app12199637.

Almeida, F. and Senapati, B. 2024. Striving for symbiosis: human-machine relations in the AI Era. 2024 *IEEE Integrated STEM Education Conference* (ISEC) (pp. 1–4). Princeton NJ, USA: IEEE.

Anderson, R. and Moore, T. 2020. The economics of cybercrime: a comprehensive review. *Journal of Cybersecurity*, 6(1): 1–16.

Bakry, A.N., Alsharkawy, A.S., Farag, M.S. and Raslan, K.R. 2023. Automatic suppression of false positive alerts in anti-money laundering systems using machine learning. *The Journal of Supercomputing, Volume*, 80: 6264–6284 (2024).

Bao, Y., Gong, W. and Yang, K. 2023. A literature review of human–AI synergy in decision making: from the perspective of affordance actualization theory. *Systems*, 11(9): 442.

Barry, C. (2024, April 16). 5 Ways Cybercriminals are Using AI: Malware Generation. Retrieved from Barracuda: https://blog.barracuda.com/2024/04/16/5-ways-cybercriminals-are-using-ai--malware-generation.

Bélanger, F., Collignon, S. and Crossler, R.E. 2021. The role of human judgment in cybercrime detection: A critical analysis. *MIS Quarterly Executive*, 20(3): 145–167.

Binns, R. 2018. Fairness in machine learning: lessons from political philosophy. Conference on fairness, accountability, and transparency (pp. 1–11). *Proceedings of Machine Learning Research* (PMLR).

Brynjolfsson, E. and McAfee, A. 2017, July 18. The business of artificial intelligence: what it can and cannot do for your organization. *Retrieved from Harvard Business Review*: https://hbr.org/2017/07/the-business-of-artificial-intelligence.

Carpenter, P. 2024, February 29. Understanding The Limits Of AI and What This Means For Cybersecurity. Retrieved from Forbes: https://www.forbes.com/councils/forbesbusinesscouncil/2024/02/29/understanding-the-limits-of-ai-and-what-this-means-for-cybersecurity/.

Commonwealth Bank. 2022, July 4. CBA introduces leading AI technology to protect more customers from scams. Retrieved from commbank.com.au: https://www.commbank.com.au/articles/newsroom/2022/07/scams-fraud-artificial-intelligence.html.

Deloitte Centre for Government Insights. (2024, October 15). Could artificial intelligence fuel the future of financial investigations? Retrieved from deloitte.com: https://www2.deloitte.com/us/en/insights/industry/public-sector/ai-financial-investigations.html.

Deloitte. (n.d.). The Upside: AI and financial crime risk management. Retrieved from deloitte.com: https://www2.deloitte.com/us/en/pages/advisory/articles/upside-transaction-monitoring.html.

Europol. 2018, March 26. Mastermind behind EUR 1 billion cyber bank robbery arrested in Spain. Retrieved from Europol: https://www.europol.europa.eu/media-press/newsroom/news/mastermind-behind-eur-1-billion-cyber-bank-robbery-arrested-in-spain.

FBI San Francisco. 2024, May 8. FBI Warns of Increasing Threat of Cyber Criminals Utilizing Artificial Intelligence. Retrieved from fbi.gov: https://www.fbi.gov/contact-us/field-offices/sanfrancisco/news/fbi-warns-of-increasing-threat-of-cyber-criminals-utilizing-artificial-intelligence.

Financial Crime Academy. 2024, November 8. Empowering Compliance: AI Solutions Redefine AML Investigations. Retrieved from Financial Crime Academy: https://financialcrimeacademy.org/ai-solutions-for-aml-investigations/#:~:text=Danske%20Bank%3A%20Danske%20Bank%2C%20a,reducing%20the%20overall%20review%20time.

Fu, D.S., Yang, D.B. and Zarifis, D.A. 2023. Human–AI Teaming: Synergy, Decision-Making and Interdependency. *Systems*.

Hadi, D.A. 2023, November 13. The dynamic between humans & AI in tackling financial crime. Retrieved from AI Magazine: https://aimagazine.com/articles/the-dynamic-between-humans-ai-in-tackling-financial-crime.

Hadi, D.A. and Sotuminu, S. 2023, November 13. The dynamic between humans & AI in tackling financial crime. Retrieved from AI Magazine: https://aimagazine.com/articles/the-dynamic-between-humans-ai-in-tackling-financial-crime.

Hasham, S., Joshi, S. and Mikkelsen, D. 2019. Financial crime and fraud in the age of cybersecurity. McKinsey & Company.

Horvatic, D. and Lipic, T. 2021. Human-Centric AI: The Symbiosis of Human and Artificial Intelligence. *Entropy*, 10.3390/e23030332.

Kase, S.E., Hung, C.P., Krayzman, T., Hare, J.Z., Rinderpsacher, B.C. and Su, S.M. 2022. The future of collaborative human-artificial intelligence decision-making for mission planning. *Frontiers in Psychology*, 13: 850628. doi: 10.3389/fpsyg.2022.850628.

Kay, A., Hutcherson, C., Keene, C., Zhang, X. and Terwilliger, M.G. 2021. How financial institutions address cybersecurity threats: A critical analysis. *Issues in Information Systems*, 63–74.

Maor, E. (2024, September 12). Evasion Tactics Used by Cybercriminals to Fly Under the Radar. Retrieved from SecurityWeek: https://www.securityweek.com/evasion-tactics-used-by-cybercriminals-to-fly-under-the-radar/.

May, R.D. 2023, November 30. Fighting money launderers with artificial intelligence at HSBC. Retrieved from cloud.google.com: https://cloud.google.com/blog/topics/financial-services/how-hsbc-fights-money-launderers-with-artificial-intelligence.

Molina, D.A., Kharlov, V. and Chen, J.-S. 2024. Towards effective human-AI collaboration in decision-making: a comprehensive review and conceptual framework. 2024 *Portland International Conference on Management of Engineering and Technology* (PICMET) (pp. 1–6). Portland: IEEE.

Nagao, K. 2019. Symbiosis between Humans and Artificial Intelligence. pp. 135–151. *In*: Nagao, K. (ed.). *Artificial Intelligence Accelerates Human Learning*. Singapore: Springer.

Nasdaq. 2024, January 16. Global Financial Crime Report. Retrieved from Nasdaq: https://www.nasdaq.com/global-financial-crime-report#TL-Nasdaq-2024-Global-Financial-Crime-Report.

Nicholls, J., Kuppa, A. and Le-Khac, N.-A. 2021. Financial cybercrime: a comprehensive survey of deep learning approaches to tackle the evolving financial crime landscape. *IEEE Access*, 9: 163965–16398.

PR Newswire. 2023, June 21. Google cloud launches ai-powered anti money laundering product for financial institutions. Retrieved from PR Newswire: https://www.prnewswire.com/news-releases/google-cloud-launches-ai-powered-anti-money-laundering-product-for-financial-institutions-301856403.html.

Reid, A.S. 2018. Financial crime in the twenty-first century: the rise of the virtual collar criminal. In R. N, White Collar Crime and Risk. Palgrave Studies in Risk, Crime and Society (pp. 231–251). London: Palgrave Macmillan.

Ren, M., Chen, N. and Qiu, H. 2023. Human-machine collaborative decision-making: an evolutionary roadmap based on cognitive intelligence. *International Journal of Social Robotics*, 1101–1114.

Reuters. 2024, November 15. New York Department of Financial Services provides AI cybersecurity guidance: what you need to know. Retrieved from Reuters: https://www.reuters.com/legal/legalindustry/new-york-department-financial-services-provides-ai-cybersecurity-guidance-what-2024-11-15/.

Sanction Scanner. 2024, September 17. The Effects of Artificial Intelligence on Anti-Money Laundering. Retrieved from sanctionscanner.com: https://www.sanctionscanner.com/blog/artificial-intelligence-and-anti-money-laundering-17.

Shokri, R., Stronati, M., Song, C. and Shmatikov, V. 2017. Membership inference attacks against machine learning models. In 2017 *IEEE Symposium on Security and Privacy* (SP) (pp. 3–18). San Jose, CA, USA: IEEE. https://doi.org/10.1109/SP.2017.41.

Socradar. 2024, August 24. AI-assisted cyber attacks examples. Retrieved from socradar.io: https://socradar.io/examples-of-ai-assisted-cyber-attacks.

Software Engineering Insights. 2024, January 16. 20 Uses of Artificial Intelligence in Day-to-Day Life. Retrieved from daffodil: https://insights.daffodilsw.com/blog/20-uses-of-artificial-intelligence-in-day-to-day-life#:~:text=Prominent%20examples%20of%20AI%20software,and%20requires%20no%20peripheral%20devices.

Thomson Reuters. 2024, April 29. SARs and Fraud in 2024: Expect more - lots more. Retrieved from Thomson Reuters: https://www.thomsonreuters.com/en-us/posts/investigation-fraud-and-risk/sars-fraud-2024/.

Uddin, M.H., Ali, M.H. and Hassan, M.K. 2020. Cybersecurity hazards and financial system vulnerability: a synthesis of literature. Risk Management, 239–309.

UHURA. n.d. The Role of AI in Anti-Money Laundering. Retrieved from uhurasolutions.com: https://uhurasolutions.com/2023/08/01/the-role-of-ai-in-anti-money-laundering/#:~:text=By%20employing%20machine%20learning%20algorithms%20to%20scrutinise%20customer%20data%20and,accuracy%20of%20their%20AML%20program.

United Nations Office on Drugs and Crime. (n.d.). Money Laundering Overview. Retrieved from UNODC: https://www.unodc.org/unodc/en/money-laundering/overview.html.

Wang, (Justin), Y., Yang, X., Ju, C., Zhang, Y., Zhang, J., Ma, v. et al. 2024. Quantum Computing in Community Detection for Anti-Fraud Applications. *Entropy*, 1026. https://doi.org/10.3390/e26121026.

Wilson, H.J. and Daugherty, P.R. 2019, October 21. Creating the Symbiotic AI Workforce of the Future. Retrieved from MITSloan Management Review: https://sloanreview.mit.edu/article/creating-the-symbiotic-ai-workforce-of-the-future/.

Wilson, H.J. and Daugherty, P.R. 2019, October 21. Creating the Symbiotic AI Workforce of the Future. Retrieved from MIT Sloan Management Review: https://sloanreview.mit.edu/article/creating-the-symbiotic-ai-workforce-of-the-future/.

Zahedi, Z. and Kambhampati, S. 2021, March 18. Human-AI Symbiosis: A Survey of Current Approaches. Retrieved from Cornell University: https://arxiv.org/abs/2103.09990.

Chapter 14

Biomedical Digital Twin as a Part of the Industry 5.0

Conceptual View

David J. Herzog,[1] *Nitsa J. Herzog*[2,*] and *Mhd Saeed Sharif*[3]

1. Introduction

Industrial Revolution 4.0 is conceptualised as a cyber-physical production space (Pivoto et al. 2021). The exponential growth of computer power has consequently brought novel techniques. Industrial Revolution 4.0 is based on the interaction of AI, Big Data processing, IoT, robotics, driverless vehicles, and 3D printers. The smart industry is extensively exploited for healthcare and biomedical research (Nollo et al. 2022), but the idea itself visibly lacks significant human and biological components. Customisation, virtual and augmented reality, along with 3D digital twins, are instrumental steps towards Industry 5.0. This next stage is expected to include constant communication between humans and Industry 4.0 infrastructure, personalisation, a green environment, and sustainable product cycles. The concept of Industry 5.0 must focus not only on 4D-5D printing, holograms, and virtual reality but also on the broader notion of a cyber-biological space and its interactions (Frederico 2021). While human-machine interaction today includes human-computer and human-robot interaction, this cannot be limited to the ideas of co-bots and personal adjustment. Cyber-biological systems potentially range from standard biosensors

[1] Computer Science, London Campus of Ulster, Solent and Roehampton Universities.
Email: davidjosef.herzog@qa.com
[2] Environmental and Engineering, Northumbria University, UK.
[3] School of Architecture, Engineering and Computing, UEL, UK.
Email: s.sharif@uel.ac.uk
* Corresponding author: nitsa.herzog@northumbria.ac.uk

DOI: 10.1201/9781003540373-14

and DNA programming to multiscale biosensing and an interactive digital twin of the biosphere (Dixon et al. 2021).

An underlying principle is a data-driven process. Data exchange between humankind and the digital realm is determined by the nature of civilization itself (Rosol et al. 2018). The contemporary paradigm shift is multiscale and reflects the interplay of "natural spheres and a technosphere". Natural Intelligence (Van Gerven 2017) created an extension, Artificial Intelligence. Regardless of its nature, intelligence's essence is recognized as algorithmic (Nelson 2001). More precisely, it has computational, algorithmic and implementation levels (Van Gerven 2017). An anti-entropy aspect of the Universe, in order to achieve expansion into all spheres of the environment, from the micro-world to the open space, developed intelligence in its earliest stages (Jacob and Shapira 2005). It opened the theoretical possibility for its "intelligent" copy.

There are discussion about eternal life, continues as a computerized behavioural clone (Savin-Baden and Burden 2019). in the machine, with the potential for physical replication (Laakasuo et al. 2021). Genetic (Herbert 2021), regenerative (Aithal 2021), hibernating, cyborg (McGee and Maguire 2007), or hive mind forms of perpetual transhuman existence are also subjects of debate. They have multiple applications as a common denominator of the modern digital revolution (San et al. 2021). Model creation, pattern recognition, data processing, smart environment and digital twinning today employ various AI algorithms by default (Rasheed et al. 2020). Figure 1 (Source: Carlos Fy from Wikimedia Commons, Free Attribution-ShareAlike 4.0 International (CC BY-SA 4.0)) demonstrates a combined AR-enabled cyber-physical object—basic elements of possible digital twinning. It permits effective control of mechanical systems through the Augmented Reality framework and digital twin information flows.

Mathematical and physical modelling, supplied with statistical tools today, is supported by computer-aided design, virtual and augmented reality (Jones et al. 2020), and blockchain (Suhail et al. 2022). It allows for running fundamental research, experiments *in silico* and proactive management with the help of the digital twin (Barricelli et al. 2019). Used by NASA for the Apollo 13 mission, the concept was formulated by David Gelernter in the early nineties, and the term was coined by John Vickers and Michael Grieves in 2002–2003 (Grieves and Vickers 2017). Digital

Figure 1: AR-enabled cyber-physical object.

twinning goes beyond modelling *in silico* and simulations by the data flow between physical and digital twins (Wright and Davidson 2020). The concept was extensively used for infrastructural and industrial products and processes (Kirchhof et al. 2020). Recently, it was extended to biomedical research and clinical management (Volkov et al. 2021).

The next step is the expansion of digital twinning into routine clinical practice. The future applications are seen as biosphere twinning, expected to be in place around 2060 (Dixon et al. 2021). Biomedical digital twins are essential for fundamental research and clinical experiments *in silico* (Bajwa et al. 2021). Coupled with organ-on-a-chip and genetic data, it helps to produce effective personalized medicines (Wu 2020). Cyber-physical models with digital twins are used for medical training (Hagmann et al. 2021). It helps to speed up research and education but raises ethical questions and creates new data protection issues (Bruynseels et al. 2018). The primary idea is to present an object, process or environment as a data aggregation (Meulen and Bruinsma 2019).

In biomedicine, the predominant focus is on the person, and the levels range from the atomic and molecular to the population and the holistic biophysical world (Kamel Boulos and Zhang 2021). The digital twins can be 1) structural, 2) anatomic (Hashizume 2021), 3) physiological, 4) behavioural and 5) complex, with the reflection of different aspects of functionality, from mechanical to biochemical, electrophysiological and behavioural (Al-Khafaji et al. 2019). These types of digital twins, made for the same biological object with different functionality, are called digital siblings (Papatsimpa and Linnartz 2021). The higher levels are often modular, where interaction with other twins and the immediate environment are included (Masison et al. 2021).

This paper outlines the main technologies and their applications for biomedical digital twins. It then provides a hierarchical overview of simulations and their cyber-biological extensions as digital twins, followed by the algorithms and techniques used in them. The final part discusses the possibility of developing systems of biomedical twins, their capabilities, and their limitations.

2. Biomedical Digital Twins: Levels And Types

Biomedical digital twins in this paper are classified on the basis of biological hierarchy: (1) omics, (2) biological cells, (3) tissues, (4) organs, (3) organismic, and (4) population. All of them differ in type and have their own digital siblings.

2.1 Omics

In the last two hundred years, biomedical studies have made significant advances on the cellular and molecular levels (Baronov 2008). Digital applications have made computational biology and bioinformatics possible. Genomics, proteomics, transcriptomics, and epigenomics work with the fundamental code of life - DNA and RNA - and their translation into proteins. There are more than 30,000 genes in the human nuclear genome and approximately 3.2 Billion nucleotides (Brown 2002). The number of protein molecules only in one eucaryotic yeast cell of Saccharomyces

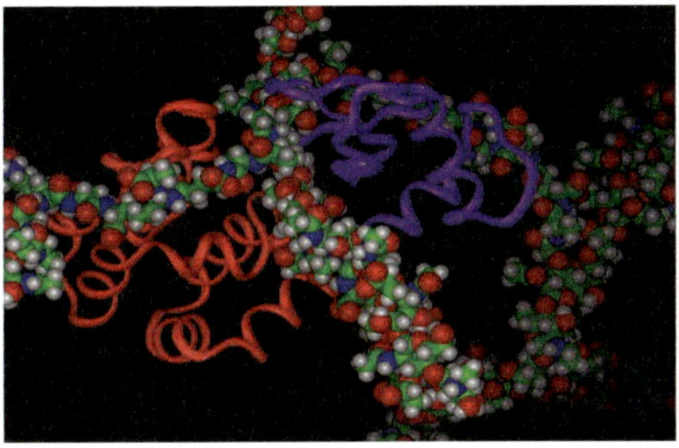

Figure 2: Computer simulation of the T4 lysozyme (rendered as a ribbon) wrapped around a bacterial cell.

cerevisiae is estimated at 42 million (Ho et al. 2018). Still, there is the current possibility of creating digital analogues of molecular complexes for elements of organelles and cells. For example, in Figure 2 (Source: EMSL, Attribution-NonCommercial-ShareAlike 2.0 Generic (CC BY-NC-SA 2.0)), we see a molecular computer simulation of the lymphocyte T4 lysozyme, which is wrapped around non-visible bacteria.

Digital twinning requires additional information stream from the object to the regularly updated digital copy. The field is highly developed today, and it is impossible to imagine modern biology without computerized tools, databases or algorithmic search and model building (Zobel-Roos et al. 2019). Digital twins in disruptive clinical research, for example, in haematology, always include genomics, analysed with machine learning (ML) and deep learning (DL) methods (Walter et al. 2021). Digital twinning is proposed for mRNA vaccine production (Schmidt et al. 2021). Interactions between biochemical molecules, especially in living cells and tissues, are complex. They require a clear understanding of reaction networks and cycles. Metabolomics is significantly enhanced by digital tools. There are specific areas, such as lipidomics and glycomics, which deal with the metabolism of lipids and glycans in cells and tissues. Databases hold tens of thousands of interconnected entries (Ren et al. 2015). Human Metabolome Database or HMDB 5.0 (https://hmdb.ca) currently holds 217,920 compounds (Wishart et al. 2023). *In vivo*, metabolomics for biological models is supported today by digital twinning (Korvink et al. 2018). Multi-omics is supposed to be an essential part of the Multiple Sclerosis Digital Twin project, MSDT (Voigt et al. 2021).

2.2 Cells, tissues and organs

The elementary organizational and operating unit of the organism is the cell (Egli et al. 2020, Gkouskou 2020). There are, on average, 3.7 × 1013 cells in the human body (Geanta et al. 2022, Roy and Conroy 2018), with around 1014 atoms in a cell and roughly 2 × 1025 organic molecules. There are more than 200 types of cells in the human body. Similar types of cells function as tissues, organs and systems. For example, the brain consists of around 1012 neurons and at least 1013 glial cells with 1015 synapses (Herculano-Houzel 2012, Ho et al. 2011) in the connectome.

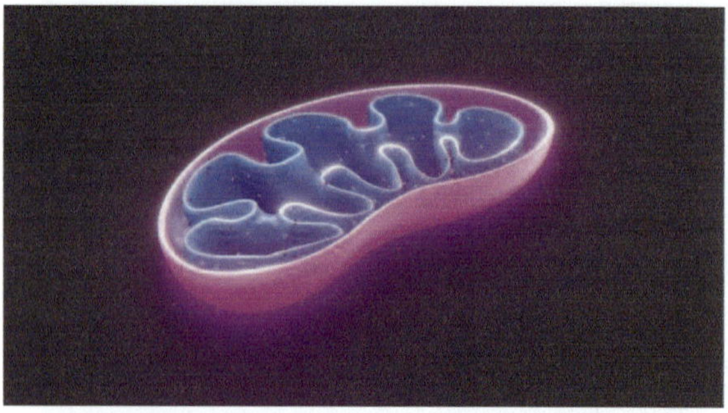

Figure 3: Mitochondria: A structural model.

An average neuron has no less than 104 synapses per neuron. Estimates also exist for the number of cells in various organs and systems. The number of osteocytes is approximately $7.11 \pm 3.72 \times 10^8$, while bone marrow contains around $7.53 \pm 2.18 \times 10^{11}$ cells. The liver has an estimated 3.61×10^{11} cells, and pancreatic islets contain approximately $2.95 \pm 0.78 \times 10^9$ cells (Bianconi et al. 2013). Digital twins of different types are used for the representation of organelles, cells, tissues, organs, tumours (Gaebel et al. 2021) and bionic prosthetics. Figure 3 (Source: Pixabey, license (CC BY-ND 2.0)) demonstrates a structural model of the intracellular organelle, the mitochondria, which can be a starting point for the organelle structural and functional dynamic simulation and, as a next step, the digital twin of the organelle.

On a higher level, the neuro-musculoskeletal (NMS) digital twin is important for creating dynamic models of interaction between patient and mechanical objects, as well as prosthetic and assistive devices (Pizzolato et al. 2019). The digital twin of whole dentition is proposed for prosthetic restoration (Dobrzanski and Dobrzanski 2020).

Normal and pathological anatomy and physiology are reflected in structural and functional digital twins. These models and simulations are important for bioprinting (An et al. 2021), personalised oncology (Hormuth et al. 2021), and prosthetics (Antonini et al. 2021). The HuBMAP Consortium created the Human Biomolecular Atlas (HuBMAP Consortium 2019), which is open to other researchers. The modular approach takes into account several types of interacting cells (Masison et al. 2021). Digital twins of tissue cultures (Moller and Portner 2021) employ a whole set of mathematical models. An extension of biological 3D tissue models is organ-on-a-chip (OOC) (Bajwa et al. 2021). The dynamic digital twin can be enriched by the data flow from the OOC. Figure 4 (Sources: National Center for Advancing Translational Sciences, Public Domain Mark 1.0) demonstrates the potential of the OOC system for creating body-on-a-chip (BOC).

There are a significant number of proposed digital twins at the organ level. The synergy model of the heart for personalised cardiology (Corral-Acero et al. 2020) opens possibilities for quick, precise, and highly individual diagnosis and treatment. Virtual liver dynamic modelling starts from the cellular level and is built up to the organ level (Holzhütter et al. 2012). The virtual patient can be supplemented with lungs to reflect anatomy, physiology, and tumour-focused treatment (Barricelli et al. 2019). Deep brain stimulation, reflected in density heat maps, requires a brain neural

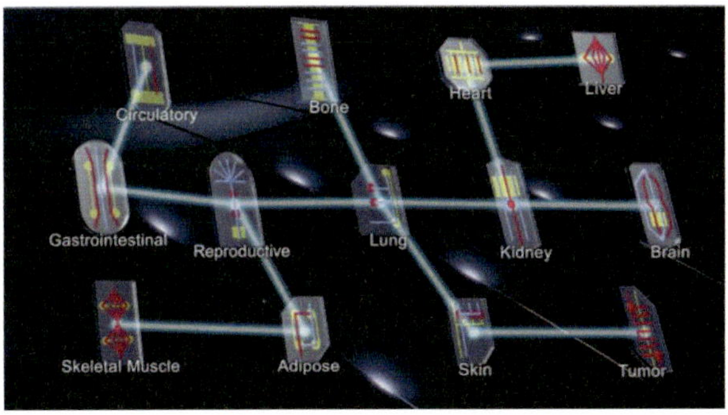

Figure 4: Several tissue chips can be connected in a system to simulate a human-body-on-a-chip.

model (Barbiero et al. 2021). The entire nervous system can be represented as a digital twin (Narcross 2021). Today, the 3D virtual model of the kidney has become standard for partial nephrectomy (Amparore et al. 2022).

2.3 Organismic and populational level

The systemic and organismic level raises the question of the whole-body digital twin. A number of pathophysiological, pharmacological, and treatment models have been proposed for routine use. Figure 5 demonstrates a still image of a short 3D intravascular blood flow visualisation. The dynamic model can serve as a basis for specific physiological digital twins. The part and whole-body musculoskeletal anatomic, structural, and functional OpenSim framework is proposed for education and research (see Figure 5 – Source: OpenSim GUI 1.1 By A Habib, Attribution-ShareAlike 3.0 Unported (CC BY-SA 3.0)).

Pathological multiorganic or whole-body processes can also be modelled and developed into a digital twin. Multiple sclerosis is dynamically modelled at the systemic level (Voigt et al. 2021). A stroke patient's digital twin is proposed for forecasting pathology progression (Allen et al. 2021). A treatment and condition

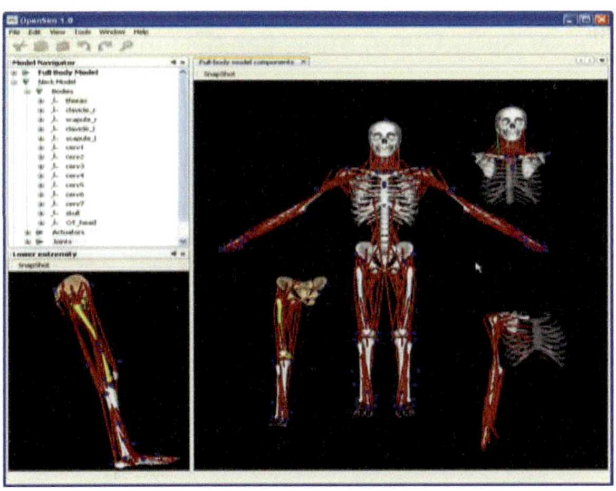

Figure 5: OpenSim musculo-skeletal modelling

Table 1: Levels of Biomedical Digital Twins.

Type	Level	Digital Solution	Digital siblings
Genome	Biochemical	Digital genetics	Close focus
Proteome	Biochemical	Digital proteomics	Close focus
Metabolome	Biochemical	Digital metabolomics	Close focus
Organelle	Subcellular	2D/3D digital twin	Structure/Function
Cell	Cellular	Digital twin	Structure/Function
Cell group	Tissue	3D digital twin	Structure/Function
Tumour	Sub-organic	Digital twin	Structure/Function
Prosthetic	Sub-organic	3D digital twin	Interactive
Heart Valve	Sub-organic	Dynamic model	Structural/Functional/Dynamic
Heart/Liver	Organ	Synergetic twin	Structural/Functional/Dynamic
Body part	Systemic	Dynamic model	Structural/Functional/Dynamic
Disease	Systemic	Dynamic model	Structural/Functional/Dynamic
Person	Organism	Dynamic model	Anatomic/Physiological
Person	Individuum	Behavioural twin	Dynamic simulation
Population	Group	Behavioural twin	Dynamic simulation
Population + environment	System	Synergy twins	Dynamic simulation

progress digital twin for a patient with sepsis has been created (Lal et al. 2020). At the organismic level, digital twinning makes personalised healthcare more accessible (Gaebel et al. 2021). Thus, Table 1 demonstrates the different levels of digital solutions in biomedicine.

At the holistic body level, behavioural circadian rhythms are integrated into digital twins (Papatsimpa and Linnartz 2021). A specific digital twin has been created for elderly healthcare management (Liu et al. 2019). In healthcare, specific dynamic models can be used for theoretical individual patient treatment, medical procedure planning, and training. Figure 6 (Source: Duke University Human Simulation and Patient Safety Center. Attribution-ShareAlike 3.0 Unported (CC BY-

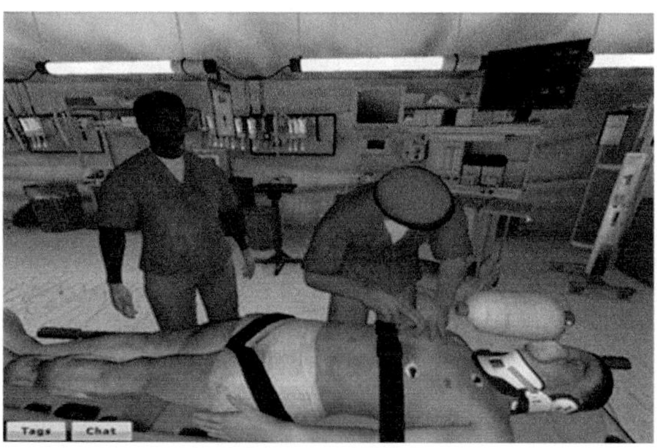

Figure 6: A screenshot from the 3DiTeams game. A player performs chest percussion.

SA 3.0)) demonstrates a screenshot from the 3DiTeams educational game. Coupling such technology with AR, VR, haptic technology, and digital twin models opens new possibilities for safe, effective, and technologically enhanced medical training.

A more abstract approach is also possible. A whole-body diagnostic digital twin has been proposed based on a modular approach using a graph model (Barbiero et al. 2021). The modules reflect different levels of the organism, and specific graph modes represent pathological conditions. This approach may require a biomedical model, body-on-a-chip (Sung et al. 2018), and its digital twin. However, the feasibility of a fully realistic human digital twin remains a question (Shengli 2021).

How far can we go in this direction if an augmented digital twin requires not only a reflection of biological anatomy and physiology but also environmental factors and interacting agents? Is it feasible to create individualised, adjustable, dynamic human digital twins based on existing clinical data or additional data collection from wearable sensors, diagnostic tools, and treatment results? It is certainly possible to limit the functionality of a digital twin to behaviour or to single public health issues, such as Covid-19 management (Barat et al. 2021) and vaccination centres (Pilati et al. 2021). Broader questions of society and environmental levels of biosecurity still await the digital twin solutions (Geanta et al. 2021, Kemp et al. 2021).

3. Data for Digital Twins: Sources and Means

The concept of the digital twin is principally based on volumetric information about the physical object or group of objects that are to be twinned. The biomedical digital twin represents structures and processes from the molecular level to the population level. There are numerous sources for data extraction. For "omics", twinning information is obtained from extensive medical and biomedical databases. Imaging and non-imaging data can be gathered through various methods, such as X-ray, molecular magnetic resonance imaging (mMRI), mass spectrometry, analytical biochemistry, molecular biophysics, and other techniques (Mathe et al. 2018). Imaging and bioinformatics tools allow for the structural and functional analysis of data. These results are utilised in clinical and pharmacological research as well as medical practice. A similar approach is applied at the cellular and tissue levels (Love 2017).

Digital twinning at these levels is crucial for histochemistry research, diagnostics, tissue bioprinting, cell therapy, and embryo and tissue models (Braun 2021). Clinical research data is essential for organ, system, and organism levels. Artificial intelligence (AI) is now employed at every level of research and data implementation, including computer vision (CV), machine learning (ML), and deep learning (DL). Electronic Health Records (EHR) (Gaebel et al. 2021) serve as a source of Big Data and personalised medical data. Today, these records are routinely processed using ML and DL algorithms. Additional information can be incorporated into databases through smart medical devices, smart diagnostic/laboratory devices, and specialised software. Computer vision analysis of diagnostic images—such as those of the skin, eye fundus, and other visualised information from magnetic resonance imaging (MRI), computer tomography (CT), and ultrasound (US)—provides the basis for personalised digital twins of organs, systems, and the whole body (Masison et al. 2021). Behavioural data from smart and wearable devices, smart environments, smartphones, and internet sources can also be integrated for clinical research, medical treatment, and even medical marketing. On a broader scale, these applications extend to public health (Boulos and Zhang 2021). Digital shadow data can also be added to EHR to generate digital twins. However, obtaining high-quality data is crucial. The quality of a digital twin depends not only on data precision but also on model accuracy, interaction quality between the digital and physical twin, and real or near-real-time dynamics (Shengli 2021). From a technical perspective, quality is determined by technological capacity and processing functionality, including the robustness of algorithms, hardware quality, and operational factors such as CPU/GPU usage and multichannel data processing. Data collected from multiple sources can be processed and analysed with AI tools (see Table 2).

The massive implementation of digital twins is expected to speed up research and allow personalised medicines and highly customised treatment. It is supposed to be integrated into R&D, coupled with EHR and wider data (Bajwa et al. 2021). Digital twinning changes the way patients are treated. Diagnostics and clinical procedures with the help of digital twins and augmented and virtual reality (AR/VR) require not only technical overhaul but also changes in clinical training and practice. At the same time, it raises questions about privacy and data protection (Bruynseels et al. 2018). Data encoding and decoding, avatar and persona usage, and anonymisation

Table 2: Data sources and means of extraction.

Sources	Means	AI tools	Area of application
Omics	Research data, thematic databases	ML, DL Computer vision	Fundamental and Clinical research
Electronic Health Records	Big Data harvesting, Smart medical devices, diagnostic software	ML, DL Computer vision, Decision Support System (DSS)	Clinical and Pharmacological research Clinical management
Public health data	Big Data harvesting	DL, ML, People interaction graphs	Public health research and management
Smart home	Smart devices, computing devices, sensors, wearables, AAL data and smart medical devices	DL, ML, DSS, Pattern recognition	Clinical research and management
Behavioural data	Internet and mobile, smart environment sensors, smart devices, computing devices, wearables	DL, ML, Computer vision	Public health management, marketing
Smart environment	Smart environment sensors, smart vehicles, smartphones	DL, ML, Computer vision, Pattern recognition	Personal and Public health management, marketing
Digital shadow	Internet and mobile data, behavioural data, smart device data	DL, ML, Computer vision, Pattern recognition	Personalized Marketing data, Personal and Public health management

are not easily integrated with dynamic digital twinning and personalised medicine (Rossant and Tam). Also, technological solutions have to be balanced with ethical requirements (Baronov 2008).

4. AI solution for Digital Twin Data

Digital twinning requires the interaction of dynamic data from the object about structure or processes/functions and data from the pre-existing model, simulation, or previous stages (Peng et al. Peng). Space and time characteristics are discrete, and ML algorithms often reduce and homogenise physical information. The data for biomedical digital twins can be obtained from biophysical and biochemical objects and processes at every level, from molecular to populational and environmental. There are certain groups of AI algorithms employed for the necessary functions or levels. Dynamic modelling can be applied to molecular, cellular, and higher levels, such as an organ or system.

4.1 AI approaches overview

Genomics, proteomics, metabolomics, and transcriptomics depend on information collection methods and quick database analysis. The gene-to-phenotype approach is also implemented in digital twinning (Bates et al. 2020). Information about the structure of molecules is derived from biochemical methods such as X-ray crystallography, mass spectrometry, cryoEM, nuclear magnetic resonance MS, electron paramagnetic resonance, and some other techniques. CV and ML methods are extensively used (Dias and Torkamani 2019). CAD helps to reflect physical objects as the digital twin. Computer vision techniques allow high-precision object digitalisation, often dynamically. MRI, various X-ray and CT methods, US, positron-emission tomography (PET), microscopy, and other medical imaging and combinations are popular methods for data retrieval (Panayides et al. 2020). The obtained information is compared against existing databases. Data processing can be done with the help of evolutionary algorithms such as genetic ones. Natural language processing (NLP) and long short-term memory (LSTM) networks are also popular methods for these tasks (Yandell and Majoros 2002, Caudai et al. 2021). Digital twin construction can benefit from the bionic approach when a digitalised biological object produces potential solutions for the technological sphere. For example, modelling the nervous system today can improve artificial nervous systems (ANS) and their functionality (Narcross 2021).

Behavioural digital twins are important for clinical management, medical education, and public health modelling (Al-Khafaji et al. 2019). They are also crucial in catastrophe medicine when healthcare specialists' intervention depends on information about the type of disaster, available resources, and public behaviour. The smart city environment allows the implementation of systemic combinations of digital twins for crisis management.

4.2 AI data preparation

Some essential matters require solutions in AI information management. Data usually requires normalization and standardization (Castiglioni et al. 2021). Normalization methods utilize a wide range of techniques for contrast-to-noise reduction.

The collected raw data preferably has to be labelled for classification and further processing. Labels are assigned based on the features and parameters of data objects. The class and value of labels can be attributed manually, automatically, or semi-automatically. There is also interactive labelling in the case of the human-in-the-loop approach (Sager et al. 2021). Automatic labelling can be done by neural networks (NN). Labelled data can then be processed and classified. Unlabelled data can be grouped using clustering technologies. The well-known clustering methods are based on C-means, K-means, K-Nearest Neighbours (KNN), and Expectation-Maximisation (EM) algorithms. There are different approaches to clustering, which can roughly be divided into hierarchical and partitional, followed by further subdivisions (Bae et al. 2020). They might also be used in computer vision for image segmentation (Panayides et al. 2020).

Unique data features can be represented as dimensions. However, the problem with Big Data is its high dimensionality. There are several ways to reduce the number of dimensions. Algorithms such as Principal Component Analysis (PCA), Linear Discriminant Analysis (LDA), Restricted Boltzmann Machine (RBM) (Salakhutdinov and Hinton 2007), and Extreme Learning Machine (ELM) are widely used for dimensionality reduction. In signal processing, for example, wavelet transform (Abramovich et al. 2000) is one of the methods of dimensionality reduction, while the Fourier Transform (FT) is exploited for the improvement of signal-to-noise ratio, e.g., noise reduction (Kazimierczuk et al. 2012). Classification and analysis of information have become more complicated in the presence of a large amount of meaningless information called "noise". The raw data often includes noise. The reduction of outliers, replacement of missing values, and removal of duplicate entries (Dempster 1971), data standardisation, and consistency control are essential for data preparation (Nakamura et al. 2020).

Clean and processed data can be used for model training, which can be done with the help of classic and deep learning algorithms. Several approaches exist for choosing the best AI model. Among them are the Least Absolute Shrinkage and Selection Operator (LASSO) regression, Ridge regression, and Elastic Net Regression (ENR) (Omran et al. 2007).

Table 3 aggregates the digital twin functions, their sources and levels with the applied AI tools and areas of applications.

4.3 AI data processing for biomedical digital twin

As we can see, the digital twin concept is closely connected to AI. Self-adaptation and self-parametrisation are recognised as core characteristics of the digital twinning process (Barricelli et al. 2019). Statistically based tools, pattern recognition, ML, and dynamic programming are important for cyber-biological systems. Data preprocessing and labelling are followed by feature extraction and analysis. Training

Table 3: AI for digital twin.

Digital Twin Function	Method/Source	Algorithm/method	Area of application	Level	Type
Data acquisition	Mass Spectrometry; MALDI; Microarray; X-ray- crystallography; X-ray; UltraSound; Digital image; Video streaming; Sensors data	Speeded-Up Robust Features; Scale-Invariant Feature Transform; Support Vector Machine; Principal Component Analysis; Convolutional Neural Network; Recurrent Neural Network;	Biochemistry; Histochemistry; Clinical research; Clinical practice; Public health	Omics Cell/tissue Organ/system Organism	Biophysical; Biochemical; Biomechanical; Behavioural
Analytical	Research data; Electronic Health Records; BLAST; OMIM; PDB; EMBL; 23andMe; Family Tree; UNIPROT; HMDB; Population statistics	Speeded-Up Robust Features; Scale-Invariant Feature Transform; Support Vector Machine; Principal Component Analysis; Convolutional Neural Network; Recurrent Neural Network;	Biochemistry; Histochemistry; Clinical research; Clinical practice; Public health	Omics Cell/tissue Organ/system Organism	Biophysical; Biochemical; Biomechanical; Behavioural
Modelling	All above	Probabilistic algorithms; Hidden Markov Model; Generalized Linear Model; Gradient Boosting Machine; Deformable model algorithms; K-means	Biochemistry; Histochemistry; Clinical research; Clinical practice; Public health	Omics; Cell/tissue; Organ/system; Organism/ population	Biophysical; Biochemical; Biomechanical; Behavioural; Clinical; Modular
Dynamic interaction	All above	Time series; Markovian models; Reinforcement learning; Optimization algorithms; Random Forest	Biochemistry; Histochemistry; Clinical research; Clinical practice; Public health	Omics; Cell/tissue; Organ/system; Organism/ population	Biophysical; Biochemical; Biomechanical; Behavioural; Clinical; Modular

previously extracted features from objects of interest leads to data modelling and recognition of new objects if they match the model. Multiple feature recognition and extraction algorithms are exploited in the recognition process. Among them is the classic "Harris" detector (Harris and Stephens 1988). More modern variants belong to the derivatives of a Gaussian (Schmid et al. 2000, Triggs 2004). Local features or key-point descriptors help to identify and describe the unique characteristics of the image. The list of those detectors and descriptors is long, and it can start from the famous Scale-Invariant Feature Transform (SIFT) (Lowe 2004), histogram of oriented gradients (HOG) (Isik 2014) and Speeded-Up Robust Features (SURF) algorithm (Bay 2006, Oyallon and Rabin 2015). One of the most difficult tasks in digital image processing is image segmentation (Kumar et al. 2018). The images can be highly variable in colouring, gradient, and texture. The process of estimating the image segmentation before it starts can help with choosing the segmentation algorithm to be applied (Liu et al. 2011). It is proposed to use combined information from the histogram of the log gradient together with the local binary pattern histogram to predict the success of the segmentation (Liu et al. 2011, Li and Allinson 2008).

In some cases, the imaging data requires image restoration and reconstruction. Image restoration deals with the improvement of the appearance of an image. The restoration methods are based on mathematical or probabilistic models of image degradation and use inverse models for image recovery (Qiu et al. 2009). GRAPPA and SENSE algorithms are examples of image reconstruction used for DL (St-Jean et al. 2020). Computer vision in medicine often goes beyond strict visual detection and requires so-called "electronic phenotyping" (Willemink et al. 2020), incorporating the influx of information about other clinical features.

"Vision" in the case of biomedical digital twins often means a complex, modular approach with the ability to use different digital siblings together or interchangeably (Corral-Acero et al. 2020). It may require a combination of information obtained by special methods, databases and datasets, as in the case of the OpenOrganelle database. Focused Ion Beam (FIB)-Scanning Electron Microscope (SEM)-FIB-SEM datasets (Heinrich et al. 2021) are available for research and model building. The special algorithm, COSEM, is responsible for the interaction with OpenOrganelle.

AI tools for digital twinning are extensively used in Diagnostic Support Systems, which can be part of the biomedical digital twin. A Diagnostic Support System is a particular variant of a Decision Support System (Boulos and Zhang 2021).

The dynamic twinning process includes significant data flow between digital and physical/biological twins. Big Data, with its Vs, such as volume, volatility, velocity, and variety, acquires value by veracity. DL algorithms are frequently named as a superior solution for Big Data in biomedical applications as well. At the same time, DL algorithms sometimes have a long processing time and, significantly, have a so-called "black box" problem (Sendak et al. 2020). This can lead to malpractice in "black box" medicine (Price and Nicholson 2019) or even to privacy problems and model hijacking (De Cristofaro 2021). One solution is to produce a "white box" (Rudin 2019). Another is to replace DL with human-readable ML. Classic algorithms can work on limited data, require less computing power and often do not need a permanent connection with the Internet or databases. However, this can pose problems for modular dynamic biomedical digital twins, and a combination of ML and DL may be required.

5. Natural Intelligence and Artificial Intelligence Interaction

Industry 5.0 conception is based on the postulate of cyber-biological space (Dixon et al. 2021). The digital twin of the object's structure, function and environment allows dynamic modelling, simulation and just-in-time management. While these tasks can be seen as technically achievable, depending on the hardware and software facilities, narrowing the space between natural and artificial intelligence faces deep-rooted obstacles. For example, the difference between NI and AI is stated as "data extraction versus meaning extraction" (Jacob and Shapira 2005). While playing chess, the human brain is capable of using general reasoning and automatic patterns, while AI needs to consider long sequences of moves (Van der Maas and Stevenson 2021). This is reflected even in the level of research: there is insufficient interaction between studies about intelligence and AI (Neubauer 2021).

There are several well-known problems with AI (Lu et al. 2018). (1) Frame problem: AI is effective only for narrowly defined tasks and ineffective for a wide range of assignments. (2) Association function problem: AI extracts numerical information from a large volume of data and recognizes it when presented again but cannot use the wide associative properties of the natural brain. (3) Symbol grounding problems: While the human brain can perform the "zebra = horse + stripes" task, it is outside of normal AI functionality. (4) Authors also state mind and body problems when the physical basis of intelligence influences its type and functionality.

This problem can be reformulated as the difference in the structure of underlying networks and the way information is handled. An initial solution for bridging the gap was proposed several decades ago. The idea of AI and NN was taken from neural science, which is reflected in the terminology. However, the difference between neurons in NN and cellular neurons in living tissue is well known, as well as the difference between synapses and types of networks. The same logic is used for natural and artificial neurons and the same algorithmic approach (Nelson 2001). However, the structure of NN and the natural brain is quite dissimilar. The number of neurons in the brain is 10^{11}, while AI is based on a much smaller number. The speed of operations for the human brain is estimated at 10^8 MIPS (Moravec 2009), thanks to multiple parallel processes. The heterogeneity of natural neurons also can be a source of significant difference. The artificial NN uses different types of neurons compared to the natural brain (Perez-Nieves et al. 2021). This neuronal diversity, according to cited authors, greatly speeds up the learning process.

NI and AI can be represented as the difference between human-readable and machine-readable information, as well as natural and formal language (Sayers et al. 2021). At the same time, human readability is much wider than language disparity. For example, the limitation of unsupervised ML is often seen as the difference between the black-box approach and high-stakes human-understandable decision-making (Legg and Hutter 2007). There is also a fundamental question of "intelligence", which, according to some authors, is not easy to measure by the Turing test or other imitation tests (Legg and Hutter 2007), so AI is not easily comparable to NI. One of the solutions for the black box problem is the possibility of a white box (Rudin 2019). In a broad context of NI and AI interaction, humans can be seen as helpers for AI tasks (Kamar 2016). On the other hand, interaction can be presented by AI-assisted human functioning, such as Ambient Assisted Living (AAL), assisted driving, and other similar technologies (Rzepka and Berger 2018). For Industry 5.0, it is possible to speak about the necessity of pursuing human-AI complementarity and Hybrid Intelligence systems (Hemmer et al. 2021). Large language models (LLM) are relatively new tools with the potential for fruitful AI and NI interaction. While LLM, such as ChatGPT, are able to produce human-like texts and perform some testing tasks, they fall short of expectations of artificial general intelligence by their nature, exploiting a natural language understanding. It is shown to fail in some basic medical tasks and is not reliable as an assisting tool (Alberts et al. 2023). However, it might be integral in creating cyber-physical space, especially when digital twinning is an essential part of it.

6. Applications, Challenges, and Future Trends

The integration of digital twin technology in healthcare represents a transformative leap, offering unprecedented opportunities for patient care and treatment. At the same time, the implementation of digital models requires extensive knowledge of the latest technologies that provide comprehensive solutions for multiple challenges accompanied by the digital twinning industry.

6.1 Applications

While the concept of a digital twin has been around for several decades, its application in healthcare has only recently become available (Xames and Topcu 2024). The gradual implementation of digital twin technology, which initially started in the industrial and manufacturing sectors, has now extended to healthcare. This transformative technology is revolutionising the way we approach healthcare. Companies began proposing virtual replicas of equipment and medical devices to optimise operation, monitor performance, and predict maintenance needs. These digital models of human organs and tissues have positively influenced the development of medical imaging technologies, leading to an increase in diagnostic performance (Lee et al. 2022). They have also improved the customisation of medical prosthetics and implants. Digital twins are now able to continuously monitor patient data from wearable devices, alerting healthcare providers to any significant changes in a patient's health. They can be used in chronic conditions, lifestyle adjustments, and medical treatments.

Digital twin models are not just limited to practical applications. They are also widely implemented for professional medical training, providing a risk-free virtual environment for learning. Digital twins are actively used in surgical simulations, where visualised digital replicas of a patient's anatomy help to choose a surgical approach and anticipate potential complications. This educational use of digital twins is shaping the future of healthcare by preparing future professionals in a safe and effective manner.

The latest trends in digital replicas of cells, tissues, organs, and entire humans provide additional ground for researchers and medical professionals to understand medical pathologies and stimulate the development of predictive and personalised medicine by using different case scenarios. Digital twins can track patient progress and simulate different rehabilitation exercises, allowing therapists to tailor programmes to individual needs. This emphasis on personalised care reassures patients and healthcare providers alike about the potential for tailored treatments (Ghatti et al. 2023). In addition, the digital clone can engage a patient in virtual rehabilitation sessions and adapt exercises through the collection of real-time feedback. Most of all, digital twin technologies facilitate drug development and actively help in the building and adjustment of treatment plans.

Recent advancements in data analytics, machine learning, and cloud computing have accelerated the adoption of digital twins in the healthcare industry through predictive analytics, automated decision-making, and operational optimisation within healthcare facilities and hospital trusts.

6.2 Challenges and solutions

The multiple benefits of using digital twin solutions are obvious. However, a number of challenges are encountered during the development and implementation of digital twin technologies in the healthcare industry that require additional attention from the government, technological companies, and health organisations (Xames and Topcu 2024, Attaran and Celik 2023, Meijer et al. 2023). The solutions are explained in Table 4.

6.3 Future trends

The forecasting reports of investments in digital twin technologies demonstrate significant growth between 2021 and 2023 [125 – 129]. Figure 7 shows the Compound Annual Growth Rate (CAGR) based on the statistical information provided by reporting agencies over a period of 4 year from 2021 to 2023.

Future digital twin technologies will expand the development of precision medicine. Virtual twins will integrate various "omics" data (genomics, proteomics, metabolomics) to provide a comprehensive view of a patient's health, leading to more precise and targeted therapies (Meijer et al. 2023). For instance, incorporating genomic data into digital twins will enable highly personalised treatment in the fields of oncology and rare genetic disorders.

Future trends will also focus on virtualising patient cohorts for clinical trials. Implementing digital twins will improve the design and efficiency of clinical trials and enhance the evaluation of new treatments. Digital clones will become a central component of telemedicine platforms, providing doctors with a detailed, real-time view of a patient's health during virtual consultations. Digital models will facilitate the future development of personalised medicine.

Table 4: Challenges in digital twin technologies with possible solutions.

Challenges	**Solutions**
Data Integration and Interoperability	Industry-wide standards for data formats and communication protocols; Implementation of interoperability frameworks; Application Programming Interfaces (APIs) and Fast Healthcare Interoperability Resources (FHIR) are utilized to streamline data integration.
Data Quality and Accuracy	Implementation of advanced data cleaning techniques; Utilization of real-time data processing; Deployment of ML algorithms for automated data validation.
Privacy and Security	Integration of data encryption methods; Implementation of robust access control mechanisms; Ensuring compliance with regulations by incorporating privacy-by-design principles in the development of digital twin solutions; Conducting regular security audits and vulnerability assessments to identify and mitigate potential threats.
Computational and Technical Challenges	Leveraging High-Performance Computing (HPC) and cloud-based resources; Investment in the development and optimization of algorithms for the modelling of complex biological systems; Development of modular and scalable architectures; Using distributed systems and decentralized data architectures for data processing and management at the required scale.
Regulatory and Ethical Considerations	Regulatory bodies' collaboration to ensure that digital twin technologies meet all necessary guidelines and standards; Establishing clear ethical guidelines and frameworks related to a person's consent, data ownership, and bias mitigation; Maintaining transparency for patients on how their data is used and the benefits and risks associated with digital twin technologies.
Cost and Resource Allocation	Funding and grant allocation from government bodies and private investors; Cost-benefit analyses to demonstrate the long-term savings and improved outcomes associated with digital twins; Collaborative projects involving academic institutions, healthcare providers, and technology companies.
Clinical Validation and Adoption	Conducting meticulous clinical trials and pilot studies to validate the efficacy and safety of digital twin solutions; Publishing results in peer-reviewed journals to prove solid evidence of the benefits of using digital twins in healthcare; Developing comprehensive training programmes for healthcare providers and staff in using digital twin technologies.

The interoperability of the health data platform and data standardisation will stimulate the seamless integration of digital twins across different healthcare providers. Enhanced regulation will ensure that AI algorithms used in digital twins are free from bias and that ethical considerations are prioritised in their development and deployment (Attaran and Celik 2023).

As soon as ethical frameworks are established, digital twins will be used to design and operate smart hospitals, optimising everything from patient flow to energy consumption and improving overall efficiency and patient experience. The twin models will help in efficient resource allocation, prediction of the demand for

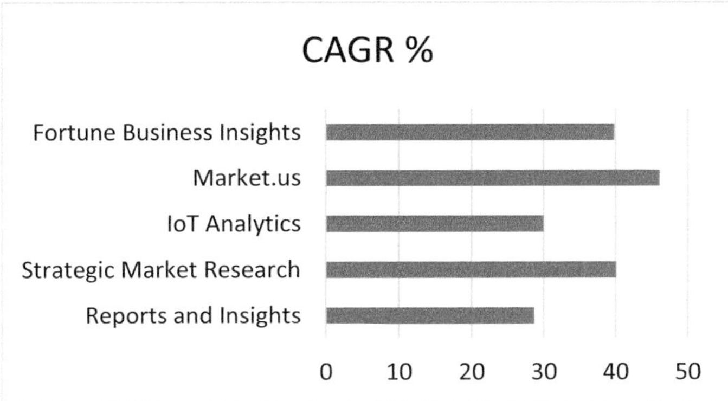

Figure 7: CAGR of the digital twin market from 2021 to 2023.

medical supplies, and optimisation of staff schedules. By identifying and addressing disparities in healthcare access and outcomes, digital twins can contribute to more equitable healthcare delivery. They will play a crucial role in public health by modelling disease outbreaks, tracking the spread of infections, and aiding in the development of preventive strategies.

7. Conclusion

Progress in Artificial Intelligence development has created new opportunities for data manipulation. With effective Big Data processing, dynamic modelling and simulations have become possible for complex objects and ensembles. The cyber-physical interactive mode requires sophisticated digital twinning. With further advances, biomedical digital twins will become not only conceivable but also a possible future part of enhanced biomedical research and healthcare practice. The current overview can be helpful for specialists in research and practical applications in the wide area of biomedicine. The technological ability to emulate real biological processes *in silico* speeds up the exploration of new diagnostics and treatments. The underlying infrastructure of Industry 4.0 opens opportunities for establishing and developing cyber-biological space, where interactions between the biological object and its digital twin will occur in near-real-time. Applications of biomedical digital twins are, in theory, possible at all scales, from the biomolecular to the planetary level. While an optimistic outlook suggests anticipated dates for the twinning of Earth's biosphere in the coming decades, significant work must be done beforehand. Necessary steps for future research are required. Current research on the challenges of biomedical digital twinning processes requires massive investment in the areas of Artificial Intelligence, Computer-Aided Design, Virtual Reality, biomedical computing and 3D bioprinting, to name just a few. Subsequent advancements will lead to a quick and robust pharmaceuticals industry, an effective and individualised healthcare system, and flexible and adaptive healthcare management. To enable this, a broad framework for research programmes must be supported by efforts in education, commercial R&D, and protective legal implementation. The enormous data flow between biophysical world objects and their digital twins raises questions about privacy and data protection. The ethical implications of considerable social overhaul, expected from the paradigm shift from Industry 4.0 to Industry 5.0, will affect every person today and future generations. The real task is to ensure that the transition to the future is not only successful technically but also fully accepted socially.

Ethical Statement

This study does not contain any studies with human or animal subjects performed by any authors.

References

Abramovich, F., Bailey, T.C. and Sapatinas, T. 2000. Wavelet analysis and its statistical applications. *Journal of the Royal Statistical Society: Series D (The Statistician)*, 49(1): 1–29.

Aithal, P.S. 2021. Marching towards technological immortality. In *Chapter* (Vol. 9, pp. 386–405). https://doi.org/10.9734/bpi/ccbms/v9/7432D.

Alberts, I.L., Mercolli, L., Pyka, T., Prenosil, G., Shi, K., Rominger, A. et al. 2023. Large language models (LLM) and ChatGPT: What will the impact on nuclear medicine be? *European Journal of Nuclear Medicine and Molecular Imaging*, 50(6): 1549–1552.

Al-Khafaji, H., Nickerson, M., Al-Rubaye, S., Abd-Alhameed, R., See, C., Noras, J. et al. 2019. IoT-fog optimal workload via deep learning inference system. *Sensors*, 19(20): 4446. https://doi.org/10.3390/s19204446.

Allen, A., Siefkas, A., Pellegrini, E., Burdick, H., Barnes, G., Calvert, J. et al. 2021. A digital twin machine learning model for forecasting disease progression in stroke patients. *Applied Sciences*, 11(12): 5576.

Amparore, D., Pecoraro, A., Checcucci, E., Piramide, F., Verri, P., De Cillis, S. et al. 2022. Three-dimensional virtual models' assistance during minimally invasive partial nephrectomy minimizes the impairment of kidney function. *European Urology Oncology*, 5(1): 104–108.

An, J., Chua, C.K. and Mironov, V. 2021. Application of machine learning in 3D bioprinting: Focus on development of big data and digital twin. *International Journal of Bioprinting*, 7(1).

Antonini, L., Berti, F., Isella, B., Hossain, D., Mandelli, L., Pennati, G. et al. 2021. From the real device to the digital twin: A coupled experimental numerical strategy to investigate a novel bioresorbable vascular scaffold. *PLOS ONE*, 16(6): e0252788.

Attaran, M. and Celik, B.G. 2023. Digital Twin: Benefits, use cases, challenges, and opportunities. *Decision Analytics Journal*, 6: 100165. https://doi.org/10.1016/j.dajour.2023.100165.

Bae, J., Helldin, T., Riveiro, M., Nowaczyk, S., Bouguelia, M.R. and Falkman, G. 2020. Interactive clustering: A comprehensive review. *ACM Computing Surveys (CSUR)*, 53(1): 1–39.

Bajwa, J., Munir, U., Nori, A. and Williams, B. 2021. Artificial intelligence in healthcare: Transforming the practice of medicine. *Future Healthcare Journal*, 8(2): e188–e194. https://doi.org/10.7861/fhj.2021-0095.

Barat, S., Parchure, R., Darak, S., Kulkarni, V., Paranjape, A., Gajrani, M. et al. 2021. An agent-based digital twin for exploring localized nonpharmaceutical interventions to control COVID-19 pandemic. *Transactions of the Indian National Academy of Engineering*, 6: 323–353.

Barbiero, P., Vinas Torne, R. and Lio, P. 2021. Graph representation forecasting of patient's medical conditions: Toward a digital twin. *Frontiers in Genetics*, 12: 652907.

Baronov, D. 2008. Biomedicine: An ontological dissection. *Theoretical Medicine and Bioethics*, 29(4): 235–254.

Barricelli, B.R., Casiraghi, E. and Fogli, D. 2019. A survey on digital twin: Definitions, characteristics, applications, and design implications. *IEEE Access*, 7: 167653–167671. https://doi.org/10.1109/ACCESS.2019.2953499.

Bates, S., Sesia, M., Sabatti, C. and Candès, E. 2020. Causal inference in genetic trio studies. *Proceedings of the National Academy of Sciences*, 117(39): 24117–24126.

Bay, H., Tuytelaars, T. and Van Gool, L. 2006. Surf: Speeded up robust features. *Lecture Notes in Computer Science*, 3951: 404–417.

Bianconi, E., Piovesan, A., Facchin, F., Beraudi, A., Casadei, R., Frabetti, F. et al. 2013. An estimation of the number of cells in the human body. *Annals of Human Biology*, 40(6): 463–471.

Braun, M. 2021. Represent me: Please! Towards an ethics of digital twins in medicine. *Journal of Medical Ethics*, 47(6): 394–400.

Brown, T.A. 2002. The human genome. In *Genomes* (2nd ed.). Wiley-Liss.

Bruynseels, K., Santoni de Sio, F. and Van den Hoven, J. 2018. Digital twins in health care: Ethical implications of an emerging engineering paradigm. *Frontiers in Genetics*, 9: 31. https://doi.org/10.3389/fgene.2018.00031.

Castiglioni, I., Rundo, L., Codari, M., Di Leo, G., Salvatore, C., Interlenghi, M. et al. 2021. AI applications to medical images: From machine learning to deep learning. *Physica Medica*, 83: 9–24.

Caudai, C., Galizia, A., Geraci, F., Le Pera, L., Morea, V., Salerno, E. et al. 2021. AI applications in functional genomics. *Computational and Structural Biotechnology Journal*, 19: 5762–5790.

Corral-Acero, J., Margara, F., Marciniak, M., Rodero, C., Loncaric, F., Feng, Y. et al. 2020. The 'Digital Twin' to enable the vision of precision cardiology. *European Heart Journal*, 41(48): 4556–4564.

De Cristofaro, E. 2021. A critical overview of privacy in machine learning. *IEEE Security and Privacy*, 19(4): 19–27.

Dempster, A.P. 1971. An overview of multivariate data analysis. *Journal of Multivariate Analysis*, 1(3): 316–346.

Dias, R. and Torkamani, A. 2019. Artificial intelligence in clinical and genomic diagnostics. *Genome Medicine*, 11(1): 1–2.

Dixon, T.A., Williams, T.C. and Pretorius, I.S. 2021. Sensing the future of bio-informational engineering. *Nature Communications*, 12(1): 388. https://doi.org/10.1038/s41467-020-20296-8.

Dobrzanski, L.A. and Dobrzanski, L.B. 2020. Dentistry 4.0 concept in the design and manufacturing of prosthetic dental restorations. *Processes*, 8(5): 525.

Egli, A., Schrenzel, J. and Greub, G. 2020. Digital microbiology. *Clinical Microbiology and Infection*, 26(10): 1324–1331.

Frederico, G.F. 2021. From supply chain 4.0 to supply chain 5.0: Findings from a systematic literature review and research directions. *Logistics*, 5(3): 49. https://doi.org/10.3390/logistics5030049.

Gaebel, J., Keller, J., Schneider, D., Lindenmeyer, A., Neumuth, T. and Franke, S. 2021. The digital twin: Modular model-based approach to personalized medicine. *Current Directions in Biomedical Engineering*, 7(2): 223–226.

Geanta, M., Tanwar, A.S., Lehrach, H., Satyamoorthy, K. and Brand, A. 2022. Horizon scanning: Rise of planetary health genomics and digital twins for pandemic preparedness. *OMICS: A Journal of Integrative Biology*, 26(2): 93–100.

Ghatti, S., Yurish, L.A., Shen, H., Rheuban, K., Enfield, K.B., Facteau, N.R. et al. 2023. Digital Twins in Healthcare: A Survey of Current Methods. *Archives of Clinical and Biomedical Research*, 7(3): 365–381.

Gkouskou, K., Vlastos, I., Karkalousos, P., Chaniotis, D., Sanoudou, D. and Eliopoulos, A.G. 2020. The "virtual digital twins" concept in precision nutrition. *Advances in Nutrition*, 11(6): 1405–1413.

Grieves, M. and Vickers, J. 2017. Digital twin: Mitigating unpredictable, undesirable emergent behavior in complex systems. In *Transdisciplinary Perspectives on Complex Systems: New Findings and Approaches* (pp. 85–113). https://doi.org/10.1007/978-3-319-38756-7_4.

Hagmann, K., Hellings-Kuß, A., Klodmann, J., Richter, R., Stulp, F. and Leidner, D. 2021. A digital twin approach for contextual assistance for surgeons during surgical robotics training. *Frontiers in Robotics and AI*, 8: 305. https://doi.org/10.3389/frobt.2021.699646.

Harris, C. and Stephens, M. 1988, August 31. A combined corner and edge detector. In *Alvey Vision Conference*, 15(50): 10–5244.

Hartmann, C.J., Chaturvedi, A. and Lujan, J.L. 2015. Quantitative analysis of axonal fiber activation evoked by deep brain stimulation via activation density heat maps. *Frontiers in Neuroscience*, 9: 28.

Hashizume, M. 2021. Perspective for future medicine: Multidisciplinary computational anatomy-based medicine with artificial intelligence. *Cognitive Computation*, 13(4): 761–769. https://doi.org/10.1007/s12559-021-09801-0.

Heinrich, L., Bennett, D., Ackerman, D., Park, W., Bogovic, J., Eckstein, N. et al. 2021. Whole-cell organelle segmentation in volume electron microscopy. *Nature*, 599(7883): 141–146.

Hemmer, P., Schemmer, M., Vossing, M. and Kuhl, N. 2021, July. Human-AI complementarity in hybrid intelligence systems: A structured literature review. *PACIS*, 78.

Herbert, M. 2021. Immortality, cancer and telomere. *Cancer Biology*, 11(2): 109–123.

Herculano-Houzel, S. 2012. The remarkable, yet not extraordinary, human brain as a scaled-up primate brain and its associated cost. *Proceedings of the National Academy of Sciences*, 109(Supplement 1): 10661–10668.

Ho, B., Baryshnikova, A. and Brown, G.W. 2018. Unification of protein abundance datasets yields a quantitative Saccharomyces cerevisiae proteome. *Cell Systems*, 6(2): 192–205.

Ho, V.M., Lee, J.A. and Martin, K.C. 2011. The cell biology of synaptic plasticity. *Science*, 334(6056): 623–628.

Holzhütter, H.G., Drasdo, D., Preusser, T., Lippert, J. and Henney, A.M. 2012. The virtual liver: A multidisciplinary, multilevel challenge for systems biology. *Wiley Interdisciplinary Reviews: Systems Biology and Medicine*, 4(3): 221–235.

Hormuth, D.A., Jarrett, A.M., Lorenzo, G., Lima, E.A., Wu, C., Chung, C. et al. 2021. Math, magnets, and medicine: Enabling personalized oncology. *Expert Review of Precision Medicine and Drug Development*, 6(2): 79–81.

https://iot-analytics.com/digital-twin-market-analyzing-growth-emerging-trends/ (Accessed 02/08/2024).

https://market.us/report/digital-twin-market/ (Accessed 02/08/2024).

https://www.fortunebusinessinsights.com/digital-twin-market-106246 (Accessed 02/08/2024).

https://www.reportsandinsights.com/report/digital-twin-market (Accessed 02/02/2024).

https://www.strategicmarketresearch.com/market-report/digital-twin-market (Accessed 02/08/2024).

HuBMAP Consortium. 2019. The human body at cellular resolution: The NIH Human Biomolecular Atlas Program. *Nature*, 574(7777): 187–192.

Isik, S. 2014. A comparative evaluation of well-known feature detectors and descriptors. *International Journal of Applied Mathematics Electronics and Computers*, 3(1): 1–6.

Jacob, E.B. and Shapira, Y. 2005. Meaning-based natural intelligence vs. information-based artificial intelligence. In *The Cradle of Creativity*. Shaarey Mishpat, Jerusalem.

Jones, D., Snider, C., Nassehi, A., Yon, J. and Hicks, B. 2020. Characterising the digital twin: A systematic literature review. *CIRP Journal of Manufacturing Science and Technology*, 29: 36–52. https://doi.org/10.1016/j.cirpj.2020.02.002.

Kamar, E. 2016, July 9. Directions in hybrid intelligence: Complementing AI systems with human intelligence. In *IJCAI* (pp. 4070–4073).

Kamel Boulos, M.N. and Zhang, P. 2021. Digital twins: From personalised medicine to precision public health. *Journal of Personalized Medicine*, 11(8): 745. https://doi.org/10.3390/jpm11080745.

Kazimierczuk, K., Misiak, M., Stanek, J., Zawadzka-Kazimierczuk, A. and Koźmiński, W. 2012. Generalized Fourier transform for non-uniform sampled data. In *Novel Sampling Approaches in Higher Dimensional NMR* (pp. 79–124).

Kemp, L., Aldridge, D.C., Booy, O., Bower, H., Browne, D., Burgmann, M. et al. 2021. 80 questions for UK biological security. *PLOS One*, 16(1): e0241190.

Kirchhof, J.C., Michael, J., Rumpe, B., Varga, S. and Wortmann, A. 2020. Model-driven digital twin construction: Synthesizing the integration of cyber-physical systems with their information systems. In *Proceedings of the 23rd ACM/IEEE International Conference on Model Driven Engineering Languages and Systems* (pp. 90–101). https://doi.org/10.1145/3365438.3410941.

Korvink, J.G., Badilita, V., Bordonali, L., Jouda, M., Mager, D. and MacKinnon, N. 2018. Nuclear magnetic resonance microscopy for in vivo metabolomics, digitally twinned by computational systems biology, needs a sensitivity boost. *Sens. Mater.*, 30: 157–166.

Kumar, S.N., Fred, A.L. and Varghese, P.S. 2018. An overview of segmentation algorithms for the analysis of anomalies on medical images. *Journal of Intelligent Systems*, 29(1): 612–625.

Laakasuo, M., Repo, M., Drosinou, M., Berg, A., Kunnari, A., Koverola, M. et al. 2021. The dark path to eternal life: Machiavellianism predicts approval of mind upload technology. *Personality and Individual Differences*, 177: 110731. https://doi.org/10.1016/j.paid.2021.110731.

Lal, A., Li, G., Cubro, E., Chalmers, S., Li, H., Herasevich, V. et al. 2020. Development and verification of a digital twin patient model to predict specific treatment response during the first 24 hours of sepsis. *Critical Care Explorations*, 2(11).

Lee, E.L., Barrett, M., Prince, K., Oborn, E., Li, O. and Thomas, P. 2022. Digital twins and service innovation in designing the Hospital of the Future.

Legg, S. and Hutter, M. 2007. Universal intelligence: A definition of machine intelligence. *Minds and Machines*, 17: 391–444.

Li, J. and Allinson, N.M. 2008. A comprehensive review of current local features for computer vision. *Neurocomputing*, 71(10–12): 1771–1787.

Liu, D., Xiong, Y., Pulli, K. and Shapiro, L. 2011. Estimating image segmentation difficulty. In *Machine Learning and Data Mining in Pattern Recognition: 7th International Conference, MLDM 2011, New York, NY, USA, August 30–September 3, 2011. Proceedings* (pp. 484–495). Springer Berlin Heidelberg.

Liu, Y., Zhang, L., Yang, Y., Zhou, L., Ren, L., Wang, F. et al. 2019. A novel cloud-based framework for the elderly healthcare services using digital twin. *IEEE Access*, 7: 49088–49101.

Love, B. 2017. *Biomaterials: A systems approach to engineering concepts*. Academic Press.

Lowe, D.G. 2004. Distinctive image features from scale-invariant keypoints. *International Journal of Computer Vision*, 60: 91–110.

Lu, H., Li, Y., Chen, M., Kim, H. and Serikawa, S. 2018. Brain intelligence: Go beyond artificial intelligence. *Mobile Networks and Applications*, 23, 368–375.

Masison, J., Beezley, J., Mei, Y., Ribeiro, H.A., Knapp, A.C., Sordo Vieira, L. et al. 2021. A modular computational framework for medical digital twins. *Proceedings of the National Academy of Sciences*, 118(20): e2024287118.

Mathe, E., Hays, J.L., Stover, D.G. and Chen, J.L. 2018. The omics revolution continues: The maturation of high-throughput biological data sources. *Yearbook of Medical Informatics*, 27(1): 211–222.

McGee, E.M. and Maguire, G.Q. 2007. Becoming borg to become immortal: Regulating brain implant technologies. *Cambridge Quarterly of Healthcare Ethics*, 16(3): 291–302. https://doi.org/10.1017/S0963180107070387.

Meijer, C., Uh, H.W. and El Bouhaddani, S. 2023. Digital twins in healthcare: Methodological challenges and opportunities. *Journal of Personalized Medicine*, 13(10): 1522. doi: 10.3390/jpm13101522.

Meulen, S. and Bruinsma, M. 2019. Man as aggregate of data. *AI and Society*, 34(2): 343–354. https://doi.org/10.1007/s00146-018-0843-1.

Moller, J. and Portner, R. 2021. Digital twins for tissue culture techniques—concepts, expectations, and state of the art. *Processes*, 9(3): 447.

Moravec, H. 2009. Rise of the robots-the future of artificial intelligence. *Scientific American*, 23.

Nakamura, Y., Higaki, T., Tatsugami, F., Honda, Y., Narita, K., Akagi, M. et al. 2020. Possibility of deep learning in medical imaging focusing improvement of computed tomography image quality. *Journal of Computer Assisted Tomography*, 44(2): 161–167.

Narcross, F. 2021. Artificial nervous systems—A new paradigm for artificial intelligence. *Patterns*, 2(6): 100265.

Nelson, E. 2001. Mathematics and the mind. *Advances in Consciousness Research*, 33: 89–94.

Neubauer, A.C. 2021. The future of intelligence research in the coming age of artificial intelligence–With a special consideration of the philosophical movements of trans-and posthumanism. *Intelligence*, 87: 101563.

Nollo, G., Pilati, F., Tronconi, R. and Rigoni, M. 2022. Industry 4.0 at the service of public health against the COVID-19 pandemic. *Disaster Medicine and Public Health Preparedness*, 16(5): 1735–1736. https://doi.org/10.1017/dmp.2020.426.

Omran, M.G., Engelbrecht, A.P. and Salman, A. 2007. An overview of clustering methods. *Intelligent Data Analysis*, 11(6): 583–605.

Oyallon, E. and Rabin, J. 2015. An analysis of the SURF method. *Image Processing Online*, 5: 176–218.

Panayides, A.S., Amini, A., Filipovic, N.D., Sharma, A., Tsaftaris, S.A., Young, A. et al. 2020. AI in medical imaging informatics: Current challenges and future directions. *IEEE Journal of Biomedical and Health Informatics*, 24(7): 1837–1857.

Papatsimpa, C. and Linnartz, J.P. 2021. Personalized circadian light: A digital siblings approach. In *Intelligent Environments 2021* (pp. 61–70). IOS Press.

Peng, G.C., Alber, M., Buganza Tepole, A., Cannon, W.R., De, S., Dura-Bernal, S. et al. 2021. Multiscale modeling meets machine learning: What can we learn? *Archives of Computational Methods in Engineering*, 28: 1017–1037.

Perez-Nieves, N., Leung, V.C., Dragotti, P.L. and Goodman, D.F. 2021. Neural heterogeneity promotes robust learning. *Nature Communications*, 12(1): 5791.

Pilati, F., Tronconi, R., Nollo, G., Heragu, S.S. and Zerzer, F. 2021. Digital twin of COVID-19 mass vaccination centers. *Sustainability*, 13(13): 7396.

Pivoto, D.G., de Almeida, L.F., da Rosa Righi, R., Rodrigues, J.J., Lugli, A.B. and Alberti, A.M. 2021. Cyber-physical systems architectures for industrial internet of things applications in Industry 4.0: A literature review. *Journal of Manufacturing Systems*, 58: 176–192. https://doi.org/10.1016/j.jmsy.2020.11.010.

Pizzolato, C., Saxby, D.J., Palipana, D., Diamond, L.E., Barrett, R.S., Teng, Y.D. et al. 2019. Neuromusculoskeletal modeling-based prostheses for recovery after spinal cord injury. *Frontiers in Neurorobotics*, 13: 97.

Price, W. and Nicholson, I. 2019. Medical AI and contextual bias. *Harvard Journal of Law and Technology*, 33: 65.

Qiu, C., Lu, W. and Vaswani, N. 2009, April 19. Real-time dynamic MR image reconstruction using Kalman filtered compressed sensing. In *2009 IEEE International Conference on Acoustics, Speech and Signal Processing* (pp. 393–396). IEEE.

Rasheed, A., San, O. and Kvamsdal, T. 2020. Digital twin: Values, challenges and enablers from a modeling perspectiveESS.2020.2970143.

Ren, S., Hinzman, A.A., Kang, E.L., Szczesniak, R.D. and Lu, L.J. 2015. Computational and statistical analysis of metabolomics data. *Metabolomics, 11*, 1492–1513.

Rosol, C., Steininger, B., Renn, J., & Schlogl, R. (2018). On the age of computation in the epoch of humankind. *Nature Outlook*, 563(7733), 1–5. https://doi.org/10.1038/d41586-018-07445-7.

Rossant, J. and Tam, P.P. 2021. Opportunities and challenges with stem cell-based embryo models. *Stem Cell Reports*, 16(5): 1031–1038.

Roy, A.L. and Conroy, R.S. 2018. Toward mapping the human body at a cellular resolution. *Molecular Biology of the Cell*, 29(15): 1779–1785.

Rudin, C. 2019. Stop explaining black box machine learning models for high stakes decisions and use interpretable models instead. *Nature Machine Intelligence*, 1(5): 206–215.

Rzepka, C. and Berger, B. 2018. User interaction with AI-enabled systems: A systematic review of IS research.

Sager, C., Janiesch, C. and Zschech, P. 2021. A survey of image labelling for computer vision applications. *Journal of Business Analytics*, 4(2): 91–110.

Salakhutdinov, R. and Hinton, G. 2007, March. Learning a nonlinear embedding by preserving class neighbourhood structure. In *Artificial Intelligence and Statistics* (pp. 412–419). PMLR.

San, O., Rasheed, A. and Kvamsdal, T. 2021. Hybrid ana. *IEEE Access*, 8: 21980–22012. https://doi.org/10.1109/ACC lysis and modeling, eclecticism, and multifidelity computing toward digital twin revolution. *GAMM-Mitteilungen, 44*(2), e202100007. https://doi.org/10.1002/gamm.202100007.

Savin-Baden, M. and Burden, D. 2019. Digital immortality and virtual humans. *Postdigital Science and Education*, 1: 87–103. https://doi.org/10.1007/s42438-018-0006-5.

Sayers, D., Sousa-Silva, R., Höhn, S., Ahmedi, L., Allkivi-Metsoja, K., Anastasiou, D., Beňuš, Š., Bowker, L., Bytyçi, E., Catala, A. and Çepani, A. 2021. The Dawn of the Human-Machine Era: A forecast of new and emerging language technologies.

Schmid, C., Mohr, R. and Bauckhage, C. 2000. Evaluation of interest point detectors. *International Journal of Computer Vision*, 37(2), 151–172.

Schmidt, A., Helgers, H., Vetter, F.L., Juckers, A. and Strube, J. 2021. Digital twin of mRNA-based SARS-COVID-19 vaccine manufacturing towards autonomous operation for improvements in speed, scale, robustness, flexibility and real-time release testing. *Processes*, 9(5): 748.

Sendak, M., Elish, M.C., Gao, M., Futoma, J., Ratliff, W., Nichols, M. et al. 2020, January 27. "The human body is a black box" supporting clinical decision-making with deep learning. In *Proceedings of the 2020 Conference on Fairness, Accountability, and Transparency* (pp. 99–109).

Shengli, W. 2021. Is human digital twin possible? *Computer Methods and Programs in Biomedicine Update*, 1: 100014.

St-Jean, S., De Luca, A., Tax, C.M., Viergever, M.A. and Leemans, A. 2020. Automated characterization of noise distributions in diffusion MRI data. *Medical Image Analysis*, 65: 101758.

Suhail, S., Hussain, R., Jurdak, R., Oracevic, A., Salah, K., Hong, C.S. et al. 2022. Blockchain-based digital twins: Research trends, issues, and future challenges. *ACM Computing Surveys (CSUR)*, 54(11s): 1–34. https://doi.org/10.1145/3472070.

Sung, J.H., Wang, Y.I., Narasimhan Sriram, N., Jackson, M., Long, C., Hickman, J.J. et al. 2018. Recent advances in body-on-a-chip systems. *Analytical Chemistry*, 91(1): 330–351.

Triggs, B. 2004. Detecting keypoints with stable position, orientation, and scale under illumination changes. In *Computer Vision-ECCV 2004: 8th European Conference on Computer Vision, Prague, Czech Republic, May 11-14, 2004. Proceedings, Part IV* (pp. 100–113). Springer Berlin Heidelberg.

Van der Maas, H.L., Snoek, L. and Stevenson, C.E. 2021. How much intelligence is there in artificial intelligence? A 2020 update. *Intelligence*, 87: 101548.

Van Gerven, M. 2017. Computational foundations of natural intelligence. *Frontiers in Computational Neuroscience*, 11: 112. https://doi.org/10.3389/fncom.2017.00112.

Voigt, I., Inojosa, H., Dillenseger, A., Haase, R., Akgün, K. and Ziemssen, T. 2021. Digital twins for multiple sclerosis. *Frontiers in Immunology*, 12: 669811.

Volkov, I., Radchenko, G. and Tchernykh, A. 2021. Digital twins, internet of things and mobile medicine: A review of current platforms to support smart healthcare. *Programming and Computer Software*, 47: 578–590. https://doi.org/10.1134/S0361768821040142.

Walter, W., Haferlach, C., Nadarajah, N., Schmidts, I., Kuhn, C., Kern, W. et al. 2021. How artificial intelligence might disrupt diagnostics in hematology in the near future. *Oncogene*, 40(25): 4271–4280.

Willemink, M.J., Koszek, W.A., Hardell, C., Wu, J., Fleischmann, D., Harvey, H. et al. 2020. Preparing medical imaging data for machine learning. *Radiology*, 295(1): 4–15.

Wishart, D.S., Oler, E., Peters, H., Guo, A., Girod, S., Han, S. et al. 2023. MiMeDB: The Human Microbial Metabolome Database. *Nucleic Acids Research*, 51(D1): D611–D620.

Wright, L. and Davidson, S. 2020. How to tell the difference between a model and a digital twin. *Advanced Modeling and Simulation in Engineering Sciences*, 7(1): 1–3. https://doi.org/10.1186/s40323-020-00147-4.

Wu, Q., Liu, J., Wang, X., Feng, L., Wu, J., Zhu, X. et al. 2020. Organ-on-a-chip: Recent breakthroughs and future prospects. *Biomedical Engineering Online*, 19(1): 1–9. https://doi.org/10.1186/s12938-020-00822-0.

Xames, M.D. and Topcu, T.G. 2024. A Systematic Literature Review of Digital Twin Research for Healthcare Systems: Research Trends, Gaps, and Realization Challenges. *IEEE Access*. DOI: 10.1109/ACCESS.2023.3349379.

Yandell, M.D. and Majoros, W.H. 2002. Genomics and natural language processing. *Nature Reviews Genetics*, 3(8): 601–610.

Zobel-Roos, S., Schmidt, A., Mestmacker, F., Mouellef, M., Huter, M., Uhlenbrock, L. et al. 2019. Accelerating biologics manufacturing by modeling or: Is approval under the QbD and PAT approaches demanded by authorities acceptable without a digital-twin? *Processes*, 7(2): 94.

CHAPTER 15

XAI-driven Insights

Unravelling London's Housing Market Trends and Predictions

Rizwan R. Khan and *Nitsa J. Herzog*★

1. Introduction

An article from The Times Money Mentor (Josh 2024) highlighted the divergent views of banks and consultancy firms on future London house prices. In such an unpredictable market, this project aims to analyse the determinants of house prices in London using explainable AI (XAI) methodologies to produce reliable forecasts. The solution will be deployed on a web platform to serve a wide range of stakeholders, filling a significant research gap, as no other studies have employed XAI for London house prices. In the current macroeconomic environment, with high interest rates and persistent inflation, predicting housing prices in London is both intriguing and challenging. Although platforms like Zoopla and Rightmove exist, they do not offer robust forecasting capabilities, and many consultancy forecasts lack transparency in their methodologies.

Various price prediction methods, both statistical and analytical, are available. This project focuses on AI models due to their higher accuracy compared to traditional methods (Fourkiotis and Tsadiras 2023). Explainable AI (XAI) enhances stakeholder understanding of model decisions, ensuring transparency and ethical adherence (Karamanou et al. 2022).

The primary intent of this project was to utilize machine learning algorithms to address the uncertainty faced by house buyers in London regarding house price estimation. With mortgage interest rates at record highs and fears of a housing market crash, it is crucial for property buyers to make informed decisions. This project aims

Faculty of Engineering & Environment, Northumbria University London Campus, UK.
* Corresponding author: nitsa.herzog@northumbria.ac.uk

DOI: 10.1201/9781003540373-15

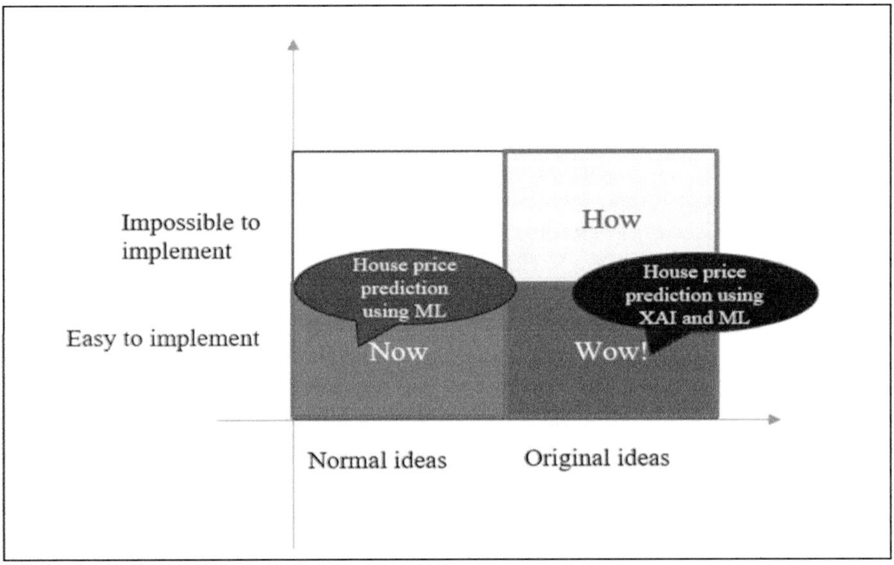

Figure 1: How-Now-Wow Matrix.

to provide an interpretable and transparent predictive model, beneficial to buyers, sellers, and policymakers.

Through Figure 1, How-Now-Wow matrix (Gray 2011), we can compare that our idea of using XAI for House Price Prediction is novel and thus falls under "easy to implement" as techniques are available, but the earlier projects have not implemented this idea.

1.1 Research hypothesis

The research hypothesis posits that deploying a house price prediction system using publicly available data, machine learning models, and explainable AI will provide valuable insights to all stakeholders in the London housing market. The project will use government and open-source data to build and deploy a predictive model accessible via a user-friendly website.

1.2 Research questions

This project addresses the following research questions:

- What are the key factors influencing housing prices in London?
- How can machine learning and XAI be integrated to provide useful insights?
- How will XAI-driven insights benefit buyers, sellers, and policymakers?
- How well can machine learning models predict housing prices?
- How does data variety influence different machine learning algorithms?
- What are the current approaches to house price prediction, and how can this research enhance existing standards?

2. Literature review

A house is a fundamental necessity for every human being, providing comfort and security. The housing market is a vital component of the economy, particularly in developed nations. London's housing market, in particular, holds significant importance in the UK economy. It contributes to GDP, generates employment, attracts foreign investment, creates wealth, and serves as a funding source for the financial services sector. Therefore, forecasting housing prices in London is not only relevant but also beneficial for various stakeholders in the housing market.

2.1 House prices in London

House prices in London frequently make headlines and become subjects of political discussion due to their unique status. Compared to other cities, London house prices stand out significantly, often exceeding those in other parts of the UK by a large margin.

The affordability crisis in the London market is stark, with the average house costing 12 times the average London salary (Lamont 2023). Burrows and Knowles (2019) studied changes in London from 2007 to 2017, highlighting significant socio-spatial transformations and increasing financialisation of housing, reshaping London into a "plutocratic city" where even middle-class households struggle to afford housing in many areas.

As noted by Santarelli (2024), "The London housing market presents a dynamic landscape with both challenges and opportunities. As buyers and sellers navigate these complexities, staying informed and considering a range of factors will be key to making strategic decisions in the ever-evolving real estate market." Thus, our forecasting application/website will be crucial in providing valuable price forecasts.

2.2 Websites for property search

Platforms like Rightmove and Zoopla enable real-time property searches but focus on asking prices without offering future projections. These prices reflect neighbourhood characteristics based on sellers' listings, lacking macroeconomic indicators. Our research aims to bridge this gap by using price-paid data that includes cash sales and properties not listed on these websites/apps. By incorporating macroeconomic data and leveraging machine learning analysis, our research will provide robust trend predictions.

2.3 Significance of macroeconomic factors

Macroeconomic factors such as monetary policy and mortgage rates have long-term impacts on the housing market. Duan et al. (2021) and Plakandaras et al. (2018) emphasise the importance of capturing these variables. Plakandaras et al. found that monetary policy significantly influences house prices over the long term, while housing supply shocks have minimal impact.

2.4 Significance of neighborhood factors

Proximity to transportation, parks, and services significantly affects house prices within a city (Heyman and Sommervoll 2019). Hodgson (2019) noted that properties within 500 metres of a station have experienced nearly 10% annual value growth since the financial crisis.

2.5 Traditional statistical methods

House price prediction methodologies have evolved significantly with advancements in technology and big data platforms. Hedonic modelling, which decomposes house values based on individual components, gained popularity in the 1970s following Rosen's work. This approach measures the relationship between sale prices and housing characteristics along with neighbourhood properties. However, it must account for spatial effects, as residential properties in the same area share similar structural and locational attributes (Basu and Thibodeau 1998).

2.6 Emergence of complex techniques

Numerous machine learning techniques exist for house price prediction. Nguyen and Cripps (2001) compared multiple regression analysis (MRA) and artificial neural networks (ANN), finding that ANN performed better with sufficient training data. Hasan Selim (2009) also demonstrated the superiority of ANN in predicting house prices in Turkey. Consequently, this project will employ a combination of linear regression and ANN. These techniques can handle non-linear relationships and detect complex interactions.

Lohith et al. (2023) showed that Random Forest (RF) outperformed other regression models in terms of accuracy and stability. We will use Python to implement these machine learning models. Geerts et al. (2023) reviewed 93 articles on house price prediction, highlighting the popularity of various methods over time.

2.7 Need for a hybrid model

Given the numerous models for house price prediction, relying on a single model may not yield optimal results. Akyüz et al. (2022) demonstrated that hybrid models combining clustering and regression outperform standalone models. Sharma et al. (2023) predicted house prices using multiple techniques, including Linear Regression, Gradient Boosting Regressor, Histogram Gradient Boosting Regressor, and RF Regressor algorithms. Accordingly, we will employ a hybrid approach and test various machine learning techniques to predict London house prices.

2.8 Challenges and limitations of machine learning models

While machine learning models are accurate, they often lack transparency. Deeks (2019) highlighted the need for interpretable models to ensure reliability. Black-box methods like neural networks fail to explain their decisions, necessitating transparent models in critical applications like housing price prediction.

2.9 XAI techniques for transparency

To address the transparency issue in machine learning, Explainable AI (XAI) techniques can be used to elucidate model behaviour and decisions. Few empirical studies have explored nonlinear relationships between housing prices and neighbourhood factors at an individual level (Pérez-Molina 2021). Dou et al. (2023) recently used the SHAP model to investigate these effects in Shanghai, illustrating the potential of XAI in housing price prediction.

2.10 Need for London housing price prediction

Previous studies on nonlinear relationships in housing prices may not apply to London. Although XAI has been used to predict house prices in Scotland (Karamanou et al. 2022), no such model exists for London. Ng (2015) implemented regression models for London house prices, but more advanced techniques are needed. Law et al. (2019) used satellite images for prediction, but their overreliance on imagery limited accuracy. Our model will incorporate multiple techniques and factors to improve accuracy and reliability.

AWONAIKE (2022) used XGBoost but lacked XAI capabilities and did not include neighbourhood factors. A comprehensive literature review of six theses and 21 journal articles revealed no precedent for an XAI-based house price prediction model for London. This underscores the need for our project, which will combine complex machine learning techniques and XAI for accurate and interpretable predictions. Table 1 summarizes the state-of-the-art literature used in this section.

3. Research Methodology and Design

3.1 Research method/design

The research process consists of several stages to ensure a comprehensive and efficient approach to house price prediction. The initial stage involves identifying gaps in previous methods to improve efficiency. Subsequent stages include data collection, preparation for training, implementation of Explainable AI (XAI), and deployment of the predictive model on a website. Refer Figure 2 for the complete methodology and design of the project.

3.2 Data Collection

The project utilizes publicly available data to maintain transparency. Data is categorized into three types as seen in Figure 3 below.

- House Price Data: Historical data from HM Land Registry (2000–2023).
- Neighbourhood Data: Public transport and supermarket locations from sources like Transport of London and geolytics.com.
- Macroeconomic Data: Includes GDP growth, unemployment rate, employment rate, inflation rate, and Bank of England rate, sourced from the Office for National Statistics.

Table 1: Analysis of previous House Price Prediction Projects; Research across the globe.

Category	**Author**	**Geography**	**Methods**	**Prediction Model Type**	**XAI used? (Yes/No)**
Journal	Xu and Zhang (2023)	Ten major cities, China	Univariate neural network model	Neural network (Classification)	No
Journal	Lu et al. (2011)	London, U.K	Geographically Weighted Regression	Regression	No
Journal	Law (2017)	London, U.K	Multi-level hedonic price approach	Regression	No
Journal	Brown et al. (1997)	London, U.K	Regression	Regression	No
Journal	Bork and Moller (2014)	U.S.A.	Dynamic Model Averaging	Regression	No
Journal	De Aquino Afonso et al. (2019)	Brazil	Random Forest and Neural Networks	Random Forest and Neural Networks	No
Journal	Alzain et al. (2022)	Saudi Arabia	Artificial Neural Networks	Neural Networks	No
Journal	Dou et al. (2023)	Shanghai, China	XGBoost, SHAP	Decision tree and XAI	Yes
Journal	Imran et al. (2021)	Islamabad, Pakistan	SVR, and Deep Learning Network	Regression and Neural Networks	No
Journal	Pérez-Molina (2021)	San José, Costa Rica	MLRE and CARM models	Regression	No
Journal	Xu and Zhang (2021)	100 cities in China	Nonlinear autoregressive (NAR)	Neural Networks	No
Journal	Yin (2023)	London, U.K	Multiple linear regression	Regression	No
Journal	Pai and Wang (2020)	Taichung, Taiwan	LSSVR, CART, GRNN	Regression and Neural Networks	No
Journal	Wang et al. (2022)	Guangdong, China	Regression	Regression	No
Journal	Peng et al. (2021)	Toronto, Canada	GCN and LSTM	Regression and Neural Networks	No
Journal	Phipps and Li (2019)	Windsor, Canada	Quigley's hybrid price model in Microsoft Excel	Regression	No
Journal	Temur et al. (2019)	Turkey	ARIMA, LSTM, HYBRID mode	Hybrid	No

Table 1 contd. ...

...Table 1 contd.

Category	Author	Geography	Methods	Prediction Model Type	XAI used? (Yes/No)
Journal	Alfiyatin et al. (2017)	Malang, East Java, Indonesia	Regression analysis	Regression	No
Conference Paper	Sanyal et al. (2022)	Boston, U.S.A	Regression	Regression	No
Conference Paper	Ahtesham et al. (2020)	Karachi, Pakistan	XGBoost	Decision tree	No
Journal	Karamanou et al. (2022)	Scotland, U.K	XGBoost, SHAP	Decision tree and XAI	Yes
Master's Thesis	Sjöblom (2023)	Finland	XGBoost	Decision tree	No
Master's Thesis	Hartikainen (2023)	Denmark	XGBoost and XAI	Decision tree	No
Master's Thesis	STANG (2023)	Germany	XGBoost	Decision tree	No
Bachelor's Thesis	Ng (2015)	London, U.K	Regression	Regression	No
Bachelor's Thesis	Hansson and Holmqvist (2023)	Stockholm, Sweden	XGBoost	Decision tree	No
Master's Thesis	Komagome-Towne (2016)	Pasadena, California, U.S.A	Multiple linear regression, KNN, tree-based methods	Regression, Decision tree, Neural networks	No

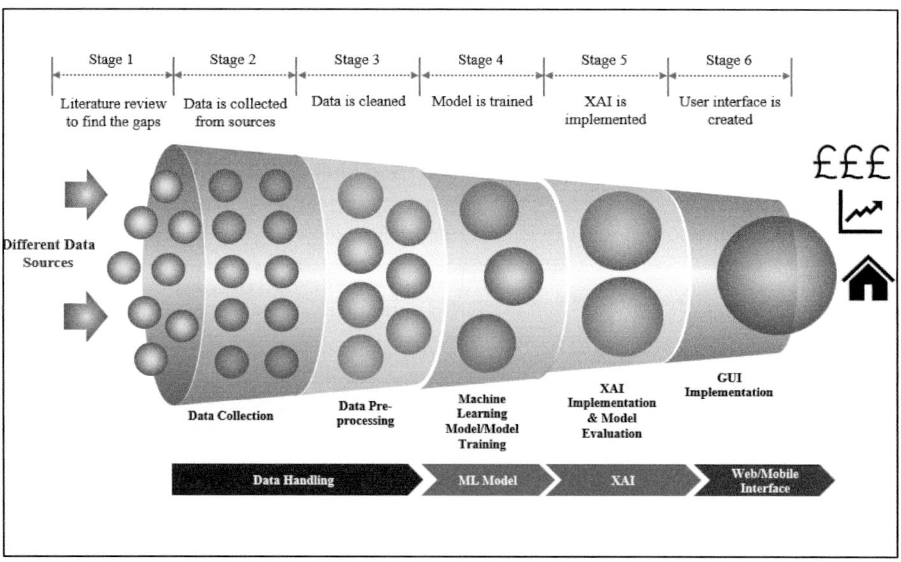

Figure 2: Stages for the proposed project.

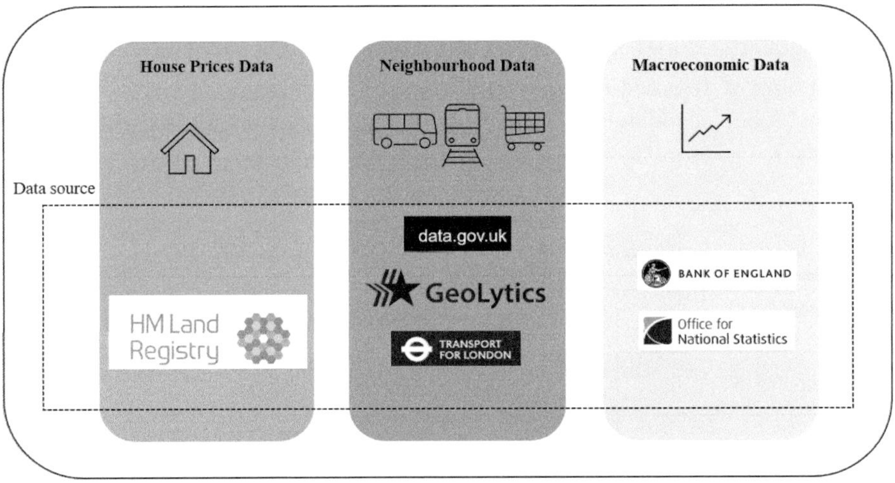

Figure 3: Data collection sources.

3.3 XAI – SHAP and LIME

SHAP and LIME are widely used XAI algorithms.

SHAP, based on game theory, makes machine learning models interpretable. It uses Shapley values to estimate each player's contribution in a cooperative game, ensuring fair distribution. Although computationally intensive, SHAP provides fair contributions and was enhanced for efficiency by Lundberg and Lee in 2017.

SHAP is preferred over LIME for its stability and less sensitivity to high-contribution features, despite being computationally expensive (see Table 2). Google Colab Pro+ aids in handling SHAP's computational demands due to its robust theoretical properties.

Table 2: SHAP versus LIME.

Criteria	SHAP	LIME
Theory driven	✓ Supports Shapley values and consistency property	✗ Fails to be consistent
Time expensive	✗ Computation of marginal costs makes it expensive	✓ Time affordable
Require training data	✓ Strong theoretical properties make it stable	✗ Instability; kernel width can make it unstable

3.4 Data pre-processing

Data pre-processing involves several steps to prepare the data for model training:

- Duplicate Removal: Ensuring no duplicates exist in the dataset.
- Outlier Detection and Handling: Using the IQR to detect and manage outliers.

- Dataset Purging: Limiting data to 10 years for manageability.
- Exploratory Data Analysis (EDA): Identifying trends and relationships.
- Handling of Text and Categorical Features: Encoding non-numerical variables using label encoding for efficiency. Encoding techniques are reflected in Table 3.

Table 3: Encoding techniques.

Encoding Technique	Description
Ordinal encoding	Each category is assigned (unique) an integer value. The integers can be ordered. It can impose an ordinal relationship.
Label encoding	Converting categorical to numerical values. Each class is converted into values 0 to n-1.
One-Hot Encoding	Every level in the categorical variable is compared with a fixed reference level by transforming single variables. The observations can thus indicate either the absence (0) or the presence (1) of binary values (Dahouda and Joe 2021).
Hash encoding	Hashing algorithms are used to generate hash values of fixed length.
Dummy encoding	Transforms categorical features into a set of binary variables
Target encoding	It is a Bayesian technique in which the mean of the target variable replaces the target variable.

3.5 Model training and selection

Various machine learning algorithms are used, including XGBoost, Random Forest, Gradient Boosting, and Decision Tree.

3.5.1 XGBoost

XGBoost is an open-source implementation of a gradient-boosting tree algorithm. It is a type of ensemble learning model where several models are combined to find a solution. For the feature characteristics of the algorithm, refer to Table 4.

The model constructs multiple Classification and Regression Trees (CART). A CART differs from decision trees in that the leaf only stores decision values, whereas a CART stores the real score associated with each leaf. The model predicts

Table 4: XGBoost features.

Feature	Detail
Parallelization	Model is devised to train with multiple CPU cores
Regularization	Has regularization penalties to avoid overfitting
Non-linearity	Can detect and learn from non-linear data patterns
Scalability	Can process billions of examples using fewer resources

each tree separately and then combines the prediction results of each tree to achieve the final prediction value. A decision tree is taken as the base learner, multiple weak learners are constructed, and the model is trained continuously along the descending direction of the gradient (Hachcham 2023).

3.5.2 Random forest regressor

The Random Forest algorithm was included in this project, as Adetunji et al. (2022) concluded that this model had acceptable predicted values with an error margin of ±5 when used on the Boston housing dataset, which had 506 entries and 14 features.

This algorithm is a collection of decision trees, where each tree consists of a data sample drawn from the training set with replacement. For regression, the individual decision trees are averaged.

3.5.3 Gradient boosting regressor

Kumar et al. (2020) found that the Gradient Boosting algorithm has higher accuracy while predicting house prices.

It is an ensemble of decision trees, and instead of building one tree, it predicts the desired outcome based on an additive regression model that uses decision trees as weak learners (Ye et al. 2009). Each model attempts to improve on the error from the previous one, making the model more reliable and robust.

3.5.4 Decision tree regressor

Zhang (2021) compared SVR and Linear Regression with Decision Trees and concluded that Decision Trees are more effective for house price forecasting.

A Decision Tree is a non-parametric supervised learning algorithm. It uses a hierarchical tree structure, which consists of a root node, branches, internal nodes, and leaf nodes. A Decision Tree starts with a root node, and the outgoing branches from the root node feed into internal or decision nodes.

3.6 Model optimization

Initially, the models are run using default parameters. However, to achieve maximum performance, optimisation of algorithms is essential. This is performed using hyperparameters tuning.

Below approaches are utilized in building our project:

- Grid search: In Grid Search, a list of hyperparameters and performance metrics are supplied, and the algorithm works through all possible scenarios to find the best fit. While effective, it is computationally intensive and time-consuming.
- Random search: Random Search selects groups of hyperparameters randomly in each step. It works well if there are a small number of hyperparameters.

The above two approaches are easier to implement using the computational efficiency of Collab Pro+ platform.

There are other techniques below which were not explored in this project due to scope and time constraints.

- Bayesian optimization: It is a sequential model-based approach. Initially, it builds a model over the unknown objective function and iterates by improving the sampling method in the next experiment. It consists of a surrogate function that selects evaluation points (Ramachandran et al. 2020).
- Gradient-based optimization: This technique is applicable for neural networks to compute gradients to hyperparameters and optimise them by applying the gradient descent algorithm.

Metrics like R-Square, RMSE, MSE, and MAE are used to compare and select the best regression models.

3.7 Deployment architecture

The deployment structure bridges the gap between user interaction and machine predictions, using Django as the framework.

3.7.1 Django overview

Django is a Python-based open-source web framework that employs the Model View Controller (MVC) framework, suitable for larger applications and beginner developers. Django's MVC pattern allows efficient handling of user interactions.

ML Deployment using Django (see Figure 4):

- Build Django Application: Create a user interface for system interaction.
- Train Machine Learning Model: Train the selected model using the steps outlined.
- User Input: Accept user input for house price prediction.
- Display Results: Show output using the ML prediction algorithm.

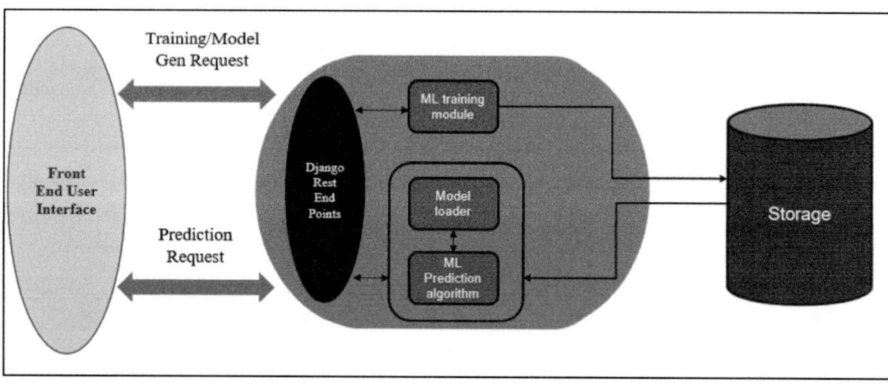

Figure 4: ML Deployment using Django.

3.8 Ethics consideration in the context of explainable AI (XAI) implementation

The rise of Artificial Intelligence (AI) in fields like house price prediction has brought about transformative changes in decision-making processes. However, the opacity of many AI models, especially complex ones like ensemble methods and deep learning, raises critical ethical, legal, social, and security (PELSS) concerns. Explainable AI (XAI) addresses these issues by making AI models more transparent, interpretable, and accountable. Explainable AI focuses on making AI systems understandable to human users, providing clear insights into how decisions are made. In the context of predicting house prices, XAI ensures that models do not merely offer accurate predictions but also allow stakeholders to comprehend the reasoning behind these predictions.

XAI plays a crucial role in addressing ethical challenges in AI, such as bias, fairness, and transparency. By revealing how models make decisions, XAI ensures that predictions do not perpetuate existing biases or lead to unfair outcomes.

- Bias Detection and Mitigation: XAI tools can identify which features most influence the model's predictions, enabling developers to detect potential biases. For example, if the model heavily weights demographic factors in a way that leads to discriminatory predictions, XAI can highlight these issues, prompting corrective actions such as re-balancing the training data or adjusting model parameters.
- Fairness and Accountability: XAI enhances accountability by allowing developers and stakeholders to scrutinise predictions for fairness. Techniques like fairness metrics and counterfactual explanations can be employed to ensure that predictions do not unjustly favour one group over another. This transparency supports ethical AI practices by ensuring that all stakeholders can understand and challenge the basis of AI decisions.
- Informed Consent and Transparency: XAI provides clear, understandable insights into how personal data is used in predictions. Users and stakeholders can be informed about the factors influencing predictions, enhancing transparency and fostering trust in the AI system. This aligns with ethical standards that emphasise the need for transparency in AI-driven decision-making.

4. Data Analysis and Implementation

The roadmap for model design and implementation is reflected in Table 5.

4.1 Data collection and data cleaning

Data is collected from open-source platforms and government data and saved in csv files in local machines. Data is cleaned in this stage to perform Exploratory Data Analysis (EDA) and the creation of data frame for the purpose of model training. It is necessary to remove outliers as it can affect machine learning. Outliers are detected and removed using interquartile range.

Table 5: Implementation Roadmap.

Step	Description
1	Data Collection
2	Data Cleaning and Visualization
3	Model Selection
4	Model Optimization
5	XAI Implementation
6	Deployment

4.1.1 Neighborhood dataframe creation

In this part of the data collection, a data frame is created to store transaction details, including postcode information and neighbourhood data, such as the distance to the nearest railway station, bus stops, and supermarkets, as shown in Table 6.

Table 6: Neighborhood Dataframe Infographic – Tier1.

Data Category	Description
Price Paid Data	Data on prices of homes sold
Railway Stations Data	Information about nearby railway stations
Bus Stops Data	Data on the location of bus stops
Supermarket Data	Data on the proximity of supermarkets

4.1.2 Macroeconomic dataframe creation

In this part of the data collection, a data frame stores data for macroeconomic indicators for the UK, as seen in Table 7. After this stage, a Tier 2 data frame is created that stores price-paid data with neighbourhood data from the previous stage. Macroeconomic data is added, and thus, the data frame has both neighbourhood and macroeconomic indicators in a single data frame.

Table 7: Macroeconomic Indicator Dataframe Infographic - Tier2.

Data Category	Description
Neighbourhood Data (Tier 1 Dataframe)	Data from the first Neighbourhood Dataframe
Bank Rate/Mortgage Rate	Interest rate and mortgage rate data
Unemployment Data	Data on unemployment rates
Employment Data	Data on employment figures
GDP Data	Gross Domestic Product information

4.2 Exploratory data analysis and visualization

In this section, we undertake an in-depth exploratory data analysis (EDA) to uncover critical patterns, trends, and relationships within the dataset that will inform our

London house price prediction model. EDA is not merely a precursor to model building but a crucial phase that can reveal hidden insights, guide feature engineering, and ultimately improve model performance. The analysis will be guided by key questions such as: What are the main factors influencing house prices in London? Are there any notable spatial or temporal patterns? How do features interact with each other? Our approach is systematic, combining statistical summaries, visualizations, and domain knowledge to build an understanding of the data landscape.

4.2.1 Data understanding and cleaning

The first step in our analysis involves gaining a thorough understanding of the dataset. This process starts with data loading and initial inspection to identify the key features available, their data types, and the presence of any missing or anomalous values. Key steps include:

1. Inspecting Data Types and Basic Statistics: Utilize Python's pandas library to explore data types and basic descriptive statistics (mean, median, standard deviation) for numerical features. For categorical features, inspect unique values and their frequencies to understand the data distribution.
2. Handling Missing Values and Outliers: Examine missing values using visual tools like heatmaps and imputation techniques where necessary. Outliers, especially in price-related features, should be identified through box plots and statistical tests. Depending on the context, outliers may need to be corrected, transformed, or excluded to ensure robust model performance.
3. Feature Engineering: Create new features that may add predictive power to the model. For example, extract year, month, and season from date fields to capture temporal trends. Distance from the city centre, proximity to public transport, and socio-economic indices can be engineered from geospatial data to enhance the dataset.

4.2.2 Univariate analysis

Univariate analysis focuses on examining each feature independently to understand its distribution and characteristics:

1. **Price Distribution Analysis**: Plot the distribution of house prices using histograms and kernel density plots. Identify skewness, kurtosis, and any multimodal tendencies in price distribution. Often, house prices are right-skewed, suggesting the need for log transformation to normalize the data.
2. **Feature Distributions**: Use histograms and density plots to examine the distributions of key features such as property size, number of bedrooms, and age of the property. Visualizing these distributions helps identify any need for data transformation, such as standardization or normalization.
3. **Categorical Variables**: Use bar charts to explore the distribution of categorical variables such as property type (e.g., flat, house, terraced house) and boroughs. Understanding the distribution of categorical features aids in later stages of model encoding and feature importance analysis.

4.2.3 Bivariate analysis

Bivariate analysis investigates the relationships between house prices and individual features. This step aims to identify which factors have the strongest correlation with house prices and might serve as important predictors.

1. **Correlation Analysis**: Compute Pearson or Spearman correlation coefficients between numerical features and house prices. Visualize these correlations using heatmaps to quickly identify which features have the strongest linear relationships.
2. **Scatter Plots**: Utilize scatter plots to examine relationships between price and key numerical features, such as property size or distance to central London. Look for patterns, clusters, or trends that may inform the modelling process.
3. **Box Plots for Categorical Features**: Use box plots to visualize the relationship between house prices and categorical variables like property type or location (borough). This will highlight which categories tend to command higher prices and help identify potential groupings that could be valuable in feature engineering.

4.2.4 Multivariate analysis

Multivariate analysis extends our exploration to consider the interactions between multiple features simultaneously, which is critical for capturing the complexities inherent in real-world housing markets.

1. **Pairwise Plots**: Use pair plots to explore relationships between several key features and house prices, revealing potential multicollinearity or complex interactions. This step helps identify which feature pairs are most closely related and might need special attention during modelling.
2. **Heatmaps and Cluster Maps**: Create heatmaps to visualize correlations between all pairs of features, identifying clusters of features that are highly interrelated. Cluster maps add an extra layer of insight by showing hierarchical relationships between features.
3. **Dimensionality Reduction**: Techniques like Principal Component Analysis (PCA) can be employed to visualize high-dimensional feature spaces and identify the most informative features. This step is particularly useful for understanding the overall structure of the data and the relationships between features.

4.2.5 Spatial and temporal analysis

Given the geographic and temporal nature of house prices, spatial and temporal analysis is critical to uncover trends that are not apparent in purely numerical data.

1. **Geospatial Visualization**: Heatmaps, scatter plots, and choropleth maps are used to visualize price distributions across London. This spatial analysis can reveal how location, proximity to landmarks, and neighbourhood characteristics affect house prices.

2. **Time Series Analysis**: Average prices over time are plotted to identify trends, seasonality, and cycles. Time series data are analysed using rolling averages and decomposition techniques to separate seasonal effects from long-term trends.
3. **Interactive Plots**: Interactive visualizations are employed using libraries like Plotly or Folium to explore spatial-temporal patterns dynamically. These plots can help stakeholders intuitively grasp how house prices vary across both space and time.

4.3 Modelling

In this section, we delve into the modelling phase of the London house price prediction project. The goal of this phase is to develop predictive models that can accurately estimate house prices based on the features identified during the Exploratory Data Analysis (EDA). To achieve this, we will explore a variety of machine learning algorithms, each with unique characteristics that make them suitable for different aspects of prediction tasks.

We start by establishing a baseline model using Linear Regression, which provides a benchmark for comparing the performance of more complex models. Subsequently, we will implement a range of advanced algorithms, including Decision Tree Regressor, Random Forest Regressor, Gradient Boosting Regressor, and Extreme Gradient Boosting (XGBoost). For the initial phase, all models will be tested using their default parameters, providing a fair comparison of their out-of-the-box performance. Further optimization and fine-tuning of these models will be addressed in the subsequent sections.

4.3.1 Linear regression (Baseline Model)

Linear Regression serves as our baseline model. It is a simple yet powerful algorithm that assumes a linear relationship between the input features and the target variable, house prices. The model predicts prices by fitting a straight line (or hyperplane in higher dimensions) through the data, minimising the residual sum of squares between observed and predicted values.

- **Why Use Linear Regression?**

  Linear regression is chosen as the baseline because of its interpretability and ease of implementation. It helps us establish a benchmark accuracy that more sophisticated models must exceed. Additionally, linear regression offers insights into feature importance through coefficients, helping to understand the underlying data structure.

- **Implementation**

  The model is implemented using the `LinearRegression` class from Python's `scikit-learn` library. After fitting the model on the training data, predictions are made on the test set, and evaluation metrics such as Mean Absolute Error (MAE), Mean Squared Error (MSE), and R-squared (R^2) are recorded.

4.3.2 Decision tree regressor

Decision Tree Regressor is a non-linear model that splits the data into subsets based on feature values, creating a tree-like structure of decisions. Each node represents a decision based on a feature, and each leaf node represents a predicted house price.

- **Why Use Decision Tree Regressor?**

  The Decision Tree Regressor is highly interpretable and can capture complex non-linear relationships between features and the target variable. It allows us to see how different features influence predictions, making it a valuable tool for understanding data-driven decisions.

- **Implementation**

  Using the `DecisionTreeRegressor` class from `scikit`-learn, the model is trained with default parameters. The performance of the Decision Tree Regressor is compared against the baseline to assess the improvement in capturing non-linear patterns in the data.

4.3.3 Random forest regressor

Random Forest Regressor is an ensemble learning method that builds multiple decision trees and merges them to obtain more accurate and stable predictions. By averaging the results of many trees, Random Forest reduces overfitting and improves generalisation.

- **Why Use Random Forest Regressor?**

  Random Forest Regressor is robust to outliers, handles missing data well, and can capture complex interactions between features. It often outperforms single decision trees by reducing variance and improving predictive power.

- **Implementation**

  The model is implemented using the `RandomForestRegressor` class from `scikit`-learn. With default parameters, a number of trees are trained and averaged to provide the final predictions. The model's performance is evaluated and compared to other algorithms to highlight its strengths in capturing feature interactions.

4.3.4 Gradient boosting regressor

Gradient Boosting Regressor is an ensemble technique that builds trees sequentially, where each new tree corrects the errors of the previous one. Unlike Random Forest, which builds trees independently, Gradient Boosting focuses on minimizing the errors through iterative optimization.

- **Why Use Gradient Boosting Regressor?**

  Gradient Boosting Regressor is powerful in capturing complex patterns in the data and often delivers superior performance compared to other tree-based methods. Its ability to fine-tune each step in the sequence makes it an excellent choice for prediction tasks requiring high accuracy.

- **Implementation**

  We use the `GradientBoostingRegressor` class from `scikit-learn` with default settings. The model's sequential learning approach is evaluated to see how well it performs compared to other models, particularly in terms of reducing residual errors in house price predictions.

4.3.5 Extreme gradient boosting (XGBoost)

Extreme Gradient Boosting (XGBoost) is an advanced implementation of Gradient Boosting that includes enhancements like regularization, which prevents overfitting, and optimized computation that makes it faster and more efficient. XGBoost is known for its excellent predictive performance and is widely used in competitive modelling scenarios.

- **Why Use XGBoost?**

  XGBoost is particularly well-suited for high-dimensional data and is known for its scalability, speed, and superior handling of missing values. Its built-in regularization mechanisms make it a strong contender for achieving high predictive accuracy without overfitting.

- **Implementation**

  The `XGBRegressor` class from the `xgboost` library is used to implement this model. The model is run with default parameters, and its performance is assessed in comparison to other models. Given its proven track record, XGBoost often sets the bar for predictive accuracy in regression tasks.

4.3.6 Model evaluation and comparison

Each of these models is evaluated using a consistent set of performance metrics, including mean absolute error (MAE), mean squared error (MSE), and R-squared (R^2) on the test data. This allows us to objectively compare the models based on their ability to predict London house prices accurately. Key findings from this initial round of testing are displayed in Table 8, which summarises the default model comparison scores. These insights will inform the next stage of the process, where we will focus on hyperparameter tuning and optimisation to enhance model performance further.

Table 8: Default Model comparison scores.

Default Model	R-squared	RMSE	MSE	MAE
Linear Regression	0.260	271325	73617192326	191584
eXtreme Gradient Boosting (XGBoost)	0.530	216040	46673438837	143841
Random Forest Regressor	0.660	184666	34101668716	120770
Decision Tree Regressor	0.270	268447	72063746775	172318
Gradient Boosting Regressor	0.460	232387	54003658847	153994

4.5 Model optimization

Model optimisation is a pivotal step in the machine learning workflow, aiming to refine models to achieve peak performance and generalisability. For the London house price prediction project, three key regression models were subjected to a rigorous optimisation process: Extreme Gradient Boosting (XGBoost), Random Forest Regressor (RFR), and Decision Tree Regressor (DTR). Each model underwent hyperparameter tuning, performance evaluation, and feature importance analysis to maximise predictive accuracy. This chapter explores the optimisation journey of these models, comparing their improvements and highlighting the factors influencing their performance.

4.5.1 XGBoost model optimization

XGBoost (Extreme Gradient Boosting) is renowned for its high efficiency, scalability, and superior performance on structured data. The optimization process aimed to leverage these strengths to refine predictions of house prices in London.

Steps Performed:

1. **Hyperparameter Tuning**: A systematic approach using Grid Search and Random Search was employed to fine-tune critical hyperparameters, such as learning rate, max depth, number of estimators, and subsample ratio. This process aimed to minimise errors while maintaining model robustness.
2. **Performance Evaluation**: The optimized XGBoost model was evaluated against the default model, focusing on key metrics: Mean Squared Error (MSE), Root Mean Squared Error (RMSE), Mean Absolute Error (MAE), and R-squared. The optimized model outperformed the default configuration, demonstrating substantial gains in accuracy.
3. **Cross-Validation**: To validate the optimized model's performance, k-fold cross-validation was conducted, ensuring that the results were consistent and not the product of overfitting.
4. **Visualization of Actual vs. Predicted Values**: The comparison of actual versus predicted values for 250 random samples visually confirmed the model's improved predictive alignment, revealing tighter clustering around the ideal line.

Inference:

- **Key Features**: The optimised XGBoost model identified estate type, year, count of supermarkets within 2 km, latitude, longitude, and district as pivotal determinants of house prices. These features align well with the known market dynamics of London's real estate sector.
- **Performance Improvement**: The optimisation led to a 17% reduction in MSE, a 9% decrease in RMSE, an 8% reduction in MAE, and a 15% increase in R-squared compared to the default model. Against the baseline linear regression model, XGBoost demonstrated significantly superior performance, with MSE, RMSE, and MAE lower by 47%, 27%, and 31%, respectively.

These improvements underscore the efficacy of XGBoost in capturing complex, non-linear relationships inherent in the housing market.

4.5.2 Random Forest Regressor (RFR) model optimization

The Random Forest Regressor, an ensemble learning technique that builds multiple decision trees and averages their predictions, was also optimised to enhance its predictive power. Known for its robustness and ability to handle large datasets, RFR was a strong candidate for model optimisation.

Steps Performed:

1. **Hyperparameter Tuning:** A comprehensive search was conducted to identify the optimal number of trees, maximum depth, and minimum samples required for splits and leaf nodes. This tuning aimed to balance the model's complexity and predictive accuracy.
2. **Performance Evaluation:** Despite tuning, the optimised RFR showed a minor decline in performance compared to the default model, indicating that further parameter adjustments might be necessary.
3. **Feature Importance Analysis:** The optimised RFR revealed that estate type, location, supermarket count within 2 km, and postcode had a substantial impact on house prices, aligning closely with market expectations.
4. **Visualization of Actual vs. Predicted Values:** Visualisation of predictions versus actual values indicated that while the model captured broad trends, there were noticeable deviations, particularly in high-value predictions, suggesting potential overfitting or sensitivity to certain features.

Inference:

- **Key Features:** The RFR consistently highlighted estate type, location, and proximity to amenities as key drivers of house prices, providing valuable insights into the factors influencing the London property market.
- **Performance Challenges:** Despite optimisation, the RFR's performance was slightly lower than the default model, and the extensive computation time due to high data volume proved impractical for ongoing use. The RFR struggled with the large dataset, taking up to eight hours on high-performance platforms like Google Colab Pro+, which ultimately limited its feasibility for practical application.

4.5.3 Decision Tree Regressor (DTR) model optimization

Decision Tree Regressor, a straightforward model that splits data into branches based on feature values, was optimised to evaluate its effectiveness in predicting house prices. While simpler than ensemble models, DTR offers interpretability and quick training times, making it a valuable tool for initial analysis and feature selection.

Steps Performed:

1. **Hyperparameter Tuning:** Key hyperparameters, such as maximum depth, minimum samples per split, and minimum samples per leaf, were adjusted to

balance model accuracy and complexity. The goal was to prevent overfitting while maintaining sufficient depth to capture key trends in the data.

2. **Performance Evaluation:** The DTR optimization focused on achieving a balance between model complexity and performance. Although the optimized DTR did not match the accuracy of XGBoost, it served as a useful benchmark for understanding feature interactions.
3. **Feature Importance Analysis:** DTR optimization highlighted similar influential features as those seen in XGBoost and RFR, including estate type, location, and nearby amenities, underscoring the consistency of these factors across different modeling approaches.
4. **Visualization of Actual vs. Predicted Values:** Visual analysis of DTR predictions revealed broader error margins compared to ensemble models, with significant variance in high-price predictions, reflecting the model's sensitivity to outlier data.

Inference:

- Key Features: DTR consistently identified estate type and location as top predictors of house prices, reinforcing their importance across all models.
- Com**parative Performance**: While the optimised DTR model showed some improvements over its default settings, it lagged significantly behind the more sophisticated XGBoost and RFR in terms of accuracy. The model's simple structure, while offering clear insights into feature importance, proved insufficient for capturing the complex interactions driving house prices.

4.5.4 Final model selection and rationale

As shown in Table 9, the rigorous optimization of XGBoost, Random Forest Regressor, and Decision Tree Regressor made it clear that XGBoost was the most suitable model for predicting London house prices. The optimized XGBoost model not only delivered superior performance metrics but also demonstrated greater resilience and efficiency, handling large datasets with relative ease.

While Random Forest and Decision Tree Regressor provided valuable insights and served as benchmarks, their computational demands and performance limitations rendered them less practical for this application. Consequently, XGBoost emerged as the optimal choice, offering a robust combination of accuracy, interpretability, and feasibility.

Model optimization significantly enhances the predictive accuracy and reliability of machine learning models. By fine-tuning hyperparameters and

Table 9: Optimized Model comparison scores.

Optimized Model	R-squared	RMSE	MSE	MAE
eXtreme Gradient Boosting (XGBoost)	0.610	197368	38953942063	131680
Random Forest Regressor	0.620	193327	37375511303	127629
Decision Tree Regressor	0.530	216538	46888989114	142628

rigorously evaluating performance, we identified XGBoost as the most effective model for predicting London house prices. The optimization process underscored the importance of selecting models that not only perform well but also align with practical considerations, such as computational efficiency and interpretability, ensuring that the AI system is both powerful and actionable in real-world settings.

4.6 XAI implementation using SHAP

Explainable AI (XAI) is increasingly vital in machine learning, offering transparency and interpretability in predictive models. For this project on London house price prediction, SHAP (SHapley Additive exPlanations) was implemented to provide insights into the decision-making process of our optimized models, primarily focusing on the XGBoost algorithm. SHAP provides a robust framework for understanding complex models by quantifying the contribution of each feature to individual predictions, thereby bridging the gap between model accuracy and human interpretability.

The choice of XGBoost for SHAP implementation was driven by practical constraints; attempts to apply SHAP on the Random Forest Regressor (RFR) repeatedly led to system crashes, even on high-performance platforms like Google Colab Pro+. Therefore, XGBoost, which offered the best trade-off between performance and computational efficiency, was selected for the SHAP analysis, allowing us to derive meaningful, actionable insights from the model.

Steps Performed:

1. **Install and Initialize SHAP:** SHAP was installed and initialized within the Python environment, setting up the framework for extracting interpretability insights from the XGBoost model.
2. **Visualize SHAP Summary Plot for Global Interpretability:** The SHAP summary plot was used to visualize the impact of all features across the dataset, highlighting which variables had the most significant influence on the model's predictions.
3. **Create Force Plot:** The force plot was generated to illustrate how individual features contribute to a single prediction. This visualization showcases the push and pull effect of each feature on the predicted house price, making it easier to understand the underlying logic of the model.

Inference:

1. **Key Features Influencing House Prices:** The SHAP analysis identified estate type, location (latitude and longitude), the count of supermarkets within 2 km, and postcode as the most critical factors in determining house prices in London. These features consistently influenced the model's output, aligning with known market drivers such as location desirability and access to amenities.
2. **SHAP Value Interpretation:** Variables that increase the predicted house price are highlighted in red, while those that decrease the value appear in blue. Features with larger SHAP values have more substantial effects, represented

by larger arrows. This colour-coded representation simplifies the interpretation, making it clear which factors are driving up or pulling down property values.

3. **Feature Effects on SHAP Values:** Estate type and property type were found to have positive effects on SHAP values, indicating that these factors tend to push house prices higher. Conversely, factors like town characteristics and transaction category often exert a downward pressure on prices.

4.6.1 SHAP visualizations

The force plot provides a detailed visualisation of how each feature influences an individual prediction, showing the cumulative effect of positive and negative contributions. The top value in the plot represents the predicted house price, with arrows indicating the direction and magnitude of each feature's impact. These plots offer a comprehensive view of how the model arrives at a specific prediction, making the model's behaviour more transparent.

For instance, in high-value predictions (95th and 90th percentiles), property type and estate type were dominant factors that significantly influenced SHAP values. In contrast, for lower percentiles (75th and 50th), the influence was mixed, with certain features pushing the SHAP values up and others, like town and transaction category, pushing them lower. This granular view helps stakeholders understand which factors are driving house prices in different market segments.

The SHAP waterfall chart further decomposes the SHAP values, illustrating how individual variables affect the model's prediction step by step. In the given Figure 5, estate type and property type have the most significant positive impact, boosting the predicted house price by over 130,000 units and 60,000 units, respectively. This suggests that these factors are major determinants in increasing house prices.

Conversely, variables like town and transaction category exert a notable negative influence, pulling the SHAP value down by approximately 45,000 and 33,000 units, respectively. This indicates that these factors contribute to lower house prices in the model's prediction.

Additionally, latitude and deed date show a positive impact, while longitude has a minor negative effect. These location-specific variables emphasize the importance of geographical position, with certain aspects, such as deed date, adding value to the predicted house price.

Supermarket count within 2 km and rail distance also significantly affect the SHAP values, indicating that proximity to these amenities has a substantial influence on property values, either positively or negatively. On the other hand, variables like district and nearest bus stop distance have a negative effect, reducing the SHAP values slightly.

Overall, this visualization helps identify which features consistently push property prices up or down, giving insight into the key drivers of value in the housing market model.

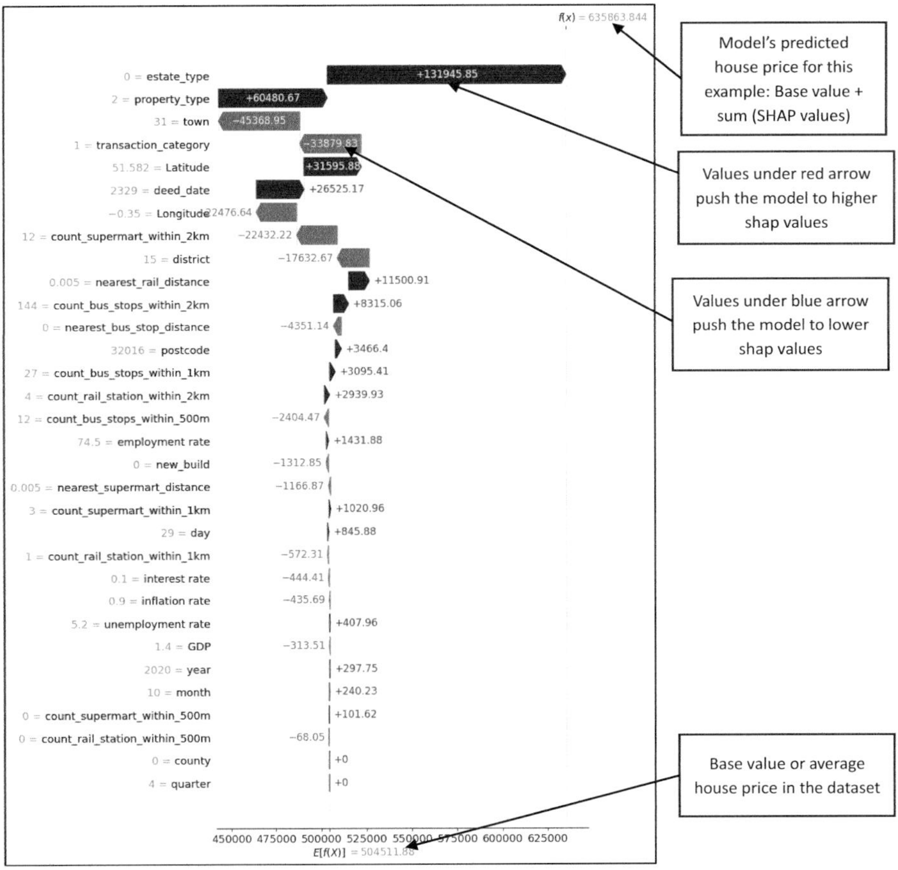

Figure 5: Waterfall Chart in SHAP.

SHAP dependence plots provide further insights by showing how individual features impact SHAP values across the dataset. Several key observations were made:

1. **Supermarket Proximity:** SHAP values increase as the count of supermarkets within 2 km rises, highlighting the importance of nearby amenities in driving property prices higher.
2. **Property Type:** Certain property types were consistently associated with higher SHAP values, indicating a strong influence on price, particularly for premium properties.
3. **Proximity to Railway Stations:** Closer proximity to railway stations correlates with higher SHAP values, suggesting accessibility and connectivity as critical drivers of higher house prices.
4. **Minimum Railway Stations Required:** At least one nearby railway station is needed for higher predicted prices, emphasizing the importance of transportation links.

5. **Employment Rate:** Interestingly, the employment rate showed little to no effect on SHAP values, indicating that economic factors such as employment levels may be less influential than physical characteristics and amenities in determining property prices.

4.6.2 Feature importance: mean absolute SHAP value

The feature importance plot using mean absolute SHAP values provides a ranked view of the most influential features across all predictions. Estate type, location variables (latitude and longitude), and supermarket proximity consistently emerged as top factors, reinforcing their critical role in the London property market. This ranking helps prioritise features for further analysis and potential policy implications.

4.6.3 Additional points on XAI using SHAP

The application of SHAP in this project highlights the broader benefits of XAI in enhancing the interpretability of machine learning models:

1. **Transparency and Trust:** SHAP enhances transparency by providing clear, visual explanations of how models make decisions. This builds trust among stakeholders, including property developers, investors, and policymakers, who can see exactly how predictions are generated.
2. **Model Validation:** XAI tools like SHAP can be used to validate model behaviour, ensuring that the model's decisions align with domain knowledge. For instance, the identification of location and amenities as key drivers of house prices corroborates existing market understanding, reinforcing confidence in the model.
3. **Bias Detection and Mitigation:** SHAP can help detect biases in model predictions by highlighting feature impacts. If a model disproportionately relies on certain features that should not heavily influence pricing (e.g., postcode biases), this can prompt corrective actions to adjust the model.
4. **Enhanced Decision-Making:** By elucidating the factors that drive predictions, SHAP empowers decision-makers with actionable insights. For example, understanding that proximity to supermarkets significantly boosts house prices can guide urban planning and development strategies.
5. **Scenario Analysis:** SHAP allows users to explore "what-if" scenarios by adjusting feature values and observing their impact on predictions. This capability is particularly valuable in real estate, where stakeholders can simulate the effects of changes in property characteristics or neighbourhood amenities on house prices.

Thus, the implementation of XAI using SHAP has been instrumental in unpacking the complex predictions of the XGBoost model for London house prices. SHAP provides a comprehensive, interpretable view of how individual features drive model predictions through visualisations such as force plots, waterfall charts, and dependence plots. This level of interpretability not only enhances trust and transparency but also offers valuable insights that can inform strategic decisions in the real estate market. SHAP's ability to make black-box models explainable highlights its importance in the broader context of AI, where understanding and mitigating the impact of algorithms on real-world outcomes is increasingly critical.

5. Discussion and Evaluation

This section provides a comprehensive evaluation of the machine learning models used to predict house prices in London. It discusses the models' performance, the rationale behind model selection, and the implementation of explainability techniques to interpret the models' decisions. The chapter also highlights comparisons with existing literature and addresses the ethical, legal, and social considerations handled throughout the project.

5.1 Machine learning model's performance and model selection

The selection of an appropriate machine learning model is a critical step in any predictive modelling project. This study initially tested multiple models, including Linear Regression, Random Forest Regressor (RFR), Decision Tree Regressor, and XGBoost. The initial evaluations with default parameters indicated that the Random Forest Regressor provided the best performance in terms of accuracy. However, challenges in optimising this model led to the eventual selection of XGBoost for final implementation.

5.1.1 Random Forest Regressor (RFR) challenges

Random Forest, a powerful ensemble learning method, initially showed promising results in its default configuration. However, the process was met with significant computational challenges when hyperparameter tuning was attempted on Google Colab Pro+. The hyperparameter tuning process, intended to enhance the model's predictive accuracy further, failed to complete even after approximately eight hours of continuous execution on Google Colab Pro+, a premium computing environment. This failure was attributed to the large volume of data (millions of rows) and the high dimensionality (33 columns), which strained the computational resources available.

Despite showing potential in initial tests, the optimised Random Forest model's performance fell short compared to its default settings. These results underscored the computational infeasibility of Random Forest, given the scale of the data and the resources available. Consequently, the study pivoted to XGBoost, which offered a more feasible balance of performance and computational efficiency.

5.1.2 XGBoost as the optimal model

XGBoost (Extreme Gradient Boosting) emerged as the optimal model for this study. Not only did it deliver superior accuracy compared to other models tested, but it also demonstrated compatibility with the available computing resources. XGBoost's performance, even with default settings, outperformed Linear Regression, Decision Tree, and the Random Forest Regressor under optimised conditions. This led to the decision to use XGBoost for the explainability analysis using SHAP (SHapley Additive exPlanations), further solidifying its role as the primary model for the project.

Tables 8 and 9 present a comparative analysis of the performance of all tested models, highlighting XGBoost's dominance in both default and optimized configurations.

5.2 Machine learning model explainability

Explainability is a cornerstone of this research, as it provides stakeholders with transparency into the model's decision-making process. Given the complexity and black-box nature of XGBoost, SHAP was utilised to unpack and visualise the contribution of individual features to the model's predictions. SHAP helps translate complex model outputs into comprehensible insights, offering a clear narrative of how different factors influence the predicted house prices.

5.2.1 Implementation of SHAP

Due to the computational limitations encountered with the Random Forest model, SHAP was applied exclusively to XGBoost, which was both the best-performing and most computationally feasible model. SHAP summary plots and force plots were generated to provide a global view of feature importance and individual prediction explanations. Key findings from the SHAP analysis include:

- **Estate Type and Property Location:** Estate type and location (latitude and longitude) were identified as the most influential features affecting house prices in London. These variables consistently exhibited high SHAP values, pushing predictions towards higher price ranges.
- **Property Type and Supermarket Proximity:** The number of supermarkets within a 2km radius also played a significant role, reflecting the importance of neighbourhood amenities in house price determination. Property type further influenced SHAP values, illustrating how structural factors and design styles impact valuations.
- **SHAP Force and Waterfall Plots:** Force plots and waterfall charts provided localized explanations of individual predictions, visually demonstrating how specific feature values contributed to price forecasts. For instance, estate type and property type showed strong positive effects, while other variables, such as town or transaction category, pushed predictions lower.

Figure 6 showcases the SHAP values for important features, reinforcing the findings of this study and enabling stakeholders to gain confidence in the model's decisions.

5.2.2 Comparison with other studies

This study's results are compared with findings of state-of-the-art literature (see Table 10). Across various geographical contexts and datasets, XGBoost consistently emerged as a leading predictive model for housing prices, underscoring this algorithm's robustness and adaptability.

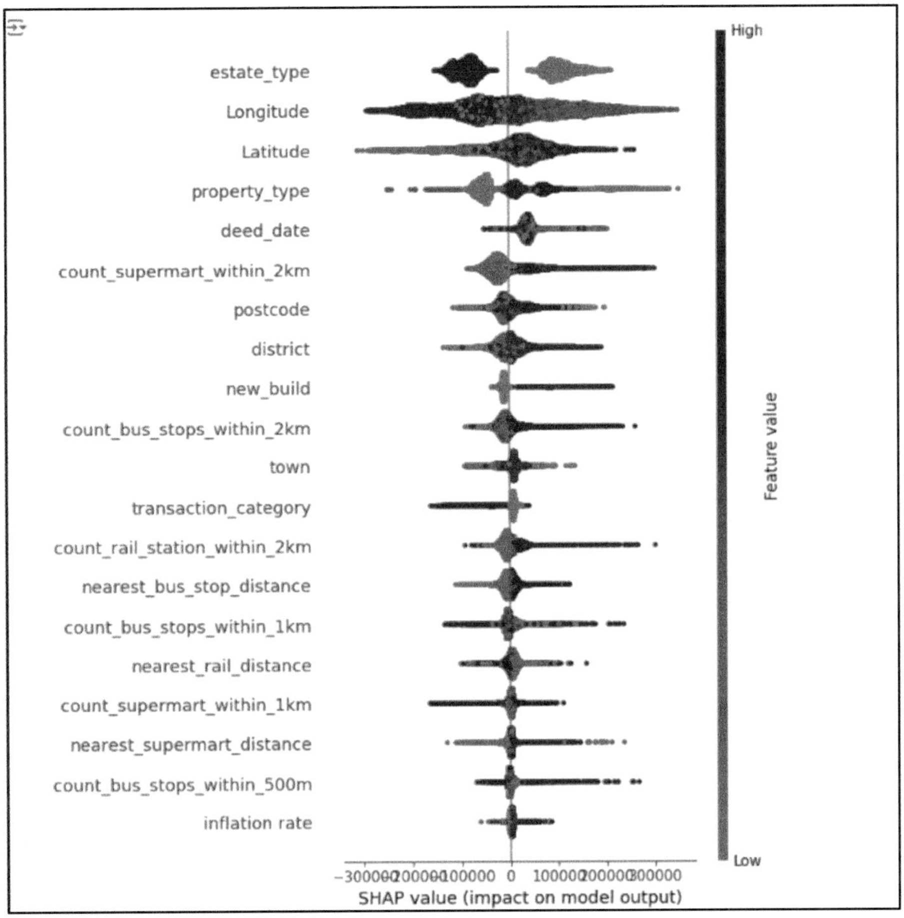

Figure 6: SHAP value for important features.

5.3 Discussion on expectations and observations

Throughout this study, the models generally met expectations in terms of performance and interpretability. The transition from Random Forest to XGBoost was a strategic decision driven by computational constraints, but it ultimately led to a model that not only performed well but also offered greater transparency through SHAP. Observations confirmed that real estate and location-specific factors remain paramount in predicting house prices, aligning with both market intuition and empirical evidence.

These observations illustrate the practical challenges and deviations from expectations encountered throughout the project (see Table 11). The study not only met its primary goals but also provided valuable insights into the complexities of model optimization, explainability, and deployment. The experience underscores the need for flexibility and adaptability in addressing real-world challenges and improving the overall effectiveness and usability of predictive modelling systems.

Table 10: Comparison of results with previous studies

Author	Research area	Findings	Our study
Zhang (2023)	Compared KNN, Ridge Regression, RF, and XGBoost on residential property sales in Ames, Iowa	Found XGBoost to be most effective. SHAP could unravel complexity of XGBoost	We also found XGBoost to be most effective and used SHAP to make our model transparent.
Ghatnekar and Shanbhag (2023)	Compared SVM, Linear Regression, RF on Boston and California dataset	Concluded that XGBoost generated most accurate predictions.	Our study found XGBoost to be effective for optimal solution.
Dou et al. (2023)	Applied XGBoost with SHAP in Shanghai	Showed that neighbourhood factors including public amenities account for 46% effect on forecasting house prices.	We found that more than 97% is contributed due to neighbourhood factors.

Table 11: Expectations and observations.

Category	Expectations	Observations
Macroeconomic Factors	Based on the literature review, macroeconomic factors were anticipated to have a significant impact on house prices.	In the tested models, macroeconomic factors did not emerge as a prominent feature. This discrepancy suggests that their impact may be less pronounced or indirect in this specific dataset context.
Neighbourhood Factors	Expected that neighbourhood factors would significantly influence house prices, as supported by previous research.	Research confirmed the importance of neighbourhood factors, with influence varying across districts. Proximity to amenities and local infrastructure proved influential, aligning with expectations.
Model Optimization	Anticipated that model optimization would be manageable on Google Collab Pro+, handling computational demands effectively.	Google Collab Pro+ struggled with the dataset scale, especially for Random Forest and other models requiring extensive optimization, underscoring the need for more robust computational resources for large-scale data.
SHAP (SHapley Additive exPlanations)	Expected SHAP to be straightforward to interpret, enhancing transparency and understanding of model predictions.	While SHAP provided valuable insights, some plots were challenging for novice users to interpret, indicating a need for improved accessibility in visualizations to aid broader user comprehension.
Deployment	Django was expected to be an easy-to-learn and implement framework for building the prediction system.	Django required considerable development time due to its complexity and learning curve, making the system implementation more time-consuming and less intuitive than initially anticipated.

6. Conclusions and Recommendations

This research has made significant strides in the domain of house price prediction by integrating XAI with machine learning models. By focusing on the application of XGBoost and SHAP, the study has advanced the understanding of how various factors influence house prices and provided a practical tool for users. The deployment of a web-based prediction system not only validates the model's effectiveness but also ensures that the insights are accessible to a wider audience, bridging the gap between complex data analysis and practical, real-world applications.

This study makes several significant contributions to the field of house price prediction through machine learning and explainable artificial intelligence (XAI):

1. **Framework for House Price Prediction:** The research introduced a robust framework by integrating macroeconomic and neighbourhood data into a single data frame. This comprehensive dataset, after rigorous pre-processing, was used to build and evaluate machine learning models. The framework demonstrated how diverse data sources can be synthesised to enhance predictive accuracy.
2. **Extensive Literature Review:** An extensive review of over 21 journals, articles, conference papers, and six theses highlighted XGBoost as the most accurate algorithm for house price prediction. The literature review also revealed a gap in the use of XAI techniques, which this research addressed by implementing SHAP for the first time in this context.
3. **Use of SHAP:** The research showcased the implementation of SHAP (SHapley Additive exPlanations) to elucidate the predictions made by the XGBoost model. This contributed to the understanding of how various features affect house prices, thus enhancing the model's transparency and interpretability.
4. **Website for House Price Prediction:** Moving beyond theoretical and experimental work, the research developed a user-friendly website that allows individuals without data science expertise to predict house prices in London. This practical application of the research ensures that valuable insights are accessible to a broader audience.

The research limitations include geographic factors, house characteristics, neighbouring environments, and some computational constraints during model optimisation. The research was geographically restricted to Greater London, meaning the findings are specifically relevant to this region. A broader geographic scope could provide more generalised insights. Due to time constraints, the analysis did not include detailed house features like the number of floors, energy utilisation, and specific amenities. Incorporating these factors could refine the model's accuracy. Key neighbourhood features, such as the presence of hospitals, schools, and restaurants, were not explored due to computational and time limitations. Also, the study limited its analysis to a subset of machine learning models, including Linear Regression, XGBoost, Random Forest Regressor (RFR), Decision Tree (DT), and Gradient Boosting Regressor (GBR). Moreover, computational constraints prevented the optimisation of RFR and GBR, which could potentially become more efficient.

Future recommendations can focus on eliminating the research limitations discussed above. Web scraping data from platforms like Zoopla and Rightmove could offer additional insights and enable comparisons with existing predictions. Expanding the research to include the development of a mobile application would improve accessibility and usability, making the prediction system available to users on various devices.

References

Adetunji, A.B., Akande, O.N., Ajala, F.A., Oyewo, O., Akande, Y.F. and Oluwadara, G. 2022. House Price prediction using random forest machine learning technique. *Procedia Computer Science*, 199: 806–813. https://doi.org/10.1016/j.procs.2022.01.100.

Afonso, B., Melo, L., Oliveira, W., Sousa, S. and Berton, L. 2019. Housing prices prediction with a deep learning and random forest ensemble. *ResearchGate* [Preprint]. https://www.researchgate.net/publication/335527230_Housing_Prices_Prediction_with_a_Deep_Learning_and_Random_Forest_Ensemble.

Aggarwal, S., Saini, L.M. and Kumar, A. 2008. Price forecasting using wavelet transform and LSE based mixed model in Australian electricity market. *International Journal of Energy Sector Management*, 2(4): 521–546. https://doi.org/10.1108/17506220810919054.

Ahtesham, M., Bawany, N.Z. and Fatima, K. 2020. House price prediction using machine learning algorithm - the case of Karachi City, Pakistan. 2020 21st International Arab Conference on Information Technology (ACIT), Giza, Egypt, pp. 1–5, doi: 10.1109/ACIT50332.2020.9300074.

Alfiyatin, A.N., Febrita, R.E., Taufiq, H. and Mahmudy, W.F. 2017. Modeling house price prediction using regression analysis and particle swarm optimization case study: Malang, East Java, Indonesia. *International Journal of Advanced Computer Science and Applications*, 8(10). https://doi.org/10.14569/ijacsa.2017.081042.

Ali, S., Abuhmed, T., El-Sappagh, S., Muhammad, K., Alonso-Moral, J.M., Confalonieri, R. et al. 2023. Explainable Artificial Intelligence (XAI): What we know and what is left to attain trustworthy artificial intelligence. *Information Fusion*, 99: 101805. https://doi.org/10.1016/j.inffus.2023.101805.

Alzain, E., Alshebami, A.S., Aldhyani, T.H. and Alsubari, S.N. 2022. Application of Artificial Intelligence for predicting real estate prices: the case of Saudi Arabia. *Electronics*, 11(21): 3448. https://doi.org/10.3390/electronics11213448.

Awonaike, A.A. 2022. Estimating UK house prices using machine learning. PhD Thesis. University of East London.

Bailey, J.R. 2022. Don't underestimate the power of self-reflection. *Harvard Business Review* [Preprint]. https://hbr.org/2022/03/dont-underestimate-the-power-of-self-reflection.

Basu, S. and Thibodeau, T.G. 1998. Analysis of spatial autocorrelation in house prices. *The Journal of Real Estate Finance and Economics*, 17(1): 61–85. https://doi.org/10.1023/a:1007703229507.

Baturynska, I. and Martinsen, K. 2020. Prediction of geometry deviations in additive manufactured parts: comparison of linear regression with machine learning algorithms. *Journal of Intelligent Manufacturing*, 32(1): 179–200. https://doi.org/10.1007/s10845-020-01567-0.

Bloomberg - Are you a robot? (2023, June 19). https://www.bloomberg.com/opinion/articles/2023-06-19/london-house-prices-what-i-learned-from-buying-a-home-in-a-down-market?embedded-checkout=true.

Bork, L. and Møller, S.V. 2014. Forecasting house prices in the 50 states using dynamic model averaging and dynamic model selection. *International Journal of Forecasting*, 31(1): 63–78. https://doi.org/10.1016/j.ijforecast.2014.05.005.

Bove, C., Aigrain, J., Lesot, M. and Detyniecki, M. 2021. Contextualising local explanations for non-expert users: an XAI pricing interface for insurance. ResearchGate. https://www.researchgate.net/publication/360222734_Contextualising_local_explanations_for_non-expert_users_an_XAI_pricing_interface_for_insurance.

Brown, J.P., Song, H. and McGillivray, A. 1997. Forecasting UK house prices: A time-varying coefficient approach. *Economic Modelling*, 14(4): 529–548. https://doi.org/10.1016/s0264-9993(97)00006-0.

Burrows, R. and Knowles, C. 2019. The "HAVES" and the "HAVE YACHTS." *Cultural Politics: An International Journal*, 15(1): 72–87. https://doi.org/10.1215/17432197-7289528.

C3.ai. (2023, September 19). Shapley values. C3 AI. https://c3.ai/glossary/data-science/shapley-values/.

Campbell, S. 2024, February 24. Django Tutorial for Beginners: Features, architecture & History. Guru99. https://www.guru99.com/django-tutorial.html.

Code of Good Practice. 2004. The British Computer Society. https://www.inf.ed.ac.uk/teaching/courses/pi/2013_2014/notes/1/cop.pdf (Accessed: December 6, 2023).

Colab paid services pricing. (n.d.). https://colab.research.google.com/signup#:~:text=Subscribing%20to%20Colab%20Pro%20or,additional%20compute%20units%20every%20month.

Creating your Personal Development Plan (PDP). 2019. The London School of Economics and Political Science (LSE). https://info.lse.ac.uk/staff/divisions/Human-Resources/Assets/Documents/OLL/PDP-Guidance-230719.pdf.

Dahouda, M.K. and Joe, I. 2021. A deep-learned embedding technique for categorical features encoding. *In IEEE Access*, 9: 114381–114391, doi: 10.1109/ACCESS.2021.310435.

Deeks, A. 2019. The judicial demand for explainable artificial intelligence on JSTOR. Columbia Law Review, 119: 1829–1850. https://www.jstor.org/stable/26810851?seq=4&saml_data=eyJzYW1sVG9rZW4iOiI4OWUwZWNmZS0yNjU3LTRlZDgtYWMxNi0yMmQxMmE4ZDY5ZDIiLCJpbnN0aXR1dGlvbklkcyI6WyIyYjFlM2Y1Ni02ODk3LTQ1NzMtOTFlYi1jZGJhZTQ5ZmJkZDIiXX0.

Dou, M., Gu, Y. and Fan, H. 2023. Incorporating neighborhoods with explainable artificial intelligence for modeling fine-scale housing prices. *Applied Geography*, 158: 103032. https://doi.org/10.1016/j.apgeog.2023.103032.

Duan, J., Tian, G., Yang, L. and Zhou, T. 2021. Addressing the macroeconomic and hedonic determinants of housing prices in Beijing Metropolitan Area, China. *Habitat International*, 113: 102374. https://doi.org/10.1016/j.habitatint.2021.102374.

Farooq, M.S., Tahseen, R. and Omer, U. 2021. Ethical guidelines for AI: a systematic literature review. *VFAST Transactions on Software Engineering*, 9(3): 33–47. https://doi.org/10.21015/vtse.v9i3.701.

Farooq, M.S., Tahseen, R. and Omer, U. 2021. Ethical guidelines for artificial intelligence: a systematic LiteratureReview. *VFAST Transactions on Software Engineering*, 9(3): 33–47. https://www.researchgate.net/publication/355788500_Ethical_Guidelines_for_Artificial_Intelligence_A_Systematic_Literature_Review#fullTextFileContent.

Fiok, K., Farahani, F.V., Karwowski, W. and Ahram, T. 2022. Explainable artificial intelligence for education and training. *The Journal of Defense Modeling and Simulation*, 19(2): 133–144. https://doi.org/10.1177/15485129211028651.

Fourkiotis, K.P. and Tsadiras, A. 2023. Comparing machine learning techniques for house price prediction. In IFIP Advances in Information and Communication Technology (pp. 292–303). https://doi.org/10.1007/978-3-031-34107-6_23.

Garcia-Canadilla, P., Sanchez-Martinez, S., Crispi, F. and Bijnens, B. 2020. Machine learning in fetal Cardiology: what to expect. *Fetal Diagnosis and Therapy*, 47(5): 363–372. https://doi.org/10.1159/000505021.

Geerts, M., Vanden Broucke, S. and De Weerdt, J. 2023. A survey of methods and input data types for house price prediction. *ISPRS International Journal of Geo-information*, 12(5): 200. https://doi.org/10.3390/ijgi12050200.

Ghatnekar, A. and Shanbhag, A.D. 2021. Explainable, multi-region price prediction. 2021 International Conference on Electrical, Computer and Energy Technologies (ICECET), Cape Town, South Africa, pp. 1–7, doi: 10.1109/ICECET52533.2021.9698641.

Gray, D. 2011. How-Now-Wow Matrix – Gamestorming. https://gamestorming.com/how-now-wow-matrix/.

Hachcham, A. 2023, August 11. XGBoost: Everything you need to know. neptune.ai. https://neptune.ai/blog/xgboost-everything-you-need-to-know.

Hannah, S. and Georgie, F. 2023. Will house prices keep falling in 2024? Times Money Mentor, 20 December. https://www.thetimes.co.uk/money-mentor/buying-home/will-house-prices-fall-uk.

Hansson, M. and Holmqvist, M. 2023. Improving house price prediction models: exploring the impact of macroeconomic features. Bachelor's Thesis. Uppsala University.

Hariharan, S., Robinson, R., Prasad, R.R., Thomas, C. and Balakrishnan, N. 2022. XAI for intrusion detection system: comparing explanations based on global and local scope. *Journal of Computer Virology and Hacking Techniques*, 19(2): 217–239. https://doi.org/10.1007/s11416-022-00441-2.

Hartikainen, K. 2023. Property valuation with interpretable machine learning. Master's Thesis. Aalto University.

He, S.Y. 2020. Regional impact of rail network accessibility on residential property price: Modelling spatial heterogeneous capitalisation effects in Hong Kong. *Transportation Research. Part a, Policy and Practice*, 135: 244–263. https://doi.org/10.1016/j.tra.2020.01.025.

Heyman, A. and Sommervoll, D.E. 2019. House prices and relative location. Cities, 95: 102373. https://doi.org/10.1016/j.cities.2019.06.004.

Hodgson, J. 2019, September 4. Living near the Tube: house prices within 500m of a London Underground station mostly likely to weather property market's Brexit jitters | Homes and Property. Evening Standard. https://www.standard.co.uk/homesandproperty/property-news/living-near-the-tube-house-prices-within-500m-of-a-station-mostly-likely-to-weather-property-markets-brexit-jitters-a132976.html.

Imran, I.U., Muhammad, Zaman, Atif. 2021. Using machine learning algorithms for housing price prediction: the case of islamabad housing data. *Soft Computing and Machine Intelligence Journal*, 1(1). https://koreascience.kr/article/JAKO202122260767075.page.

Inflation and the 2% target. (2024, March 21). Bank of England. https://www.bankofengland.co.uk/monetary-policy/inflation.

Intaver Institute: Project risk management and risk analysis software (no date). https://riskyproject.blogspot.com/.

Introduction to Boosted Trees — xgboost 2.0.3 documentation. (n.d.). https://xgboost.readthedocs.io/en/stable/tutorials/model.html.

Josh, K. (2024, March 5). Will house prices fall in 2024? Times Money Mentor. https://www.thetimes.co.uk/money-mentor/buying-home/will-house-prices-fall-uk.

Kaluža, M., Kalanj, M. and Vukelić, B. 2019. A comparison of back-end frameworks for web application development. *Zbornik VeleučIlišTa U Rijeci*, 7(1): 317–332. https://doi.org/10.31784/zvr.7.1.10.

Karamanou, A., Kalampokis, E. and Tarabanis, K. 2022. Linked open government data to predict and explain house prices: the case of Scottish Statistics Portal. *Big Data Research*, 30: 100355. https://doi.org/10.1016/j.bdr.2022.100355.

Komagome-Towne, A. 2016. Models and Visualizations for Housing Price Prediction. MSc Thesis. California State Polytechnic University.

Krupitzer, C., Noack, T. and Borsum, C. 2022. Digital food twins combining data science and food Science: system model, applications, and challenges. *Processes*, 10(9): 1781. https://doi.org/10.3390/pr10091781.

Kumar, B., Ashritha, B., Teja, CH. and Vineeth, M. 2020. House price prediction using gradient boost regression model. *International Journal of Research and Analytical Reviews* (IJRAR), 7(1): 52–53. https://www.ijrar.org/papers/IJRAR2001569.pdf.

Lamont, D.L. 2023, February 20. What 175 years of data tell us about house price affordability in the UK. Schroders. https://www.schroders.com/en/global/individual/insights/what-174-years-of-data-tell-us-about-house-price-affordability-in-the-uk/.

Law, S.S. 2017. Defining street-based local area and measuring its effect on house price using a hedonic price approach: The case study of Metropolitan London. *Cities*, 60: 166–179. https://doi.org/10.1016/j.cities.2016.08.008.

Law, S.S., Paige, B. and Russell, C. 2019. Take a Look Around. *ACM Transactions on Intelligent Systems and Technology*, 10(5): 1–19. https://doi.org/10.1145/3342240.

Lohith, O., Jha, A. and Tamboli, S.C. 2023. Comparative analysis of random forest regression for house price prediction. *International Journal of Creative Research Thoughts*, 11. https://ijcrt.org/papers/IJCRT2306866.pdf.

London's future first time buyers. 2024, February 29. https://www.savills.co.uk/research_articles/229130/355591-0.

London's parasitical housing market is driving away young families. (2023, April 20). Financial Times. https://www.ft.com/content/d6bc22ed-d6d8-464b-b706-b4d478c6baf1.

Lu, B., Charlton, M. and Fotheringhama, A.S. 2011. Geographically weighted regression using a non-euclidean distance metric with a study on london house price data. *Procedia Environmental Sciences*, 7: 92–97. https://doi.org/10.1016/j.proenv.2011.07.017.

Lundberg, S. and Lee, S. 2017. A unified approach to interpreting model predictions. ResearchGate. https://www.researchgate.net/publication/317062430_A_Unified_Approach_to_Interpreting_Model_Predictions.

Nationwide. 2021. Transport Special Feature. In http://www.nationwidehousepriceindex.co.uk/.

Ng, A. 2015. Machine learning for a london housing price prediction mobile application. Bachelor's Thesis. Imperial College London.

Nguyen, N. and Cripps, A. 2001. Predicting housing value: a comparison of multiple regression analysis and artificial neural networks. *Journal of Real Estate Research*, 22(3). https://core.ac.uk/download/pdf/7162826.pdf.

North, A. 2024, February 14. UK House Price Index - Office for National Statistics. https://www.ons.gov.uk/economy/inflationandpriceindices/bulletins/housepriceindex/december2023.

Özöğür Akyüz, S., Eygi Erdogan, B., Yıldız, Ö. and Karadayı Ataş, P. 2023. A novel hybrid house price prediction model. *Computational Economics*, 62(3): 1215–1232.

Pai, P.-F. and Wang, W. 2020. Using machine learning models and actual transaction data for predicting real estate prices. *Applied Sciences*, 10(17): 5832. https://doi.org/10.3390/app10175832.

Peng, H., Li, J., Wang, Z., Yang, R., Liu, M., Zhang, M. et al. 2021. Lifelong property price prediction: a case study for the toronto real estate market - white rose research online. *IEEE Transactions on Knowledge and Data Engineering*, 35(3): 2765–2780. ISSN (2021) IEEE [Preprint]. https://eprints.whiterose.ac.uk/178229/.

Pérez-Molina, E. 2021. Exploring a multilevel approach with spatial effects to model housing price in San José, Costa Rica. Environment and Planning B: Urban Analytics and City Science, 49(3): 987–1004. https://doi.org/10.1177/23998083211041122.

Phipps, A.G. and Li, D. 2019. Calibration and evaluation of Quigley's hybrid housing price model in Microsoft Excel. *PLOS ONE*, 14(4): e0215954. https://doi.org/10.1371/journal.pone.0215954.

Plakandaras, V., Gupta, R., Katrakilidis, C. and Wohar, M.E. 2018. Time-varying role of macroeconomic shocks on house prices in the US and UK: evidence from over 150 years of data. *Empirical Economics*, 58(5): 2249–2285. https://doi.org/10.1007/s00181-018-1581-x.

Plumplot. 2024. Inner-London house prices in maps and graphs. https://www.plumplot.co.uk/City-Inner-London-house-prices.html.

PPTMON. https://pptmon.com/?s=london&post_type=post&lang=en.

Ramachandran, A., Gupta, S., Rana, S., Li, C. and Venkatesh, S. 2020. Incorporating expert prior in Bayesian optimisation via space warping. *Knowledge-based Systems*, 195: 105663. https://doi.org/10.1016/j.knosys.2020.105663.

Regional Performance: Cycles and Inflection points. (2024, February 29). https://www.savills.co.uk/research_articles/229130/353667-0.

RMSE (Root Mean squared Error). (2024, May 1). Oracle Help Center. https://docs.oracle.com/en/cloud/saas/planning-budgeting-cloud/pfusu/insights_metrics_RMSE.html.

Rosen, S. 1974. Hedonic prices and implicit markets: product differentiation in pure competition. *Journal of Political Economy*, 82(1): 34–55. http://www.jstor.org/stable/1830899.

Rowe, W. (n.d.). Mean square error & R2 score clearly explained. BMC Blogs. https://www.bmc.com/blogs/mean-squared-error-r2-and-variance-in-regression-analysis/.

Santarelli, M. 2024, February 14. Will the London housing market crash in 2024? Norada Real Estate Investments. https://www.noradarealestate.com/blog/london-housing-market/.

Sanyal, S., Biswas, S.K., Das, D., Chakraborty, M. and Purkayastha, B. 2022. Boston house price prediction using regression models. 022 2nd International Conference on Intelligent Technologies (CONIT), Hubli, India, pp. 1–6, doi: 10.1109/CONIT55038.2022.9848309.

Selim, H. 2009. Determinants of house prices in Turkey: Hedonic regression versus artificial neural network. *Expert Systems With Applications*, 36(2): 2843–2852. https://doi.org/10.1016/j.eswa.2008.01.044.

Sewell, A. 2023. Lesson study. https://www.structural-learning.com/post/reflective-practice.

Sharma, H., Harsora, H. and Ogunleye, B. 2024. An optimal house price prediction algorithm: XGBoost. Analytics, 3(1): 30–45. https://doi.org/10.3390/analytics3010003.

Sharma, S., Arora, D., Shankar, G., Sharma, P. and Motwani, V. 2023 House Price Prediction using Machine Learning Algorithm. Erode, India: IEEE. https://ieeexplore.ieee.org/document/10084197.

Sjöblom, S. 2023. Machine Learning for Predicting the Prices of Dwellings in Small and Large Cities of Finland. Master's Thesis in Information Systems. Åbo Akademi University.

Soltani, A., Heydari, M., Aghaei, F. and Pettit, C.J. 2022. Housing price prediction incorporating spatio-temporal dependency into machine learning algorithms. *Cities*, 131: 103941. https://doi.org/10.1016/j.cities.2022.103941.

Stang, M. 2023. Real estate valuation in the age of artificial intelligence – modern machine learning algorithms and their application in property appraisal. MSc Thesis. University of Regensburg.

Štrumbelj, E. and Kononenko, I. 2010. An Efficient Explanation of Individual Classifications using Game Theory. https://jmlr.org/papers/v11/strumbelj10a.html.

Temür, A.S., Akgün, M. and Temür, G. 2019. Predicting housing sales in turkey using arima, LSTM and hybrid models. *Journal of Business Economics and Management*, 20(5): 920–938. https://doi.org/10.3846/jbem.2019.10190.

The Insider @ Houst. 2022. How is The Londing Housing Market Landscape in 2023? Houst. https://www.houst.com/blog/london-housing-market.

Turing. 2022, July 22. Why is Python best adapted to AI and machine learning? https://www.turing.com/kb/python-best-adapted-to-ai-and-machine-learning.

Unemployment - Unemployment rate - OECD Data. (n.d.). theOECD. https://data.oecd.org/unemp/unemployment-rate.htm.

Wang, L., Wang, G., Yu, H. and Wang, F. 2022. Prediction and analysis of residential house price using a flexible spatiotemporal model. *Journal of Applied Economics*, 25(1): 503–522. https://doi.org/10.1080/15140326.2022.2045466.

What is a Decision Tree? | IBM. (n.d.). https://www.ibm.com/topics/decision-trees.

What is Random Forest? | IBM. (n.d.). https://www.ibm.com/topics/random-forest#:~:text=Random%20forest%20is%20a%20commonly,Decision%20trees.

Xu, X. and Zhang, Y. 2021. House price forecasting with neural networks. *Intelligent Systems With Applications*, 12: 200052. https://doi.org/10.1016/j.iswa.2021.200052.

Xu, X. and Zhang, Y. 2023. Residential housing price index forecasting via neural networks. *Neural Computing and Applications*, 34(17): 14763–14776. https://doi.org/10.1007/s00521-022-07309-y.

Yakub, A.A. 2020. Journal of Critical Reviews the effect of adopting micro and macro-economic variables on real estate price prediction models using ANN: a systematic literature review. Teknologimalaysia. https://www.academia.edu/43512098/Journal_of_Critical_Reviews_THE_EFFECT_OF_ADOPTING_MICRO_AND_MACRO_ECONOMIC_VARIABLES_ON_REAL_ESTATE_PRICE_PREDICTION_MODELS_USING_ANN_A_SYSTEMATIC_LITERATURE_REVIEW.

Ye, J., Chow, J., Jiang, C. and Zheng, Z. 2009. Stochastic gradient boosted distributed decision trees. Association for Computing Machinery. https://doi.org/10.1145/1645953.1646301.

Yin, M. 2023. Model for predicting london house prices. Highlights in Business Economics and *Management*, 5: 124–133. https://doi.org/10.54097/hbem.v5i.5039.

Zhang, Z. 2021. Decision trees for objective house price prediction. 2021 3rd International Conference on Machine Learning, Big Data and Business Intelligence (MLBDBI), Taiyuan, China, pp. 280–283, doi: 10.1109/MLBDBI54094.2021.00059.

Zhang, Y., Xu, F., Zou, J. and Petrosian, O. 2021. XAI Evaluation: Evaluating Black-Box Model Explanations for Prediction. IEEE Conference Publication | IEEE Xplore. https://ieeexplore.ieee.org/document/9472817.

What is Hyperparameter Tuning? - Hyperparameter Tuning Methods Explained - AWS. (n.d.). Amazon Web Services, Inc. https://aws.amazon.com/what-is/hyperparameter-tuning/#:~:text=Hyperparameter%20tuning%20allows%20data%20scientists,the%20model%20as%20a%20hyperparameter.

Zhang, L. 2023, August 7. Housing price prediction using machine learning algorithm. https://www.pioneerpublisher.com/jwe/article/view/392.

Index

L

M

N

O

P

Q

R

S

T

X

Y

For Product Safety Concerns and Information please contact our EU representative GPSR@taylorandfrancis.com Taylor & Francis Verlag GmbH, Kaufingerstraße 24, 80331 München, Germany